By James D. Hornfischer

The Last Stand of the Tin Can Sailors: The Extraordinary World
War II Story of the U.S. Navy's Finest Hour

Ship of Ghosts: The Story of the USS *Houston,* FDR's Legendary
Lost Cruiser, and the Epic Saga of Her Survivors

Neptune's Inferno: The U.S. Navy at Guadalcanal

Service: A Navy SEAL at War *(with Marcus Luttrell)*

The Fleet at Flood Tide: America at Total War
in the Pacific, 1944–1945

The Fleet at Flood Tide

JAMES D. HORNFISCHER

Bantam Books  *New York*

The Fleet at Flood Tide

America at Total War in the Pacific, 1944–1945

Published in the United States by Bantam Books, an imprint of Random House, a division of Penguin Random House LLC, New York.

BANTAM BOOKS and the HOUSE colophon are registered trademarks of Penguin Random House LLC.

Title-page photo: U.S. Navy

LIBRARY OF CONGRESS CATALOGING-IN-PUBLICATION DATA

Names: Hornfischer, James D., author.
Title: The fleet at flood tide : America at total war in the Pacific, 1944–1945 / James D. Hornfischer.
Other titles: America at total war in the Pacific, 1944–1945
Description: New York : Bantam Books, [2016] |
Includes bibliographical references and index.
Identifiers: LCCN 2016027323 (print) | LCCN 2016027474 (Ebook) |
ISBN 9780345548702 | ISBN 9780345548719 (Ebook)
Subjects: LCSH: World War, 1939-1945—Campaigns—Pacific Area. |
United States. Navy. Fleet, 5th—History—20th century. |
Spruance, Raymond Ames, 1886–1969. | Turner, Richmond Kelly,
1885–1961. | Tibbets, Paul W. (Paul Warfield), 1915–2007. |
World War, 1939–1945—Amphibious operations, American. |
World War, 1939–1945—Naval operations, American. | World War,
1939–1945—Aerial operations, American.
Classification: LCC D767 .H598 2016 (print) | LCC D767 (ebook) |
DDC 940.54/5973—dc23
LC record available at https://lccn.loc.gov/2016027323

Printed in the United States of America on acid-free paper

randomhousebooks.com

2 4 6 8 9 7 5 3 1

First Edition

Book design by Virginia Norey

There were in morals two requisites for a lawful war,
a just cause and the chance of victory. The cause was now,
past all question, just. The enemy was exorbitant.
—EVELYN WAUGH, *Men at Arms* (1952)

Contents

Maps and Diagrams xi

Military Designations and Abbreviations xiii

Preface: Total War xvii

Prologue: Cashiered in Algiers xxi

PART ONE
Sea

1. Engine of Siege *3*

2. On the Western Warpath *20*

3. In Turner's Train *37*

4. A Charge for Ozawa *65*

5. The Outer Colony *71*

6. A Rumor of Fleets *81*

7. OBB and UDT *88*

8. Heavy Weather *99*

PART TWO
Land

9. Heavier, Higher, Faster *111*

10. D Day *116*

11. Trail, Attack, Report *144*

12. Tank Attack *153*

13. The View from the Mountain *163*

14. First Contact *170*

15. War of the Wind Machines *178*

16. Fast Carriers Down   194

17. To Build a Better Airfield   204

18. Beyond Darkness   212

19. Smith versus Smith   233

20. Satan's Breath   247

21. The Dying Game   263

22. Sniper Ship on a Cave Shoot   268

23. Beyond All Boundaries   279

24. Atop Suicide Cliffs   290

25. Regime Change   301

26. Steel Like Snowflakes   318

27. The Will to Lose Hard   332

PART THREE
Air

28. Secrets of New Mexico   347

29. Going Critical   366

30. Everybody's Business   384

31. Divine Winds   393

32. Methods of Death on the Wing   410

33. Opportunity and Madness   416

34. Prompt and Utter Destruction   429

35. Clear-cut Results   440

PART FOUR
Earth

36. Eight Bells for an Empire   461

37. The War Wearies   482

Acknowledgments   505

Notes   507

Bibliography   541

Index   569

Maps and Diagrams

Central Pacific Advance (endpaper)

Chain of Command, Fifth Fleet   24

Annual U.S. Naval Production by Type   53

Assault on Saipan, June 15   119

Battle of the Philippine Sea,
June 17–20   180

Progress on Saipan, June 16–22   209

Progress on Saipan, June 23–July 9   235

Assault on Guam, July 21   313

Assault on Tinian, July 24   320

U.S. Army Air Forces in the Pacific, May 1945   405

Operation Downfall (Operations Olympic and
Coronet)   418

Military Designations and Abbreviations

Command Abbreviations

COMINCH: Commander in Chief, U.S. Fleet

CINCPAC: Commander in Chief, Pacific Fleet

COMFIFTHFLT: Commander, Fifth Fleet

COMFIFTHPHIB: Commander, Fifth Amphibious Force

COMPHIBPAC: Commander, Amphibious Forces, Pacific

COMSUBPAC: Commander, Submarines, Pacific

COMGEN: Commanding General

CTF: Commander, Task Force

CTG: Commander, Task Group

BatDiv: Battleship Division

TransDiv: Transport Division

2/8 Marines (e.g.): 2nd Battalion, 8th Regiment

U.S. Aircraft

B-17: Boeing Flying Fortress, a heavy bomber flown by the USAAF

B-24: Consolidated Liberator, a heavy bomber flown by the USAAF and Navy (as the PB4Y)

B-25: Consolidated Mitchell, a medium bomber flown by the USAAF

B-29: Boeing Superfortress, a heavy bomber flown by the USAAF

C-54: Douglas Skymaster, a transport flown by the USAAF and Navy (as the R5D)

F4U: Chance-Vought Corsair, a land- and carrier-based fighter flown by the Navy and Marine Corps

PBM: Consolidated Mariner, a flying boat used for long-range reconnaissance

SB2C: Curtiss Helldiver, a carrier-based dive-bomber

SBD: Douglas Dauntless, a carrier-based dive-bomber

F6F: Grumman Hellcat, a carrier-based fighter

FM-2: Grumman Wildcat, a carrier-based fighter

OY-1: Stinson Sentinel, a liaison/observation plane

P-47: Republic Thunderbolt, a land-based fighter-bomber flown by the USAAF

P-51: North American Mustang, a land-based fighter flown by the USAAF

TBM/TBF: Grumman Avenger, a carrier-based torpedo bomber

VB: naval dive-bomber squadron

VF: naval fighter squadron

VMF: Marine Corps fighter squadron

VT: naval torpedo bomber squadron; may also indicate a variable timed proximity fuze

Japanese Aircraft

Betty: Mitsubishi G4M Type 1 land-based bomber

Emily: Kawanishi H8K Type 2 flying boat

Frances: Yokosuka P1Y1 *Ginga* land-based bomber

Frank: Nakajima Ki-84 *Hayate* Type 4 fighter

Hamp: *see* Zeke

Irving: Nakajima J1N *Gekko* Type 2 twin-engine night fighter and reconnaissance plane

Jill: Nakajima B6N *Tenzan* carrier-based torpedo bomber

Judy: Yokosuka D4Y *Suisei* carrier-based dive-bomber

Kate: Nakajima B5N Type 97 carrier-based torpedo bomber

Mavis: Kawanishi H6K Type 97 flying boat

Nate: Nakajima Ki-27 Type 97 fighter

Oscar: Nakajima Ki-43 *Hayabusa* Type 1 fighter

Tony: Kawasaki Ki-61 *Hien* Type 3 fighter

Val: Aichi D3A Navy Type 99 carrier-based dive-bomber

Zeke: Mitsubishi A6M *Zero-Sen* Type 0 carrier- and land-based fighter

Zero: *see* Zeke

U.S. Warship Types

BB: battleship, 35,000–48,000 tons

CA: heavy cruiser, 10,000–17,000 tons

CL: light cruiser, 6,000–10,000 tons

CV: aircraft carrier, 27,000–34,000 tons

CVE: escort carrier, 7,800 tons

CVL: light aircraft carrier, 11,000 tons

DD: destroyer, 1,600–2,500 tons

DE: destroyer escort, 1,200 tons

OBB: old battleship (pre–World War I era), 27,000–33,000 tons

U.S. Amphibious Craft

amtank: *see* LVT(A)

amtrac: *see* LVT

APD: a destroyer or destroyer escort converted as a high-speed
  transport; used to deliver up to company-sized elements of Marine
  Raiders, Army Rangers, and Navy Underwater Demolition Teams
  to enemy beachheads

DUKW: a six-wheeled amphibian truck with a 2½-ton capacity for
  cargo and personnel; the name is not an initialism but a model code
  assigned by the manufacturer, GMC

LCM: Landing Craft Medium; a lighter with capacity for a 30-ton
  medium tank or 60,000 pounds of cargo

LCPR: Landing Craft Personnel, Ramp. Replaced by the LCVP, its
  slightly larger, more-numerous successor, after 1942

LCT: Landing Craft Tank; a large lighter with capacity for multiple
  tanks and trucks and large quantities of gear and supplies

LCVP: Landing Craft Vehicle Personnel; a small landing craft used for
  personnel, with capacity for 36 troops or 10,000 pounds of cargo

LSD: Landing Ship Dock; a large vessel for cross-ocean transport
  of troops, vehicles, and cargo, with capacity for 240 soldiers or
  eighteen medium-tank-laden LCMs

LST: Landing Ship Tank; used to transport troops, vehicles, and
  equipment

LVT: Landing Vehicle Tracked (aka "amphibian tractor," or "amtrac");
  a lightly armored tactical vehicle capable of carrying troops and
  equipment over reefs and onto beaches

LVT(A): Landing Vehicle Tracked (Armored) (aka "amtank"); an
  amtrac armed with a 75 mm or 37 mm main gun

Ground Units (USMC as of March 1944)

squad: 13 men, led by a sergeant

platoon: three or four squads, about 40–50 men, led by a lieutenant

company: four platoons, about 250 men, led by a captain

battalion: three rifle companies plus a headquarters company; about
  900 men, led by a lieutenant colonel

Battalion Landing Team: reinforced infantry unit used in amphibious
  assaults, 1,100 men, led by a lieutenant colonel

regiment: three infantry battalions plus one weapons company and
  headquarters and service companies; about 3,300 men, led by a
  colonel

Regimental Combat Team: two Battalion Landing Teams, reinforced
    infantry units used in amphibious assaults, led by a colonel
division: three infantry regiments plus one artillery regiment, an
    engineer battalion, and a special troops battalion; about 17,000 men,
    led by a major general
corps: two to five divisions, led by a lieutenant general
army: two to five corps, led by a general
SFC: shore fire-control party, aka "Charlie"

Total War

On the morning of June 15, 1944, when swimming tractors carrying four regiments of Marines crabbed over a fringing reef and dropped into the lagoon off Saipan's western shore, the punishment phase of the Pacific war began. Thirty months of furious struggle had been the prologue to this, the largest amphibious naval operation to date. Midway had been the stopper. Guadalcanal to Bougainville, the first assaults. Tiny Japanese garrisons in the Gilberts and Marshalls fought sharply on strips and curls of coral in early 1944. On Saipan, multiple U.S. divisions went ashore outnumbered. The terror and nihilism of the ensuing four weeks produced a reckoning on a far larger scale.

The battle for the Marianas posed the first major test of the U.S. Pacific Fleet as an integrated transoceanic striking force. Its appearance there drew out the Japanese carrier fleet en masse and provoked the war's greatest naval air engagement, the Battle of the Philippine Sea, as well as a major submarine and air campaign. On Saipan, for the first time in the Central Pacific, U.S. troops faced a large population of civilians, native and Japanese alike. What happened at this unprecedented intersection of cultures would transform the character of the war effort—and stand as a rationale for the pitiless strategic air campaign that the United States staged from the Marianas.

Japanese soldiers had been demonstrating their preference for death over surrender since 1942. But a deeper madness revealed itself on Saipan, where Americans confronted the horror of civilians—women, children, entire families—leaping to their death from high cliffs into the sea. The Japanese army had terrorized them so thoroughly that they, too, preferred suicide to capture. They blew themselves up with hand grenades and killed their own kids. When the tragedy repeated itself on Tinian and Guam, it was clear that the horror had been no accident of local circumstance.

American commanders were quickly alive to the implications of this cruel perfidy. They viewed it as a preview of what awaited them farther to the west. In response, with a subtle cue from their commander in chief, they passed a threshold into total war. To force voluntary surrender from a people who would resist to the end entailed the crossing of a moral threshold. The delirious death-chasing of the Japanese in the Marianas so impressed Franklin D. Roosevelt that he authorized release of a statement, following a major Allied planning conference in September 1944, that served to condone and perhaps even activate a totalistic and utterly merciless approach to war-making. In the Marianas, for the first time, the Army Air Forces used air-dropped napalm on a large scale. Tanks equipped with flamethrowers, and infantry squads carrying liquid fire, turned Operation Forager, as the invasion of the Marianas was known, into an inferno for the doomed. Once the Twentieth Air Force had finished transforming the Marianas into nests for its B-29 Superfortresses, the Japanese home islands reaped a harvest of ashes.

Though the Navy had been wargaming a Central Pacific offensive for decades, the globe-spanning ambition of U.S. Army airpower ensured the fleet would come to the Marianas. With Henry "Hap" Arnold, Curtis LeMay, and Paul Tibbets, among others, eager to strike at the heart of Japan, Douglas MacArthur finally had to cease protesting the Navy's choice of trans-Pacific routes. The Central Pacific drive acquired an irreversible momentum as the carriers of Raymond A. Spruance's Fifth Fleet, under Marc A. Mitscher, and Richmond Kelly Turner's amphibious forces delivered this conquest. The powerful triad of naval power, amphibious heavy lift, and strategic air forces opened an air corridor to Japan that would culminate in history's first uses of atomic weapons. The war would have endured beyond 1945 had Saipan, Tinian, and Guam not been taken.

This narrative is generally fixed at the level of How Things Work, following infantry battalions, naval task groups, air squadrons, and other combatants up and down the line with the goal of illustrating how their power combined in the Marianas to win a hemispheric total war. But a shadow story line runs in parallel: the story of boundaries being broken at every turn. The question of morality in warfare is vexing. Is there a moral way to kill someone? Is a bullet preferable to starvation, starvation to incineration? By law or by norm, who is a legitimate target in a war in which one side will not yield? The innocent deserve to stand in the foreground of this picture. When civilians are on the battlefield, what line separates those who may be killed from everyone else? What limits on conduct should be imposed on commanders caught up in a struggle to the death? Should one nation's pattern of conduct in war guide the strategy and tactics of the other side? Afterward, what rights may a conqueror claim and what tribute may he demand? The moral questions will be left for the reader to answer, but they must be put on the table lucidly, for they arise from any illustration, sufficiently intensive, of the means by which the Marianas were assaulted and defended, and the ends to which they were used.

Though this book contains deep portraiture of Japanese civilians who suffered this whirlwind, my treatment crystallizes around three important U.S. line officers whose work gave shape to the endgame of the Pacific war: Raymond Spruance, commander of the Fifth Fleet; Kelly Turner, commander of Fifth Fleet amphibious forces; and Paul Tibbets, founding commander of the world's first atomic striking force. Some readers may quibble that Major General Curtis LeMay deserved Tibbets's place in this construct, but given that part of my story is the astonishing revolution in weapons technology that was born at Los Alamos and turned loose from the Marianas, the commander who had a hand in developing them, and then actually undertook to deliver them, thereby fulfilling the strategic destiny of the Mariana Islands, is rightfully the third leg of this stool.

Surrounding these men is a host of others of varied ranks who played important subsidiary roles: Holland Smith, Turner's corps commander on Saipan and several subsequent campaigns; Marc Mitscher, commander of Task Force 58, the fast carrier force; Draper Kauffman, founder of the Underwater Demolition Teams; David McCampbell, the Navy's leading ace and an important air group leader; and LeMay, the second commander of the Twentieth Air Force's Marianas-based XXI Bomber Command. Their work brought about the supremacy of U.S. naval aviation, the coming of age of the Marine Corps, the debut of Navy underwater demolition (a byword for today's Navy SEALs), and the aborning atomic age, finally "weaponized" by a Navy captain who flew with Tibbets to Hiroshima. Douglas MacArthur, whose messianism vexed the Navy all along, commanded the stage in the end. With his deft handling of the surrender and occupation of Japan, working by, with, and through a defeated emperor, MacArthur as much as anyone else shaped the legacy of the war beyond its end.

Raymond Spruance had only modest influence at the level of strategic planning. Chester Nimitz, the commander of joint forces in the Pacific

Ocean Areas, was the driver of the war strategy formulated in Washington. But Spruance emerges as the indispensable man in the story of the conquest of the Western Pacific. As both planner and fleet commander, Spruance held a purview that was high enough to indulge his tendency to see war foremost as an intellectual test, but he always situated himself close to the contested shore, where he could grasp its human element in intimate terms. Through all altitudes of perspective, his prevailing attitude of cool rationality, methodically applied, stands in contrast to the frenetic, desperate death cult that was Imperial Japan. Spruance's emotional austerity and analytical mind reflected the same science-mindedness that animated both the Manhattan Project and the Army Air Forces' strategic planners, whom Spruance empowered by his victory. Spruance helped deliver to Japan the storm of atomic warfare, and his men were the first to have a hand in mitigating it, orchestrating the evacuation of American POWs while his medical teams tended to the victims of *"atombomben* disease" at Nagasaki. Their conduct foretold America's rehabilitative approach toward its defeated foes.

The rectitude of President Harry S. Truman's decision to drop the two atomic bombs has become a sacred belief among military history enthusiasts and even among many historians. I wish to avoid a wiser-than-thou pose, for a full consideration of the stakes of the war and of the decisions made in its midst should recommend humility on the part of all. Neither triumphalism, condemnation, nor apology does intellectual or emotional justice to the brute reality of this savage war, the outcome of which could not have been known in the moment. For the narrative historian, re-creating those moments is the aim. I want readers to appreciate how fallible, striving human beings responded to them. In the Marianas campaign, and from there onward, America mastered the vast geopolitics of the Pacific. But all history remains a human story.

The capture of the Marianas was ten weeks into history, and the Philippines were at issue, when the U.S. State Department's director of Far Eastern affairs, Joseph L. Grew, made a broadcast to the nation on Navy Day 1944 paying tribute to the fleet. "No dream castle ever erected could have surpassed the construction in these three years of the greatest, most powerful and certainly the most efficient and effective navy that the world has ever seen," he said. It was Grew's resolve—though not everyone's—to fight Japan to the end, to ensure that its predatory militarism would not rise again. When the Fifth Fleet—that dream castle, that Grand Fleet—came to the Marianas, the means to that end were in hand.

Prologue

Cashiered in Algiers

The confectioner's son was sweet on flying and wanted to know everything about it: "Did you ever loop the loop? Does a tailspin make you dizzy?"

It didn't matter what the answers were. The twelve-year-old swooned at the sight of the World War I veteran when he arrived in his father's office. The aviator jacket, whipcord breeches, leather helmet and goggles: Paul Tibbets thought, *Here is an honest-to-God hero in the flesh.* And to think he was soon to be the man's partner!

The kid's father was a marketer for the Curtiss Candy Company. He had hired Doug Davis for some promotional work. The pilot would take to the skies in his Waco Model 9 and barnstorm the racetrack at Hialeah, and then Miami Beach, anyplace crowds were gathered, to publicize the launch of Curtiss's new chocolate bar. He would shower the world with Baby Ruths.

In the 1930s Florida boom, civil aviation was in a golden age, and so was Paul Tibbets's dad. Having taken the job with Curtiss, he had moved his family from Quincy, Illinois, three years earlier. His timing was right. Real estate developers had conjured Miami Beach out of the sand dunes in the 1920s. After hurricane winds carried much of it away in 1926, the area was on the mend, new residents and holiday revelers returning on Clyde Line steamships or driving Packards and Pierce-Arrows. Business was good. Tibbets & Smith Wholesale Confectioners was the largest candy distributor in the state.

For their mission over Hialeah, Davis and Tibbets père decided they needed an assistant. Paul would help with the payload. They showed him how to tie a little paper parachute to each of the wrapped confections. Then Davis said he would need someone to go aloft with him to toss out the candy while he flew the plane. "I can do that," Paul said in a snap, and they were off to the airfield on Thirty-Sixth Street.

The Waco Model 9 was the most beautiful thing Paul Tibbets had ever seen, with biplane wings painted bright red, fuselage white, trimmed in royal blue—the colors of a Baby Ruth wrapper. He spent that night rigging hundreds of parachutes, finishing so revved up by anticipation that he could not sleep. The next day, when Davis opened up the throttle, thundered down the runway, and began climbing, Paul Tibbets looked down upon his home city, Miami, and considered himself the luckiest kid in the whole land sliding by below.

That was the day his aviation career began. Sixteen years later, in Algiers, North Africa, Major Paul Tibbets stood at a crossroads, contemplating its end.

It was February 1943. Mere months ago, he had counted himself among a club of aviation supermen who thought their airmanship would bring them home no matter what. He had led the very first heavy bomber raids from England into Hitler's Europe. In August 1942, Tibbets was at the head of a flight of B-17s bound for Rotterdam when the flak and fighters struck. He watched as one of his bombers got hit, caught fire, and traced a steepening arc of smoke down to the ground. No parachutes blossomed as John Lipsky and his crew of ten went into the earth.

On the next mission, a raid on German installations near the border between Belgium and France, he nearly joined Lipsky. While returning to England, Tibbets's formation was jumped by Messerschmitts. The yellow-nosed interceptors came in from three directions, but what commanded his attention was a little horizontal slash coming at him from dead ahead. Tibbets yanked at the controls to escape the swarm of tracer bullets, and they flashed by in a blur. Then the windscreen spidered and the cockpit shook, and he felt a hammering wallop on his right side as shrapnel peppered his legs and feet.

His copilot, sitting to his right, got it worse. Lieutenant Gene Lockhart's left hand was torn away, and the stump sprayed blood into what was left of the instrument panel. As Tibbets fought to keep his Flying Fortress on course, it shuddered from hits. Then, as Lockhart faltered, Tibbets felt other hands fighting him for mastery of the controls. It was a colonel from another bomber group, a friend on board for a ride-along. In a full-on panic, the colonel pulled at the yoke, grabbing at knobs and switches.

At risk of losing his feel for the wounded plane—the delicate balance of power to his four engines, his touch with the hydraulics—Tibbets struggled to fend off the interference. He used one arm to hold level flight and the other to put pressure on Lockhart's wound. As cold wind howled through the cockpit, he shouted at the colonel to lay off. But the man wouldn't back off. Though he was well liked and respected, the officer was beyond all reason now. Releasing his grip on Lockhart's wrist, Tibbets planted his left foot on the floor and with his opposing elbow launched a sharp backward jab into the chin of the man, who staggered to the floor, dazed.

Just then, the gunner manning the top turret, above and behind them, took a grazing hit to the head. He slumped down from his Plexiglas dome, landing unconscious but alive on top of the colonel. The German pilot who had stung them must have had fuel enough for only one pass. No more bullets came. Tibbets held his place in formation, exhaling in relief when the English Channel came into view.

Lockhart's vitals stabilized and the colonel returned to his senses, spending the next half hour helping tend to the wounded crew. On final approach at Polebrook, the colonel took over the right seat and popped flares, summoning ambulances as the gunner and the copilot clung to life. Later, after his release from the base hospital, he confessed to Tibbets, "I sure as hell goofed on that one. Paul, you did the right thing. If I ever do it again, I hope the same thing will happen." They remained friends, but Tibbets learned unforgettably how good men can falter under fire.

That series of raids, well planned and successfully carried out, put Paul Tibbets in the conversation as one of the finest bomber pilots and squadron commanders in the Army Air Forces. He was shortly promoted to lieutenant colonel, and when his 97th Bombardment Group moved to North Africa at the end of 1942, he was selected for a staff job at Twelfth Air Force headquarters in Algiers, where he served under Major General Jimmy Doolittle, the revered leader of the 1942 carrier raid on Tokyo that would forever bear his name. And it was there, in Algiers, that Tibbets's fiery pride would push his career to a crossroads.

The moment of truth arrived while Tibbets was seated at a table in a starkly furnished conference room. The Twelfth's operations officer, a colonel named Lauris Norstad, presided over a discussion of upcoming missions. Running an air force from fields scattered on the edge of the Sahara, supplied by single-track mountain railroads, constantly tested their skills in planning. That was Norstad's forte. On this day, though, when he announced plans to bomb the Tunisian seaport of Bizerte, an Axis supply base in North Africa, he stepped on his aviators' toes. Norstad declared that the missions would be flown at low altitude, just six thousand feet. "It was his habit to announce his plans with the expectation that the other officers would nod their agreement and limit their suggestions to a minor detail or two," Tibbets would write. Norstad had expected the usual rubber stamp. Instead, he got straight talk born of brute experience, untempered by tact.

How many bombers could dance on the muzzle of a German 88? The man widely reputed as Europe's hottest B-17 pilot feared that he knew. Aware that the port was protected by antiaircraft guns that were especially lethal at the proposed altitude, Tibbets reacted instantly. "We just can't do it," he said. When Norstad asked him why not, Tibbets snapped, "I've been there. I know: If we send them in at six thousand feet, they'll be wiped out!"

Norstad considered his impertinent aviator coldly, then said, "It appears that Colonel Tibbets has been flying too much. He may be suffering from combat fatigue." If "fatigue" meant learning to live and work with mission loss rates as high as twenty percent, or deadening one's heart to the weekly loss of close friends, then Tibbets might have known something akin to it. But suggesting more was too much. "This handsome desk jockey with the eagles on his shoulders was calling me a coward," Tibbets wrote.

His response was as quick and reflexive as his work to save his crew over northwestern France had been. Tibbets rose from his chair and said, with fists clenched, "I'll tell you what I'm prepared to do, Colonel. I'll lead that raid myself at six thousand feet—if you will come along as my copilot." He rated Norstad as a shrewd and capable planner, but no flier. In his estimation, Norstad had gotten ahead more on a talent for fastening himself to star performers than on earning the claim to be one himself—"an intelligent opportunist" is the label Tibbets would use for "one of the most vain and egotistical officers I had ever met." Tibbets had his share of those traits, too, but he could explain with logbook precision how he had earned them. He could not tolerate a paper pusher telling him or his men how to fly.

Tibbets fully expected Norstad to decline, and when the colonel did not disappoint him, a satisfied Tibbets sealed the doom of Norstad's proposal by coolly detailing the target's extensive flak defenses and their deadly effects at six thousand feet. Wisdom and experience having carried the argument, if not yet the day, the meeting adjourned.

Whispers of the showdown passed around headquarters, and rumors came that some kind of punishment might be coming Tibbets's way.

Shortly he was summoned to see General Doolittle. The legendary pilot had a bombshell to drop.

"Larry Norstad wants to court-martial you. I can't stop him."

Doolittle was a master of all airframes, a wizard at the yoke, but politics was not his game. Norstad was adept at it. One of the star performers he had cultivated was Hoyt Vandenberg, a brigadier general who held two relevant distinctions: He was the nephew of a U.S. senator—and he was Doolittle's own chief of staff. Norstad and Vandenberg were close. With Vandenberg holding political clout in Washington and Norstad keenly attuned to the best ways to use it, Doolittle was powerless to stop the ambitious, back-scratching duo from delivering a comeuppance to Tibbets.

But the architect of the Tokyo raids held a hidden ace, and in fact he had already thrown it on the table by the time Tibbets reported to his office. As Tibbets was absorbing the news of the pending court-martial, Doolittle told him, "I've just received a message from Hap Arnold. He wants an experienced bombardment officer to come back to the States and help with the development of a big new bomber. I've recommended you for the job." The transfer was quickly approved, and Doolittle told him to pack at once; his own staff car was standing by. And just like that, Paul Tibbets was going home.

Seven days later, crossing continents and oceans on lumbering military transport planes, Tibbets landed at Homestead Army Airfield in Miami. He had arranged to stop over to rest before reporting to Washington as ordered. He needed to see his mother. Enola Gay Tibbets had worried constantly about him ever since he entered the dangerous business of flight. His father thought he was crazy for abandoning an early ambition to become a doctor. Home now from war, he understood their concerns. His nerves felt tight; he flinched at the sound of sirens. He took comfort in the words of reassurance his mother often gave him, words that were surely as much a prayer: "I know you will be all right, son." As she set about putting back onto him the thirty-seven pounds he had sweated out overseas, Tibbets reflected on his days as a candy bomber over Hialeah's track, the childhood lark that had propelled him into a life above the clouds. Like any bomber pilot, he understood the accidental nature of any given man's survival, and the capricious way of military life in other respects. With his career-risking encounter with politics in his rearview mirror, he began to see the setback as an opportunity. He was eager to meet with General Henry "Hap" Arnold, the commanding general of the Army Air Forces. With that prospect in view, loafing around Miami soon got old.

The bomber Doolittle had mentioned was the B-29 Superfortress. Then in testing, it dwarfed in size and capability the plane Tibbets had made his name flying. It was so revolutionary that Arnold felt it should move Allied war strategy. The very-long-range bomber had the potential to be a war winner. The need for the B-29 was so great that the Army was rushing it through the evaluation process. Paul Tibbets, with his ticket punched to Washington, would have a conductor's seat on this freight train of a program and its ocean-spanning mission in the Pacific.

When he reported to Washington in February 1943, Tibbets discovered that the program to build the world's largest bomber aircraft was in shambles. On the eighteenth of that month, Boeing's chief test pilot and director of flight research, Edmund T. Allen, had taken off from Seattle in an experimental model XB-29 and suffered an engine fire. For all his savvy, the engineer couldn't extinguish the flames. Quickly they reached the fuel tanks in the wing. That was the end. Allen lost control of the burning plane and crashed into a meatpacking plant on Seattle's industrial south side. Allen, his copilot, nine crew technicians, and twenty people on the ground became casualties of the Army's overambitious schedule. "I don't know whether we'll ever have a B-29," Major General Eugene Eubank lamented to Tibbets.

The plane hadn't even been fully tested yet when the Army ordered it into quantity production in May 1941. Boeing, Bell Aircraft, and the Glenn L. Martin Company collaborated to move heaven and earth, but inevitably flaws remained. The men and women on the assembly line were inexperienced. Bomb bay doors and nose wheels wouldn't retract. Generators had faulty wiring. Interior light switches triggered warning horns. Fuel relays malfunctioned, starter switches started the wrong engines, and electrical shorts burned wires and insulation. The Chrysler-built Wright 3350 engine tended to overheat and catch fire. Every day, problems arose that required painstaking, methodical assault. Twelve-hour shifts weren't enough when the problems took all day and night to fix.

With development at Boeing slowed to a crawl, Tibbets got orders to report to Orlando for a time-killing ground assignment, but then he arranged a return to flying, entering advanced instrument flight training at the 19th Transport Group in Milwaukee. Far from the war, flying lumbering cargo planes that were as likely to carry crates of Baby Ruth candy bars as bombs, he found life decidedly prosaic. Tibbets, ever the combat pilot, wondered when he would see the war again. But for a multiengine aircraft specialist, it proved to be more of an opportunity than he at first realized. Flying with the crackerjack pilots of the transport group was an education that few bomber pilots got. Tibbets had fancied himself as an expert in precision flying, but the rigorous training he received on instruments, and the endless dry runs through emergency situations, expanded his grasp of what a large plane could do. At the end of the tour, he would receive a card certifying that he had met all requirements and was authorized to fly a plane "any time under his own authority."

"I walked out of that office feeling like Mr. God," he wrote. "No one other than pilots of the Nineteenth had such personal clearance authority. I could now take off under zero-zero conditions, if I wished, and no base operations officer could stop me."

In spite of himself and the conspiracies of fortune, he was finally becoming the kind of pilot he had always imagined Doug Davis to be. At some point, Tibbets imagined, the war effort might have use for a pilot like that.

On June 13, 1944, off Saipan, an F6F Hellcat is ready for launch from the USS *Lexington*. The battleship *North Carolina;* carrier *Enterprise,* a light carrier; and a *South Dakota*-class battleship are visible in the distance. (USN)

1

Engine of Siege

Almost two years underway, the war in the Pacific, the Navy's war, was not yet total. Indeed, some were calling it a phony war. Such a term had been applied to the eight-month period of stasis in Europe between the declaration of war by the Allies and their first major operations on Germany's Western Front in 1940. In the Pacific, the year 1943 had been, for the Navy, a year of rebuilding and waiting.

The invasion of Guadalcanal, the first Allied offensive of the war, launched in August 1942, had been carried out on a shoestring, using a back-of-the-envelope contingency plan. The six-month campaign of attrition ended in U.S. victory in February, but nine more months would pass before the Marine Corps attacked another Japanese-held island. While General Douglas MacArthur's troops wore down the Japanese in New Guinea and the Army's Kiska Task Force retook the Aleutians, the Navy endured an interval of gathering and adjustment, of preparation and planning, recruitment and training, construction and commissioning. Mostly the latter, and the shipyards would tell an epic tale.

The lead ship of the *Essex* class of aircraft carriers joined the fleet on New Year's Eve 1942. The 34,000-tonner would emerge as the signature ship of the U.S. Navy's combat task force. Four more would be launched before 1943 was out. A pair of *Iowa*-class battleships reached the Pacific that year, too, as four more of the 45,000-ton behemoths took shape in the yards. A horde of new destroyers and destroyer escorts—more than five hundred of them—were launched in the year's second half alone. But the greatest economies of scale revealed themselves in the building of merchant ships. President Franklin D. Roosevelt had directed the Maritime Commission to produce twenty-four million tons of cargo shipping in

1943. The surge was so great that it might have strained the wine industry's capacity to make bottles to smash against prows on launching day. Surprising shortages cascaded through the supply chain. When grease was rationed for the exclusive use of combat units, a shipyard in Beaumont, Texas, found a substitute to use in lubricating the skids of their ramps: ripe bananas. Personnel officers, short on applicants, hired women and minorities to work in the yards and looked inland from the traditional recruitment fields of the coasts on the hunch that farmers with wits enough to survive the Dust Bowl might be useful in building ships. Coming out of the Depression, no one missed the chance to earn a better wage.

It was this outpouring of manpower and industry that enabled the Navy's long-envisioned drive through the Central Pacific to begin. Since 1909, the "Pacific problem" had been an important object of study, premised upon the Navy's need to retake the Philippines after a Japanese attack. Since 1933, Ernest King had favored a path through the Marianas, which he considered the "key to the Western Pacific." As commander in chief of the U.S. fleet, based in Washington, Admiral King had been pressing the Joint Chiefs to approve an invasion of the islands ever since the end stages of the Guadalcanal campaign. The size and difficulty of the island objectives seized to date—mere apostrophes of coral with little elevation or terrain—paled next to the Marianas, which lay within what Japan considered its inner defensive perimeter.

In November 1943, as Admiral William F. Halsey's South Pacific forces attacked Bougainville, Vice Admiral Raymond Spruance's Central Pacific Force began its oceanic march, falling upon the tiniest and humblest of objectives: Tarawa, a coral atoll in the Gilberts. The sharp, bloody fight was won quickly by the men of the Second Marine Division. The Marshall Islands campaign was next. Spruance took the fleet there in January, delivering the Fourth Marine Division and elements of the Army's Seventh Division to conquer Kwajalein, an infamous prison island that had been the site of many executions of captured Allied pilots and sailors.

When Nimitz, delighted, asked Spruance for his thoughts about what to do next, Spruance proposed jumping ahead immediately to capture Eniwetok, an anchorage in the western Marshalls. It would be the farthest advance by American forces in the whole war. Spruance said he could do it, but only if the carriers handled an important preliminary matter first. Any ships assaulting Eniwetok, he said, would come within aircraft striking range of the greatest Japanese base in the Central Pacific. Spruance proposed sending the fast carrier task force to strike it. Its name was Truk.

The stronghold had never before been glimpsed, much less attacked. Located in the Caroline Islands, Truk was a massive, multi-island lagoon. Its gigantic outer barrier of coral heads traced a triangle that held eighty-four coral and basaltic islands, most of which were substantial enough to mount antiaircraft artillery. Four of the inner islands had airfields. The lagoon's harbors and anchorages were deep enough for major warships, and the base's capacity to support such assets, and its location on the boundary of the Central and South Pacific areas, recommended it as a forward naval base, fleet headquarters, air base, radio communications hub, and supply base as well. From Truk, the Imperial Navy could muster in defense of almost any point on the perimeter of its so-called Southeast Area, all the way into the deep South Pacific.

The question of how finally to deal with Truk would be decided only after Spruance's raid was over. Two options were on the table. The U.S. Joint Chiefs of Staff had approved two offensive paths across the Central Pacific: Either the Navy would assault Truk directly and seize it by June 15, to be followed by landings in the Marianas on September 1; or the Navy would bypass it, leaping straight to the Marianas, with D Day on Saipan set for June 15.

Nimitz thought Truk would have to be taken, but his amphibious planners considered it beyond their means. Truk's barrier reef was a dangerous obstacle to assault, and its enormous radius kept the inner harbor out of range of naval gunfire from outside. The atoll's principal islands themselves, Eten, Moen, Param, Fefan, and Dublon, were within mutually supporting range of each other and thus formidable objectives. The more Nimitz and his people looked at it, the less they liked the odds.

On February 12, Spruance and Mitscher led nine aircraft carriers to sea from Majuro, an anchorage in the Marshalls. Their mission was to stick an arm into the hornet's nest that was Truk and rate the potency of its sting. If the raid, code-named Operational Hailstone, went well, no Japanese planes would remain on Truk to interfere with the landings on Eniwetok. The results would bear, too, on the choice of the next strategic objective.

Though Spruance had a reputation as a battleship man, he had won his greatest fame leading carriers. In June 1942, in the Battle of Midway, he exercised tactical control over the *Enterprise, Hornet,* and *Yorktown* while their aviators destroyed four Japanese carriers. For the loss of the *Yorktown,* the United States won a victory that would resound in history. Elevated thereafter to serve as Admiral Chester Nimitz's chief of staff, Spruance commanded a desk at Pearl Harbor. It wasn't until August 1943 that he returned to sea to command the Central Pacific Force. Its fast carrier element acquired its muscular size nearly coincidentally with Spruance's rise. It dwarfed in every dimension the carrier group he had led at Midway. The *Essex*-class carriers were made mighty by their association with an air group of ninety planes, made up of a fighter squadron, a dive-bomber squadron, and a torpedo bomber squadron. By 1944 these squadrons used best-in-class aircraft, the F6F-3 Hellcat, the SB2C-1 Helldiver (or the older SBD-5 Dauntless), and the TBF-1c Avenger, respectively.

The argument about how to employ the Navy's multiplying roster of carriers—singly, as in the past, or in groups—was settled not so much by persuasion or battle experience as by the surging output of the yards. As far as combat tactics went, the standard assumption that they had to hit, then run, because they were impossible to save against a determined air attack, was yielding to a new reality. Quantity was not merely a luxury but a revolution. By concentrating their aircraft and flak defenses, the carrier task force could hold an air attack at bay. Their planes had radio transponders that enabled specially trained fighter direction teams to recognize them and direct them using long-range search radars. New shipboard combat information centers collated and communicated this critical information. With common doctrine governing the use of combat air patrols, ship formations, and air defense tactics, the carrier task force acquired a flexibility that multiplied its reach and staying power. Several groups of three or four carriers, operating together, could quite well take care of themselves. Approaching Truk, Spruance and Mitscher were about to prove it.

They had arranged their nine carriers in three task groups, each steaming just over the horizon from the next. Spruance flew his three-star flag in the battleship *New Jersey,* riding in a great circle with the carrier *Bunker Hill* and the light carriers *Monterey* and *Cowpens.* Over the horizon to his north was the group built around the *Enterprise,* the *Yorktown,** and the light carrier *Belleau Wood.* To his south came the *Essex,* with the *Intrepid* and the light carrier *Cabot.* Deployment in groups allowed concentration or dispersion as a mission might require. Typically the force could be seen in its totality only in an anchorage. At sea, such a spectacle required a few thousand feet of altitude.

Ninety minutes before sunrise on February 16, the fleet closed to within ninety miles of Truk and, on order from Mitscher, as tactical commander of the carriers under Spruance, turned into a force-five wind and began

---

* The replacement for the original carrier *Yorktown* (CV-5), which had been lost at Midway.

launching planes. One by one, with the release of chocks and the roar of Wright radial engines, a swarm of F6F-3 Hellcats took wing over the spray of onrushing whitecaps.

At the break of morning light, the leaders of each of the five participating fighter squadrons led their flights in a wide turn to the west and circled, allowing the others to join up. After the seventy Hellcats had gathered, they turned out on a heading that would take them west, harbingers of a two-day operation to neutralize Truk as a threat to U.S. ambitions in the Pacific.

The swarm had droned along for less than an hour when their target appeared before them. Illuminated by the sun just above the eastern horizon, it resembled a cluster of mountains contained in a huge coral-fringed tub. Truk's barrier reef, a round-cornered triangle, encompassed a lagoon. As they came nearer, twelve planes from the *Bunker Hill* flew high cover at twenty thousand feet, while two divisions of four ranged more widely as scouts. Two dozen Hellcats from the *Enterprise* and the *Yorktown,* Mitscher's flagship, formed the low-attack group. Like-sized contingents from the *Intrepid* and *Essex* came in at medium altitude. The boss of the *Bunker Hill* air group, Commander Roland H. "Brute" Dale, flew separately as the strike coordinator. His job was to make sure the remaining forty-eight planes, his strikers, found the right targets to strafe, assisted by three other air group commanders who served as target observers.

Twelve planes from the *Intrepid*'s Fighter Squadron Six circled the atoll at a distance, waiting for their high cover to reach its station. A pilot from this group, Lieutenant (j.g.) Alex Vraciu, was mystified to find no Japanese planes in the air to intercept. Little did the U.S. pilots know that the base's naval commander had just relaxed his guard, a decision that was almost coincident with the arrival of enemy carriers off his shores. For the previous two weeks, Truk had been on high alert, ever since American search planes reconnoitered it on February 4. Knowing that his pilots were exhausted, Vice Admiral Masami Kobayashi, commander of the Fourth Fleet, had ordered most of them to shore leave in the barracks district located across a causeway from the main airfield at Dublon. The subsequent lapse in air search allowed Spruance to approach Truk undetected and left a sizable portion of the available fighters on the ground when the American swarm arrived overhead before sunrise.

On a fighter sweep, U.S. Navy tactical doctrine boiled down to this: Keep your Hellcats high. Concentrate them in force. Clear out the enemy fighters first. Then get after the airfields. Don't circle and tarry; it only gives the enemy a chance to scramble. Save for the initial five or so minutes of circling necessary to allow the Hellcats assigned to high cover to take station, this was exactly what Dale and his pilots did, if not necessarily in that order. It wasn't until Fighting Six was pushing over to strafe that they discovered that some enemy fighters were airborne after all. Pacific Fleet intelligence had estimated that not fewer than seventy-five fighters would be on hand to defend Truk, along with twenty-eight scout bombers, twelve torpedo planes, twelve medium bombers, five large patrol planes, and fifty-eight floatplanes, a total of 190 aircraft. "Not fewer than" proved to be the operative words. The Japanese pilots indeed did in the end get to their planes. U.S. fliers would count more than three hundred of them in the air and on the ground during the day.

As flak puffed the sky around him, Alex Vraciu, with his wingman, Lou Little, found himself in the tail of a spiral of Hellcats bearing down on Moen Island, the site of one of Truk's principal airfields. Ten Hellcats ahead of him were into their dives when, to be safe, Vraciu looked back over his shoulder. No rookie, he knew the clouds offered nooks and crannies for enemy pilots to use as cover for ambush. His caution likely saved his life. There he saw it at last, the dim form of a Mitsubishi A6M Model Zero, known as a Zeke, diving, its cowling and wings twinkling with gunfire.

Vraciu pulled back his stick, and Little followed him into a climb. Turning sharply toward the enemy plane, Vraciu maneuvered to bring the plane into his gunsight, then fired a burst that forced the pilot to break off and dive. That's when he noticed the enemy planes above him—a gaggle of dozens that included every model the Japanese flew. The fight was on.

Alex Vraciu was just one among many similarly situated young pilots, full of ambition, in thrall of their tribe, in the grip of their squadron's logo and mojo and full of stories about the wise old hands who had forged them. He entered pilot training while he was still a senior at Depauw University in Muncie, Indiana. Joining his first squadron at North Island, San Diego, Vraciu was singled out as a talent by the commander, Butch O'Hare, who made the rookie his wingman. The skipper proceeded to hand down the lessons of air combat as they had been taught to him—via the "humiliation squad."

This powerful pedagogy threw new pilots fresh from training into mock dogfights against a cadre of experienced veterans. As O'Hare had learned from fighter ace legends such as John S. "Jimmie" Thach and Jimmy Flatley, now Vraciu faced his own learning curve. Flying against

O'Hare, a Medal of Honor recipient, Vraciu performed well enough to raise eyebrows. And so O'Hare brought him into a new program to develop night fighting tactics. In a "bat team," a pair of Hellcats flew with a radar-equipped Avenger to hunt enemy planes flying at night. And it was on just such a mission, one night off the Marshalls in November 1943, that O'Hare was killed while defending the *Enterprise* task group against a night air attack. His loss stoked Vraciu's Pearl Harbor fever. The desire for revenge became the driving force of his life wearing wings. He was already an ace by the time the carriers reached Truk.

Sizing up the enemy formation, Vraciu knew that he had enough airspeed, about 250 knots, to lose any enemy fighter that latched onto his tail. The fast and sturdy Grumman fighter could outturn a Zeke at high speed. By diving down to gain speed, he could execute a chandelle, pulling up in a steep climbing turn that would cause his pursuer to shoot past him. By making a barrel roll, Vraciu could pounce down on the Zeke as it flew by. Vraciu had him right where he wanted him, this pilot who settled in on his tail.

As Vraciu's opponent tried to follow him through the chandelle, the Zeke lost its grip on the air and spun out at the top of the turn. Vraciu was lining up a killing deflection shot when he noticed more enemy fighters turning down on him from above. His zeal gave way to prudence. He declined the shot, letting the enemy pilot dive out and escape while he figured out a better way to win.

Vraciu was pleased to find Lou Little faithfully holding on his wing. By scissoring back and forth in opposite interweaving S patterns, he and his wingman made the enemy think better of getting on their tails. Known as the Thach Weave after its creator, Jimmie Thach, the skipper of Fighting Three, the tactic allowed two fighter pilots to cover each other's vulnerable six o'clock position against more maneuverable aircraft such as the Zeke. In this way Vraciu gradually coaxed the enemy to descend. Once the Japanese yielded the advantage of altitude, Vraciu noted, they seemed to lose their resolve. Gaining the tail of three Zekes in succession, he set them on fire and watched the brown-and-green-mottled aircraft splash into the lagoon. The morning belonged to the Americans. After a sharp ten-minute engagement, Vraciu noticed more than a few Japanese pilots swinging down slowly, suspended from silk. Some of them were still wearing pajamas.

The fighter sweep swarmed over the great atoll, devouring Japanese planes in the air and on the ground. Led by Fighting Six's exec, Lieutenant G. C. Bullard, Vraciu's squadron made twelve passes over the strip, burning row upon row of planes. Firing on a Zeke and setting it afire, Teddy Schofield of Fighting Five followed the enemy pilot in a descent toward the airfield on Eten Island. The Japanese flier was probably wounded, for he didn't square his wheels on touchdown. His plane rolled enough to catch a wingtip on the runway, then started cartwheeling. Turning over and over, the Zeke rolled across a hangar apron, igniting three parked torpedo planes, and as Schofield watched, rooting hard for a few more turns, the Zeke came to rest, a wreck, just short of a big four-engine plane parked at the end of the flight line.

Lieutenant Bullard of the *Intrepid* was not among the pilots who joined up at the rendezvous area. En route to it, he had spotted a Japanese light cruiser hustling toward the atoll's northern exit, North Pass. Rallying his division, he led a low-altitude strafing run. A burst of flak from the ship hit his Hellcat, and his engine lost power. Turning out to sea, the pilot descended and slowed, finally easing his fighter into the wave tops and jerking to a halt in an explosion of white spray. As it began to sink, he struggled free of the cockpit. Another pilot dropped a life raft and winged over to occupy the attention of the cruiser and its gunners. Strafing the ship, he set fire to its floatplane as it sat on a catapult. That excitement gave Bullard enough of a diversion to paddle toward a small islet about five and a half miles west of North Pass. He eventually made it, and he spent his considerable free time there spelling his name in rocks for the benefit of his eventual rescuers. Just a few miles away, several Japanese destroyers could be seen, apparently waiting to rendezvous with the light cruiser fleeing the harbor. These ships meant to make a break for it.

Mitscher's air plan was engineered in time and motion to produce a continuous flow of planes over a target, the effect of which could be simply expressed: *Never give your enemy an even chance.* Strikes were staggered at short intervals, with each carrier on pace to launch about six of them during the day. The predawn fighter sweep was barely thirty minutes off the decks when the next strike, heavy with bombers, took to the sky. This one targeted shipping. Each wave consisted of about nineteen Helldiver or Dauntless dive-bombers, nine Avenger torpedo bombers, and a dozen Hellcats. Pilots were instructed to prioritize aircraft carriers, battleships, heavy cruisers, light cruisers, submarines, oilers, auxiliaries, and destroyers, in that order. Aircraft installations and fleet-servicing facilities were secondary targets.

Some forty ships were caught in the harbor, but the news of their discovery was disappointing—none were prizes. The commander in chief of the Japanese Combined Fleet, Mineichi Koga, had divined what was coming after American search planes had flown over the base two weeks before. The superbattleship *Musashi,* reported to be at Truk prior to the Marshalls landings, had withdrawn to Palau. So had all the carriers and heavy cruisers. But it is the nature of a storm to show an implacable disinterest in the things it is on course to hit.

Arriving by midmorning, the U.S. pilots struck Japanese auxiliaries anchored near Truk's central islands and flung fragmentation clusters into the aircraft dispersal areas. Fuel storage was saved for the final wave so that other targets would not be obscured by smoke. Commander Dale alerted an inbound flight of Helldivers and Avengers from the *Bunker Hill* to the presence of a Japanese cruiser about twenty miles southwest of the atoll. They found the *Naka* right where Dale had reported her and left her sinking, bow and forward turret awash.

The rest of the afternoon saw the destruction of Japanese warships escaping through North Pass. The leader of the exodus was the *Katori,* an old cruiser. With the destroyers *Maikaze* and *Nowaki* and the minesweeper-trawler *Shonan Maru,* she was attempting to spirit herself away to Japan with an armed merchant cruiser, the *Akagi Maru,* that was carrying more than six hundred personnel. At 10:38, Admiral Mitscher picked up their chatter and alerted his group commanders of this new target.

The discovery was of interest to Spruance as well. He directed the battleship *Iowa,* the heavy cruisers *Minneapolis* and *New Orleans,* and four destroyers to leave the carrier formation, ring up full speed, and join the chase. He had decided to lead it himself. What developed was a race to the kill between Mitscher's pilots and their boss's boss.

More than a few men on Spruance's staff thought it was a hell of a thing for a fleet commander to take tactical command of a surface combat squadron. Normally, Spruance was discretion personified. The fifty-seven-year-old never fancied himself a tactically minded officer. He was a strategist, a thinker, a student of the big picture. These gifts had made him a star as an instructor at the Naval War College, and later as the right hand to Nimitz in the year after Midway. Many thought him the smartest officer in the Navy. One who knew him well said, "I remember being told once that the very great mathematician, Sir Isaac Newton, only wrote his books to prove to others what he, himself, saw at a glance. It was this way with Admiral Spruance. It was his genius which led him invariably to the heart of a problem." His elevation to command the Central Pacific Force, soon to be re-named the Fifth Fleet, had been a reward given by Nimitz out of loyalty, confidence, and concern for the national interest.

As a child in Baltimore, Spruance had grown up lonely. His mother, the dominant parent, was remote. A thoroughgoing intellectual, Annie Ames Hiss had a searching, hungry mind and an ambition that led her to travel and study internationally, enabled by the quiet complaisance of Spruance's father. She was said to feel "that everyone should have a family but that one was too many," and so, when his brother Philip was born with a mental handicap, the strain of it led her to send Raymond to live with his three maiden aunts in East Orange, New Jersey. By the time of his enrollment at the U.S. Naval Academy, he was socially withdrawn, a bit awkward, and conditioned to comfortable, quiet self-sufficiency. Though he deplored military routine and found the Annapolis curriculum trade-schoolish and technical, his intellectual hunger didn't keep him from finishing twenty-fifth among the 209 midshipmen in the class of 1906. Joining the fleet, he soon made a name for himself as an engineering specialist.

Spruance was an ascetic, unusually conscious of fitness and diet. He went on long walks in order to regulate himself; physical fitness correlated with sharp thinking, he thought. He mixed a fine drink, but he seldom had one himself except when the right moment and company persuaded him to flavor his orange juice with rum. His friends, though diverse in back-ground, generally had the traits of gentlemen: proper and correct, with en-gaged and interesting minds. Standing with him on the flag bridge of the *New Jersey,* his chief of staff, Captain Charles J. "Carl" Moore, was just such company. Now fifty-four, Carl Moore had served as engineering officer on Spruance's first command, the destroyer *Bainbridge,* in 1913. Moore, who was professorial in bearing, was a meticulous planner and a superb writer of operation orders. By 1944, these elaborate documents acquired the heft of book manuscripts as the fleet grew in size and task forces in complexity. Moore's driven, task-oriented manner often collided with Spruance's need to detach so as to keep his mind uncluttered. When he sat down to read a novel, he permitted few interruptions. Though Moore was often impatient with him, Spruance serenely insisted on the privilege. In bitter moments, the hardworking chief of staff was inclined to think his boss lazy.

Captain Moore knew the admiral's heart and mind, though perhaps not quite well enough to grasp what the present adventure off Truk was all about. Considering the power of the U.S. aerial armada overhead, he did not see the need to take battleships and cruisers hunting. He felt that this joyride was the product of something even worse than laziness: poor planning. The detachment of the battlewagons was not a surprise in itself—the operation order had provided for the possibility. What no one had anticipated, least of all his own dumbstruck staff, was that Spruance himself would descend to lead them.

As he watched Truk's mountain-range-in-a-bathtub profile ease closer on the *New Jersey*'s port bow, Moore suspected it had more to do with the legend of Truk itself than with the value of anything they might actually sink. Perhaps, Moore thought, Spruance found it irresistible to risk a 120,000-ton battle line on a close run near Truk because, as was a matter of general knowledge around Pearl Harbor, Nimitz himself often expressed the ambition to fly his flag over the Japanese bastion. It would be just like Spruance to give the Navy's biggest guns a role in the task. A traditionalist, Spruance had always considered battleships to be the heart of the fleet. His two years in command of the USS *Mississippi* ending in 1940 were possibly the proudest of his career. At a time when the power of a naval squadron had little to do with its largest guns but was flown about piecemeal, fastened to the bellies of planes controlled by swarms of flying men, Spruance clearly could not resist the chance to seize a last chance to touch a glorious age.

Leading the westward chase, the *New Jersey* was pushing past twenty-five knots when planes from the *Essex* set upon the battered Japanese convoy. Strafed by Hellcats and popped with a near miss from a Dauntless, the *Maikaze* was left limping, her hull seeping oil. A short distance away, some Avengers found the *Katori* circling with the *Akagi Maru*. They glided down and dropped, landing two bombs on the cruiser's afterdeck, which raised an internal explosion and roils of yellow smoke. When the planes were gone, the pall of smoke rose five hundred feet into the air. It was a beacon to Spruance, thirty miles out and closing.

Dale made a quick turnaround on the *Bunker Hill* and was just airborne again when a Japanese pilot found Spruance and stalked his squadron of heavies through holes in the clouds. Targeting the *Iowa,* he released a bomb that hit the water about a hundred feet off the battleship's starboard side. The close call led Captain Moore to suggest that Spruance order the group into a circular antiaircraft formation, but the admiral dismissed him abruptly. "We're not out here fighting aircraft. We're out here fighting surface vessels. I want to remain in column." That was how any battleship man had learned to fight. And so they plunged along, the *New Jersey* lead-ing the *Iowa, Minneapolis,* and *New Orleans,* with the *Izard* and *Burns* screening on her bows and the *Charrette* and *Bradford* on either beam.

With most of the ships in the lagoon afire, swamped, or sunk, the pilots striking Truk sought out smaller craft to strafe. Patrol boats and fancy yachts stood in for worthier targets. A pilot from the *Enterprise,* noticing burning enemy ships north of the atoll, announced, *"Any strike leader, there is a damaged Japanese cruiser just to the north of the lagoon. Come sink it."* This brought an immediate response from an in-charge older voice, Admi-ral Mitscher: *"Bobcat leader, this is Bald Eagle. Cancel your last. Do not, re-peat, do not sink that ship. Acknowledge."*

Translation: *Stay out of Admiral Spruance's way. The boss wants his kill.*

The *Izard* and *Burns* quickly ran down the *Akagi Maru.* Her captain tried to evade them, veering left and right, but the zigzagging only helped the destroyers overtake her and stop her with gunfire. The *Burns* then joined the *Bradford* in firing on the *Katori,* which was already down by the stern and listing to starboard. Spruance ordered the *Minneapolis* and *New Orleans* to close and finish her.

The *New Jersey* passed the *Shonan Maru* close to port and riddled the minesweeper with five-inch rapid fire from eight hundred yards. Almost instantly the ship's cargo of ordnance and powder was revealed, blowing up with a detonation so intense it left behind a single small, empty boat amid wreckage. One man was seen clinging to it, and two more held fast to a ladder floating in the water.

The *Maikaze,* crippled, had managed to fire a spread of torpedoes at the *New Jersey.* The sight of four wakes boiling in his direction brought startle-ment and humiliation in equal measure. This exercise, Moore said, was sheerest folly. Without a signal officer, a plotting team, or liaison to the fire-control or gunnery departments, he felt Spruance's staff had no busi-ness conducting surface battle. As the torpedoes passed astern and two more bubbled across the *Iowa*'s wake, Spruance turned to his flag secretary, Charles F. Barber, eyes twinkling with amusement, and said, "That would have been embarrassing." But Carl Moore wouldn't leave it at that. He suggested to Spruance that he turn over control of the force at once to the cruiser commander, Rear Admiral Robert C. Giffen, whose staff was well drilled in tactical surface action. The suggestion was moot; Spruance had anticipated the recommendation. Giffen's cruisers were already putting an end to the brief fight, and Spruance had already decided to give Giffen command once it was over. The *Minneapolis* lashed out at the overmatched

Katori, which was engulfed by blue splashes from the *Minneapolis* and orange ones from the *New Orleans.* The *Iowa,* too, found the range. When she finally went, turning on her beam ends away from the direction of the *Iowa*'s fire and capsizing, she was gone in two minutes or less, her crew a total loss. The scrappy *Maikaze* was next. She was still popping away with her after turret when Spruance's flagship turned loose her own secondary battery. A large explosion amidships produced a sheet of flame that ran forward and aft until the destroyer was burning from stem to stern. She broke in half and sank.

Spruance and Moore found themselves upset by the brutal ends delivered to the Japanese ships. Ashore at Tarawa several months earlier, they had seen war up close and whiffed its waste and loss. "I'm getting rather hardened to seeing bombs and shellfire on the beach, with gas dumps and magazines blowing up high into the air," Moore would say. "But to see fine ships explode and burn and sink without a chance to retaliate is new to me, and a little depressing if not actually sickening. As Raymond said, it is war at its worst."

The last of the Japanese destroyers, the *Nowaki,* escaped over the horizon as the *New Jersey* fired some last sixteen-inch salvos at her. But her luck survived and she vanished in the glare of the late-day sun and haze. By four o'clock she was gone from the radar scopes, too.

Once upon a time the great Lord Horatio Nelson, seeing his fleet rebuffed by enemy shore batteries, declared, "A ship is a fool to fight a fort." No more. The carrier task forces of 1944 had more than enough clout to exploit the universal weakness of a ground fortification: One always knew right where it was going to be. A carrier force could strike here or there, out of nowhere. Under cover of radio silence, overcast skies, and a saddling fog, it could move in undetected and strike so hard that no return blow was possible. A revolution in naval mobility was under way, and arguments would revolve about it through the months ahead. Though he lacked an aviator's wings, Spruance had been a principal player in the revolution. By any measure, it was lights out for Japan's great Central Pacific base. That the victor at Midway had delivered the manhandling of Truk from the bridge of a battleship would irk the Navy's aviation evangelists, but as long as Spruance had Mitscher and his carriers with him, he would always have a claim to being a carrier man. And that would annoy them even more.

Sandwiches were going around to the crews at their stations when a flight of Dauntlesses approached Spruance's column on an opposite course. A straggler, evidently following them, banked into a turn and flew toward the *Iowa*. The officers standing on the battleship's port bridge wing, including Captain John L. McCrea as well as his exec, gunnery officer, and senior aviator, recognized the plane as a friendly and ordered their talkers to pass the word: "Friendly plane. Track but do not fire." The *Iowa*'s gunnery officer announced over the intercom, "Friendly plane." But these words were misheard. The crews of several gun mounts on the port side, undeceived by their own eyes, opened fire. As the plane came closer, the pilot was seen slumped to one side of the cockpit. Passing dangerously close to the battleship's upper works, quickly losing altitude, the Dauntless fell off on one wing and crashed about five hundred yards to starboard. Lieutenant Paul E. Tepas had been looking to make a message drop to advise the battleships of the results of the recent air search. Neither the pilot nor his rear seat gunner, Harold F. Leach, survived.

The tragic incident was an hour old when the *Iowa* reported a single target to the west. The *Burns* was ordered to investigate. At length the destroyer's lookouts sighted a small target backlit by the setting sun. It was a Japanese submarine chaser, just four hundred fifty tons. She promptly began firing at the *Burns* with her forward three-inch gun. The destroyer replied, leaving the small vessel sinking by the stern. Approaching a scattering of survivors in the water, the captain of the *Burns,* Lieutenant Commander D. T. Eller, radioed his division skipper, in the *Izard,* to ask, "Shall I bring back some souvenirs?" In short order the *Burns*'s whaleboat was lowered over the side and its coxswain was steering toward the human flotsam. There were perhaps sixty sailors in the water. Almost all of the swimmers refused to cooperate, fighting all efforts to get them on board. Some vigorous persuasion got six of them to change their minds. After they were rescued and the whaleboat was hoisted back on board, Eller decided the fate of the majority by way of cold military logic. "In view of the probable rescue of survivors by the Japanese and their return to further action, and of their refusal to be rescued by ship's boat or lines, three depth charges set on depth fifty feet were dropped in the survivor area to destroy them."

Spruance did not personally exult in any of this, but he did order his ships to hoist their largest ensigns, known as "victory flags," as they finished circling the stronghold. If his pursuit of a heavy metal battle line fantasy proved to be quixotic, giving way to the brutish reality of a messily conducted mercy killing, so be it. Philosophers' ideals about "proportionality in killing" were starting to seem quaint. This had long ago ceased to be a gentleman's war.

★ ★ ★

After dark, Marc Mitscher's three carrier groups were biding time east of Truk when the *Intrepid* made radar contact with a single plane low on the water to the southwest. The Japanese snooper skirted the perimeter of Rear Admiral Alfred E. Montgomery's task group for about half an hour before disappearing to the west. Shortly a second plane appeared. Orbiting briefly beyond antiaircraft gun range to the east, it, too, vanished. Singly and in small groups, snoopers would haunt Mitscher through the night. Another pair of planes came close enough for screening ships to loft several volleys of radar-directed antiaircraft fire, which seemed to chase them off. Then, just before midnight, another soloist appeared on the scopes and closed the task group.

It came in low and so purposefully that trained eyes determined that the pilot had a radar fix on them. At twenty miles, the fighter director team in the *Enterprise* vectored a radar-equipped Hellcat from the *Yorktown* to intercept. The U.S. pilot gained tail position and pressed the chase for seven miles but never actually spotted the enemy. Worse than that, as the night fighter closed with its own task group, Montgomery had to order his anti-aircraft gunners to hold fire. It was just past midnight. As the Hellcat pilot studied his scope, hunting for the bogey amid the electronic interference of "sea return" and searching the darkness ahead for a telltale spout of exhaust flame, the Japanese torpedo bomber, last seen just four miles out, became a phantom. A commander now had to assume the worst.

Montgomery ordered his ships to execute an emergency evasive turn. Too late. A torpedo out of nowhere hit the *Intrepid*. The blow to the starboard quarter bent and jammed the rudders, opened the steering compartments to the sea, and produced a shock wave strong enough to toss a pair of Dauntlesses overboard and throw a sleeping Alex Vraciu out of his rack. Six sailors in nearby compartments were killed outright by concussion, and six more were lost, never to be recovered, when their twenty-millimeter gun tub was shorn from the hull and fell into the nighttime sea.

Once Captain Thomas L. Sprague's crew had restored steering control via the ship's engines, Mitscher ordered the *Intrepid* to form up with the cruisers *San Francisco* and *Wichita,* the light carrier *Cabot,* and four destroyers and set course for Eniwetok. At sunrise, after Spruance brought the *New Jersey* and company to join the *Bunker Hill* group, Mitscher began opening the range from Truk. The fast carrier task force, seemingly omnipotent by day, had been tagged by a dashing Japanese pilot whose torpedo plane was last seen on radar hauling away to the west, fading from the scope. At noon on February 17, after sending two last morning air strikes over the lagoon, Spruance and Mitscher agreed that it was time to go home.

The strike on Truk, that acid test of the Navy's Central Pacific war strategy, would be fodder for a hundred ready-room bull sessions, a wellspring of exploits for veteran pilots to lord over newcomers fresh from the humiliation squads. For a cost of twenty-five planes in combat and eight operational losses, as well as the dozen men lost on the *Intrepid*—a total of forty-one killed and seventeen wounded—Mitscher's pilots destroyed more than two hundred Japanese planes, burned seventeen thousand tons of stored fuel, and sank forty ships: three light cruisers, four destroyers, nine auxiliaries, and two dozen cargo ships small and large. If Spruance had missed a trophy haul of imperial capital ships, his success in both planning and execution impressed the toughest of all tough customers, the commander in chief of the U.S. fleet, Admiral Ernest J. King. Spruance's staff operations officer would write, "King was well pleased, not only with Spruance's excellent planning but with the almost perfect timing of his forces in the execution of these plans. He considered the operation a noteworthy example of the results that may be expected when good staff work is implemented by efficient fleet operations under superior leadership." In a dramatic stroke, King's men had killed the potency of that hard syllable, *Truk,* long spoken like a gulp in the throat. The fast carrier task force had come of age.

The captain of the *Minneapolis,* Richard W. Bates, indulged in an extensive personal comment in his after-action report. After remarking on the Japanese military character in a tone of both warning and admiration, and marveling at the totality of surprise that Spruance had managed to spring, he wrote, "What lesson then does all of the above indicate? Simply this: that the fortunes of war are blowing heavily in our favor at present and that we should take advantage of this fact by maintaining immediate and continuous offensive pressure against the enemy, exploiting this command of the sea to the fullest, to the end that we may advance our own position ever farther westward at minimum cost to ourselves."

On February 18, Spruance was making rendezvous with his fleet oilers when two regiments of troops assaulted Eniwetok's two principal islets, supported by Mitscher's *Saratoga* carrier task group. The assaulters from the Fourth Marine Division and the Army's Seventh Infantry Division finished quickly, overwhelming the eight thousand Japanese defenders, who were distributed piecemeal across the atoll, for a loss of just 372 killed and sixteen hundred wounded. The plan broke with the tradition of attacking flanking positions before moving to a main event. But Nimitz favored surprise, which denied the enemy time to build up his defenses. He had kicked off the Marshalls campaign by sending his amphibious forces straight to the group's largest and most important island, Kwajalein, bypassing preliminary objectives.

Spruance was making plans to address the next item on his operation order—an air raid on a Japanese seaplane base, at Ponape east of Truk—when a dispatch arrived that delivered the verdict on his recent performance. It was time to make preparations to assault the Mariana Islands. Nimitz ordered the fast carriers to strike the group's three largest islands, Saipan, Tinian, and Guam, on February 21. Japan's greatest base, Truk, would be bypassed, not invaded. The success of Operation Hailstone suggested that no island, no fort, could stand against the power of the fast carriers. It was time to push west.

Spruance and Mitscher exchanged blinker light dispatches between their flagships, the *New Jersey* and the *Yorktown,* exchanging views on how to carry out this foray into *mare incognitum.* U.S. naval forces had never gone so far west in strength, and never at all since Jimmy Doolittle's Tokyo raid in April 1942. Impressed with Mitscher's returns, Spruance finally advised him to go it alone. The carrier commander would take his three groups northwest to the Marianas while Spruance returned to the Marshalls to accept a promotion to four-star admiral and begin planning Operation Forager, as the culminating stage of the Central Pacific drive was known. Late on the eighteenth, with refueling complete, the *New Jersey* left the *Bunker Hill* task group and set course eastward with a lone destroyer as her escort. At Majuro, Spruance would turn his attention to Forager's plans. Mitscher's carriers would prepare the way for it. Air strikes on the three target islands would commence in three days.

2

On the Western Warpath

Though strategy is always a function of geography, it is a seldom-noted fact of the Pacific campaign that the best path across the Central Pacific was prescribed not only by physical geography and the location of the enemy's bases, but by anemology, the science of winds. Islands were assets in direct proportion to their utility as air bases, and air bases had value only if their runways aligned with the east-northeasterly trade winds. As one of the Pacific Fleet's masters of amphibious warfare, Rear Admiral Harry W. Hill, would observe, such islands "could almost be counted on the fingers of two hands. These, naturally, the Japs had developed as bases, and there were no more! So when we moved across the Pacific, and needed an air base, there was no alternative. We simply had to take one away from the Japs. It's just that simple, and so badly misunderstood by so many historians."

A few of these island airdromes—notably Mili, Wotje, Maloelap, and Jaluit in the Marshalls—had been bypassed because alternatives were near. But the trade winds had ensured a bloody destiny for Guadalcanal, Tarawa, Kwajalein, Roi, and Eniwetok to date. Owing to the state of the art in bomber design and the vast potential of the B-29, struggling through development, the most prized island asset of all was to be found south of Tokyo, within range of these new silvery airframes hauled along by a quartet of Wright R-3350 Duplex-Cyclones: the islands of the Marianas group.

It had been nine long months earlier, in May 1943, at the Trident Conference in Washington, that the joint U.S.-British Combined Chiefs of Staff had promulgated "The Strategic Plan for the Defeat of Japan." The plan articulated the goal of "the actual invasion of Japan following an overwhelming air offensive from bases in China." The Combined Chiefs approved a schedule to launch "an effective bomber offensive against vital targets on the main islands not later than fall of 1944. Only such an offensive can, at a sufficiently early date, reach and destroy the vital elements of Japan's transportation structure, and the nerve centers of her economic, military, and political empire." With this plan, the global mission that Hap Arnold had envisioned for his B-29 Superfortress fleet was cemented into policy. Pacific islands were not considered up to the task of basing such an enterprise—at least not at first. The U.S.-British Combined Chiefs of Staff concluded in August 1943 that only bases on the Chinese mainland had the capacity to house bombers.

Six months later, at the Cairo Conference, the idea of taking the Marianas was first put on the table, among many options given to the Combined Chiefs. General George C. Marshall did not at first share the Navy's interest in carrying the Central Pacific drive through the Marianas, but the stalemate broke when Hap Arnold voiced support of just such a move. By aligning with Navy priorities in the theater, the Army Air Forces secured for itself a primary role in the worldwide plan to bring down the Axis. The B-29 wings needed a strategic base in the mid-Pacific.

To bring the air war to Japan, Arnold had thought at first, for expediency's sake, to base his B-29s in China. This was in deference to his president, who was eager to help Chiang Kai-shek's nationalists as soon as possible. But the AAF chief knew that better bases would be needed if his planes were to sustain an aerial assualt. Chinese airfields would be hard to supply and vulnerable to ground assault.

All along, Arnold and his key planners, foremost among them Major General Haywood Hansell, the head of the USAAF's European strategic command and a principal author of "The Strategic Plan for the Defeat of Japan," preferred that the B-29s operate from the Marianas. The Army had coveted the islands as theater air bases well before the Superfortress was in the picture. With the arrival of the long-legged bomber, the Marianas acquired a new value. Even as MacArthur urged the Joint Chiefs to cancel the entire Central Pacific campaign and put all energies into his effort in the Southwest Pacific, the Army—in the persons of Arnold and Hansell—emerged as an unlikely Navy ally in the debate about where to strike next. In November 1943, King prevailed: The Joint Chiefs agreed that B-29 strikes should be staged against Japan from the Marianas in December 1944. Hap Arnold would be well pleased to let King's naval infantry conquer some better real estate for him.

The layout of the Pacific's island landforms held an inescapable strategic logic in the age of the long-range bomber. And so, eager to push the time-table and pleased to find the Army and Navy in agreement on something at long last, the Joint Chiefs authorized the Central Pacific drive to continue in parallel with MacArthur's offensive.

Truk, bypassed, could be isolated and left to die on the vine with enough attention from land-based bombers. With D Day in the Marianas coming on June 15, Arnold would soon have a new nest for his Superfortresses.

As the fast carriers were pounding northwest for their preparatory strikes on the Marianas, one of Admiral Mitscher's aides found him at his usual perch on the open-air wing outside flag plot, his tactical control center on the flagship. He was seated on a stool, feet perched high on the gyro-compass stand. Mitscher wasn't given to expression, so the aide was struck by his smile of satisfaction as he looked out over the *Yorktown*'s flight deck. Noticing his visitor, Mitscher volunteered, "I was just thinking, at home the trout season opens today."

Such reverie was normal for a commander idling between combat missions. Born in Hillsboro, Wisconsin, and schooled in Washington, D.C., Mitscher survived a terrible underperformance at the Naval Academy and began his career, appropriately, in the domain of mavericks—aviation. In 1916 he earned his wings as one of the first three dozen naval officers to do so. As "aviator number 33," he spent the next twenty years promoting the interests and capabilities of a separate naval air force. He spent the first two years of the war in Washington at the Bureau of Aeronautics, the Navy agency that oversaw carrier aviation, working under his friend John Towers, aviator number 3, who was a vocal advocate for the most aggressive possible use of the fast carrier groups. In the battle that stood as the denouement of the first six months of the war, Midway, Mitscher had been captain of the carrier *Hornet*. His performance was another disappointment. When through poor leadership and poor navigational tradecraft most of the *Hornet*'s air group failed to find the Japanese carriers, disaster ensued. The *Hornet*'s Torpedo Squadron Eight went its own way and was destroyed nearly to a man over the Japanese fleet. In a profession in which reputation can rise and fall like the price of a penny stock, the fiasco might have been a career ender for Mitscher. A saying credited to Captain Arleigh Burke, who was soon to become Mitscher's chief of staff, always applied: "The difference between a good officer and a poor one is about ten seconds."

* * *

The phenomenon of one person's confidence in another derives from a whole series of successful acts, but it can be destroyed at a blow. After Midway, Mitscher lost a chance to command a carrier task force and served out a punitive tour leading a wing of patrol planes at Pearl Harbor. His time on the sidelines might have ended his career. But he got a second chance when Nimitz sent him to serve as Halsey's land-based air commander in the South Pacific. There, in April 1943, good fortune had given it to Mitscher, and to the fighter squadrons of his command, to carry out the interception mission that killed Admiral Isoroku Yamamoto, commander in chief of the Japanese Combined Fleet. Redeemed by the success of his P-38 Lightning drivers, he was tapped nine months later to take over the CentPac fast carrier force after his predecessor, Rear Admiral Charles A. Pownall, was relieved for his lack of aggression in the Marshalls. John Towers, the commander of Pacific Fleet air forces, was furious with Pownall and Spruance for leaving the carriers "immobilized" in support of landings. After the light carrier *Independence* took a torpedo, Towers lobbied for Pownall's ouster. He wanted that battleship man, Spruance, gone, too; Towers, it was said, coveted his job.

Spruance had been satisfied with Pownall, and Mitscher was not his first choice as a replacement. Very likely Spruance didn't consider him an intellectual peer. But after the dismantling of Truk, it was hard to miss the way Mitscher got the best out of his men. He stayed close to his pilots and made their concerns his own. He observed the *Yorktown*'s flight operations whenever he could, watching his pilots enter the pattern, approach, catch the wire, respot, and get hauled to the elevator and taken below, around and around again. They were "his boys." He talked to them constantly. In every decision he made, their well-being was foremost in his mind. Mitscher would cultivate in his second life a relentless culture of competitive performance among flag officers in command of his task groups. He and Spruance developed a respectful partnership. "Their personalities were completely different," Burke said, "but they were warm friends and they did understand each other perfectly."

The carriers and fast battleships were the public face of the Navy. But the Pacific Fleet had another branch that was equally critical. Though Mitscher's combatants were peerless as destroyers, they were not conquerors. The job of conquest fell to another Navy entirely, one whose job was to assault and hold the galactically remote islands that formed the only solid ground in the oceanic theater.

Spruance's element of amphibious warships—to be known as the Fifth

CHAIN OF COMMAND, FIFTH FLEET
(formerly Central Pacific Force)

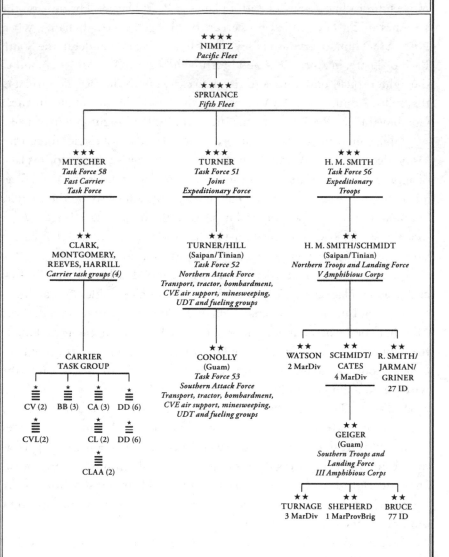

★★★★
NIMITZ
Pacific Fleet

★★★★
SPRUANCE
Fifth Fleet

★★★
MITSCHER
Task Force 58
Fast Carrier
Task Force

★★★
TURNER
Task Force 51
Joint
Expeditionary Force

★★★
H. M. SMITH
Task Force 56
Expeditionary
Troops

★★
CLARK,
MONTGOMERY,
REEVES, HARRILL
Carrier task groups (4)

★★
TURNER/HILL
(Saipan/Tinian)
Task Force 52
Northern Attack Force
Transport, tractor, bombardment,
CVE air support, minesweeping,
UDT and fueling groups

★★
H. M. SMITH/SCHMIDT
(Saipan/Tinian)
Northern Troops and Landing Force
V Amphibious Corps

★★
WATSON
2 MarDiv

★★
SCHMIDT/
CATES
4 MarDiv

★★
R. SMITH/
JARMAN/
GRINER
27 ID

CARRIER
TASK GROUP

⬚ CV (2)   ⬚ BB (3)   ⬚ CA (3)   ⬚ DD (6)

⬚ CVL(2)   ⬚ CL (2)   ⬚ DD (6)

⬚ CLAA (2)

★★
CONOLLY
(Guam)
Task Force 53
Southern Attack Force
Transport, tractor, bombardment,
CVE air support, minesweeping,
UDT and fueling groups

★★
GEIGER
(Guam)
Southern Troops and
Landing Force
III Amphibious Corps

★★
TURNAGE
3 MarDiv

★★
SHEPHERD
1 MarProvBrig

★★
BRUCE
77 ID

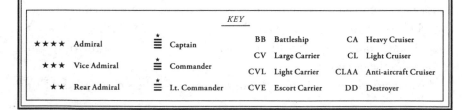

KEY

★★★★   Admiral

★★★   Vice Admiral

★★   Rear Admiral

⬚ Captain

⬚ Commander

⬚ Lt. Commander

BB   Battleship

CV   Large Carrier

CVL   Light Carrier

CVE   Escort Carrier

CA   Heavy Cruiser

CL   Light Cruiser

CLAA   Anti-aircraft Cruiser

DD   Destroyer

Amphibious Force, or just Fifth Phib—was a swarm of ugly ducklings. "Queer types of craft," their commander, Vice Admiral Richmond Kelly Turner, called them. Nameless except for their Scrabble bag of acronymage, they were equally drab in appearance: shoe boxes with bow ramps, armored swamp buggies, and swimming six-ton cargo trucks. Accompanied by a dedicated cadre of supporting warships, a sluggish fleet of old battleships and miniature aircraft carriers, the waddling seaborne boxes were suited for carriage and cargo, not seakeeping or speed. They did not lend themselves to dramatic photographic portraiture. Functional and blue-collar efficient, the troop-carrying vehicles were ferried to their targets fastened to davit cranes or stored in the holds of considerably larger ships, to be released at the target to charge the dug-in enemy. They were the wage laborers of the fleet who carried its power ashore. Turner and his group commanders understood its nature. The logo they chose for the Fifth Amphibious Force was a sinuous dragon, crazed and slashing, risen from the heart of the sea.

When Turner arrived at Pearl Harbor on August 24, 1943, to take his post under Spruance as commander of the Fifth Phib, he was in the process of turning their en-masse use into a refined military art as he drove Nimitz's island-hopping land grab across the Central Pacific. With his arrival at the Makalapa headquarters, it was as if a brisk wind had entered the building. Carl Moore wrote home, "Turner is here and he is not any more open minded than ever, but I am glad he is here, as he moves and I like movement."

This was understatement. Turner moved, yes. And he argued. He demanded, shouted, and demanded some more. Heaven help the junior officer who got facts wrong in Turner's presence, because he usually knew his junior's business as well as that officer did. "Kelly Turner was a strange individual in that he liked to test his officers," Colonel Robert E. Hogaboom, his chief of staff during the Marshalls campaign, said. "He would give identical assignments to two different officers without letting either of them know, and then let each of them bring the solutions to him and he would weigh them." According to one of Turner's top deputies, Rear Admiral Harry W. Hill, "He was intolerant of mistakes and bitter in his denunciation of the offender. He was a terrific driver of himself as well as those under him, and was inclined to ride roughshod over anyone who opposed him."

Turner was easy to misread. "On first meeting, he suggests the exacting schoolmaster, almost courtly in courtesy," wrote Holland M. Smith, the

Marine general who as Spruance's corps commander knew Turner as well as anyone did. "He is precise, affable in an academic manner, and you are tempted, in the first five minutes of acquaintance, to make the snap judgment that he is a quiet, softly philosophic man. Nothing could be farther from the truth. Kelly Turner is aggressive, a mass of energy and a relentless taskmaster. The punctilious exterior hides a terrific determination. He can be plain ornery. He wasn't called 'Terrible Turner' without reason."

And yet there was a deep-seated warmth beneath the bluster. Of all people, the gentlemanly Raymond Spruance was one of Turner's closest personal friends. A native of Stockton, California, Turner had been Spruance's shipmate on the battleship *Pennsylvania* before World War I. As teaching colleagues and neighbors at the Naval War College in Newport, Rhode Island, the two men struck up a close friendship. Though poles apart in personality, Spruance and Turner considered each other intellectual peers. Turner, who finished fifth in the Naval Academy's class of 1908, was fond of Spruance's two children and seemed to regret that he had none of his own. When Spruance was given the Central Pacific Force, he knew exactly whom he wanted at the helm of his amphibious arm: Kelly Turner would command the tractor fleet and his old friend Holland Smith his troops. Spruance had known Smith since the Marine general's days as commander of the Atlantic Fleet Marine Force; Spruance, as commandant of the Tenth Naval District in Puerto Rico, had worked with him during Caribbean exercises. He had decided long ago: When war came, these would be his men.

Turner's elevation to major command was another case, like Marc Mitscher's, of forgiveness opening a way forward from early career error and ill will. When he directed the Navy's War Plans Division in 1940, Turner was one of the Navy's fiercest partisans, maneuvering within the war-planning bureaucracy so as to shut down Army interference with the Navy's preferred strategies and policies. As a member of the Joint Board, an Army-Navy agency that reported directly to the president and that handled war planning before the creation of the Joint Chiefs of Staff, Turner gained a position of outsized influence. He served as a member of both the Joint Planning Committee, which wrote the overall war plans specifying which campaigns would be pursued, and the Joint Board, which gave approval to them. In this way he acquired the authority to conceive and also to execute, empowered with an effective veto over ideas he didn't favor. According to Carl Moore, who served on several boards and committees with and under him, Turner had a particular distaste for strategies and ideas that originated with his rival service. Turner stoked what Moore called the "violent friction" between the Army and Navy, heating up subjects ranging from the division of command authority between the services to the allocation of aircraft among combat theaters. "The general result was that there was tremendous delay, friction, and difficulty in anything that the Joint Board tried to do unless Turner approved of it," said Moore.

Conceived by midlevel naval and military officers under the loose supervision of the secretaries of Navy and War, a war plan known as Rainbow Five was promulgated in May 1941 and verbally approved by President Roosevelt. It was the product of decades of arguments between Army and Navy planners about the best way to wage a worldwide two-front war. Evolving from a strategic blueprint for defeating Japan, the Orange Plan, which was the product of a renaissance in strategic planning that began with America's emergence as a Pacific military power after the Spanish-American War, Rainbow Five codified the earliest designs of the Orange Plan, including an amphibious advance through the Central Pacific beginning with landings in the Gilberts and Marshalls as a prelude to dealing with Truk in the Carolines.

That Turner's career survived for him to carry out the Rainbow Five offensive in late 1943 was something of a miracle, following the disasters of the early Pacific war. As the Navy's head of war plans, Turner had controlled the dissemination of intelligence, both data and its analysis, from Washington to the field. When it was revealed after the Pearl Harbor attack that Hawaii's Army and Navy commanders had not received important information, including the fact that Japanese agents in Honolulu had reported to Tokyo the berthing locations of U.S. warships at Pearl Harbor prior to December 7, 1941, Turner, though he had been the agent of this disastrous stovepiping, used his position to sidestep the crosshairs of inquiry. In July 1942 he left Washington for good when he was assigned to command the landing forces that took Guadalcanal. There, another first-order disaster would be among the first entries in his war diary: With the loss of four cruisers and a thousand men in the Battle of Savo Island, he stood again on the precipice of professional oblivion.

A congressman whose son had been killed in the battle railed in Congress about the defeat. These contretemps held up Turner's promotion to vice admiral, according to Richard L. Conolly, one of Turner's amphibious group commanders. Navy Secretary Frank Knox sent Rear Admiral

Conolly to Capitol Hill to spread the message that Turner had done a fine job, all told, and deserved his promotion. When Savo Island was brought up, Conolly said, "Whether or not Turner was entirely responsible for that is something that will be decided by history. I'm not here to sit in judgment on him and I don't know too much about it. But whatever he has done since, and what he did in putting through that landing at Guadalcanal, was a marvelous piece of work. If he made a mistake, you've got a lot more to consider on the positive side of the ledger." Turner's promotion went through soon thereafter. For such a high master of bureaucratic aikido, there was little sport in shifting responsibility to junior commanders and working to make sure his superior, Frank Jack Fletcher, absorbed the wrath of the Marine Corps over the Navy's lackluster performance in the South Pacific campaign's first days.

In his final review of Turner's conduct, Admiral King exonerated both him and his counterpart, Rear Admiral Victor Crutchley, RN, in charge of cruiser dispositions that fateful night. "Both found themselves in awkward positions and both did their best with the means at their disposal," King wrote to Chief of Naval Operations Harold R. Stark. Perhaps King had relaxed his famous rigor because everyone knew a man of Turner's talent and vigor was needed as the Navy faced a steep learning curve in global naval war. King did not have the luxury to wield the ax. Commanders would never improve if they were not permitted to learn from failure. Mitscher had done so, to the nation's reward. Turner would be allowed to grow into higher command as well.

When Terrible Turner showed up at Pearl Harbor in August 1943, Carl Moore was surprised to find him friendly and solicitous. "I could talk to him about most anything," Spruance's chief of staff said, "and he frequently came to me about matters that he didn't want to talk to Spruance about." After his success taking the Marshalls, Turner was thoroughly exhausted. "Kelly was operating under a forced draft," Admiral Nimitz said. "There were times during this period when I wanted to reach out and shake Kelly." But Spruance promised to handle him when things got tough, and he did. He understood something of the darkness Turner was dealing with.

Turner had admitted his alcoholism to Spruance's wife, and his bouts of drinking, long a concern of Spruance, began to alarm his contemporaries as they witnessed them. But there was no denying he was a star. One of his former staffers wrote to Turner from Washington at the end of February 1944, "Nine out of ten people around here want to go to work for you, so don't be surprised if you start getting fan mail." A comment often attributed to Ernest King went, "When they get in trouble, they send for the sons-of-bitches"; in that way and more, Kelly Turner was a leader whose time had come.

No one else in the Navy quite seemed to match his high-speed intellect, tireless capacity for work, and creativity in the old discipline of amphibious warfare. Spruance, the big-picture thinker, understood that he needed Turner and his stickling, process-driving way. Spruance would say of him, "He is able to handle a mass of details that leave me completely muddled." He had long known Turner to be deeply interested in the future of naval warfare, be it carrier aviation or amphibious operations. During a 1939 exercise off Puerto Rico, Spruance had spied his old friend standing in the surf wearing swim trunks, signaling the coxwains of a pair of experimental landing craft to punch their throttles into the heavy surf. Watching the two boats ride up onto the beach and then retract under their own power back into the surf, Spruance saw Turner's commitment to doing new things at a time when budgets weren't friendly to innovation. Turner knew there were no new ideas under the sun. He would look in admiration upon the amphibious operations undertaken by the British and the Japanese before him, knowing that they, too, were not pioneers but students of an art that dated to the American Revolution and indeed all the way back to antiquity. He was not too proud to borrow ideas from history, even recent history; some of his prototypes were inspired by his enemy. The Japanese had used some interesting new types of boats in China, he noted. The largest ship in the amphibious navy, the Landing Ship Dock, or LSD, was developed on a Japanese model.

But Turner's contributions were numerous, and they fell into three distinct areas, as he would explain. The first was "technical equipment"—vehicles—which ranged in size from the larger transports and landing ships that served as "lift" to the smaller "connectors" that carried troops ashore—amphibious tractors, known as amtracs or alligators, swimming tanks, and various smaller landing craft. The second contribution he called "heavy power," a seagoing assault force of mechanized infantry large and well armed enough to attack from the sea, then stay and keep what they had taken. This, simply put, was the United States Marine Corps, whose hard-charging force commander in the Pacific, Holland Smith, would emerge as Turner's closest partner in arms. The third contribution was the use of warships for shore bombardment, both preparatory fires that preceded the landings and close-support fires that backed up the troops once they were ashore. The old battleships had not gone out of fashion yet, not even after Pearl Harbor.

Technical equipment, heavy power, and naval bombardment were major fields unto themselves. But even with their successful practice, Turner knew he would have to sustain and support the troops for the time they needed to get ashore and make their conquest. Stores of oil, rations, ammunition, and medicine had to be carried to the beach in proper sequence by tractor, lighter, winch, and crane. Shore parties had to land pallets and sleds and deliver them to fighting men under fire. Naval and air support had to be brought to bear at the right time and place, and not a moment too late. The assault forces would push off the beach to set up a defensible perimeter and leave room for the next wave, but never so fast as to outstrip the supply train. Constructing a smoothly running machine out of all those parts required Turner and everyone under him to master hundreds of fine points of men, matériel, process, and control. Although he had a directing hand in everything, he always remained a student at heart.

The strike on Truk suggested that the Fifth Fleet's carrier power was strong enough to kick in forbidden doors, then linger safely and break things for a while. Whether its amphibious echelon could take large islands such as Saipan or Guam was another question, however. It was very much on Spruance's and Turner's minds as Admiral Mitscher's pilots filed out of their ready rooms and prepared to turn themselves loose on the Marianas for the first time.

Destruction of Japanese planes and facilities was not the most pressing goal of the strike's first wave. Aerial photography was. Because the Pacific Fleet had no photos of the Marianas that were less than twenty years old, the carrier pilots would be giving ground commanders their first hard information in nearly a generation on what their men would face on Saipan, Tinian, and Guam. And so Mitscher's strike groups included several Avengers that were equipped as photoreconnaissance planes. Carrying photographer's mates instead of rear gunners, they circled and swooped as the strafers went in, taking aerial exposures of the coastlines, defenses, and other facilities on Saipan and Tinian and assessing the damage inflicted by the attacks.

Late on the afternoon of February 21, a Japanese search plane from Tinian, the headquarters of the Imperial Japanese Navy's land-based First Air Fleet, spotted Mitscher's task force about three hundred miles east of the Marianas. Mitscher radioed Spruance, "WE HAVE BEEN SIGHTED BY THE

ENEMY. WE WILL FIGHT OUR WAY IN." Aware of the damage that a single plane had done to the *Intrepid* off Truk, Carl Moore took Mitscher's announcement to his boss and asked if it might be prudent to cancel the raid. Spruance disagreed.

Though the First Air Fleet mustered twenty torpedo-armed Mitsubishi G4M medium bombers, known as Bettys, among other modern aircraft, the pilots were mostly students who could do little against the U.S. task force at night. On the night of the twenty-first, three waves of Japanese bombers found Mitscher's task force and attacked. Easily deterred by radar-controlled antiaircraft fire, which claimed a dozen planes, they were rated as "very definitely B squad material." Sporadic air attacks continued after sunrise. Though none of the planes scored, the nuisance of evasive maneuvers delayed Mitscher's plan to launch before dawn.

On the morning of the twenty-second, the weather was so heavy that the pilots of the TBM Avengers had to use their onboard radar to locate Saipan and Tinian. Flying amid heavy squalls, Mitscher's air groups roamed, laying waste to whatever they could find. Aviators from the *Monterey,* pouring down upon Tinian, found fifty "new and shiny" planes, mostly Bettys, stretched along both sides of the northern airfield's runway and service aprons. They burned at least six before smoke washed away the view. Six U.S. planes were shot down in these attacks, including a pair of Hellcat pilots from the *Yorktown,* Lieutenant Woodie McVay and Lieutenant (j.g.) A. F. Davis, who were last seen disappearing into the clouds to strafe Aslito Field.

When reports reached the carrier task force that pilots had ditched offshore, the submarine USS *Sunfish,* on lifeguard duty west of Tinian, was summoned to search. But faced with torrential downpours and nearly continuous radar contacts with Japanese planes and ships, the sub managed to spend just three and a half hours on the afternoon of February 23 investigating five of the six sets of coordinates that were relayed to her, while struggling to establish two-way VHF radio contact with friendly aircraft.

In two days of raids, Task Force 58 pilots would claim seventy-two planes destroyed on the ground and another fifty-one in the air, as well as several cargo ships caught in harbor. But the photographic intelligence was more valuable still. Shot from various altitudes and angles, the aerial photos would not be adequate for a proper mapping to scale with accurate elevations, but they met the need for a general orientation.

Saipan, fourteen miles long by six miles wide, was Japan's administrative headquarters in the Marianas. Since Japan had seized the archipelago under the League of Nations mandate following World War I, the island had been the site of a large colonization project. Japanese civilian workers had joined the native Chamorros in working a thriving sugar plantation there. Garapan, on Saipan's west coast, was the island's humble capital. Its major seaport, Tanapag Harbor, near Garapan, was a supply and fueling point for ships bound to and from Japan. A large airfield in the south, Aslito Field, provided air defense of the island and a stopover for pilots island-hopping between Japan and the South Pacific. The west coast of Saipan was bounded by a fringing coral reef. The north and east coasts had no coral but were bordered by sharp cliffs. The southeast coast was a gaping concavity that formed a large bay. South of Tanapag Harbor on the west coast, the village of Charan Kanoa had a large sugar refinery and a railway that linked it to the fields. In February, Nimitz's intelligence staff estimated that the island had a garrison six to eight thousand strong, twenty-five thousand Japanese civilians, and another three thousand native Chamorros.

Nimitz's interest in the craft of intelligence ran deep. The new command he set up in Hawaii in September 1942, known as Intelligence Center, Pacific Ocean Areas (ICPOA), had faced vituperous opposition from careerist intelligence officers in Washington going back to the run-up to Midway. After borrowing space at the headquarters of the Hawaii naval district's supply office, Nimitz realized he needed Army cartographic capability, too. Maps designed to show tides, currents, and oceanographic features might not be useful to commanders needing to study land areas, so he integrated the 64th Engineer Base Topographic Battalion at Fort Shafter into his operation. With Army participation, the Oahu-based intel shop became a joint operation and gained another letter in its acronym. Under command of Brigadier General Joseph Twitty, JICPOA became a highly dynamic and growing organization. One of its analysts, Donald "Mac" Showers, said, "We had only one objective: that was to win the war."

The first officer in charge of JICPOA's cryptanalyst section, Commander Joseph J. Rochefort, was widely rated a genius and received well-deserved credit for the codebreaking feat that had enabled the ambush at Midway. The Estimates Section, which divined enemy intentions based on radio intercepts and cryptanalysis, expanded to include sophisticated photoreconnaissance and interpretation units. The first aerial reconnaissance photographers were pilots who held cameras out of their cockpits as they flew. As the years advanced, professionally trained photographer's mates used stereoscopic techniques based on using two cameras, by which multiple planes flying at the same altitude and speeds could produce imagery of great accuracy, as well as oblique coverage that, clouds permitting, showed the elevations of ground features as well as the existence of cliffs and caves. Nimitz eventually moved his photo interpreters from their offices in a Kodak film-processing shop in downtown Honolulu into CINCPAC's intelligence nerve center, located on Makalapa Hill near his own bombproof headquarters. There, in a complex of labs and drafting rooms, a team of landscape architects, geologists, and Army and Navy engineers under Captain Howard J. Dyson, USN, studied aerial photos through illuminated magnifying glasses and stereoscopes to produce contour maps, rubber relief models, and larger-scale target grid maps of the islands. These were printed on eight-inch-square sheets, laminated and stapled as booklets, and given to pilots, ship captains, and ground commanders to help them coordinate their work.

Nimitz's eyes in the sky were complemented by eyes under the sea. Anticipating a Japanese buildup in the Marianas after Mitscher's strike, he and his top submarine man, Vice Admiral Charles A. Lockwood, deployed a line of submarines in a blocking position north of the islands. Since the fall of the Marshalls, the Japanese high command had ordered reinforcement of the Marianas, even though they were unsure where the next landing would be. On February 22, a convoy of five Japanese ships approaching Saipan crossed paths with the USS *Tang*. Her skipper, Lieutenant Commander Richard H. O'Kane, attacked and sank two cargo ships. The *Sunfish* put down a pair of freighters on February 23, and then O'Kane got three more. But with MacArthur making mischief in New Guinea, pushing toward the Philippines, the Japanese Combined Fleet leadership suspected their base at Biak would be the next target of an American invasion.

The Japanese, less adept than the Americans in the use of intelligence and hobbled by the unending dysfunctional feud between their army and navy, found some unlikely sources in the ongoing spy game. In January 1944, FBI agents had burst into the safety deposit vault in the Bank of New York branch at the corner of Sixty-Third and Madison and taken into custody, kicking and scratching, one Velvalee Dickinson. She was a dealer in antique dolls whose correspondence with ostensible foreign customers contained an elaborate cryptogram of double-talk. Her references to antique dolls were flagged by wartime censors to the FBI, and with good reason: They actually indicated the presence and operational status of U.S. warships she had seen in West Coast harbors. But such baroque schemes did little to help the Combined Fleet commander in chief, Admiral Miniechi Koga, see the future—in fact, in the spring of 1944 his own days were distinctly numbered.

On March 22, as Kelly Turner and his staff were fixing D Day at Saipan for June 15, Spruance, flying his flag on the *New Jersey,* led three groups of Task Force 58 from Majuro to strike Palau in support of MacArthur's advance on Hollandia, New Guinea. The mobility of carrier power was never more impressive as Mitscher carried out this round-trip of six hundred nautical miles, launching the first attacks against Palau on March 30. The next day his carriers hit the western Carolines, about three hundred fifty miles south of Guam. The principal result of these attacks—beyond the immediate harvest of twenty-nine minor auxiliary ships and 214 aircraft destroyed or damaged on Yap and Woleai, at a cost of twenty-five U.S. planes—was to force Admiral Koga once again to pull the Combined Fleet beyond the reach of U.S. carriers. Koga and his staff left Palau on March 31, boarding a pair of flying boats for Davao. En route, his plane ran into a typhoon and was never seen again. The Japanese naval command, jarred by the death of the Combined Fleet commander, remained convinced that Biak, off New Guinea, would be invaded next.

On April 7, following the Palau raid, Spruance and Mitscher returned to Majuro in the Marshalls. King considered it "almost miraculous" that the carriers had run the gauntlet from New Britain to Palau and back unscathed by land-based aircraft. Nimitz joined them to discuss the fleet's continuing support of MacArthur. Then the Pacific Fleet and Central Pacific Fleet commanders flew to Pearl Harbor to join Turner in planning the Marianas operation. After their departure, Spruance's flag was hauled down from the foretruck of the *New Jersey* and broken again in the heavy cruiser *Indianapolis,* moored alongside. There was no rest for Mitscher's pilots. Three days later, on April 13, Task Force 58 sortied again from Majuro in three groups to support MacArthur's landings at Hollandia. Beginning on April 21, the carriers operated in the Southwest Pacific for four days, then hit Truk again for good measure en route back to the Marshalls.

By now, Truk's mystique was gone. The swagger that the great Japanese base once seemed to have was stolen by the naval aviators who had neutralized it. In April, on board the *Lexington,* the "West of Tokyo Missionary Society" was chartered to celebrate the raid on Palau, which was situated west of the Japanese capital's line of longitude. In this "zealous attempt to convert the reluctant and retiring Japanese fleet," the charter read, "the missionaries, by their enlightening bombs, converted over thirty heathen ships to scrap iron." The first membership card was issued to Jimmy Doolittle, made an honorary missionary for his Tokyo raid. Admiral Mitscher was given the second card as "chief ministering missionary." The skipper of Air Group Sixteen, Commander Ernest M. Snowden (a son-in-law of the Army's top aviator, Hap Arnold), was given the title "chief evangelist."

But the élan of the naval air corps didn't save one of its best, Alex Vraciu, from taking a faceful of flak on the April replay of the Truk raid. The ace had managed to return to sea after the damaged *Intrepid* went to the West Coast for repairs. With nine air-to-air kills on his résumé, he wangled a transfer to the *Lexington*'s air group. Diving on one of the atoll's airfields, his Hellcat took a hit from ground fire. Fragments shredded his hydraulic lines and spidered his windscreen, showering him with bulletproof glass. Shaken but still airborne, he returned to the Lady Lex, only to find his landing gear jammed. Vraciu was forced to ditch alongside a destroyer, which promptly picked him up.

Chatting with the captain in the pilot house as the small ship pitched along in the screen, Vraciu asked permission to send a message to the *Lexington*. The captain agreed, and Vraciu scribbled a dispatch to his old friend Gus Widhelm, Mitscher's air operations officer. "GUS," the shutter lamp flashed, "GET ME OFF THIS DANGED ROLLER COASTER OR I'LL VOTE FOR MACARTHUR SO HELP ME."

When no response came after an hour, Vraciu began to wonder about his friend's sense of humor—and his future in naval aviation. Then it came—directed to the ship's captain. "IN ORDER TO CONSERVE AIRCRAFT, DESIRE YOU RETAIN MY BIRDMAN UNTIL WE REACH ULITHI, AT WHICH TIME WE WILL TRANSPORT HIM BACK VIA RUBBER BOAT."

Widhelm allowed forty-five minutes for Vraciu to ponder this before signaling the destroyer to come alongside and give the pilot a high line back to his carrier. As Vraciu glided to the hangar deck, Widhelm stood grinning ear to ear. He took Vraciu to see Mitscher and introduced him as "the character who sent that message." Mitscher adored his aviators for their maverick spirits. If President Roosevelt was informed of the electoral preferences of the Navy ace, or if Mitscher imposed any discipline because of it, the record does not say.

Shortly after Nimitz's final planning directive concerning the Marianas invasion reached his principal commanders on March 28, Spruance's Central Pacific Force received a new name: the Fifth Fleet. When the Joint Chiefs of Staff formally approved Operation Forager, MacArthur saw the end of his long-cherished plan to roll up the South Pacific once and for all with the longed-for conquest of Kavieng and Rabaul. He was further aggrieved by orders to give back to Nimitz all the transports and cargo ships that CINCPAC had allocated to him for the canceled operations. The Navy's most important show was getting on the road.

Spruance's fleet—composed of Mitscher's carriers, Turner's amphibs, and Holland Smith's troops—would strike into hostile waters to commence prelanding air strikes and the bombardment of Saipan on June 13.

3

In Turner's Train

From the harbor at Kahului, Maui's inland roads led through fields of sugar and pineapple, and then to a plantation where amphibious warriors were grown. At Camp Maui, a sixteen-hundred-acre training range leased from agriculture interests and private estates, the men of the Fourth Marine Division worked through the lessons of their recent history on Kwajalein. A hundred miles to their southeast, on the Big Island of Hawaii, in the saddle between the snow-topped volcanoes of Mauna Kea and Mauna Loa, the troops of the Second Marine Division reckoned with their own worst blooding under fire at Camp Tarawa, named for the costly November 1943 battle in the Gilbert Islands, the first step on the Pacific Fleet's Central Pacific warpath.

The men of the two Marine Corps divisions assigned to carry out the invasion of Saipan were intensely history-minded. The first draft of that history had been written in their blood, and they pored over its curriculum, for it would have personal consequences. What had happened to them under fire impressed them, taught them, and changed them. The peculiar field craft of amphibious assault separated them from other troops. There was an art to mastering the transient ribbon of territory where sea meets land. In sixty days' time they were going to have to prove their mastery anew.

The 27th Division of the United States Army was part of the order of battle of Major General Holland M. Smith's Fifth Amphibious Corps, too. The idea that, for the first time, a Marine general would command an echelon at that high a level, with an Army division reporting to him as well, was something of a turning point for the naval infantry service, as Holland Smith saw it. "I cannot describe the exultation that swept through Marine ranks when it became known that for the first time we were to operate in the field as organic units instead of a joint command," he would write. "We were a Marine field army, commanded by a Marine general, going into action independently against the Japanese, and the opportunity to enhance the prestige of the Marine Corps was so great that it stirred every man in my command. No more of that odious 'secondary force' talk at the Naval War College."

Neither Major General Thomas E. Watson nor any of his commanders in the Second Marine Division forgot Tarawa. The landings there had spiraled into a near disaster following a terrible misjudgment during planning. Anticipating five feet of water over the reef, planners had failed to forecast the local neap tide. When the landing craft reached the reef, they found their hull bottoms grounding on the coral fringe. The troops were forced to disembark there, five hundred yards from the shore. Marooned on the reef, they had to wait for a ride with nowhere to take cover. Under heavy fire, many ended up frogging helplessly in the deepwater lagoon with full packs. By the time the assault waves got to shore through a murderous cross fire, it was only by high-caliber leadership at the company and platoon level that the operation kept a pulse. If a captain got killed, a lieutenant knew exactly what to do; the same with sergeants and corporals. Colonels got an education, too. As Turner's chief of staff at the time, Robert E. Hogaboom, said, "There was a conviction on the part of those that were leading the Second Division that they were going to overrun the island fairly quickly." Optimism got people killed. The best antidote was hard-minded realism.

Realism was the principal product of the training range. Hawaii's diverse terrain, from mountains to desert-dry hillsides to large coastal areas, from spiny basaltic lava to the dusty plantation roads of the Parker Ranch, offered plenty of space for live-fire exercises, artillery and mortar drills, tank maneuvers, camouflage school, night assaults, jungle training, demolitions, judo, and flamethrower practice. For all the excellent features of the training area, it lacked one key feature. "Unless you know your enemy, you do not know how to face the enemy. You must know his ways," a man with the Fourth Division said. "They taught us in training that the Japanese were persistent. In other words, they didn't care about life, but we do. So we had to understand that you did not give your enemy an opportunity." There was no way to simulate the experience of combat with a living enemy. Everyone understood the Hawaiian exercises as playacting.

They had to be ready for anything; the intelligence people couldn't tell them exactly what they would face on Saipan. The aerial photographs were not the bonanza Turner had hoped for. Between the heavy blanket of cloud cover and the inexperience of the pilots, who by training and instinct cared more about avoiding enemy fire than they did about providing a platform for the picture taker in the rear seat, only partial coverage was gained of Saipan and Tinian. It would not be supplemented for weeks. "As we all settled down at Pearl to study our problem, it was apparent that we had a tough assignment on our hands," said Rear Admiral Harry Hill, Turner's deputy in the amphibious force. Intelligence estimates of Japanese strength had grown to nine to ten thousand. But the sense lingered that the island's mountains, caves, and coral crags held surprises.

All Kelly Turner knew to do was to continue perfecting his control over the variables within his reach. With a major, multi-island campaign behind him in the Marshalls, his Expeditionary Force was ready for more. His fifty-six attack transports and twenty cargo ships had the capacity to move four divisions at once. This was the capacity Admiral King had asked of the Joint Chiefs of Staff. But its power derived as much from the virtues of precision and timing as it did from its roster of hulls and the size and muzzle velocity of its supporting guns.

The spectacle that was an amphibious exercise was on display all around Hawaii and the California coast. Motorists driving the highway from San Clemente to Oceanside witnessed the exercises from time to time. Odd vehicles waddling ashore, troops and cargo piling out, under the eyes of observers on the cliffs above, watching everything and keeping score. Major commands were working overtime to train Turner's cadre of sea warriors. Coronado was a nest of amphibians, with its Landing Craft School, Naval Gunfire Liaison School, and Air Liaison School. Transport quartermasters, responsible for loading cargoes, learned their trade at Camp Elliott, north of San Diego. The crews of the jack-of-all-trades Landing Ship Tanks, or LSTs, trained at Camp Bradford at Little Creek, Virginia, instructed by veterans of the North Africa landings. Nearby, the Amphibious Training Base at Little Creek was a schoolhouse for the crews of a variety of amphibious landing craft that carried infantry, tanks, vehicles, and personnel. Turner's amphibians hailed from the Navy, Coast Guard, Marine Corps, and Army alike, all joined by their unique fieldcraft. The Army, which called its seagoing small-craft drivers engineer-amphibians, considered the ocean a rather tempestuous extension of land. As one training manual put it, "Engineer-amphibian soldiers must become 'water conscious' just as line soldiers are terrain conscious. They must learn

very thoroughly the business of using bodies of water as roads to transport
our troops, equipment, and supplies toward the enemy. It will be your duty
to carry across the ground forces, to keep them supplied, and to evacuate all
the wounded and all the prisoners and any equipment worth saving for
repair. Our work must continue until such time as the bigger boats can get
in and docks can be built. That may be a long time. . . . You will move
across through a tunnel, protected on both sides by the Navy, with the roof
made safe by the fliers of the Air Force. You will have your own guns
aboard your own craft, and that craft will be armor plated. You will attempt to catch the enemy by surprise. All this is simple common sense.
Your job is to get live men over there—not to land corpses."

The experience of Tarawa nagged at Kelly Turner. Mounting invasions
from the sea was difficult enough without neglecting to investigate readily
knowable facts, such as tides. As Turner wrote in his Tarawa after-action
report, "We must never make another amphibious operation without exact
information as to depths of water or without the ability to eliminate obstacles before the landing." With this, the Navy's leading student of ship-
to-shore movement would bring about a revolution in warfare.

Of late, Turner had taken an interest in a new kind of military occupation that would help his amphibians do their job: underwater demolition.
The Navy's so-called frogmen were specialists in swimming reconnaissance and in the use of explosives to clear obstacles in the shallows and on
the beach. Their unique mission of scouting invasion beaches would be
known as hydrographic reconnaissance: measuring water depths over reefs
and through lagoons in order to determine where men could actually walk
without being pulled under by their packs, and where tanks could swim
without wallowing and flooding out. If these specialists had been better
employed at Tarawa, Turner believed, several hundred Marines might not
have drowned or been picked off while struggling through the lagoon. The
Navy had been training Naval Combat Demolition Units (NCDUs) in
Florida since late 1943, but Washington had been sending most of them to
Europe. Thirty-two NCDUs had gone to England to prepare for the invasion of Normandy. But Tarawa sounded the call in the other hemisphere.
At Fort Pierce, Florida, a special camp was dedicated to training volunteers for this demanding line of work. In the Pacific, Turner meant to
make the Navy's echelon of frogmen his own.

On the afternoon of April 20, 1944, the aircraft carrier *Essex* arrived at
Pearl Harbor after refitting on the West Coast. Down the gangways from
the hangar deck to the landing on Ford Island came a crew of some three

hundred special passengers. They were there at Turner's summons, the full complement of Underwater Demolition Teams (UDT) 5, 6, and 7. Their commander was a wiry, bookish lieutenant commander named Draper Kauffman. Soon after his arrival he was taken by car to see Admiral Turner at his headquarters.

Turner greeted Kauffman with more than the usual pleasantries, for Kauffman was, to him, more than merely an innovator whose work promised to give a new dimension to the amphibious force. Kauffman's father, Rear Admiral James L. "Reggie" Kauffman, served on the staff of CINCPAC and was Turner's next-door neighbor on Oahu. By virtue of his father's position, Kauffman had entrée wherever he went. But nepotism, both Kauffmans would insist, was never in play. Indeed, Draper wouldn't have been able to establish and command the Navy's first Underwater Demolition Teams but for his decision expressly to defy his father's advice in the first place. Before America had even entered the war, the 1933 Annapolis graduate, denied a regular U.S. Navy commission because of his poor eyesight, put on a uniform and went out to find the war. He found it in service to the British crown.

Kauffman spent part of 1940 deployed to France as a driver in the American Volunteer Ambulance Corps. One day, on a dangerous mission that would herald an early career full of them, he volunteered to drive eight wounded soldiers to a French hospital that had been overrun by the Germans. Reaching a forward French outpost, he explained his purpose to the sentries and was directed down the winding road toward the front. That's where he encountered the heavily armed German squad that captured him. He spent four weeks in a prison camp at Lunéville, where the American nonbelligerent made for an inconvenient POW. The U.S. naval attaché in Paris, contacted by Admiral Kauffman, negotiated for Draper's release. But he wasn't done with the war. Returning to London in August, he arranged to take a special commission in the Royal Navy reserve. The German aerial blitz of England was on, and Kauffman put his explosives expertise to use saving the lives of civilians under siege.

Unexploded bombs left behind by the Luftwaffe had paralyzed the city's traffic. Some were duds. Others were live but armed with extended time fuzes, set to blow after an unknowable programmed interval, sometimes as long as weeks. One Thursday night, Kauffman was resting in his hotel room when a German air raid came. A bomb plunged through the surface of the street just outside without exploding. A British bomb disposal team was summoned. Their final moment on earth was marked by a heavy *whump* and a storm of dust that killed them to a man. The next morning Kauffman's unit of Royal Navy reservists was asked for volunteers. None stepped forward. The next day they were asked again, and Kauffman was among the twenty who raised their hands. A British officer approached Kauffman. "Young man, are you frightfully keen for this type of duty?" His answer—"No, sir"—was the one they wanted. Anyone answering "yes" was deemed too crazy to serve in bomb disposal, a specialty that required sober, methodical discipline in every move.

It was unglamorous work. Approaching a bomb site—most bombs went as deep as thirty feet into the ground—Kauffman first had to excavate a hole down to the bomb. Shoring up the sides of the pit, he went to work on the fuze. He quickly found himself in a battle of wits with the Luftwaffe's clever armorers. They rigged their bombs with antiwithdrawal devices that detonated the bomb if the fuze was removed, and trembler mechanisms that triggered an explosion when they detected a vibration. Kauffman learned to defeat the latter by drilling small holes into the top of the fuze and injecting a heated liquid that hardened as it cooled, freezing the trembler in place. He noticed that the Germans reliably identified the type of fuze by the last digit of the bomb's serial number, presumably for safety in their own handling. While he worked, he adopted the safeguard of staying in telephone contact with a colleague situated at a safe remove, reciting aloud his every step in order to keep others from repeating a fatal mistake. As he graduated to "more sporting propositions"—defeating magnetic- and acoustic-fuzed parachute mines that the Germans dropped into harbors, and disarming photoelectric booby traps that triggered a bomb when their insides were exposed to light—Kauffman realized that a certain glamor had attached to his trade. Bystanders leaned in, watching with admiration as the disposal teams loaded the inert weapons into flatbed trucks for a police-escorted sprint to the disposal area known as the bomb cemetery.

After the Blitz ended in May 1941, it wasn't long before Kauffman's countrymen got wind of his skills. On November 1, the U.S. Navy Bureau of Ordnance asked the Brits for his release. At first Kauffman resisted, fearing banishment to a life of idleness serving in a peacetime fleet. But the BuOrd chief, Rear Admiral William H. P. "Spike" Blandy, told him, "If you think the United States Navy is not at war, Draper, I suggest you consult your father. Our ship the *Reuben James* was torpedoed yesterday by a German submarine." Kauffman was ordered to start the Navy's first bomb disposal school in a vacant corner of the Washington Navy Yard.

Draper Kauffman would build a career on the power of volunteering. He believed that the quality of experience one has as a member of any team depends on the caliber and motivation of the people one serves with. He believed in volunteering not only as a means of service but as a route to associating with top people. By way of that association, one became one's best self.

Allowed to handpick the first students to join his bomb disposal school, he took the cream of the Navy's reserve officer programs at Northwestern and Columbia universities. A week after the war came to Hawaii, Kauffman was called to handle an unexploded Japanese bomb just outside the iron door of the ammunition depot at Fort Schofield. His performance in disposing of it on December 15 earned him a Navy Cross. Word got around. When Admiral Halsey requested "daisy cutter" air-burst fuzes after witnessing what such devices had wrought against his men on Guadalcanal, Kauffman's people got into the fuze design business. Within fifteen days, they had produced two hundred fifty of them for the South Pacific forces. This brought howls from the Bureau of Ordnance, but Admiral Blandy was happy to compound that insult by requiring his design staff to attend Kauffman's school. When the school was relocated to American University, the Navy leased space on fraternity row to accommodate it. The location seemed to suit the style of the swashbuckling, nonregulation cadre that would in time evolve into the Navy's SEAL teams.

One day Kauffman was visiting Admiral King's headquarters when a captain on King's staff buttonholed him and asked, "Have you ever seen pictures of the obstacles the Germans are building on their beaches in France?" Kauffman said he hadn't. "They're putting obstacles in five feet of water that will stop the landing craft there and the soldiers will have to get out in six feet of water. Do you know how much an infantryman's pack weighs?"

"No, sir."

"Well, neither do I, but this I do know: They'll all drown. I want you to put a stop to that. Go see my aide."

Questions filled Kauffman's mind: *How? When?* But the officer, Captain Jeffrey Metzel, whose nickname was "Idea-a-Minute Metzel," was taking no questions. His aide handed Kauffman a sheaf of photos from Normandy. The beach approaches to Hitler's Atlantic Wall were littered with giant concrete polyhedrons. Kauffman figured he would soon be bound for occupied France to do something about it. He had plenty of experience in bomb disposal, but none using bombs for their designed ends.

And with that mandate, Kauffman got to work setting up a school that trained people to blow up obstacles on an enemy-held beach ahead of an invasion. Time was of the essence. Once again, his orders gave the free-wheeling reservist the license to choose his own path. He could have any place he wanted as a training base, and he could have anyone he wanted for his command.

For his inaugural class at the training camp in Fort Pierce, Florida, Kauffman recruited from his bomb and mine disposal schools as well as the Naval Construction Battalions, or Seabees. "He was a great salesman," a UDT officer, Robert P. Marshall, would say. "He came up and put on a sales pitch to a group of us at Camp Peary about this extra-hazardous duty and how we'd be immediately immersed in combat of a serious nature, and there was no extra pay. It played well and several hundred of us signed up for the demolition and some preliminary training began at Camp Peary under some lovable Marines who were just delighted to take these Navy guys and put them through the ropes." After four or five weeks, everybody was sent down to Fort Pierce. Kauffman's first echelon of trainees arrived at the UDT training base, south of Vero Beach, in July 1943.

Kauffman's interest in innovation was in line with his sense that the future would be very different from the present. He was not one to be told that a physical infirmity could hold him back from achieving something and believed in the power of self-improvement. When he realized he was terrible at a lectern, he established a public speaking club at the Naval Academy and later took the Dale Carnegie course from Dale Carnegie himself. He preferred to plead for forgiveness rather than permission, and to chase red herrings rather than cut red tape.

For the training program at Fort Pierce, Kauffman realized he needed people with the gifts of initiative and flexibility. He meant to give them plenty of chances to cultivate those virtues. Wanting men who were physi-cally fit, he asked the Army's Scouts and Raiders organization to prepare a physical conditioning course. It was said that Kauffman's "Hell Week," a grinding 24/7 ordeal of mental and physical duress, would separate the men from the boys, because the men would have enough sense to quit and return to the fleet, leaving Kauffman with the boys.

Because he knew that their missions would be perilous, and that Navy support for the unconventional teams was never high, he encouraged in the UDT a high degree of esprit de corps. And he had another priority as well: mastering and applying leading-edge scientific and technical research.

When he asked BuOrd to send him the best explosives expert the U.S. military had, one name was proffered: George Kistiakowsky. Kauffman would call him the Mad Russian, though he had been born in the Ukraine. He was fascinated with Kistiakowsky. He considered the chemist "a very wild sort of a character." The forty-three-year-old hardly fitted the typical image of an Ivy League professor of chemistry, though he held just such an endowed post at Harvard. Kistiakowsky was an expert in thermo-dynamics and chemical kinetics. His talents and training had earned him membership in President Roosevelt's Office of Scientific Research and Development, where he headed the section responsible for explosives and propellants. Kistiakowsky, to say the least, knew explosives better than even Kauffman did. He understood them not as hammers but as knives. When the two men sat down to talk demolition, it was a convergence of edge-of-the-bell-curve mastery of theory and of application. And of non-regulation-like minds as well.

Kistiakowsky had all sorts of ideas about using explosives, from what specific types to employ for a task to creative ways to package and deploy them. He invented natural and synthetic explosives, edible explosives, shaped explosives, and the industrial processes to produce them. He knew the properties of shock waves and hydrodynamic theory. Kauffman did not waste the chance to bring leading-edge applied chemistry to his uncon-ventional type of warfare. According to Kauffman, it was Kistiakowsky who developed the idea of stuffing a rubber fire hose with small blocks of tetratol explosives and fuzing it with a length of primacord and a fulmi-nate of mercury cap. Teams of swimmers could carry such a device to shore and lay it in an obstacle-strewn shallows. The chemistry was such that when detonated, it produced an instantaneous explosion across the full length of the hose. The cap set off the primacord, which transmitted in a flash to the tetratol. If the fire hose was as long as, say, a football field, a small team of combat swimmers could use it to raise a giant wall of seawa-ter and maybe clear a whole beach slope of those fiendish concrete polyhe-drons, opening the way for boats to carry in the Marines.

One evening after dinner at Kauffman's house, the two men cut short their salon on bombcraft and adjourned early. As Kistiakowsky returned to his motel, they agreed to meet on the beach at Fort Pierce at five o'clock the next morning to get to work. But when the time came, Kauffman waited and waited, and as the sun rose his partner still failed to appear. Fearing he was ill, Kauffman drove to the motel and found that he had checked out. When Kauffman, incensed, called the Bureau of Ordnance to report his missing chemist, a staffer told him, "Now just calm down, young man. I don't want you to say a word about this to anybody."

"Well, a lot of people down here know all about it. What do you mean not to say a word?"

"Just exactly that. I want no conversation on this subject whatsoever." And just like that, Kauffman's explosives guru was gone. Kauffman might have figured Kistiakowsky for a ghost. A degree of mystery and secrecy would forever after touch the UDT teams and their descendant organization. A replacement was finally sent to Fort Pierce. He was good, Kauffman found, but he was nothing like the brilliant Mad Russian. For the time being, Kauffman's inquiries into the true state of the art of shaped charges and hydrodynamic waves would have to wait. Turner was pushing him hard in other directions anyway. A major operation was aborning, and Kauffman needed to keep his pipeline full at Fort Pierce in any event.

The Naval Combat Demolition Units, as the UDTs were initially known, trained in six-man teams. Kauffman didn't particularly care if they showed proper military discipline. "We were the despair of the executive officer of the base," Kauffman would say. Every day brought new cases of breached courtesies and violated decorum. "He was right and we were wrong, but I didn't have the time to indoctrinate these kids as well as teach them what I thought had to be taught." Kauffman made a promise to all of his enlisted men: "I will do everything in my power to ensure that no officer graduates from this school under whom I would not be happy to go into combat." Then he told his officers: "I will do everything in my power to ensure that no enlisted man graduates from this school whom I would not want to lead in combat." Yet he tried at the same time to keep superior attitudes from infecting his ranks. Complete secrecy, he thought, might be an antidote to braggadocio. He kept a clamp on any information that so much as suggested the existence of his command.

At Fort Pierce, a morning run through the obstacle course was followed by lectures ("Theory of Explosives," "Combined Operations," "Capping and Priming"), as well as swimming, diving, rubber boats, more lectures, signaling, seamanship, gunnery, engineering, dinner, and an exhausted collapse into secure quarters. Wearing a uniform of combat greens, including field shoes and helmets, Kauffman's students paddled rubber boats up the muddy, weed-choked Indian River to blast obstacles day and night. They studied small-craft handling, nighttime navigation, communications, silhouette recognition, and coastal reconnaissance, with explosive hose, assault problems, and marking and sounding channels added later.

Kauffman adapted some of his curriculum from the all-services Scouts and Raiders Group, which trained just south of the inlet, and from an Office of Strategic Services (OSS) maritime outfit as well. Explosives were the main course. Swimming was treated at best as a side dish, a deficiency that later would be cast in bright relief. Said Bob Marshall, a frogman with UDT 5, "At that time we didn't expect to really do much swimming. We expected to be boated in, jump out in the water, demolish any obstacles or antiboat mines that we found, and then get back in the boats and go out." Kauffman turned down the Momsen escape lung after a man died in a pool during an experiment with one. "All we had were face masks," Marshall said. "Old, tired rubber, retread rubber masks, not nice supple rubber like they have now. You would have to file them and shape them to the contour of your face. Dark blue navy swim trunks, issue trunks. Canvas shoes, knee pads, and gloves, to crawl across the reef. We had a standard pistol belt around us to which was attached a large knife, and that was the only weapon we had. We normally had a first aid kit attached to that belt. We also wore a standard issue life belt which had two CO^2 cartridges in it that you could push, or you could blow it up by hand if you wanted to."

The Japanese had specially trained underwater teams as well. They sent them to search the wrecks of the British capital ships *Repulse* and *Prince of Wales* off Malaya for codebooks, but according to a Japanese intelligence officer, they were limited to five minutes of air at a depth of sixty meters, and using "inferior diving technique" they came away with nothing. Kauffman understood the limitations of his underwater tradecraft, but he looked to his cadre to improve it. "We wanted to use our students as members of our staff and we wanted them to dream up every possible improvement in the techniques that we were using."

Kauffman had promised his men a life of danger, and he had little doubt he could deliver. But along the way he also felt nagged by the idea that he was teaching people to do something that would prove impossible to do in combat. He had no clue where he might be asked to do it, and he was sure the enemy would have a voice in his after-action reports.

As the first chairman of the Joint Army and Navy Experimental and Testing Board (JANET), he arranged for a demonstration at Fort Pierce that ratified the need for extensive and detailed underwater reconnaissance and demolition. The skipper of the Fort Pierce base, Captain Clarence

Gulbranson, was impressed. He wrote to Admiral King: "We must think in terms of overpowering use of material. If one thousand pounds just does the job, use eight thousand pounds. Some observers recommended that estimated quantities of explosives should be multiplied by ten." He recommended exploring fitting landing craft with 155 mm guns and using the surplus of hundred-pound bombs stored at naval depots everywhere for clearing wire. Gulbranson urged the use of self-propelled rafts and "stingrays," radio-controlled drone boats, to deliver explosives to deal with the heaviest steel obstacles. The UDT leadership was blast happy.

In the last week of December 1943, Kelly Turner proposed hauling Kauffman's entire operation to Pearl Harbor's Waipio Amphibious Operating Base "to lead the way in the advancement of practical methods and the development of tactical plans for underwater demolitions on coral reefs and beaches in connection with amphibious operations." There it would be easier to keep tactical tradecraft current, to bring experiments quickly to the fighting front, and to organize and train the teams.

All of this was a prelude to the arrival of the *Essex* in Hawaii that spring.

When Kauffman sat down with Turner at Pearl Harbor in April 1944, he first learned of the plan to put his fledgling teams into service in the Marianas. On a sheet of paper, Turner drew a rough outline of Saipan, without naming it, and sketched the reef that fringed the west coast as far out as a mile.

"Now, the first and most important thing you'll do is reconnaissance to measure the depth of the water," Turner said, indicating the lagoon. "I'm thinking of having you go in and reconnoiter around eight."

"Well, Admiral, it depends on the phase of the moon," Kauffman said, assuming all along his work would be done at night. This sparked Turner's famous Irish temper.

"Moon? What the hell has that got to do with it? Obviously by eight o'clock I mean zero-eight-hundred."

Kauffman gasped. "In broad daylight, sir? Onto somebody else's beach?"

"Absolutely. We'll have lots of fire support to cover you."

And so he would. Nimitz's commander of cruisers and destroyers—Kauffman's own father—would have more than the usual high level of interest in seeing the mission well conducted. A detachment of UDT had already operated at Kwajalein, scouting for obstacles while tethered to their boats and wearing heavy boots and helmets. The commander of that unit, Lieutenant Commander John T. Koehler, was made Kauffman's exec and given the task of building a training base at Maui for Operation Forager. Turner wanted five full-blown teams, each with a hundred men: three for Saipan and Tinian and two more for Guam. An old four-stack destroyer, redesignated as an auxiliary personnel destroyer, or APD, was assigned to each team for high-speed transport. Though Kauffman was in command of the overall UDT organization, he was also named commander of Team Five. Lieutenant Commander Jack Burke would take Team Seven, also bound for Saipan.

With a sullen "Aye, aye," Draper Kauffman was dismissed. He returned to Maui, where the arrival of the UDT was met with some excitement. When the trainees who would form Team Seven got to their camp, a fire burned down the base galley and mess hall, leaving the frogmen to prepare their meals in fifty-five-gallon drums and enjoy them in the dust-driving wind. But there was no time to worry about it. Full dress rehearsals for Operation Forager would not be long in coming, and there was much work to do.

First, they had to forget much of what they had learned at Fort Pierce. The emphasis turned to endurance swimming and demolition and away from rubber boat work. Boots and helmets got a goodbye and good riddance. Swim trunks, fins, and face masks were the new uniform of the day, in line with the innovations of some of Koehler's men at Kwajalein. To blast reefs, the UDT would use small landing craft to bring explosives through high surf to the reef's edge. Throwing two lines, each with a grappling hook, to secure the craft to the reef against the drag of the grounded anchor tied astern, they loaded each swimmer with twenty-five-pound packs of explosives. Depending on the extent of the coral, they could either blast it out altogether or blow a channel through it.

When he learned that the Fourth Marine Division's tank drivers wanted a path through the lagoon to the beach no deeper than three and a half feet, Kauffman came up with a new way to reconnoiter the reef-bound waterways. He contacted the supply officer at Pearl Harbor and requested fifty-five miles of fishing line. The officer thought he was crazy. The technique became known as "string reconnaissance," and it would change the way the Navy's frogmen profiled a lagoon. The frogmen of Team Five turned themselves into measuring sticks, painting black rings and dashes every six inches around their legs and torsos all the way up to the full height of their raised arms. To record their measurements of water depth, they attached one end of each line to a flag buoy that would be anchored just outside the reef. Tying knots in the line every twenty-five yards, the swimmers would pull the string across the lagoon, thereby creating a grid that could be counted off by numbering the knots. Sounding the water depths at each knot, they would jot down the readings with a grease pencil. While the team commander directed them from a small craft that was little more than a motorized floating mattress, the UDT would make a hydrographic profile of the bottom, plotting its depth on a grid that covered the lagoon. The operation, carried out in broad daylight under direct enemy observation from shore, would rely on the fact that men in the water are difficult targets to hit. The individual teams were free to devise their own methods, but this was the technique favored by Kauffman and Team Five.

Admiral Nimitz's operation plan, released on April 23, laid out the Fifth Fleet's scheme of maneuver for the invasion of Saipan. All of its many aspects derived from the manner in which boots would hit the beach. The two Marine divisions would make the initial assault landings abreast on the west coast, sending two regiments to land on each of four beach areas, designated north to south as Red, Green, Blue, and Yellow, centered on the sugar-mill town of Charan Kanoa. Raymond Spruance, as commander of the Fifth Fleet, would direct all forces involved in the operation—Navy, Marine Corps, Army, and Coast Guard. This included the four supporting carrier task groups as well as the land-based air forces that would in time be stationed ashore. Kelly Turner was in overall command of the amphibious fleet, known as the Joint Expeditionary Force. Turner's task force was split into two major echelons, a Northern Attack Force to take Saipan and Tinian and a Southern Attack Force for Guam. Each was an independent amphibious force with transports, landing craft, and battleships and cruisers for fire support. On D Day, June 15, the Northern Attack Force would carry the Second and Fourth Marine divisions to Saipan, followed by the Army's XXIV Corps Artillery and other supporting units, including the Army's 27th Infantry Division as a reserve. Once those troops had secured Saipan, they would take a brief period of rest and replenishment, then leapfrog over to Tinian, just a few miles to the south. At a later date, to be determined by circumstances, the Southern Attack Force, under Vice Admiral Richard L. Conolly, would stage from Guadalcanal and assault Guam with the Third Amphibious Corps under Major General Roy S. Geiger, USMC. Kelly Turner would personally command the Northern Troops and Landing Force while his deputy, Rear Admiral Harry W. Hill, took over control of the Saipan amphibious forces at H Hour, 8:30 A.M., on D Day, June 15. Sailing with Turner in his flagship, the *Rocky Mount,* was Lieutenant General Holland M. Smith, USMC, who would be in command of all troops, both Army and Marine, once they had gone ashore.

As spring flowered, the tempo of the Hawaiian training exercises accelerated until they nearly matched the pace of combat itself. The three regiments of the Second Marine Division mounted up and invaded Maui, conducting several weeks of maneuvers on the beaches at Ma'alaea Bay, below the tent cities and drill fields of the Fourth Marine Division camp on the lower slopes of Haleakala. Afterward, the Fourth took its turn pouring ashore at Ma'alaea, while the Second and elements of the 27th Infantry Division moved to Maui's wilder and more remote eastern coast to train on a full-scale mock-up of Saipan's beaches, complete with dummy towns and accurately drawn "phase lines" marking their expected progress inland. The difficult boat work of ship-to-shore movement took constant rehearsal. Filing up from the compartments belowdecks to their boat stations, going over the side, hurrying down the net into the heaving landing craft to beat the stopwatch, and away. Then the interminable hours circling, getting wet, hungry, and bored. All of the variables were accounted for save the vagaries of enemy action and weather, both unknowable and, veterans knew, likely to throw all plans into the limbo of desperate improvisation.

More than seven hundred amphibious tractors, officially designated Landing Vehicle Tracked but better known as LVTs, amtracs, or alligators, were available. Used at Guadalcanal to haul supplies, amtracs had been used profitabily at Kwajalein, crawling over obstructing reefs. The innovative vehicles were available in several varieties, all derived from the "swamp buggies" developed in the 1920s for hurricane rescue and salvage work by a Florida inventor and entrepreneur, Donald Roebling.

Their concept was revolutionary at a time when the Navy had been planning to send troops ashore over the bows of ships' boats. For years the Marine Corps had been trying to improve the process, rehearsing with new types of craft designed to run their bows up onto the beach to deliver troops and offload heavy equipment and vehicles without need of lighters, piers, or cranes. But funding was short and the designers at the Bureau of Ships resisted change. Spruance would write to a friend, "The idea that the Navy had 'only casual interest in the landing of men from ships upon alien shores' is not so. The Navy in conjunction with the Marines had practiced amphibious landings for many years so far as inadequate ships and equipment would permit." But the Navy owned the inadequacies.

Holland Smith, among others, was relentless in pushing a revolution in amphibious ships and warcraft. In prewar exercises, he argued constantly with Ernest King, then the commander of the Atlantic Fleet, on the subject. During exercises in the Caribbean in late 1940, the officer in charge of an amtrac unit, Captain Victor Krulak, USMC, was seized by a zeal to impress and motored his LVT alongside the battleship *Wyoming* to embark a skeptical Admiral King. Setting out and driving his amtrac onto a reef, Krulak was mortified to find that one of his tracks had been knocked loose on a coral head. As the amtrac floundered in the lagoon, a furious King offered Krulak "a few plain words—words not intended to contribute to my long-term peace of mind"—then jumped overboard in his dress whites and impatiently sloshed ashore. This incident foretold years of mechanical problems for the gangly alligator and a continuing controversy over its use. But Smith, overseeing this exercise, remained committed to the amtrac's potential and took a lesson from King in the art of vitriol while advocating for its acceptance. It had been his combative way that first drew Raymond Spruance's eye to Smith.

The first Marine Corps production model amtracs, designated by the Navy as the LVT-1, could make eighteen miles per hour over land and seven on the water. But the fact that every one of them broke down daily and needed repairs threw a wet blanket over the service's eagerness to install them throughout the force. By 1944, when Kelly Turner was assessing their utility for Operation Forager, the worst of the kinks had been pressed out.

During the first two weeks of May, the ports of Kahului on Maui and Hilo on the Big Island were closed to all shipping as supplies and men were loaded from the docks onto the transport ships of the Fifth Amphibious Force. A division had three regiments, and each one filled four transports and needed a cargo ship for its gear. Each Marine division put its tanks on board LCMs (Landing Craft Medium), which in turn were loaded onto Landing Ship Docks (LSDs) for conveyance overseas. That was only the beginning of the lift capacity required by a Marine division. To carry its seven hundred amtracs, DUKWs, artillery pieces, antiaircraft guns, aviation engineers, and other garrison forces, each division would need fifty-six LSTs (Landing Ship Tanks), the forward three-quarters of which was basically a garage, suitable for diverse cargoes, including small craft of all varieties.

Three days were allotted for loading Turner's attack cargo ships (AKAs) and two days for the attack transports (APAs). The workload was massive at Hilo, the staging area of the Second Marine Division, and at Kahului, home of the Fourth Marine Division. Eighteen hundred rounds of eight-inch naval projectiles (260 pounds apiece) and 6,480 rounds of six-inch were distributed among ten ships that would stand ready to replenish the cruisers that would bombard Saipan. Six more were stuffed to the gunwales with drums of aviation gasoline (150,000 gallons' worth), as well as lube oil and box after box of .50-caliber aircraft ammunition—1.5 million rounds. This strenuous labor was hampered by a shortage of dock cranes, booms, winches, and mooring. Unexpected alterations in ship design foiled loading plans, too. Changes in the location of cargo hatches and revisions in the placement of booms and cranes pushed transport quartermasters into a game of constant improvisation. Not only did they need keen spatial awareness, they had to know the tactical plan. The rule of last in/first out required that ammunition and water be the final items placed in the holds. But the puzzle was always complex. The need to weight-balance a fully loaded LST might require artillery pieces to be separated from their prime movers, the large tractors that towed them, and the shore parties who served the assault forces needed to know those particulars. They might be a matter of life and death for the men on the beach.

A scarcity of ammunition ships in the Pacific—only six were available—forced Turner to look to his LSTs to haul ordnance, too. At Pearl Harbor's Naval Ammunition Depot, twenty-six of them were preloaded with 5-inch naval projectiles and 4.5-inch rockets. Others were given a standard load of ammunition for the troops: seventy-one tons' worth, almost half in the form of belted .30-caliber ammo—nearly a million rounds per ship—as well as sixteen hundred grenades, two hundred 2.36-inch bazooka rockets, fourteen hundred 60 mm mortar rounds, four hundred fifty 81 mm mortar rounds, three thousand rounds for 37 mm guns, four hundred fifty rounds for 75 mm howitzers, five hundred pounds of TNT, five hundred more of C2 explosive, and two hundred M1 bangalore torpedoes.

Operation Forager's final tune-up would be a series of exercises in the middle of May. Turner had decided to test a couple of late brainstorms. Adding offensive firepower to the amphibious force itself was much on his mind, for he feared the dangerous interval of time after the preparatory bombardment stopped and before the landing craft hit the beach. So he was more than intrigued when tests in Hawaii suggested that self-propelled artillery and tank guns could be fired from LCMs, as long as the weather and surf were right.

ANNUAL U.S. NAVAL PRODUCTION BY TYPE

	1942	1943	1944
Aircraft carriers	1	15	8
Battleships	4	2	2
Battle cruisers	0	0	2
Heavy cruisers	0	4	2
Light cruisers	8	7	11
Escort carriers	13	50	37
Auxiliaries	184	303	630
Destroyers	81	128	84
Destroyer escorts	0	306	197
Submarines	34	56	77
Patrol & mine craft	743	1,106	640
Landing craft	9,488	21,525	37,724

Source: Bureau of Naval Personnel, Information Bulletin, February 1945

Earlier in the year, Spruance had shot down an idea to refit some captured Italian battleships with heavy mortars and park them off islands under invasion. He had even less interest in a variation that involved barges as large as twenty thousand tons, equipped with no machinery except that which controlled the barge's stem-to-stern battery of stabilizable guns, mortars, and fire-control systems. The mad scientist behind this idea, Captain R. C. Parker of CINCPAC's analytical section, proposed that these monstrosities be towed in and beached. "Then, from a fixed and steady gun platform, give the Jap defenses on Boola Gaboola a hell of a shellacking, controlled initially by air spot, and later by beach parties. After the party is over, tow them off to use again if you can. If not, lift off their guns and equipment to put in another hulk, leaving the old hulk on the beach. You don't lose much by it. Being a fixed platform, neither moving nor zigzagging nor rolling, and using guns for high-angle fire, they will be able to concentrate their fire on a pinpoint, or walk a barrage across the island with the accuracy of a safety razor." Parker signed the memo with the annotation, "No royalties on this idea claimed."

There were more cost-effective ways to deliver heavy fire ashore to protect the troops in that critical period following the first footfall on the beach. An Army colonel hit upon the idea of crossbreeding a self-propelled howitzer and an amtrac. Thus a variant of the LVT known as the LVT(A), or amtank, was born. The first version was equipped with a 37 mm howitzer, and an "upgunned" model had a 75 mm howitzer in an open-topped mount—with eight times the hitting power of a light tank. Mere weeks before the invasion force left for the Marianas, the first prototypes of this version would be given to the Army's 708th Amphibian Tank Battalion, attached to the 23rd and 25th regiments of the Fourth Marine Division.

The Navy created a variant of the stalwart Landing Craft Infantry (LCI), fitting it with three 40 mm Bofors guns and mounting launching racks for 4.5-inch rockets on its two forward troop ramps. In addition to this so-called LCI gunboat, Turner approved an experiment proposed by Admiral Hill to install batteries of large mortar tubes on Landing Craft Tanks (LCTs). Its rapid rate of high-trajectory fire recommended the mortar barge for use against targets on large islands such as Saipan, where rough terrain and the reverse slopes of mountains promised cover for enemy artillery and mortar crews. The only way to get at them was with high-angle plunging fire. And so these specially outfitted amphibious craft joined the exercise, too. Several LSTs were fitted to carry on their decks

LCTs bristling with 4.2-inch mortars as well as the standard load of seventeen amtracs in their wells.

Two days before the amphibious task groups left Pearl Harbor for exercises, Turner put Kauffman in overall command of all three UDTs in addition to direct command of Team Five. As the day approached, Kauffman called on Admiral Turner with a special request.

"Sir, I'd like to borrow a couple of battleships and cruisers and destroyers, just for a weekend."

"What in hell would you like to borrow my battleships and cruisers and destroyers for? Or perhaps I should say your *father's* battleships, cruisers, and destroyers?"

"Well, sir, you speak of this very heavy fire support the UDTs are going to have. I would guess that this would be a very unusual experience, to be swimming in with eight-inch guns firing almost a flat trajectory right over our heads." Kauffman thought such a concussive ordeal required a dry run.

Turner decided that a live-fire exercise off the uninhabited island of Kaho'olawe would be helpful not only for the UDT but for the commanders of his ships as well. The Marines had proposed—and Nimitz had approved—the establishment of a shore bombardment range on that island, where the gunnery teams in the old battleships and cruisers underwent intensive training with Marine Corps fire-control experts.

On the night of May 13, major elements of the Northern Attack Force were steaming toward Kaho'olawe when the winds whipped up and the seas became heavy. It was after two A.M. when the lead ship of the center column of LSTs, pushing along at nine knots, was raised high on a swell. The LST-485 was carrying a company of Marines from the Second Battalion, Eighth Regiment. They were berthed mostly in the troop compartment, but a few were carried inside the cluster of amtracs in the ship's hold, and a few more were sleeping on deck as well as inside the heavily laden LCT that was secured to the main deck, serving as a sort of minibarracks. When the bow of the LST hit the trough of the swell, the heavy load of mortar ammunition in the piggybacked LCT shifted, breaking its lashings and throwing it through the port-side rail. As it careened over the side, the LCT carried away a pair of steel 20 mm gun tubs and the ship's gangway. Thus an entire platoon from the 2/8 Marines, still asleep inside, was thrown into the sea. Nineteen of these men drowned. As other landing ships in the train turned to looking for survivors, several were caught broadside to the waves, causing two more to lose their LCTs due to the force of shifting ammunition. When the transports returned to Lahaina Roads that night, Turner decided to cancel the LCT gunboat experiment. A board of investigation quickly found that the excess weight of the ammunition was the cause of the mishaps.

Tragic though these losses were, the exercises off Kaho'olawe were fruitful as Turner, in collaboration with Admiral Kauffman, refined the practice of shore bombardment. Their innovation was the concept of the shore fire-control party. Each of these groups, which were formed from division signal companies, included two officers and eleven Marines divided into two elements: a forward observer team, led by an artillery lieutenant, and a naval gunfire liaison team, led by a Navy ensign or junior-grade lieutenant who advised an individual Marine battalion. Operating from a jeep equipped to communicate directly with ships, the forward observer team made its way around the front line, directing the warship's fire by radio. They were also given a turn watching from afloat, seeing their world from the viewpoint of ships offshore. The exercises gave everyone a ringing, stinging, true-life picture of how the component parts of Turner's alligator navy would operate at the point of attack. As he prepared to tackle Saipan, Turner revealed a creative attitude that could have been reduced to a creed: The only thing worse than a bad idea that gets implemented is a good one that is never broached.

After her turn at the firing range, the battleship *Colorado* closed with the southwest beaches of Kaho'olawe to rehearse close-in fire support for demolition teams. Having launched two spotting planes for gunnery observation, she hadn't been firing for fifteen minutes when the ship quaked with a sickening shudder, going aground on an uncharted pinnacle rock about three miles west of Kaho'olawe Light. The crew tried to "lighten ship" by pumping fuel and water overboard, more than five hundred tons' worth, and passed a towline to the *McDermut*. As the destroyer backed her engines, the 32,000-ton battleship didn't budge and the line finally parted. The *Colorado*'s deckhands passed a heavier wire line to the *McDermut,* and it snapped, too. The destroyer came alongside and secured herself directly to the battleship with wire and manila lines, then tried to back full, assisted by the *Colorado*'s own engines. This was fruitless as well. By the time they quit in the late afternoon, the battleship had taken a four-degree starboard list from serially flooded compartments.

The salvage crew's last play would rely on the natural power of the moon over the seas. The destroyer dropped anchor, with a towline running to the battleship that was kept under strain, and awaited the next high tide.

When it rolled in and peaked around midnight, an additional foot of seawater under her shredded keel allowed the *Colorado* to float free of the pinnacle. Fully waterborne again, she limped at a walking speed to Pearl Harbor for repairs.

On May 17, Turner sent both of his Marine divisions and the boats that served them to Ma'alaea Bay, Maui, for a full-scale rehearsal of the landings. His first assault echelon, the slow-moving tractor groups containing the LSTs and their embarked amtracs, would get underway for the Marianas on May 24. On D Day, June 15, the Second and Fourth Marine divisions would land on Saipan's western coast, two regiments from each division on four adjacent beaches. There was little time to waste. Maui was well situated for a realistic rehearsal, but because it was well populated, no live ammunition could be fired there. But live gunfire was not the order of the day. Timing was.

At the kickoff of the exercise, the landing craft, amtracs, and LCVPs disembarked and formed up in the assembly area, circling with other landing craft, all of them empty. Upon a signal from a transport, the coxswain gunned the motor and pulled alongside for loading. "So-called 'doping off' will not be tolerated," the commander of the assault transport *Arthur Middleton* warned. "Boat performance may make or break the entire operation." The next few minutes were a blur of activity. Deckhands on the transport dropped the fenders and manned the boat hooks while the coxswain throttled down, easing close and aiming to avoid at all cost a damaging impact with the transport's sturdier hull. While he bobbed alongside, a bowline was secured to the sea painter. Then a cargo net was lowered into the LCVP's cargo space, held taut as the troops began their descent into the boat that would carry them to the fight.

Meanwhile, the tractor groups, consisting of the thirty-four LSTs carrying assault troops loaded in amtracs, took position about twelve hundred yards behind the line of departure for each beach. Eight LSTs carried each division's artillery, two more had antiaircraft guns, and two more the corps artillery. Two Landing Ship Docks (LSDs) loaded with LCMs carrying tanks stood in the rear, prepared to send the tanks ashore on call from the assault commander.

After dropping their amtracs into the swells, the assault LSTs withdrew seaward as the amtracs and LCVPs arranged themselves in the rendezvous area, circling, rising, and falling in lazy oscillations. The lane into each of the four beaches, color-coded Red, Green, Blue, and Yellow, was marked by a landing craft known as a control vessel, or LCC, anchored at the line of departure, centered in the lane leading in to each regiment's beach. Called to the line of departure via a flag signal and a redundant voice radio call from the LCC, they rallied to the colored flag. On cue from Turner, the group control officer assigned to each division ordered the first wave to begin their run to the beach.

It was a point of no return. With the first wave committed, there was no going back. The machine was running, Turner's great dragon uncoiling to strike. The second wave, leaving the rendezvous area, formed up at the line of departure and jumped off without cue at a fixed interval, every four to six minutes. The third wave followed, and the fourth. The remainder of the amtracs stood by, awaiting a request from the regimental commander on a given beach once he was set up ashore.

As soon as the troops were away, the transport crews busied themselves with opening hatches and hauling topside priority items needed ashore: drums of water and fuel, crates of ammunition, barbed wire for use against the expected counterattack meant to throw the assaulters into the sea. The efficiency of the boat work, from the ship-to-shore movement to quick and accurate distribution of ammunition, water, medical supplies, and other critical disposables, would determine the success of the landing. History taught dire lessons from amphibious operations that had failed for an inability to manage the unique battlefield of this narrow membrane of sand. In 1915, landing on the Gallipoli peninsula, the British were thrown back in their attempt to take Constantinople, with a quarter of a million casualties. The prospect of such a failure still haunted an amphibious commander's dreams.

The dispersion of the units in Turner's exercise meant most everyone was late receiving the plan. A thirty-five-knot wind gave them a trial run in rough-water operations, and heavily laden amphibians struggled to reach the shore. Commanders judged the exercise ragged and poorly conducted, compounded by the impossibility of briefing everyone in advance. A battalion commander with the Sixth Marine Regiment considered the rehearsals a "disaster." He noticed that the amtrac drivers had trouble staying on course because of their difficulty seeing through the slits in the armor plating that partially blocked their view forward. So he imposed a simple innovation: He had his amtrac commanders tie lengths of cord around the shoulders of their drivers. Using the cord as a bridle, they administered directive tugs to steer from the vessel's open bay, peering forward over the shield.

Kelly Turner and Holland Smith were "at dagger's point" over how to employ their amtracs. The Fourth Division's chief of staff, Brigadier General Graves B. Erskine, was determined to use them not just for supply but as tactical combat vehicles. The alligators, he believed, could surge over reefs and straight onto shore, overrunning beach obstacles, taking the whole beachhead in a rush, then serving as tanks in support of the infantry. "I wanted to go ashore and run as far as possible in the amtracs, even though we lost some amtracs: You saved a hell of a lot of time, and if you could get beyond their machine gun defenses, it should be easier to continue." Smith liked the idea, as did Major General Harry Schmidt of the Fourth Marine Division. But Turner didn't like it, and Major General Thomas E. Watson of the Second Marine Division had doubts, too. He feared his troops would be vulnerable in the lumbering vehicles. Once they crawled ashore, their high silhouettes would mark them as easy targets. He didn't like the idea of exposing them to direct fire, even if amtanks were on hand with the first wave.

When the rehearsal was finished, the tractor fleet returned to Oahu. In Pearl Harbor's West Loch, the waterfront ammunition depot was a hive of activity as yard workers removed the heavy mortar ammunition that had precipitated disaster off Kaho'olawe. On board the LST-43, within a tarpaulin-draped tank lighter that was lashed to the deck, the men of Echo Company, Second Battalion, 23rd Marines, were stripped to their skivvies, lazing in their racks, reading, chatting, letting the afternoon go by as carbon-arc welds sparked, stevedores turned to, and boats and small craft gurgled past against a backdrop of Hawaiian sugar.

And then it happened: a great heave of concussion, a swirl of flame, a wave of heat, and a hurricane of burning canvas, paper, bedding, seabags, and clothing. Robert Graf, a Marine with the 2/23, opened his eyes to see the tarpaulin covering the LCT falling away, revealing the ship's bulkheads afire under the noonday sky. Lashed all across the deck were large cargo drums filled with high-octane gasoline. There was an explosion, then another, one far, one near. Graf looked in vain for attacking Japanese aircraft as his LST was swallowed in smoke and the sky rained metal. Men who had been seated on the fuel drums vanished in blinding flames. As Graf joined the surge of troops fleeing the ship, he noticed that the epicenter of the firestorm was several ships over from his. An explosion on board that ship seemed to have ignited everything within the umbrella of its discharge. Five more LSTs, all of them fully combat loaded, were on fire near the depot.

Hundreds of Marines and sailors from the six burning LSTs escaped by diving into the harbor, leaving their weapons, gear, and clothing behind. Burning oil fouled the efforts of survivors to swim. As boats in the harbor maneuvered to rescue them, or to make their own escape, some of them blundered into and over the swimmers, dragging them under with their screws. Swimmers were hit by falling shrapnel, or inhaled flames and stopped and sank.

Admiral Hill would call "superhuman" the efforts of the crews from the other LSTs and the firefighters to get the inferno under control. At the height of the effort, Admiral Turner himself boarded a yard tug to oversee the effort. Arriving at the ammunition depot, seeing a tug backing away from the flames at the dock, he shouted to a startled petty officer, "Go back in there and stay or I will shoot you." The man did as ordered.

More costly than the loss of six ships were the deaths of 163 men and disabling injuries to almost four hundred others. There were quickly rumors of sabotage and spies, and suspicions were cast upon the civilian welding corps. As the able survivors received new clothing, field equipment, weapons, and such, Graf wrote that there was scuttlebutt that "we were hurt much too badly to carry off the coming invasion." But the second board of inquiry undertaken by Turner's command in as many weeks would judge the disaster accidental, rooted in the carelessness of Army work parties off-loading 4.2-inch mortar ammunition from the LST-353, per Kelly Turner's orders. The charred hulks were hauled from the West Loch and quickly replaced by eight new ships, reassigned from the South Pacific. The hardest-hit companies filled out their ranks from the replacement pool.

A few days before the tractor groups were to leave Pearl Harbor for the Marianas, the regimental weapons company from the 24th Marines threw a beer bash on a grassy bluff overlooking the Pacific. As an orchestra ensemble played by a bonfire, promotions and decorations were handed out, and then a particularly legendary battalion commander, Lieutenant Colonel Evans Carlson, who had helped establish the Marine Raider units, lined up for chow with the men and visited with them, which was out of the ordinary for a colonel but in line with his style. After Kwajalein, his men were as ready as ever.

There was rest for top brass as well. With planning for Operation Forager complete, Raymond Spruance took a stateside leave, returning to

Monrovia, California, to the surprise of his wife, Margaret, and their daughter. In their company, he cherished his isolation and privacy. His daughter was impressed by his tranquil state of mind under the load of the burdens she knew he carried. He abruptly turned any conversation about the war to other subjects. Still, prevailing upon his sense of duty, she persuaded him to say a few words about the war to the local Rotary Club. Spruance accepted, on one condition: that he not wear his uniform. Margaret told him of a sixteen-year-old boy in the neighborhood who idolized him specifically because of that uniform. "When you appear up there in your worn old civilian clothes, he'll think you're just another old man," she said. At the luncheon, deeply uncomfortable at being treated like a celebrity, Spruance gave his audience a crisp briefing on the war's progress. Afterward, he was eager to leave when the mayor introduced him to an elderly man, an invalid. Though Spruance wasn't interested in small talk, the housebound gentleman proved to be a scholar of geopolitics and military strategy, and Spruance visited with him for hours during his time there, enjoying the company of another student of his craft.

When Spruance returned to Pearl Harbor the following week, he found that his friend of long standing, Kelly Turner, looked ragged. He had been drinking heavily. He had complained about his exhaustion following the Marshalls campaign. Now he seemed deeper into his self-destructive pattern. Nimitz could barely tolerate him in this state, but whenever he was ready to come down on Turner, Spruance would step in the way, saying, "Let me handle him." And he did. With Spruance's friendship came a deep well of understanding, accommodation, and forgiveness. He was determined to keep Turner in the war.

In Nimitz's view, the war thus far had passed through three phases. In the first, Japan expanded and the United States rebuilt, securing its lines of communication to Australia and stopping the Japanese expansion at Midway. The second phase began with the August 1942 Guadalcanal offensive and lasted until mid-1943, with the capture of the southern Solomons. The third phase, from the invasion of Tarawa to the conquest of the Marshalls in February 1944, established U.S. tactical and numerical superiority and saw the penetration of Japan's outer imperium. In a memo to his commanders dated May 29, 1944 (subject line: "Tactical Foresight"), Nimitz wrote:

> The cautious tactics of the Japanese Navy in this present phase are
> logical for them. It would be poor strategy for them to fight a de-

cisive action with their weaker fleet in the defense of outer lines, if they have hopes of bettering their chances by delay. Delay works in their favor to some extent because distance in war is like a lever-age [*sic*]; one can carry more weight close to his body than he can at arm's length. As we progress, our lines of communication grow longer, more widespread, and more vulnerable, while theirs grow shorter, more concentrated, and (up to a certain point) more read-ily protected. For each mile that the fighting fronts shift to the westward, it takes more U.S. tankers and cargo ships, more convoys and escorts, more air patrol, more staging bases, more garrisons, and more logistic support of all kinds to support our combatant effort at the greater distance. Conversely it takes less for them. Thus, paradoxically, by pushing the battlefront closer to their homeland, we are in a sense helping them to surmount their heavy losses in shipping. Furthermore any possible reverse to our fleet would be the more serious the further to the westward it oc-curred. . . . There would have been no well-defended bases and navy yards to shelter our fleet and repair its damage, no replace-ments for carrier planes lost, and no areas dominated by our land based aviation where we would have been protected and the enemy endangered.

The fleet, in other words, was becoming its own island, garrison, and air force. It had to be utterly self-sustaining, even as it stood out like a bird on a wire. Pushing deeper into Japanese waters, it faced risks that surely grew. But the counterbalance to those risks was the potential for a true strategic breakthrough. For if the Marianas could be taken, the B-29 Superfortress, struggling through its birth pangs, would at last come within range of Japan. "They probably realize," Nimitz wrote, "that their cities and AA defenses cannot 'take it' to the extent that the Germans can, although it would probably be difficult for us to develop from any bases in the Western Pacific the sustained intensity of bombing that the bases and resources of Great Britain are enabling the Allies to develop from there."

On May 24, reconnaissance planes from the Army's Seventh Air Force reported the Japanese feverishly upgrading their defenses in the Marianas. And worse news followed: The Pacific joint intelligence staff increased its estimate of Japanese combat strength on Saipan by a factor of two-thirds, from nine or ten thousand men to fifteen to eighteen thousand. Coastal batteries and antiaircraft guns were proliferating, and the shoreline was trimmed with miles of trenches. But Kelly Turner was not prepared to tolerate a delay in the timetable. His LST fleet might explode, and so might his intelligence estimates. Still, his tractor flotillas knew only one direction: west.

The next day, the landing ships carrying his amtrac horde—the slowest of the amphibious task units under his command—hauled clear of Hospital Point and turned west under escort. They were twenty-four hours behind schedule; Turner had been forced to make at least that concession to the disaster. But he would see to it that the day lost after West Loch would be made up underway to the assault area.

4

A Charge for Ozawa

He fastened himself into his cockpit before dawn and roared aloft from Tinian. First Lieutenant Takehiko Chihaya, a reconnaissance pilot from the land-based First Air Fleet, flew south to Truk, where he refueled, then took off again, navigating east by southeast to Nauru and refueling again before tackling the final northerly leg of his long journey to Majuro. Arriving over the base, Chihaya looked down upon the collected power of the U.S. fast carrier task force at rest and started his camera shutter clicking. It was May 30, 1944.

When he returned to Tinian, Chihaya hurried his film to the darkroom, where the chemical processes summoned an image of major elements of the great Fifth Fleet gathering for war. There were five fast carriers, two escort carriers, three battleships, three cruisers, ten destroyers, two transports, and sixteen tankers, plus another pair of carriers, with escorts, heading to sea.

Six days later the pilot returned to Majuro to update his sighting. The U.S. order of battle had grown. Chihaya spotted the better portion of three task groups: six *Essex*- and *Enterprise*-class fast carriers, two *Independence*-class light carriers, six escort carriers, six battleships, eight or more heavy cruisers, sixteen or more destroyers, ten tankers, and a large number of other ships. "The exploits of these scout planes ascertained where the enemy was, but we could not guess where he would go. To Saipan or Palau, it still remained uncertain," wrote Ryonosuke Kusaka, the Combined Fleet chief of staff.

Though the Japanese cipher bureau never managed to break America's naval codes, it had little trouble solving the encryption used in merchant ship communications. In this way they detected the buildup of transport vessels in Hawaii, as well as a surge of air units westward from the United States. The Japanese had responded to the fall of the Marshalls by preparing defenses along the wide perimeter connecting the Marianas, the western Carolines, and western New Guinea. They considered this line, one of their analysts would say, as a trip wire for a "fight to the finish."

The fleet commander who was charged with winning that fight was one of the most experienced hands in the entire Imperial Japanese Navy: Vice Admiral Jisaburo Ozawa. Well regarded for his intellect, bearing, and dignity, he had held major commands afloat since before the outbreak of war. After relieving Chuichi Nagumo of command of the Japanese fast carrier force in November 1942, Ozawa took over the newly established First Mobile Fleet, which comprised the Combined Fleet's principal carrier striking power. This placed not only the carriers but the supporting battleships and cruisers under his command. Though he came up as a specialist in surface warfare and torpedo tactics, he was an earlier advocate of carrier power. He knowledgeably rated the U.S. fast carrier force as nearly twice as strong as his own in surface-ship strength, and more than twice as strong in the air. His carrier force carried four hundred fifty planes in nine hulls. There was Ozawa's 37,000-ton flagship, the *Taiho,* the 32,000-ton *Shokaku* and *Zuikaku,* the 25,000-ton *Junyo* and *Hiyo* (converted ocean liners), and the light carriers *Ryuho, Chitose, Chiyoda,* and *Zuiho.* The Imperial Navy's gun club was powerfully manifested in five battleships—the incomparable sisters *Yamato* and *Musashi,* the largest in the world, and the *Nagato, Kongo,* and *Haruna*—as well as thirteen heavy cruisers, six light cruisers, and twenty-seven destroyers, serviced by six fleet oilers. Twenty-four submarines rounded out his roster of combatants.

Ozawa's flagship, *Taiho,* was formidable, the first Japanese carrier with a bomb-resistant armored flight deck. But Ozawa's force was hampered by an overriding weakness: the lamentable state of training of his pilots. Because of his fleet's appetite for scarce fuel reserves, Ozawa was forced to base at Tawi Tawi, the westernmost island in the Sulu Archipelago, southwest of Mindanao. He had wanted to remain as long as possible at Lingga Roads on Sumatra, where it was possible to train his men. But with the prospect of a long-sought decisive battle looming, Combined Fleet headquarters insisted that the carriers advance toward the U.S. fleet. "Plan Z," a scheme to confront the Americans with the entire strength of the Combined Fleet in a decisive battle, would be put into effect as soon as the American fleet manifested its next objective. Tawi Tawi was well within range of the western Carolines, deemed the likeliest site for a major fleet action, but was still within a day's cruise from the oil storage farms at Tarakan.

But shortly after Ozawa arrived at Tawi Tawi on May 16, he found himself in a bind. His arrival quickly attracted notice. Aggressive patrols by U.S. submarines kept his carriers bottled up in harbor. And with fuel scarce and no suitable airdromes in the area anyway, Ozawa's pilots stopped training and began to lose their fighting edge. So while the First Mobile Fleet fielded powerful new planes, including the Nakajima B6N Tenzan (the "Jill") and the Yokosuka D4Y Suisei (or "Judy")—successors to the vaunted Kate torpedo bomber and Val dive-bomber, respectively—their potential would be difficult to tap. Making matters worse, the seasonal trade winds in the Southwest Pacific were too weak to enable regular flight operations for these new high-performance planes. The bottleneck on the fuel supply made it hard for the First Mobile Fleet to live up to its middle name. And even in the home islands, the scarcity of fuel reserves was so great that training of pilots there "virtually ceased." Yet the great ambitions of Imperial Headquarters stood. Its operational policy, intact since September 1943, required that the entire battle fleet be thrown against the U.S. Pacific Fleet, whenever and wherever it appeared, in order to destroy it "with one blow." Given the fuel limitations Ozawa faced, this was a remarkable flight of magical thinking, more a sentiment than a strategy, its hollowness already indicated by Japan's failure to execute it when the U.S. Navy appeared in force at Tarawa, Kwajalein, Truk, Majuro, and Eniwetok. But so it stood.

On May 23 the new Combined Fleet commander in chief, Admiral Soemu Toyoda, who replaced Koga after the plane crash, had issued the general order designating Palau and the western Caroline Islands, home of the important bases of Yap and Woleai, as "decisive battle areas" where Japanese naval strength would be concentrated. A directive from Combined Fleet headquarters committed the full strength of the First Mobile Fleet and First Air Fleet to resist the Americans. "The decisive battle will be fought as close as possible to the forward base of our mobile fleet," the chief of staff instructed Ozawa.

Toyoda's senior officers flew to Saipan, where they received copies of the order from Toyoda's chief of staff, Vice Admiral Kusaka. It was clear that carriers alone would not stop the Americans. A battle plan derived from Plan Z, known as Operation A-Go, counted on the First Air Fleet to wear down the Americans prior to Ozawa's arrival in the battle area. Admiral Kakuji Kakuta's land-based squadrons were expected to destroy fully one-third of the U.S. carrier force. This ambitious plan was complicated by the need to fight MacArthur, too. The siege in the southwestern Pacific forced the transfer of about half of the First Air Fleet's planes in the Marianas to western New Guinea. The dispersion of Japan's forces among its principal bastions was an intractable problem, preventing the type of force concentration that was necessary to successful defense. The mobility and rapid pace of U.S. aircraft carrier operations contributed to this result. Casting shadows in all directions, it had spooked the Japanese into confusion, if not paralysis.

Scattered across the Central and Southwest Pacific from the Philippines to the Marianas, the First Air Fleet, as of June 1, had about six hundred planes organized into twenty-one air groups. A fully modern combat air fleet, it featured the usual array of Zekes, Jills, and Judys, as well as twin-engine Nakajima J1N "Irving" nightfighters and Yokosuka P1Y1 "Frances" twin-engine bombers. But it lacked experienced personnel. The constant shuffle of men and matériel between theaters, and the persistent shortage of fuel, hampered pilot readiness. Mitscher's February carrier strike on Saipan compelled Kakuta to deploy his 263rd Air Group, nicknamed the Leopards, to Guam, and the 261st Air Group, the Tigers, to Saipan. However, about half of those pilots were fresh from flight training, with no live-fire aerial gunnery or dogfighting training. It was all they could do to fly in formation. When these newcomers began a series of hops from the home islands to Iwo Jima and then out to the Marianas, they had to rely on a guide aircraft for navigation. Of twelve aviators who left Matsuyama, Japan, on February 28, flying new Model 52 Zekes, only one made it to Saipan. But reinforcements trickled in. At the end of March, twenty-five of the most experienced fliers from the Leopards were transferred from Guam to Peleliu. On March 31, a U.S. air strike caught them in the open while their planes were being refueled, and eighteen of the twenty-five veterans were killed. When the news reached Guam, the rookies were devastated. "The air battles over Saipan and Peleliu took away our experienced pilots, leaving us cubs to fend for ourselves. Losing the older pilots hurt because we had no one to show us the ropes," said Tomokazu Kasai, a member of the Leopards.

If there was to be a final, decisive battle with the Americans, Toyoda preferred that it be fought "as near the standby area of our Mobile Fleet as possible," or so said a May 3 order from the Naval General Staff to the Combined Fleet. "Surprise operations will be carried out insofar as is possible and the enemy's spirit of attack will be broken," the order stated. This seemed to eliminate the Marianas, the most easterly reach of Japan's "fight to the finish" perimeter, as a priority for defense.

The lone voice on the Combined Fleet staff arguing that the Americans would move against the Marianas was an intelligence officer named Yoshitaka Nakajima, who detected a pattern in intercepted U.S. Navy telegraphy. It was not what anyone wanted to hear. When Captain Toshikazu Ohmae, on Ozawa's staff, asked Kusaka how the fleet would defend the Marianas, the Combined Fleet chief of staff said that the dire fuel situation ruled them out as a decisive battle area until the latter half of 1944. If the Americans attacked, the 31st Army's commander, Lieutenant General Hideyoshi Obata, would order his garrisons to resist as fiercely as they could at the beach while land-based aircraft were shifted there from Palau. Toyoda's greater interest was Biak, which MacArthur's troops invaded on May 27. A major operation was underway to reinforce the island. Toyoda hoped the magnitude of it would lure the U.S. fleet to a decisive battle there. But Nimitz wasn't taking the bait.

As it happened, Nimitz had had the excellent fortune to have a copy of Plan Z fall into his lap. In early April, after the two flying boats bearing Combined Fleet commander in chief Mineichi Koga and his staff had gone down off Cebu, Filipino fishermen recovered from the flotsam a leatherbound portfolio bearing the Imperial Japanese Navy seal. It contained a document titled "Secret Combined Fleet Order No. 73." Signed by Koga and dated March 8, 1944, it was delivered to an American officer working with Filipino guerrillas. After days of pursuit by Japanese troops of the guerrillas, who had also taken captive Koga's chief of staff, Shigeru Fukudome, as well as custody of Koga's body, an American officer working with the guerrillas bargained with the Japanese. If they would back off the pressure and stop killing civilians, Koga's body would be returned. The deal gave the American officer, James M. Cushing, the breathing room to spirit the documents out of the country.

MacArthur's intelligence headquarters, recognizing the value and provenance of the documents, sent them quickly to Nimitz, whose linguists at JICPOA prepared a translation that would be distributed to Spruance and his principals. Although the document outlined more a general strategic concept than a fully detailed campaign plan—it did not specify the exact manner of the Japanese fleet's deployment—it did confirm that the next American invasion, be it in the Southwest or Central Pacific, would bring out Ozawa in force.

Until then, the Japanese decided to hedge their bets, scattering the land-based planes of the First Air Fleet piecemeal through the theater: 134 were sent to the Palaus, 67 to Truk, 35 to Saipan, 67 to Tinian, and 70 to Guam. If the Americans did attack the Marianas, those 172 land-based planes allocated to the three principal islands there would have to suffice until the carriers arrived. Ozawa would need four days to get within striking range.

As May neared its end, the increasing frequency of sightings of American submarines off the Philippines and in the Marianas compelled Japanese naval intelligence to warn that the next U.S. objective was the Marianas. But Toyoda's command persisted in believing that the western Carolines would be the site of the showdown. Did not the withering air attacks on Truk, boldly launched by Spruance in February and repeated in April, indicate this? Commander Chihaya's report of large U.S. carrier forces at Majuro was consistent with a leap into the Carolines, as was the cipher bureau's analysis of American radio transmissions.

On June 6, 1944, news of the Allied landings in northern France hit newspapers worldwide. Reactions within the Fifth Fleet ranged from elation to laconic indifference. Carl Moore's outlook no doubt reflected that of Spruance's entire staff: "In a very short time we will have our own hands full, and I rather expect we shall forget that there is a Europe." At a press briefing on the command ship *Rocky Mount,* Holland Smith seemed appropriately amnesiac about anything other than the objective directly in front of his men: "We have learned how to pulverize atolls, but now we are up against mountains and caves where the Japs can dig in, and a week from today there will be a lot of dead Marines."

Like other news of ill winds, developments in Normandy were not widely reported within Japanese ranks. When, a few days later, Commander Chihaya made another long-range, multileg sortie to spy on Majuro, a chill went down his spine. The American anchorage was empty.

5

The Outer Colony

As U.S. submarine wolf packs roamed at will, the sea lanes to the Marianas were the despair of Chuichi Nagumo. Once he had commanded the pride of the Imperial Navy, its carrier fleet, the vaunted Kido Butai. But his star had fallen fast after after his run-in with Raymond Spruance at the Battle of Midway. With Jisaburo Ozawa running the carrier task force now, Nagumo flew his flag over the threadbare naval garrison on Saipan.

When a convoy brought three regiments of Japanese troops from Manchuria to the Marianas in late February, the submarine *Trout* discovered it and set an ambush. The *Sakito Maru,* bound for Saipan with the 18th Regiment, was sunk, and a Guam-bound transport was damaged. Of the four thousand men in the regiment only 1,720 made it ashore, a third of them hospital cases. One of them was the commander of a rear-echelon medical company, Captain Sakae Oba. After his ship went down, the twenty-nine-year-old officer was hauled into a life raft and transferred to a destroyer that carried him and other survivors to the pier at the seaplane base at Garapan, Saipan's capital. Wearing tattered, oil-soaked fatigues, Oba was hospitalized briefly, then sent to a temporary barracks at a middle school. There he was ordered to take command of a makeshift company-sized command, 225 men, half of them drawn from the survivors of his own medical aid company and the rest an admixture of underequipped orphan soldiers. They were ordered to join a defense construction battalion working to emplace guns in the hills above Garapan. Oba's company of medics, engineers, and tank crewmen, few in possession of all their gear, were a motley group. He and his only other line officer, a cheerful soul named Lieutenant Banno, arranged for quarters and uniforms for them and dutifully set to work. Because of the volume of hard rock and coral they en-

countered, and shortages of building materials, the pace of work flagged to
less than half the estimate.

Oba set up his medical aid group in a valley just inland of Makunsha, a
village on Saipan's west coast about halfway between Garapan and Marpi
Point. There, in a thatched-roof treatment room, he had hospital space for
twenty-four stretchers, as well as two large caves for supplies and several
smaller ones for living quarters. By mid-May, their aid station was as complete as it would ever be, for the submarine stranglehold continued.

In the first week of June, U.S. subs struck Japanese convoys bringing
reinforcements to Saipan. The *Pintado* and *Shark* sank three large cargo
ships with terrible losses to their embarked soldiery. The Japanese Navy's
failure to safeguard the army's passage to the Marianas aggravated tensions
between Nagumo and Lieutenant General Yoshitsugu Saito, commander
of the army's 43rd Division and the senior Japanese Army officer on Saipan.
One of Saito's 43rd Division regiments, the 118th, arrived at Garapan at
less than half strength. At sea, even the most battle-hardened regiment was
as helpless as a cruise ship of tourists. All the air forces available to Admiral
Nimitz couldn't have done as much in three days against a division of soldiers entrenched ashore as Lockwood's wolf packs did in three hours
against their transports afloat.

Cargo ships bringing in construction materials fared no better. The
constriction of his lines of seaborne supply led the chief of staff of General
Saito's higher headquarters, the 31st Army, to warn Admiral Nagumo,
"Unless the units are supplied with cement, rebar, barbed wire, lumber,
etc., which cannot be obtained in these islands, no matter how many soldiers there are they can do nothing but sit with folded arms. The situation
is unbearable." Saito often lamented to Nagumo that without heavier
naval escort, the convoys would never get through. He made do with
what he had.

The largest artillery Saito had were eight British-built six-inch guns,
nine 140 mm and eight 120 mm dual-purpose guns, and four 200 mm mortars. Saito ordered them dispersed through the island's interior heights,
housing them in concrete blockhouses and pillboxes as well as in camouflaged open positions. A pair of the six-inchers were to be installed in casemates on Saipan's southwestern cape, Agignan Point, and the remaining
four split between Nafutan Point, the southeastern promontory, and Laulau Point, overlooking Magicienne Bay in the east. These, along with
several 140 mm dual-purpose guns, would be mounted belowground,
impossible to spot from offshore. On the slopes of Saipan's highest peak,

Mount Tapotchau, as well as a smaller peak to its west, the Japanese installed clusters of mortars, 75 mm mountain guns, and 150 mm howitzers,
which Saito's artillerists preregistered on all potential beachheads. Smaller
field guns were set in pillboxes and blockhouses on high bluffs and other
prominent points. These, Saito hoped, would produce a lethal enfilade on
the beaches, supplementing the mortars, large artillery, and howitzers.
Along most beaches, defensive trenchworks were dug in parallel, one just
up from the high-tide line and a second a few hundred yards inland, to
hold infantry and machine guns in positions protected by ridges, ravines,
and coral sinkholes. The trenches, rifle pits, and machine gun positions facing Magicienne Bay were protected by heavy wire entanglements.

Unlike the outer bases in the Marshalls and Gilberts, the Marianas had
a sizable nonmilitary population. For the twenty-eight thousand civilians
who worked in maritime commerce on Saipan—native Chamorros and
Japanese alike—life had few consolations after the war came calling. General Saito pressed into service all available hands, including women, children, and the aged, to build an airstrip on Saipan's west coast between the
capital of Garapan and the sugar processing center at Charan Kanoa. They
turned out with spades and saws and went to work on tree roots. They
hauled rocks and stones and set up bucket relays to carry fill from the
beach. The most loyal of them boasted of their blisters as evidence of their
service to the throne. But Japan's style of colonial administration, part par-
anoid, part predatory, did not take long to manifest, rankling and terror-
izing residents. Arrests, disappearances, resettlements, and executions for
treason dated to the start of the war, but the mood on Saipan was darken-
ing fast.

Manuel Sablan, the sixteen-year-old son of a Chamorro post office
worker, earned forty-five yen a month working as a messenger for the Japanese police. From that privileged position he was a close witness to the
growing oppressiveness of the garrison. He came to resent the crude regi-
mentation it imposed. The Chamorros were a lawful people. Before the
war came, just two police officers patrolled Garapan's streets on any given
night to protect a population of ninety thousand. The seven o'clock curfew
was an insult to their culture. And that wasn't the worst of it. The Chamorro natives were not allowed to speak their own language. Catholic
priests were forbidden to say Mass. Schools were closed. Trivial offenses
against military discipline brought a month in jail without a hearing.
Chamorros who knew English were arrested and interrogated. The Japanese Army drove families from the city and sent them to live in the farm-

lands while their homes were torn down and used for building materials. With his father deceased, it was especially hard for Manuel Sablan to see his mother and younger brothers evicted from their Garapan home and relocated to a farm near Aslito Field, in the island's south.

Mistreatment and abuse by foreigners had been the Chamorros' lot throughout history. When Ferdinand Magellan visited the Marianas in 1521, natives paddling canoes greeted him with gifts of freshly harvested fruit. Visiting his ships, some of them took a liking to pieces of loose iron they found, and because they had been raised in a communal culture, they helped themselves to it. Magellan, enraged, responded by sending a punitive raid that burned down a village. Thereafter he referred to the Marianas as "the Islands of Thieves." A century later, having been renamed in honor of Queen Mariana of Austria, who had sponsored Catholic missionaries there, the islands and their inhabitants faced disaster when the Chamorros rose up against the Spanish overlords. Rebellion and reprisals, coupled with repeated outbreaks of disease, reduced the Chamorro population from forty-five thousand to five thousand. Slowly, immigration from the Caroline Islands replenished the population. But the imperial chess game continued. In 1898, after the Spanish-American War, the Americans claimed Guam as a prize in the peace settlement that also put them in control of Puerto Rico and the Philippines. The following year, Spain sold the other Mariana Islands to Germany. They served as a minor trading post for Kaiser Wilhelm II before Japan declared war on Germany during World War I and exploited the withdrawal of the German East Asia Squadron from the hemisphere. In October 1914, when the battleship *Katori* dropped anchor off Garapan, the Marianas had a new ruler. The kaiser was too busy in Europe to contest Japan's bloodless conquest. From 1914 to 1922, when civilian government based on Palau was instituted under the League of Nations, the Japanese Navy ran the Marianas, thereafter known as the "Mandated Islands," more or less like their U.S. counterparts in Hawaii.

Thirty years of acquaintance with Japanese imperialism were a master class for the Chamorros in the meaning of the in-vogue term "Greater East Asia Co-Prosperity Sphere." Prosperity there surely had been. Tapping the Marianas for sugar, copra, and coconut, the Japanese turned the islands into a major axle in an old-fashioned mercantile machine. The Chamorros were subservient partners in a caste system run primarily by the military, but also by the managers of firms such as the South Seas Trading Company (*Nanyo Boeki Kabushiki-gaisha,* or "Nambo" for short). Many of them served in labor battalions, whose industrious company was salted with convicts shipped from the home islands. Even many Japanese resented this state of affairs. Shizuko Miura, eighteen, had worked for Nambo on Tinian before the arrival of the boisterous aviators of the First Air Fleet disrupted her quietude. "The streets belonged to the drunkards," she said, "these soldiers of the naval flying corps, who sang such gloomy and desperate songs." When she could stand it no longer, the poorly educated but enterprising young woman moved to Garapan to work for another firm.

The people remained unaware of the war until the February U.S. carrier raids. Afterward, everyone learned to follow the rules and avoid asking questions. Manuel Sablan's job as a police messenger gave him certain privileges, foremost among them being allowed to stay in Garapan. Informants were encouraged to report all activity that might be subversive.

During the first week of June, without fanfare, the Japanese decided to evacuate the wives and children of the privileged. Two ships, the MV *Santos* and MV *America,* were moored in Tanapag Harbor near Garapan when Manuel Sablan was sent to pack the belongings of the wife of the police chief. Shortly after they set sail, word came that the *America* had been torpedoed and everyone on board killed. One of Shizuko Miura's four sisters, Toeko, was on one of those ships. With news of its loss, she wrote, "Garapan seemed to die. Everything changed." Proprietors and workers alike appeared stuporous, vacant-eyed, as their stores were shuttered in mourning. As Japanese military tightened control, rumors spread that if the Americans ever landed, they would be coming for the women and children.

When Sablan heard that two U.S. pilots had been captured in a rubber boat off the northeastern shore, he bicycled to the jailhouse and saw a truck unloading four blindfolded men, hands tied behind their backs. "They were white and extraordinarily big," Sablan said. "Their hair was gold. I never found out much about those Americans. We went back to the jail about a week later and they were gone." An old Japanese man said they had been shipped to Japan.

Later, two more Americans arrived. They were pilots, it was said, shot down and captured at Truk. Again Sablan wanted to see them. He said, "One of the Chamorro police officers, I believe it was Antonio Cabrera, told us not to go, but we went anyway. We sneaked in and we saw the two Americans in two different cells. One was sitting in the corner holding his stomach as if he were in pain. The other one was just walking around the cell, smiling and talking, though he had a bullet wound in his arm." One of the Americans was quite tall, the other a bit shorter. The shorter one had the wounded arm.

The countrymen of the captive American aviators returned on June 11, when the preparatory air strikes began. Shizuko Miura was at her second-story office in downtown Garapan when she heard the wail of warning sirens and the bark of antiaircraft artillery. "When I gazed at the sky for the enemy planes," she recalled, "I uttered a cry unconsciously. It was a great formation which seemed to consist of hundreds, no, many thousands. One formation after another." As waves of bomb-laden fighter aircraft set upon the town and its harbor, windows rattled and buildings shook.

Leaving the office and running down the stairs to an underground bomb shelter, Shizuko and her fellow employees trembled before the onslaught of Task Force 58. For thirty minutes they huddled in hiding while it continued. Then she could stand it no longer. Plagued by the uncertainty of what might come next, Shizuko left the shelter. Momentarily relieved to see the blue sky, even though it was filled with American aircraft, she rushed up the stairs to her office. Looking out the window, where the sun glowered brown through the smoke, she saw two planes spinning in flames toward the sea. Assuming they were American, she cried out without realizing it, *"Banzai!"*

Previously the enemy pilots had spared private homes and concentrated on naval facilities. Now, facing gunfire from buildings all through the militarized island capital, the Hellcat pilots unleashed themselves on the city. With Japanese planes resisting mostly as soloists, attacking without coordination, it could scarcely be called a battle. A Task Force 58 fighter sweep was simply an ordeal to be endured and, hopefully, survived.

With the whereabouts of the Japanese carriers still largely a mystery, Raymond Spruance had hesitated to approve the fighter sweep ahead of the heavier air strikes that were planned for June 12, D Day minus three. At first he signed off on it provisionally: His planes would fly only if the Japanese carrier fleet had not been spotted by June 10. But Marc Mitscher argued that the strike should proceed regardless of enemy surface contacts. Even if his carriers sent the whole house against the Marianas, he said, they were more than prepared to defend themselves with two hundred Hellcats in reserve. And so Mitscher's "Plan Johnny," named for the young officer on the operations staff who conceived it, went forward.

On the afternoon of June 11, from a position east of Guam, the fighter pilots of Task Force 58 marched to their flight decks, with each group given an airfield to hit. The *Hornet* task group drew Guam and Rota. The *Bunker Hill* task group attacked Tinian, concentrating on the airfield at Ushi Point. The *Enterprise* task group took southern Saipan and its most dangerous hive, Aslito Field. David McCampbell and his company from the *Essex* covered Saipan's heavily settled west coast, from Charan Kanoa to Marpi Point. Behind a pair of wayfinding TBF-1c Avengers equipped with extra rubber life rafts, the commander of Air Group 15 led the rendezvous of thirty-nine Hellcats from the *Essex, Cowpens,* and *Langley* and set course for Saipan, a two-hundred-twenty-mile flight.

Arriving over the island at twelve thousand feet, with the early afternoon sun skylighting his canopy overhead, McCampbell pushed over into his first dive over Tanapag Harbor. While the seven bomb-carrying Hellcats dropped their instantaneous-fuzed 350-pounders on the seaplane ramp, strafers took apart targets on the water: large seaplanes at their moorings, a small cargo ship, and shore installations as far up the coast as Marpi Point. There, an oil storage tank was left spouting a tower of pitch-black smoke that leaned over to the southwest and churned for an hour and a half before dying.

After the first pass, the Japanese lit smoke pots on the eastern shore, producing a thick haze that flowed across the island on the easterly winds. But McCampbell's pilots still found targets of opportunity. Flying in sections of two and divisions of four, they strafed without interference from enemy planes, though flak was plentiful and accurate. On the initial run over the harbor, one of McCampbell's youngsters, Lieutenant (j.g.) L. T. Kenney, was hit by flak and continued straight into the water. He was one of a dozen Hellcat pilots lost that day.

Out to sea, several miles northwest of Marpi Point, the action was brisk. The skipper of Fighting Fifteen, Commander Charles W. Brewer, destroyed a pair of dark green Kawanishi H8K "Emily" flying boats, then spied three Zekes west of Garapan, but they were turned into charcoal streaks before he could close them. Squadron exec James F. Rigg, after burning an Emily moored in the harbor, saw a Japanese fighter low on his five o'clock. Banking around and spiraling down, he got on its tail as the Tojo skidded from left to right, and he fired bursts into its wing roots until it came apart at the seams. Regaining altitude, Rigg found a Zeke coming at him head-on. It was a game of chicken that only a man behind a bullet-proof windscreen could love. Both planes held course until a collision was but a few seconds away; then the Zeke pulled up, exposing its belly. Rigg peppered its engine nacelle, and the Zeke turned and lost control, crashing into the water.

Task Force 58, June 1944
VADM Marc A. Mitscher, commanding

Task Group 58.1: *Hornet* (RADM J. J. Clark), *Yorktown, Belleau Wood,* and *Bataan*

Task Group 58.2: *Bunker Hill* (RADM A. E. Montgomery), *Wasp, Cabot,* and *Monterey*

Task Group 58.3: *Enterprise* (RADM J. W. Reeves), *Lexington, San Jacinto,* and *Princeton*

Task Group 58.4: *Essex* (RADM W. K. Harrill), *Langley,* and *Cowpens*

With their debut over the Marianas, McCampbell's air group was on the long march to becoming the highest-scoring naval air unit in the Pacific. The skipper was flying low cover for his strafers when he scored his first kill of the war. Three miles southwest of Saipan, McCampbell saw a Zeke dive through the cloud ceiling behind him. When the Japanese pilot pulled up in a high wingover to his left, the American turned toward him, gained his tail, and dropped him into the water.

McCampbell's pilots had little difficulty with Japanese fighters over Saipan, destroying seventeen. Flak was the greater threat. Over Aslito Field, the *Lexington*'s Fighting Sixteen lost one of its best. Lieutenant (j.g.) Bill Burckholter, an ace with six kills, was hit on a strafing run. Descending to make a water landing about six miles east of Nafutan Point, he made an upwind descent, dropping his tail so that it touched the swells first, easing the plane into the sea upright. Throwing open his canopy, he climbed onto the port wing, only to find that his parachute had deployed. The bulk of his inflated life jacket kept him from reaching the buckles that released his harness. And when he found that his chute had snagged in the cockpit, Burckholter was effectively chained to his sinking plane. Within thirty seconds he was underwater, never to come back up.

Conditioned to expect American air attacks at dawn, the Japanese seemed surprised by the afternoon sweep and suffered for their inattention to patrol and search. "When there was no raid early in the morning," Kusaka wrote, "we usually thought there would be no attack that day. . . . The damage was the greater because of our incautiousness." The young trainees of the First Air Fleet paid the price. From Orote Peninsula on Guam to Marpi Point on Saipan, the fighter sweep winnowed the ranks of the student-heavy Japanese air unit. A flight of Hellcats from the *Hornet,* set upon by Zekes over Guam, got less than they bargained for, destroying twenty-three in a briskly fought scrap. The *Cabot* and *Monterey* fighter squadrons cleared the air of interceptors over Tinian, exposing a flight of twin-engine Betty bombers that had just rolled to a stop after landing. The opportunistic Americans dived down to the deck and burned nine.

"It was noted that the enemy fighters were never seen to employ team-work or effective defensive or offensive tactics but specialized in acrobatics, many times low over the water, which resulted in at least one Nip diving into the sea unable to pull out of a split S practically on the deck," a Navy analyst would write. "The net result of the sweep was to destroy or seriously damage approximately one hundred and fifty aircraft in the air or on the ground, a blow which not only safeguarded Task Force 58's entrance into the area and facilitated the first day's bombing program, but placed the enemy in a position of requiring drastic steps toward reinforcement."

It was late afternoon on June 11 when Shizuko Miura heard the all-clear siren wail. With the naval hospital abandoned, the walking wounded sought shelter elsewhere, and many came to her office. Trained in first aid through service in a women's auxiliary, she applied bandages and disinfectant. There were eight patients at first, then sixteen, all bleeding from shrapnel and .50-caliber bullet wounds. In the street for a break, she came upon a soldier named Goto, sobbing as he sat by the bodies of two soldiers. "For eighteen years since my birth, until war came to Saipan, I had never seen a dead man's face," she wrote. "So I might not have known death. But before my eyes, these two soldiers lay dead as if to teach me: 'Look! This is death itself!'" She thought of her older brother, Shinichi, an army tank crewman and a veteran of the Manchuria fighting, who, miracle of miracles, had been transferred to Saipan to serve with a tank unit quartered at Charan Kanoa. She had seen him earlier that spring as his tank passed through town. He looked older, sun-weathered. His armored vehicle was painted with kanji representing the word "Swallow." Looking across the sound, just six miles to her south, she wondered how her parents and sisters on Tinian were faring. She was sure her parents were doing the same from their farmhouse there, anxious about their daughter so close abroad. Having entertained the notion of her own death, having entertained it beyond the point of fear, she silently exulted, *Mother, Shizuko is full of spirit!*

When the planes went away, the streets buzzed with soldiers, and work parties carried the stretcher cases to refuge higher in the hills. Smoke rose above Garapan and Tanapag Harbor. Just as the army had warned, here came the foreign devils, hungry for rape and conquest, bent on the consumption of the young. That was the message Japanese officials spread among the populace, and Shizuko heard the grim warnings and trembled.

Out to sea, about two hundred miles to the southwest, Marc Mitscher's four carrier task groups were readying another blow.

6

A Rumor of Fleets

Before first light on June 12, McCampbell took to the skies again to exploit the smashing success of the fighter sweep. The whole *Essex* air group was with him now, including the torpedo and bombing squadrons. On the way in, McCampbell spotted the white truck lights of a ship on the sea, winking in betrayal on the black velvet below. He ordered a section of Hellcats from the *Cowpens* to work it over. Confronted with their two dozen fifties, the Japanese ship captain quickly got smart about light discipline.

Over Saipan, finding no enemy planes, McCampbell circled to cover the Avengers and Helldivers as they piled in to hit enemy gun and troop positions also using the idle time to note and report the surf conditions at the landing beaches. Returning to the *Essex,* he found his squadron unscathed save three Hellcats pockmarked by small-caliber fire. McCampbell was getting ready to strike Saipan again when he received an order to hit a new target. His force of twenty-eight Hellcats, and the same number of Helldivers and Avengers, would divert and pursue a Japanese merchant ship convoy reported northwest of the island. Gaining altitude, McCampbell ordered his pilots to form a scouting line twenty miles wide to search the ocean below. Sixty-five miles north of the island, McCampbell found three columns of cargo ships, led by an old destroyer and ringed by thirteen small patrol craft. It was a brutal sunrise for these sailors.

As the half-moon retreated in the west, the sky was filled with the low hum of American pistons. Then the Hellcats appeared, wings trailing dot-dot-dot puffs like semaphore as they let fly with tracer and ball. Around and around they went, each plane making six runs apiece. McCampbell called it the rotary mower drill. The old destroyer and a small merchantman were quickly in flames. Every one of the escorts took lead; two were torn open and sunk by .50-caliber fire alone.

Then the bombers took their turn. As McCampbell watched from a high cover position at twelve thousand feet, he could see how the chaotic swirl of evading ships would make it hard to untangle the damage claims of his pilots. The largest *maru,* straddled by a bomb salvo, stopped dead in the water. Then she was strafed severely enough to start fires in her superstructure. A small cargo ship, shot up badly, was attacked by a Helldiver, which straddled her close off her bows with a brace of bombs. The explosions shredded deck plates and lofted fragments and debris. Another cargo ship took a near miss from a bomb just off the port beam, slowing her enough for an Avenger to close in a glide-diving attack and drop four more that buckled her plates, leaving her to sink. A five-thousand-tonner, taking two wing racks of rockets, burned from bridge to stern. Japanese ship construction was no match for the violent forces carried by McCampbell's posse of ship-killing specialists.

Circling the convoy twice to confirm damage and catalog targets for follow-up attacks, McCampbell led his flight back to the *Essex* while the Japanese ships pushed west, trailing oil. He would claim five vessels sunk, four probably sunk, and twenty damaged, six of them seriously. There was no knowing the casualties to personnel, but about thirty members of one surviving Japanese crew, about half of them civilian fishermen, crawled ashore on Anatahan, a volcano island about ninety miles north of Saipan, where they disappeared into the jungle, their war essentially over, to subsist on forage.

Later in the afternoon, Air Group 15 returned. Commander Brewer led a dozen Hellcats and fifteen Helldivers, all bearing bombs, and set upon the survivors, a formation of six small cargo ships and five escorts led by a destroyer. For the latter, a newcomer to the convoy, this escort assignment was a rude awakening. She was set upon and whipped by .50-caliber slugs. Diving on one of the cargo ships, Brewer dropped his external fuel tank like a bomb, hitting her with it and washing her decks with burning fuel. Of the thirty ships in the original convoy, half were either confirmed sunk or counted as probables, six were badly damaged, and nine more damaged. Seven survivors were eventually recovered and taken to the *Essex,* where as POWs they confirmed the horrific details. The day belonged to Task Force 58, striking at will with little resistance from the overmatched students of the First Air Fleet.

The next morning, McCampbell's group took one last swing against the fleeing, brutalized convoy, then joined the strikes against Saipan's airfields and air defenses. One thing he and his pilots learned: Although small ships were devilishly hard to hit, they did have the virtue of sinking when you hit them. It was far harder to kill an airfield. You could shoot down and burn planes, you could strafe and kill men. But putting a fifty-acre stretch of dirt and coral permanently out of business, unusable by planes that might fly in tomorrow from other bases, was nearly impossible. Carrier air attacks were neither heavy nor sustained enough to outstrip the capacity of working parties to fill craters.

Antiaircraft guns were the thorniest targets of all. Not only were they inclined to defend themselves, but destroying them required tremendous accuracy. The Navy's number crunchers had worked it all out. The odds against a dive-bomber pilot's directly hitting a gun revetment twenty-five feet in diameter was three hundred to one. The odds fell to six hundred to one in glide-bombing attacks, and ten thousand to one via level bombing from high altitude. The advent of wing-mounted rockets improved a pilot's chance of a hit to twenty-one to one. The Navy discovered a law of diminishing returns with larger ordnance: A five-hundred-pound bomb had to land within twenty feet to disable a gun in a revetment; a two-thousand-pounder had to hit within thirty feet. Smaller bombs had much to recommend them. "For even a thirty percent chance of making a direct hit on one of the guns in a two-gun emplacement, a hundred bombs must be dropped via dive bombing, and a hundred thirty-five in glide bombing. The only practicable way of achieving anything like this concentration is by the use of small bombs." Temporary suppression—neutralization as opposed to outright destruction—was the most realistic goal of an air attack. That end, the Navy found, was most reliably achieved with a few hundred .50-caliber rounds from an unladen Hellcat on a strafing run.

For the strikes that ran through the day on June 13, the *Lexington* task group launched almost every plane it had: sixty-two Hellcats, fifty-three Helldivers, and twenty-two Avengers, many of the latter armed with rockets. Under high scattered cirrus they formed up. Against a buzz saw of flak they chewed over Aslito Field. The rocket-firing Avengers were vulnerable while making glide attacks. Medium antiaircraft guns, mobile and deadly, were especially threatening to the large, slow planes. A pilot from Torpedo Seventeen, Lieutenant (j.g.) Frank M. Delgado, destroyed a hangar north of the airstrip and caught a large fragment from a 75 mm shell during pullout. He and his two aircrewmen escaped the plane, leaving it to crash and burn. As they drifted on the winds, south and west toward the sea, Japanese gunners along the beach fired on them. The last anyone saw of Delgado, his parachute had collapsed under fire when he was still four hundred feet above the water. None of the three men were recovered in spite of careful searching by the Navy.

Commander Robert H. Isely, the skipper of the *Lexington*'s Torpedo Sixteen, was leading a rocket attack against gun positions near Aslito Field when his Avenger became a torch during its glide. He went in straight. No parachutes blossomed as Isely's plane crashed at the southern edge of the airfield. Thereafter, the use of rockets by lumbering torpedo bombers was loudly protested in the ready rooms of the carrier task force, for the numbers portended rough times ahead once the carriers began striking well-defended heavy industry. In June 1944, antiaircraft fire replaced aerial interception as the greatest danger to U.S. pilots. In the first three weeks of the campaign, strikes on gun positions would cost Mitscher nineteen planes over Saipan, thirty-five over Guam, and seventeen over Tinian, for a loss rate of 1.25 aircraft per hundred sorties.

For the moment, Spruance and Mitscher were in firm possession of the seaways around the Marianas. With their four groups operating as close as forty miles east of Guam, the air strikes continued on June 13. Meanwhile, Kelly Turner's amphibious force was plunging westward about six hundred miles to the east, having departed Eniwetok in a majestic dawn procession seventy-two hours before.

The command ship *Rocky Mount,* bearing Turner and Holland Smith, led the immense company of the Fifth Amphibious Force, with seventy-one thousand invasion troops embarked. After his minesweepers cleared Mellu Pass, the destroyers of Captain Jesse Coward's antisubmarine screen departed Roi Anchorage, Kwajalein, before eight A.M., forming up around the heavies. The old battleships *Tennessee, California, Maryland,* and *Colorado* cleared the pass, then the escort carriers *Kitkun Bay* and *Gambier Bay* and the APDs *Gilmer, Clemson,* and *Brooks,* carrying Draper Kauffman and his UDTs. The bombardment group overtook the tractors along the way. Forming a circular cruising disposition, with the *Kitkun Bay* as the guide in line abreast behind the battleships, they slugged along at ten knots, radios scrupulously silent, destination Marianas.

Turner's fleet was like a great wave surging invisibly through midocean waters. It was difficult to take its measure until it was just about upon you.

From the standpoint of the U.S. troops embarked, the naval forces that carried and protected them assembled mysteriously, like schools of fish appearing from beyond range of sight in the deep. "This one morning I came up out of the hold after a night's rest," said Donald Boots, a Fourth Marine Division engineer, "and I couldn't believe what I saw. It was a mass of ships. I'd never seen anything like that in my life! We'd always talk—some of our guys—and we said, 'See how important we are? Right here, we're in the center, and we got the whole U.S. Navy protecting us.'"

At intervals, the tedium of breaking swells at thirteen knots gave way to the frantic rigmarole of antiaircraft and damage control drills. Occasionally a submarine contact enlivened the moment and a destroyer peeled off for an exploratory foray, sonar pinging and hatches dogged shut.

The operation in Normandy, seven days along, had seen an Allied invasion force cross one hundred twenty miles of sea, using modern harbors sustained by a major seafaring nation's infrastructure. Operation Forager was something far more ambitious. Staging from Eniwetok, already a continent's distance (2,700 miles) from Pearl Harbor, the Fifth Amphibious Force would traverse a thousand miles on this final leg.

In a sense, the long distances were Turner's friend. Combined Fleet headquarters suspected a major movement was underway, but until submarines or aircraft made an actual sighting, they could not know for sure. They were not convinced the Marianas were the objective until the morning of the thirteenth, when Spruance detached seven fast battleships from carrier escort duty to bombard gun positions on Saipan's southwestern beaches. The *Washington,* flagship of Rear Admiral Willis A. Lee, led her divisionmates *Indiana* and *North Carolina,* joined by the *Iowa* and *New Jersey,* and the *South Dakota* and *Alabama.* The mightiest gunfighters in the fleet approached Saipan's western shore and split off by division. Opening fire at eleven, they kept at it until midafternoon, covering minesweepers that went in to sweep the shallows.

While all ships reported optimistically on the results of their gunnery, none of the fast battleships had trained at Kelly Turner's Kaho'olawe gunnery schoolhouse, and their results showed it. Though the barrage was prodigious—2,400 sixteen-inch and 12,500 five-inch shells—the high muzzle velocity and flat trajectory of their fire made it difficult for them to hit targets situated on anything other than a coastline or a forward slope. And so the large farmhouses and sugar mills of Charan Kanoa burned, but hardened gun emplacements were unscathed. A wag in the task force called it "a Navy-sponsored farm project that simultaneously plows the fields, prunes the trees, harvests the crops, and adds iron to the soil." But it did little for the Marines who would charge this hostile shore and take it from enemies secured in blockhouses and just over the next hill.

Though the invasion force itself had not yet been spotted, the vigor of Spruance's activities on June 13 finally convinced the Japanese Naval General Staff that Saipan was the objective of the next U.S. landing. Still, Admiral Toyoda was careful about activating the Marianas battle plan, Operation A-Go. The fuel problem meant he couldn't afford to move his fleet in error. When Toyoda got news of U.S. minesweepers working Garapan harbor and a pack of fast battleships pounding sand, it was clear that Saipan was the American objective; A-Go could commence. As Ozawa and his First Mobile Fleet put to sea, the Japanese halted their effort to reinforce Biak. As nine aircraft carriers prepared to depart Tawi Tawi with their consorts, a close watch would be kept on Saipan.

The Combined Fleet chief of staff, Kusaka, was buoyant. Ozawa's sortie, as he saw it, was no desperate measure. It was a magnificent trap: "If the First Mobile Fleet sortied too early, the enemy might stop its landing operation, or retire," he wrote. "Therefore it was necessary to make sure the enemy would land troops after conducting air raids and warship bombardment. Then the enemy would be in a fix, having no choice but to try to save their own soldiers."

The trap would be sprung, he wrote, "when there came to be no retreat for the enemy."

With the U.S. Fifth Fleet booming into the southern Marianas, Rear Admiral Lockwood, knowing his Japanese counterparts would be stalking Spruance, instructed his submarine wolf packs to decamp from their hunting grounds close to the islands and seek out less crowded waters. He had no wish for the presence of his boats to hinder Spruance's destroyers from their pursuits or to see his own subs get caught in a rain of American depth charges. By many indications, farther afield to the west, new game was in the brush.

From their patrol stations off Truk, off Palau, in the Surigao and San Bernardino straits in the Philippines, off Okinawa and the Bonins, forty-eight Pacific Fleet submarines roamed with the mission of intercepting enemy ships approaching the Marianas. Six more boats from Rear Admiral Ralph W. Christie's Southwest Pacific command, supporting MacArthur, were in the Sulu Sea and the southwestern Philippine Sea. "The setup looked excellent and we sat back to admire it," Lockwood would write. "All exits from the Inland Sea and Tokyo Bay were covered, as well as normal areas along the coasts of the Empire."

At first light on June 13, the *Redfin* sounded the alarm. Spruance's white whale was off Tawi Tawi: The sub reported six Japanese carriers, four battleships, five heavy cruisers, one light cruiser, and six destroyers. The American boat was unable to gain position for an attack, but that was no terrible thing. The contact report that she radioed to Brisbane was of far greater value. It was Ozawa, no doubt about it. Three days earlier, another sub, the *Harder,* had reported three battleships in the same area, including a giant of the *Musashi* class. "The Japanese had been pried out," Mitscher's chief of staff, Arleigh Burke, wrote. "They were going to do something. Maybe they would attack, maybe they would feint, maybe they would go home. We didn't know."

Within days, all the mysteries at hand, including all rumors of fleets, would at last have their solution.

7

OBB and UDT

In the predawn darkness of June 14, Kelly Turner's weapons of mass destruction approached Saipan from the east in a circular cruising disposition, and at 2:25 A.M. general quarters sounded. As the moon glowed through the overcast, the search radars of Rear Admiral Jesse Oldendorf's bombardment group registered the island, fourteen miles to the west. Seen from overhead, it resembles nothing so much, to a modern eye, as a standing profile of the monster Godzilla, tramping east toward Hawaii.

When Oldendorf, in the heavy cruiser *Louisville,* led the *Tennessee, California, Maryland,* and *Colorado* around Saipan's northern cape, twelve miles off Marpi Point, Japanese shore batteries met him with a trio of two-gun salvos. He pushed on. Turning south to approach the landing beach, he formed up in column parallel to shore, eight miles out, while Rear Admiral Walden L. Ainsworth led the other group, including the *Pennsylvania, New Mexico,* and *Idaho,* around Nafutan Point, transiting the three-mile channel that separated Saipan from nearby Tinian.

The epitaph for the Pacific Fleet's squadron of old battleships, or OBBs, was written while the pyres at Pearl Harbor were still warm. Though salvaged and modernized within months after the attack, there was no overcoming the mechanics of their antiquated design. With their twenty-one-knot top speeds, they were too slow to run with the carriers or to anchor their own striking forces. They were useless in pursuit except to consume farmloads of fuel at flank speed; they could not maneuver with the swift cruisers and destroyers that operated with them. The ancient craft of shipbuilding never stood still, and before the war had even begun the OBBs were surpassed in speed, size, and firepower by newer ships. Designed for the Great War, the old battleships would have seen their role reduced to the symbolic—icons of another day's fleet—had Kelly Turner not transformed them into specialty players with an essential role in his traveling show: floating corps artillery for the alligator navy. Now bombardment was their game. They were students and masters of all its varieties and forms. Harassing fire, supporting fire, neutralization fire, destruction fire, interdiction fire. Each served a distinct, definable purpose, and each had a chapter in the new manual of the trade. Some of their fire would be prearranged, delivered by schedule; much more of it would fly on call from the shore.

In the gun pits of the battlewagons, turret crews kept up a constant cycle of cleaning and inspection. Firing locks and breeches were taken apart every day, cleaned, and lubricated with castor oil. Guns were boresighted daily, carefully aligned with the scopes that trained and elevated them. After test firing, the great barrels were scrubbed clean of residue with cylindrical wire brushes. And the crews practiced and practiced. "If everything was really moving, you could fire a gun every thirteen seconds," said Leo Vrana of the USS *California*.

First light came at 4:25. Forty-five minutes later, just before sunrise, the fantail catapults on the *Tennessee* threw two floatplanes skyward for gunnery spotting. As Ainsworth's cruisers opened fire on gun positions in the cliffs of Nafutan Point, Japanese crews manning the weapons hidden in the greenery revealed themselves with licks of orange flame as they fired in return. On board the light cruiser *Honolulu,* a VIP observer, Samuel Eliot Morison, seconded to the fleet from the Harvard history faculty, watched transfixed. Twenty minutes later, with their eyes in the sky on station, the battleships began to roar.

The *California* worked over her schedule of targets—trenchworks and guns—from Afetna Point northward. Spruance always insisted on wielding the shears of a "Spruance haircut" himself, from a place where he could see the results personally. At six o'clock, he got his front-row seat on the action when his flagship, the *Indianapolis,* joined Rear Admiral Howard F. Kingman's Fire Support Unit One, anchored by the battleships *California* and *Tennessee*.

In the north, the *Montpelier* targeted coastal defense batteries around Marpi Point, while the *Cleveland* locked her directors on large dualpurpose antiaircraft guns installed on a cliff-side mesa south of the Marpi Point airfield. Her first salvos fell short, but she spotted her aim up the cliff until the blasts of her six-inch were hitting the buildings on top of it and walking through the gun galleries the Japanese had dug into the cliff's rocky face. Taking no return fire, the *Cleveland* worked slowly southward, methodically targeting pillboxes and emplacements along the beaches on Kagman Peninsula's northeast coast. Switching then to indirect fire, she fired across the valley at the neck of the peninsula, and lofted salvos across it, enfilading fortifications near Laulau on Magicienne Bay, using aircraft for spotting. When the *Cleveland* drew so close to Kagman Peninsula that the sheer bluffs of its southeast face cut into her line of fire, she spotted up and loosed several volleys at long range into Nafutan Point. For nearly an hour that morning, the *Cleveland* worked the water's edge all the way around Magicienne Bay, hammering its northside beaches with close-in direct fire. Then she withdrew to the east to haul aboard and reservice her spotting planes. And so it went, ship by ship, as the Navy began the process of reducing the great fortress of Japan's inner defensive line target by target, spot by spot. A thousand miles west of the nearest forward base, Eniwetok, and many miles more from the next naval ordnance depot, there was no ammunition to waste.

The morning fireworks were a showcase of the bombardment force's mobility and heavy power, both of which it exploited fully as its ships maneuvered to gain commanding firing positions against strongpoints unreachable by ground artillery. But the bombardment's effectiveness was difficult to rate. Though an illusion of total destruction arose whenever a target was swallowed by smoke, its true effect would be reflected in the activity level of the enemy in the area after the dust settled. The canary in that particular coal mine on the morning of June 14, the day before D Day, would be Draper Kauffman and the men of his Underwater Demolition Teams.

The UDT were among several wrinkles that Turner and Holland Smith had in store for D Day, set to roll less than twenty-four hours hence. Some were technical: ranks of LCI gunboats, advancing ahead of the amtracs, firing rockets in swarms. Some were organizational: a new way to organize the Marine divisions and their weapons, based on the concept of the battalion landing team. This was an eleven-hundred-man unit, two or three of them to every regiment, whose nucleus was a regular infantry battalion, muscled up with additional integrated elements: an artillery battery, an amphibious assault vehicle platoon, a combat engineer platoon, a light armored reconnaissance company, a tank platoon, a reconnaissance platoon, and other units as a mission might require. Other wrinkles were tactical.

Turner had an entire transport division set aside, carrying a whole Marine regiment, to execute a false landing off Tanapag, the large harbor town north of Garapan. With the feint, he hoped to freeze Japanese forces in place well up the coast from the actual assault area. During planning, the Marines sprang a little surprise of their own. It was intended to deceive the U.S. Navy.

Holland Smith's chief of staff, Brigadier General Graves Erskine, proposed the idea of embarking a battalion of Marines in rubber boats and, in dark of night, towing them with landing craft to the beach on the north coast of Magicienne Bay, on the side of the island opposite where the main landings would take place. Lieutenant Colonel Wood B. Kyle's First Battalion of the Second Regiment (1/2) would go in light and mobile. Carrying no weapons heavier than their rifles and a few 60 mm mortars, they would move rapidly inland from Laulau before dawn and assault Saipan's highest peak, Mount Tapotchau, three times the height of Iwo Jima's Mount Suribachi. The 1/2 would take it, and then hold on against the inevitable counterattacks, resupplied by parachute drop, until units of the Second and Fourth Marine divisions had fought their way to the top of the island.

"This was the song and dance I gave," Erskine said. The audacious administrative caper was calculated to appeal to Spruance and Turner, for the fast conquest of key objectives was always a priority, promising as it did to free the Navy from the dangerous, exposed job of supporting a ground operation. Erskine knew his proposal would never survive review by his higher headquarters, but the plan was not essential. What mattered were its men. "I wanted at least one extra reinforced battalion, but the Navy claimed they were short of ships."

Holland Smith was in on the gambit. During discussion, he played the role of skeptic and inquisitor with zeal and zest, claiming that he agonized through many sleepless nights over the tactical problem of putting the 1/2 up the heavily defended mountain before reluctantly canceling the mission—but not until the Navy had assigned additional shipping for a Marine Corps brainstorm it decided it liked.

And so, just as Erskine had calculated all along, Colonel Kyle's battalion was thrown into the general reserve, right where Smith and Erskine had wanted it all along. The shipping stayed, too. Erskine would call it "a beautiful maneuver," adding, "In our planning we had to do a lot of things like that, in order to get what we really felt we needed to carry out the operation." The Marine Corps had built a maverick reputation on the battles it fought in the halls of the Pentagon against the Navy's perceived quest to sideline and humiliate it in various ways. At Saipan, the Marines had a last laugh. They hadn't won a "special operations" victory so efficiently since Lieutenant O'Bannon roamed the Barbary Coast.

As the sun rose on June 14, D Day minus one, Draper Kauffman and his two Underwater Demolition Teams left their cramped crew spaces in the APDs *Gilmer* and *Brooks* and began their part in the action, piling into four landing craft that came alongside the ships. Each of the thirty-six-foot-long LCPRs took sixteen swimmers, each assigned to survey the approach to a particular beach. The Japanese had not reckoned with a volume of preparatory fires reaching such a crescendo. Nor were they expecting to discover, as day broke, swimmers sidestroking toward them, led by officers embarked in flagships no more glorious than a motorized black mattress, puttering in via an electric motor toward the well-defended shore.

Kauffman and his teams were minimally equipped as usual, wearing trunks, swim shoes, a face mask, and a sheath knife. They didn't have fins or snorkels. Each pair carried a buoy, a reel, a Plexiglas slate, and a grease pencil as well. Though they had trained in the use of oxygen–beryllium chloride rebreathers, they didn't carry those, either. The gear was cumbersome. Most of Kauffman's team leaders decided to toss their bulky radios, too, in favor of a faster swim. And so they crossed the reef and entered the lagoon using a basic sidestroke known as the "invasion crawl." It was less exhausting than an overhand crawl and produced minimal splash.

Kauffman was resigned to the idea that their chances of coming through unbloodied were poor. Team Five, under Kauffman, would reconnoiter the Red and Green beaches; UDT 7, under the command of Lieutenant Richard F. Burke, would take Blue and Yellow. Quietly estimating that his casualties would run as high as fifty percent, he kept his third team, UDT 6, in reserve, prepared for the worst.

As the LCPRs approached the reef, Japanese fire splashed around them. The frogmen began rolling over the gunwales into the water, one pair every twenty-five yards. Each duo dropped a red buoy, anchoring it to the point marking the seaward origin of their route, in order to orient them for the return. When enemy shell splashes began walking in toward the buoys, the Team Seven exec, Sidney Robbins, instructed the crews to stop placing them. He also decided then and there to abandon the use of the string reconnaissance technique that Kauffman had taught them. *This was not going to be easy,* he thought. The less they carried, the greater their chance of surviving the gauntlet ahead. Shortly after 8:30, Kauffman and his buddy, a frogman named Page, switched on their small outboard electric motor and began their puttering daylight run toward the beach.

The motorized mattresses were humble flagships, but Kauffman wanted his team leaders to keep some semblance of awareness and potential control over their eight dispersed swimming pairs. Kauffman was soon to consider them "the dumbest idea I'd had in a long time. They were the most magnificent targets." In briefings, he had heard about the large sharks and man-eating giant clams known to be in the area. But he had advised his men to take no precautions against them, because greater threats loomed: Japanese coastal guns, beach pillboxes, and mortars, for starters.

A low ceiling of gun smoke hung over the strand as the bombardment continued. Just inland of the Red beaches, oil storage tanks were burning fiercely. The *California*'s neutralization fire was meant to keep enemy gunners from shooting at the UDT, and also to interdict Japanese troop movements down from Garapan. But even after rehearsing with real live ships at Kaho'olawe, Kauffman wasn't prepared for this. When he saw splashes in the lagoon landing perilously close to his men, both ahead of and behind them, he thought the Navy needed work on its marksmanship. He radioed his executive officer, Johnny DeBold, and said, "Blow Pistol, this is Blow Gun. For God's sake tell the support ships they're firing short."

Slowly and calmly DeBold answered, "Skipper, those aren't shorts, they're *overs*. They're not ours!"

Kauffman's reply fell flatly from his mouth. "Oh."

The UDT commander's many gifts did not include sharp eyesight. He was significantly shortsighted, in fact, so his buddy Page served as his seeing eye. But Page was color-blind. As they motored in, Page told Kauffman what he was looking at and Kauffman told him what color it was. That became the running joke, at any rate, but it was true. To Kauffman's amazement, all of his men closed to within fifty yards of the beach, and most went in even nearer than that, under continued heavy fire.

On the *Indianapolis,* on station more than a mile west of Afetna Point in order to cover the lagoon reconnaissance, Raymond Spruance was serenely watching his flagship's secondary battery pound the Blue beaches when incoming return fire began landing nearby. As large splashes rose close aboard, Captain E. R. Johnson maneuvered sharply back and forth, keeping broadside to his enemy while trying to anticipate the fall of shot. But the *Birmingham,* astern Spruance's flagship, seemed to command greater interest from the shore gunners. Her ample battery of fast-firing six-inch/47s probably marked her as the greater threat. As she eased along at five knots, plunging fire straddled her like a pair of calipers two hundred yards off both beams. Two more shells followed quickly, raising splashes just twenty-five yards to port. Captain Thomas B. Inglis backed his engines, then increased his RPMs, backing faster, just then to be straddled seventy-five yards dead ahead, and then again still closer off the starboard bow. Noticing a shore battery on the heights above Garapan—three-inch guns, he thought—the captain ordered his gunnery officer to bring the secondary battery to bear. The first salvo produced a spout of white and yellow smoke that marked a direct hit. But the torrent of incoming fire continued. Japanese ordnance whistled through the cruiser's masts, over, astern, ahead, and to port. Shells pierced the large square bedspring of her air-search radar antenna. Inglis thought it was mortar fire until one shell burst close enough aboard to throw hot fragments into one of his 40 mm mounts, wounding two crewmen and starting a small fire. Remnants of the shell's base plate, found aboard, had rotating bands, indicating it had been fired by a heavy antiaircraft gun. He felt like a ball tumbling around war's roulette wheel, not yet settling in a pocket painted red.

Shortly after nine, the *California* stood in Japanese crosshairs with a bit less luck. Salvos from 105 mm howitzers or large mortar tubes landed a pebble's toss off the port side, and others off the port bow; several more passed close overhead. Then she took a direct hit. Falling nearly vertically, the shell hit the main battery fire-control platform, killing one man and wounding nine. It was well that the *California* was more than three times the *Birmingham*'s size, but the damage was substantial nonetheless. Her forward search and gunnery radars were knocked out of action, and for fifteen long minutes the main battery sat mute while control was switched to other stations.

On the bridge of the *Birmingham,* Captain Inglis took a moment to admire the courage of the UDT as they methodically sounded the lagoon. "This was all close under the gunfire of the Japanese, and within easy range of their machine guns emplaced on the beach itself. Therefore, their work was about as hazardous as anything that can be imagined." As splashes played among the frogmen and their landing craft, the *Birmingham*'s spotters found a battery just north of Charan Kanoa's sugar mill and took it under fire. A huge explosion marked its destruction, part and parcel of the detonation of a neighboring ammo dump. Closer to the water, Japanese soldiers could be seen moving among several gun positions. The crews of

Kauffman's LCPRs, using the two .30-caliber machine guns mounted on either side of the forward ramp, laid suppressive fire close over the heads of the swimmers. But there was little to be done against gunners they could not see.

The volume of incoming fire persuaded Kauffman to abandon his floating mattress experiment. The writing was on the wall for that oddball scheme as soon as he realized the morning naval bombardment hadn't helped him much. Kelly Turner, to his chagrin, would find his instructions to his fire-support ships—target the beachfront first, then walk fire slowly inland—largely unexecuted. The first salvos started too far inland to neutralize the waterfront defenses. The commanding officer of the *California,* Captain Henry Poynter Burnett, had not been properly briefed, for he was under the misapprehension that Kauffman's men would actually land. "Due to faulty communications, this ship was not so informed and considerable protection of their activities thus was unfortunately lost," he admitted. As the salvos plowed farther inland, Japanese snipers and machine gunners near the beach were left unhindered. Larger guns located on Afetna Point, jutting through the surf between Green Beaches Two and Three, could enfilade the entire landing area, to the north and south. Somehow surviving an early-morning plastering by Oldendorf's fire-support ships, Japanese crews located there kept their sights on Kauffman all morning long. So the UDT commander and his guide, Page, opted to ditch their awkward floating command post three hundred yards out. "We anchored it there and swam in because it would have been ridiculous to take the mattress in any further," Kauffman said.

Lacking direct radio contact with the bombardment ships, the frogmen were poorly prepared to deal with surprises. Sid Robbins of Team Seven was startled to find that mortar teams had made a firing position out of a cluster of a dozen Japanese barges moored to the pier at Blue Beach One. Because of the intensity of the barrage that came down upon them, Robbins's swimmers weren't able to reconnoiter Yellow Beach One at all. After several attempts, this detachment returned to the *Brooks* with casualties that seemed light under the circumstances: just two men seriously injured.

Kauffman was mystified by the absence of airpower supporting him. Just after sunrise, the *Wasp* had sent a large strike with the ostensible mission of covering the UDTs, but the air coordinator routed them to other targets, and it was wise that he did, for Oldendorf's heavies were in full voice then. The Avengers of Torpedo Fourteen hit gun positions around

Aslito Field and tried to burn nearby sugarcane fields with phosphorus incendiaries. The remaining Helldivers, joined by Hellcats, attacked targets on Nafutan Point, where photo interpreters noticed six-inch shore batteries, the largest on the island.

At ten o'clock, a large flight of Hellcats was scheduled to sweep the full two-mile length of the four landing beaches. The mission would likely have scattered, killed, or suppressed most of the enemy soldiers working the waterfront and filled the gap in the pattern of supporting naval gunfire close to the water. But to Kauffman's chagrin, the fighters never appeared. Their no-show likely had to do with confusion arising from the fact that Turner's commander of support aircraft, Captain Richard F. Whitehead, had not yet arrived as of D Day minus one. He would not join Turner on the *Rocky Mount* until the day of the landings. That left an air support coordinator in the *Tennessee* to make sure the mission was carried out. But the battleship had a long list of scheduled fires to manage, and the air mission seemed to give way to other priorities on a day that was loaded with them.

Kauffman's losses were light under the circumstances. Six men from Team Five were injured—internal damage from hydraulic concussion. Only one frogman was killed. This was Robert Christensen, a first-class petty officer who was one of the best-liked men on the team. He was shot in the head while helping Ensign Bill Running supervise his platoon from their floating mattress. Team Seven had five wounded, but they, too, lost only one man, Albert G. Weidner. He was the coxswain on Lieutenant Burke's own LCPR, blown from the wheel when the boat took a direct hit after dropping off its swimmers at the reef. Burke escaped serious injury, but a Navy crewman from the *Brooks* was killed as well.

At 11:30, the *Birmingham,* her barrels radiating hot as a forge, checked fire after dealing more than thirteen hundred six-inch rounds and nearly twelve hundred five-inch rounds into Saipan. Around this same time, Kauffman ordered all his swimmers back to the reef, where their landing craft would be waiting for them. It proved to be an unpopular order, for two of his men were unaccounted for. But with mortars dropping around his boats, he had no wish to lose any of his critical information on the reef and the lagoon. Team Seven had lost one of its landing craft already, and Admirals Turner and Hill, as well as General Smith and his division and regimental commanders, were counting on a complete report. The *Gilmer* and *Brooks* poured smoke onto the water as the frogmen climbed aboard their LCPRs. The *Tennessee, California, Indianapolis,* and *Birmingham*

threw their final salvos, then hauled clear to recover their planes and prepare for what was sure to be an even harder trial the next morning, when
four Marine regiments would storm ashore.

Kelly Turner continued to doubt the wisdom of allowing the amtracs to
ride inland, and he worried, too, about the chances of getting tanks over
the reef and through the lagoon. That was until the leadership of UDT 7
appeared on the *Rocky Mount* and presented him and General Smith with
the fruits of their morning of work. Draper Kauffman reported to Rear
Admiral Harry Hill, Turner's deputy, and the commanding general of the
Second Marine Division, Tommy Watson.

Kauffman brought good news. There was about two feet of water over
the reef, and the depth of the lagoon did not surpass eight feet. He reported
that the reef was flat enough to be passable by amtracs and DUKWs, and
that while stores of barbed wire, concrete, and posts on the beach suggested
the Japanese had had plans, no man-made obstacles or mines were in the
lagoon. Equally valuable, Team Seven had located off Blue Beach One a
natural channel large enough for LSTs. Little work was needed to make
it serviceable, aside from marking it with buoys. Blasting such a route
through the reef after the landings would have been difficult given that the
dense, sand-cemented coral polyps did not seem likely to disintegrate into
a smooth ramp but to fracture into a mess of boulders and craters needing
further demolition.

The UDT also found that the route the Marines had planned to use for
their waterproofed tanks, set to paddle ashore following the assault waves,
would lead them to disaster. It was potholed, and the water was too deep
for these jury-rigged amphibs, which were never designed to swim and
drowned out easily. Kauffman believed he had found a better way, a
smooth path that crossed the lagoon in front of Red Beach Three diago-
nally onto Green Two. The Marines didn't know what to make of Kauffman, with his professorial airs, thick glasses, and careful manner of speech.
"He had none of the rough, tough appearance of an Underwater Demolition Team man," said Colonel Robert E. Hogaboom, General Smith's operations officer. "But there was no question about his competence and his
willingness and his courage." Kauffman passed along the positions of
enemy guns and snipers, and he marked the nest of mortar barges for special attention by Oldendorf's fire-support group.

That night Kauffman had his handiest draftsmen make charts based on the lagoon soundings. When the invasion force arrived before the next sunrise, the commanders of the amtrac and tank battalions and transport groups would have hand-drawn maps delivered to them.

During the evening, Admiral Hill summoned Kauffman to see General Watson. The Second Marine Division boss asked, "What in the hell is this I hear about your changing the route for my tanks?" He had wanted them to swim in across Red Two.

"General, they'll never get through there," Kauffman said, showing him his charts.

"Well, all right. But, young man, you're going to lead that first tank in, and you'd better be damned sure that every one of them gets in safely, without drowning out."

And now, considering Kauffman's report and his calm, overriding confidence, Kelly Turner began to think that the idea of sending twenty thousand Marines ashore in these newfangled swamp buggies might just work out after all.

8

Heavy Weather

On the same morning that the USS *Redfin* first reported a Japanese carrier task force off Tawi Tawi, the submarine *Cavalla* surfaced eight hundred miles northwest of Saipan into a seascape littered with broken cork. By afternoon, the barometer dropped and the wind began to run. The chop became so rough, and his boat's pitching, yawing, and rolling so great, that the skipper, Herman J. Kossler, decided to submerge into gentler depths. The seas above him were so heavy that he could make just as good speed underwater toward his patrol station off the Philippines. But his more immediate purpose was to serve dinner. He took her down to calm the boat, let his seasick crew recover, and make possible a civilized evening meal.

Past midnight and into the dark of morning on June 14, Kossler surfaced again to find himself on the edge of a typhoon. Against mountainous seas and unrelenting winds, he struggled to hold the boat's trim. Once, then again, waves crested high and crashed over the bridge, their dregs draining straight down the open hatch of the conning tower. No sailor minded getting wet, but if Kossler allowed his machinery to flood or his electronics or radio to ground out, his first war patrol would be valueless to the larger cause of fixing the location of the enemy fleet. So he endured another hour on the surface, trying fruitlessly to send a weather report to Admiral Lockwood. Then he took the *Cavalla* down again.

Three times throughout the day he ascended to periscope depth to observe the sea condition, and each time the piling waves broached him, leaving him with a struggle at a shallow depth to get his boat upright again. When Kossler surfaced late in the afternoon, one of his main engines was flooded and the barometer was falling freely. The storm seemed to be moving north. He decided to resume traveling on the surface toward his patrol station and not worry about sending the weather dispatch. When the sun was low in the west, he received a message from another boat, the *Flying Fish,* which the *Cavalla* was to join near the strategic bottleneck of San Bernardino Strait. Kossler set course for his rendezvous at the best speed he could manage, twelve knots. When it was clear that the storm really was gone, he risked an increase in his revolutions, pushing to sixteen knots to make up for lost time.

Raymond Spruance, Marc Mitscher, and their staffs were more than casually interested in what Lockwood's submarines were finding. The sightings to date left little doubt that the Combined Fleet was headed their way. The question was what precisely to do about it—stand and defend, or sortie and hunt?

Arleigh Burke, Mitscher's chief of staff, was no aviator, but understood the tactical significance of the prevailing winds out of the east. He knew that the constant need to turn eastward in order to launch and recover planes would draw the carrier task force in the direction of the wind. If circumstances carried them too far east, Task Force 58 could easily find itself running short on sea room. The carriers might end up having to maneuver between islands, which might delay important air operations in those moments when restricted waters made it impossible for the carriers to keep an easterly heading. Burke suggested to Mitscher that he steam aggressively to the west in order to meet the Japanese far enough from the Marianas that they would preserve their freedom of movement in a subsequent air battle. Mitscher forwarded this plan to Spruance—who disagreed entirely. The mission of the task force, Spruance replied, was to cover and support Turner's landings. He would not expose the amphibious force by taking the carriers west. Mitscher protested in vain but finally abided by his superior's desire.

A debate had been raging from Washington to the Central Pacific about how aircraft carriers should be employed. Spruance, more than most, understood the nuances at hand. He knew his decisions would face sharp scrutiny, for even his victory at Midway had come with recrimination. Far from making him a star in the eyes of his peers, it stoked their envy and second-guessing. Though many would credit the nonaviator for the greatest victory in naval aviation's history, he was startled to find the second-guessing coming from high places.

In November 1942, after a briefing at Pacific Fleet headquarters, where Spruance was serving as Nimitz's chief of staff, Spruance approached

Edwin T. Layton, the head of the Joint Intelligence Center. Layton would reveal the whole story to Spruance's biographer:

> As we talked, I realized that Admiral Spruance was more tense, more keyed-up (by his questions) than I'd ever before observed. He then told me that he was very much disturbed by a [Naval] War College analysis of his actions during the Battle of Midway—specifically his withdrawal *eastward* during the night of 4 June; that the War College analysis had been forwarded with a heavy-handed endorsement by Ernie King to Nimitz—that the study stated Spruance's withdrawal to the eastward was the wrong decision—that he should have continued *westward* during the night to be in a position to attack, effectively, Japanese forces from first light 5 June.

When Spruance asked Layton if he had collected any intelligence that might illuminate the matter, the JICPOA boss produced captured Japanese charts showing that had Spruance done what the War College mandarins wanted, he would have run straight into the teeth of the Combined Fleet's heavy surface forces at night. It would have been a grievous mistake. Layton wrote,

> "We went over each item with care, then reviewed them as he made notes. He then told me to take them up to Admiral Nimitz; that he now had the basis for a definite rebuttal to [NWC president] Admiral Pye's criticisms and fault-finding and that 'the weight of a score of years had been lifted from his shoulders'! You can imagine, if you will, his delight to be vindicated in a course of action he unswervingly knew (in his heart) had been the correct one—and which he felt (in his heart) had been criticized *unfairly* and *unjustly*."

Speed and surprise were the carrier's great strength over an island base. Spruance had proved this at Truk, at Kwajalein, at Eniwetok, and again with the fighter sweeps against the Marianas. An island never went anywhere, and the radius of its reach was readily understood. But though Spruance valued surprise, he did not overrate mobility. Now, as at Midway, he understood his duty to the ground forces and felt the responsibility not to be caught out of position chasing phantoms when the enemy fleet appeared. While setting the ambush at Midway, he had stayed within air-supporting distance of the island he was charged to protect. Though the opportunity to surprise Japanese carriers did not seem to exist, he would do the same thing now.

In early May, King and Nimitz met in San Francisco and devised a scheme of command whereby Spruance and Halsey would alternate as task force commanders, with Mitscher and Rear Admiral John McCain as their respective underlings in command of the fast carrier task force. The rotation of Halsey and Spruance would ensure an ongoing study in contrasts along the doctrinal divide. When Spruance and Mitscher had command, their forces would be known as the Fifth Fleet and Task Force 58. When Halsey and McCain took over—this was to take place in the fall—the names would change to the Third Fleet and Task Force 38. "Instead of the stagecoach system of keeping the drivers and changing the horses," Halsey would write, "we changed drivers and kept the horses. It was hard on the horses, but it was effective. Moreover, it consistently misled the Japs into an exaggerated conception of our seagoing strength." The arrangement ensured continuity on one hand—Spruance and Halsey would have the same ships—and a regularly scheduled sea change in the mindset of the man controlling how those ships were used. That is, Halsey felt, the carriers should be free to fly in pursuit of a sighted enemy.

The difference in opinion rose anew every time U.S. carriers engaged in battle, from the Coral Sea up to Midway, down to Guadalcanal and back up to the Gilberts and Marshalls. Spruance was perfectly comfortable using the carriers defensively, by staying close to important strategic objectives and employing the talents of the likes of McCampbell, Vraciu, Brewer, and Rigg as an iron dome. But Halsey and John Towers, Nimitz's ambitious, willful aviation chief, believed that any failure to exploit the freewheeling, mobile striking power of the carrier task force was first-degree professional malpractice.

Now what to do about these sightings of the First Mobile Fleet? Some scoffed at Spruance's belief that his carrier task force could be end-run by the Japanese were it to go west. Mitscher and just about every member of his command belonged to this skeptical camp. Mitscher's fiery task group commander, Rear Admiral John J. "Jocko" Clark, would write, "If carriers are properly utilized, it is not possible for surface ships to make an end run around them." To which Spruance might have replied: *That's right, "proper* *utilization" requires that we not run out of position.* Equipped with air groups with striking ranges out to four hundred fifty miles, Task Force 58 would indeed be hard for an enemy to skirt, but Spruance knew it was possible and that the Japanese had divided their forces to attempt end runs before, at the Coral Sea, Midway, and Guadalcanal.* They were coming to appreciate the rigidity of Japanese thinking. Operation Forager's stakes were such that any setback to it would harm the war effort. So against the back-biting of his carrier bosses, he resolved that Task Force 58 would continue to hold fast in its patrol area west of the islands.

Spruance's views on command generally leaned away from impulse and aggression. "Leadership," he once wrote,

> comprises a number of moral qualities among which may be mentioned: force; initiative; determination; a strong sense of justice; loyalty, both to superiors and subordinates; good judgment; generosity; self-possession; energy; decision. The qualities of leadership inspire loyalty in one's subordinates; and this loyalty, accompanied by confidence in the commander's professional ability, gives him such an enthusiastic support from them that he is, in times of crisis, able to demand and accomplish what might appear to be the impossible. History abounds with instances where great leaders have inspired such confidence and enthusiasm. . . . Alexander the Great, Hannibal, Caesar, Frederick the Great, Napoleon and Nelson. It requires both the moral qualities and the brains and knowledge to make a greater leader. Both may be improved by application, study and reflection.

And by agitated pacing, too. In moments of decision, Spruance paced the flag bridge of the *Indianapolis,* thinking aloud to anyone who was on hand. When the volume of message traffic, orders, and dispatches threatened to clutter his big-picture view, he left the bridge and walked the cruiser's long decks. In the aftermath of Midway and other surprise attacks—notably the one that was sprung on his professional judgment by his cherished professional alma mater in Newport—Spruance had plenty of reasons to pace the decks as the dance of carriers began.

---

* In October 1944, at the Battle of Leyte Gulf, Halsey would run his carriers so far out of position as to make Spruance's point.

★ ★ ★

Holed up in a cave in a hill behind the Garapan police station, Manuel Sablan was awestruck at the shellacking the capital had taken. The city was a ruin. "When we came out of the cave that evening, not a building was standing," he said. Among the casualties, apparently, were the two American pilots whom Sablan had seen in the Garapan jail. Another prisoner told him, "The roof came down on one of them during the shelling, and the other one was beheaded by one of the Japanese." One of the captives was later found dead with a .50-caliber slug in him. The other, Lieutenant (j.g.) Woodie McVay from the *Yorktown,* had survived the heavy strafing by his fellow aviators, only to meet a grimmer fate. Four Japanese police officers hauled him out of the jail and seated him on the ground with his hands tied behind him, then two of the cops produced swords. The witness to this scene, a prisoner at the jail named Neratus, who hailed from Palau, couldn't bring himself to watch. He heard several thuds of blade on flesh and was then ordered to burn the body. McVay was still barely alive as Neratus carried him twenty-five yards to a pile of wood. Neratus waited until his labored breathing stopped before lighting the pyre, then took the cross and chain from the pilot's neck and fashioned a marker with it before fleeing into the woods.

Shizuko Miura's small office in Garapan could hold twenty stretcher cases, and it stayed full as people came and went in the day after the air attacks. But when the warship bombardment began, the office was a more dangerous place to be, and the wounded were hauled outside and laid in trenches. Around Saipan, in the streets, airfields, hillsides, cane fields, and army headquarters, people asked: Where was the navy? Returning from her office to her sister-in-law's home after the all-clear siren had sounded, Shizuko found the authorities urging her to retreat to the mountain. There was a cave up there that could hold a thousand, it was said. The civilians and the wounded must head to the hills at once. The soldiers were coming down from the hills, hauling boxes of ammunition toward their threatened shore.

The bombarding warships lay distant on the water, low and sleek, like predators. When a round fell near, she thought the dugout trench might collapse, burying her with all her patients. She thought, *The time to die has come.* "My mind became clear all the more and I was not afraid at all," she would write. When she learned there were two dead soldiers in the dugout, she ran to the office and retrieved blankets to use as shrouds. As she busied herself with this task, others comforted the wounded and prepared them to be borne to the mountain at night.

But for Shizuko, night came early. "There arose suddenly a terrible sound, when it became quite dark before my eyes." One of Kelly Turner's ships must have found her location. Concussion hit her like a hammer. There was a brief, ringing silence. Then she heard someone ask, "Is everybody safe?" Her hands checked her body. Soldiers called out for each other. She tried to calm herself. *Everyone is okay.* Then she heard more distant voices, coming from the office. She scrambled from the trench and ran to her building. It had been destroyed entirely. Fragments of iron were scattered about, the warehouse storing their food in shambles, buried under jumping flames. She noticed that her skin had been burned, and grief overtook her. Garapan was a ruin. The long dry season, no rain for months, had left everything vulnerable to the flames. "The town is a sea of flame. This is the end of Garapan Town."

From his headquarters on Flores Point, by the seaplane base at Tanapag, Admiral Chuichi Nagumo effectively acquired a new title. He could now best be referred to as the *ostensible* commander of Japanese naval forces on Saipan. The strikes on Aslito Field, against Garapan and Charan Kanoa, shredded his wired communications and utterly scrambled his ability to communicate with his subordinates. Situated in his own headquarters in an elementary school at the southern edge of Charan Kanoa, General Yoshitsugu Saito, commander of the 43rd Division and the senior army officer on the island, was uprooted from his headquarters soon after the battleships began to roar. His staff insisted he find a safer place, so he removed to a hillside cave where another unit, the 47th Independent Mixed Brigade, already had its headquarters. Thus began a migration of command posts that would render Saito, too, virtually a figurehead.

His was a piecemeal command overseeing an unfinished defense. Though howitzers and large mortars were sited all through the island, hidden in coral caves and ravines safe from aircraft and naval artillery, the Japanese could have done much more with even just a few extra weeks. At Nafutan, concrete casemates awaited installation of five-inch dual-purpose guns that lay in storage near Garapan. In the capital's naval station, four dozen more such weapons, 120 mm and larger, sat on railroad flatcars or languished in warehouses. Beach defenses were well established. Trenchworks offered cover for infantry. A second defensive line faced the strand from higher ground a few hundred yards inland, exploiting ridges and cliffs. Pillboxes and blockhouses were planted in enfilading positions on points and headlands at the ends of the western beaches. These held guns as large as 47 mm. Deeper in, and in cliffs facing the shore, coastal defense batteries were set up in casemates and open positions. Several 200 mm antiboat guns were operational, their crews instructed to hold their fire until the landing force was inside the reef line. Saito's instructions were to resist at the beach. Any troops who got through the gauntlet of heavy artillery and got ashore would face a prompt counterattack.

The Japanese defenses were organized in four sectors. The northern third of the island, from Tanapag to Marpi Point in the north, was the domain of the 135th Regiment under Colonel Eisuke Suzuki. Tanapag Harbor was the locus of the navy's sector, represented by a regiment-sized Special Naval Landing Force, plus a battalion from the 136th Regiment. The central sector, ranging from the southern outskirts of Garapan south to Afetna Point and east as far as the island's mountainous central spine, was the responsibility of the rest of the 136th Regiment, under Colonel Yukimatsu Ogawa. Last, the southern sector, from Afetna Point across to Magicienne Bay and including Aslito Field, belonged to Colonel Yoshiro Oka's 47th Independent Mixed Brigade. A reserve consisting of four companies of the 136th Regiment and 9th Independent Mixed Brigade was bivouacked in the southeast near Laulau. A forest near Chacha Village concealed forty-four medium and light tanks belonging to Colonel Takishi Goto's 9th Tank Regiment, available to counterattack against either shore. The Imperial General Staff was outwardly confident in the Saipan garrison. "More than once I was told by the officers of the General Staff that Saipan was absolutely invincible," wrote Toshikazu Kase, with the Japanese foreign ministry.

Carrying a litter, marching with a procession of walking wounded toward a rumor of refuge in a cave to the east, Shizuko Miura saw the dead sprawled everywhere among the ruins, soldiers and townspeople alike. The army men, she noticed, made up the majority of them. Young troops, newly arrived and few with weapons, wandered lost through the bombardment. The navy had been on Saipan longer, and so its people must have had shelters to escape to, she thought.

She was impatient with the slow pace as her ad hoc medical triage team and its platoon of wounded, forty or fifty souls, moved toward the outskirts of town. Soon the smoke that covered their movements began to drain them. The heat and fouled air began to make breathing difficult. As the sun began to set, they reached the cave, only to find it already full of refugees. A scattering of empty food containers suggested they had been there awhile.

A naval officer presented himself, instructing the girl to take the group to the fire department. She considered it a risky move. But short of gathering somewhere, there would be no way to organize or communicate. So the group returned to the march. In Garapan, houses on both sides of the street were on fire. The heat wore on them. The air did not nourish their lungs. They yearned for water. The soles of her sneakers melted.

The city firehouse stood as if in mockery of itself. "The firehouse bell, which there was no point in ringing, hung from the belfry against a red sky," Shizuko wrote. Such was the color of the heavens, an angry scarlet, that she couldn't tell whether it was night or day. At length a warrant officer appeared and continued their lesson in the confusion of the hour. He ordered them to turn around again and head for the mountains, where, he said, there was in fact a cave large enough to shelter them. Before leaving again, she stole a moment to take a short detour to look at her own home. The humble structure was, surprisingly, intact, perhaps saved from fire by the surrounding marshes, she thought. The enemy fleet seemed hell-bent upon burning the entire town. The flashing of warship batteries was incessant, their low roll washing ashore asynchronously, like heavy thunder. And so the small diaspora of wounded trudged east again, their lives in flames.

By the time they made it to the cave near Mount Tapotchau, it was past eleven o'clock at night. The huge natural fortress of stone had room for many hundreds, but no medical supplies or medicine. With so many people on hand, the shortage of water became a pressing crisis, too. The wanderers and the wounded had no choice but to settle in and make do.

Out to sea, beyond sight of shore, the *Indianapolis* idled in formation with the *Tennessee,* the *California,* the *Birmingham,* and four destroyers. During the afternoon of Garapan's destruction, Spruance's flagship had held a funeral service for the Team Seven frogman, Al Weidner, and another sailor, E. J. Parsons, who had died aboard ship. During the night, a host of newcomers quietly arrived, most of them unaware of the debt they would owe to the frogmen and fire-control men who were preparing their way. Kelly Turner's tractor battalions and transport groups took their stations outside the transport area and began arraying themselves in the dark.

PART TWO

Land

Riflemen from the Second Marine Division assault Garapan, the principal city of Saipan, as buildings burn following naval and artillery bombardment. (USMC)

9

Heavier, Higher, Faster

He had been the scourge of Hitler's freight dispatchers and harbormasters, and the bane of the Afrika Korps. A veteran of dangerous missions over occupied France and North Africa, Paul Tibbets was bound to suffer an emotional letdown while serving essentially as an airline captain while the world burned from war. Piloting transport planes, he sometimes felt his career was banging along a potholed side road. The milk run from Milwaukee to New York would be hardly less stimulating than the hop across the Atlantic to resupply Marrakesh, but both routes offered consolation to someone with the right professional outlook: They were links in the chain of the war effort, and someone had to haul the cargo. In three months of service as a "trash hauler," Tibbets logged more hours in a four-engine plane than he had in any other airframe to date, cultivating and testing his professionalism and patience. As ever, they would pay him a reward.

In the late summer of 1943 he received orders to report to Wichita, Kansas, the site of a Boeing plant that was building the troubled B-29 Superfortress. The Army hadn't quit on the program. The crash of the test flight in Seattle led not to cancellation of the new long-range bomber, but to a reevaluation of and a doubling down on it. The B-29 was larger and faster than Boeing's redoubtable B-17, with a higher service ceiling and a heavier payload. Its wingspan was 141 feet to the B-17's 103, its length 93 feet against the B-17's 75. Many innovations were built into it, including a centrally directed and remote-controlled Sperry defensive armament system that put four turrets of .50-caliber machine guns in the hands of one man, and a pressurized interior that allowed the crew to work comfortably in shirtsleeves. Engineers believed the early problems were fixable, merely growing pains of a complex new machine. Assembly line workers were green; that was why bomb bay doors and nose wheels wouldn't retract, and generators did not generate owing to faulty wiring, and interior light switches sometimes triggered warning horns, and fuel relay switches and indicator lights malfunctioned, and engine starter switches turned over the wrong engine. With more than sixteen hundred Superfortresses already on order by the Army Air Forces and a war to win in two hemispheres, the program managers and their military overseers decided to proceed on faith that the problems could be worked out during production.

Eighty miles north of Wichita, at Smoky Hill Army Airfield, Tibbets put in sixteen-hour days assisting with crew training, preparing them for the rigors of overseas deployment and combat. If the complexity of the plane vexed the assembly line, it was just as difficult to bring new crews up to speed. There was a great deal for these young men to learn, and precious flew flyable aircraft in which to train. Tibbets himself had a hard time finding a qualified B-29 driver to check him out in the aircraft. But once he did, he was in the aircraft's thrall. After three high-speed taxi runs—tearing down the runway, lifting off, and touching down again—Tibbets had the sense "it was just another flying machine with characteristics that were not too different from those with which I was familiar." On the next run, he grasped the cluster of four throttle levers farthest to his left and pushed them all the way forward. The bomber's engines surged ahead at full power. As the aircraft took to the air, he was the candy man's bombardier all over again.

After his yearlong tour developing the B-29 and training its crews, Tibbets took a transfer in March 1944 to Grand Island, Nebraska, home of a Superfortress unit headed by his old commanding officer in England, Frank Armstrong. There Tibbets started a school to train B-29 flight instructors. His tenure was brief. He was soon ordered to Alamogordo, New Mexico, to study the vulnerability of the plane against enemy fighters at high altitude.

It might have seemed fitting that the man who ended up in the Pacific for his refusal to fight at low altitude should study the alternative in depth. At thirty thousand feet, aerodynamics was "an entirely different ball game," Tibbets would write. In thinner air, the slightest misstep at the controls could cause a plane to lose control or stall. That meant it would be dangerous, if not reckless, for pilots at high altitudes to fly in the same type of tightly packed defensive formations the B-17s used in Europe. And that raised the question of how bombers might defend themselves against fighter attack.

Conducting live simulations against P-47 Thunderbolts at extreme altitudes, Tibbets began to have doubts about the survivability of a fully loaded B-29 against a skillfully flown fighter above thirty thousand feet. In one test, he flew a bomber that had none of its machine guns installed and discovered that the weight saving—three and a half tons' worth—changed the B-29's flight characteristics entirely. It was a function of hundreds of physical factors involving airfoils and engine horsepower, but the long and short of his experiment was that he could climb higher and faster, and maneuver more easily, too, without a suite of guns. He found that at altitudes between thirty thousand and thirty-five thousand feet, his big plane could turn much more tightly than a P-47 could. This meant the lumbering bomber could escape a plane chasing it by turning sharply, forcing the pursuer to disengage.

In April, in line with the directives from the Cairo Conference, a major new command, the Twentieth Air Force, was established to carry out the strategic bombing of Japan. General Hap Arnold, the USAAF chief of staff, commanded the unit personally from Washington, placing it effectively under the control of the Joint Chiefs of Staff, of which Arnold was a member. This administrative setup was purposeful; Arnold saw the B-29's mission as strategic in nature and did not want local commanders enlisting his new bomber in tactical operations. The first Superfortresses of the 58th Bombardment Wing arrived in southern Bengal, not far from the port of Calcutta, on April 2. A week later, the Joint Chiefs of Staff approved Operation Matterhorn, a plan to bombard Japan from secret airfields in China. The plan took two months to become operational. On June 5, Brigadier General Kenneth B. Wolfe's XX Bomber Command carried out its first raid, sending ninety-eight Superfortresses from eastern India to hit railroad yards in Bangkok, Thailand. By the middle of the month, the forward bases in China were ready to stage the first attack against mainland Japan.

On the night of June 14–15, 1944, as Kelly Turner's amphibious force was arriving off Saipan, the first blow fell against mainland Japan. Seventy-five B-29s took off from bases near Chengdu, China, and set course for the Yawata iron and steel works on Kyushu. After all the complexities of staging from China, Hap Arnold wanted results. But the strike was a flub. Forewarned by their agents in China, who closely monitored the movements of the new American bombers, the Japanese blacked out their cities in northern Kyushu. Not a single bomb hit the steelworks, and seven B-29s were lost. With this raid, the flaw in Operation Matterhorn became manifest: logistics. A strategic bombing campaign would not prove feasible when the airlift supporting it—ferries of bombs, supplies, and fuel—had to fly from Calcutta to Kunming and then to the forward bases in China, hurdling the Himalayas coming and going. The Army Air Forces calculated that it would take a force of twenty-eight bomb groups, each with twenty-eight B-29s, flying five missions a month for six months to reduce Japan to the point of surrender or occupation. But each of those groups would need two hundred B-24 Liberators as transports, stripped down for maximum cargo carriage. A total of four thousand B-24s would be needed to support the campaign. They were hungry planes, too: Three out of every four tons of supplies shipped to Calcutta would go toward maintaining the air bridge, not supplying the B-29s at the point of the spear.

The Navy had long shared the Army Air Forces' enthusiasm for pushing to the Chinese mainland. Nimitz believed that seizing ports and bases in China would "give a wholly new impulse to the Pacific War," enabling a vigorous bombing effort against Japan's home islands, a tightened blockade, and a renewed Chinese ground offensive against the Japanese Army in Asia.

When Raymond Spruance first told Carl Moore that the Joint Chiefs had recommended an invasion of the Marianas, Moore reacted with disbelief. "I was furious," Spruance's chief of staff said. "I couldn't understand what the idea was. I didn't know why. Nobody ever told me why they were going to the Marianas. . . . I fought with Spruance violently for a couple of weeks before he cracked down on me and told me for God's sake to shut up and play the game and quit bucking it, fighting the problem. Because I was sure that something was all wrong, that we had worked this idea out about China and that was the only possible way we could bomb Japan." But after Hap Arnold's people crunched the numbers, there was no denying that the cost-benefit analysis ran quickly to the red. It was thus once again that the needs of the Army Air Forces encouraged strategic clarity at Pearl Harbor.

The War Department touted the Yawata raid to boost morale at home, the Pentagon boasting that the Twentieth Air Force was "an aerial battle fleet, able to participate in combined operations, or . . . to strike wherever the need is greatest." This overstated the strained program's capabilities; in fact, General Arnold's global striking force had yet to find a base from which it could deliver the "overwhelming air offensive" the U.S. Joint Chiefs of Staff had in mind for Imperial Japan.

★ ★ ★

During the night, on final approach, all hands in Kelly Turner's four transport divisions had been impressed by the flashes of bombardment silently lighting the horizon ahead. Drawing closer to Saipan, they whiffed its acrid waste, sharp on nostrils and tongues. On June 15, the eastern sky was brightening over the light southeasterly swells. Each transport division embarked a Marine regiment, approached Saipan's hundred-fathom line, and entered the outer transport area off the western shore.

An officer in one of the transports, a veteran of Sicily and Salerno, looked at the black form of Mount Tapotchau, backlit by twilight, and said, "That silhouette is made to order for a night landing under a good moon. Every natural landmark stands out. Perfect, I say, except she's coral-bound. That's the gimmick."

The Fifth Amphibious Force, having finished its oceanic transit, prepared to make its power felt on land. On board the LCI gunboats, the smallest commissioned ships in Turner's task force, all hands turned to, unpacking and loading their abundance of rockets. Marines in the transports and amtracs and LSTs checked their weapons, breathed deeply to calm their nerves. Draper Kauffman and his UDT reviewed the results of their lagoon reconnaissance. Kelly Turner signaled to Harry Hill, "TAKE CHARGE. GOOD LUCK." In the dawning daylight of "the other D Day," transports began lowering boats.

10

D Day

The drone of radial engines manifested over Saipan before six A.M., when the commander of the *Enterprise* air group, Bill "Killer" Kane, arrived on station to serve as air coordinator of the day's flying circus covering the assault. His first order of business was to direct an air strike set for H Hour, 0830. With him: a dozen Hellcats to provide combat air patrol over the landing force and eight Avengers to encourage Tojo's submarines to keep a respectful distance.

Surveying the armada below—the transports bearing three divisions, battleships worthy of Jutland, the sheer numerosity of Turner's tractor fleet, dropping from davits and gathering in the assembly areas—Kane had little sense that his day would come to an early end. As he flew over the transport area, the air bursts began. Anxious gunners in Turner's invasion fleet had his range. One of the shells was close enough to fill Kane's cowling with steel. Riddled by friendly fire, his engine began to smoke and he began spiraling down to the sea. He had enough horses to keep his nose up and manage a water landing. He would be rescued later and returned to his carrier. But his forced relief from duty by that spooked antiaircraft crew served to promote James D. "Jig Dog" Ramage, skipper of Bombing Ten, to Kane's post as air coordinator. He would look after the H Hour air strike and the subsequent close support of the troops. Circling at two thousand feet, in awe of the spectacle below, he, too, kept a respectful distance.

Though Harry Hill had immediate command of landing operations, Kelly Turner made sure to retain certain privileges of overall command. He had thought through the location of every ship in the plan. His talent, his admirers said, was a meticulous, hands-on approach to crafting a war plan; in Washington, at Main Navy, he had practiced the state of the art at the level of high strategy. The invasion of Saipan marked his return to the tactical; his talent poured forth into crafting the plan. "He carried it in his own mind," Hogaboom said. "He rarely had to refer to the plans, although the plans were voluminous. He supervised, himself, the actual maneuver and the actual position of the ships as they approached a position at D Day. He was determined to meet his D Days. He was determined to meet his H Hours." What followed from there would be up to the Marines.

It wasn't yet six when Turner issued the order he always deemed his due: "Land the landing force." The dispatch set his numerous assembly into motion. The bow ramps of LSTs swung open, releasing amtracs to roll forward. LSDs opened their stern gates and began disgorging LCMs bearing waterproofed tanks, which, tightly packed in the well deck, slid down the ramp and entered the sea, bouncing once or twice, then motoring smoothly atop the swells. After reporting to the control officer at the line of departure of their assigned beach, they would stand by until they were needed, on call, not belonging to any particular wave. The amtracs approached the transports, cargo nets draped over the side, and Marines began mounting up.

North of the main assembly area, another group of transports milled at sea. Carrying a regiment from each of the two Marine divisions, they were assigned to make a feint, a diversionary landing that Turner hoped would freeze Japanese troops in place and prevent them from moving south from Tanapag into the Charan Kanoa landing area.

At 6:30, two hours before H Hour, the transports of the diversionary force began hoisting out their boats off Tanapag. More than a hundred LCVPs formed in the assembly area and then came alongside the transports to simulate the embarkation of troops of the Second Regiment of the Second Marine Division, and the 24th Regiment of the Fourth, as well as a battalion of the 29th Marines. For several minutes the boats remained alongside the transports, rising and falling beside the nets, then shoved off for the rendezvous area while smoke boats and control vessels took positions near a plausible line of departure. The setup consumed more than an hour, in the hope that the Japanese were watching from shore. On a signal from the commander of the control group, the charade ended. The landing boats reversed course and returned to the transports to be hauled back aboard. Generals Watson and Schmidt would use them as their floating reserve.

It was seven A.M. when the LST group carrying the two assault regiments of the Fourth Marine Division stopped outside the rendezous area and began launching amtracs. Crabbing down the nets from the transports, armed men filled the tractors. The sense of it was vivid, the feeling of starting in. Robert Graf checked his cartridge belt, heavily loaded with ammo; shifted the straps of the weighty bandoliers that pinched his shoulders; vetted his first aid kit and two canteens of water; tested his pack, loaded with items he might never use or that might save a life, one could never tell which. With all its useful things, the pack was heavy enough that, under fire, it might plausibly claim his own. On his right leg were a Ka-Bar in its sheath and a throwing knife holstered like a gun. His gas mask went over the shoulder, its bulk hanging in the way as he reached for his rifle, checking its action, and grabbed a life belt. He looked up from his kit. "Now our group was standing, waiting to start."

Lieutenant Carl Roth came over and looked him over as his quadriceps burned, spun him around to survey his gear. Like all platoon commanders, Roth wore no insignia—it only encouraged snipers—and was underarmed, carrying a carbine instead of an M-1 Garand. Roth led his men into the hold of the LST-84, where they found their amtracs. They were Army vehicles belonging to the 708th Amphibian Tank Battalion. The tractors were ready for them, engines running, fumes fouling the air. The Marines piled in and took their places. Waiting and listening, then waiting some more, they finally heard the grinding of gears, telling them at last that they would soon be on their way. They heard the crash of the bow doors opening and the propulsive sensation of rolling forward. Down they went, out the ramp. Nosing down, the LVTs dropped into the Pacific. The coxswains raced their engines, whose whining revolutions belied their pedestrian's speed toward the line of departure.

The Army crews were largely veteran tankers, hastily retrained as demand for amtrac personnel surged. The one hundred LVTs of their battalion had been hastily refitted, up-armored with extra steel plate at the destroyer base in San Diego—half an inch on the bow and cab, a quarter inch on the sides and the ramp. It was seven o'clock when the amtracs carrying the 25th Marines were underway to the assembly area. Ten minutes later, the LSTs embarking two regiments from the Second Marine Division dropped ramps and released their alligators.

Looking toward shore from the line of departure, three thousand yards out from the reef, each coxswain drew a bead on the major landmarks that

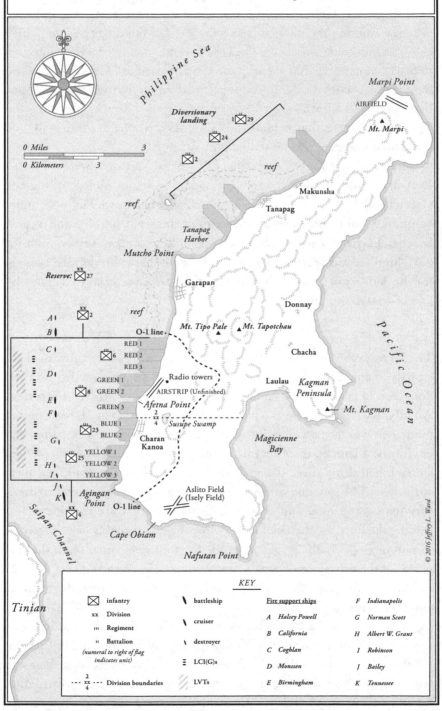

ASSAULT ON SAIPAN, *June 15*

Philippine Sea

Marpi Point

AIRFIELD

▲ *Mt. Marpi*

Diversionary
landing   1 ⊠ 29

⊠ 24

⊠ 2

reef

Makunsha

Tanapag

reef

reef

Tanapag
Harbor

Mutcho Point

Donnay

Reserve: ⊠ 27

Garapan

A
B   ⊠ 2   *reef*   O-1 line

RED 1
C   ⊠ 6   RED 2
RED 3

Mt. Tipo Pale ▲   ▲ Mt. Tapotchau

Chacha

D   GREEN 1
⊠ 8   GREEN 2
E   GREEN 3

Radio towers
AIRSTRIP (Unfinished)
Afetna Point

Laulau   *Kagman
Peninsula*

▲ *Mt. Kagman*

F
2
⊠ 23   BLUE 1   4
G   BLUE 2   *Susupe Swamp*

Charan
Kanoa

*Magicienne
Bay*

H   ⊠ 25   YELLOW 1
YELLOW 2
I   YELLOW 3

J
K   *Agingan
Point*

⊠ 4   O-1 line

Aslito Field
(Isely Field)

Cape Obiam

Nafutan Point

Tinian

© 2016 Jeffrey L. Ward

Pacific Ocean

Saipan Channel

KEY

⊠ infantry	\ battleship	**Fire support ships**	F *Indianapolis*
xx Division	\ cruiser	A *Halsey Powell*	G *Norman Scott*
׀׀׀ Regiment		B *California*	H *Albert W. Grant*
׀׀ Battalion	\ destroyer	C *Coghlan*	I *Robinson*
*(numeral to right of flag
indicates unit)*		D *Monssen*	J *Bailey*
	≡ LCI(G)s	E *Birmingham*	K *Tennessee*
2
--- xx --- Division boundaries
4	LVTs		

showed him the way. Three in particular stood out. There was Mount Ta-potchau, straight ahead to the east. The pier at Garapan was up the coast to the left; the dock at Charan Kanoa jutted out between Green and Blue beaches, fronting the town and its gable-roofed buildings. As they drew closer, details came into focus. The beach, a ribbon of crushed coral just ten to fifteen yards deep. Shrubs atop the beachfront bluff. Groves of trees on higher slopes farther inland. A coastal road and a narrow-gauge rail line that connected Saipan's west-coast towns, Charan Kanoa, Garapan, and Tanapag. The clearing behind the Green beaches held an airstrip, and three high towers of a radio station sat to its north.

The Sixth and Eighth regiments of General Watson's Second Marine Division would go ashore on the left, north of Charan Kanoa, at Red and Green beaches. The 23rd and 25th regiments of the Fourth Division, under Schmidt, would land on the right, south of the town, on Blue and Yellow beaches. Each of the regiments' battalion landing teams was responsible for a six-hundred-yard section of beach, this being the width deemed optimal for the delivery of a Marine battalion's concentrated force as well as its life-line of waterborne supply.

The largest units of troops—divisions and regiments—were governed ab-stractly, maneuvered by generals on rubber topographic models and sel-dom seen in person unless embarked on board ship or arrayed for review. An infantry regiment had about thirty-three hundred men. Its basic unit of maneuver was the battalion. Fortified with heavy weapons companies and engineers, a battalion landing team, under the command of a lieutenant colonel, had thirty-three officers, two or three Navy surgeons, and forty corpsmen. The key line officers were the captains of the two-hundred-fifty-man companies, and their principals in turn were the lieutenants leading the forty-six-man platoons. Below them—arguably of even greater importance—were the sergeants of the thirteen-man squads and the cor-porals of the fire teams of four. Companies, platoons, and squads, large to small, were the units that most powerfully shaped and held the fortunes and memories of individual men.

Robert Graf ducked low while waves crested the bow of his amtrac, tor-rents of salty spray washing over the Marines inside. The gunner up front got the worst of the sea shower. "Being low in the water, we were unable to see much of what was going on," Graf said. "Slowly we went forward until we were in our assigned departure area. We started our circling, waiting."

He had time to think of his parents and two sisters, and of the inferno that had nearly engulfed him at West Loch. His unit, Easy Company, Second Battalion, 23rd Marines, was going ashore on Blue Beach Two. He wasn't sure it would go well.

Overhead, carrier planes were reporting on station. Turner's plan called for a sweep against enemy positions to take place at H Hour minus 90, and now it began, a droning horde mustered not by Mitscher but by the escort carriers of the support groups. Each of the eight small flattops in the two CVE task units put up eight FM-2 Wildcats and a quartet of Avengers, wings sagging with a load of eight five-inch high-explosive rockets and a dozen hundred-pound bombs tucked in their bellies. Specialists in troop support, they bore down fast, roaring over the amtracs, the reef, and the gentle lagoon. The Wildcats strafed the beach head-on, followed at thirty-second intervals by the Avengers, which attacked in pairs, two planes to a beach. They let fly their rockets, dropped their frags, and retired across the island.

Saito's guns were still silent. There was nothing for his inland artillery and mortars to shoot at yet. Captain Whitehead, Turner's commander of support aircraft, was eager to keep things that way. To stop a Japanese counterattack on the landing area, he passed what was known about the locations of Japanese gun and troop positions to Commander Ramage, the air coordinator from the *Enterprise*. But the carrier pilots struggled all day long to find targets through the cloak of smoke that rose after the naval bombardment. The Japanese had gone to ground under ingenious schemes of camouflage. The air strikes lacked the volume and sustenance required of an effective area bombing attack. Turner meant it more to demoralize and suppress the defenders than to wipe them out. His belief that planes could do what ships couldn't might have been the optimism of a man who had never flown a strike aircraft under fire. If the enemy could not move beneath this storm of lead and shrapnel, they usually found the where-withal to hunker down and endure, looking to survive until a more opportune hour.

After thirty minutes, the air strike ended and the planes returned to their carriers. Admiral Hill took over as preparatory naval gunfire re-sumed. The *California* drenched Red Beach with everything she had, but after pouring white phosphorus rounds inshore of Red Beach One, she ceased fire when some of her shells burst prematurely, casting smoky streaks of the incendiary chemical over the assembly area. There, a control boat dropped a flag, and a column of LCI gunboats motoring along the line of departure executed simultaneously ninety-degree turns and set out toward shore. With a dozen of them allocated to each beach, surging along in a single rank, they would offer the final salvo of preparatory fire before the amtracs went in. Diversely configured with 20 and 40 mm guns, rails bristling with 4.5-inch rockets, the gunboats were a mile and a half out when mortars and artillery began falling around them. The incoming fire surprised Captain Inglis in the *Birmingham,* on station with the *Indianapolis* on the division boundary line, firing at targets on Green Beach. Inglis had not expected so many Japanese guns to remain in action. The gunboat crews pulled the pins on their rockets, five hundred at a time, and threw the switches that armed the launchers.

On another signal from the control boat, the first wave of amtracs came to the line of departure. The first wave was anchored in the center by a seven-vehicle wedge of LVT(A)s. The amtanks were arrayed like an arrowhead pointed toward the enemy. Flanking the wedge to each side was a rank of six troop-carrying LVTs. Without fanfare, the coxswain in Robert Graf's amtrac opened the throttle and his engine's song went from gurgle to growl to roaring whine. Led by an LVT(A) serving as the wave guide, flying a numbered flag at the point of the wedge, the first assault wave, nineteen vehicles strong, followed the LCI gunboats in the Second Division landing area. From Red Beach One in the north to Green Beach Two in the south, the full two-regiment line consisted of seventy amtanks and forty-eight LVTs carrying eight Marine infantry battalions to shore. The second wave departed the line four minutes later, followed by the third wave six minutes after it. As Graf's amtrac passed the *Norman Scott,* a voice on the destroyer's PA system called out, "God bless you all!"

Inglis had not seen its like, this parade of ferocious small ships motoring toward the reef in formation, followed at close intervals by rank after rank of amtanks and amtracs. As he looked out to sea, the spectacle of the LCI gunboats in their rush, leading the first wave of troop-laden alligators, took his breath away. He had what he called a "$6.60 orchestra seat, close enough to see the anxious but determined expressions of the faces of the Marines in the landing craft."

When the LCI gunboats were just fifty yards from the reef, the signal to fire came. Within three seconds five hundred rockets were airborne. The parade spectacle vanished in the backwash of smoke. A gray carpet covered the waters beyond the reef, and though the winds pushed it seaward, it was heavy enough to obscure the landing area from view. No targets of opportunity were apparent. All the gunboat rocketeers could do was smother their assigned sectors in high explosives. After two salvos were off the rails, five shifted from beach to bluff.

Carrier planes struck inland targets. Flying low over the first wave, fighters showered the alligator fleet with brass cartridges. When the LCIs were finished, their long single rank opened like a double pocket door, half splitting away to the left, half to the right. Through the opening came the first wave of amtracs, churning through smoke toward the reef. "As the troops came abreast and passed us," one gunboat crewman wrote, "an eerie silence fell. All that could be heard was the whine of the amtracs."

Lieutenant Roth told his platoon, "Lock and load your pieces. Fix bayonets." There were crisp metallic sounds as eight-round clips went into their rifles and bolts were snapped forward, pushing the first shell into the chamber. Robert Graf turned on his safety, reached over his shoulder, took his bayonet from his pack, and fitted it on the end of his rifle, keeping the butt on the deck and muzzle skyward. As the beach drew closer, perceptions grew sharper.

In the Fourth Marine Division's landing area, amtracs carrying the 23rd and 25th Marines moved past the *Tennessee* to either side. The battleship hit the sugar mill with her main battery, then enfiladed the southernmost beach, Yellow Three, concentrating on gun positions near Agingan Point. "The beaches were a mass of smoke," Captain A. D. Mayer would write, "but the Mark Eight radar operator could effectively observe the salvo landing on the beach on his radar screen, and control same." But pinpoint accuracy was an illusion on an A scope. Two days earlier the *Indiana* had put sixty-three high-capacity sixteen-inch shells into that strongpoint, but still the Japanese were in business. Tests had revealed that the burst of a sixteen-inch high-explosive projectile would shock but not destroy emplacements built from sand and coconut logs. "These bursting projectiles would have great disruptive effect but doubtful penetrating power," Admiral Hill said. The Marines would pay the price.

To hold formation, the amtrac drivers kept an eye to their periscopes, watching ahead while also checking the line to each side. Holding steady amid the waves and slow-moving tide, worrying (but not too much) about the high-angle barrage the Japanese were sending them, the drivers consulted one another on the radio, keeping their line tight. Crawling toward Green Beach One, Marshall E. Harris was talking to his best friend from radio school, Robert B. Lewis, in an amtank nearby. He was asking him if they'd drifted too far left when Lewis's voice vanished beneath an explosion. Harris felt a concussion, then heard another explosion. Turning his periscope to the side, he saw black smoke and fire on the water. "Flames boiled out of blackened, bent metal hatches—Bob's tank." His platoon commander, Lieutenant Michael, motioned to him to keep going. He never saw Lewis again.

As the cleated tracks of the amtracs mounted the reef, their hydrostatic transmissions dropped automatically into low gear, enabling the heavy vehicles to haul themselves up and over. The surf could make things dicey. Off Red Beach, large swells were crashing hard over the reef. A coxswain had to time his approach such that the wave cupped his transom and carried them onto the reef. He would have to keep moving, for the next swell would bid to roll him over or swamp his engine while he was still on the coral. As the amtracs clawed over the reef, the *California,* off Red Beach, and the *Tennessee,* off Yellow, shifted to targets farther inland, beyond the map line that Holland Smith had set as the first day's objective for his Marines. Known as the O-1 line (for "Objective One"), it roughly paralleled the beach about fifteen hundred yards inland. The *Birmingham* kept watch off Afetna Point while the *Norman Scott, Monssen,* and other destroyers moved close, released by Admiral Hill to the freelancing counterbattery missions that destroyermen relished. Two thousand yards offshore, between the boat lanes leading to Blue and Yellow beaches, the *Norman Scott* fired on gun positions near Blue Beach One. As her captain, Seymour D. Owens, watched the first wave of amtracs go in, an artillery shell landed close off the forecastle, wounding three men. Hammering the bluffs to keep the enemy's heads down, the destroyers kept at it until the first amtrac wave was about three hundred yards from shore, then trained out to the flanks. Dropping into the calm lagoon waters, the amtracs began the last leg to shore.

The volume of incoming fire grew; neither the aircraft nor the naval fire support had an answer for what the Japanese had installed on Saipan's reverse slopes. "There was a loud explosion to our right," Robert Graf wrote, "and we saw one of our craft exploding, bodies flying through the air."

Carl Roth said, "Unlock your pieces. Good luck. Keep low, and get inland as fast as you can and get off the beach. They're zeroing in on it." Turner had overestimated the threat of beach defenses—pillboxes with machine guns, fire trenches, antitank trenches, and the like. Artillery and mortars located inland were the problem. He had underrated them. The clouds obscuring the early reconnaissance photos hid the guns from Nimitz's analysts. They revealed themselves against the first waves.

Control officers off Blue and Yellow beaches reported the first waves of the Fourth Marine Division ashore at 8:43. Five minutes later an air observer reported the Second Marine Division's amtracs piling onto Red and Green beaches, though not always in the right place. Heavy fire poured into the first wave from the shrub-topped bluff behind Red Three. Heavier fire enfiladed them from Afetna Point, far to the right. The volume of it startled the drivers, and even the slightest flinch at the wheel caused them to veer left, carrying in the Sixth Marines farther north than they were supposed to be. The same problem beset the Eighth Regiment, only worse, owing to a northward-carrying tide. Both of its battalions landed on Green One, causing congestion and a dangerous massing of forces there, as well as a void on Green Two, just to the south. The architect of the Second Marine Division's confusion was a battery of heavy machine guns and antiboat guns on Afetna Point. Having somehow survived the morning bombardment by the *Birmingham* and *Indianapolis,* it enjoyed a run of terrible glory. Head still down, filled with silent prayer, Robert Graf heard the smooth tenor of the engine change as his tracks bit into the ground. His platoon was on the beach.

As the critical hour began ashore, the naval fire support shifted inland, leaving the amtracs to their own devices. The bow gunners trained their fifties on the thin ribbon of sand and scrub ahead as the mortars and artillery continued their incessant high-angle fall. General Saito's artillerymen and mortar teams were in impressive form given the plastering that had been leveled upon them from air and sea. Lofting shells on tall parabolas from crevices, ravines, and the back sides of hills, they began taking a toll on Turner's force. The beach where Easy Company of the 2/23 went ashore, Blue Beach Two, took a particularly brutal deluge. "More and more shells came pounding at us and more tractors were hit," wrote Graf. "Bodies, both whole and in pieces, were scattered about." He saw men mortally wounded but still alive, floating with the aid of life jackets. The Marines left no man behind, except by necessity at H Hour, when the imperative to get off the beach was existential. The whole operation depended on it. Already, with the arrival of the second wave, the boat lane was a bottleneck, with a huge inflow of machines grinding through it.

Amtracs had their appeal, foremost their armor plate, which was proof against all but the closest artillery rounds. But many veteran Marines preferred the old LCVPs with their bow ramps, which when dropped allowed them to make a quick low rush forward out of the hold. Amtracs, in contrast, required them to stand up and dismount over the side, and that meant exposing themselves to enemy fire. When Donald Boots hit the beach, enemy gunners were waiting. The platoon sergeant and gunnery sergeant of his pioneer company were shot dead along with a few other men. As bullets zipped overhead, his platoon, deprived of their leadership, dropped to the beach and pressed themselves into the crushed coral for cover. Boots moved left, bounding into a large shell crater with several other men as machine gun fire whipped overhead. When the mortars came, Boots didn't think he would survive.

"It was really tragic to watch the effect of this mortar fire on our own troops," said Captain Inglis.

> The Japanese were extremely accurate, and as they walked this shellfire up the beach, this shellfire falling at about ten yard intervals, our Marines at first stood up under the fire without flinching, continued their operations of sorting out and transporting to front lines the equipment which had been landed and which was lying on the beach. After the first two or three shells had fallen it was quite apparent to us that the Marines were beginning to flinch under the fire and at first they threw themselves on the ground and then eventually, after this fire was continued, broke and ran. Through high powered optical instruments we could almost see the whiskers on men's faces, and the whole impression that I received was something unreal, something that you might see in the *London Graphic,* for instance, as sketched in the imagination of an artist. It seemed almost too dramatic and too close to be realistic.

Though the largest Japanese coastal guns had been easy for the Navy to destroy, as they were sited conspicuously in fixed emplacements vulnerable to direct fire, and beach positions evaporated quickly in the initial barrage, the inland positions were trickier even when ship commanders could see where the fire was coming from. "The mobilization of that mass of field artillery and mortars on the reverse slope of the hills back of the beaches was a complete unknown to us when we landed," Hill said.

Captain Inglis felt a mounting frustration. "We tried our best to determine the source of this fire, but the Japanese, being past masters in the twin arts of playing possum and camouflage, had very successfully concealed their batteries from observation and the source of the fire could not be determined from observation from the ship, or from the spotters ashore, nor from observation from aircraft, nor from photographs taken by aircraft." There were many eyes on D Day, but none were all-seeing. It remained to the assaulters to push forward and deliver themselves from death.

The Second Armored Amphibian Battalion, a Marine outfit, hit Red Beach One promptly at H Hour. General Watson, who hadn't wanted to use his regular amtracs as fighting vehicles on land, had his men debark from the troop-carrying LVTs immediately, to begin the fight in the footprint of the tides. As LVTs unloaded elements of the Second Battalion, Sixth Marines, high on the beach, the unit's seventeen LVT(A)-4 amtanks sought routes inland, to serve as a sort of mobile amphibious armored striking force. Their crews were freelancers as soon as they went ashore, and thus they acquired a fearsome responsibility: to use their thin-skinned "armored pigs" to hold the exposed far left flank of the entire two-division landing beach. This meant facing off against anything the Japanese might send them from the north. Turner had anticipated this; the whole purpose of the feint he had carried out off Garapan was to let the first two battalions of the Sixth Marine Regiment get ashore and dig in before a counterattack came.

"I never will forget the concussion of the battleships' guns and the power and compression that blew over us," remembered R. J. Lee. The driver of his amtank was looking to push inland off the beach, but with a deep trench just behind the shrub line there was no way forward. He threw the pig into reverse and backed out to the water's edge, where he unlimbered the 75 mm cannon and began blasting to cut a navigable lane. The Japanese had built only the simplest of defensive works, thanks to the efforts of U.S. submarines to strangle their source of supply. But their trenches, foxholes, and log obstacles near the beach were made reasonably effective by the pressure of artillery and mortar fire coming from the highlands far away. Marine amtanks on Red Beach struggled to get over the bluffs behind the beaches. Lee had gotten off perhaps four shots when Japanese artillery found his range. The open turret took a direct hit. Before the smoke washed everything black, Lee saw his platoon leader and two of his sergeants dead.

"Let's get the hell out of here before she blows up," another sergeant said to the five survivors. The amtank's seven-cylinder radial aircraft engine, owing to the aviation gasoline that fed it, was always a fire hazard. They shimmied through the escape hatch into the water and turned and charged the beach, weapons held high. Lee looked to his right and saw one of his crew, Gus Evans, rifle raised over his head, take a bullet to the face and go down. He was reaching for him when he, too, was hit. Two head shots—one a ricochet, the other penetrating the helmet but somehow retaining only enough force to knock him cold. "Lights out for me," Lee said. "I heard my four-year-old son calling, 'Get up, Daddy, get up, Daddy,' and by the grace of God and my son I made it back to the beach."

On Red Three, a trio of amtanks under the command of Lieutenant Philo Pease found a path through a grove of trees and made it up onto the bluff. Crossing a narrow road, they approached a trenchworks. The lead vehicle tried to cross it but came to grief, stuck fast, treads clawing the air. According to the driver, S. A. Balsano, Japanese soldiers were "on us like flies." There was no way forward, or back, either, for the rear amtank was stuck, too. Lieutenant Pease realized their only hope was to get moving again, or artillery would surely find them. He saw that the second amtank in his column, the one right behind him, might be able to pull the third one free of its snag. He ordered his crew to stay with their stranded lead vehicle and try to break it free while he ran outside, exposing himself in order to help the commander behind him to rig a tow cable. As a cluster of enemy troops approached, one of Pease's crew, Leroy Clobes, stuck a light machine gun through the side hatch and leaned into the trigger, scattering them. Balsano, the driver, jammed his Thompson through the front hatch and jackhammered away. Then they realized that the foreign voices they had heard were coming from the trench beneath them.

Pease reached the amtank behind him only to find himself going to the assistance of a dead man. A Japanese soldier had drawn a bead on the other commander and shot him dead where he stood. Ducking low under fire, Pease inherited the job of attaching the cable. The enemy rifleman chambered another round and took him down next. A corporal in Pease's amtank, Paul Durand, took command, shouting, "Shoot all the sons of bitches you can!" Nearby he spotted a straw house that seemed to harbor an enemy squad. Traversing the 75 mm gun onto it, he blew it right down. At that point a Japanese light tank appeared and put a 37 mm round through the hull of the third amtank in line, killing the driver. Marine bazookamen put the enemy armored vehicle out of business in turn, but here, exposed under merciless direct fire, was the root of General Watson's worry all along: Amtracs were sitting ducks. Lieutenant Pease's surviving crew were lucky. Inspecting their stranded amphibian later, one of them found a magnetic mine fastened to the undercarriage. Somehow it had failed to explode.

South of them, Green Beach One was chaos, its six-hundred-yard frontage hopelessly congested after the arrival of two full battalions. The commanders of the first wave's amtanks tried to deepen the beachhead by driving inland. Their advance was conspicuous to the well-spotted mortarmen and artillery gunners in the hills. Coming under heavy plunging fire, several of the amtanks became bogged down in a rice paddy. Two others, driven by Sergeant Benjamin R. Livesey and Sergeant Onel W. Dickens, pushed on. Crossing the end of the single runway paralleling Green Beach, they turned up a dirt road leading north past the Japanese radio station. The road was little more than a cart path, barely wide enough for two-way traffic. Along it they clattered, fortunate to evade the incoming fire. A Japanese machine gun nest, then another, revealed themselves with spitting tracers. The armored amphibians turned the fury of their 75 mm howitzers and .50- and .30-caliber machine guns onto them, to overwhelming effect. Passing through a banana grove, Livesey realized its value as cover and stopped there as the mortars continued to fall. As the crew crouched low, they heard the chatter of small arms fire as Japanese soldiers opened up on them from down the road. "We scrambled back into our tank," Livesey said, "and scanned ahead into the grove of trees, using our gun sight and binoculars to spot a building with some Japs moving around inside it. We opened fire with everything we had."

Their 75 mm main gun was loaded with high-explosive and incendiary rounds. Several hits produced larger explosions followed climactically by a mushrooming fireball that marked the demise of a Japanese fuel dump. Livesey ordered his driver forward and shot up the area for effect. About a hundred yards on, he came upon a clearing and stopped again, breaking out water for his crew. As Dickens's amtank rolled up alongside, Livesey and his men dismounted to talk with them. No other Marines had yet made it that far inland. "We were alone and isolated," Livesey said, "but enjoying our success." They were picking through the wooden crates that constituted their magazines, counting their remaining shells, when, down the road, four behemoths of foreign origin loomed into view.

The Japanese medium tanks were in a single column, moving toward the landing beach. They did not seem to see the Americans hustling to remount. Once buttoned in, Livesey and Dickens turned out after them, unlimbering their 75 mm guns and opening fire. His ammunition passers were scrambling to find armor-piercing shells when the enemy column turned and came directly at the Marines. "It was us or them," Livesey said.

Neither side's vehicle was a match for the other's main gun. Livesey's vehicle shook from a hit to its engine compartment, but June 15 was his day; the shell was a dud. Gales of machine gun fire washed over them. Though the 75s liked to jam and did, the gunners and loaders kept their breech blocks smoking, and Marine Corps marksmanship was equal to the moment. Destroying three of the enemy tanks in succession, they stopped the Japanese armor just fifty to seventy yards away. Livesey watched one of the enemy tankers pile out of his hatch and start running for the hills, a good thing given that Livesey's ammunition passers were nearly down to smoke shells. He threw a few rounds after the enemy squirter, but as artillery and mortars in the hills began bracketing them again, he and Dickens and their crews opted to bail out. As they set out on foot to the beach, mortar shrapnel killed one of Dickens's men, Private Leo Pletcher. The free-lancing foray by Livesey and Dickens would earn each of them a Navy Cross. More important, it relieved pressure on the vulnerable Second Marine Division foothold by blunting an armored assault that might have fallen upon the beach.

The fighting on the left flank continued stiff and sharp. The Sixth Marines were able to force a shallow beachhead no more than a hundred yards deep, as far as the coastal road behind Red Beach. But pillboxes and machine gun positions checked their progress. An enemy tank on the beach that everyone had thought was disabled opened fire with its 37 mm gun on the LVTs that were bringing in the Sixth Marines' reserve unit, the First Battalion, under Lieutenant Colonel William K. Jones. One of the vehicles that got hit was carrying the staff of Jones's boss, the regimental commander, Colonel James P. Riseley. Many of them were badly wounded. Soon after landing, Riseley learned that the commander of his Third Battalion, Lieutenant Colonel John W. Easley, had been hit, too.

As Riseley was setting up his regimental command post near the center of Red Beach Two, as many as two dozen Japanese troops charged down the beach from the north. They reached the rear area of the regiment's Second Battalion, where wounded Americans were laid out in stretchers under tents near the beach. The Marines rallied, established a firing line, and annihilated the Japanese force. But the close-run assault proved that no one was safe in a battle of infiltration. On the day, the commanders of all four of the Second Marine Division's assault battalions were wounded in action: Raymond L. Murray of the 2/6 (hit along with his executive officer), Henry P. Crowe of the 2/8, John C. Miller of the 3/8, and Easley of the 3/6.

After nightfall, the task of closing the gaps in their lines would be a matter of life and death.

To break the pressure of the counterattack, Riseley ordered the First Battalion to pass through the Third Battalion area and renew the push toward the O-1 line. Riseley would have given the job to no one other than the 1/6's commander, Lieutenant Colonel Jones. He would call him "the best damn battalion commander in this division, or any other division." At the moment, Jones was the only officer of his rank physically able to lead an assault on that high ground. The 1/6 had taken a hundred casualties on the way to the beach. Coming ashore, the survivors had replaced their soaked equipment and gear by harvesting from those who had fallen ahead of them. Jones rallied them forward.

With units scattered and intermingled thanks to the whirligig movements of amtracs in surf and tide, and with the heavy fire urging survival ahead of record keeping, it was difficult to count the wounded. The first casualties were brought to the beach for loading onto LVTs at about 10:40. The total number of killed and wounded that day would total more than two thousand, most of the casualties inflicted by artillery and mortar fire. But an untold multitude emblematized by Lieutenant Colonel Easley refused to report to triage for fear of being removed from the company of their men at the front.

Of course, the problems facing the Eighth Marines, just to the south of the Sixth, made Lieutenant Colonel Jones's advance hazardous. He would make it with his right flank exposed. The amtracs carrying the Eighth Regiment ashore had wandered left under fire from Afetna Point and by the steady pull of an unreadable current, putting both the Second and Third battalions ashore on Green Beach One. This left Green Two, adjoining dangerous Afetna Point, empty of American troops. The Japanese crews manning the gallery of stubbornly surviving antiboat guns there had a field day as a consequence. Facing no direct pressure from assault, they enjoyed their choice of targets.

The mission of the 2/8 Marines, the wayward amphibians, was to turn south and use its three companies to conquer from land the beach they were supposed to have taken from the lagoon. There were two complications with this. First, they would be advancing straight toward the left flank of the 23rd Marines, who had landed on Blue Beach, and would risk hitting them every time they fired their weapons ahead. Second, because they would be moving south while their adjoining battalion, the 3/8, pushed east in order to stay even with Jones's 1/6, they would risk losing contact with their neighboring unit and allowing a gap to open that Japanese infiltrators could exploit to deadly effect in their rear.

The answer to the first problem was shotguns. Lots of them. The entire regiment's allocation of Winchester Model 12s went to Company G of the 2/8. With a six-shot capacity, the Model 12 was excellent in close combat, capable of being "slam fired" simply by pumping its action with the trigger held down. Its short range and wide dispersion of shot made it ideal when the assaulters didn't want their misses carrying too far.

As Company G advanced over the dunes, it confronted a network of mutually supporting pillboxes housing antitank guns, covered by riflemen in open trenches. But they caught a surprising break. The Japanese, rather than holding fast behind their cover, preferred charging into the open, bayonets and swords held high. And as the Marines approached Afetna Point, the antiboat guns installed there did not turn on their attackers, but continued firing at ships in the lagoon. Marine combat engineers worked around and behind the guns and finally, by application of flamethrower, bazooka, and satchel charge, did what the Navy had not. Only after Afetna Point was neutralized would it be possible to use the boat channel the UDT had discovered off Green Beach Two. Using it, the LCMs could drive directly ashore without having to unload their waterproofed tanks at the reef to make a perilous swim.

In the south, the fall of artillery and mortars wrought havoc. Unlike General Watson, Harry Schmidt had wanted his men to ride in their amtracs all the way inland to the O-1 line, where the troops would debark and set up a perimeter in defense of their foothold. But the plan fell apart under live fire. On the division's far left, the Third Battalion of the 23rd Marines became bogged down in Charan Kanoa, fighting Japanese troops concealed in the town's beachfront. Firefights in the streets slowed their progress and clogged the beach as more waves landed behind them.

On the farthest southern extreme of the Fourth Marine Division area, heavy fire from Agingan Point forced the First Battalion of the 25th Marines to leave their amtracs at water's edge. After an hour ashore, this unit held the critical flank only to the skin-deep extent of a dozen or so yards. At least four large Japanese artillery pieces, emplaced on the high ground about eight hundred yards inland, were able to bring flanking fire to bear against the beach. Veteran hands in the Second Marine Division would

Adm. Raymond Spruance was uneasy around photographers. The Fifth Fleet commander was seldom photographed smiling. Here is an exception. (USN/Alfred J. Sedivi, courtesy of U.S. Naval Institute)

Vice Adm. Richmond Kelly Turner off Saipan, June 15, 1944. The brilliant, volatile officer was indispensable as Spruance's amphibious force commander. (USN)

Maj. Gen. Holland A. Smith, known as "Howlin' Mad," cherished his status as the first operational corps commander to hail from the U.S. Marine Corps. His great pride in this was at the heart of his bad relationship with the Army. (USN)

Vice Adm. Marc A. Mitscher, commander of Task Force 58. A main battle fleet of such unprecedented power surely deserved a more imposing name, but understatement was the Nimitz way. (USN)

Sailors enjoy a swim at Majuro, May 1944, while Fifth Fleet
carriers lie at anchor, awaiting the launch of Operation Forager. (USN)

The logo of Turner's Fifth Amphibious Force highlights its Central Pacific track record—
and suggests its dynamic approach to warfare. (USN)

The Navy's first frogmen, the swimmers of the Underwater Demolition Teams, reconnoitered lagoons and blew out reefs to clear the way for Turner's assault troops and supply train. (USN)

Cdr. Draper L. Kauffman was the innovative commander of the first UDT teams. Here his father, Rear Adm. James L. Kauffman, presents him with a gold star in lieu of his second Navy Cross, for action in the Marianas. (USN)

Rocket-equipped LCIs
hammered Saipan ahead
of the first assault wave.
(USN)

From the bow ramp of an LST, an amtrac launches with trailer in tow. (USN)

Amtracs off Saipan, June 15, 1944. Derived from the "swamp buggy" designed to rescue Floridians from hurricanes, the LVTs were indispensable in landing invasion troops on heavily defended shores. (right: U.S. Coast Guard; below: USMC)

Spruance's flagship, the *Indianapolis,* lets loose a salvo as the first wave goes in. Cruisers and other Navy ships supported the landings and provided call fire throughout the operation. (USN)

Once on the beach, the men of the Second and Fourth Marine Divisions faced ferocious bombardment from Japanese mortars and mountain guns. (USMC/Sgt. James L. Burns)

Dauntless dive-bombers from the *Lexington* cover the landings,
struggling to suppress Japanese guns well concealed in caves
and ravines. (USN)

Marines take cover behind an amtrac to assault a
Japanese position as an oil dump burns in the
background. (USMC)

Maj. Gen. Thomas E. Watson (above), commander of the Second Marine Division, and Maj. Gen. Harry Schmidt, commander of the Fourth Marine Division, were well regarded for their work on Saipan. (USMC)

Marines turn a captured mountain gun against the Japanese capital at Garapan. (USMC)

Marines in action on Saipan. (USMC)

Using bazookas and grenades, Pfcs. Lauren H. Kahn (left) and
Lewis M. Nalder destroyed three tanks during a Japanese attack on
the beachhead on D Day plus 1. (USMC)

Japanese light tanks were no match for Marine
bazookas and field pieces. (USN)

A Marine feeds a battlefield refugee. (USMC)

Wounded in action amid Saipan's sugarcane, a Marine
is carried away to triage. (USMC/Cpl. E. G Wilbert)

Marines use flamethrowers to root Japanese soldiers from a cave. One of them emerges (below) holding a stick of dynamite. When he tries to throw it, the Americans shoot him dead. (above: USMC; below: USMC/Robert B. Opper)

Maj. Gen. Ralph Smith, commanding general of the 27th Infantry Division, gives a cup of water to a wounded Japanese soldier at Aslito Field, Saipan. (U.S. Army Signal Corps)

An unexploded battleship projectile offers a resting place for this Second Division rifleman. (USMC)

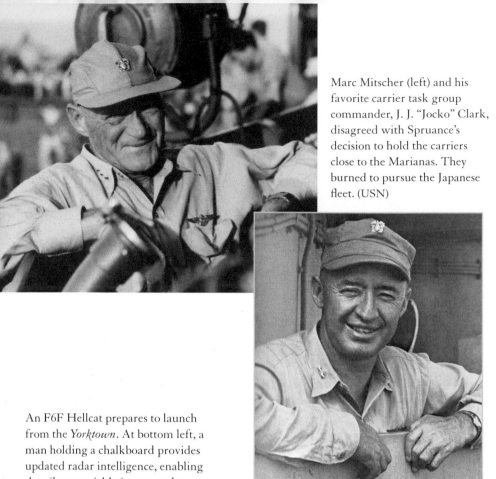

Marc Mitscher (left) and his favorite carrier task group commander, J. J. "Jocko" Clark, disagreed with Spruance's decision to hold the carriers close to the Marianas. They burned to pursue the Japanese fleet. (USN)

An F6F Hellcat prepares to launch from the *Yorktown*. At bottom left, a man holding a chalkboard provides updated radar intelligence, enabling the pilot to quickly intercept the incoming enemy planes. (USN)

David McCampbell, commander of Air Group 15 on the *Essex,* was revered for his surpassing competence as an aviator, aerial marksman, and leader. By the end of 1944 he had assured his standing as the top-scoring U.S. Navy fighter ace of the war. (USN)

Ens. Claude S. Plant was one of McCampbell's high scorers. (USN)

In spite of a balking engine, Lt. Alex (j.g.) Vraciu of the *Lexington*'s VF-16 still managed to destroy six planes in the Marianas Turkey Shoot. This photo, taken immediately after he landed on June 19, became a national sensation. (USN)

A cameraman stationed on the light carrier *Monterey* captures a Japanese plane falling to antiaircraft fire on the afternoon of June 19. (USN)

have recognized their dire position after the ordeal at Tarawa. In the early hours, the issue seemed in doubt. The battleship *Tennessee* had been blasting the strongpoint but had not yet silenced it.

As the 1/25 faltered, its leading waves pinned down and picked apart, some of their amtracs turned around and fled without unloading their ammunition, mortars, or machine guns. The Marines often mistrusted the Navy, but as a partner in arms they considered the Army equally dubious. To many a Marine, fairly or otherwise, the Army LVT crews were doubly suspect as drivers of watercraft who took paychecks from a rival service. As he was going over the side, a Marine remarked to an amtrac driver, "So you're just gonna drop us off and get the hell out of here, huh?" The driver, Merlin Fontenot of New Orleans, replied in his Cajun fiddler's brogue, "That's right. We're going to get the hell out of here and go and get some more of you boys and bring them right back on in!" And he did, and did again.

Courage could arise from an ability to let go of fear for your own life and limbs. To those who saw not the future but only the present, it was often easier to do the necessary thing. It could seem that what happened to one happened to all, and thus the life of another man could be just as valuable as one's own. This was Donald Boots's view. "I was so caught up in the life of another person that you become a part of that person. You would do something that maybe the world doesn't understand. . . . You do things because you became one with the people close to you. You went on liberty together; you looked out for one another; you traveled around together, you bunked together. When it came time to sit in place before the enemy, you were still there. There was a closeness there that death could not separate. I don't have the words to explain it."

Japanese infantry on Agingan Point tried to counterattack the Fourth Division right flank. Air strikes and supporting fire from the *Tennessee* kept them from massing for good effect. With the backs of his men to the sea, the commander of the 1/25, Lieutenant Colonel Hollis Mustain, requested that tanks be landed as soon as possible, along with an additional rifle company from the regimental reserve. Mortar and artillery fire rained mercilessly upon his men, as well as the battalion to their left, where cover was scarce. The key to surviving was to move inland as fast as possible.

Up the beach from Mustain's embattled flank, another battalion managed to drive in their amtracs all the way to the railroad embankment, about five hundred yards inland. Farther up the coast, on Blue Beach, Robert Graf's Second Battalion, 23rd Marines, under the command of Lieutenant Colonel Edward J. Dillon, pushed inland a few hundred yards before debarking from the LVTs and taking to foot. Their progress forward would be halting.

Admiral Turner, with direct command of all firing ships now, required them to shoot either on his direct order or at the request of shore fire-control parties. On board the battleships this produced unending frustration, as the targets they were given could seldom be spotted from the ship or from spotting planes overhead. Studying the island through binoculars off the Second Marine Division beaches, the *California*'s gunnery officer called it "a rare treat when gun flashes or possible targets of opportunity made themselves seen." Aerial observers were constantly foiled by the enemy's skill at camouflage and by the roil of smoke and dust scrubbing over the island. "Several times the planes reported no targets or activity in an area only to have it come to life a short time later."

Shortly after nine, the *Tennessee* was blasting the Yellow and Blue beaches when she took a blow from an unexpected quarter. Three six-inch projectiles fired from Tinian struck her unengaged starboard side. A twin five-inch/38 mount took a direct hit, killing eight of its ten-man crew and starting an oil fire. Another shell hit her side plate, blasting a three-by-three-foot hole just above the waterline. The third shell crashed through the main deck, shredding bulkheads, doors, and air ducts before coming to rest in the vegetable storage locker, stopped cold by a crate of potatoes. Twenty-six men were wounded in addition to the fatalities in the gun mount.

A little before ten, Turner reported that Japanese tanks were on the move south from Garapan. The battleship *California,* supporting a battalion of the Sixth Marines, had eyes on the threat, and Captain Burnett ordered his five-inch batteries to engage, breaking up the formation and destroying two of the tanks. The rumbling of activity on the Second Division's left flank was ominous, but Burnett could do nothing more about it without word from either a forward observer or the battalion naval liaison officer. He was left to make do with what little his own spotters could see. After an hour of frustration, the news reached him that his "Charlie" (as the forward observers or shore fire-control parties were known) had been a casualty at the beach.

As each battalion had just one Charlie, the *California*'s battalion, the 2/6, was out of luck. No one was on hand to set up an observation post, lay wires to headquarters, or set up on a radio frequency shared with Burnett and his staff; to orient the map and determine whether its landmarks were within range of the battleship's guns; or to keep track of the movement of friendly troops. As a result, the *California* was left shooting far beyond the combat front, hitting targets reported by spotting planes. Captain Inglis of the *Birmingham* found himself spending much of the day idle. On D Day, the wicked barb that had been directed at the fast battleships—"a Navy-sponsored farm project"—applied to some of Oldendorf's ships, too.

With twenty thousand Marines ashore and progress stalled in spite of an overwhelming advantage in potential firepower, there seemed to be, at this hour, reason to fear for the success of the landings. As the fourth wave went ashore, Japanese artillery and mortar fire converged viciously on the reef, swallowing it in a storm of sea spray. Noting some amtracs milling about, Inglis thought the assault was faltering under fire. Inland from Blue and Yellow beaches, the differences in terrain and enemy resistance turned the Fourth Division's planned forward rush into a series of separate actions by the amtrac companies. "The suspense at that moment was terrific," Inglis said, "but was soon relieved by a report by radio from the amphibious tanks that they had reached and crossed the airstrip paralleling the beach line about a hundred yards inshore and just north of the town of Charan Kanoa." This Fourth Division element, thirteen amtanks from the 708th Amphibian Tank Battalion, had managed to maneuver through the town, skirt the marshy tidal wetlands of Susupe Swamp, and reach the O-1 line, where by midmorning they held high ground commanding the Green beaches.

By eleven, the transport group that had conducted the feint off Tanapag was back in the main transport area preparing to send ashore the Second and 24th regiments as their respective division reserves. Answering the call from battalion commanders, Admiral Hill ordered the LCMs to begin carrying in their tanks. Just as the Marine commanders had asked, Draper Kauffman went with the first wave, using the route he had surveyed across Red Beach Three. In the Fourth Marine Division sector, several platoons of medium tanks clanked ashore on Blue Beach Two and threw themselves into support of Mustain's 1/25. The tanks arrived on his far right flank just as two companies of Japanese troops, some four hundred men, appeared from Agingan Point, bidding to push the battalion into the sea. But an open-field charge was the wrong tactic to use against Marine armor. With infantry support, the tankers turned loose against the exposed enemy mass, stilling it at close range. Though other tank companies lost vehicles to high surf off the Yellow beaches, causing LCMs and swimming tanks to broach and flounder, Mustain's line companies were able to push off and expand their toehold enough to open up some beach for resupply and the evacuation of casualties. All of this came without the loss of a single tank.

On the left flank, far to the north, Admiral Hill saw how Japanese batteries were causing trouble for the Sixth Marines and requested intensified air search to deal with them. He reported to Turner that the regiment's east-facing line, now anchored by Jones and his 1/6, was swinging north to face Japanese troops gathering near Garapan. Here, too, Marine forward observers were not yet in place, so there was little that warships could do to help. They could not see the Japanese guns, and their observation planes were causing as many problems as they were solving. Though Admiral Mitscher had sent the *Hornet* and *Essex* task groups, under John J. "Jocko" Clark and William K. Harrill, on a two-day side trip to strike Iwo Jima and Chichi Jima in order to keep planes based there from interfering with the landings, his remaining two groups kept up a steady pace of air strikes against both Saipan and Tinian. The greatest danger they faced was the risk of collision with the spotting planes. When Turner complained of the interference, barking to the commander of the *California*'s fire-support group, "Get those planes out of the way," the battleships quickly found other targets: Japanese troops massing inland of Charan Kanoa, near Susupe Swamp, and more tanks on the flank of the Sixth Marines. The *California* fired five-inch air bursts at the latter, breaking up an armored formation, then, on order from Oldendorf, turned its guns on Mutcho Point and Afetna Point, strongholds from which some notably persistent defenders were enfilading the entire Second Marine Division beachhead. It was only after the *California* had retired to seaward to recover her spotting planes that the Charlie assigned to that battleship made contact. "It was unfortunate that on so vital a day the Shore Fire Control Party had so little use of our secondary battery," the gunnery officer noted. More long and trying days lay ahead.

The battle of artillery—Japanese mountain guns and mortars versus Oldendorf's fire-support ships—was the Saipan campaign's first critical fight. Kelly Turner was coming to a fuller realization of something that had bothered him since Tarawa: that saturation naval bombardment was futile, squandering both time and ordnance. He would compare the effort to destroy his well-entrenched enemy with general area fire to the prolonged artillery bombardments of the Great War. "Beyond a certain point, both became ineffective and wasteful," he would write. Although heavy naval gunfire tore away most of the wiring that formed the physical grid of General Saito's communications network, the shaken defenders dug in amid Saipan's interior hills, valleys, cliff sides, and crevices and held on. The island would have to be taken as contested ground always was: by men on foot carrying guns.

Two miles off the landing beach, Admiral Spruance watched with satisfaction in the *Indianapolis* as the menagerie of landing craft from later waves passed close aboard, the troops inside them standing and waving broadly as they went in, high spirits all around. The Marines' own artillery, loaded in DUKWs, was rolling ashore, too. The fleet flagship ranged across a mile-long north-south line, throwing shells at inland targets. "Whenever we reached the southern end of our little run, mortar shells dropped around us," Carl Moore said. One landed particularly close, grazing the starboard bow. Spruance never made a show of his physical courage, but his Japanese radio intelligence officer, Commander Gil Slonim, would write, "He was the essence of ice water as we watched the bombardments of fixed positions ashore. . . . As the shells whizzed through our rigging, many of us sought shelter; and quickly. Not Spruance, who remained unhelmeted in the wing of the flag bridge watching the point-blank range operations, the flagship stopped dead in the water, with keen intellectual interest."

When Draper Kauffman returned to the *Cambria* after his excursion ashore with the first wave of tanks, Admiral Hill ordered him to report to the shore party commander. It seemed the Marines wanted a channel blown through the reef to allow tank-carrying landing craft to drive straight in. Kauffman and his Marine liaison officer, Lieutenant Gordon Leslie, hitched a ride in an amtrac to the beach, huddling with paper and pencil trying to figure how much tetratol to use for the job. When they reached the sand, they hopped over the side and became immediate objects of curiosity, wearing blue "coral shoes" and face masks slung around their necks. As the Marines dug foxholes and occasionally traded fire with Japanese, one of them sauntered over, offered the frogmen a blank, quizzical look, then shouted to another rifleman. "We don't even have the *beachhead* yet and the goddamn tourists have already arrived!"

After about hour and a half of going foxhole to foxhole, Kauffman and Leslie found the shore party commander. He pointed out where he wanted the channel, adding, "I want it very, very badly and very, very quickly." To blast a channel three hundred feet long by forty feet wide, they figured they would need more than a hundred thousand pounds of tetratol. Planting such a volume of explosives in twenty-pound packages would be no small task even in the absence of surf, but that's what three full teams of UDT were for. In the early days they were not known for underdoing things. "Each package had to be secured firmly to the coral reef which was hard to do with the surf constantly pounding over it. Then the five thousand packs all had to be connected together by explosive cord or primacord so that when we fired it would all go simultaneously," Kauffman said. The tourists would return that night to do the job.

Shortly after two, the destroyer *Monssen,* while delivering counterbattery and call fires off the northern landing beaches, relayed to Admiral Turner a message from the Sixth Marines on Red Beach Two. "Casualties are piling up and we have inadequate supplies. Blood plasma needed." Medical evacuation was a continuing challenge. By midafternoon, one hundred forty-two Marines were reported killed in action, and more than seven hundred casualties were received aboard transports offshore. But that was far from the total count. Hundreds more men were bleeding and suffering in the seagoing wagon train set up to carry casualties to safety. The Fourth Division was so hard-pressed that it made no casualty report at all on D Day.

Three hospital-equipped LSTs waited off the beaches, all three to be swarmed by amtracs and filled to capacity—two hundred souls apiece—before midday. The overload meant misery for stretcher cases waiting ashore. They had to be loaded into amtracs, then driven out over the reef to the transport area for direct transfer to larger ships. When heavy seas made it impossible to transfer them from bow ramps, the wounded suffered a rough trip as their stretchers were lifted and swung aboard by cherry-picker cranes. Each of Turner's attack transports had a medical team of four to six officers and thirty or so corpsmen, but that wasn't enough. Regular sailors, Seabees, and embarked troops turned to, helping those in need.

"On one of these LSTs, ammunition was being unloaded from the starboard side while casualties were being received on the port side," wrote Turner's top surgeon.

> The medical personnel of this LST were bewildered by the sudden influx of such large-scale critical personnel casualties to the extent that a systematic handling of the casualties was not carried out. In one instance, a very severe wound of a shoulder involving

complete destruction of the joint was evacuated from an LST to an APA without so much as even a dressing over the wound. Not to mention failure to splint the extremity. . . . If an LST was not able to evacuate its load of casualties in time to transfer them to a transport prior to dark, the casualties were obliged to stay aboard overnight. As a result of this, several chest and abdominal wounds were kept on LSTs and away from life saving surgery for periods of up to thirty-six hours or more. . . . The departure of transports on D plus 2 imposed a large problem of medical supply and evacuation ashore. However, the large initial quantities of medical supply landed by the divisions tided them over during this critical phase.

The mountain artillery and mortar fire reached a murderous crescendo just before dusk. From the control boat off Yellow Beach, an officer remarked: "To me it looked awfully serious; I didn't really know how well we had this business under control but I could see flashes of the hits along the beaches which I knew were full of men. It looked awfully serious to me." And yet the force beachmaster, Commander Charles E. "Squeaky" Anderson, was undaunted. A colorful figure known for his excitable way and high-pitched, obscenity-laced Swedish twang, Anderson commanded the respect of most everyone who knew him. He had come to America penniless, making his way to Alaska, where he was naturalized and learned the salmon cannery business. He came up the hard way, learning to solve problems with the materials at hand. "He was a real man," said Harry Hill. Draper Kauffman marveled at his courage: "He walked up and down the beach, never ducking or taking cover, a thoroughgoing fatalist. Impeccably shined black shoes, black socks held up by garters, a pair of Marine green trousers, ripped off halfway above the knee, and an open shirt. A funny old man, but very competent."

Anderson was in charge of every crate that came or went ashore. He specialized in meeting the needs of the Marines, whose regimental shore party commanders were his most vital opposite numbers. He informed Admiral Hill late in the afternoon that the Yellow beaches were still too hot for the unloading. Despite the casualties his beach parties took, they continued directing the flow of men and equipment, diverting traffic to adjust to the effects of tides and enemy gunfire. "Anderson was everywhere," Hill said, "but came out unscathed. He really had a guardian angel watching over him. The story of those beach parties should some day be told—they have been the forgotten heroes of the war." According to Colonel Jones of the 23rd Marines, what saved his bloodied regiment were two segregated companies of African American troops from the Army beach parties, who kept the way open for the tanks as they rolled ashore late on D Day.

Landing with the 24th Marines, Lieutenant John C. Chapin found that most of his unit, Company K of the 3/24, had become scattered. Under bombardment, he and his platoon sergeant ran forward through a gasoline dump littered with blackened and burst fuel drums, a surreal landscape of shredded trees, dismembered buildings, and the bodies of those who had passed there ahead of him and many of their enemy, too. The dead were everywhere, thrown down like dolls by a violent hand. About six hundred yards southeast of Charan Kanoa, in the assembly area of the Fourth Division reserve, he rounded up a few of his men and decided to make his stand. He dived to ground in a trench and began digging in as well as he could. He left his platoon sergeant there to oversee the construction of their lines at the place Chapin had chosen, then set out with his corpsman to reconnoiter the area and try to round up his wounded. "It was vital that we locate and give first aid to as many of them as possible before dark," he wrote. "During the night we wouldn't be able to move around, and by dawn they would either have died of their wounds or have been killed by the Japs. So the two of us stumbled urgently around in the gloom, searching for the wounded. There was no time to bother with the dead."

Plenty of men had gotten lost. Robert Graf had become separated from Easy Company during an advance that faltered under shattering artillery fire. As dusk fell, he was alone and traveling light, approaching Susupe Swamp. He had ditched his pack, put his bayonet sheath onto his cartridge belt, and stuffed his rations into his dungarees. He spotted to his left a group of six men, including Sergeant Max Klein of his company, but otherwise he saw few familiar faces in this area of the Second Battalion, 23rd Marines. The group decided to avoid the risk of running into the Japanese positions that were believed to infest the swamp bank. They advanced through the waist-high waters instead. Some distance along, Graf noticed, sliding off the bank ahead, "several of the most gruesome things that I had ever seen. They looked like alligators but we had not been briefed on any. By God, if they were the lizards that they told us about they were big." He feared they might be poisonous, but after discussing with his team the wisdom of opening fire, they opted not to attract attention to themselves. So, bayonets at the level, they started in reverse, retreating the way they had come. As heavy shells continued to strike the ground around them, forcing them to take cover in shell holes and trenches, Graf found that his group had withdrawn all the way back to the outskirts of Charan Kanoa. According to Colonel Jones, the town's sugar mill changed hands seven or eight times on the first day as the Japanese held out against repeated assaults, supported by mortar teams hiding in the swamp.

"The damned artillery fire made me very uptight," Robert Graf wrote. "Bursting shells blew our minds apart as we could not fight back. As far as we knew, the guns were several miles back in the hills, yet they fired in pre-arranged patterns so that a shell landed in each sector under fire. Laying in a previous shell hole might not necessarily prove wise, as the pattern could be repeated. It was just dumb luck if you lived or died." Few members of Easy Company, Graf would find, had been lucky. When he reached battalion headquarters, someone he knew called him over, expressed amazement he was still alive, and told him the story of how Japanese artillery had fixed on them. Lieutenant Roth was among the dead, the man said, killed instantly by the shellfire. Graf was so badly shaken that he checked in to battalion headquarters and stayed there awhile, heaving from the impact of everything he had seen since the fire first began raining down on him, long ago in West Loch.

Around five, Turner ordered his task force to retire for the night. Only the *Cambria* remained near the anchorage. Hill's flagship was set up to serve as an air defense control center until one could be established ashore. Her combat information center would be linked to U.S. antiaircraft batteries and also to the amphibious force's fighter director ships. Radars were picking up Japanese planes venturing into the area in singles and doubles.

As darkness fell, the Marine division commanders, Watson and Schmidt, went ashore to take command of their ten-thousand-yard front. Defying a high surf at the reef that had overturned four amtracs, Watson landed with his assistant, Brigadier General Merritt A. Edson, and installed his command post on Red Beach Two. After sundown, he was forced to move. "The distant night was alive with fires, and shelling from enemy artillery and mortars was unremitting," he recalled.

> I directed Brigadier General Edson and his small control group to remain behind until our new command post could be established. The rest of our headquarters group moved northward along the beach, then struck inland across the open beach road and, moving

in the shadows of the road, finally reached the wooded area which had been selected for the new command post.

They had wanted to set it up in trenches and shelters that the Japanese had dug. Exploring them, the general and his men found that the naval bombardment had transformed these fortifications into an open grave for the defenders. The beach parties set about hauling away the dead and securing the enemy's stockpiles of dynamite and high explosives. The night would see the Japanese make probing attacks along the entire front of the Sixth Regiment.

Schmidt made his Fourth Division headquarters in a shattered palm grove near a partially buried dump of fuel drums on Yellow Beach Two. At the end of the day, his reserve, the 24th Marines, was gathered in their assembly area south of Charan Kanoa. After a notably rough start, only one regiment on Saipan, the 25th Marines, had managed to reach the first day's objective, the O-1 line. But they held it well: About forty LVT(A)s, that formidable tank army that led the way in from the sea, held defilade positions on the high ground overwatching the Blue and Yellow beaches.

Each division had a clear objective before it. The Second would hold fast on the left, repulsing any attacks down the coast while preparing to advance toward Mount Tapotchau. The Fourth would push all the way across the island, seizing Aslito Field and then turning north to roll up the eastern side of the island. But a gap yawned between the two divisions. Susupe Swamp was a nest of enemy opportunists. Though no man's position was enviable with two Marine divisions bidding to envelop him, the Japanese threatened both of their flanks. Patrols from the Eighth and 23rd Marines, situated along the division boundary, went out to search for each other but failed to make contact. To reduce the exposure of their flanks, Holland Smith approved the landing of the reserve for the 23rd Marines, its First Battalion. That unit hit Blue Beach One and spent the remainder of the day helping shore parties deal with infiltration by overrun Japanese. Sentries adopted a protocol for passwords and countersigns.

Challenger: "Halt, who's there?"
Answer: "July" (or any month of the year).
Challenger: "April" (or any other month).

The challenger or the person challenged could say "Repeat" at any time, requiring a different month to be called until each party was satisfied with the identity of the other. After five days, the operative words would change to cities, and five days after that, to states.

In the cramped confines of three hospital-equipped LSTs outside the reef, where bitter sulfa and rancid blood stained the air, succor was given the wounded. In the anchorage that night, patrol boats eased to and fro, alert for intrusions by enemy rafts, swimmers, human torpedoes, and mine layers. But Japanese ambitions were to surpass such quarter measures. The 31st Army, nominally headquartered on Saipan, transmitted to Tokyo a confident declaration: "The army this evening will make a night attack with all its forces and expects to annihilate all the enemy at one blow."

Night had fallen when Admiral Hill ordered the ships remaining in the western roadstead to execute the smoke plan. Situated upwind from the anchorage, LCI gunboats fitted with smoke generators opened up their pots and an enveloping cloud of white vapor poured forth. As dramatically as it had appeared that morning from the heart of the sea, Task Force 52 vanished again after dark, swallowed by nightfall and obscured by a shield of atomized fog oil. The morning cargo of the task force, six regiments of Marines, held fast to their foothold, stringing barbed wire around their foxholes and trench lines under the uneven brilliance of star shells. Swinging down from parachutes, they cast over the landscape shadows whose metronomic flickerings provoked the imagination. The Marines, firmly ashore, tied in their lines and awaited enemy contact.

11

Trail, Attack, Report

On the evening of D Day at Saipan, after refueling his carriers in the Philippines, the Combined Fleet commander in chief, Admiral Soemu Toyoda, announced, "On the morning of the fifteenth, a strong enemy force began landing operations in the Saipan-Tinian area. The Combined Fleet will attack the enemy in the Marianas area and annihilate the invasion force. Activate the A-Go operation for decisive battle." At sea with his task force of nine aircraft carriers, Toyoda received a dispatch from Tokyo: "The fate of our Empire depends upon the outcome of this battle. Let each each man do his utmost."

The pressure on the Combined Fleet to act derived not only from the U.S. landings, but also from the startling manner in which the war came falling on Japan proper that same day. When the B-29s based in China attacked the steelworks in Yawata, the domestic reaction was as disproportionate to the damage suffered as the reaction to the Doolittle raid had been. Saburo Sakai, a fighter ace with the elite Yokosuka Wing, would write, "Everywhere in Japan, the people talked about the raid, discussed the fact that our fighters had failed to stop the bombers. They all asked the same questions. Who was next? When? And how many bombers would come?"

News of armed Americans coming ashore in the Marianas put the lie to years of claims of sweeping Japanese victories. "The maps were unrolled, and our people looked for the tiny dot which lay not so far off our coastline," wrote Sakai. "And they looked at each other. They began to question—never aloud, but in furtive conversations—the ceaseless reports of victories. How could we have smashed the enemy's ships, destroyed his planes, decimated his armies, if Saipan had been invaded? It was a question which everyone asked, but which very few dared to answer." The next morning Sakai's unit received new orders: They were to transfer from Yokosuka to Iwo Jima. The volcanic island was six hundred fifty miles north of the land battle raging in the Marianas. The fact that such a valuable base was not also under invasion surprised Sakai, for the Japanese hadn't even begun to fortify it. "The island was barely able to defend itself!" he wrote. He joined a detachment of thirty fighter pilots slated to make the long flight to deploy there.

From the halyards of all of Ozawa's ships flew the Z flag, a signal that carried historic import. In 1905, it had been raised by Admiral Heihachiro Togo's flagship prior to Japan's victory at the Battle of Tsushima. It flew again during the Combined Fleet's strike on Pearl Harbor. Ozawa's plan was ambitious enough to justify its use again now. He would strike Task Force 58 using the advantage of his planes' longer range. By using Guam to land and refuel them after their strike, he could effectively double his reach. To attack him, American planes would have to make a round-trip, reserving enough fuel to return to the flight decks that had launched them. Ozawa was aware the Americans had fifteen fast carriers in the area, against his nine, and a bevy of escort carriers operating east of the islands. He didn't think Mitscher would venture too far west to attack him, though; Ozawa fancied land-based airpower in the western Carolines and the Palaus as a discouragement to adventurism by U.S. carriers.

If his aviators were to attack at long range, they could afford no mistakes in locating their targets. Ozawa ordered the First Air Fleet on Tinian to track the movements of Task Force 58, and to keep watch over the seas south of Iwo Jima. It would prove difficult to stand up Iwo Jima's own air force. Saburo Sakai and his fellow pilots, lacking radar and in some cases radios, had been blocked by dangerous storms off the home island. Sakai would write, "In the vast reaches of the Pacific the distance between each small outcropping of land can assume terrifying proportions. We dared not risk the loss of most of our planes. . . . We languished in our billets, listening to radio reports from our island garrisons, telling of the enemy air attacks all through the day and on into the night."

Kakuta's fliers on Tinian, battered by days of carrier strikes on their airfields, mustered little more than piecemeal counterattacks. At dusk on June 15, he put forth his best effort, sending about two dozen bombers to strike the *Enterprise* and her task group. Four Hellcats from the *San Jacinto* caught and destroyed eight of them about thirty-five miles out. A pair of night fighters from the *Enterprise* stalked in and destroyed another, as well as an escorting fighter. The rest came straight through. As red tracers flashed outward into the night, a twin-engine bomber roared past the bridge of the *Lexington,* and another came in off the port bow, banking and dipping down to make what a combat correspondent called "a lively bonfire on the smooth dark sea." But some pilots managed to release their torpedoes before meeting their death. Looking over the rail, the journalist noted a ripple on the water. A torpedo. It passed parallel to the carrier, so close that its wake disappeared from view beneath the flight deck. Another torpedo plane attacked from ahead. The *Lexington*'s guns torched it, and the enemy pilot buzzed the flight deck about thirty feet up, his flames warming the faces of everyone watching from the bridge, before crashing astern. As more torpedoes came on, the captains of the *Enterprise* and *Lexington* gamely held course head-on toward their attackers, combing the wakes.

When the radar tracks betrayed the planes as having come from Tinian, Guam, and Rota, Mitscher redirected close-support strikes bound for Saipan and threw them against its neighbor islands instead. But packed coral runways were nearly impossible to put out of business permanently. As ever, it was the threat of Ozawa's powerful carrier task force that concerned Spruance, Mitscher, and their staffs, not the scattershot attacks mounted from land bases.

For four days now the scuttlebutt had been that the Combined Fleet was on the move. Pacific Fleet intelligence assessed its strength at 450 planes, in addition to 1,285 land-based planes thought to be scattered across bases in the Western Pacific. There were rumors of a new navy interceptor, the Mitsubishi J2M Raiden or "Jack," with a maximum speed of 310 knots, able to reach its thirty-thousand-foot ceiling in fifteen minutes, and a land-based twin-engine light bomber, the Yokosuka P1Y1 "Frances," faster and longer-ranged than its predecessor, the ubiquitous Betty.

Even though they surmised that Ozawa would soon appear, Spruance and Mitscher were uncertain from which direction he would come. Three possibilities offered themselves. Ozawa could steam toward the Marianas straight from the west. He could take a northerly route around Luzon and come down from the northwest. Or he could take a southern route, skirting Mindanao, and attack from the southwest. The fuel supply, the Americans thought, recommended the southwesterly approach. According to Kelly Turner, "Before leaving Pearl Harbor, lengthy discussions were held concerning the prospect of fleet action. . . . The ideas of major commands were in complete accord that whatever happened, Task Force 58 would adequately cover the Expeditionary Force during its landing of troops."

Mitscher, of course, wanted to pursue Ozawa aggressively. Spruance did not. Arleigh Burke, Mitscher's chief of staff and a loyal carrier man (though his history was in destroyers), was aware that overpursuit could be dangerous, for if Ozawa drew Mitscher far to the west, he could send another force to make an end-around, outflanking Task Force 58 to attack the vulnerable invasion force off Saipan. "This trick was possible," Burke said, "if their main body continued a direct approach while a small, high-speed carrier unit ran close to Ulithi and attacked our forces from the southern flank or from the rear and if the U.S. fleet went too far to the west without searching its southern flank." It was a known Japanese tactic, and in recognizing it, Burke put the lie to Jocko Clark's claim that it was impossible to end-run a carrier task force. Further proof arrived in the form of a manual of Japanese carrier doctrine, captured at Hollandia that spring. It urged IJN carrier commanders to feint to the center while sending a force around the flanks. "We didn't know whether it had been received by Turner and Mitscher or not," Carl Moore would say, "but it was of a great deal of significance as far as we were concerned."

Task Force 58's operations officer, Gus Widhelm, threw down a thousand-dollar bet that the Japanese carrier fleet would offer battle. Several fighter pilots pitched in to cover it. But the question did not seem to be *whether.* It was more a matter of where and when. As the two Marine division commanders were going ashore on Saipan, U.S. submarines supplied new hints toward an answer.

All morning long, the skipper of the *Flying Fish* had had the sense that "something was in the wind" as he watched through a periscope Japanese planes circling low over the eastern exit to San Bernardino Strait, as if they were heralding an eventful arrival. Now, pushing an easterly course at twenty knots at 6:35 P.M. Marianas time, here it was: a forest of masts in San Bernardino Strait. Studying it through his periscope, Lieutenant Commander Robert D. Risser estimated the force as three aircraft carriers, three battleships, and several cruisers and destroyers. With the nearest of them at the extremity of his sight range, twelve and a half miles away, he was not able to close and attack. But he kept watch until the ships dropped below the horizon. When all was clear, Risser took the *Flying Fish* to the surface, north-northeast of the eastern exit from the strait, and began transmitting a report.

At 7:45 P.M. Marianas time, about two hundred miles east of Surigao Strait, the captain of the submarine USS *Seahorse,* by the last traces of twilight, spied the tops of four unidentified men-of-war as well as smoke from six other ships. Within ten minutes, Slade Cutter had lost sight of them in the growing darkness of a moonless night. Less than an hour later, holding a pursuit course, he made radar contact on three ships making a zigzag course at sixteen and a half knots toward Saipan to his northeast, range 27,000 yards, just over fifteen miles. It seemed a stellar opportunity, but as he attempted pursuit, chronic problems with his battery-powered engines flared anew, causing a ferocious sparking in the engine room and a loss of power that would make it impossible for the *Seahorse* to reach attack position. Lieutenant Commander Cutter surfaced and began sending a contact report. Because of "very persistent jamming by the enemy," it wasn't until four A.M. that he was able to clear it to Admiral Lockwood's station. Lockwood forwarded the report to Nimitz at Pearl Harbor, who relayed it to Spruance off Saipan.

Where was Ozawa? A third piece of the puzzle slid into place thanks to the alert periscope work of a third submarine, the *Cavalla.* Commander Kossler's boat, on her first war patrol, was en route to relieve the *Flying Fish,* an urgent task given that Commander Risser had reported his fuel running low. But when Kossler made contact at 12:30 A.M. on June 16 with a convoy of two Japanese tankers, he raced for position ahead. In the darkness before dawn, at the same time that Cutter was transmitting the *Seahorse*'s sighting report, Kossler went to radar depth and maneuvered to fire torpedoes. Then one of the two destroyers escorting the convoy turned straight for him. Kossler turned down his bow planes, and as his boat descended past seventy-five feet he could hear the swishing whine of high-speed screws crossing overhead. To the *Cavalla*'s good fortune, the Japanese ship must have been moving too fast to operate her sonar; his soundmen heard no pings, and her depth charges remained in their racks. But the destroyer's captain still managed to render some service to his emperor; by the time Kossler came back to radar depth, his targets were out of range. He surfaced before sunrise, reporting to Lockwood that he would continue on to relieve the *Flying Fish* that day. But Lockwood had other plans. "It appeared most important to chase those tankers. They undoubtedly had a fueling rendezvous with the enemy fleet. Big game might be brought to bag by following them." He instructed Kossler, "TRAIL . . . ATTACK . . . REPORT. KEEP YOUR CHIN UP." He then informed three nearby submarines of the situation. The *Cavalla* pursued the tankers at her full four-engine speed, but, forced to submerge three times by the appearance of aircraft through the next day, she would be unable to hold their scent.

As scouts and point men in a carrier battle that was likely to dwarf all others before it, Lockwood and his boats would play a critical part in determining how Spruance moved his pieces on the oceanic chessboard surrounding the Marianas. After hearing from the *Cavalla,* ComSubPac huddled with his operations staff over his charts and drew a box, sixty miles on a side, across the probable track the Japanese carriers would take. The box marked the area where Lockwood figured the Japanese task force would slow down to begin refueling at sea. He ordered four submarines to set up there, one at each corner of the box, covering 270-degree arcs sweeping thirty miles outward from the corners of the square. Dispatches flew to the *Albacore, Bang, Stingray,* and *Finback,* and their captains set course for their stations.

Lockwood figured the dispatches were causing a stir. The approach of a powerful fleet was bound to complicate the desperate real-time improvision needed to deal with a beachhead fiercely under contest. But there was little drama. On board the *Indianapolis,* steaming slowly abeam the *Tennessee* in the night retirement area west of Saipan, Spruance weighed the reports calmly. Young in his career, Spruance had a tendency to make lessons out of situations for the benefit of his staff. "He spoke only when it was absolutely necessary, and rarely, if ever, used even one unnecessary word," said a young officer who knew him before the war. "Yet every word he spoke was completely appropriate and significant to the point at hand. When he spoke to you, he looked straight into your eyes with his piercing eyes of a hawk. Yet he assured you he was benevolent and completely supporting you in your responsibilities. When he spoke to you, he immediately put you at ease." While absorbing the meaning of the submarine reports, Spruance said little, but the words he did speak changed the ambit of the campaign. The news from the *Seahorse* and *Flying Fish,* he would write, "materially altered the situation."

Spruance had at first doubted the Japanese would show up to challenge him in the Marianas. He believed the Combined Fleet's failure to confront MacArthur's invasion of Biak was telling of its spirit. The base in western New Guinea lay relatively close to their sources of strength and their lines of supply. If they hadn't attacked then, Spruance had thought, surely they would not now. But when the Fifth Fleet commander began to see submarine reports of Japanese carriers at sea near the Philippines, he changed his view. "I thought that my estimate of their strategical attitude had been all wrong," Spruance wrote Nimitz, "and that they had decided to risk everything in a determined attack on us while we were engaged in the early and critical part of a large amphibious operation." He expected the Combined Fleet to throw the whole house at him.

He took a boat from his flagship to the *Rocky Mount* and sat down with Kelly Turner and Holland Smith to review the situation ashore and settle on the best way to use the fleet to protect the beachhead. With an attack by the Combined Fleet likely, he ordered the indefinite postponement of the landings on Guam, penciled optimistically to begin on June 18. He directed Vice Admiral Richard L. Conolly's Guam invasion task force, lingering at sea, to return to Eniwetok and await further orders. General Geiger's troops would not land until Holland Smith had taken the challenge of Saipan fully in hand. The fighting there was so sharp that Smith asked permission to land his floating reserve, the 27th Infantry Division, that very day. To deal with Ozawa, the Fifth Fleet commander also decided to augment Mitscher's carrier task force with a number of cruisers and destroyers taken from Turner's fire-support groups. The transports would continue to unload off Saipan through the day on June 17, withdrawing to safer waters east of the islands after dark; only ships that were urgently needed would return to the shelf on the eighteenth. The battleships and cruisers of the fire-support unit would form a battle line twenty-five miles west of Saipan to guard against a direct attack on the landing area.

Spruance approved Holland Smith's request to land his reserve and designated Conolly's task force, en route to Eniwetok, as the new reserve for Saipan. With fleet battle a possibility, however, the last thing he could afford was to have an entire division idling afloat, exposed to attack. One regiment of the 27th would go ashore later that afternoon, artillery soon to follow.

Spruance, his agenda finished, announced that he was taking the *Indianapolis* to rejoin Task Force 58 and intercept the Japanese. He told his two chief subordinates that two Japanese task forces had been sighted and were expected to rendezvous that night. As Spruance boarded his barge back to his flagship, Holland Smith asked, "Do you think the Japs will turn tail and run?"

"No, not now," Spruance replied. "They are out after big game. If they had wanted an easy victory, they could have disposed of the relatively small force covering MacArthur's operation at Biak. But the attack on the Marianas is too great a challenge for the Japanese navy to ignore."

Mitscher was at that very time operating with his own carrier task force divided. On the night of the thirteenth, to keep land-based enemy airpower at bay, Spruance ordered him to send the *Hornet* and *Essex* task groups to strike airfields in the Bonins—Iwo Jimi, Chichi Jima, and Haha Jima. They carried out fighter sweeps on the fifteenth and sixteenth and were preparing to launch another strike the next day when Spruance ordered them to rejoin Task Force 58 west of Guam. Fury ensued on board the *Hornet*. Jocko Clark, commander of that task group, heard the reports of a major enemy fleet approaching and asked to be set free to strike it. He believed that if Spruance would let him continue to roam free, he might be able to slip behind the Japanese fleet and keep it from ever seeing port again. "An opportunity was presented that seldom comes in the lifetime of a naval officer," he wrote.

Tempestuous and fiery, Clark was already in the midst of a minor feud with with the older, quieter officer who commanded the *Essex* task group, Rear Admiral William K. Harrill. When the idea to attack Iwo Jima was first under discussion, Harrill had not wanted to do it. He argued that the storm-season weather would not cooperate (he was partly vindicated in this by the bad weather that hampered some of the raids) and said he preferred to stay close to Saipan to support the landings. Clark, in utter disdain of a commander he considered halting and indecisive, said he would go it alone if necessary. Harrill grudgingly brought the *Essex* and company along. Now Clark raised him on the Talk Between Ships (TBS) frequency to discuss how they should use the time available to them. Clark wanted to continue freelancing to the southwest, hunting Ozawa. His search planes flew three hundred fifty miles with negative results. But what reward might come from pushing that horizon out a little farther? Clark bitterly recalled Harrill's refusal. "He told me he had had enough of independent operations and was now going to make his rendezvous. Without further ado he changed course and headed off to the south, leaving me all alone." And thus one defiant turn by a U.S. carrier group commander begat another. As Clark had led Harrill north, now Harrill dragged Clark back south.

Clark wrote, "I dared not break radio silence to consult Mitscher, for this would have disclosed my position to the Japanese fleet. . . . I did not wish to find myself on a windy corner with so many Japanese airplanes that I could not shoot them all down. In addition, embarking on my own course might have embarrassed Mitscher before Spruance; I admired both men, but it was obvious to me that Spruance, not being an aviator, did not react to the advantages we had. Together, Mitscher's fifteen carriers made a virtually invincible force. If Mitscher had been in command of the Fifth Fleet, I would have continued to the southwest. But Mitscher was subordinate to Spruance, and I did not want to disturb their good working relationship. Finally, I asked myself if I were not about to take the whole world on my shoulders."

With their raid on Iwo, Clark and Harrill had closed, albeit briefly, the aircraft pipeline flowing from Japan to the Marianas. But Clark never let go of the belief that he had forfeited a larger opportunity. "We would have had a glorious naval victory, and I would have been the Beatty of the war," he told an interviewer. He was referring to the example of Vice Admiral David Beatty of the Royal Navy, who in 1916 had a similar chance to encircle an enemy squadron at Jutland. "After debating the pros and cons, my staff and I decided against striking off on our own," Clark wrote, "so I turned, following Harrill to carry out my orders."

Spruance didn't mind looking to foreign commanders for inspiration, either. He had always admired Japan's Admiral Togo, the victor at Tsushima, for the manner in which he stood patiently by in 1905, waiting for the Russians to offer battle. He considered his situation comparable, different only because of the long reach and striking power of the carriers. All things would tell in time. In a battle of waiting, reconnaissance was the better part of gallantry. Spruance directed Vice Admiral John H. Hoover, based in the Marshalls as the Commander, Forward Area, to send six flying boats and a tender to Saipan, to set up in the anchorage under Kelly Turner's command. Equipped to make radar searches at night, the PBM Mariners would range to the west to a distance of six hundred miles, all eyes and ears out for Japanese aircraft carriers.

12

Tank Attack

Before dawn on June 16, as the ships bearing the 27th Infantry Division and its train of violent freight arrived in the transport area off Saipan, all hands beheld the burning hulks of cargo ships off their port bows. Adrift on the water were the survivors, all Japanese, the fresh detritus of a naval battle in miniature that had filled the anchorage with sound and fury. The commander of the transport group, Rear Admiral Spike Blandy, detached some small ships to rescue them. There were about fifty in all, including a nine-year-old girl.

Draper Kauffman's flagship, the *Gilmer,* had started it. While serving as a radar picket outside the transport area, she registered five surface contacts approaching the beachhead from Garapan harbor. Admiral Hill instructed the *Gilmer,* "*Take appropriate action,* Shaw *to assist.*"

The *Gilmer*'s captain, Lieutenant Commander Jack S. Horner, decided to beat his bigger teammate to the kill and went to twenty knots. He thought the contacts might be friendly—wayward LCIs, perhaps—and circled them at a respectful distance to confirm their identity. Plodding and small, the bogies proved to be Japanese, wooden cargomen, just two hundred fifty tons, inbound from Tokyo with loads of cement. They were flagged as men-of-war and had 25 mm antiaircraft cannons mounted forward. Fair targets.

Horner fired star shells, then reversed course and opened fire at three thousand yards. Tracers whipped over the deckhouse as the Japanese fired in return, aiming by the spittle of American tracers. Horner ceased fire with his twenties then, leaving his three-inch main gun and trio of fifties chattering on flashless powder. By the time the *Shaw* arrived, he had four of them in duress, afire across their entire length. Twenty holes in the hull and three wounded crew were the price the *Gilmer* paid to stop the cement run and take two dozen prisoners. As Horner returned to the transport area, Japanese were probing American lines all across the front.

Turner's feint had frozen much of the Japanese 135th Regiment in their positions near Garapan. Now the Navy targeted the coast road to stop its movement south. The *California* fired more than a thousand rounds of five-inch, half of them air bursts, knocking out Garapan's radio station as well. On the division left, the Sixth Regiment was holding fast and tying in, serving as the "hinge" in the great gate of Marine regiments, nearly six miles long, that would soon begin swinging across the island. The Second Division's reserve, the Second Marines, landed two of its battalions and tied in with the Sixth Marines, holding the seacoast corner of the left flank. The battalion that was involved in General Erskine's scheme to manipulate the Navy into assigning additional transports, Lieutenant Colonel Wood B. Kyle's unit, the First Battalion, landed and fell in. The Navy's inadvertent revenge came when Kyle's allocation of heavy mortars and machine guns, stowed aboard escort carriers, reached Saipan. When Avenger torpedo bombers air-dropped them onto the Charan Kanoa airstrip, nearly the entire allocation inadequately crated, was ruined.

Farther behind the lines in the north, the artillerymen of the Tenth Marines set up among the tall stalks of sugarcane that stretched into the foothills of Mount Tapotchau. "You could move a battalion through a cane field and not see even an occasional wiggle of the cane," said Charles Pase, a howitzer man. "So this was the thing that worried us more than anything else. We had to set up where we had clear fields of fire as much as possible." Where the ground was so rough as to be physically impossible to control—areas cut with ravines, warrens of caves, and pits of coral-covered tree roots—the Marines arranged their fields of fire to cover the gaps. "You couldn't hardly slip a jackrabbit through the lines once they got them set," said Pase.

After a sleepless night, Robert E. Wolin, an amtanker with the Second Amphibious Tractor Battalion, considered being alive at sunrise "one of the great experiences of my life." He didn't wish to move from his foxhole, fearing if he did "all hell would rain down." But a senior officer happened by then, swagger stick under his arm, and said his unit was a hundred or so yards out of position. "He suggested we move south, collecting men as we went. Then he concluded: 'After all, Lieutenant, you don't want to live forever.'

"With that, fear melted away, and that's what we did. Almost every man

I have ever talked to about war will admit that at some time someone or something moved them through a barrier of fear to do what they'd been trained to do."

Inland from Green Beach, the Eighth Marines sparred with Japanese soldiers who had taken refuge in Susupe Swamp. Throughout the day they emerged from the soup to attack the Marines in singles and squads, favoring infiltration over overt assault. Shifting her fire to support the Third Battalion against this threat, the destroyer *Monssen* hit an ammunition dump hidden in the swamp, which exploded in a roar and produced flames that rose two thousand feet into the sky as the sun went down.

In the Fourth Division area, company and battalion commanders continued knitting their lines together in preparation for the big cross-island push. The barrage from Japanese mountain guns and mortars never abated. As the blasts walked up and down the beach, small groups of Japanese troops probed the front for openings. They broke through momentarily on Blue Beaches One and Two, driving Squeaky Anderson's shore parties from the Charan Kanoa pier. The area was quickly retaken, but not before the infiltrators managed to damage the pier. The dangerous gap between the two divisions closed once the 2/8 Marines rolled up Afetna Point. Then they swung inland and pushed against Susupe Swamp, vise-clamping its inhabitants against the lines of the 23rd Marines, who were no less eager to close their exposed flank.

The first two regiments from the 27th Infantry Division, the 165th and 105th Infantry, formed their lines south of Fourth Division positions, extending the right flank toward the southern end of the coast. As the soldiers got their first taste of enemy artillery, they were soon chafing to march on the airfield. But as night fell on June 16, it was in the north that events were set to explode.

Near midnight, the forward listening posts of the Sixth Marines reported movement on its front facing Garapan. On request of the new 2/6 commanding officer, Major LeRoy P. Hunt, Jr., destroyers offshore popped star shells, and by the welcome suspended light his Marines could see the shadowy forms of Japanese soldiers advancing. When the movement stopped, the listening posts whispered that the enemy was hunkered down some five hundred yards from the American lines. Lieutenant Colonel William K. Jones, commander of the First Battalion, heard their chants and shouting and thought they were "working up courage to charge. . . . Some of it sounded drunken." Then came a telltale heavy mechanical clamor. Enemy tanks were approaching his line, supported by infantry.

Jones gave permission to withdraw the listening posts. Then he passed word to the destroyers to keep the illumination rounds coming as field guns, mortars, and artillery began deluging the area in front of Jones's line companies. At Sixth Marines headquarters, Colonel Riseley directed the regimental weapons company to send its half-tracks, armed with 75 mm guns, to move to Jones's sector.

General Saito had meant the attack to take place the first night, in line with his general order to repel the invaders at the beach. Vice Admiral Nagumo was to command the attack personally. But because the naval bombardment had uprooted the communications network, the message was slow to reach field commanders and Nagumo did not appear. When a battalion from the 136th Infantry Regiment, under Colonel Yukimatsu Ogawa, stepped off from their positions south of Garapan, General Saito had already resigned himself to a lack of control, for his order contained the instruction, "The attack will be made whenever possible." Its tactical objective was to recapture the inter-island radio station near Green Beach, located about four hundred yards behind U.S. lines, where the force would consolidate and stage further attacks. It was about three A.M. when a bugle sounded and the front rank of tanks began their lumbering rush. Ogawa's troops, joined by a smaller force from the Special Naval Landing Force, raced forward in the night, sabers held high.

Their attack was supposed to be coordinated with the largest tank assault Japan had ever mustered against American forces. Colonel Takashi Goto committed the majority of his remaining forty-four tanks to the assault. These rolled forward from the west, traversing the road from Cha-cha Village that skirted north of Susupe Swamp. After just two days, the 9th Tank Regiment was war-weathered. One of its companies had advanced to attack the landings on D Day, to be destroyed nearly to a vehicle. He had two models of medium tanks—eighteen-tonners with a five-man crew and either a 47 mm or a 57 mm main gun, and light tanks with a crew of three and a 37 mm gun.

Concentrated fire from Marine howitzers killed or scattered much of the infantry riding or running along with Goto's tanks, but still the armor rolled. Captain Claude B. Rollen had placed his company's two-man bazooka teams on the line that night. When the tanks appeared, advancing in elements of four or five, Rollen's men left their foxholes and ran forward. From ranges of less than seventy-five yards, they did lethal work, often at ranges so close that the concussions of their own hits knocked them down. As Rollen stood in a foxhole at his Company B command post, a tank came right at him. He stood and raised his carbine to launch a grenade from the launcher fitted to it. As he was doing so, a Japanese bullet hit the grenade square-on, detonating it. The explosion punctured both of his eardrums. As the tank moved past Rollen, it took a hit and began to burn, but it kept on coming into the Marine lines. Colonel Jones's naval liaison officer made an urgent call to the night fire-support group. The heavy cruiser *Louisville* and destroyer *Halsey Powell* answered the call, firing on Japanese tanks as pinpointed by the 2/2's shore fire-control party, hammering the cross-island road to Chacha Village and the coast road north of Marine lines as well. By that time, the light of star shells revealed that more than three dozen Japanese tanks had already jumped off and were inside danger-close radius of the American positions.

When he learned Rollen had been hit, Colonel Jones ordered the commander of his headquarters company, Captain Norman K. Thomas, to lead a platoon forward and take over Company B on the front line. As Thomas and his thirty-six men moved out, carrying additional bazooka ammunition on stretchers, a Japanese machine gun crew swiveled their weapon toward them. Thomas's first sergeant saw it. "I hollered, 'Hit the deck!'" Lewis J. Michelony remembered, "and as I hit it, we were touching elbows, all three of us. Captain Thomas caught it first in the stomach and then in the head. I mean, I could see daylight through him." Michelony, ascending to command, saw Japanese tanks bearing down on him and in terror ordered his men to withdraw and find cover. "By that time, the tanks started following us, and their officers were chasing us with their sabers. I mean, I was scared."

As Goto's tanks penetrated Marine lines, "the battle evolved into a madhouse of noise, tracers, and flashing light," the First Battalion's executive officer, Major James A. Donovan, Jr., wrote, with rifle fire, the chatter of Browning Automatic Rifles, the pop of canister rounds, and the rush of bazookas. "As tanks were hit and set afire, they silhouetted other tanks coming out of the flickering shadows to the front or already on top of the squads." When First Sergeant Michelony saw an opening, he broke cover and rallied his platoon forward. Reaching the command post, he was impressed to see Rollen still leading his company even though he was deaf. Rollen's troopers would make good use of the bazooka rockets that Michelony delivered. With multiple teams in action, firing and hopping foxholes, it was, according to Jones, "impossible to sort claims from actual kills, with all the interlocking fires and simultaneous action." But several bazookamen, privates first class all, stood out as the principal agents of carnage.

Herbert J. Hodges, for one, did not tend to miss. He and his partner, Charlie Merritt, hit seven tanks with seven rounds. Robert S. Reed went four for four with his tube. Out of rockets, he took an incendiary grenade, ran to a fifth tank, forced open its hatch, and dropped it inside, killing the crew in a thermite flash. Another Marine, holding his cover in a foxhole as a Japanese tank rumbled past, rushed forward and jammed a log into its bogie wheels. The obstruction caused the tank to begin turning in a circle. When the commander unbuttoned his hatch to see what the problem was, the Marine climbed up and dropped a grenade into the turret. "The tank erupted like a volcano," Colonel Jones would write.

"The incident was typical," wrote Fletcher Pratt. "These were veterans of Tarawa. They never budged from their deep foxholes but let the clanking machines roll past and went for them in the weak rear." The Japanese broke through the lines of Colonel Riseley's Third Battalion as well, penetrating about fifty yards, but his men "held onto the shoulders of the penetration." The Japanese tankers didn't seem to know how to capitalize on their breakthroughs. "As their guides and crew chiefs were hit by Marine rifle and machine gun fire," Major Donovan wrote, "what little control they had was lost. They ambled on in the general direction of the beach, getting hit and hit again until each one burst into flame or turned in aimless circles only to stop dead, stalled in its own ruts or the marshes of the low ground." Lauren H. Kahn and Lewis M. Nalder of Company K knocked out two tanks with their rocket tube and, out of ammunition, destroyed a third with a grenade, saving the lives of a 37 mm gun crew situated right in the enemy's path. A platoon of Marine medium tanks rallied to the imperiled sector and put an end to the incursion. The Japanese probably had no idea they had come within five hundred yards of General Watson's division headquarters.

When the weapons company's half-tracks showed up, their heavy 75 mm guns turned the failed assault into an utter rout, destroying seven Japanese tanks as they tried to escape into the hills. The Sixth Marines, supported by regimental weapons and artillery, had destroyed twenty-four tanks in two hours of action. A captured Japanese intelligence officer would say the attack failed because the tanks "took the wrong road and did not attack down the beach road as they were ordered to do." The chief of staff of the Japanese 43rd Division credited the naval star shells, which "robbed the attack of cover of darkness. . . . In the open, on wet terrain, against American firepower, it was a huge mistake." But really the assault ended as it did because Colonel Goto had no knowledge of the location of the American positions or the extent of their strength. The day's delay in launching it gave the Marines time to establish their positions and their artillery support. The punctuation mark on the Japanese defeat was the suicides of many wounded as, chased by gusts of artillery and naval fire, they vanished into the hills.

The rise of morning revealed the gruesome detritus of the first mass armored assault on U.S. positions during the war. Seven hundred dead littered the rolling scrub inland of Red Beach, among them Colonel Goto. The 1/6 Marines suffered seventy-eight casualties, and the 2/2 on their left took nineteen more. Their artillery took heavy counterbattery fire from artillery and mortars in the highlands, losing many of its guns. If Goto had been able to plot U.S. positions as well as the Japanese in the hills had registered the Marine artillery, the result of the battle might have been different. As it was, General Saito, monitoring reports at his command post, recognized that the beach was lost. On a map he traced a new defensive line, running from a point about a half mile south of Garapan across the south slopes of Mount Tapotchau and over to Laulau Bay. The 31st Army chief of staff reported to Tokyo the lamentable disorganization of the garrison.

The tank battle was settled with brute and systemic application of superior firepower, but its aftermath was a matter of law. U.S. commanders issued orders requiring their troops to follow the protocols of land warfare, which prohibited the robbery and maltreatment of the wounded or dead; required the collection of an identity tag, one to be archived, the other left attached to the body; and mandated honorable burial in graves "that are respected and may always be found again." A Second Marine Division chaplain, David Hermin of Omaha, Nebraska, buried the Japanese with a short ceremony that included the reading of a Buddhist sutra.

The problem of civilians on the battlefield manifested as a new problem for Marines in the Pacific. Having fled the city to take refuge, they emerged from crevices and caves to surrender in desperate terror to beings who, they were told, would eat their children and defile their women. Those who stepped forward, numb with fear, wrestled with disbelief at finding themselves taken in and treated well. A stockade near Charan Kanoa would house and feed thousands of civilian refugees until larger accommodations could be built to shelter them.

The Second Marine Division had established a battalion surgical triage in a former Japanese hospital at Charan Kanoa. Its doctors and medics were busy cutting and suturing almost immediately. According to a Marine Corps historian, "At all medical installations, the rule was the same: care for the individual regardless of where he came from or to what unit he belonged. Red tape in the handling of casualties was nonexistent; the tape was all white." The magnitude of the crisis would worsen with each passing day.

Draper Kauffman and his UDT had been busy all that night stringing packs of explosives over coral heads and boulders inside the reef off Red Beach Three. Fearful that his primacord fuzes would be cut by the action of the surf against the coral, he wired the series in triplicate. The laborious work carried over into morning, when Japanese spotters noticed Kauffman's swimmers at work. "They made our last hour or so miserable with mortars," Kauffman said. "Our worst worry was that one of their mortars would hit a pack or a section of primacord and set the whole shebang off along with all of us." But good fortune shone on his frogmen. They finished wiring the shot and Kauffman himself pulled the nine fuzes, three for each circuit. During the ten-minute countdown, the UDT swam back to their landing craft to get clear.

Credit the founder of UDT for his humility: "We were not skilled artists in the use of explosives," he would say. Overkill was part of the culture. Off Saipan on the night of June 16, his teams wired the reef with the rough equivalent of more than six hundred high-capacity battleship projectiles. The explosion, when it went, was a monument to their achievements of the past six months and a marker of Kauffman's ambitions going forward. The surge of seawater that formed the base of the blast was unlike any he had seen before. A quarter mile long, it was "a wall of absolutely black water," Kauffman recalled, that went straight up and then spread. Harry Hill had never seen its like, either, and that would be a problem, as Kauffman had failed to tell him that he was about to close the circuit. The collapsing rampart of tetryl-stained seawater slammed down upon everything in the anchorage, including Hill's flagship. Basaltic slag and particulate coral drenched the *Cambria* from stem to stern.

Hill might have been willing to tolerate the godawful mess for what it did for his supply effort. "It is hard to realize the magnitude of a D Day ship-to-shore problem," he would say. Each man ashore—and there were upward of twenty-five thousand of them within the first two hours—needed half a ton of additional supplies per day. Yet air raid alerts, false or otherwise, cost Kelly Turner hundreds of hours of unloading time. With the blasting of the channel, the Blue beaches became a massive supply dump, with scarcely an inch to move. But the pontoon causeway was a terrible bottleneck, backed up with boats and barges bringing in drums of gasoline, water, and oil urgently needed ashore. "Tens of thousands of these had to be handled," Hill said, "and as we watched them being hoisted out of the holds four or six at a time, lowered into amphibious craft, it seemed a never-ending job. I asked Squeaky Anderson why we couldn't make a floating corral to hold them, using some of the creosoted piles we were also unloading, and tow the corral to an anchorage off the beach. That would greatly speed up unloading, as the chine hooks would disengage when the drums were dunked. A fine idea, but about the time we had several hundred drums afloat, the corral broke, and for the next day or two our LCVPs were chasing drums all around the anchorage, picking up escapees."

None of the benefits that flowed from the monstrous explosion Kauffman and his UDT had rigged saved him from a tongue-lashing when he answered the summons to see Admiral Hill. As soot from the frogman's reef shoes ruined the fine rug in the flag quarters, "We discussed the advisability of letting the task force commander know when I was going to fire a shot like that," Kauffman said. Turner's transport captains and quartermasters, though, were pleased with the work of the UDT. Squeaky Anderson called them "his own all-American football team." They took another twelve hours that night to make the channel usable, removing rough spots and piles with more explosives. When they were done, the oceanic roadway to the beach was open at last, and the bottlenecks at the reef and the beach began to clear.

By early afternoon, Holland Smith took leave of Kelly Turner in the *Rocky Mount* and motored to the beach, establishing his corps headquarters at Charan Kanoa, where he assumed command of all U.S. troops ashore. Three battalions of 27th Division artillery were on the way in, to be hustled into position and registered on inland targets before lunch. Two LSTs loaded with antiaircraft guns passed through the channel the UDT had blasted, as did the commanding general of the 27th, Major General Ralph C. Smith, who landed and set up his headquarters. Nuisance air attacks slowed unloading as ships were forced to get underway under cover of smoke screens, but Holland Smith was disturbed more by the stench of the carabao carcass lying in the yard of the bungalow that his staff chose as his post. His men piled it under with a bulldozer. Smith went to meet with Harry Schmidt at his Fourth Division headquarters on the beach near the sugar mill. As he heard of the progress and losses of the unit's three regiments, he knew at once that winning the fight would require taking the mountain slopes from which death tended to fall. The Japanese were ensconced on the high ground surrounding Mount Tapotchau, protected from most flat-trajectory naval gunfire in the finger ridges that descended from the peak.

"I was sixty-two when we attacked Saipan," Holland Smith wrote, "and many times during that month I felt like a tired old man under the strain of directing a campaign which required so much nervous and physical energy." Massed armor assaults, city fighting, rolling hills cut through with crevices and cliffs, the character of the terrain cleverly exploited by the Japanese, lofting artillery from positions nearly invulnerable to neutralization, infiltrators working the gaps of a ten-thousand-yard front from sundown till dawn, civilians in harm's way—this much was new. This wasn't: Americans didn't invade islands except to capture airfields. Their first objective would be Aslito Field. A battalion of the 27th Division's 165th Regiment, under the control of General Schmidt, reached its southwestern edge on the afternoon of the seventeenth.

Speed was the Marine way, for no fear was long in them but one: that the fleet would up and leave them. "I was determined to take Saipan and take it quickly," Holland Smith would write. The small perimeter of the two-division beachhead expanded like a spreading inkblot as the Americans pushed inland, and fastest in the south.

13

The View from the Mountain

If she buried herself far enough in the cave on the mountain, Shizuko Miura could almost believe the war was not there. The cave was proof against blast, for large rocks shielded the opening. Deep within, she found that the concussions of naval shells were completely inaudible. But the beam of her flashlight dispelled the illusion. It showed that the life she had known was over. Row upon row of stretchers, laid down on the long slope of rock in the back of the cave, bore the worst of the wounded who had been carried to the hills. Most were soldiers, but there were a husband and a wife, who was in labor. Shizuko's nurse training hadn't taught her how to deal with a live birth, so she resolved just to sit near them and talk about Garapan as it burned.

She didn't like the air, so she ventured to the cave entrance in order to breathe and suggested the couple do the same. He was an administrator at the South Islands Agency. She, so pale and very young, had been there barely a month from the homeland. All she wanted was water. Water, so scarce, would determine who lived and who died. On the back side of the mountain, someone said, was a farmhouse with a cistern. So Shizuko decided to go there. It would be a short walk so long as the American spotting planes left her alone.

From the cave mouth she raced down the mountain slope to the east, away from Garapan, and about a hundred meters along she came to a small hut where, inside, eight wounded men lay in the care of an army soldier. They were completely bald, their bodies swollen with fluid, bright red and hairless. They had been doused in burning gasoline in Garapan, the soldier told her. A few of them saw her and implored her for water, but the soldier said that giving it to them would kill them. They were delirious, he said, and did not know what was best for them. Shizuko feared that that described every imperial soldier she was seeing on Saipan. Some more soldiers came by, their faces expressionless and blank, "as if they had no souls," she wrote. What they indisputably lacked was rifles. How would they throw back the American devils equipped like this? Before the invasion she had seen her brother, just once, in his tank, "the Swallow." The sight of him had warmed her heart. But she remembered then that she had a farmhouse to find.

Down the east slope of the mountain, she found a farmhouse. This must be it. But the cistern was dry. She saw another house and ran to it, and another. Their cisterns were empty, too. Returning to the cave, she checked in at the hut and despaired to see that the burned soldiers' condition had worsened. A few of them moaned, "Water, water. . . ." It was unbearable to her, and, determined to find help, she set out running around the mountain to the side facing Garapan. It was daylight now, and the sight she beheld as she came around to the vista toward the west took her breath away. American ships, hundreds of them. She could see the tracers of the shells flying inland. *Every ship is flashing. Are they shooting at me?* The sight of it was so spectacular, she felt as though she were watching a film. She had no fear. The sum of her thoughts was: *How striking!* Then something else struck her. A voice, behind her.

"Woman! What are you doing? What will you do when the enemy planes see you?" The man appeared from behind a large rock. *"Bakayaro!"*—fool! He carried a gun and wore a fearsome expression. She recognized his insignia as that of a sergeant. She found herself more afraid of him, and more startled by his words, than by the sight of the enemy fleet. Withdrawing to a hollow in a slope behind some rocks, hiding from view from the air, she kept one eye on the ships, fascinated. Another soldier came along then. He was one of the expressionless ones she had seen earlier. A red-brown stain marked his breast. She didn't think his wound had been treated; there was shock in his eyes, and he did not respond to voices, not even the sergeant's powerful imperative. The soldier just walked with vacant eyes down the slope toward Garapan. "Halt!" the sergeant shouted. "That is dangerous! Hey—I will shoot!" Just then the soldier stopped and drew a saber from a scabbard at his waist. In a single stroke he drew it across his neck. Blood sprayed the ground and he fell, kicking and slapping at Saipan. No one went to his aid as his struggling slowed, and after he bled some more he became still. An American plane flew overhead and Shizuko snapped a branch from a tree and held it over her head, crouching motionless. When it passed, seeking profitable prey, she remembered what she had been looking for. She resumed her march down the slope in search of water.

The building she found next was a power plant. It had been shattered by bombs. There was a water tank nearby, an open cistern, full of water. Nearby, the bodies of two soldiers and a civilian lay rotting. She was surprised to see the civilian, for she recognized him, name of Yamashita, an agent of the South Islands Trading Company. The name registered as a fact, not an emotion, for emotions were beyond her now. Hearing the buzz of another plane, she dropped and lay motionless as if dead. The plane passed and she moved again, searching the area and finding salvation: a big empty bucket. The fortunate turn filled her with a strange confidence in her destiny. Of all the souls on Saipan, she and she alone would be safe. She filled the bucket and hauled it up the hill, struggling, taking care not to spare herself any of its weight by spilling. Returning to the cave, she went to the back, to the phalanx of stretchers, and served water to the worst of the wounded with her own cupped hands. As the bucket became lighter, she rose and spoke. "Mr. Soldiers, I am sorry, but there are badly wounded men nearby who are eager for water. I will come to you again."

Returning to the hut where the eight burned men lay, she found their condition considerably worse. She wondered what would happen if she let them drink. She stayed with them for much of the afternoon. As it went along, they began to expire, one by one. Her bucket went dry and she had no more water to give them. He tear ducts were dry as well.

The evening twilight backlit the great fleet in the west. Ships continued shooting into the mountain. Would they never run out of shells? "Then, suddenly, a strange thing happened," Shizuko wrote. "Ship guns which had been shooting into the mountain began shooting into the sky. At once every vessel cast lights like jetting fountains." Tracers produced high-angle streamers that she found profoundly beautiful. They meant one thing: Japanese aircraft were attacking, and Saipan had not been forgotten. "Friendly planes!" As a small audience formed on the mountain slope, one of the planes, flying low on the water, nosed down toward an American ship. "Oh, a sacrifice attack!" someone cried. The aircraft drew fire and began to burn. Appearing to lose a wing, trailing long orange streamers, in silence from this distance, the plane ended its mission abruptly against the sea. The surface, fouled by its fuel, awoke in flames.

The air attack that she witnessed had been launched from Yap. The bogies registered on the radars of Kelly Turner's escort carriers at sundown.

In the waters east of Saipan, eight of the small jeep carriers pushed zigzag paths. With Task Force 58 awaiting the Combined Fleet, they were all Turner had for air support. When the flight of forty to fifty planes was eighty-five miles out, coming in from the south, Rear Admirals Gerald F. Bogan and Henry B. Sallada vectored their combat air patrol to intercept. It was their first experience with task force defense, and with so many planes airborne from so many ships, confusion prevailed. Of the forty-six Wildcats that got airborne, only nine managed to intercept.

A group from the *Midway* was climbing through twelve thousand feet, thirty miles south of the carriers, when they spotted the enemy above them. A dozen Kate torpedo bombers and Judy dive-bombers formed a bottom layer, and above that there was another, with twelve to eighteen Zekes at top cover. Lieutenant Gordon A. Gabbert led the attack from below, beginning an air battle that went on until the last glow of twilight.

Virgil Green had been on combat air patrol for nearly two hours when the tallyhos of his squadronmates came. Low on fuel and returning to base, he was cursing the circumstances when, looking back over his left shoulder, the junior-grade lieutenant spied a twin-engine aircraft skirting the white boulder field of cumulus below him. He turned sharply, and his wingman, Charles Freer, followed. In the distance he could make out the swirling mite specks of other combats. But this enemy plane was alone, probably a snooper looking for the carriers. Such pilots as these were chosen for their sharp eyesight, and clearly this one had seen him. The enemy plane began a wide turn as he dived, reversing course away to the west. A tail chase ensued.

As Green and Freer broke into clear skies, the enemy descended to seek the refuge of the wave tops. Down, down, to twenty-five feet off the water, then ten, so close to the sea that the wash of the plane's twin propellers whipped up parallel foaming paths across it. The pilot and his crew of seven flew for their lives, racing south toward Guam. As he caught up with it, Green pegged the bomber as a Mitsubishi Ki-21, Type 97, code-named Sally, and he opened fire with short bursts at the Sally's starboard engine. Because his tracer rounds tumbled badly, their red firefly track was of little use in marking his actual point of aim, but the engine began to burn nonetheless. Green's engine did, too; the long run with his supercharger switched on "high blower," which improved the engine's high-altitude performance by condensing thin air in order to feed more oxygen into the carburetor, had overheated it. Out of ammunition, he throttled down to let his engine cool. Freer roared past from dead astern, riding the pursuit trail down from two thousand feet. "I was excited in a way I never had been," Freer would write. He closed with the Sally as its pilot jerked evasively left and right, firing bursts into the smoking starboard engine. Seeing that the bomber's turret could not bear effectively to the rear, Freer held directly at six o'clock, in the gap of the firing arc. As he closed to three hundred feet, the belly of the Japanese plane seemed to graze a wave top. It bounced up, then skipped again. As Freer zoomed past, the turret gunner got a fleeting shot at him. He dropped his left wing, pulled around sharply for a side pass, and fired a full deflection shot into the top of her fuselage. At this, the enemy pilot seemed to lose control. His port wing dipped. When its tip caught the water at two hundred knots, the plane cartwheeled into pieces on the hardpan of the glistening ocean.

In the Saipan transport anchorage, as Shizuko Miura watched, the surviving Japanese planes reached their target and fell upon a group of LSTs that were about to depart carrying casualties from Blue Beach. As the sun set, a Judy dropped out of the low haze and dived on the LST-84. Every ship in the group opened fire as the plane passed low over its target, dropping a bomb that missed off the starboard bow. As the antiaircraft bursts shredded the air, their shrapnel rained down, ripping into the landing ship's deck. Ten sailors fell wounded. The friendly fire ignited a cluster of gasoline drums lashed to the forecastle. A fierce fire raged brightly, then quickly faded away.

At sunset, some of the planes from the Japanese formation found the jeep carriers and attacked. With nearly four dozen Wildcats airborne, a general melee quickly began, all ships firing almost indiscriminately as they made evasive turns. In a poorly coordinated attack, a twin-engine bomber attacked the *Gambier Bay* head-on, putting a near miss off her port bow and strafing as it passed. A Judy attacked the *Coral Sea,* dropping a bomb that missed, then crashing astern under concentrated fire. A Val dived on Admiral Bogan's flagship, the *Fanshaw Bay,* hitting her with a bomb that exploded in the hangar deck, killing eleven. Everyone on board that escort carrier was lucky the aircraft torpedoes littering the space did not go up. The *Fanshaw Bay* would return to Eniwetok for repairs, and the Japanese fancied that they had given a black eye to Task Force 58.

Freer and Green returned to the *Midway.* Freer caught the first wire, taxied forward past the barrier, and cut his engine. Then it hit him, the strain of his first kill and a landing at night manifesting in the complete inability to move his legs. Nerves afire from having pushed all margins, he needed help to get out of his plane. He reported to sick bay for a taste of brandy. The doc gave him the whole bottle and told him to hit the rack.

Off Guam, as the Third Amphibious Force prepared to depart for Eniwetok, some torpedo bombers staging from Truk attacked one of Admiral Conolly's tractor flotillas. The large box formation of LSTs and LCIs, making just six knots, was an easy target. A torpedo hit the LCI-468, carrying away fifty feet of her bow and killing fifteen men. She had to be scuttled in the end. But these bruises to the southern transport force came two days—and seventy thousand troops—too late.

The urgent need remained to find the Japanese carriers. The night air-search scheme had presumed the availability of six long-range PBM Mariners. With some arm-twisting by Spruance, Kelly Turner made room in the Garapan roadstead for the five big flying boats of Patrol Squadron Sixteen. Landing by late afternoon, the Mariners moored alongside the seaplane tender *Ballard* to refuel. Later that day, when a Japanese dive-bomber visited the anchorage to strafe, the tender cast off the planes. After taxiing away to avoid the attack, one pilot somehow failed to make it back to the ship in the dark. On the eve of this critical mission, the squadron of five big flying boats had been reduced by twenty percent.

The *Cavalla,* meanwhile, was on the verge of her biggest break yet. Avoiding Japanese planes at dusk, Commander Kossler welcomed the fall of night, and at 9:15 he registered fresh surface contacts on the radar at twenty-two thousand yards, or twelve and a half miles. The pips looked like a large task force. He estimated seven major ships, including a probable carrier. Zigzagging east at nineteen knots, they were coming straight toward him, perhaps to overrun him in the night. "It was apparent that we were on the track of a large, fast task force, heading some place in a pretty big hurry." Stalking the formation from ahead, he was in an enviable position to do some damage, so he decided to submerge to radar depth and go to battle stations. But the radar receiver peeking above the waves did not tell him the whole story. The soundman reported a host of fast screws, at least fifteen different ships, evidently destroyers that were not detected by the radar. The group was a juicy target if ever there was one. But Kossler faced a tough decision. Since he had no record of previous contact with this task force, he needed to alert his command. Maneuvering for attack, though, would mean a delay in making the critical dispatch. He decided to abandon the attack and surface as quickly as possible in order to report. But first he had to survive contact with the entire heavy assembly. Holding at a depth of a hundred feet, he watched it parade by, counting masts for nearly an hour and "evading by every method I knew how."

It was nearly midnight on Saipan when the trailing pair of escorts cleared the area. Kossler let them vanish from his scope, then surfaced in the star-studded blackness and began transmitting to Admiral Lockwood. "On receipt of his message," the sub boss wrote, "we told all submarines that both Japanese forces had been reported and added instructions to shoot first and report afterward." Lockwood informed his undersea force, "The above list of enemy ships does not frighten our varsity. We have all that and plenty more ready and waiting, and they are all rough, tough, and nasty." Kossler surfaced and set out in pursuit at four-engine speed.

After midnight, destroyers lit the Garapan roadstead with their carbon-arc searchlights as the PBM Mariners' crews prepared for their long-range night mission. By one A.M. on June 18, the last of them was plowing through the swells, faster and faster until it was airborne, to spend the last hours of darkness searching for carriers far to the west.

14

First Contact

In the lonely precinct of the admiral's cabin in the *Indianapolis,* Raymond Spruance mulled over the fast-developing scenario with his staff. He had been schooled to think like the enemy, and he fancied himself a master student of the Japanese mind. "If I were the Japanese admiral in this situation," he said, "I would split my forces and hope that the forces remaining to the west were sighted in order to decoy the main forces of the opposing fleet away from Saipan, and I would get the strike forces separated in order to get into Saipan and if possible destroy the transports. I would assume that the mission was to protect Saipan, and this could be most effectively done by destroying the transports and the support forces, the [Japanese] army forces ashore on Saipan being quite adequate against the forces that had already been landed."

When Spruance was teaching at the Naval War College, the prescribed method of analysis required commanders to forecast "the enemy, his strength, dispositions, and probable intentions." The rubric seemed reasonable enough, except, as Spruance later realized, estimating probable intent entailed making dangerous assumptions. The safer and more prudent course, he would decide, was to plan within the possible range of the enemy's *capabilities,* which were more knowable, and not his intentions, ever mysterious. But during the night, new data clarified the situation so as to make moot the distinction between the two.

After three A.M. on June 18, the *Cavalla*'s sighting report of a large task force reached the *Indianapolis.* Copied by the radio department almost six hours after it was sent, the news made Spruance wonder: Was this the same Japanese task force that the *Flying Fish* had reported in San Bernardino Strait? Since the *Cavalla* had not regained contact with it,

Arleigh Burke surmised, the fleet must have continued east at high speed. But where was it now? The PBM Mariners reported no contacts after their long-range night search in the predawn hours. Thus, Ozawa had done something other than make best speed straight toward the Marianas. A dawn search by Task Force 58 planes encountered and shot down a floatplane typical of those used by cruisers as spotting aircraft. With its demise, both Ozawa and Spruance knew the other was near. Studying the projected track of the Japanese force from its last known position, Burke calculated that the Japanese should be within three hundred miles by late the following afternoon. "If we closed during the afternoon and night and the enemy wanted to fight, we'd better be ready for a night action," he said.

Mitscher notified Willis Lee of this development and asked whether his battleships would be ready. By order of Spruance, Lee's fast battleships had been detached from the carrier groups as a separate surface combat squadron in case a night action developed. Lee had proved his mastery of night surface action, having led two of his present company—the *Washington* and *South Dakota*—to a smashing night victory over a powerful enemy squadron off Guadalcanal. Lee's reply seemed to take everyone except Spruance by surprise: "DO NOT—REPEAT NOT—BELIEVE WE SHOULD SEEK NIGHT ENGAGEMENT. POSSIBLE ADVANTAGES OF RADAR MORE THAN OFFSET BY DIFFICULTIES OF COMMUNICATIONS AND LACK OF TRAINING IN FLEET TACTICS AT NIGHT. WOULD PRESS PURSUIT OF DAMAGED OR FLEEING ENEMY, HOWEVER, AT ANY TIME." Spruance had already mentioned via dispatch that he preferred not to engage in a night action. Having served as Nimitz's chief of staff during Guadalcanal, he had reason to understand Lee's hesitation, even after the experience of his finest hour. For a while, that night in November 1942, the sea battle had seemed a close-run thing as the *South Dakota* was mauled point-blank by enemy cruisers. Big ships were vulnerable even in the best of circumstances. Lee must also have feared that months of operating in separate task groups had diluted the chemistry of his captains and slowed their reflexes in nighttime gunnery action. The independent ambitions of the "gun club" had been subsumed by the diverse needs of an integrated carrier task group. Thus, while Lee said he would gladly chase cripples, he didn't relish the idea of starting the fight himself.* The fast car-

---

* Lee's restraint cast new light on Spruance's decision to freelance as a battleship division commander off Truk. He had indulged himself there as an eager amateur, far from his days as captain of the *Mississippi*. Lee's considered refusal to push his battleships into a fight off the

riers would do it if anyone did. But with the fighting on Saipan in full voice, Spruance thought it unwise to give Mitscher the freedom to roam.

On the morning of June 18, Spruance instructed Mitscher and Lee:

> Task Force 58 must cover Saipan and our forces engaged in that operation. I still feel that main enemy attack will come from the westward but it might be diverted to come in from southwestward. Diversionary attacks may come in from either flank or reinforcements might come from Empire. Consider that we can best cover Saipan by advancing to westward during daylight and retiring to the eastward at night, so as to reduce possibility of enemy passing us during darkness. The distance which you can make to the westward during the day will naturally be restricted by your air operations and by necessity to conserve fuel. We should, however, remain in air supporting positions of Saipan until information of the enemy requires other action.

Burke figured the need of carriers to turn into the wind would be so frequent that "we would be lucky if we could gain fifty miles to the west."

At 10:30 A.M., Mitscher made radar contact with Clark and Harrill as they returned from their diversion to strike the Bonins. As the fifteen carriers concentrated again, Harrill was ordered to put the *Essex* and company at Admiral Lee's disposal as a battle-line carrier group. The void of battleships in the carrier dispositions was partly filled by the light cruisers *Birmingham, Cleveland,* and *Montpelier,* which were ordered to leave their fire-support sectors off Saipan. Most carrier commanders preferred having the smaller ships in their screen, as they were four knots faster than battleships and could keep up with the carriers while maneuvering under attack. The day passed, ripe with anticipation for both sides. Late in the afternoon, nine Japanese fighters armed with bombs attacked the Fifth Fleet's fleet oiler group twenty miles southeast of Saipan. The *Neshanic* and *Saranac* each took a bomb. But the carriers remained the prize.

From the flag plot of the *Lexington,* Mitscher chafed at the restrictions that Spruance was placing upon his flattops. At night, when air operations were idle, the trade winds would not restrain him. He could push west and

---

Marianas raises the intriguing prospect that Halsey's refusal, four months later at Leyte, to turn loose Lee's heavies to confront Japanese battleships coming through San Bernardino Strait might have had the same taproot.

strike Ozawa at dawn. Mitscher blinkered a visual dispatch asking Spruance to reconsider. Spruance responded: "WE WILL PROCEED WITH MY ORIGINAL ORDERS."

After sundown on June 18, CINCPAC informed Spruance that its high-frequency direction finding (HF/DF) units had triangulated a Japanese transmission originating about 355 miles west-southwest of Task Force 58. Spruance believed that if the transmission had indeed come from Japan's most important naval task force, such a breach of radio discipline would be unlikely, and that if it were real, it might well be bait meant to draw him away from Saipan.

Unlike almost every one of his carrier admirals, Spruance saw his mission as larger than sinking enemy ships. As he explained to a journalist embarked with him in the *Indianapolis*, "This is the first time in many months that the Japanese fleet has been out in force. Of course we'd like to find it—to destroy it might shorten the war by a good deal. My first mission, however, is to protect the landing ships at Saipan. Until we know exactly where the enemy is, we must be positive that we are between his possible locations and those landing ships." The objective of Operation Forager was islands, not enemy ships. Turner's amphibs were the Fifth Fleet's principal agents for accomplishing it. Thus, insofar as Task Force 58 did not have the capacity to seize a defended island, the ambitions of the aviators would have to take a backseat to the security of the Joint Expeditionary Force.

With the advantage of local airfields on Guam, it was the Japanese who won the race for the first actionable contact with opposing carriers. At 2:15 P.M. on the eighteenth, Ozawa's search planes spotted three of Mitscher's groups. Judys fitted with belly tanks were long-legged and fast. Flying high, they were hard for U.S. interceptors to catch, giving Ozawa a valuable information advantage. He knew that three hundred eighty miles separated the carriers. The range was too great for his planes to strike on a round-trip. But if his planes landed at Guam after their attack, he could double his range by "shuttle bombing" the Americans, saving pilots the trouble of a long return flight. The airfields at Orote and Agana were the key to the plan. On board the carriers of the First Mobile Fleet, and at Combined Fleet headquarters in Tokyo, confidence swelled like a storm. "We so firmly believed in our victory that we nearly drank in celebration," the chief of staff, Rear Admiral Kusaka, wrote.

All hands awaited the klaxon signaling general quarters and the spotting of the Japanese fleet. But the night was quiet. In the *Indianapolis*, a young officer said what everyone was thinking: "If the old man pulls it off this time, they'll be naming streets after him all over the country." But Spruance had no taste for the fame the young officer envisioned, and there were limits to his willingness to chase it.

At 11:25 P.M., Mitscher raised the *Indianapolis* on the Talk Between Ships frequency and made his proposal again. "PROPOSE COMING TO COURSE 270 AT 0130 IN ORDER TO COMMENCE TREATMENT AT 0500. ADVISE." Shortly thereafter, Spruance was given an intercepted exchange of messages between ComSubPac and the submarine *Stingray*. It seemed that Admiral Lockwood and the skipper of that boat weren't reading each other. Spruance interpreted the sub's repeated attempts to send a message—unknowable though its content was—as evidence that the Japanese fleet might be nearby. It might well have been a sighting report. Actually, the *Stingray*'s captain, Samuel C. Loomis, Jr., was trying to confirm his patrol station 435 miles west of Saipan, and Lockwood was trying to tell him his transmissions were being jammed by the Japanese. The skipper was re-sending the dispatch after a fire in the sub's conning tower burned out her radio transmitter leads. "Here we are looking for the Jap fleet and we're looking like a Christmas tree," Loomis complained. "Just as well for the time being, as enemy will probably detour if we talk too much." A detour was exactly what worried Spruance. Ozawa remained elusive as the American search planes prowled the trackless void. Four of the long-legged PBM Mariner flying boats took off from Saipan around midnight to scan the Philippine Sea using the AN/APS-15 air-to-surface radar, mounted in a radome behind the cockpit. Japanese snoopers haunted Task Force 58 through the night, marking its track by dropping flares that floated on the sea. The destroyer *Burns* tried to extinguish them with depth charges, but it didn't work.

Given Ozawa's superior awareness of Mitscher's position, his well-known limitations on fuel, and the standing Japanese desire to find a decisive battle, Mitscher believed the Japanese would come straight on from the west. But Spruance regarded this type of thinking as imprudent—Mitscher had drawn a conclusion based on the enemy's assumed intentions rather than on his actual capabilities.

With no word from the Mariners, and the carrier task force's own air searches turning up empty out to almost five hundred miles, Spruance concluded that Ozawa had done something other than make a beeline toward battle. Given evidence that more than one Japanese force was on the move, and with no indication that Ozawa had concentrated, Spruance had to consider that anything was still possible.

At about 12:30 A.M., Spruance replied to Mitscher's entreaty:

> CHANGE PROPOSED IN YOUR TBS MESSAGE DOES NOT APPEAR ADVISABLE. BELIEVE INDICATION GIVEN BY STINGRAY MORE ACCURATE THAN THAT CONTAINED IN CINCPAC DISPATCH. IF THAT IS SO, CONTINUATION AS AT PRESENT SEEMS PREFERABLE. END RUN BY OTHER FAST ONES REMAINS A POSSIBILITY AND MUST NOT BE OVERLOOKED.

Too much remained unknown, and the enemy's capability was certain.

With the Fifth Fleet commander's final refusal to chase west, the second-guessing took root. Arleigh Burke was incredulous. He and his special assistant, Jimmie Thach, stayed up most of the night proposing terse dispatches for Mitscher to send to Spruance, demanding a reversal of course. "We wrote dozens of them," Thach said, "some stronger than others. Finally we wrote one that said, 'You can have my job if you won't let me run toward the enemy.' Mitscher wouldn't send that one. But I would have done it, I'm sure. Arleigh Burke would have, too."

The carrier partisans never let the matter drop. They argued that mobility was the only thing that would save carriers from heavy air attack. Offense was not just the best but the only defense. Standing on station meant death. But by mid-1944 this view was as much an antique as a Sopwith Camel. Fifteen flight decks buzzing with Hellcats was a defense; two dozen fighter aces stacked at twenty thousand feet was a defense; fighter direction teams guiding them via radar were a defense; a steel ring of five-inch mounts firing proximity-fuzed shells was a defense. And this blue and gray umbrella could open only on a foundation of tactical concentration by all air groups. Spruance achieved this by purposeful design. According to Morison, "The Turkey Shoot could never have made such a spectacular score if Mitscher had had to divide his air forces between offense and defense."

And yet in the wardroom of the *Lexington,* as a correspondent would write, "junior officers began to talk in low voices. The most daring spoke almost in whispers when they said, 'Halsey wouldn't be doing it this way.'" Halsey never would have done this, at least: as battle offered, amid all the tension and uncertainty, retire quietly to his sea cabin and resume reading a novel. Spruance did. When he reached a suitable stopping point, he put the book down, looked at some dispatches from the decoding room, then closed his eyes and slept.

Mitscher heard out his subordinates but dead-ended their complaints. Though he would later speak his piece up the chain of command, for the time being Mitscher chose to suppress the rebellion and accept the fact that four-star admirals like Spruance lived in a larger world. He let his boss sleep in peace.

From his cave headquarters on Saipan's highest mountain, Admiral Nagumo made a report to Combined Fleet headquarters. He offered five observations on the events of the previous seventy-two hours:

1. Since the enemy landed, we have carried out unsuccessful operations every night.
2. The enemy finished landing today. His forces are assumed to be about three divisions.
3. Today five enemy flying boats landed in the anchorage.
4. Landing operations at Tinian and Guam will not immediately be carried out.
5. Most of the aircraft carriers seem to have departed from here. I fear that a delay of the A-Go operations will not only cause us to miss the chance but also make it impossible for us to secure this island.

The carrier fleet he once commanded was rushing to his aid. Its first service to him was to disrupt Kelly Turner's carefully designed invasion support plan. When Spruance sortied to deal with Ozawa, he took away from the close-support mission not only the carriers, but the fire-support groups and replenishment train, too. With Oldendorf's battleships in a blocking position in the west, only one was available to provide fire support, and then only by the approval of Harry Hill. Turner kept the transports and cargo ships at sea to the east, under guard of the escort carriers.

Holland M. Smith, who had earned the nickname "Howlin' Mad" for his high-decibel approach to grievance, considered it just another chapter in the rolling siege of his Marine Corps by the agents of an implacable universe. "We were indeed orphans of the Japanese storm. . . . It needed no mastermind to appreciate the situation on Saipan after the fleet left. The only unknown and highly significant factor was time: How long would it last? The answer to this question was Spruance's success with the Japanese fleet."

Smith told Admiral Nimitz, "Marines die for their country as willingly as the Japanese. There may be Marine annihilation, but there never will be a Marine defeat. My Marines will die to the last man; they never will be taken prisoners." To his division officers he said, "If that time comes, there will be no one left alive to tell the tale. And I'll be with you."

It was 1:15 A.M. on June 19—Spruance had just turned in—when the PBM Mariners, running their spread-fingers search pattern to the west, at last found their prize. Three hundred thirty miles from Task Force 58, more than five hundred miles west of Guam, pounding east, came two groups of Japanese ships, numbering thirty and ten. The pilot, Lieutenant H. F. Arle, switched to the primary frequency and tried to send a sighting report. No station on the circuit acknowledged receipt. He tried others, to no result. Frustrated, he decided to return to Saipan and deliver the report in person. Accordingly, word of the sighting would not reach Spruance for seven and a half hours, when to his utter shock and chagrin his flagship intercepted a transmission from the destroyer *Izard* to Marc Mitscher announcing the sighting report. The protracted labors of the long-legged night search planes was so much exhaust on the easterly wind.

And injury followed insult. At dawn, one of the returning PBMs, on approach to land in the Garapan anchorage, was spotted by a quartet of Hellcats, whose pilots mistook it for a Japanese Emily. Two of the fighters riddled the flying boat with bullets, killing one of her crew. The ruined plane, after landing, was only narrowly saved from sinking, and the crew taken aboard their tender. But there was no saving the failure of the communications net. "Had the report arrived sooner," Carl Moore speculated, "Spruance and Mitscher could well have closed during darkness for a morning strike on Ozawa on June 19." Even this was a leap, given how strongly Spruance was committed to protecting Saipan.

For two years now, the way of carrier warfare had seemed to follow a particular pattern: In every battle of the war—Coral Sea, Midway, and two contests off Guadalcanal—the side to spot the enemy first was the one that won. Ozawa now held that critical advantage. His nine carriers began launching at dawn. Spruance and Mitscher faced a severe test: to see if their peerless force would be the first one in history to weather the likes of the coming storm.

15

War of the Wind Machines

Guam was a hornet's nest, and it was buzzing fiercely at dawn. The radar operators of the *Bunker Hill* task group sniffed out the spike in enemy air activity and vectored four Hellcats from the *Belleau Wood* to investigate. Lieutenant C. I. Oveland and his mates from VF-24 got more than they bargained for at the end of their ninety-mile flight.

About twenty Zekes were in the area, and it was the Americans' good fortune that they did not swarm. Four of them dived on Oveland and his gang as they arrived at fifteen thousand feet. The Americans turned and climbed to face them head-on. Oveland and Lieutenant (j.g.) R. C. Tabler each got a Zeke on the first pass as heavy flak, inaccurate but threatening, burst below. More Zekes bounced into the fray as the Americans tried to regroup, and still more were taxiing and taking off from the island's several airstrips below. During the short, vicious swirl, Oveland radioed the first word back to the task force that a large enemy gaggle was active over Guam. The *Belleau Wood* pilots got away with only one of their planes damaged—Ensign Carl J. Bennett took Plexiglas shrapnel to the back of the head. Within minutes, Mitscher's cavalry was mustering.

The commander of Task Force 58 understood the urgency of disrupting as quickly as possible whatever mischief the Japanese land-based fliers were cooking up. Jocko Clark's *Hornet* task group, steaming closest to Guam, sent two dozen F6Fs to join the fracas over the island. But Spruance and Mitscher were more concerned with Ozawa's whereabouts than with a swarm of planes over a known enemy base. Having been spotted, they were certain an air attack would not be far behind. "We were certainly due for a working over," Arleigh Burke said. Ozawa had already set it into motion. Having listened intently to reports of the air action over Guam—Kakuta's headquarters boasted of a major victory over the U.S. strikers—Ozawa began launching his first strike from three hundred eighty miles away. The *Zuiho, Chiyoda,* and *Chitose* put up sixty-one Zekes, two-thirds of them hauling 550-pound bombs, and eight Jills. Thirty minutes on, the largest element clawed skyward from the *Taiho, Shokaku,* and *Zuikaku:* twenty-seven Jills and fifty-three Judys, each with a thousand-pound armor-piercing bomb, escorted by four dozen Zekes.

As the Japanese carriers were launching, the submarine *Albacore* was in fast pursuit of the *Zuiho* group. It was moving so rapidly east, however, that Commander J. W. Blanchard could not close the range. But sometimes good luck insists on finding a man. He was about ready to quit when a second group of Japanese ships came upon him at high speed, seemingly out of nowhere. The group contained Japan's largest carrier, the *Taiho,* Ozawa's flagship. She blundered into his path while her flight deck crews were spotting more planes to launch against the Americans. As the carrier crossed just fifteen hundred yards—less than a mile—ahead of the *Albacore,* Blanchard had his tubes loaded, awaiting a solution from his torpedo data computer. He waited, and waited some more. The computer, a mechanical-analog device that sent aiming corrections automatically to the torpedoes in their tubes, had failed. With opportunity speeding by at point-blank range, Blanchard began firing his torpedoes anyway. One through six, they leaped from their tubes, and the sub dived deep.

Marking time for each of the half dozen tracks, Blanchard's soundmen listened for explosions. Hearing none as the time counted down for the first five fish, Blanchard ruefully noted his failure. The torpedoes did nothing but leave behind white tracks that traced the path for the *Taiho*'s escorts to follow straight back to the submarine. As the destroyers began dropping depth charges, it was impossible for the *Albacore*'s crew to tell whether the concussion that coincided with the timing of their sixth and last torpedo was a hit or just a coincidence as depth charges tumbled down upon them.

It was in fact a hit. The torpedo struck the hull of the *Taiho,* starting some fires that were quickly brought under control. Damage was otherwise minor. Leaving behind a destroyer to make life miserable for Blanchard and his men, Ozawa continued east, the *Taiho* soon to launch planes with her counterparts, the *Shokaku* and *Zuikaku.*

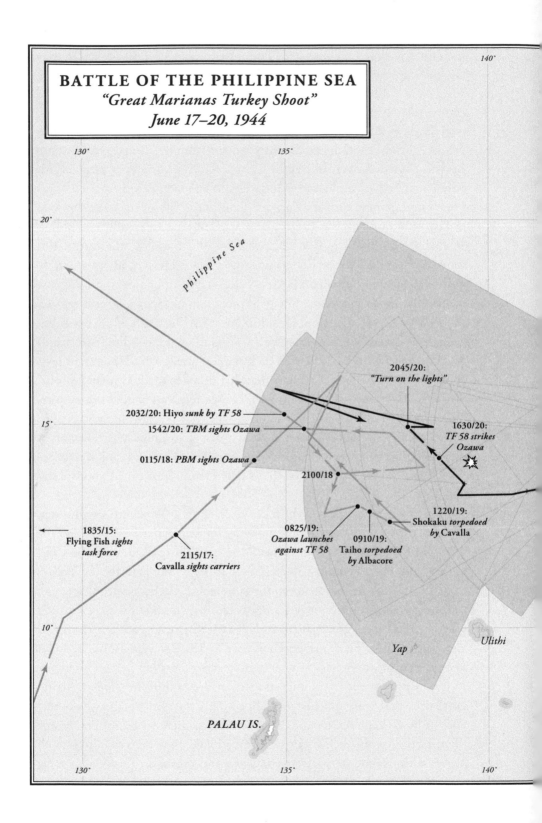

BATTLE OF THE PHILIPPINE SEA
"Great Marianas Turkey Shoot"
June 17–20, 1944

140°

130°   135°

20°

Philippine Sea

2045/20:
"Turn on the lights"

15°   2032/20: Hiyo *sunk by TF 58*   1630/20:
       1542/20: *TBM sights Ozawa*   *TF 58 strikes
                                              Ozawa*

       0115/18: *PBM sights Ozawa*

                              2100/18   1220/19:
                                               Shokaku *torpedoed
       0825/19:   by* Cavalla
1835/15:   *Ozawa launches*   0910/19:
Flying Fish *sights*   *against TF 58* Taiho *torpedoed
task force*   2115/17:   by* Albacore
                       Cavalla *sights carriers*

10°

                                        Yap   *Ulithi*

                    PALAU IS.

130°   135°   140°

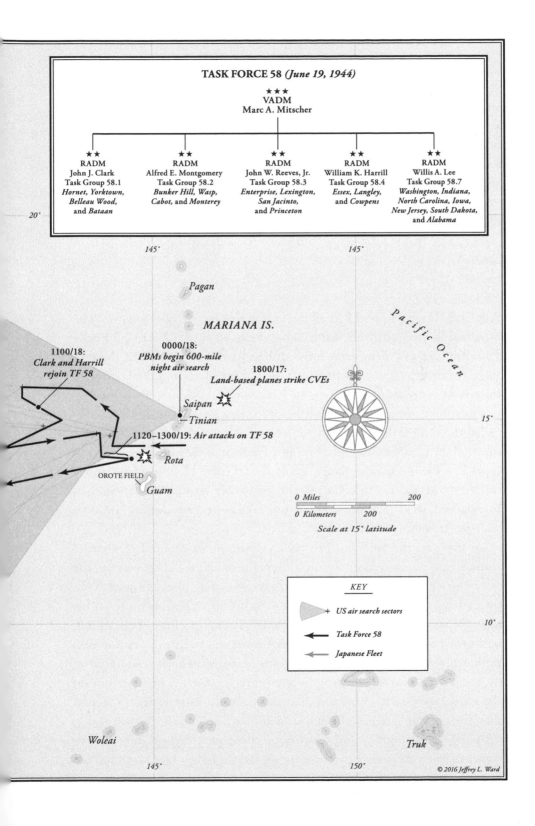

TASK FORCE 58 *(June 19, 1944)*

★ ★ ★
VADM
Marc A. Mitscher

★★
RADM
John J. Clark
Task Group 58.1
Hornet, Yorktown,
Belleau Wood,
and *Bataan*

★★
RADM
Alfred E. Montgomery
Task Group 58.2
Bunker Hill, Wasp,
Cabot, and *Monterey*

★★
RADM
John W. Reeves, Jr.
Task Group 58.3
Enterprise, Lexington,
San Jacinto,
and *Princeton*

★★
RADM
William K. Harrill
Task Group 58.4
Essex, Langley,
and *Cowpens*

★★
RADM
Willis A. Lee
Task Group 58.7
Washington, Indiana,
North Carolina, Iowa,
New Jersey, South Dakota,
and *Alabama*

20°

145°   145°

Pagan

MARIANA IS.

1100/18:
Clark and Harrill
rejoin TF 58

0000/18:
PBMs begin 600-mile
night air search

1800/17:
Land-based planes strike CVEs

Saipan

Tinian

1120–1300/19: *Air attacks on TF 58*

Rota

 OROTE FIELD

Guam

Pacific Ocean

15°

0 Miles   200
0 Kilometers   200
Scale at 15° latitude

10°

KEY

US air search sectors

Task Force 58

Japanese Fleet

Woleai

Truk

145°   150°

© 2016 Jeffrey L. Ward

* * *

The *Albacore* was diving to safety below when Admiral Spruance belatedly received the sighting report made the previous night by the flying boat now sitting at anchor off Garapan. It stated that thirty enemy ships were headed east, about five hundred twenty miles west of Guam, with another group of ten about ten miles farther westward.

"The plane made no report?" Spruance asked the officer who handed it to him.

"None received, sir. Atmospheric conditions must have blacked out their radio."

Spruance handed the dispatch back to his staff, saying quietly, "That's too bad, isn't it?"

Admiral Mitscher's pilots had all they wanted to handle over Guam. "The boys had just too many aircraft to shoot down all at once," Arleigh Burke said. But Ozawa's main strike element had yet to arrive. By 9:50, the task force radars began to show the great aerial host all around the horizon, a hundred twenty miles out.

Over the flagship's radio went the call, *"Hey Rube!"*—a signal that recalled the Hellcat drivers to return to the vicinity of the carriers. Mitscher directed them to take station at low altitude west of the task force, ready to repel low-flying torpedo planes. It would take the Hellcats about thirty minutes to get there. The enemy would get in the first attack. But Mitscher, forewarned, was preparing a welcoming committee, a powerful one, on a scale never before mustered.

At ten A.M., the radars of Mitscher's westernmost group, Lee's battleships, began registering the leading elements of Ozawa's first wave in the west. Sitting on a leather sofa in the *Lexington*'s flag plot, Mitscher wore his ball cap with its brim pulled low over his brow, a grim smile on his face. He asked his staff, "Are you excited?" Then, uttering a small sound, half growl and half laugh, he answered himself: "So am I." As the TBS radio squawked with the voices of a multitude, Mitscher's yeoman sat at the desk in the corner, making a stenographic record. The intercom on the *Lexington* carried two sharp whistles from the boatswain's pipe, and then the general-quarters alarm sounded.

As elevators rumbled and pilots ran to their planes, the fighter squadrons of fifteen carriers began layering in depth. Every Hellcat that Task Force 58 had was set to take a turn overhead to parry. Dive-bombers and torpedo planes were moving, too, except these were ordered to fly away east and orbit in safety. Their orders: "Get out of the road, and get high."

The culture of the Navy fighter squadrons encouraged speed, aggression, and initiative. The craft of killing was intrinsic to it, and though their power was collective, it was cut through with tribal rivalries that convinced every squadron it was best in class, pride of the breed. The *Yorktown*'s Fighting One called themselves the Tophatters. Commander Charlie Brewer's Fighting Fifteen, based on the *Essex,* were the Fighting Aces. The light carrier *Cabot*'s Fighting Thirty-One, the Meataxers, had their fuselages painted with a flying meat cleaver. Their motto: "Cut them down." Robert A. Winston, the air group commander of that unit, was one of the first to fly combat air patrol that morning. It was his bad luck to run low on fuel just as the first Japanese wave was approaching. After landing he noticed an uncommon atmospheric condition that caused aircraft to leave white contrails of water vapor as low as twenty thousand feet. Even with the advent of radar this was a curse to the Japanese, a sort of divine wind in reverse that easily marked their movements for the eye. While his Hellcat was serviced, Commander Winston awaited his next turn to spot, biding his time by watching the incoming white lines converge with white lines going the other way as the Hellcats reached interception altitude.

The *Essex* task group, on duty to provide air cover to Lee's battleships, steamed farthest to the west, fifteen miles to Lee's north, the tall masts of the battlewagons barely visible on the horizon. Situated forward, Rear Admiral Harrill's three carriers were first in line when the Japanese approached. As a result, Fighting Fifteen was among the first to intercept. Brewer led eight Hellcats toward the bogies. As he reached twenty-four thousand feet, he called "Tallyho" on a flight of sixteen Judys, flanked on both sides by four Hamp fighters. Above and astern of them flew a gaggle of sixteen Zekes.

Looking to cash in his advantage in altitude, Brewer placed his two four-plane divisions in position for an overhead run. He chose as his target the leader of the first group of dive-bombers. Riding down from their flank, Brewer and his wingman, Richard E. Fowler, bored in close and opened fire at eight hundred feet. The Judy exploded. Passing through its flaming debris, Brewer pulled up and shot another Judy from below, sawing off parts until its wing separated, leaving the plane to spin, burning and falling like a leaf. The squadron leader spied a Zeke now and pushed over in pursuit. Fowler was no longer with him, but he gained position behind the plane and fired into its wing roots. Veering away as the Zeke began to burn and plunged, Brewer survived a pass from a plane that dived on him unseen. Turning sharply away, then back again, through a series of maneuvers, he worked his way onto the Zeke's tail. Each time Brewer fired, the skilled enemy pilot juked and twisted violently, half rolling onto his back, then pulling through and whirling around into barrel rolls and wingovers, sideslips, and skids. The best Japanese pilots fought like aerobats. Their maneuvers were quick, sharp. But the Hellcat was built to beat them. Above 160 knots, it rivaled the nimble Zeke in maneuverability. And so Brewer stayed in high blower, slashing at the Zeke's fuselage, wings, and cockpit until it caught fire. Releasing into a wild, tight spiral, the enemy plane plummeted into the sea.

His fuel running low, Brewer formed up with his division and set course back to the *Essex*. Ensign Fowler rejoined him now, having split off after Brewer's second kill. He ended up matching his flight leader, with four kills that morning. But neither set the day's record for Fighting Fifteen. Lieutenant (j.g.) George R. Carr, leader of the other division that flew with Brewer, shot down five. As they turned away from the fight, Brewer noted with relish that the Japanese formation was no longer whole. His boys had done their part in scattering them, culling their numbers by twenty planes.

Willis Lee's battleships were ringing up full speed now as they steamed east in a circular antiaircraft disposition. In the *Indiana,* riding at their center as guide, radar operators noticed that the large group of bogies had dispersed into three smaller gaggles. Gun crews were preparing to deal with them.

One of the Navy's top experts in fleet air defense, Lloyd Mustin, disliked tracers as a means of fire control. He regarded the "hose pipe method," also called "gunner's delight," as virtually useless when crews weren't intensively trained. An optical illusion took hold when gunners fired on targets moving perpendicular to their line of sight. "Any gunner who thinks he is using tracer control at a thousand yards or more is sure to be shooting low and behind," Mustin said. "The physics of the thing [is] unanswerable." But another discipline of physics offered a novel solution. "Proximity-detonated" fuzes, triggered to explode by miniature radar transmitters, were a technological marvel. They were known in the fleet as "variable-timed," or VT, fuzes—a euphemism meant to obscure the actual mechanism of the device, first used successfully in combat by the cruiser *Helena* in the South Pacific in January 1943. Screwed into five-inch projectiles that were lethal to seventy yards, VT fuzes were the state of the art in task force air defense.

Shipboard gunners were forbidden to fire at targets within the circle of a task group, as the rain of metal was liable to be dangerous. The crews of the 20 mm and 40 mm mounts were permitted to fire at planes inside the formation only if their elevation was above the line of fire of surrounding ships. But if the Navy's leading fighter ace had anything to say about it, those instructions would be entirely moot.

When Alex Vraciu jogged up the steps from the ready room to the *Lexington*'s flight deck, he found a dozen Hellcats lined up, fueled, armed, and waiting. "No one kicked the tires," he said. "It was just climb aboard and go." He was on the standby alert team, ready to supplement the CAP at the first sign of trouble. As he got airborne, the fighter direction officer's voice crackled over his radio, "Vector two-fifty, climb to angels twenty-five, pronto!" Vraciu didn't wait around for the rest of Fighting Sixteen. "It was a running rendezvous on the climb," he said.

Air-search radar put to use by a competent fighter direction team changed the game of task force air defense, multiplying significantly the advantage in proficiency enjoyed by the U.S. pilots on an individual basis. Normally, combat air patrols had to cover large swaths of sky. With shipboard search radar doing its thing, fighters could beeline in swarms straight to their target, attacking while their fuel tanks were still full. The contrail effect helped in that task, too.

Jimmie Thach was glad to have a single task consuming all the energies of the Hellcat squadrons. "We weren't doing any striking ourselves, so we could put all our effort and use all the deck space for fighter operations for defense. There's no use keeping fighters on the hangar deck for tomorrow if you might get hit today. You want to be sure you don't get hit. This is the principle on which we operated."

When Alex Vraciu tried to throw his engine into high blower to intercept, he realized his plane was sick. Hellcats were so plentiful—Grumman was producing five hundred a month, most all of them sent to the Pacific—that a liberal replacement policy was in effect. Planes with the slightest sign of a worn engine were buried at sea without ceremony. But it was his bilge-level luck to find that his plane was lame at the start of what promised to be the sortie of his life. Struggling to climb, Vraciu watched helplessly as the squadron's skipper, Paul Buie, riding behind a brand-new Pratt & Whitney radial engine, surged high and far ahead with his own division of eight. Soon they were out of Vraciu's sight, bound for an intercept in just eight short minutes. Sixty miles from the *Lexington* were seventy Japanese planes stacked between sixteen and twenty thousand feet. But Vraciu would have to wait his turn. He cussed his luck as a film of oil began collecting on his windscreen. An engine leak! He eased back on the throttle, and his seven divisionmates stayed with him as a matter of course. As Commander Buie piled into the enemy formation, the force fighter direction officer in the *Lexington* ordered Vraciu's division to return and orbit the task group.

He had barely begun to comply when the fighter director raised him again, directing him back to the west. "There was something in his voice," Vraciu said, "that indicated he had a good one on the string." Another wave was inbound, seventy-five miles out. Vraciu figured to catch them at the midpoint.

As this was happening, David McCampbell was getting airborne with a second wave of Hellcats from the *Essex*. Matching Charlie Brewer's gaudy score would be a tall order, to be sure, and a conversation for another day. But the air group commander knew a rich chance when he saw one, and he figured the setup promised to keep the squadron's artists busy decorating his fuselage. Leading eleven other Hellcats, he climbed to intercept the enemy about forty-five miles from his ship.

Waging a full-on task force defense, Mitscher had to forget about closing and attacking Ozawa. All fifteen carriers were putting up a maximum defensive effort, cycling their Hellcat squadrons in a constant rotation: launch, land, rearm, reservice, and relaunch as quickly as possible for what promised to be a prolonged battle through the day. Sustaining the aerial dance required Mitscher to hold his carriers on an easterly heading into the wind—and straight toward the Mariana Islands air bases that the Japanese were planning to use to land and rearm their own planes. He hoped he had gone far enough west by night to have sea room to hold the necessary easterly course. If he had to turn to another heading, or if he were forced to thread between or around the islands, he would have trouble launching and recovering planes. As the Japanese carriers shot their bolt at him that morning, they were virtually immune to attack. "Every time we launched a plane we had to run away from them. The wind was just that way," Burke said. He could not close the range. It would be up to his fighter squadrons to win by way of defense.

From the time he rolled out of his rack at four every morning, David McCampbell was focused on his mission. He never ate breakfast. He took a glass of orange juice; that was it. Then he went to work in the ready room, filing reports, studying intelligence, and running his pilots through recognition drills. He was professional through and through. He seemed to take no joy in his work. But he was good at it. Every day he made sure his pilots spent thirty minutes, maybe more, working on silhouette recognition. The intelligence staff flashed on a screen a series of black forms depicting the full arsenal of both nations' planes and ships. The images were shown fleetingly, and pilots were expected to know in a blink exactly what type they were. As a journalist would soon famously observe, "To see what is in front of one's nose needs a constant struggle," and it took repetitious training to discern reality in the world at three hundred knots.

The intelligence officer then briefed the pilots on target locations, fleet movements, types of AA weaponry, and the latest capabilities of enemy planes and armaments. Was it any wonder McCampbell was a smoker? He smoked in the ready room, and he smoked in his plane, even above eighteen thousand feet, where he had to wear a mask delivering pure, flammable oxygen under continuous pressure. Inside his cockpit, his plane captain had riveted a small aluminum pocket to hold his cigarette packs and saw to it that it was always filled for missions. For this reason, and surely others, McCampbell allowed only two men on the *Essex* to serve as crew chiefs to his Hellcat.

The record of VF-15's Fighting Aces would be the product of the disciplined systemization of McCampbell's rigor. From his first days training them at a naval air station in New Jersey, he was an enthusiast of extreme aerial aggression. He disdained the Thach Weave, a defensive maneuver that was necessary in its time but did not suit a fast-stepping fighter squadron equipped with the magnificent F6F. A fighter pilot should never be on the defensive, McCampbell thought. He expected every enemy pilot he saw to be his match. "You could never know when you might run into a real top-notch fighter pilot. So I always gave them the benefit of the doubt and I engaged them in that fashion. I expected him to give his best, and I gave my best. That didn't make me more cautious. I knew that I was a pretty good shot, so I was just doing what I had trained to do. If I found that he had a tendency to run, maybe I would be more aggressive. If he was more combative, I'd be less aggressive and pay him more respect." He prided himself on his aerial gunnery. And he made sure his squadronmates had confidence in one another. Before setting out for the Pacific, he asked his trainees, until recently completely green, to vote on the men they wanted to go into combat with, voting positively instead of negatively. The top forty vote getters went with him to war.

Climbing to intercept, McCampbell lost two pilots to balking engines. Lieutenant Commander Rigg and another pilot punched out, leaving the air group commander to re-form with ten. McCampbell climbed to twenty-five thousand feet and ordered four of his pilots to fly high cover. That left him and his wingman, and another division of four, to do the dirty work at the point of attack. Six pilots. McCampbell considered Roy Rushing one of the good ones. He flew the best way his surname suggested, and always tight on McCampbell's wing. To preserve radio silence, the two pilots communicated with hand signals and slaps of Morse code on the dashboard. Sometimes McCampbell had to wave him back, get him to loosen up. But he was always right there, ever aggressive but never freelancing.

Ahead, the heavens streamed with eastbound white contrails. Their sources resolved as black specks, then silhouettes that McCampbell recognized as Jills, Judys, and Zekes. Coming nearer, his veteran eye discerned the geometry of the formation and profitable angles of attack. He called "Tallyho" and pulled his Hellcat's stubby nose toward the first section of Judys, while his other section went after the Zekes. He had nearly a mile in altitude advantage and meant to use it wisely.

McCampbell picked out the flight leader but built up too much speed in his dive to draw on him. He settled for another Judy halfway back on the formation's left. He planned to finish his run by passing beneath his target and through the formation to the other side, pulling up and hitting another plane from below, then executing a chandelle and starting another pass from the other side. But this plan had to change as soon as he pulled the trigger. His marksmanship was perfect, and the first Judy exploded in his face. The flash of fire and storm of metal parts forced him to evade, pulling up. As he passed over the formation, he winced: He had exposed himself to a belt-fed greeting from most every tail gunner in the Japanese formation. As bullets flew by, he wondered when he would ever get clear.

When the Hellcats began making their runs, the flight leader of the Judys and his wingman began fishtailing. These evasions were minimally effective and served mainly to reduce their airspeed. This made it possible for the U.S. pilots to make successive passes from the side, maintaining an advantageous attacking position ahead of the enemy gaggle. McCampbell sawed away at its numbers. On four passes he destroyed four planes. On his fifth pass, he worked his way to his favorite attacking position, behind his target at its seven o'clock. He easily destroyed the lead plane's wingman. Swinging around for another pass, McCampbell closed the leader from below at eight o'clock. When he pressed the trigger now, however, he found that only one of his six guns was working. He kept at it, carefully spending the last of his belted fifties, and the enemy plane caught fire and spiraled down, out of control.

The Zekes flying with the bomber formation, McCampbell noticed, were doing nothing to provide high cover. Some of the enemy fighters might have been armed with bombs themselves, he thought. No doubt they were preoccupied with the problem of their own survival. Claude Plant of McCampbell's division had already shot down two when he saw another Zeke attacking a Hellcat two thousand feet below him to the right. Ensign Plant banked over and gained the Zeke's tail, firing a long burst from above that stitched the enemy plane up the back and through the cockpit and engine. Parts of the stabilizer broke away and flames poured from the forward fuselage. With the pilot slumped at his stick, the Zeke spun out of control. Piling into another pair of enemy fighters, Plant fired bursts that caused one of them to lose control and spin like a leaf, down and down, into the water. By now another Zeke was maneuvering on Plant, managing to settle on his tail. The American did everything possible to shake him, but it was no use. His Hellcat spasmed from the impact of cannon rounds, and machine gun bullets smacked the armor plate behind his seat. By the time another F6F shot the enemy fighter off his tail, Plant's aircraft had collected a hundred fifty holes. He formed up with his savior, passing a gesture of thanks as his radio was out of action. Both shot-up planes made it back to the task force.

But Mitscher's pilots couldn't get them all. Lee's battleships were about two hundred miles west of Tinian when the Japanese survivors of the Hellcat swarm broke through. Around 10:40, about thirty aircraft bore down on his heavies from astern. Lee ordered four of his destroyers to drop back and provide a trip wire for his force, and the cruisers at the rear of the formation opened fire first.

It was Ozawa's misfortune to have his largest strike fall upon the stoutest target in the entire Fifth Fleet, Willis Lee's fast battleship squadron. That was precisely Mitscher's design: a flak trap. He deployed them far to the west, covered by the *Essex* task group. Forewarned by radar as well as by the jubilant radio chatter of Hellcat pilots, the battleships were ready.

Twelve to fifteen Jills, low on the water, closed on the *Alabama*'s starboard quarter. Converging tracers from the ship knocked one plane into the sea. Three others broke off, tracing a circle to close on the *South Dakota* from ahead. The pilot released his torpedo while evading, and, falling with a wobble, the weapon hit the water nose down and dived while tracers from the *Alabama* and *South Dakota* met the plane and shot it down.

Lee kept his ships' sterns to the Japanese, steaming eastward as the carriers conducted air operations, changing course slightly only when needed to bring full broadsides to bear. Riding at the center of the formation, the *Indiana* was a magnet for attacking pilots. Two Jills came at her from ahead. One of them dropped a torpedo that nose-dived into the sea and exploded. As the pilot pulled up and away to the left, the *Indiana*'s gunners hit him. He turned his burning plane back toward the battleship as if to sell his life dearly, but he crashed short of her. Another Jill closing from the *Indiana*'s starboard quarter had its tail carried away by gunfire, snapped into an uncontrolled spiral and smacked down on the sea, leaving a puddle of flames. A minute later, another torpedo bomber pressed in low on her starboard beam. It got within a hundred yards before catching fire and crashing into the *Indiana* at the waterline. The crumpled aircraft sank fast, leaving a divot in the *Indiana*'s torpedo belt and a glistening swirl of fuel on the face of the sea, to be washed away within moments in the rolling cataract of the battleship's wake.

The Japanese pilots attacked alone, or in pairs and trios. A Zeke glided in behind the heavy cruiser *Minneapolis* and dropped a bomb that landed so close to starboard that its explosion blasted shrapnel straight through her hull, the hot fragments igniting bedding and clothes in an officers' stateroom. A dive-bomber managed a pair of near misses on the cruiser *Wichita* and continued into a cross fire of leviathans. Swarming tracers from the *Indiana,* steaming in the formation's center, and the *North Carolina* brought down the pilot, who crashed on the sea ahead of them.

A pair of Judys dived sharply on the battleship *South Dakota,* strafing as they came. Dropping their bombs, they pulled up sharply and passed over the starboard bow. As one plane took hits and crashed into the sea, one of the bombs struck home, hitting near the wardroom and blowing a nine-by-ten-foot hole in the overhead of a battle dressing station. When a medical party reached the site, they found ten sailors dead in the wreckage. Two more would die after hours of "energetic treatment" by the ship's doctors. In all, twenty-seven *South Dakota* crewmen were killed, and the same number wounded.

Because the Japanese were attacking from the south and southwest, the battleships riding on the northern arc of the circle had little shooting to do. Doctrine forbade them to fire across the formation. The *South Dakota* and *Alabama* were on the hot spot, and it was they who sent skyward the greatest volume of steel. Nervous trigger fingers and intermingling friendly and hostile planes led the *South Dakota*'s sky control station to repeatedly direct fire at friendly planes. More than a few Hellcat drivers flirted with disaster by chasing Japanese planes near Lee's disposition.

Alex Vraciu was among the swarm of F6F pilots who pressed their luck in the neighborhood of the battleships. Locating a group of at least fifty enemy planes, Vraciu rocked his wings and peeled away to attack a Judy at the edge of the formation. His adrenaline had "hit high C," he said, when he found himself nudged aside by another Hellcat pilot with similar thoughts. Turning away and diving beneath the formation to size it up, Vraciu thought, *There are enough cookies on this plate for everyone.* Counting the throng of Judys, Jills, and Zekes, he radioed his count to the *Lexington,* then worked his way into position to attack some Judys.

Easing down on them from behind, he picked a plane that was wildly evading, its rear gunner firing away. Vraciu nudged his stick, adjusting until the dive-bomber sat beneath the pipper of his Mark 8 gunsight. His six machine guns tore into the plane and it fell away smoking. He pulled up and away again and lined up a pair of Judys, burning them one after the other, the last of them from close enough to see the results personally. He watched the rear seat gunner peppering at him for a moment before the man vanished, sucked down by his dying plane's sharp plummeting arc. "For a split second, I almost felt sorry for the little bastard," Vraciu would say of his third kill within minutes.

> The enemy planes had been pretty well chopped down, but a substantial number remained. It didn't look like we would score a grand slam. I reported this information back to base. The sky appeared to be full of smoke and pieces of planes. And we were trying to ride herd on the remaining attacking planes and keep them from scattering. Another meatball broke formation up ahead and I slid over onto his tail, again working in close because of my oil-smeared windscreen. I gave him a short burst, and it was enough; it went right into the sweet spot at the root of his wing tanks. The pilot control cables must have been hit, also, because the burning plane twisted crazily, out of control. . . .
>
> In spite of our efforts, the Jills were beginning to descend to begin their torpedo runs, and the remaining Judys were at the point of peeling off to go down with their bombs. I headed for a group of three Judys in a long column. By the time I had reached

the tail-ender, we were almost over our outer screen of ships, but still fairly high. The first Judy was about to begin his dive and as he started to nose over, I noticed black puffs beside him in the sky. Our five inchers were beginning to open up. Foolishly maybe, I overtook the nearest one. It seemed that I barely touched the trigger and his engine started coming to pieces. The Judy started smoking, then torching alternately, off and on, as it disappeared below.

The next one was about one-fifth of the way down in his dive— trying for one of the destroyers—before I caught up with him. This time a short burst produced astonishing results. Number six blew up with a tremendous explosion right in front of my face. I must have hit his bomb. I have seen planes blow up before, but *never* like this. I yanked the stick up sharply to avoid the scattered pieces and flying hot stuff, then radioed, "Splash number six! There's one more ahead, and he's headed for a BB [battleship] but I don't think he'll make it." Hardly had the words left my mouth than the Judy caught a direct hit that removed it immediately as a factor to be worried about in the war. He had run into a solid curtain of steel from the battlewagon.

Looking around at that point, only Hellcats seemed to be remaining in the sky. Glancing backward to where we had begun, in a pattern thirty-five miles long, there were flaming oil slicks in the water and smoke still hanging in the air. It didn't seem like eight minutes—it seemed longer. But that's all it was—an eight-minute opportunity for the flight of a lifetime.

It was a rout. The Hellcat jockeys seemed likelier to be hit by falling brass cartridges ejecting from the wings of their section leaders ahead than by bullets fired by a Zeke or a Hamp behind.

Returning to the *Lexington,* Alex Vraciu began his circling descent into the landing pattern and became the target of trigger-happy gun crews on the surrounding escorts. As tracers flew his way, he unloaded a blur of obscenity into his radio mike. Little did the pilot know that among the general confusion of pilots circling, trying to identify which carrier was theirs, a certain hysteria arose briefly when it was reported that at least one Japanese pilot was trying to land on a U.S. carrier. But Vraciu made it down safely.

Normally the routine was all rush and hustle. Fighter pilots ran down to their ready rooms, stopping for a sip of pineapple juice at the canteen before unloading what they remembered of their mission to an intelligence officer. After receiving a quick debriefing and checking notices on the blackboard, they returned to the flight deck, ready for another chance to boost their own and their unit's score. "From their attitude," observed a war correspondent, "it would have been reasonable to guess they were engaged not in a battle at all but in some especially fast and exciting game, like polo or hockey."

As the task force flagship, the *Lexington* carried an unusually large collection of journalists. They mobbed Vraciu as he filled out his maintenance paperwork. One of them had seen him flash six fingers to Mitscher on the flag bridge as his Hellcat rolled past the island. He was asked to repeat the gesture for a camera. Vraciu the impaler looked up, smiled broadly, and held up six fingers to show his score. His plane handler then noticed something truly remarkable: his ammunition usage for the day. To bring down six planes, Vraciu had fired a total of only 360 rounds—just ten bullets per gun for each kill. His efficiency was as much a mark of pride as the hand-painted red sunbursts that would adorn his Hellcat below the canopy track. The wardroom revelry was boosted by the knowledge that Fighting Sixteen was still winning its bet with Gus Widhelm, Mitscher's air operations officer. Such a field day, and the enemy fleet had not even been engaged yet. Some felt sure they would win their money.

Shortly after noon, Willis Lee's staff passed word that all contacts on their radars were friendly, and the order went around to unload all guns. But a handful of Japanese pilots were patient and enterprising enough to stick around and find Mitscher's carriers. Around noon, a half dozen Judy dive-bombers found the *Bunker Hill* task group and played cat and mouse with its gunners among the clouds. Finally one of the dive-bombers fell upon the *Wasp*, Captain Clifton Sprague commanding, and scored a hit that killed a man and wounded four. The *Bunker Hill* took a near miss that riddled her bustling hangar deck, killing two and wounding eighty-four.

Returning to the *Essex*, skirting the dangerous skies over the battleship group, David McCampbell saw the bomb hit the *South Dakota* as well as the long trail of fires and oil slicks on the water marking the graves of Japanese pilots and aircrew along the path of their approach. Antiaircraft gunners were bound to be stirred up. Passing well to the north, McCampbell found his task group and entered the pattern to land. His Fighting Aces had had a productive morning, claiming sixty-eight kills. And the day was far from done.

16

Fast Carriers Down

Submarines were lonely, the only vessels in the fleet to operate for days and weeks completely on their own. This added urgency to their crises and weight to all their mistakes. And what a mistake it had been, long into the night before dawn on the nineteenth, when the *Cavalla*'s officer of the deck neglected the search radar and let a plane catch them napping. Closing without warning, an aircraft of undetermined nationality buzzed them close overhead. When Captain Kossler saw him in the control room, the young officer was white as a ghost.

When the next plane came calling before sunrise, less than two hundred miles from Yap, the radar was alertly manned. Kossler detected it six miles out and dived. It had been a frustrating night. He had never managed to close the major enemy task force he had seen and quit his pursuit around two A.M. Unable to get through a report to that effect, Kossler resumed course for his Philippines patrol station. Surfacing after sunrise, he transmitted his news.

Three hours underway, a situation developed. Through his periscope, Kossler saw four aircraft low on the water, about fifteen miles to the west. His soundman then reported ship engine noises on the same bearing as the planes. The captain kept a careful periscope watch in that direction, and the soundman monitored the hydrophones.

Lee's battleships were just facing Ozawa's air assault when Kossler spotted masts. "The picture," he wrote, "was too good to be true." There were four ships, and one was a carrier, distinguishable by the bedspring radar transmitter atop the island superstructure. The carrier was landing planes. Kossler could see the forward part of the flight deck crowded with aircraft. It was the *Shokaku*. Kossler could never have caught her in pursuit. The good fortune to have her change course and double back upon him was the result of Ozawa's decision to stop closing with Mitscher's carriers and strike from standoff distance. The carrier was holding position now, steaming slowly as she recovered planes. She thus made herself vulnerable, terribly so.

Kossler was leery of the destroyer riding nearest him, but he knew it was time to calculate and accept certain risks, given how quickly the problem was developing. After letting his exec and gunnery officer take a look to confirm his identification, he maneuvered for a shot with his bow tubes.

He closed to twelve hundred yards before firing, setting the first torpedo to run at fifteen feet. The fish rushed from the tubes at timed intervals. When the fifth one was clear, he flooded his tanks. The sixth was fired with the *Cavalla* in fast descent. The countdown to glory was short. Fifty seconds on, there came a heavy detonation, followed by two more at eight-second intervals. Kossler, thrilled to have scored, threw his rudder left and rigged for silent running.

Too soon the destroyer was over him. A salvo of four depth charges popped ahead, above, and to port. Quickly two more destroyers joined her, and in the next few hours the trio would roll more than a hundred depth charges overboard, half of which came close enough to make Kossler sweat. The Japanese escorts never used active sonar, he noted, and eventually they lost the scent. Soon his hydrophones registered only one destroyer close by, and as the explosions of depth charges receded, his soundman reported other "water noises," loud ones, in the direction of his prospective kill. Kossler hazarded to ascend, raising his periscope for a look.

The "water noises" told a grim story, the tale of a Japanese aircraft carrier fighting for her life. When the three torpedoes hit, the *Shokaku*'s hangar deck was full of aircraft being refueled and rearmed. A great fire feasted upon them, spreading hungrily after an explosion concussed the ship violently enough to raise her elevators by three feet. As the carrier took a hard list to starboard, Captain Hiroshi Matsubara ordered counter-flooding on the port side to correct it, but the sea cocks remained open too long, and the mass of water caused the ship to heel back over to port.

Shokaku's damage control crew were among the most experienced in the Combined Fleet. They had saved her twice: once at the Battle of the Coral Sea, then again at Santa Cruz. Closing the fuel lines to the hangar deck, they hoped to contain the flames. But with the ship's pumps out of action owing to a shipwide power failure, the flooding could not be stemmed. The conflagration was so bad near the fire mains on the hangar deck that firefighters dared not approach them. Portable extinguishers and bucket brigades were useless. Meanwhile, the flooding was swamping the ship's forward compartments. Her bow began to settle. Through the ship spread flammable vapors.

By two thirty in the afternoon, the fires, fed by stockpiles of aircraft fuel tanks and oxygen bottles, had engulfed the hangar deck, slowed little by the fire screens dividing the hangar into makeshift compartments. As the bow continued to submerge, the sea lapped over the forecastle, and Captain Matsubara ordered all hands to report topside for roll call and to prepare to abandon ship. The light cruiser *Yahagi* closed with the stricken carrier to assist. But the fires and explosions prospered, and the free-surface effect turned suddenly lethal. The great momentum of the water shifting laterally through large compartments belowdecks reached a critical point. Upending the ship, it caused the crew on the flight deck to fall over and begin sliding forward, many of them to drop through an open elevator to their death in the inferno below. Around this same time a series of four catastrophic explosions rocked the ship. At 3:10 the carrier's nose dived beneath the water and she stood straight up and with a "groaning roar" disappeared. "Survivors remaining in the water began to sing with 'blood tears' the *Shokaku*'s ship song," a Japanese historian wrote.

Her death throes continued to register on the *Cavalla*'s hydrophones. When Kossler came to periscope depth and swung the well-greased cylinder of mirrors through an arc to the north, he saw only the gray void of a rain squall that had taken over the area. It was almost eight P.M. by the time he dared to surface. Clearing the area at three-engine speed, he began transmitting a message to ComSubPac.

Easing through the debris field, the *Yahagi* and *Urakaze* found an alarming scarcity of survivors, fewer than six hundred of them, which meant more than twice that number had been lost, the final count being 887 petty officers and crewmen, plus 376 men from the air group. Among the survivors was Captain Matsubara, who, having been washed from the bridge as the ship dived under, ordered away the rescue boats that eventually came for him, only to be hauled aboard a cutter that took him, to his shame, to safety in the *Yahagi*.

The disaster would soon cumulate as a full-on catastrophe. Ozawa's flagship, the *Taiho,* was recovering from its own torpedoing that morning. The hit by the *Albacore* had ruptured fuel oil lines, and fumes had been accumulating so intensely that she was forced to send her returning aircraft to the *Zuikaku*. Damage control teams thought they had a remedy: the ship's ventilation system, the absence of which may have doomed the *Sho-kaku*. The *Taiho*'s damage control officer ordered it turned on and all hatches and doors opened to allow fresh air to disperse the fumes. This allowed fuel vapors to spread throughout the ship.

In spite of the loss of the *Shokaku*, Ozawa was not yet ready to retire. He believed hundreds more Japanese planes were en route to attack the Americans. Vice Admiral Kakuta, commander of the First Air Fleet, had radioed him to say that many of Ozawa's carrier planes had landed on Guam. If that was in fact the case, few of them were in one piece.

At about 3:30 P.M., more than six hours after the torpedo hit the *Taiho*, the catastrophe arrived as an explosion shook the guts of the flagship. The flight deck rose up and the sides of the ship were breached. The wounded carrier was stopped dead, in mortal distress. Her escorts pulled close.

When rescuers found him, Ozawa made the usual protest about leaving his ship before his staff persuaded him to accept transfer. A destroyer came alongside and took the admiral, who had retrieved the portrait of his emperor, to the heavy cruiser *Haguro*. A second explosion occurred at that point—only a bomb or torpedo stowage could have produced such a blast. Fatally wounded, the carrier sank, stern first, around 5:30, taking down more than sixteen hundred officers and men.

By midafternoon, almost every plane Ozawa had thrown at Spruance had been destroyed or turned away by Mitscher's pilots. But radars in the task force found another large bogie before three P.M. While still 135 miles out, it split up and began inching toward Guam. These planes weren't coming to attack. They were inbound to land.

Spruance and Mitscher had believed all along that Ozawa would not risk a late-day strike and a nighttime return to base. More likely, they thought, he would stage planes into Guam for a morning attack. Their prediction was on the money. Kakuta had ordered every plane under his command to gather at Guam. Though his land-based contribution would amount to a mere fifty planes, they might make for a powerful force when joined with Ozawa's air groups. But the Americans were ready for them. At twenty-four thousand feet, Dave McCampbell was inbound hot, leading a dozen Hellcats from the *Essex* toward trouble.

Under scattered light cumulus, his trio of four-plane divisions approached from the northeast to find Japanese planes circling Guam's airfield on Orote Peninsula. There were sixteen to eighteen Zekes, he estimated, brand-new light-gray-painted planes with belly tanks, and forty or more brown-green dive-bombers—Vals, he thought. The Japanese pilots were looking to land.

McCampbell had started a corkscrewing descent to twelve thousand feet, with Ensign Raymond L. Nall flying on his wing, when another U.S. fighter group arrived in the area, broadcasting their own tallyho. Hearing this, McCampbell pushed his throttle into high blower. Scattered in twos and fours, the enemy planes were descending, wheels down, when the boys from Fighting Fifteen fell upon them. McCampbell raced to the kill.

Targeting a group of four Zekes, McCampbell and Nall missed on their first high-side run, but both pilots scored on their second pass. While pulling out, they found a pair of Zekes diving and firing right at them. McCampbell didn't have enough airspeed to get away, so he turned straight at the Japanese pilots as a hail of machine gun fire raked him and Nall. Bullets tore away part of his wingman's elevator; McCampbell took hits to his tail and wing. They were lucky not to get it worse.

Seeing that Nall's battered Hellcat couldn't stay with him, the air group commander dropped back and tailed his wingman, scissoring in a wide S pattern across his wake. When the two Zekes tried another run on Nall, McCampbell turned out and shot one of them down, leaving the other pilot to split-S down and out, heading for Orote. Instructing Nall to return to the carrier, McCampbell set out in pursuit. Catching up to the Zeke and giving it a burst, he watched as it executed a slow barrel roll so aerodynamically perfect that he never had to adjust his point of aim. He gave it another burst and the plane fell away toward the airfield, trailing smoke. At that point, McCampbell cashed in his chips, heading for the rendezvous area designated for lone aircraft.

While waiting for another pilot to join up, McCampbell spotted two parachutes on the water, drifting like great jellyfish near Cabras Island. As two cruiser floatplanes were descending to land and rescue the crews, McCampbell saw several Zekes making firing passes on them. Joining up with two other pilots from Fighting Fifteen, Lieutenant Commander George Duncan and his wingman, Ensign Wendell Twelves, he winged over to save the rescuers. After an initial high-side run on the Zekes, a sharp, turning dogfight developed in which Duncan and Twelves shot down five planes, the last one catching fire before it went in, skipping across the water, leaving behind a trail of flames.

As the enemy dispersed, the *Essex* pilots, joined by another from the

Enterprise, formed up and returned to their carriers. Looking around as they flew east, McCampbell counted seventeen fires or oil slicks on the water within a mile of Guam's Apra Harbor. He was back aboard ship by five thirty, without the loss of a single pilot. The squadron's claims that morning totaled thirteen Zekes and two Vals, plus six probables—a healthy return, but soon to fade amid a tragic loss that occurred on their last sortie of June 19.

McCampbell was circling to land on the *Essex* when the commander of Fighting Fifteen, Charlie Brewer, outbound with another group of Hellcats, called the ship. *"Is this all the planes I get for this flight?"* he asked. Brewer had six in addition to himself. Their mission, late in the day, was to take one last slash at the stream of aircraft Ozawa was ferrying in to Orote Field.

McCampbell keyed his mike and replied, *"Charlie, there's lots of Japs over Guam, so when you go in, you'd better go in high and fast and stay that way."*

Brewer's sweep had no sooner begun to orbit over Guam when one of his pilots, Lieutenant John R. Strane, tallyhoed a lone aircraft approaching from the west as if to land. Brewer's men were hungry to match McCampbell's mark. Leaving four Hellcats high, under James Rigg, to cover them, three of Brewer's Hellcats jumped the Judy torpedo bomber and destroyed it. Almost immediately, a flight of Zekes—a big one, four divisions of four—were diving on the Americans from astern.

McCampbell had always urged caution—*Treat the enemy as if he is as skilled as you*—and was always scrupulous about keeping a few pilots high until the absence of enemy could be confirmed. According to McCampbell, Rigg's quartet had not maintained a proper covering position; their formation was "slightly strung out," the action report would state. So Brewer and his wingman, Ensign Thomas Tarr, and the other duo, Lieutenant Edward W. Overton and his wingman, Ensign Glenn Mellon, turned to meet the attack head-on. Each of the pilots had more than he could handle. Four Zekes took each of the F6Fs.

Brewer, climbing to meet them, fired on the leader, who continued his dive, crashing in flames on the ground. Tarr claimed another one, and his victim hit zero airspeed, zero altitude in much the same way. From this point on, the U.S. pilots were fighting for their lives.

When he was finished with his firing pass, Overton found he had been hit. His belly tank was on fire. Having passed through the first division of

Zekes, he released the burning steel teardrop and lined up on the leader of the following element, flaming him. Then Overton began taking hits in his port wing. As it briefly flared up, he realized his wingman, Mellon, was gone. Zekes were everywhere now. Overton could see planes catching fire and crashing, and he did his part amid the whirlwind, pouring a long deflection shot into a Zeke tailing another Hellcat, causing the enemy plane to roll over and hit the water. He won a head-on bout with a Zeke, firing until it smoked and dived away below him. Another enemy plane appeared and he stitched its fuselage and it flashed by. By the time Mellon rejoined him, the odds had seemed to improve. The Japanese pilots were attacking singly and none too effectively. Then suddenly they were gone. There were no Zekes in the sky, and none visible on the runway below. Had they gone to another airdrome? This battle was over.

Overton tried to raise Brewer to inquire about a rendezvous, but the skipper did not respond. Eventually two Hellcats joined up with Overton. At length he spotted another section of four. Their radios were out, but they joined up, too. Circling the area in search of survivors, he found no signs of life, no telltale stains of green dye on the sea marking the location of a downed pilot in the water. As the sun set and an overcast gathered, he decided to quit the search. It was getting too dark to see. He turned east to return to the *Essex,* where he landed an hour before dusk.

No one ever saw Charlie Brewer or his wingman, Tarr, again. One pilot from the squadron reported seeing an unidentified plane—it could have been Brewer—pull up as if to wing over or loop, then shudder and fall off. But since a definite identification was impossible, the skipper and Lieutenant Tarr were listed as missing in action.

Brewer's fate was topic number one when Rigg returned to the *Essex* after landing on the *Enterprise,* his Hellcat full of holes. McCampbell questioned Rigg sharply about the loss of the two pilots, becoming angry when the VF-15 exec had no answers. "He was supposed to stay up high and protect Charlie Brewer and his wingman," McCampbell would say, "and Charlie told him he was going down on this plane. He must have had to go down quite a ways, and Jimmy Rigg never knew what happened to him. His main job was to offer protection for him in that case, and yet he didn't know what happened."

Wondering about the fate of Brewer, whom he considered his best Hellcat pilot, McCampbell recalled an earlier mission during which, after a long diving run, his windscreen had fogged from the drastic change in air temperature and pressure. McCampbell thought it possible that Brewer, in the tunnel vision of pursuit, his forward view blocked by condensed fog, had flown straight into the water.

The bitter tonic of the day's last flight did not diminish the triumph that was June 19. American pilots would soon boast of their victory as a "turkey shoot." Also to be known as the Battle of the Philippine Sea, it would be among the naval aviation community's finest hours. McCampbell's Fighting Aces had won bragging rights on the biggest day of all. Fighting Fifteen's claims of 68.5 kills and 12.5 probables topped the illustrious company of Task Force 58. Six pilots from the squadron claimed four or more planes. McCampbell led the field with seven destroyed and a probable. In the *Lexington*'s Fighting Sixteen, Alex Vraciu claimed six kills and his fellows scored forty more, plus five probables. This pushed VF-16's aerial combat record to 134 kills, tops in the Navy at the time. Vraciu, with eighteen victories, was now the leading Navy ace. When Vraciu reported his six kills to Commander Buie, the skipper said, "Congratulations. You're grounded for running off on your own." Vraciu was crestfallen. He felt he had done the best he could without a working supercharger. But after Buie spoke to the fighter direction officer who had guided Vraciu and his faltering plane to a secondary intercept, the commander appeared in Vraciu's stateroom bearing a bottle of good whiskey as a gift.

The task force's antiaircraft gunners combined to make a triple ace that day, with sixteen aircraft destroyed. The work of the ships was by no means equal. The gunners in the *Washington,* riding on the northern arc of the disposition, got few clear lines of sight, firing just once, a twelve-second flurry of twenty-seven five-inch shells. The *South Dakota* simply shredded the air: 859 five-inch shells, nearly ten thousand 40 mm shells, and more than eleven thousand 20 mm shells. The *Alabama* and *Indiana* added four hundred five-inchers apiece. A handful of the *Indiana*'s 4,654 40 mm shells were fired at a torpedo plane astern. More than a few of them curved into the graceful form of the cruiser *San Francisco,* wounding two. "Regrettable, but could not be avoided," was the cold verdict of the battleship's captain. "An enemy plane was making an attack on this ship, and it was essential that it be taken under fire. . . . All planes that actually approached this ship in a position to attack were destroyed," he claimed. The *Indiana* in turn had five of her crew wounded by other ships' gunfire. The extent of the blizzard of fire thrown skyward was suggested by the air-burst fragments covering the *Hudson*'s decks from stem to stern. The destroyer also took a direct hit on the bridge from a five-inch shell, killing two and wounding six. In the *Indianapolis,* steaming with the *Bunker Hill* group fifteen miles from the major action, Spruance and his staff had seen the attack on Lee's battleship group as a distant spectacle, dying planes painting black streaks across sapphire skies. Just four pilots got through to menace the fleet flagship. The *Indy* managed to shoot down a Jill. "His torpedo went one way, he another, and one of his wings another," Carl Moore exulted. "You should have heard the cheers."

The victory of June 19 encouraged U.S. naval commanders to a new boldness in their planning. With enemy air forces resoundingly walloped, Kelly Turner could stand for another day to rely on the little jeep carriers for fighter cover and close support. And Mitscher believed he had earned the license he coveted to roam west and destroy Ozawa's carriers. He recalled his Avengers, Dauntlesses, and Helldivers from their long day of orbiting in safety in the east. When they landed, their pilots were sent below to catch up on their rest. Everyone knew they faced a decisive day of battle in the morning.

Early that night, on Admiral's Harrill's request, Spruance detached the *Essex* task group to refuel. They would remain behind in the Marianas to rendezvous with the fleet oilers, then cover Saipan and hit Guam and Rota while Mitscher took his other three groups west in pursuit of Ozawa. The Fifth Fleet commander sent Mitscher his long-coveted dispatch: "DESIRE TO ATTACK ENEMY TOMORROW IF WE KNOW HIS POSITION WITH SUFFICIENT AC-CURACY." Spruance figured that if the Mariner flying boats located Ozawa, there would be no need to use carrier planes for searches. The carriers could save their air groups for strike missions, steaming west in pursuit as far as air operations would permit. Around this same time the *Indianapolis* intercepted an encoded radio dispatch. It was from the Japanese carrier *Zuikaku,* apparently relaying a brief message from the captain of the *Shokaku.* "You could sense that it was being handled as a pretty hot potato and had the highest priority used in Japanese naval traffic," Spruance's language officer, Gil Slonim, wrote. "We were unable to read the message. However, we realized that it carried extreme urgency." Slonim considered the dispatch evidence that the *Shokaku* had been attacked and perhaps damaged. Shortly after nine P.M., Spruance and Mitscher received a message from ComSubPac verifying that supposition and more. The *Cavalla's* torpedo attack on a carrier had apparently been successful.

Vectored by radar, trained to a sharp edge, and available in abundant numbers, the submarines had been brilliant in support of the carrier task force. Shortly after ten, Mitscher changed course west and accelerated to twenty-three knots. He didn't know how long Spruance would allow him to chase. As far as he was concerned, it was a matter of now or probably never. The Japanese carriers had fired their bolt. After dark and through the following day, the First Mobile Fleet would be the hunted.

17

To Build a Better Airfield

As aerial combat defaced the skies to his southwest, General Saito found himself in a nearly impossible position. The commander of Japanese Army forces on Saipan had no wired communications with his units on the island, and they had none with one another. And he had no line of supply. His soldiers would live off their cave stores, then off the land. The American beachhead, meanwhile, was swelling with supplies and reinforcements. He had no air forces to parry the constant air attacks or blunt the naval bombardment. And the craggy, tangled terrain was as difficult for his men as it was for the Americans, freezing them in place even as it provided them with stout natural fortifications. The island's single most commanding feature, Mount Tapotchau, was like a towering hub in the wheel of his disparate garrison, both a fortress and an obstacle to his ability to maneuver.

Faced with an aggressive advance by two Marine divisions fortified by two U.S. Army regiments, Saito was forced on June 19 to relocate his headquarters for a second time. On the day before the landings, he had fled the schoolhouse at Charan Kanoa in favor of a hillside cave about five hundred yards northwest of a promontory known as Hill 500. He had watched the landings from there, until the U.S. advance uprooted him once again. The day of the air battle, he established his third headquarters on a ridgeline overlooking Chacha Village in Saipan's east, in a natural cave in a pit protected by huge slabs of rock. The ample stores of food there, and proximity to his largest force of reserves, marshaled near the village, recommended it.

Howlin' Mad Smith meant to keep Saito dancing. In the afternoon he urged Kelly Turner to land the third and last regiment of the 27th Division. Schmidt's Fourth Marine Division had made fast progress across the island's southern plain, reaching the coast of Magicienne Bay and swinging north on June 19. The rough terrain made it hard to keep his lines closed as the regiment moved forward. Though tanks were on hand, platoons and companies, isolated in many draws and ravines where armor could not go, had to shoot their way through.

John Chapin's platoon from K Company, Third Battalion, 24th Marines, was not alone in taking severe casualties along the way. Slogging forward to tie in his flank with the neighboring 23rd Marines, the lieutenant led his men past an American tank, disabled and burned out with a dead Marine lying beside it. As his men dug foxholes along a narrow-gauge railway running toward the bay, he set up a command post in a farmhouse, emplacing his machine guns with fields of fire commanding the tracks. Only a few yards away, he noticed a monstrous projectile lying on the ground, a dud, a big one from a battleship—a sixteen-incher, he figured. *Suppose a Jap throws a grenade and sets that thing off?* he wondered, but it was an idle thought and he was fast asleep before he finished puzzling it out. Sheet tin was in short supply for shelter from the nightly rain, leaving men to sleep only in sprints. Chapin had sensed that the brass hats at headquarters had no idea what life was really like on the front. Over the radio, their impatient inquiries regarding the battalion's rate of advance, its objectives, and its boundaries with other units suggested how poorly his leadership understood the divergence between the portrait of a map and reality in the field.

Chapin was surprised to find a colonel on the line, studying the terrain of the long draw just east of Mount Tapotchau known as Death Valley and making plans to support the 23rd Regiment's assault on it the following day. He was a leader of proven pedigree, Evans Carlson, of South Pacific Marine Raiders fame. "His presence there and his study of the ground were in marked contrast to the absence of the high brass on other occasions," Chapin would write. Headquarters could never know in advance what improvisions would be necessary in the moment. Holland Smith had not planned for his men to use oxcarts to haul ordnance, but when human energies flagged, terrain loomed at angles, and vehicles broke down, native livestock filled the bill. "Saipan possessed large numbers of these powerful, heavy brutes," wrote Lieutenant Frederic Stott of the 1/24, "and by nightfall the platoon owned a train of half a dozen two-wheeled carts with the necessary oxen. The sight of the platoon advancing with this primitive baggage train was reminiscent of many an old-time battle painting—minus the camp followers. Improvised whips and cattle calls soon appeared, and a few of the 'experts' even rode their steeds in the attack, as long as all was quiet." The Marines built picketed enclosures to hold the oxen at night, but one night the animals broke loose and, according to Stott, the Marines "awoke to find two of them pawing up the center of a company CP, their horns locked. For the moment it was more fearsome than the Japs, and one man was carted away suffering from distinctive hoofprints."

On the morning of June 20, units of the 25th Marines began passing through Chapin's battalion to take up the offensive. The 24th were ordered to plant their stakes and rest. Their transfer to division reserve status did not impress Japanese snipers, however, whose harrowing enfilade from positions unknown continued unpredictably. But Chapin used the opportunity to rest his weary mind and take in the spectacle of a Marine regiment on the assault. Hill 500, the dominant terrain feature in the area, was just a quarter mile away, and as the 25th Marines stepped off, "The whole panorama was spread out before us," Chapin wrote. Under heavy fire, expertly coordinating their advance with tank support, laying smoke and pouring burning napalm into the cave entrances, and stepladdering main gun rounds up and down the hill, the Marines were able to storm to the top. Once again, as the hill fell, General Saito was on the run.

The relentless pace of the Fourth Marine Division's advance across Saipan was the by-product of the usual hardwired Marine urgency. The sprint to Magicienne Bay paid quick dividends, blocking Japanese reserve forces from the most important strategic asset on the island: Aslito Field. Its triangle of crisscrossing coral runways, and others like it on Tinian and Guam, were the prize of the Marianas. Nimitz's base development plan for Saipan directed the construction of three airfields, to be given to the Army once the island had been secured. The air complex, joined with similar facilities planned for Tinian and Guam once they were taken, would comprise the largest air base in the world. It fell to the Army, not the Marine Corps, to take the airfield, and that was only appropriate, for Army priorities were foremost among the reasons the Americans were there.

The Seabees and the Army's aviation engineers had a herculean task before them. They turned their shoulders to the airfield project with relish, sending the first site survey parties before the area was even clear of Japanese snipers. A Navy technical air intelligence team captured twenty-four intact Zekes and thirty spare engines. The airfield—soon to be rechristened Gardiner Conroy Field after the late commander of the Army regiment that took it—needed just simple bulldozer work in order to handle single-engine planes. Nimitz's plan called for it to be ready for its first Army aircraft by June 20. But the Boeing B-29 Superfortress was its reason for being. The Army general assigned to command the eventual garrison on Saipan, Sanderford Jarman, said, "I knew the primary job was to push the very long-range bomber program as rapidly as possible." The big aircraft needed a robust and expansive habitat. General Jarman had three top priorities: construction of airstrips, docks for unloading, and roads linking the two. "Everything else was secondary," he said.

The first bomber runway was to be 8,500 feet long, surfaced with asphalt. Though initial surveys had indicated Saipan had two feet of topsoil, it turned out to be only a few inches atop hard limestone. Blasting was necessary. Seabees and Army aviation engineers did Draper Kauffman one better, using about five tons of dynamite a day to smooth the mile-and-a-half-long bomber strip while developing quarries to obtain coral and rock fill, which was used to fill sloughs and ravines to a depth of more than twenty feet. During their first ten days ashore, sporadic Japanese air raids from Iwo Jima and other land bases required nighttime blackouts that shut down work. But with thirty-two thousand Army and Marine ground troops fighting to seize the island and twelve thousand Army Air Forces personnel ready to effect its transformation, the rapid pace would resume.

The Army would be responsible for maintaining the ground defense garrison and for operating the resident bomber groups and a fighter command to defend them, as well as for establishing an extensive antiaircraft infrastructure: ten batteries of 90 mm guns, ten more of 40 mm and eighty quad-mount .50-caliber machine guns, and harbor defenses based on 155 mm artillery. The island would be densely planted with air-search radars. Among the associated tasks, water storage was a top priority, supporting five gallons per man per day, as were electric power and refrigeration. The Navy would develop and expand the harbors at Garapan and Magicienne Bay, installing fuel tank farms linked by pipelines to tanker moorings, as well as storage for avgas, motor gas, and diesel. At the beach, pontoon piers would extend the existing facilities for unloading and supply. The Marine Corps would boost the garrison by sending frontline units there for rehabilitation and training.

As the Seabees went to work on the airfield under occasional fire, they were fortunate that their construction effort coincided with the arrival of the first battery of the XXIV Corps Artillery from Oahu. From their firing positions south of Susupe Swamp, they could suppress their Japanese counterparts across much of Saipan and even reach across the strait to hit targets on Tinian, well within range to the south.

By the evening of June 20, the wheeling movement had been completed, leaving both Marine divisions facing north. With Aslito Field in American hands, Mount Tapotchau loomed, a tower of needled coral, jutting lava rock, and limestone crags that multiplied the threat of the Japanese entrenched within.

In Yokosuka Harbor in Tokyo Bay, on board the light cruiser *Oyodo,* flagship of the Combined Fleet, popular opinion among staff ran strongly toward allowing Jisaburo Ozawa to make his own decisions about how to fight the battle in the Marianas. But Admiral Toyoda's chief of staff, Kusaka, feared that a dangerous psychology could overtake a commander in the midst of combat. He envisioned Ozawa wishing to avenge his honor, and that of the fleet, by pressing a hopeless cause against Task Force 58. "It is very difficult for a commander to decide on retreat even when a battle seems decided," Kusaka would write. "He tries to do things that are impossible, swayed by a sense of responsibility."

Kusaka lobbied for Admiral Toyoda to recall Ozawa to fight another day. Kusaka fancied he was relieving a colleague of a burden. "When ordered to retreat by those of higher rank, he can make up his mind to do so with ease," he wrote. But more important than that was the rock-bottom duty of high command to avoid strategic disaster. Kusaka believed that ordering a commander in Ozawa's position to withdraw might ultimately "prevent a reckless man from carrying out a campaign in a daredevil manner."* Combined Fleet headquarters had itself been guilty of overconfidence, holding out lofty hope, for example, that Kakuta's land-based squadrons, predominantly trainees, would show far better against Mitscher's varsity than they did. Headquarters seemed to have been unaware of the poor state of readiness in the First Air Fleet until the evidence came falling down in flames. As Kusaka himself would later observe, "The task force without planes was, as it were, a living corpse."

---

* His words were not likely meant in the particular, for Ozawa was admired and considered to have sound judgment.

PROGRESS ON SAIPAN, *June 16–22*

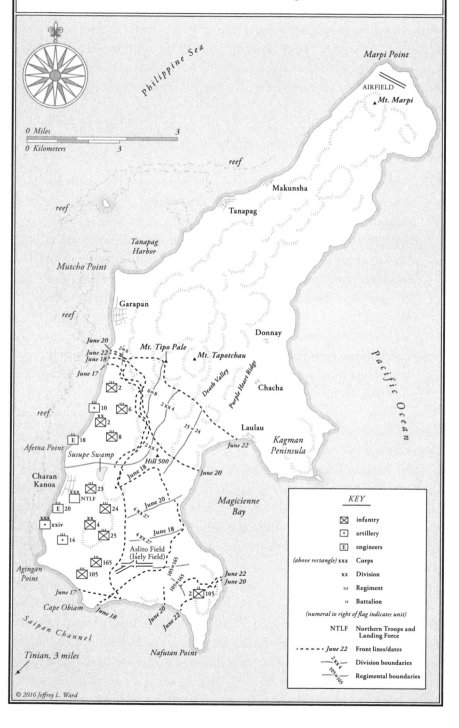

Philippine Sea

Marpi Point

AIRFIELD

▲ *Mt. Marpi*

reef

Makunsha

reef

Tanapag

Tanapag Harbor

Mutcho Point

Garapan

reef

Donnay

Pacific Ocean

June 20
June 22
June 18

2=6

Mt. Tipo Pale

▲ *Mt. Tapotchau*

June 17

⊠ 2

6=8

Death Valley

Purple Heart Ridge

Chacha

⊡ 10   ⊠ 6

2 xx 4

reef

⊠ 2

25 = 24

Laulau

Ⓔ 18   ⊠ 8

2 xx 4

June 22

Afetna Point

Susupe Swamp

Kagman Peninsula

Charan Kanoa

▲ Hill 500

June 18   June 20

⊠ 23

June 22

xxx NTLF

4 xx 27

Magicienne Bay

Ⓔ 20   ⊠ 24   June 20

⊡ xxiv   ⊠ 4   June 18

⊡ 14   ⊠ 25   4 xx 27

Aslito Field (Isely Field)

⊠ 165

105=165

Agingan Point

⊠ 105

June 22
June 20

105=165

June 17

2 ⊠ 105

105=165

Cape Obiam   June 18

June 20   June 22

Saipan Channel

Tinian, 3 miles

Nafutan Point

KEY

⊠	infantry
⊡	artillery
Ⓔ	engineers
(above rectangle) xxx	Corps
xx	Division
ııı	Regiment
ıı	Battalion

(numeral to right of flag indicates unit)

NTLF — Northern Troops and Landing Force

– – June 22 — Front lines/dates

2 xx 4 — Division boundaries

105=165 — Regimental boundaries

0 Miles   3

0 Kilometers   3

© 2016 Jeffrey L. Ward

★ ★ ★

Warrant Officer Saburo Sakai, the ace pilot from the Yokosuka Wing, had gotten news of the catastrophe, and on June 20 he made another attempt to reach Iwo Jima through the barrier of gray weather. "Our officers were desperate," he wrote. "They knew all too well the need for help at Saipan. But what could we do? A mass assault by our fighters would have only a temporary and meaningless effect, for Saipan lay nearly six hundred miles south of Iwo."

Piecemeal night attacks against the American beachhead by Iwo-based twin engine bombers were "only flea bites," Sakai wrote.

> And every night perhaps one or two planes limped back with fuselage and wings holed, the crews desperately tired, their eyes haggard from watching their friends going down, one after the other, even before they were within attack range. The few pilots who returned to the island told us of fighters coming in after them in almost total darkness, and finding their planes unerringly in the gloom, of tracers bursting bright as day when all the guns on the American ships opened up on them. Brilliant explosions, cobwebs of spitting tracers which seemed to be impenetrable walls of fire blocking their path as they swung into their bombing runs. In a few days there were hardly any of the twin-engined Mitsubishi bombers left on the island.

Carrier-based pilots were no better off.

Before sunrise on June 20, his air group reeling from the loss of Commander Brewer, David McCampbell led sixteen Hellcats to Guam. Leaving four planes high to provide cover, he led them south along the west coast, but they found no willing opponents. At first sight of the Hellcats, four Zekes scattered among the cloud forms. McCampbell caught them again on his flight back north and released some pilots to the chase. Lieutenant Bert Morris claimed a probable. After two more circuits over Guam, McCampbell buzzed Rota, strafing a cargo ship, then returned to the *Essex*.

The rousing triumph of the previous day left one nagging question: Where were the enemy carriers? "Through the whole of yesterday's fight, no one ever actually sighted the Japanese ships," a combat correspondent wrote. Through midafternoon, every air-search mission that Mitscher sent west came up empty. After history's biggest naval air battle, doubts persisted whether Gus Widhelm was entitled to collect on his thousand-dollar bet with his pilots, for no one could point to any hard proof that they had waged battle against Japanese naval aviators.

On the twentieth, Ozawa and his surviving carriers flew west with the wind. There was little life or fight left in them now, and with Mitscher and fifteen carriers bent on catching them, they would be fortunate to see a harbor again.

18

Beyond Darkness

At the start of the operation, while stationed in the *Indianapolis* as an observer, Rear Admiral John McCain had said to Raymond Spruance, "Every commander must be a gambler." Spruance considered this and replied, "If this were so, then I am one of the professional variety—I want all the odds I can get stacked in my favor." And so no effort was spared in the search for Ozawa and his elusive carriers. In the darkness after midnight on June 20, fifteen Avengers from the "bat team" on the *Enterprise* were flung skyward to conduct a long-range armed search.

The search planes flew west for a hundred miles, then broke up into seven sections flying five-degree sectors for two hundred miles. "The two fleets had been widely separated at dusk on the nineteenth," Arleigh Burke said, "and we knew the Japanese would try to put as much distance as they could during that night. We knew that if we were not able to strike them the next day, they would have been able to escape us completely. Our planes had to cover a huge area." Mitscher figured the Japanese could reasonably go north toward Japan, or northwest toward Taiwan, or west to the Philippines, or southwest back to the South China Sea. The searchers found nothing.

Early in the morning, a pair of Avengers from the same squadron sighted part of Ozawa's retiring force at an extreme range, three hundred ninety miles, and kept contact for an hour. Strike groups launched from the *Enterprise* and *Hornet* at six A.M. didn't have enough fuel to reach this force. Mitscher's carriers plunged westward, eager to prevent the extreme range from opening up any wider.

The afternoon hunt was taken up by Hellcats, longer-legged than the torpedo bombers. At noon, a dozen F6Fs from the *Lexington* armed with single five-hundred-pound armor-piercing bombs, escorted by eight *San Jacinto* Hellcats, flew north by northwest out to a record-breaking four hundred seventy miles. "We did everything we could possibly think of to extend the range of our air group: making sure everybody knew what the most efficient airspeeds were; the best altitude to fly with the winds that were then prevailing; the most efficient rates of climb; the bomb loads—all the little details," Burke said. They made a twenty-mile down leg and returned empty-handed. "We hoped against hope that the enemy fleet might be so foolish as to remain within striking distance of our carriers after most of their carrier planes had been destroyed," Burke said. "There was a very slight chance that the enemy ships were escorting their damaged carrier which the submarine had hit, at a slow speed back to the Empire. . . . We asked if we could continue the pursuit and we were granted such permission. However, our destroyers were running low on fuel and we had to prepare to fuel them the next morning if it was possible."

At 3:42 in the afternoon, a radio in the *Lexington* came to life with a garbled report from an unknown plane. "Someone had sighted something, but where, or what, or who, could not be determined from the first transmission," Burke said. It was Lieutenant Robert S. "Stu" Nelson of Torpedo Ten. Amplifying reports clarified the picture: The Japanese force was composed of battleships, carriers, cruisers, oilers, and destroyers, disposed in three groups. Two of them were steaming west at twenty knots, and one was limping north at ten knots. The report indicated the carriers had no planes on their decks.

As the turning earth eased the sun ever closer to the horizon, Mitscher faced the dilemma of whether to strike or not. "If the Japanese ships were where we thought they were, our aircraft would barely have enough fuel to make an attack and return to their ships. This would require the utmost conservation of fuel by the pilots and did not allow for any high-speed, high-altitude operations that might be necessary during the actual attack," Burke wrote. Navigation over open water was hazardous enough by daylight. Surviving air-to-air combat over an enemy task force, then returning more than two hundred miles with no fuel to spare in total blackness, was a nightmare for a pilot. Mitscher would not send them lightly, for he regarded the pilots as sons. Should he risk their lives for a chance at a strategic blow?

According to Burke, Spruance had planned to release Lee and his battleships to undertake a nighttime pursuit, aiming to catch Ozawa by morning. But Burke indicated that Spruance finally thought better of it, deciding to keep the entire force tactically concentrated. However, Spruance's ops officer, Captain Emmet P. Forrestel, said it was Lee who declined Spruance's suggestion on the night of June 20. Lee couldn't have caught Ozawa anyway. In the early evening, his battleships were at least three hundred thirty miles from the Japanese force. Even with a ten-knot speed advantage, Lee would have been about a hundred miles behind after an all-night, all-day chase.

It took Mitscher less than ten minutes to make his decision. He alerted his task group commanders, with an information dispatch to Spruance, that the carriers would launch everything they had and that they would recover their planes after dark. "Mitscher warned the pilots to conserve their fuel and also that they would probably return at dusk or in dark, and to be prepared for that situation," Burke said, adding that Mitscher believed this would be "the last time that the Japanese could be brought to grips and that their navy might be destroyed once and for all."

All day long Alex Vraciu had been in and out of the *Lexington*'s ready room, expecting to launch. When news of the sighting came, he and his division had just been released from ready alert. But at once all pilots were rushed back in to begin working up a plan for the late-day strike. "The flight was so long that we had to go half scale on our plotting boards," he said. "We figured our Hellcats would have enough fuel for this mission, but seriously doubted that the bombers would be too pleased. They would be running on fumes on the return." Vraciu had served in the bat team, but few others had night flying training. Air Group Sixteen rushed to the flight deck for a 1624 launch. Within minutes came the order, "Start engines." It took just twelve minutes for the carrier to get her deckload of eleven Hellcats, seven Avengers, and fifteen Dauntlesses aloft, contributing to the total of 226 strikers mustered from the task force. Jocko Clark in the *Hornet* had his flag secretary send a blinker message to his friend Captain Sol Phillips in the cruiser *Oakland*: "TELL TOKYO ROSE TO STAND BY FOR A RAM." Four hundred eleven airmen were on the way to deliver it.

The Hellcats—fast and powerful, in need of less flight deck to get airborne—took off first, reversed course, and climbed toward the low westering sun. It was a running rendezvous. The fighter pilots flew slowly, and twenty miles along the dive-bombers and torpedo planes caught up. Vraciu and his wingman, Ensign Homer W. Brockmeyer, had a hard time staying with the strike planes, which hauled four five-hundred-pound bombs apiece, and the even slower Dauntlesses, which carried single thousand-pounders. The Hellcat pilots had to fly in a weaving S pattern so as not to leave them behind.

Each carrier air group flew subject to one general order: Get the carriers first. As they droned along, other strike groups became visible all around. Shortly after launch came a correction to the sighting report. The original coordinates were one degree off in latitude, meaning the target was sixty miles farther out than initially thought. Hearing this, the skipper of the *Enterprise*'s Bombing Ten, James D. Ramage, felt certain that his entire squadron of Dauntlesses, shorter of range than the others, was on a one-way trip, bound to "take a bath." He kept his fuel mixture lean and cruised as slowly as possible.

The monotony of the flight toward the deepening red horizon broke after about two and a half hours, when the tiny white traces of ship wakes became visible below. This was Ozawa's B Force, whose nucleus, Rear Admiral Takaji Joshima's Second Carrier Squadron, contained the aircraft carriers *Junyo*, *Hiyo*, and *Ryuho*, as well as the battleship *Nagato*. Following the element from the *Yorktown*, the *Belleau Wood*'s Air Group 24 was among the first to arrive. With no air coordinator on hand to assign targets, the pilots were on their own. Flying past his target to the west, Lieutenant (j.g.) George P. Brown turned 180 degrees and led his element to attack with the setting sun behind them, the better to blind any Japanese gunners who might take an interest. As they broke through a cloud layer at a fifty-degree angle, Brown and his two squadronmates, Benjamin C. Tate and Warren R. Omark, set up an "anvil" attack. Straight from the ship killer's playbook, the tactic involved dropping torpedoes against a target from three different head-on bearings, leaving the captain no way to turn that would avoid putting his ship broadside to at least one of the fish. Omark and Tate broke left and Brown went right, widening out to make runs on the *Hiyo* from three different quadrants. These TBFs were the only ones in the task force to be armed with torpedoes, and Brown and company meant to make the most of it.

As he settled on his run against the carrier's port bow, Brown began taking hits. Antiaircraft fire tore away parts of his port wing and punched through his fuselage. When a fire started in his wing fuel tank, the flames swirled up so hot that his radiomen and gunner had to bail out. But Brown stayed with it. The *Hiyo* was turning sharply left when his torpedo fell from his plane just two hundred feet above the water. His two crewmen splashed down in time to watch Brown continue his run, painting a smoke trail with his burning plane over the full length of the enemy carrier until he vanished in the distance. Tate and Omark passed fore and aft, respectively, of the *Nagato* as they closed on the *Hiyo* to starboard. They would credit Brown for diverting her gunners for several critical seconds, allowing them to close the range and drop their torpedoes. Tate broke left, retiring between the *Hiyo* and the battleship, and antiaircraft fire riddled his cockpit. Bullets tore away the top of his control stick, right there in his hands, and jammed his rear turret. Omark broke right, crossing behind Tate, and his turret and tunnel gunners, R. E. Ranes and J. E. Prince, claimed to have had a straight-on view as the foaming oxygen trail of their torpedo touched the carrier, about a hundred fifty feet back of the bow. The underwater explosion rocked the ship and raised gouts of black smoke.

Jig Dog Ramage, flying slowly to spare fuel, arrived with his flight from the *Enterprise* and spotted Ozawa's oilers around 6:45 P.M. Noticing some other U.S. planes preparing to attack them, Ramage broke radio silence to advise his fellow Dauntless pilots not to spend themselves on support vessels when fleet carriers were to be had. He then took the liberty of reaching out to the other air group: *"Unknown Strike Leader from Forty-one Sniper. The carriers are dead ahead. What are you trying to do? Sink their merchant marine?"* Miles to the north, Ramage saw black smoke standing in the sky at his altitude. It suggested quite a fracas, and in mere minutes a major element of Ozawa's First Mobile Fleet appeared below and ahead, just to starboard of his west-northwesterly line of flight. About twenty miles out, it contained a large carrier of the *Shokaku* class. This was the *Zuikaku,* now Ozawa's flagship, the lone survivor of what had been the First Mobile Fleet's premier carrier squadron. Shorn of the *Shokaku* and *Taiho* by submarine attack, the A Force was the northernmost of his three carrier groups now. With attacks underway, all ships were turning in evasive action.

As Ramage skirted a towering cumulus cloud to his left, a greater spectacle greeted him. It was Ozawa's B Force. With a fine view of the enemy below, surveying the rich landscape of targets at sixteen thousand feet, Ramage chose this group as his target. He fingered his mike.

"Forty-one Sniper to all bombers. The first division will dive on the largest CV. The other sections will dive on the small jobs unless the big one is still not hit. Out." Actually, two ships in this group rated as "big ones." The *Junyo* and *Hiyo* were sisters, and the *Ryuho* was the smallest of the three. Ramage's division and five TBFs led by Lieutenant Van V. Eason targeted the *Ryuho.* Ramage ordered his exec, Lieutenant Louis L. Bangs, to take six Dauntlesses and attack the *Hiyo.* But soon Bangs sighted the *Junyo,* and he

decided to divide his flight into two sections. He took two other pilots and prepared to attack the *Hiyo,* while the other trio split off to attack the *Junyo*.

Flying with Ramage's section, Lieutenant (j.g.) Don "Hound Dog" Lewis began working through his checklist as he prepared to line up on the *Ryuho*. He switched between fuel tanks to maintain the weight balance of his plane. He noted the direction of the wind. He checked his bomb release, then flipped on his gun switches and reflector sight. "I was scared. I couldn't really believe this was happening to me. I went over my checkoff list again, closed my formation. In a few minutes, I could see them. Yes, even as I thought this, I could make out several black forms ahead way below and partly concealed by some clouds. They were already starting to maneuver. Some were going in circles, others were zigzagging. Their formation was well spread out, just the opposite battle procedure from our task force."

Many pilots saw that their fuel was below half a tank when they arrived over their targets. They knew they had no time or avgas to waste. They chose their targets quickly and dived to the attack. Helldivers from the *Yorktown* and *Hornet* hit the *Zuikaku* and set her on fire. Avengers from the *Enterprise* piled in and attacked *Ryuho,* grazing her with near misses. After the Hellcat squadron from the Fighting Ten pushed over the strafe ahead of them (their flight leader, Commander William R. "Killer" Kane, had been shot down by U.S. ships the day of the Saipan landings), Ramage led his element into a pushover, and in seconds they were diving nearly vertically. His Dauntless gained airspeed until, at ten thousand feet, he pulled his split flaps open. A pair of large perforated wing flaps (also known as dive brakes), these spread open, one up, one down, and served to hold the aircraft's speed within a performance envelope that made control of the plane possible. Ramage heard his rear gunner, David J. Cawley, call out Zekes overhead, and then his twin thirties chattered. The timing of the braking effect happened to throw off the aim of a Zeke that was making a run on him. An enemy fighter shot beneath him, narrowly missing a collision. But Ramage's attention was all forward, complete tunnel vision, as his reflector sight framed his target.

Keeping his plane trimmed as it fell through five thousand feet, Ramage checked his aim by firing his two cowling-mounted .50-caliber machine guns at the *Ryuho*. As the tracers disappeared into the carrier's forward elevator, he adjusted for the wind and the movement of his target, moved the pipper to just ahead of the carrier, and released. Ramage and the two pilots who followed him seemed to miss. The fourth pilot in his stack,

Schaal, claimed a hit on the port side. It wasn't fifteen seconds before Cawley was yelling into his mike, "Skipper, look back. She's burning from asshole to appetite!" More likely he was looking at the other carrier, the *Hiyo,* because Lieutenant Bangs's section did not miss.

Diving down on the *Hiyo* behind Bangs, Don Lewis saw a plane smoking profusely to port and hoped it wasn't a friendly. "I heard Japs talking on our radio frequency. They were counting, then more talk. They were excited. Who wasn't?" An American voice issued a tallyho: *"Enemy aircraft, four o'clock, angels five."*

Lewis could hardly stand the way time stood still.

> Never had a dive taken so long. The wind was from my left. I was overshooting. I corkscrewed toward the left and then back again. It helped. The carrier below looked big, tremendous, almost make-believe. I had a moment of real joy. I had often dreamed of something like this. Then I was horrified with myself. What a spot to be in. I must be crazy. I was straight up and down now in my dive. I was right in the middle of all those white puffs, and for the first time I could see where they were coming from. From each side of the carrier below seemed to be a mass of flashing red dots. It had been turning slowly to port. It stopped, and I noticed a larger red flash, which was a bomb hit on the side and well forward, but unmistakably a hit.
>
> I figured it must have been scored by "Banger," as we called Lou Bangs. The carrier below had stopped moving. Who could ask for more? I thanked whoever it was who laid on the last one, as it had stopped the carrier right up and down in my sights.

Lieutenant Bangs would claim a hit on the carrier's stern. The bomb exploded among some aircraft that were spotted there, and many of them tumbled, shattered, into the water. Lieutenant Cecil R. Mester followed him to similar effect, laying a bomb on the fantail. In their wake came Don Lewis. As he poured down through three thousand feet, he tried to hold his aiming point to the right in order to compensate for wind. It seemed to Lewis that the carrier had stopped moving, as perhaps it might have after taking two hits aft, perhaps damaging her screws. "It was completely enveloped in a sort of smoke haze," he wrote. "It was hard to stay in my dive this long. Under some conditions, a person can live a lifetime in a few seconds. It was time. I couldn't go any lower. Now!"

As his thousand-pounder fell free, Lewis pulled out and felt the Gs take hold of him. His eyes watered and his ears hurt. He looked back toward his target and was disappointed that the volume of smoke and flame wasn't greater. He had hoped a carrier, with all the fuel and ordnance it carried, would be a more visually rewarding target. Then he realized his semi-armor-piercing bomb would have penetrated belowdecks, where its explosion would not show spectacularly. In fact, it hit close to the *Hiyo*'s island superstructure, and upon exploding killed a great many people stationed there. Lewis closed his dive flaps and accelerated to 280 knots, pulling out to the southeast and retiring low on the water at a thousand feet. "I couldn't seem to go fast enough." His target would be reported "dead in the water, down at the stern, and listing to starboard."

Forewarned by scout planes of the incoming strike, Ozawa's carriers, their air groups eviscerated, managed to scramble about forty Zekes and Nakajima A6M3 Hamps to challenge the Americans. They were on station at high altitude to defend their carriers, and by all accounts they did so aggressively and skillfully. The Avenger pilots from the *Lexington,* led by Lieutenant Norman A. Sterrie, targeted the same group as well. Following in the second section of three planes, Warren McLellan was processing some radio chatter reporting enemy fighters nearby when suddenly tracers swarmed him, whipping tight and flashing all around. One of them had McLellan dead to rights from below and behind. Some of the bullets penetrated his center main gas tank, and its self-sealing rubber liner failed to hold. Within seconds his cockpit was awash in flames, bathing the pilot in smoke and hydraulic fluid. McLellan pulled back on the stick to evade, but there was no saving his TBF. Though his gloves and flight suit protected him from the flames, the heat in the cockpit quickly became unbearable. As his two aircrewmen were preparing to bail out, he wriggled up out of his seat to stand, leaned out of the cockpit as far as possible, planted his feet on the instrument panel, and launched himself into the void. Eleven thousand feet above the Japanese carrier group, McLellan fell free. Elapsed time since the first bullets had hit him: about ten seconds.

Eager to avoid the brutish ordeal of enemy pilots spraying bullets at him and his chute, he stayed in free fall down to a few thousand feet before pulling his rip cord ring. As silk billowed above him, he was transfixed by the sight of a Japanese carrier on fire. He thought he had seen his bombs strike. Below him, in the water, there was a large splash. He figured it must be his plane. As it rocked in the swells, taking on water, a Zeke dived down and strafed it. Swinging slowly down, carried by the breeze, McLellan and his two crewmen alighted in the water. Events were so dizzying that the pilot neglected to prepare for a water landing until the swells rose up and met him. Working fast, he took off his parachute harness before hitting, but he couldn't find the buckle that fastened the small life raft to his chute, and as the chute was becoming waterlogged and beginning to sink, he had to let it go. It carried his life raft under with it. He was left to float on the swells—close enough to the Japanese task force to be able to witness the action.

The heavy cumulus made it hard for the shepherds to stay with their sheep. Vraciu and Brockmeyer descended below the clouds in order to keep the dive-bombers in view. Their first indication that enemy fighters were offering battle was the sight of a TBF Avenger burning and its crew piling out. This was probably McLellan and company. Then all of a sudden Zekes were all around them—"good pilots who knew what they were doing," Vraciu said. The rest of his squadron, seven Hellcats on high cover, had no idea of the dogfight developing beneath the clouds. The two pilots were quickly fighting for their own lives, without help, able to do nothing for the attack planes they were there to escort. Vraciu and Brockmeyer were forced to do what F6F jockeys in 1944 seldom did except by rare necessity: employ that 1942-vintage survival drill known as the Thach Weave. Vraciu was turning back from the extremity of one of his wide, counter-turning S-weaves when he noticed that his wingman hadn't swung back past him as he should have. Vraciu quickly saw why. A Zeke hugged Brockmeyer's tail, peppering his Hellcat. Vraciu winged over sharply, closed with the enemy fighter, and burned it. Over the radio he heard Brockmeyer say faintly, "I'm hit." His plane, streaming smoke, lost altitude and kept losing it until it crashed on the sea. He must have been too badly wounded to bail out. Vraciu knew then that he would be a fool to continue fighting. He dived out, pouring on speed low on the water to escape the enemy gaggle.

As several dozen Zekes pressed their attacks, Tom Bronn and the rest of Lieutenant Sterrie's flight closed ranks to allow their turret and stinger gunners to bear. The stinger, a .30-caliber gun available to the radioman in the lower fuselage of the TBF, covered a forty-degree firing arc below and to the rear. "Things were popping and cracking pretty good for a while," Bronn wrote in his action report. The fighters continued attacking until the shipboard antiaircraft fire forced them to break off. All the pilots had faced enemy AA before, but these barrages had a new twist. "Instead of the usual ugly grayish black bursts when the shells reached their intended altitude, we were seeing bursts in very vivid colors encompassing every color of the rainbow," Bronn said. The colored smoke used for optical spotting "looked more like a Fourth of July fireworks display than enemy fire."

Carrying four five-hundred-pound bombs, the *Lexington* Avengers started their glide-bombing runs as soon as the last Dauntless from their air group pushed over. The sun was still visible on the horizon when Sterrie approached the *Junyo* and the *Hiyo*. "All of the enemy ships were taking evasive action as we dove," Bronn said. "The carrier that we had selected accommodated us very nicely by making a rudder change just prior to our drop. This resulted in the ship being on a relative steady course for a few seconds before it changed direction." He saw one of Sterrie's bombs hit the flight deck and another explode alongside the ship. Gliding down from astern his target, Bronn released his four bombs, continued on for a few seconds in his dive, then leveled out and sped away low. At ten thousand feet, pilots had full daylight even after sunset. But with every foot of altitude they lost, time effectively passed, and quickly. By the time the strike planes finished their runs down low, the sun was below the horizon.

Bombing Sixteen paid for their lack of close fighter escort. After making their attacks, a flight of nine Dauntlesses and three Avengers was heading for the rendezvous point, eight to ten miles east of the enemy task force, to return to their carrier. Flying at low altitude, just a few hundred feet, they passed between a pair of Japanese cruisers who took them under heavy fire. After evasive maneuvering dispersed them, three of the Dauntlesses found themselves alone. Then a flight of eight or more Zekes fell upon them from above and to their left. The Japanese pilots took turns making high-side runs on the American dive-bombers. With the Dauntlesses' rear seat gunners putting up vigorous protective fire, at first the Zekes declined to press their attacks. But the third enemy pilot showed more mettle, closing with a Dauntless flown by Lieutenant (j.g.) J. A. Shields and riddling its cockpit. Shields was seen to shudder and slump over his stick. The gunners in the three planes filled the Zeke with hundreds of rounds as it passed by, but the plane did not burn. The Japanese pilot managed to climb away, but then fell off on one wing and crashed. As Shields's plane nosed over toward the water, his gunner, C. A. LeMay, continued firing wildly in a plane out of control. In the last seconds, he stood up from his gunner's seat as if to bail out, but the plane hit the water at an angle that allowed no survival.

Adrift on the swells, Warren McLellan watched ten Zekes circling in the distance as if prepared to land. He saw a Japanese carrier a mile away, afire from stem to stern, listing so badly he didn't think it could stay afloat.

Only the stricken *Hiyo* fit such a description. She was the worst off of Oza-wa's escaping carriers. Brown's two crewmen, after ejecting, splashed down to a front-row seat on the carrier's demise. They felt her explosions, three of them, deep in their guts. The carrier slipped stern first under the waves, taking the lives of two hundred fifty officers and men. The rest of her crew, about one thousand, survived to be rescued by destroyers.

Some unknown distance away from him, McLellan's turret gunner, John S. Hutchinson, had seen it, too—a carrier listing to starboard, a de-stroyer alongside to take off her crew, then sinking by the bow, her stern out of the water. Another ship to the east burned so furiously he couldn't tell its type. About thirty minutes after dark—sunset fell at 7:38—McLellan saw a massive explosion in the forward half of the ship and a tower of flames hundreds of feet high. His radioman, Selbie Greenhalgh, saw a third carrier steam past him, a big one, in good condition. It was probably the *Zuikaku,* for her crew had gotten the lucky ship's fire under control.

McLellan wasn't sure how long he could float. Without a life raft, the pilot was clinging to a survival pack that grew heavier by the moment. About eight hours along, once it was fully soaked through, he realized it was useful only as ballast. Removing his .38-caliber pistol and a Very flare gun, he surrendered the pack and everything else in it to the depths of the Marianas abyss.

His Mae West was only half inflated, leaving him up to his chin in water. He couldn't see far, but he could see this. He would call it "my only hope of getting out of this mess." It was coming right at him: a Japanese cruiser. "I was trying to decide which way to swim to get out of its way when it turned and went to one side." It passed so close that he could see the white and brownish-olive-drab color of the crew's uniforms, even in the near dark-ness. The excitement was short-lived. The Japanese ships, at speed, quickly cleared the area. The quiet was broken only by the underwater explosions that continued to concuss his abdomen as the dead *Hiyo* passed into the deep.

Alex Vraciu felt he had failed McLellan—him and every other bomber pilot and aircrew that got wet for lack of fighter cover. Five dive-bombers, in addition to McLellan's TBF, were shot down. "It was a botched-up hop as far as our fighters were concerned," Vraciu would say. Though there were twice as many Hellcats as Japanese fighters in the area, fewer than half of the F6Fs on high cover ever managed to engage. Many of them dived against ships, strafing ahead of the bombers. Still, twenty-six Zekes and Hamps would end up being claimed as kills, with tail gunners claiming four of these. But a far greater price remained to be paid for Mitscher's decision to launch late in the day. The pilots, many with wounds, all of them exhausted and low on fuel, still had to fly more than two hundred miles home, in the dark, over open ocean.

On course toward the rendezvous area, Alex Vraciu joined up on a damaged Avenger. He wasn't sure what carrier he was from, but as he pulled alongside he noted a little numeral 3 on the tail. The Avenger's running lights were flickering, suggesting its electrical system was failing, and the weapons bay doors were stuck open and dragging. The pilot seemed in fine spirits. He traced a question mark with his finger, the standard query about fuel, and Vraciu nodded, indicating he was good. He had learned long ago to conserve fuel where possible. When his skin wasn't at risk from enemy bullets, he fed his powerful Pratt & Whitney R-2800 like a miser. It was a habit of years. He had gotten used to running on a lean mixture himself. The other pilot signaled that he didn't think he had enough in his tanks to get back. The sun's last light was just about gone.

Other planes appeared nearby now, all pushing east on lean mixtures, low on the water. As Avenger number 3 turned as if to join up with them, Vraciu heard voices on the radio. "I've got only twenty-five gallons of fuel left. I've got to ditch." . . . "I've got thirty-five myself, but I might as well go down with you." He could do nothing for them except to fix his position, return safely to the *Lexington*, and perhaps testify to what he had seen. There was safety and survival in numbers. He left them to their fortune. "It was dark by that time and I gave them all a heartfelt salute."

Clear of hostile skies, Tom Bronn reached the rendezvous area, where he found Lieutenant Sterrie circling at a thousand feet. He joined up with him and three other planes, and the quintet headed out on the easterly course that Sterrie had plotted while waiting for the others. Shortly after starting east, Bronn noticed his oil pressure was low and alerted Sterrie to the problem. Bronn's radioman, Linson, heard the message, but with the intercom out, he had no way of talking to his pilot. He crawled forward to the center cockpit and handed Bronn a written message saying, "If you want us to bail out blink the arm-master switch three times, or twice to get set for a water landing." All possibilities were on the table.

Vraciu was alone now. Far from his wartime home, he found himself dehydrated and thirsty. In the darkness, he thought about the bubbling fountain in the *Lexington*'s ready room. Anything to distract him from what he was hearing on the radio. "Some of the guys were breaking down sobbing on the air. It was a dark and blank ocean out there. I could empathize with them. But it got so bad that I had to turn my radio off for a while."

Jig Dog Ramage was harder of heart. He was disgusted with "the most miserable case of radio and air discipline imaginable. It would have been all right if people with genuine emergencies sounded off, but it seemed like many just transmitted in panic." He had no illusions in this perilous moment. Life or death would be a matter of discipline and focus.

"Fatigue is a peculiar thing," Arleigh Burke would say. "There are very few people who suffer from combat fatigue who realize its importance. They will try harder, they will try to do more, and the harder they work, the more tired they get and the less they can do. So they bend all their efforts until pretty soon they just plain don't give a damn. They'll land in the sea. They'll wash themselves out. They'll risk their men and not understand why. They're just so tired they can't think clearly. This happens to high commands, too, and all the way down to the lowest and newest seaman." For the returning pilots, fatigue was as dangerous an enemy as a Zeke at six o'clock.

Following his section's successful torpedo attack on the *Hiyo,* Lieutenant Tate narrowly survived attacks by a pair of Zekes, then took refuge in the clouds. Continuing east and finally breaking into the clear, he joined up on a TBF that was badly shot up, its entire underside blackened by fire. The pilot was George Brown. He was badly wounded and bleeding. Tate tried to get him to follow, but the pilot was losing altitude and having trouble holding course. With the survival envelope narrow and dwindling, Tate couldn't afford to stay with him. He had to leave Brown behind. Sometime later, Lieutenant Omark also encountered Brown. He led him for a while, but since the wounded pilot had no lights and was flying erratically, Omark lost him while tunneling through a cloud.

In the *Lexington,* suspense gripped Mitscher as he waited for the strike to return. Around seven P.M., reports began reaching the flagship that, correlated and totaled, suggested that four Japanese carriers had been hit. "Mitscher sat on his windy bridge rubbing his chin from time to time," a correspondent wrote. "Between seven and seven thirty he smoked three cigarettes, taking them carefully from his leather case and lighting each with a wooden match, cupped under the box, on the first attempt."

To improve the odds of the pilots finding their roosts, Mitscher had dispersed his three task groups more widely than usual. Expanding the task force's radius would make it an easier target for the fliers and allow carrier captains more sea room to maneuver during aircraft recovery. Winds were variable, and captains would struggle to hold course into the breeze. Tired pilots did not need their landing circles to intersect. Mitscher was about to do something else as well. He would enact an important rescue protocol—so important that he had not told his pilots about it in advance. The less they knew about it, the better he thought it would work.

Lieutenant Sterrie picked up the *Lexington*'s homing signal about sixty miles out. The so-called YE-ZB beacons broadcast letter codes to different pie slices around the compass, indicating a pilot's position relative to his carrier. Alex Vraciu did, too, a steady and strong letter A, confirming an easterly homeward bearing. It was around 8:30 P.M. when Vraciu saw the lights.

Beams bright and white stabbed the sky ahead. He thought, *My God, I'm heading for Yap.* He thought it had to be the enemy base. "I kept thinking about all these revolting things the bomber pilots used to say, that fighter pilots couldn't navigate. I thought, *Well, it's coming home to roost now.*" He knew aircraft carriers kept strict blackout conditions at night so as to avoid detection. It could only be the enemy base.

Mitscher had started the fireworks show as soon as the first returning plane appeared on the radar. He passed the order over the TBS radio to his chief of staff, relaying it in a manner that would ring in the history of naval aviation: *"Bald Eagle, this is Blue Jacket himself. Turn on the lights."*

Not some of the lights. All of the lights. Running lights, truck lights, and glow lights tracing carrier flight decks. Star shells on parachutes fired by five-inch guns of the screen, flashlights brandished by crew on deck, and twenty-four-inch carbon arc searchlights pointed straight up to touch the stars. Grateful for the reprieve from nighttime blackout discipline, nervous sailors and officers lit cigarettes. No one's sense of reprieve was greater than Vraciu's. When the fighter pilot heard, *"Land at nearest base. Land at nearest base,"* he realized he might not have blundered into enemy territory after all.

It would become a matter of dispute whether the order to turn on the lights was inspired by circumstances or was planned. Some claimed Mitscher made a desperate decision spurred by the emergency. Others would say that this was a legend, that illumination was standard operating procedure for night recovery. Arleigh Burke considered it a surprise.

Regardless, the plan's blinding reality hit the returning pilots as a shock, and then as a gift from heaven. That was why Mitscher had said nothing about it in advance. Picturing his pilots in extremis, low on fuel, exhausted, perhaps gravely wounded, he had wanted them to navigate home as best they could, using all the focus and precision of attention that comes from a belief that one's own calculations are a matter of life and death. "Their desperation to pull that trick would engage all their effort, conscious and otherwise, to bring them close," Arleigh Burke said. Then the light show would guide them the rest of the way in.

Some destroyers laid their searchlights flat over the sea to illuminate the surface so that pilots could ditch more safely. They were relieved to find that the swells were calm. "We stood open-mouthed on the deck for a moment at the sheer audacity of asking the Japs to come and get us, then a spontaneous cheer went up. To hell with the Japs around us. Let them come in if they dare! Japs or no Japs, the Navy was taking care of its own; our pilots were not expendable!" Robert Winston, commander of the *Cabot*'s Air Group 31, would write.

"The planes were instructed to land on any carrier where they found themselves, and the carriers were instructed to accept any planes," Barber said. Landing signal officers waved in the first few planes as quickly as they could, swinging their fluorescent batons, but it didn't take long before the volume overwhelmed them. Pilots crowded all available landing circles. As the LSOs began to wave pilots off, forcing them to circle around it, the affair became something of a free-for-all. Some pilots struggled to distinguish searchlight beams terminating in carrier flight decks from equally bright beacons offered by destroyers and cruisers.

Vraciu recognized the unique, broad-based island superstructure of the old *Enterprise* as she steamed alongside his new *Lexington*. With fuel to spare, the experienced night flier decided to orbit a few times. *Let the pilots who are short on fuel get aboard first,* he thought.

As he led five Avengers into the *Lexington*'s pattern, Lieutenant Sterrie found himself dodging other pilots who were cutting into the landing circle. One of them was Omark from the *Belleau Wood*. His tail hook snagged a wire on the task force flagship, and it pulled his TBM to a stop. The plane handlers swarmed him, detaching the cable and muscling his plane forward, soon to find that he had but a single gallon of gasoline left in his tank.

Sterrie climbed back up to a thousand feet to avoid the traffic. The change of altitude consumed the final sips of fuel for one of his pilots. Lieutenant Buzz Thomas had to ditch. Sterrie was better off. Dropping to five hundred feet again, he located the *Lexington,* entered the pattern, and landed.

Lady Lex's flight deck was closed by the time Tom Bronn returned. Fuel gauge sitting on empty, he made two more passes, hoping the fouled

deck would clear. He wasn't sure he had enough left to find another carrier. If he had to make a water landing, he might as well do it with power
to spare. He toggled the armament master switch twice, causing a light to
blink that signaled a water landing to his crew. His gunner, Banazak, took
off his parachute harness and unlocked the escape hatch. Linson climbed
into the middle cockpit.

> Up ahead and to my port I saw one of our TF Destroyers. By now,
> I had the flaps down. The landing gear remained in the up posi-
> tion. I made my last change of direction toward the destroyer,
> blinking my running lights with the hope of attracting someone's
> attention, and allowed the plane to settle slowly down toward the
> water. The reflection from the exhaust flames from the engine be-
> came brighter and brighter against the water as we came closer to
> the surface of the water. The plane hit and crashed to a stop with
> water spraying up over the cockpit and the wings of the plane. For
> a moment it seemed like the plane would go right up on its nose,
> but then it settled back and actually floated for a matter of sec-
> onds.

Bronn and Linson climbed onto the starboard wing, and Banazak climbed
out to port. They removed a hatch in the fuselage and pulled out their life
raft.

> Our next task was to inflate the raft and board it hopefully before
> the plane fell out below us. There was no moon and at the mo-
> ment no artificial source of light. It was dark! Unfortunately we
> inflated the life raft upside down and had no time to do anything
> about it then as the plane sank away from us. We were holding on
> to the raft and decided we would be better off to inflate our life
> jackets that we each were wearing. This solved the problem of
> staying above the water for the moment. I had a flashlight that
> was attached to my life jacket. I started waving the light as high
> above the water as I could reach and blew the whistle as loud and
> long as I could. We were in the water only a few minutes when we
> heard a voice from the destroyer call out, "Hold on! We'll be right
> back."
>
> I think that it was about at this point that the energy level of all
> three of us had reached the empty point on our own gauges.

> We had been in the water about twenty minutes when we saw a second ship approaching. We could see search lights from the deck of the ship playing out over the ocean in all directions.
>
> We started the flashlight and the whistle routine again with a few shouts mixed in. Finally the lights honed in on us. I can tell you that at that point there were three very wet but happy flyers. The ship turned out to be the light cruiser, USS *Reno*. It put a whale boat over the side and came out and picked us up and took us aboard.

By the time the crowd in the air had thinned out to his satisfaction, Vraciu found his fuel gauge in dangerous territory. He entered the landing circle and fixed his eyes on the glowing paddles of the landing signal officer. Pilots were indoctrinated to obey those paddles without question. When the LSO gave the signal, Vraciu cut his power instantly, on faith, allowing his plane to drop to the deck, tail hook catching one of the arrester cables that stretched across the flight deck. After his plane stopped, the flight deck crew detached the cable and he taxied to park beyond the woven net of cabling that protected planes parked farther forward. Meanwhile, the LSO was busy waving in the next plane.

The first six aircraft to approach the *Lexington* touched down safely, but the seventh, a Helldiver from the *Hornet,* came in too high and got a wave-off. "Because he was wounded, out of gas and dead tired, the pilot ignored it and cut his motor a moment later than he should have," a *Life* magazine correspondent wrote. "The plane consequently missed the cables. It was instead stopped by parked planes at the bow. Riding into one of these, its propeller killed a rear seat gunner, who a few seconds before had felt himself safe at last from the most hazardous flight he had ever undertaken. Searchlights were turned on the wreck from the bridge. Within ten minutes another corpse, that of a deck hand, had been pulled out of the wreckage." This tragic mishap accounted for the wave-off Brown received, and the next one, too. He gave up and decided to find another carrier.

On the *Bunker Hill,* another Helldiver missed the wires and crashed into the barrier, coming to rest nose down, pilot and crew, natives of the *Hornet,* uninjured. As a flight deck crew scrambled to pull them out, a TBF from the *Cabot* lost control on landing, crashing into the Helldiver and flipping onto its back, killing three and injuring four more. On the *Enterprise,* two planes narrowly escaped disaster when they tried to land simultaneously. One plane caught the second cable and the other the fifth, nearly a miracle.

Lieutenant George Brown's, with the *Hiyo* to his name, was among the seventy-nine planes lost for "operational reasons." Most of these planes went down from fuel exhaustion, either ditching in the sea or crashing on their flight decks. Their number fairly dwarfed the seventeen planes lost to enemy fire during the attacks. A total of 177 pilots and aircrew were as yet missing.

At about 11:30, two and half hours after the first planes appeared as winking green and red lights in the night sky, aircraft recovery was complete. Mitscher asked Spruance for permission to turn west and trace the path of the returning planes, looking for castaways. Spruance promptly approved. Task Force 58 shaped a course westward through the night and into the next day, following the path of the returning fliers.

But Warren McLellan and his crew remained a dramatic special case, adrift three hundred miles from home, in the vicinity of the enemy fleet. The pilot had become separated from the other two men, and as he continued survival-floating throughout the long night, he didn't know whether they were alive. About every three hours, hoping to be seen by friendly forces, McLellan fired flares from the Very pistol he had saved as well as a few rounds from his .38-caliber pistol. He blew his whistle and flashed a pocket light intermittently. At one point during the night, his hand touched a fish. "Not a huge one but big enough to scare me," he said. He was more worried about the saltwater making him sick, and the effects of dehydration as his tongue swelled.

"I needed a miracle. I began to realize that I would not leave a legacy to this world. I had not accomplished much in life—twenty-two years old, no family of my own and none in sight." Back home, what they were calling the Great Marianas Turkey Shoot had already made the papers. When his mother told his father about it, his father said, "I know it, for I dreamed about it last night." McLellan said he could feel them praying for him that night, back home in Fort Smith, Arkansas.

The next morning, June 21, the castaway heard the muscular drone of single-engine Grummans. It was his own squadron, VT-16, coming to find him. McLellan popped a dye marker, and they must have seen it. One of the planes made a low-level pass, dropping an inflatable raft. McLellan crawled in, covered himself with a sail that was stowed in the boat, and went to sleep.

It was midafternoon, twenty-two hours along, when he was awakened by a Hellcat roaring by on a low-level run. Shortly behind it came a Navy flying boat, which landed and picked him up. After he got back to the task force, he was taken to see Admiral Mitscher. "When I told him what I had seen he thanked me and said, 'I believe we sank two carriers.' And I thanked him for caring enough about downed aviators to send rescue planes over three hundred miles to get five people out of the water. Two crewmen from another torpedo plane and me and my crew were rescued. That night we lost about forty-two men."

"Pilots were picked up right and left, until our personnel losses were only a small fraction of what we had feared the night before," wrote Robert Winston. "This decision resulted in the rescue of fifty-nine of the pilots and air crewmen who had hit the Japs so hard and who would otherwise have been lost." The Navy would finally put the recovery rate at 77 percent: 143 of 177 missing men, including four of the eleven survivors who were shot down near the enemy fleet.

Tom Bronn made his reunion on the *Lexington* by transfer from the *Reno* to a destroyer, and then by breeches buoy back to the carrier. He found Lieutenant Sterrie on the hangar deck and asked him about their losses. Sterrie smiled and said that Warren McLellan and his crew had been picked up, hale and healthy, and that the rest of their division had made safe water landings around the task group or on other carriers.

Searching for a place to land, Jig Dog Ramage had found his home ship, the *Enterprise,* but her flight deck was closed. He and his squadronmates had been forced to find other flight decks, too. The *Wasp* took five, the *Bunker Hill* another, and when Ramage at last found a clear flight deck and landed, he was whisked belowdecks and learned he was a guest on the *Yorktown.* On board that ship he found some familiar faces, including Hound Dog Lewis. There, as elsewhere, there were no celebrations. The men of the *Yorktown*'s air group were despondent, in fact. "They lost a lot of their aircraft, and it was quite an unhappy situation," Ramage would write. His own squadron had lost but a single plane. It belonged to Lieutenant Bangs, who had ditched near the task force, earning a cut on his forehead that would need six stitches from a doctor on a destroyer. The commander of the *Enterprise*'s fighter squadron, Killer Kane, crash-landed as well, to be fished out by a cruiser's floatplane the following day.

Ramage was assigned a bunk in a compartment belonging to two pilots who were still missing. He was picking at a late-night plate in the *York-town*'s wardroom when an old friend, Captain John Crommelin, a legendary naval aviator, visited him, exuberant. "Looks like you guys got them pretty good today!" Ramage wasn't sure. "Captain, I think these reports you're getting are very exaggerated. I think we got two carriers out there." Ramage told him what his rear gunner had seen: one carrier burning and one apparently sinking. "That was all that I could personally vouch for, and I really hadn't seen that." Crommelin said there were reports of more sinkings. Ramage said he doubted it. Briefing the task group commander, Rear Admiral J. W. Reeves, Ramage said he suspected the claims were optimistic. He had various complaints in the moment. In time, he would see the larger truth. After the two days of almost constant action, Japanese naval aviation was no more. Admiral Ozawa had just thirty-five carrier aircraft left to him, according to Nimitz's estimates. Ninety-seven U.S. planes did not return from the mission.

The manner of the U.S. victory in the Battle of the Philippine Sea resounded in ways that could not be measured by aircraft counts. As Robert Winston of the *Cabot* air group would attest, "I doubt if any other high command in any other nation would have risked what ours did in order to save their pilots. All of our pilots realized this, and it has done much for pilot morale. This is one reason why our pilots don't hesitate to tackle much larger enemy formations at any time, because they know that the high command will spare no effort to see that they are picked up."

It took some time for the task force to reconstitute itself, as destroyers returned to station from search and rescue duty. On the twenty-first, a morning air strike against Ozawa was canceled when scout planes discovered the range was too great. Spruance had detached the *Indianapolis* from the *Lexington* task group and joined Admiral Lee and his battleships. Spruance wanted his surface combatants in position to sink any cripples that might be left behind. And as at Truk, he was evidently keen to participate firsthand. When air searches turned up negative, he concluded there were no cripples to be had. And with the Japanese undoubtedly not eager for a fleet action, he ordered the battleships and carrier task groups to retire and refuel in the vicinity of the Marianas. On the morning of June 22, the *Lexington* made visual contact with Harrill's *Essex* task group, approaching in the company of the fleet oilers. Dave McCampbell and his boys covered the returning carriers as they refueled, conducted burials at sea, and transferred personnel who had been rescued the previous day and night.

At Spruance's direction, the *Indianapolis* joined the *Essex* task group as it continued air operations off Saipan. To their northwest, the *Lexington* and company took station with Lee, ready to make an impressive nuisance of themselves against anything looking to interfere with Holland Smith's men from land, sea, or air. The campaign ashore would not be short. It would need naval support for the long haul. And so Jocko Clark went north with the *Hornet* and company to hit Iwo Jima again. The *Bunker Hill* group, meanwhile, got underway for Eniwetok to reprovision, refuel, re-bomb, and replace lost aircraft.

Spruance's conduct of the great two-day air battle stirred predictable controversy in high places. His detractors were irate that six enemy aircraft carriers had been allowed to escape. Some of them—not likely more than casually appreciative of the progress the Marines were making on Saipan and the strategic value of the workmanlike fleet that supported them—bent the ear of Admiral Nimitz and demanded Spruance's relief. But the Fifth Fleet commander had no regrets, and Nimitz didn't, either. With a major assist from Lockwood's subs, Task Force 58 had rendered the Combined Fleet's carrier force nearly as powerless as it would have been at the bottom of the ocean in pieces, while ensuring that Kelly Turner's amphibious force was protected. With the apparent destruction of three Japanese carriers and 476 aircraft for the cost of 130 planes from Task Force 58 and not a single ship, Spruance knew that the Battle of the Philippine Sea was a decisive win in support of an important strategic objective. Spruance always knew where his duty lay.

As the *Indianapolis* stopped her engines off Saipan on the afternoon of June 23, her anchor taking hold inside the hundred-fathom line, he went to see Turner to discuss progress ashore. Later that night the fleet flagship weighed anchor and fell in with the battleship *Colorado* and a pair of destroyers, on call again for fire-support duty as Holland Smith's men pushed inland from the previous week's contested shore.

19

Smith versus Smith

The return of major elements of Task Force 58 to the waters around Saipan was a victory parade without ticker tape. The arrival of cruisers and battleships to the daily host offshore allowed the normal menagerie of auxiliary and service vessels to return to the roadstead as well, powerfully covered as they were now against the threat of air attack. Holland Smith exulted in the knowledge that the threat of abandonment by the fleet was gone. It was a matter of morale as much as anything else.

While the fleet was away, his men had done some fast, bloody work, cutting the island in half at its midsection and isolating the valuable southern plain with its invaluable capital asset, Aslito Field. Save for a pocket of holdouts desperately hiding within the natural ramparts of Nafutan Point, the southern part of the island was under American control. The nine battalions of the three regiments of the Fourth Marine Division, with a fine view of Magicienne Bay, were preparing to push up the island's east coast. The bulk of the Second Marine Division, meanwhile, held south of Garapan.

Mount Tapotchau remained the anchor of the Japanese defense of Saipan. With its many nooks and crannies of limestone, tree roots, and coral, it promised to be among the most daunting objectives of the campaign.

On the morning of the twenty-first, Smith issued an attack order that would put the Fourth Division on the O-5 line by the end of the day on June 22. It was an ambitious plan, requiring elements of all three divisions to advance with a unified front. The O-5 line was anchored in the east by the coastal village of Laulau, on Magicienne Bay's northern shore, and traced an arc north and west that encompassed Mount Tapotchau and terminated on the west coast about a thousand yards south of the outskirts of Garapan. The Fourth Division advance, broad, fast, and sweeping, would be covered by flanking fires from the Second Division until the loom of Mount Tapotchau got in their way. By that time, the 27th Division, having secured the airfield, would have advanced far enough north to join them for the northward push, sandwiched between the two Marine divisions.

A natural chauvinist for the Corps, Holland Smith considered doing business with the Army as the cost of serving as a corps commander. Ever since the November 1943 Gilberts campaign, he had disdained the 27th's leadership, culture, and fighting spirit. At Makin, one of its regiments, the 165th Infantry, was slowed to a crawl by an enemy garrison of fewer than three hundred men. After Colonel Gardiner Conroy, the namesake of Saipan's southern airfield, was shot and killed by a Japanese sniper on D Day, his body was left where it had fallen for two days. "To me this callous disregard of a soldier's common duty to his commanding officer was an ominous commentary on the morale of the regiment," Smith wrote.

On Saipan, it was all coming to a head. The commanding general of the 27th Infantry Division, Major General Ralph Smith, felt his men had plenty of work left to do in the south before piling into the northward push. After four of his battalions had driven the Japanese from the airfield, the enemy melted into the crags around Nafutan, where they prepared their last stand. Facing counterattacks even in daylight, the division found its progress slowed by sporadic rifle fire and ambushes. He wanted to leave behind at least two battalions to mop up Japanese resistance in Nafutan Point, and his chief of staff called Holland Smith's headquarters to say as much. That evening, Ralph Smith asked permission to leave an entire regiment—three battalions—at Nafutan. Holland Smith agreed to leave two battalions in the south, but because he did not specify the regiment from which they were to come, and gave his Army division no written orders that night, Ralph Smith seemed to take it to mean that he had personal discretion over the matter. He proceeded to designate not two battalions but the entire 105th Regiment for the job at Nafutan, ordering its commander to begin the assault against the holdouts not later than eleven A.M. on June 22.

After the mission kicked off, Ralph Smith and several of his staff drove to the front areas of the two Marine divisions, then proceeded to visit Holland Smith at his command post. After a staff conference, the two general officers met in person. Holland Smith expressed disappointment with the progress at Nafutan, saying he had been told that an officer on Ralph

PROGRESS ON SAIPAN, *June 23–July 9*

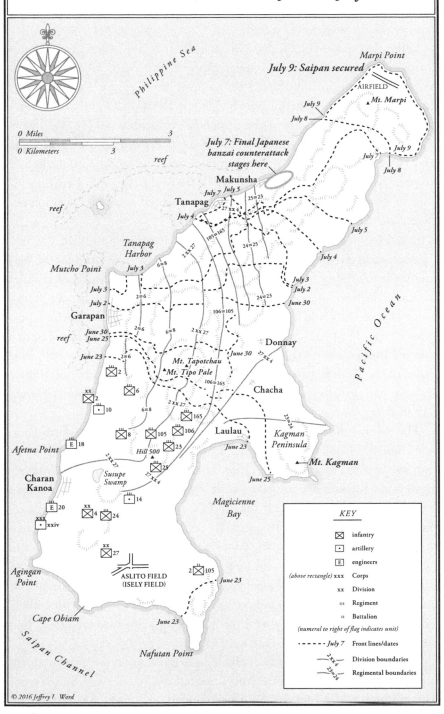

Philippine Sea

Marpi Point

July 9: Saipan secured

AIRFIELD

▲ Mt. Marpi

July 9

July 8

July 7: Final Japanese
banzai counterattack
stages here

July 9

July 7

July 8

0 Miles 3

0 Kilometers 3

reef

Makunsha

July 7 July 5

reef

Tanapag

25=23

July 5

July 4

27 XX 4

105=165

24=25

July 4

Mutcho Point

Tanapag
Harbor

July 3

6=8

2 XX 27

Mt. Tipo Pale

July 3

July 3

July 2

July 2

June 30

Garapan

2=6

106=105

24=23

June 30

June 25

reef

2=6

6=8

2 XX 27

Donnay

June 23

2=6

June 30

27 XX 4

⊠2

⊠6

Mt. Tapotchau

106=165

Chacha

XX

⊠2

∙10

6=8

⊠165

2 XX 27

⊠8

⊠105

⊠106

Laulau

Kagman
Peninsula

Afetna Point

E 18

⊠23

June 23

23=24

Hill 500

⊠25

▲ Mt. Kagman

Charan
Kanoa

Susupe
Swamp

23=24

June 25

⊠14

Magicienne
Bay

E 20

XX
⊠4

⊠24

Agingan
Point

XXX
∙xxiv

XX
⊠27

ASLITO FIELD
(ISELY FIELD)

2⊠105

June 23

Cape Obiam

June 23

Saipan Channel

Nafutan Point

Pacific Ocean

KEY		
⊠		infantry
∙		artillery
E		engineers
(above rectangle) xxx		Corps
xx		Division
⑊		Regiment
⑊		Battalion
(numeral to right of flag indicates unit)		
- - -		July 7 Front lines/dates
2 XX 4		Division boundaries
23=24		Regimental boundaries

© 2016 Jeffrey L. Ward

Smith's staff had suggested they simply starve out the Japanese rather than go in after them. Ralph Smith assured him that he would encourage a more aggressive attitude. To all who were in attendance, the meeting seemed routine. Voices were never raised.

Later that afternoon, Ralph Smith called on the Fifth Amphibious Corps chief of staff, Brigadier General Graves B. Erskine. At a large wall map, Erskine pointed out how well the push into Kagman Pensinula was going but indicated that the weary Fourth Division might need Army help. Ralph Smith noted that the peninsula's breadth would make it hard for his two available regiments to cover their sector. Erskine agreed. He told Smith that the entire 105th Regiment, less one battalion detached to mop up Nafutan, should join the corps' offensive. Erskine and Smith concurred, stipulating that the Army formation would take up a position between the two Marine divisions on the front.

Ralph Smith remained concerned with the situation in the south, where the six hundred men of his 2/105 would have to cover the front facing Nafutan. One battalion could generally cover six hundred yards of combat frontage; the front at Nafutan was about three thousand yards long. Ralph Smith warned Holland Smith on the afternoon of June 23 that airfield personnel might be at risk, because a single battalion would be hard pressed to prevent infiltration. Such exposure would be most untimely as the vanguard of the 318th Fighter Group, twenty-two P-47D Thunderbolt fighter aircraft, had just staged in to Aslito Field from the escort carriers *Manila Bay* and *Natoma Bay* to begin operations.

The Army pilots were a boisterous group, traveling with a nonregulation supply of Canadian Club hidden in their gunny sacks. Stuck aboard ship for three additional days because Japanese holdouts were still freelancing around the airfield, the pilots were finally confronted by the *Natoma Bay*'s captain, who said that if they didn't stow their whiskey and square themselves away they would spend the rest of the war in his brig. When they bade the Navy farewell, the last pilot catapulting off the ship forgot to release his brake. His P-47 went screeching down the flight deck, leaving a stinking trail of burned rubber before he got airborne. Within hours, at Gardiner Conroy Field, ground crews were fastening rockets to the undersides of their wings and they were hitting artillery positions on Tinian that were in range to threaten Saipan's airfield.

That night, a Japanese assault all along 27th Division lines in the north inflicted six hundred casualties and knocked out fourteen of Smith's sixteen medium tanks. Holland Smith responded by sending Major General

Sanderford Jarman, who had been tapped to command the Army garrison after the end of combat operations on Saipan, to appeal to Ralph Smith "as one Army man to another, on the ground that the reputation of the Army was suffering through his lack of offensive spirit." Numbers were elusive, but to date the landing forces had reported nearly 7,300 casualties, more than eighty percent of which were Marines. Army forces were only now seeing the worst of the fighting. The two Marine divisions had taken more than 6,100 casualties, as against 320 for the newly integrated Army division. In a letter to Carl Moore dated May 13, 1945, Spruance wrote, "I doubt if the Army's slow, methodical method of fighting really saves any lives in the long run. It merely spreads the casualties over a longer period. The longer period greatly increases the Navy casualties, when Jap air attacks on ships are a continuing factor. However, I do not believe the Army is at all allergic to losses of naval ships and personnel."

Holland Smith's opinion of the Army was at ebb tide. Having seen them struggle to tie in with the Marine regiments in the eastern shadow of Mount Tapotchau and fail to clean out Nafutan Point, he doubted their competence across the board. His operations officer, Colonel Robert E. Hogaboom, detailed their inadequacy right down to the platoon and company level: "Any objective examination is bound to conclude that that outfit did not function effectively. . . . They fired at everything and anything. They fired all night long. There was not a sign of a Jap anywhere in sight. It was a total lack of fire discipline, a total lack of anything like professional military conduct, and apparently General Ralph Smith tolerated it."

Smith actually had no clear idea what the 27th faced as its unluckiest battalion, the 3/106, prepared to assault the single most difficult objective on the island. The sheer cliffs to the west made it impossible for Lieutenant Colonel Harold I. Mizony to keep his companies in contact with the Marine units that were themselves preoccupied with the caves and crags of the mountain. As the unit moved north, its left flank lay exposed to direct observation and fire from Japanese troops ensconced in the caves and interlinking trenchworks of Mount Tapotchau. On his right flank, the series of hilltops known as Purple Heart Ridge was no less daunting. The complex of defensive works had been meant to anchor General Saito's effort to repel an invasion coming ashore on Magicienne Bay. According to a captured Japanese intelligence officer, Saito had been sure, right up until D Day, that landings would take place there on the eastern shore. It was the poor luck of the 3/106 to confront a fortress engineered to repel a division or more. Unbeknownst to Holland Smith's intelligence staff, Saito had ordered a four-thousand-man regiment to make a stand at the north end of the draw. This fireswept area between mountain and ridge would become known as Death Valley.

As mortars, machine guns, field pieces, and Japanese medium tanks turned on the lone Army battalion, so many officers were wounded that L Company's commander, First Lieutenant Charles H. Hallden, was forced to take command of three of the battalion's four rifle companies, at least one of which was so heavily hit that it was rendered combat ineffective. Tank support was scarce, and repeated requests to division artillery to hit the ridges were refused because of the presence of American troops higher up on the mountain. Holland Smith's intelligence officer believed the 27th confronted nothing more than "a few scattered riflemen."

At this time, the 23rd Marines, to the east of Death Valley, on the right flank of the 106th, were turning east to advance into Kagman Peninsula. As the regiment pivoted on the 24th Marines, holding closer to the coast, its left flank moved fast to keep up with the line's rotation. There was no way the Army units in the center, so deeply preoccupied, were going to move forward fast enough to hold the Marine regiment's left flank, not when they were facing counterattack and often confused about their orientation in the rough terrain. West of Chacha Village, a battalion of the 165th Infantry was struggling to handle enemy fire from three different directions. All of this led to confused expectations. To keep the eight-hundred-yard gap on their fast-swinging flank from widening, the 23rd Marines were forced to slow their advance into Kagman Peninsula while their reserve battalion came up to fill the void.

Holland Smith ultimately felt that the 27th's problems were both organic and a matter of faulty leadership. According to Erskine, Ralph Smith had admitted to him before the Marianas campaign, over dinner in Hawaii, "I don't think I am really a combat commander. I've been highly trained for staff work, and that's where I feel my abilities could best be used." There was no disagreement with that at corps headquarters on Saipan. Holland Smith had sent Colonel Hogaboom to visit Nafutan Point. Hogaboom was shocked by the posture of the Army in the south. "I went out and met the regimental commander and he was about three thousand yards behind the front lines. I went up to the battalion headquarters and it was about a thousand yards behind the lines. I finally got up to a company that was actually involved in the attack and met the company commander and he was practically in tears, saying that he had been ordered to withdraw for the night. He had taken a hill and here he was ordered to drop back to some other position for the night. The troops were not being personally led."

On the afternoon of June 23, the assault on the mountain began in earnest. With a reputation for skill in hard tasks, having cleared the hornet's nest at Afetna Point in the first days after the landings, the 2/8 Marines were charged with taking the mountain. That battalion was joined in this project by the First Battalion of the 29th Marines, which operated under command of the Eighth Regiment. The commander of the 1/29, Lieutenant Colonel Rathvon "Tommy" Tompkins, was newly arrived. In the fighting that led to the wounding of his predecessor, his battalion had taken a beating. Bitter firefights around Susupe Swamp had claimed the lives of many, including one Warren G. Harding, a private with Tompkins's unit, who held a machine gun position, alone, to cover his decimated platoon as it tried to reorganize under counterattack. Their head count was down to under fifty percent when the assault began. Sharp, rough, and steep, the terrain was no place for tank or jeeps. It would have to be captured by infantry.

On June 23, Tompkins started up the mountain with the 2/8 on his right. Two routes led toward the crest. He decided to attack through a densely wooded valley, then up the steep southern face, while the 2/8, under Major William Chamberlin, skirted its southern slope, then veered left to assault it from the east. Though they were supported for a time by elements of the Sixth Marines, which held a subsidiary peak about a thousand yards west of the mountain, the 1/29 became bogged down in the woods, halted beyond reach of supporting fire by impassable terrain and enemy troops hidden in coral caves. On the right, the 2/8 moved rapidly to the cliff that marked the eastern terminus of Tapotchau's crescent-shaped peak. Chamberlin ordered one of his platoons to scale the cliff, and it did so without opposition. His success encouraged Tompkins to attempt a breakout, and on his command his companies turned around and marched back to the east, passing through Chamberlin's lines until they, too, faced Mount Tapotchau's summit from the east. As the Japanese launched a series of probes against the U.S. position, sharp firefights pushed them back with perhaps forty casualties, and the Marines just three. As mortars rained along the cliff, the concentration of parabolic fire forced the 2/8 to fall back from its exposed position.

The sun was beginning to set by the time Tompkins's men were ready to climb the mountain. As 81 mm mortars popped smoke rounds on the mountain slopes, and 105 mm howitzers of the Tenth Marines blasted suspected enemy positions, Tompkins's riflemen began the ascent. Skirting a pinnacle east of the mountain, they passed through a saddle, then began climbing the slope toward the summit.

Atop Hill 500 in the Fourth Division area of operations, Lieutenant Fred Stott and the men of A Company, First Battalion, 24th Marines had a panoramic view of Tapotchau's southern slopes. To the east, an expanse of sugarcane stretched into Kagman Peninsula. Scanning this landscape with field glasses, Stott could see little sign of an enemy presence. It had been almost four days since his platoon had seen any sizable number of Japanese. Half in jest, his communications officer wagered that a jeep could drive all the way around the island without taking a nick, but no one had volunteered to take him on. The reality in the field was more forbidding than distant appearances suggested.

Before daylight the XXIV Corps Artillery unleashed itself on a grand scale, preparing the southeastern foothills with rolling blankets of high explosives that left a thick gray haze on the land. Marines preferred the support of field artillery to naval gunfire, which was usually slow to respond to immediate imperatives. Under new restrictions meant to save ammunition, a battalion could request fire twice daily unless there was an emergency, and every request had to go first to Admiral Turner's headquarters, which would assign it to a ship that had enough ammunition on hand to take the job. Sometimes the response took hours. With the arrival of a squadron of "grasshopper" observation planes at Gardiner Conroy Field, a more efficient way of working was at hand. The OY-1 Stinson Sentinels were flying around the clock as of June 21. With artillery spotters embarked, the grasshoppers stayed airborne in shifts throughout the day, keeping a radio link to an air officer attached to Corps Artillery. Soon, artillery barrages as practiced and perfected by "Big Army" were a daily occurrence. Everyone in the rear areas came to appreciate how the 155 mm long tubes bounced them on the floor of their slit trenches, giving far worse to General Saito's men wherever more than a handful dared to gather. The Corps Artillery were stout shoulders upon which ground troops' progress into the hills and ravines of Saipan's midsection would stand.

Though all U.S. troops were having trouble keeping their lines tight in the warrens, valleys, and foothills of the interior island and living with almost constant exposure to attack from the flanks and rear, Holland Smith's low opinion of the 27th Infantry Division persisted. On the morning of

June 24, he sent Ralph Smith a telegram expressing disappointment with the unit's combat performance. The Army general was quick in bringing the heat on Colonel Russell G. Ayres, commander of the 106th Infantry: "Your failure to maintain contact with unit on your left is most embarrassing. Advance on your left at once."

This pressure from division headquarters compelled Lieutenant Colonel Mizony of the 3/106, struggling through Death Valley, to commit one of his companies to a virtually suicidal advance. When he ordered Captain William T. Heminway to push forward beneath Mount Tapotchau's fortified gallery of cliffs, he said, "Bill, I hate to do it, but I've got to send you out there."

Heminway said, "Don't apologize, Hi. I know how it is. So long, Hi. It's damned nice knowing you." Fifteen minutes later, he and seventeen others from K Company were dead.

This pointless sacrifice was too little, too late, for Holland Smith was already on the way to see Kelly Turner. From Blue Beach he boarded a landing craft for the short, bouncy ride to the *Rocky Mount*.

When the two flag officers met, Smith requested the authority to relieve the 27th Division commander, saying he had ignored his orders relating to Nafutan Point and that his delays at the front were jeopardizing the whole operation. Though the Marine leadership underestimated the bitter opposition the 27th confronted in Death Valley, and though Marine units, too, were frequently unable to keep contact at their flanks because of the stark terrain, Turner was sympathetic. He feared Nimitz was impatient with his progress. He didn't want a postponement of the Tinian or Guam landings to indict his own leadership. Turner suggested to Holland Smith that they take their case to Spruance. Smith would call it "one of the most disagreeable tasks I have ever been forced to perform. Personally, I always regarded Ralph Smith as a likable and professionally knowledgeable man. However, there are times in battle when the responsibility of the commander to his country and to his troops requires hard measures. Smith's division was not fighting as it should, and its failure to perform was endangering American lives."

Spruance and his staff met with his two principals in the flag quarters of the *Indianapolis* for an hour or more. According to Carl Moore, Smith told Spruance that General Jarman, the garrison commander designee, was "disgusted" with the 27th Division's performance and said he could make it fight if he were given command. Though the Marine Corps would minimize the challenges faced by the Army on Saipan, there was little appetite within the Fifth Fleet for thorough, charitable adjudication. Carl Moore would say the discussion "bid fair to be rather endless." At the end of it, Spruance asked Moore to draft an order directing Holland Smith to relieve Ralph Smith of command and appointing Jarman in his place. Moore showed it to Holland Smith, Turner, and Spruance, "and they all agreed that that was about what they wanted to say." The Fifth Fleet commander signed the memorandum and had it sent to Admiral Nimitz.

So began a controversy that threatened to hamper the integrity of Nimitz's entire ground command. The Army's resentment over the relief of Ralph Smith would bleed into the U.S. media as war correspondents told the story, aired their views, and received public rebuttals in turn. But the intensity of the furor would seem to vary inversely with its military significance. The relief of division commanders was hardly unknown in war, and Smith's relief did nothing to suppress the heavy fire raining down on the Army's brave troops in Saipan's most lethal firetrap.

From a distance, the Japanese appeared overmatched. The commander of the XXIV Corps Artillery, Brigadier General Arthur M. Harper—one Army officer who would thrive under Holland Smith's leadership— considered the Japanese skill with artillery suspect. Though General Saito's artillery and mortars retained considerable power and asserted it, Harper noted that "it smacked of infantry attachment, sector assignment, a paucity of volume, poor adjustment, and lacked persistence." Above and beyond the technical nits that he picked lay a broader problem: "The Japanese are a dangerous enemy but they are clearly defective in command leadership and not prepared to meet a modern army on a battlefield," he wrote. His assessment, even if correct, was of little comfort to platoon commanders in the field. The energy of a battle was best observed at the front.

Only there could one see how the fighting was coming to a breaking point. At a time when captains and lieutenants were carrying the ball, there was little time to worry about the feelings of generals. From headquarters, it was always hard to discern the activity of units smaller than a battalion, and even then, a War Department study noted, "When the record sums up an action by saying, 'The Third Battalion fought its way forward against heavy resistance for five hundred yards,' only the man who has himself experienced combat is likely to realize what this can involve, and what the phrase conceals."

What it concealed were the travails of Lieutenant Fred Stott, a platoon commander in an understrength company, struggling to hold several hundred yards of rough, uneven, and increasingly wooded terrain near Chacha. His company, like the two others in his exhausted battalion, had only two effective officers. The loss of field-grade officers was constant on Saipan. Even rear areas were not safe from enemy infiltration. And sometimes the predators were completely noncorporeal, merest shadows, pressing their assault through men's imaginations.

Deep behind U.S. lines, in the the area of the XXIV Corps Artillery, a soldier named in reports only as "Private Costanzo" fell asleep in his foxhole well past midnight and paid the price for his proclivity for nightmares and a tendency to walk in his sleep. Startled by night terrors, all at once he was up and running among the gun pits of B Battery. Someone shouted a command to halt, but he did not do so. Three men jumped him and dragged him into a foxhole. Gripping knives, and thinking he was Japanese, they stuck him in the left arm, left chest, and back, penetrating near the heart. Costanzo would survive. But the madness of the incident must have been nearly as disorienting to Constanzo's confused assailants as it was to the man himself. As he was taken to an amtrac on Blue Beach and transferred to a hospital ship, there could have been no doubt that Holland Smith and his staff had little sense of the mounting visceral terror that was overtaking Costanzo's unit and others and the consequences that it might have. Safety was relative and varied by platoon, and so, too, notions of success.

On June 24, once more under pressure in an imperiled headquarters, General Saito was forced to pull up his stakes yet again. With the Fourth Marine Division giving him no rest, he left his well-concealed cave above Chacha Village and relocated higher up on the mountain. His fourth headquarters in less than two weeks was situated in a large cave set in an east-facing sheer white cliff on the east side of a spine that ran north from Tapotchau's peak. He considered it his best-prepared command post yet. But he would not reside there long. Already the Second Marine Division was planning to take the mountain's highest peak.

The 2/8 Marines and the 1/29 Marines began the assault on the peak on June 25. An experimental rocket detachment assigned by division headquarters to support the Eighth Marines proved that the 4.5-inch barrage rocket was a devastating area weapon. The rocket launchers, mounted in trios on two-and-a-half-ton trucks, could let fly a salvo of six in two seconds. They silenced any area they touched. But without roads to make possible their use, the men of the two mountain-bound battalions had to make do with what they could carry.

Lieutenant Colonel Tommy Tompkins, commander of the 1/29, led a team of scout-snipers up the cliff from the south and east and audaciously gained an exposed secondary peak near the summit. The position was both commanding and vulnerable. "We had no place to go and were fully exposed up there," one of the Marines said. Japanese mortars zeroed in quickly on them, and so did the infiltrators. About thirty yards below the ridge a machine gun was chattering, pouring fire on American troops in the valley below. Meanwhile, incoming mortar rounds were hitting just off the ledge. "There had to be casualties in the troops just below the top of the mountain when we were banzaied that first night. I remember hearing a Marine calling out 'My life's blood!' a number of times"—a call-and-response challenge.

Concerned that their flank was not protected, and knowing that Japanese troops were near, Colonel Clarence R. Wallace, commander of the Eighth Marines, ordered Tompkins to come down, but he and his men were determined to hold the peak even if it became their Alamo. Tompkins replied, "If you want me to move off this mountain tonight, send me a herd of mountain goats. We'll drink the milk from them and ride them down the mountain. That's the only way we will get down it tonight."

"It was frustrating as we had no way to communicate," said Mort Hamilton of the 1/29. "We had no radio and could not get on our knees or stand to send semaphore. We had to be content with firing on Japs below us with small arms. All in all, it was a very perilous situation for us." Thinking to set up a supporting position for his .30-06-caliber light machine gun, Hamilton's Browning Automatic Rifle man, Harry Neal, tried to make a sprint to a secondary peak about thirty yards away, but he didn't get far. A bullet struck the BAR man in the shoulder and spun him around, then another round caught him in the other shoulder. "Sharp shooting by some Jap," Hamilton said. "Harry got back to the top, where he was attended to in a small cave."

After nightfall, Tompkins abandoned his bravado and sneaked back to his battalion lines below. The next day he returned under cover of smoke, leading two of his three rifle companies from the 1/29 on a single-file march to the crest, while the third company held in the valley to cover their rear. When Tompkins reached the summit again, climbing over the ridge, he nearly piled on top of Mort Hamilton. He opened his blouse and dumped some grenades on the ground. Hamilton understood the message: "We were there to stay." They dug in, building up a skirt of large rocks to create a stronghold just in time to repel a rush from Japanese soldiers, who came running up from a position beneath them, around the open eastern side of the peak. The assault continued throughout the next day as the enemy machine gun below the ridge, never seen, chattered on. The end came when two squads of Marine demolition men and flamethrower teams moved up and evicted the last Japanese occupants of Saipan's highest peak. After holding fast for about two days at the pinnacle, Tompkins and his men patrolled the ridgeline, securing the high ground for the protection of the troops down in the valley.

Below, stretching nearly three miles to the southeast, Kagman Point was yielding quickly to the Fourth Marine Division. As Schmidt's troops overran long trenches sited so as to enfilade the beach at Magicienne Bay, they were glad they had not landed there. Five-inch dual-purpose naval rifles, heavily greased and wrapped in burlap, lay on skids nearby. Lieutenant Fred Stott, who had taken command of C Company of the 1/24 after its skipper was killed by an artillery round, had been part of the conquering push. He rested, sleeping and stirring awake to stare at a world that he now understood would spin very well whether he happened to live or die.

He was heartened to see a battalion from the 27th Infantry Division trundle by. "Having apparently finished with their assignment on Nafutan Point, seemingly endless lines of dusty 'dogfaces' came trudging up the winding road," he wrote. "Marine 'love,' 'admiration,' and 'respect' for the Army is well known in all the branches of the service, but on that day the appearance of the soldiers brought nothing but thankful smiles to our faces. Combat is a quick leveler of many differences, and whenever we worked directly in conjunction with the Army troops we had no complaint."

His men were served a deluxe meal of "ten in one" rations, supplemented for protein with fresh-killed chickens, ducks, and pigs ("which failed to evade tackling Marines"). They relished the quartermaster's windfall—razor blades, shaving cream, and toothbrushes—as well as a bounty of time to use them. "From the heights at the end of the peninsula we gazed back with contentment on the land we had conquered. It stretched out for many miles, some level, some alternately dipping and rising abruptly. Somehow the map hadn't told us that Saipan was such a large land mass."

On the night of June 26, the company phone rang and Stott and his platoon were ordered to break camp and prepare to get back on the move. In some ways, the rest was anything but therapeutic. For some, it gave the nerves a chance to quake. "It often happens that there is far more apprehension when behind the front than when on it," Stott wrote, "so we were unconsciously relieved when a distant Nambu machine gun opened up without damage and our return was complete." The first patrols uncovered no Japanese nearby. "But several accurate bursts from hidden machine guns confirmed our fears that once again we were seated under an enemy position which possessed superior height and observation; except that machine guns rather than artillery now constituted the major danger, and most of us preferred the machine guns."

Saito's new headquarters was less than a mile from where Lieutenant Stott's platoon rested. From his new location in the cave on the sheer white cliff, Saito would direct, as best he could, a defensive fight that would be unlike anything that American troops had seen during the entire war. The worst of it all lay ahead.

20

Satan's Breath

The surprise assault on Aslito Field began in the deep night of June 26, when Japanese troops trapped at Nafutan Point launched their bid to break out. Pouring through the threadbare lines of the 2/105, the lone battalion on guard to prevent infiltration, they launched themselves against the airfield in the last hours of darkness. As they did so, it wasn't clear whose ox was being gored: Holland Smith's for requiring that a single battalion secure a hot area, or Ralph Smith's for failing to ensure that the unit covered its sector efficiently. Such considerations were academic to airfield ground crews cast in the role of infantry and yelling for reinforcements.

Captain Sasaki, commander of a battalion of the 47th Independent Mixed Brigade, picked five hundred men to lead the attack. They were on their own. Plans to ferry in reinforcements by sea had failed. Eleven barges full of troops from Tinian were preparing to leave Sunharon Harbor, near Tinian Town, after dark, only to be met and dispersed by the destroyer *Bancroft* and the destroyer escort *Elden*. A similar gambit staged from Tanapag had failed that same night, too, courtesy of two LCIs from the alligator navy that prevailed in a firefight against barges armed with 37 mm field guns and even, reportedly, torpedoes.

Sasaki's plan envisioned no survivors. After assaulting the airfield, anyone left walking was to drive north, assemble at Hill 500, his old brigade headquarters, and await instructions. Perhaps he meant them to link up with Saito's main force near Tapotchau. If cornered, his survivors would make a last stand, defending to the end the ground upon which they fell. "Those who cannot participate in combat must commit suicide," Sasaki wrote. The password among his forces that night was *Shichi Sei Hokoku*—

"Seven Lives for One's Country." It was a signal to fight to the end. And with that they set out from Nafutan Point.

Marching in double file, Sasaki's assault force escaped detection by the thinly spread observation posts and fell upon the 2/105's battalion headquarters. The attackers piled in. In a short but fierce fight that cost them twenty-seven of their own before being driven off, four Americans died and twenty more were wounded. The surviving Japanese regrouped and headed toward the airfield, where they stuck bayonets into aircraft fuel tanks to set them alight. One P-47 was burned to a skeleton and several more were damaged.

The Army aviation engineers at Gardiner Conroy Field filled in as first responders, using bulldozers as combat vehicles and brandishing carbines with skill. They were soon joined by artillerymen and Marines from the rear area, who rallied to the threat. The attackers were scattered and killed after claiming their first ground kill against the Army Air Forces. Holland Smith would claim that the Army battalion could have blocked this late-night incursion by advancing just two hundred yards toward the tapering neck of the point, thus reducing by half the frontage it had to defend. But actually the Japanese breakout made easier the grotesque task that lay ahead for U.S. troops: routing the Japanese from Nafutan's coral caves.

The next day, the 2/105 pushed into Nafutan Point to deal with its last holdouts for good. When all was burned out and done, the bodies of about five hundred fifty Japanese troops lay within their zone. Some of the dead had been killed during the earlier fighting; others, in defeat, were obedient to Sasaki's final order.

Some units developed a battle drill that proved effective in neutralizing smaller caves. It employed a squad of fourteen men supported by a flame-throwing tank known as a Satan, a modified M3A1 light tank that mounted a Canadian-made Ronson flame projection system in lieu of a main gun. The squad was divided into three groups of four. One group was a BAR team. Another group carried a pair of bazookas. The third was devoted to protecting the tank. The remaining pair of soldiers was a communications team maintaining radio contact with the tank. The drill went like this: The BAR men moved up from one flank, getting close to the mouth of the cave and setting up a firing position with their M1918 automatic rifles. Covered by their heavy .30-06 fire, the two bazooka teams followed them forward, bounding straight up to the mouth of the cave. The tank and the other four-man team circled to the far side of cave, seeking a position with a clear line of fire into its mouth. While the tank hosed the cave with burning napalm, the bazookas launched their rockets deep into its rear, and the BAR team stood ready to cut down anyone who came running out. Where rough terrain forbade the use of Ronson-equipped tanks, portable flame-throwers, white phosphorus grenades, and demolition charges were used instead. It was a grim task, an ugly trade. Practiced slowly and methodically, it could not be beaten.

"We got a hell of an education on Saipan," said George Charland, a BAR man with the 23rd Marines. "We made ample use of the flame-thrower as that was a weapon that put terror in them." It had been used on Tarawa before, but never on a larger battlefield where the terrain gave the enemy places to go. And so the fire breathers had to improve their mobility, too. Enter the Satan: Squirting thickened gasoline with pressurized carbon dioxide, it was experimental and unperfected. When the spark plugs got fouled, soldiers would ignite the spewing flame oil by the readiest means, including handheld cigarette lighters. Often, troops could only stare as the terrible vehicles went to work. "How many of their lives were saved by fire we'll never know," a Satan driver said. "The super hot flames reached sixty to eighty yards, deep within caves, and lapped over the top and sides of cliffs. If the flames didn't make contact, concealed troops were often asphyxiated. Captain Ed Bollard and Lieutenant Brenden just shook their heads in disbelief over how precious life could become so cheap in this enlightened age."

It was late on the night of the twenty-eighth when Fred Stott and his company made contact with the Second Division, whose leading elements stood atop Saipan's highest mountain. The gap between them had been their worst obstacle, for any Japanese who ventured into it were off-limits from being shot at, owing to the risk of friendly fire. In the tangle of Saipan's central highlands, the logic of a clear aerial view was unavailable to the Marines and soldiers who hung out their lives with every step, taking hills, crossing ravines, picking through cages of tree roots to seal suspicious caves. The pointillistic nightmare of this slow, brutal death struggle was immune to capture in action reports. And often when a target presented itself, there were frustrating reasons that it could not be engaged. "We sat and sat and watched these woods, unable to deliver any effective fire, for every time we requested permission to open up, it was denied on the grounds that the Army was advancing and would soon be occupying that hill. So we sat and watched the Nips flit safely back and forth amongst the trees while our distaste for the terrain grew hourly." Regiment and division could do little to save a company or platoon that found itself in a tactical vise grip. It was entirely academic that day that Major General George W. Griner took command of the 27th Division from Sanderford Jarman. Little had changed. For the men on the line, the only way out was through.

One of Stott's squads, exploring a deep cave, found evidence that it had served as a Japanese command post. They rolled up a half-track and a tank and took it apart with gunfire. Possibly this was General Saito's fourth headquarters, the one situated in the stark white cliffs. He had abandoned it the previous night after suffering badly from its exposure to cruisers and destroyers patrolling off the island's east coast. His next headquarters took shape in a crude cave in a small, jungle-wrapped depression south of Radio Hill.

As the front line pushed north, passing Mount Tapotchau to the east, the island narrowed like a funnel, pushing the Fourth Marine Division up against the unoccupied void of the Army's zone of operations. On the left flank, Lieutenant Chapin's outfit, Company K of the 3/24, found itself facing a wooded ridge that was swarming with Japanese. "They were in the Army's zone, and the doggies hadn't yet come abreast of us to clean them out. (How many times did we run into that situation?) So we kept waiting to get hit by a wave of fire from the ridge. Nothing happened, however, and we eventually turned off the road and met up with an Army outfit."

Pushing west to seal the gap, Chapin's platoon faced two ridges: a big one, their main objective, and a smaller one that was more of a low hill. Chapin heard gunfire on his left. It was his hard-charging partner platoon, under Lieutenant Mike Minnick. They got hit and took some casualties, but in the moment, Chapin had little idea of what was going on. It was all he could do to hold together a single functioning platoon. He had led it ashore fifty strong. Now it was down to twelve men.

Reaching the top of the first, smaller ridge, Chapin stopped and ordered his men to dig foxholes. Suspecting that the open terrain before him invited use by Japanese tanks, he summoned a 37 mm gun from Third Battalion. As his men were painstakingly emplacing it with a favorable field of fire, the order came—"Stand by to move!"—and they pulled up stakes and got rolling again. Cursing his luck, Chapin went to his company CP and learned why they had to move. "After spending all day working their way up abreast of us, the doggies on the company's right flank were withdrawing to their original jumping-off place. This was just dandy. Now we would have a huge gap on our right." He knew the Marine company on his left would not pull back. So his company commander resorted to hex-map gymnastics to cover the potential exposure, stretching as far as possible to the right to maintain contact and prevent infiltration. The 24th Marines, technically in reserve, devoted two whole battalions to protecting their open left flank and yet still never made solid contact with the Army. By nightfall, four battalions from the Fourth Division had been forced to turn west to face the pocket on the flank created when the rest of the division outran the Army. By darkness on June 29, the gap between the right element of the 27th Infantry Division and the 23rd Marines was about four hundred yards. A detachment of engineers came up to help Chapin fill in his sector, and the next morning they were moving again, jumping off to assault the large ridge ahead. The influence of Saipan's terrain was far more important than the identity of any division officer.

Two weeks had passed since Captain Sakae Oba, the commander of the Japanese Army medical aid station in the hills west of Makunsha, went to ground to survive the frightful American onslaught. His thatched-roof operating room had been destroyed, forcing him to shelter his wounded in caves once used for supplies. Four medics and an army doctor, Captain Kenji Ishikawa, divided their time among the caves. Ishikawa was the only other captain in the regiment to have lived through the sinking of their transport off Taiwan back in March, and the only survivor of Oba's twelve original doctors.

By June 30, Oba's aid station was less than four miles from the leading edge of the enemy advance. The Americans owned the mountain and were rumbling up the west coast toward Garapan, too. Robbed of their observation posts in high terrain, the Japanese had no way to monitor the advance and few weapons to strike back at it. Ishikawa complained to Oba, "We're supposed to be a field hospital, but we don't even have enough supplies to keep our wounded alive. None of us has even seen an American, yet we're destroyed as a unit. What kind of a war is this?" It was a war of subsistence combat. They were surviving on water drawn from a cistern near the ruins of a house at the base of the cliff, foul-smelling brine that they purified by boiling.

A soldier scrambled up to the cave entrance where Oba was standing, bowed stiffly, and produced a message from a dispatch case. "Orders from regimental headquarters," he said. Signed by Colonel Eisuke Suzuki, commander of the 135th Regiment, the order directed the medical aid unit to

move out that night and march south to the town of Donnay on Saipan's
east coast. Oba knew that the move would put them on a collision course
with the Americans as they pushed north. He was a veteran of Manchuria
and relished the prospect of battle. *Tonight or tomorrow morning,* Oba
thought, *I will strike my first blow against the American enemy. And if I should
die it will be with a bloodied sword in my hands.* He assembled his men outside the cave at sunset for a briefing with an officer senior to him.

Major Hanai, with his sharp nose and thin face, struck Oba as "an offi-
cious little man." But he had a speech to give, and it was designed to rouse
the majority who shared Oba's state of mind:

> The ungodly enemy has succeeded in getting ashore. But his back
> is to the sea. His weaponry, which has won him a foothold, is no
> match for Japanese courage. Even now, our force, inspired by
> their dedication to our Emperor, are regrouping to drive the for-
> eign devils into the sea. Tonight, we will take part in that honor-
> able battle. We will halt this barbarous attack that is an insult to
> our Imperial forces. Our role will be in coordination with other
> units of the Imperial Army. We will establish our headquarters
> just north of Donnay, then prepare to join our comrades in deal-
> ing a death blow to the American devils.

The group rose to its feet as one: *"Dai Nippon, banzai!"*

Oba and Ishikawa were with the first group of a hundred to move out
east along a cross-island road. They set out at eleven P.M., followed by other
groups at fifteen-minute intervals. About a mile along, Oba's group found
a narrow dirt road running south and took it. The road fringed a spiny
ridge that rose toward Mount Tapotchau, separating the overgrowth-
covered ridge from a cane field on the left. A few miles farther, by the light
of American star shells hanging in the sky, Oba made out movement ahead.
It was a ragged mass of people walking toward him. Women toted their
infants on their backs; soldiers, wounded and blank-faced, trudged along
without weapons. There was no place left for them in this hell. At intervals
American artillery, firing for harassment, crashed into the jungle around
them. Most of it landed in the distance, but twice during the night shells
landed close enough to jar the group with their concussion.

At two A.M., Oba stopped at an east-west road and studied his map with
a flashlight. He saw that if he turned left and headed down the slope, he
would come to Colonel Suzuki's rendezvous area north of Donnay. Ma-

chine gun fire rattled in the middle distance to their south. Proceeding down the slope, he encountered three soldiers who told him that another group, under cheerful Lieutenant Banno, was just ahead, in a canyon about two hundred yards away. Oba joined him and they organized their forces. Then they stepped off the road, posted guards, and settled down for a few hours' sleep. They were up and moving again before first light.

In the limestone ramble to their south, Oba sensed activity. He grabbed the arm of a sergeant named Bito and told him to take his rifle and come with him to investigate. Just a few meters off the road, the tangle was thick enough to slow their movement to labored individual steps. Ahead and to their right, Oba heard a rustle of movement. He and Bito dropped to their stomachs. Pistol in hand, he watched and waited, ready to ambush whoever or whatever came. When soldiers appeared in a clearing just thirty yards away, his finger tensed on the trigger, then relaxed. They were Japanese, a whole platoon. Visible by morning twilight, they crashed through the undergrowth, crossed the dirt road, and disappeared into the cane field to the east. Moments later a cacophony of gunfire erupted in their direction. The *crack-crack* of rifle fire, the heavy percussion of American machine guns, and the thump of mortars preceded the most horrific sight of all: a wash of midnight-black smoke and flames rising above the bush line.

Oba and his comrade withdrew, hopeful that their group would avoid this enemy and their inferno. He had barely had time to settle his nerves when the roar of an aircraft descended from overhead. A floatplane buzzed them close, banked, and disappeared to the south. A few of his men fired on the plane with their rifles, but Oba ordered them to stand down and take refuge in a cave off the ravine. The plane came back a few minutes later, circling at a more respectful altitude.

Within minutes, the first heavy shell rent the air outside the cave, exploding at the north end of the ravine. As the U.S. plane stood off, relaying corrections to a warship offshore, Oba lay, just as Banno did, in a cave nearby, covering his ears to protect against the overpressure. Another salvo landed closer, like a localized earthquake. Its fury was matched by the anger that Oba felt. *This is no way to fight a war. How can we be expected to fight when we can't move a hand or a foot outside the caves? There is no honor in hiding like frightened children.* The next salvo had his number, dialed in with machinist precision by the pilot orbiting on high. A blast and a flash sent red-hot steel whipping at the entrance to his cave. Oba heard someone scream. Able to see nothing, he went into a panic, fearing he had been struck blind. But as the smoke washed away, he realized his eyes still worked. He wriggled toward the screaming and found the source. One of his men had a large piece of shrapnel, hot as a griddle to the touch, stuck in his lower abdomen. He was among dozens who were felled by the power of this distant warship, which risked little from return fire now that the mountain and its hidden artillery pieces had been seized by the enemy. When the bombardment ended, Oba learned that almost half his unit had been killed or badly wounded. Lieutenant Banno and his group got away unharmed, but most of their gear was lost. Captain Oba found his counterpart, Ishikawa, dead among the throng. His last surviving doctor had died trying to drag another man to safety.

It was perhaps a subtle sign of the continuing interservice rivalry that on June 30, Gardiner Conroy Field was renamed in honor of a Navy pilot, Commander Robert H. Isely, the *Lexington*'s late torpedo squadron commander, killed during the initial air strikes on the airdrome. That day Isely Field sent forty P-47s to hit targets on Saipan, Tinian, and Rota, while four dozen Hellcats from the *Essex* and *Enterprise* task groups lent close support to troops. Holland Smith was determined to keep Saito under pressure. He ordered the Second and 27th Divisions to catch up with General Schmidt's fast-moving Fourth Marine Division.

It was to the Marines' chagrin that no pilots from their own service were on hand to support them. As was usual, the men of the Corps felt disregarded or at least poorly understood. But on Saipan, all the ground pounders were. Flying at two hundred knots, few pilots could understand with any useful granularity the subtle geometry of the land rushing beneath their wings. Saipan's rough landscape forced front lines to curve in ways that made it hard for pilots to find safe angles of attack. The response times of pilots were too various to allow proper coordination. An air-ground liaison officer with the 105th Infantry said the average time lag for the missions he requested was more than an hour. Delays were doubly costly when artillery, otherwise very effective, had to stand down when an air strike was coming. The world could change within these critical minutes. There were seldom enough planes "in the net" to assist as quickly as the troops needed, and even then, bombs dropped from low altitude could not be counted upon to do the right thing when slamming into uneven or rough terrain.

The troops had little grasp of a pilot's problems. Once on Saipan, a ground commander requested a group of TBF Avengers to hit a Japanese pillbox in a ravine. "This seems logical," the Pacific Fleet commander of support aircraft, R. F. Whitehead, wrote, "except that an attack in this direction would have been crosswind, up sun, and pullouts made directly into the face of a 1,500-foot mountain. The ground troops could not understand why the group leader insisted on changing the direction of attack." Such diverse frustrations were no doubt behind the fact that during the whole Marianas campaign, only one bomb in three was spent in direct support of ground troops. Pilots preferred to hit targets that could hit them back: enemy airfields and antiaircraft guns. As a result, the swarm of U.S. aircraft over Saipan seldom eased the immediate problems of troops on the ground.

In an ideal world, Lieutenant Chapin would have known in advance how many enemy soldiers confronted him on the large ridge directly to his front. But Death Valley was not a map exercise or a live-fire drill. It kept its secrets from pilots and intelligence analysts. And so when Chapin's quarter-strength platoon was ordered to conduct a reconnaissance, his men were on their own. Almost always, platoons and squads got along on their grit. Chapin launched the probe at seven A.M. sharp on July 1, encouraged by the monotonal syncopation of distant mortar tubes.

The one road on Saipan that could support military traffic was the twenty-foot-wide thoroughfare linking Charan Kanoa to Garapan. But it and others had nearly disappeared under the daily mashing of wheels, treads, and boots, lubricated by rains. Few of them were much better than oxcart trails, and Chapin and his men did not use them as they pushed in loose column up a steep divoted slope. There was an explosion close ahead. One of his squad leaders, Sam Fothergill, let out a cry and fell. A friendly mortar had fallen short. Chapin rushed forward and found his corporal going gray in the face. Though a corpsman managed to stabilize him until the stretcher came, the platoon was down to eleven men now, and Fothergill would not make it home. The eleven-man platoon pushed on.

At the top of the ridge, they found the detritus of a well-established and populous Japanese position: spent cartridges, bags of rice, cans of salmon. On the far side, looking north and west, he gained some perspective. A panoramic view of a valley spread below. *Where is the Army?* Chapin wondered. He sent part of his platoon to secure the rest of the hilltop, then took two BAR men and picked a spot from which to observe and provide covering fire from the commanding position. Looking back upon the wooded stretch of tangle to his southwest, he hoped that units from the 27th Infantry were out there somewhere, hidden in its midst. It would have eased his mind to know his flank was secure. That was when one of his men ran to him to say he had shot a Japanese officer and taken from him some maps showing the enemy's defensive positions. Chapin called for a runner and ordered him to take the maps back to the company command post. As he was returning to the hilltop, another of his men appeared and announced breathlessly, "They shot Sully!"

Chapin rated Sullivan as one of his best sergeants, squad leaders, and teachers. Considerably upset, he assembled a patrol and began working northward through a maze of rocks, trees, and creepers. Several hundred yards along to the north, they found Sully in the company of several Marines. Lifting his shirt, Chapin could see through the dirt a pasty white patch that was bleeding profusely. Sullivan had been shot in the belly. "We were miles from any stretcher and he obviously couldn't walk," Chapin wrote. "The Japs were close by but, as usual, we didn't know where they were. There was only one thing to do: I posted some of my men to keep guard around us and had the others whack off some saplings with their machetes. Then I told a couple of the men to peel off their dungaree jackets. We put the saplings through the sleeves, buttoned up the fronts, and had a crude stretcher on which to evacuate Sully." In the rough terrain, they judged that four men would be needed to get him back to company headquarters. They worked the stretcher under him, and the casualty detail began humping back the way they had come. One bullet, five men gone. For Chapin's platoon, the equation was unsustainable. His unit was far beneath even the strictest definition of "combat ineffective." But completing the mission was his route to survival, and he led the rest of his platoon, just five men now, to search the area.

Amid the tangle, working around ramparts of rocks and roots, he discovered crevices that looked large enough to hold enemy soldiers. Chapin shouted Japanese commands to surrender until he realized that he was merely broadcasting his whereabouts to every enemy soldier within fifty yards. He had just summoned a flamethrower to light up a crevice when, about twenty feet away, an automatic weapon rattled. Chapin shouted to the man on his left, but there was no answer. He hollered for two of his men to throw grenades and called one of his men forward, but as he hunkered down for cover, the fire only seemed to increase. "I began to get very worried. Here we were, completely isolated from the rest of the company, only a half dozen of us left, our left flank man had disappeared, and now we were getting heavy fire from an uncertain number of Japs who were right in our middle and whom we couldn't locate."

When the fire abated, Chapin put on a mask of calm and decided to make a slow withdrawal back to the hilltop, report to his company commander, and call up another platoon to assist. He left a sergeant in charge and descended the hill, locating Lieutenant Schauss's platoon about fifty yards away. He had just reached them when gunfire exploded and grenades began popping again on the hilltop.

With all the noise, Chapin wasn't able to yell orders to his men. So he got low, made himself small, and began running back up the hill, dropping near the top and continuing in a crawl. When he heard an enemy presence about ten yards ahead, he spread all of his grenades on the ground in front of him, crabbed forward a bit farther, sandwiching himself for cover between some rocks, and started tossing them. He was holding a live grenade in his hand, its pin removed, when there was a flash of light between the rocks and he was knocked onto his back. Disoriented, unsure of his wounds, he realized he was still gripping the grenade. He summoned enough strength to heave it toward the enemy, then dragged himself back to cover and called for a corpsman.

A medic found him and bound up the hole in his side, then asked him if he was able to help get himself off the hill. Fearing the enemy might overrun them at any moment, Chapin was willing to try. "They raised me up, and with them supporting me under each arm, we started down the hill. It was a grim descent—every bump seemed to jar me through and through, and sometimes we would stumble over vines and rocks and we worked our way down the steep slope." When they reached Schauss's platoon, Chapin rested while a jeep was called to take him to company headquarters. There he was cheered to find a doctor who had once been his roommate at Camp Pendleton. They cut off his dungarees, made an incision, explored his abdomen, and announced good news. Just by a hair, the bullet had missed everything—kidneys, ribs, lungs. An ambulance came and Chapin was lifted onto a litter. He was loaded aboard with several other casualties and evacuated to Isely Field. "How it had changed since the last time I'd been on its perimeter! Then it was a shambles and we were driving to gain control of it. Now much of the debris and wreckage of the Jap installations had been cleared away; the runways had been repaired; and the field was swarming with U.S. planes: P-47s, TBFs, and R5Ds. The transport planes were really impressive in size."

The doctor had arranged an air evacuation for the wounded young officer. His stretcher was carried to a military transport and loaded, stacked in tiers with others on either side of the fuselage. Presided over by an Army flight nurse, he watched the cargo door slam shut, heard the engines roar, and soon the plane was trundling down the packed coral runway and climbing into the air. "Goodbye to Saipan forever." The fight in the tangle went on, prosecuted by others, yard by contested yard.

When the submarine *Cavalla* approached Saipan's anchorage, her radars sensed the large host of ships nearby. The scope was cluttered with returns. Captain Kossler exchanged blinker-light greetings with the destroyer *Philip* and fell in behind her. The destroyer's skipper warned Kossler about floating wreckage endangering navigation around the embattled island. It would have been easy for a sub driver to miss a piece of dangerous flotsam, the spectacle ashore was so impressive and commanding. Sunrise revealed a violent tableau for the crew of the submarine: Turner's tractor navy, grimly at work.

Kossler called it "a scene which we will not soon forget."

> Practically every type of ship in the book was in sight. A large column of smoke hung over the northern end of Saipan, caused mostly by an oil fire near the town of Garapan. Gunfire and bomb explosions could be seen on Saipan, and bomb and shell bursts could be seen on Tinian. We had expected to fuel in Magicienne Bay, but as we neared the island, ships of all descriptions came into sight, anchored off what was left of the sugar mill on the southwest side of the island. . . .
>
> We were only a mile from the beach and had a ringside seat for one of the toughest fights our Marines had had to date. Units of our fleet bombarded Saipan all day without a letup and their marksmanship was amazing. The island seemed to tremble under the blasting they gave it. The dive bombing of our planes was thrilling to watch, and to top it off, at times you could see our Marines ashore with their tanks and flamethrowers giving the Japs hell.

The submarine had surely done this, too, and spectacularly. Both the skipper and his crew knew they had scored, though it was not yet known that they had sunk one of the most important ships in the Japanese fleet, the *Shokaku*. For the time being, the *Cavalla* was enjoying a humbler distinction: being the first U.S. sub to enter Garapan harbor after its conquest.

Spruance, Turner, and Hill came aboard upon arrival, followed by journalists eager to ask Kossler questions. The session lasted an hour, but the crew was far more interested in watching the exhibition ashore than in suffering through a press briefing.

On July 2, when Kossler took the *Cavalla* for refueling, the crew of the oiler that serviced them, the *Suamico,* explained how Japanese planes came over and attacked at night, and how enemy artillery let loose on the anchorage from Tinian sometimes, in spite of the suppressive fire that American warships blanketed them with. Impressed by this information, Kossler kept his machine guns manned, but he still granted his crew two hours of swimming call. Everyone needed a chance to forget the war for a while.

Before five P.M. the sub was underway again. Refreshed with seventy thousand gallons of fuel oil, a new radar transformer, assorted engine repairs, a touch-up of gray paint, and her topside thoroughly greased, the *Cavalla* steamed west back to her own war. The morale of the crew surged powerfully. "The reception we received on arriving at Saipan, and the services while there, left us feeling damn glad we are Americans, and mighty proud to be members of the United States Navy."

In the *Indianapolis,* Carl Moore had had almost two weeks to get used to what he could see from the transport area, and even buffered by distance it struck him as a raw and terrifying novelty. "This campaign is a stiff one, as we all anticipated," he wrote his parents.

> I can watch it all from a grandstand seat, literally as well as figuratively. It is fire and explosions and burning airplanes, disaster and narrow escapes. We listen to the rumble of artillery, ship and shore, and do a little shooting ourselves, get shot at, sometimes, mostly by our friends, and watch results of bombardment. We think of the Marines and soldiers crawling through the dirt, getting shot at, while we sit down at a white tablecloth for lunch. Clouds of dust rise continuously over our end of the island, and our observers come back to the ship covered with it. Today I can hardly keep my eyes off the beach and get any work done. It is fascinating and terrible.

And there promised to be more of it, for two more islands remained to be taken.

Spruance was ashore now. Having stayed as close to the beachhead as the skipper of the *Indianapolis* could tolerate, he took a boat to the Saipan beachhead and was taken to see Holland Smith. He appreciated the fast progress the troops had made, even as the invasions of Tinian and Guam loomed, to be dealt with almost simultaneously.

On July 2, General Smith took Spruance for a tour. They piled into a jeep and were driven to the top of Mount Tapotchau. The centrally located peak impressed him as an obstacle to everything the troops wanted to accomplish. Spruance reported to Nimitz, "The difficulties of the mountainous backbone of Saipan have to be seen at first hand to be appreciated. The Japs have taken full advantage of the terrain for defensive purposes. This accounts for much of the length of time being taken to capture the island."

Afterward, Spruance and Smith were joined at lunch by the officer who was to serve as corps commander of Guam operations, Marine Major General Roy Geiger, and his artillery commander, Major General Pedro del Valle. Time was not on their side; aerial reconnaissance showed that heavy fortification of the Japanese defenses on Guam was in progress and that the Japanese were repairing airfields as quickly as U.S. pilots could crater them.

Guam's 18,500-man Japanese garrison was the usual amalgam of partial-strength units from different service branches. The commander of the Imperial Army's 29th Infantry Division, Lieutenant General Takeshi Takashina, had little left from this veteran unit, which had once been part of the Kwantung Army in Manchuria. These remnants, two battalions from the 18th Regiment, were survivors of the same submarine ambush that had left Captain Oba swimming ashore on Saipan. The rest of the 11,500-man army complement consisted of elements of the 38th Infantry, 48th Independent Mixed Brigade, and 10th Independent Mixed Regiment. They were joined by five thousand naval troops from the 54th Naval Guard Force (or Keibeitai), as well as two thousand naval airmen who were constituted as infantry to defend the important airfield on Orote Peninsula.

These troops were bolstered by the personal presence of Lieutenant General Hideyoshi Obata, commander of the 31st Army, who had returned from the Palaus during the battle for Saipan. Though he left the defense of Guam to General Takashina, he oversaw a formidable defensive installation that included nineteen eight-inch naval coastal defense guns, eight six-inch and twenty-two five-inch dual-purpose guns, and a suite of antiaircraft weapons suited to protecting major harbor installations and airfields.

As Rear Admiral Richard Conolly's UDT swimmers would discover, the landing beaches on the west coast near Agat were studded with log-cabin-sized coconut-log cribs filled with chunks of coral, which threatened to block amtracs from coming ashore. One benefit of delaying W Day, as the Guam landing date was known, was additional time to prepare to deal with complexities such as these.

Spruance agreed that W Day, set for July 21, should be confirmed as soon as possible. Bad weather was stirring up. Typhoon season was near. The price of a delay at Guam or at Tinian, where J Day was scheduled for July 24, would cascade through the roster of future Pacific operations.

Spruance had no doubt that the forces were ready. Geiger's Third Amphibious Corps had the Third Marine Division and the First Provisional Marine Brigade as an assault force. Conolly, commander of the amphibious naval task force, known as Task Force 53 or the Southern Attack Force, commanded bombardment and heavy lift forces that were comparable to what Turner had at Saipan. Nimitz wanted Geiger to storm Guam on July 15 with the forces available. He saw no reason to wait for the designated reserve, the Army's 77th Infantry Division, to reach the Marianas. When he expressed this opinion to Spruance, and in no uncertain terms, Spruance pushed back. He understood that it would be reckless to land troops on Guam until an adequate corps reserve was in place. The Fifth Fleet commander would not see the combined expertise of Holland Smith, Geiger, Turner, Conolly, and their staffs so lightly dismissed. "If their views as to military forces needed are to be overruled . . . the decision should be made by higher authority on the basis of the effect of the delay upon the conduct of future operations." These were bold words. "Tell Admiral King to call me," Spruance might as well have said.

Nimitz got the message. W Day was set tentatively for July 25, and when it turned out that the 77th could ship out sooner than thought, the date was advanced to July 21, right where it had been at the start. Though Kelly Turner, worn out after Saipan, worried that more troops would be needed, Geiger and Conolly feared the effect of any delay on the readiness of troops who had been embarked at sea for several weeks. Conolly said, "It was going to be very difficult to get them up to the proper pitch again."

The landings at Tinian would kick off just seventy-two hours later, and the veterans of Saipan would handle it. For the weary men who would have just weeks to recover and prepare, such a quick follow-on would surely be a trial. General Schmidt of the Fourth Marine Division would serve as corps commander at Tinian, while Major General Clif-ton B. Cates stepped up as division commander. Disillusioned with the Army after the contretemps with Ralph Smith, they had no interest in having the 27th Infantry Division as their reserve. Spruance passed along to Nimitz their dim view of the Army outfit, as if CINCPAC didn't al-ready know: "Its quality is poor, the date of the completion of the cleanup of Saipan is indeterminate, and time will be required when the fighting is over to rehabilitate and reequip all three of these Saipan divisions." Spruance rated Tinian as a challenge but thought that a single regiment from the 77th might suffice as a reserve for Tinian, too. As the plan was drawn up in the end, the Fourth Marine Division would handle the ini-tial assault, with the Second Division coming in behind them.

Spruance spent the afternoon touring Isely Field, where steel matting had been used to extend the main airstrip. He wrote Nimitz that Saipan reminded him of Maui before military aviation came to the Valley Isle. They both knew very well that the future of the Marianas lay with the Army and its B-29s.

21

The Dying Game

In the heat of early July, Shizuko Miura was thirsty. She had ventured from her cave to look for water, fresh to drink or dirty to boil, when she ran into some Japanese soldiers gathered around a field radio. A captain, holding the receiver, looked somber as he listened to the voice on the other end. It sounded deep and hoarse. As a lieutenant next to him scribbled on a notepad, the captain looked up and said, "The commander in chief is giving an order."

Shizuko strained to listen, but all she could make out was a reference to Makunsha, a village on the island's west coast. Then the radio connection was lost. The soldiers looked at one another with grave foreboding. One of them bowed down, held his head, and cried out. Miura asked the captain, "Has something happened?"

He replied, "Yes. The order has been given for the dying game."

All three U.S. divisions had been on the move that day, launching coordinated attacks meant to straighten out their lines as a single front clear across the island. It would never quite happen, partly because the Fourth Marine Division just never stopped moving. They had overrun Donnay and were squeezing into the narrow end of the island now. Their fast advance forced Shizuko and her surviving patients to evacuate the field hospital at Donnay, and so they scrambled to haul litters back to the hills, settling into a warren of caves in a large, rocky bowl.

Located north and east of Makunsha, the basin was big enough for the battalion-sized ranks of the wounded, but it was only sparsely forested and offered little shelter from snooping planes. A gallery of caves beneath its fringing lip of rock served as a command post.

Shizuko Miura had never heard this term before. "The dying game?" she asked the captain. "What does it mean?"

"Well, Saipan is now surrounded by the enemy and our forces are being annihilated. So we all must die. We will all die together," he said.

The meaning of this didn't register, except to impress her that Japan must be losing this battle and that reinforcements, long hoped for, were unlikely to come. Her brother, she had learned, had been killed on June 16 in a tank battle near Garapan. Since receiving this news, she saw every soldier as a manifestation of him and decided she would treat soldiers' wounds as long as she lived.

"What has happened at Makunsha?" she asked.

"Headquarters is moving there," the captain said. The top headquarters, belonging to the navy, she had heard, was in a cave somewhere in the shadow of the mountain. It surprised her that it would move from the forbidding heights of Tapotchau toward the vulnerable coast.

The bombardment that afternoon was fierce. Two American cruisers were off Garapan. The *Indianapolis* was firing on the outskirts of the occupied town. The *Louisville,* using her spotting plane, was shooting farther inland and north. It was probably salvos from that ship that had crashed down upon Captain Oba. One of them nearly found Shizuko Miura, too. A large explosion shook the slope nearby and showered her with rocks. When the smoke and dust settled, four medical orderlies lay dead nearby, cut to pieces.

After dark, Shizuko ventured from the cave to draw water with some others. The captain had said nothing more about the death order, but everyone seemed to know about it, judging by the mood. Finding a small stream, she was able to see her face by the reflected light of the moon. It was filthy and blackened. As she splashed herself clean, her mystical self-assurance took hold again, a sort of waking dream. "I had confidence that only I would be safe in the enemy's midst. I believed I could run about freely among them. I was different from the soldiers."

Returning to the field hospital with water, she supplied it to her patients and found that cartons of crackers and cans of food had been produced from storage that she had not been aware of. Seeing this bounty, she was indignant that her patients had not been given more to eat before now. They needed sustenance. An old man was without a leg. A soldier with no lower jaw and a hanging tongue slavered constantly. A wounded soldier wore a ceremonial sash for a dressing. Fastened around his abdomen, it was embroidered with messages from family members and soaked with his blood. She passed out the food by the captain's instructions—a pouch of crackers and a tin of salmon for every patient—and then he pointed to three crates painted red and told her to open them. She discovered that they contained hand grenades. She was ordered to pass these out, too, one for every eight patients.

There was silence as the captain stepped up on a rock ledge and called for attention. He seemed to reflect for a moment, then spoke in a loud voice. "By order of the high commander, this field hospital shall move to Makunsha in order to join the last general attack. Every soldier who can walk shall go with me. But to my great pity, I will leave here the comrades who cannot walk. You, die gloriously as soldiers of Japan."

Shizuko recoiled at the cruelty of it at first. The older soldiers spoke of their children, the younger ones of their parents. Such talk was generally considered effeminate, and some of the troops hardened their talk of home with crude language and jokes. But as the only woman present, she discovered that she had a special status. Then she realized the captain was right, and a great commander, too, for at such moments, she thought, tenderness could rob one of the courage to do what had to be done. "Captain, I will stay here," she said. "I am resolved to kill myself together with my patients."

The captain looked at her sharply and said, "You are one of the volunteering nurses of the army in this hospital. It is the high commander who gave the last general attack order. This is an army. You can walk, so you shall join us. This is my order." She would have to go without her patients, for no one left in the field hospital was well enough to walk.

In the middle of the night of July 1, General Saito abandoned his field headquarters south of Radio Hill and withdrew to another rocky hideaway inside a draw that ran for about two miles down to the northeastern limit of Garapan. His command was truly broken now, well beyond his control. The 136th Infantry was isolated on the east slope of Mount Tapotchau. The 135th Infantry had been pushed off the mountain by the Second Marine Division. Then, under pressure from the Fourth, it withdrew to the island's northeast coast, near Talafofo. Their withdrawal took place a day sooner than Saito had wanted. This exposed the left (eastward) flank of his forces holding the coast. They risked being cut off now.

At his new command post, Saito heard a proposal that the garrison end it all in a last glorious charge to the death. He tabled this idea, ordering instead that the scattered units be gathered along the coast to construct defensive positions in the narrowest portion of the island. "You must chew the American force to pieces!" His staff envisioned re-forming a line running from a point north of Tanapag all the way to Talafofo on the coast. But the picks and shovels needed for the task were in storage elsewhere and he couldn't risk men to procure them, even at night.

Caught in a vise of gunfire from the sea, Saito's headquarters continued to take casualties. On July 3 he relocated to yet another site, in a valley just east of Makunsha. So much death had taken place there after two weeks of bombardment and air attack that it was already known as the Valley of Hell. "We felt this was an unpleasant hint concerning our future," a captured account read.

The Second Marine Division had moved little at all while their Fourth Division counterparts swept to Magicienne Bay, turned north, and began their fraught, fractious drive up the island's central spine. Accordingly, they maintained the tightest lines on the whole island. At night, the company commanders of the Sixth Marines found that patrolling forward was the best remedy to infiltration and counterattack. Patrols ventured out every night to secure the first thousand feet to their front. They almost always ended up in a firefight. It was said that Lieutenant Charles Tacovsky's regimental scout-sniper platoon spent more time behind Japanese lines than their own. It was only after the Army and Marines had hit their stride in the east that the advance on Garapan could begin.

Garapan's defenses were sparse. A Japanese POW who had commanded an antiaircraft battery near the shattered capital said that his unit of one hundred fifty men was down to thirty or forty, and the elite First Yokosuka Special Naval Landing Force, originally eight hundred strong, had just a hundred survivors, who had since been ordered into the hills to hide and harass. General Watson's men needed about a day to break their lines. Crossing the island from the east, elements of the 27th Division had cut off any hope for many Japanese units to join Saito in the north. At 1:30 A.M. on July 4, a company-sized Japanese element stumbled into the regimental command post of the 165th Infantry. Army troops fired on them in a murderous slaughter. Among the twenty-six dead was the commander of the 136th Regiment, Colonel Yukimatsu Ogawa, whose body yielded valuable maps as well as orders from General Saito to establish a new stronghold near Makunsha.

The U.S. Navy was eager to use the harbor to bring in supplies and repair damaged ships. But a complication arose: Two small islands in the harbor held Japanese snipers. Admiral Hill's staff asked Draper Kauffman if his UDT could take care of it. Kauffman was embarrassed to admit that he didn't think he had three men who had ever fired a rifle before. A company of Marines did the job, then cleared the wrecks in the harbor of bombs.

Looking down on Garapan from the highlands, Shizuko Miura could see American troops marching through town and piling out of craft at the government pier. Watching the pacification of the waterfront, she was numb. "I didn't feel they were a terrible enemy. I saw them as if I were seeing a film." A Japanese tank lay disabled near the pier. If it belonged to her elder brother, surely he still lay dead in it. She thought of the others she considered brothers, the soldiers in her care. Those who were able to walk were gathering in the hills near the basin. Under cover of trees, many were wounded, arms bound in slings, leaning on rough-hewn staves scavenged from the forest. She could see their movements by the moonlight glinting on their helmets. She went to them and said her farewells. They said, "Thank you, Miss Nurse," "Goodbye, Miss Nurse, and thank you for your kindness."

In the distance, she heard a series of sharp cracks. Plaintive voices called names, and then there were more cracks and dull pops. Grenades. She began running toward the sound of this miserable rapture, but the captain held her back. The company of the displaced Donnay field hospital was ready to move. It was arrayed along a mountain trail leading down through slopes of sugarcane toward the west coast. She closed her eyes and tried to ignore the sound of the concussions as she fell in on the march toward Makunsha.

22

Sniper Ship on a Cave Shoot

At sundown on July 4 on Saipan, it was the afternoon of July 3 in Washington, D.C. Independence Day would be a sober celebration. Allied forces in Normandy were seeking their breakout while contending with counterattacks. General George C. Marshall was preparing to warn his president that Japanese advances in China threatened not only the new B-29 bases near Chengdu but the collapse of China itself. In the Marianas, Kelly Turner and his generals were rushing to finish their task so the big new silver warbirds would have a place to roost. Jocko Clark and a division of cruisers had ruined another sunrise for Saburo Sakai and his squadronmates on Iwo Jima, razing its buildings and leaving its commander begging for reinforcement. On Saipan, some exhausted Marines found themselves firing at shadows from their hillside overwatch of Garapan. When an officer appeared, demanding to know who had shown such a lack of discipline, no one replied. He said he expected to see a dead enemy soldier for every spent cartridge. At that point, the companies in the area began firing en masse. "It was our way of celebrating the Fourth," one of them said. "Next day, there were no dead Japs but a lot of dead cows."

Off the west coast of the island, the Navy was pouring it on the enemy wherever they could be found, looking to preempt General Saito's explosive prideful finale. On hand to provide call fire to the Second Division, the *Montpelier* had spotted Japanese troops on the beach north of Tanapag and turned her forties on them. Loitering offshore, the light cruiser then covered Marines as they advanced. For the first time, the ship was close enough for her men to see enemy troops. Though a light cruiser like the *Montpelier,* almost five times the displacement of a destroyer, had to stay outside the two-hundred-fathom curve, six to eight miles offshore, in order to avoid hazards to navigation, her lookouts could see the Marines moving north in ones and twos. "They appeared near exhaustion and were not seen to be carrying packs, but they still had their rifles and they still could fight," a ship's officer wrote.

That night the destroyer *Philip* drew sniper ship duty. The unit she was supporting, a battalion of the 25th Marines, had chased some Japanese troops into desperate refuge in caves along the coast. Marines loved destroyers best. Heavier ships were slower to respond to their requests for call fire. Destroyers responded fast. If they were handled well, they could turn the tide of battle. It was about nine thirty when Colonel Mustain's 1/25 Marines raised the *Philip* on a field radio. A forward observer was in a good spot, huddled in the dark, under cover on Hill 767.

He said, "We are going to spot you pretty close to our front lines. We can hear the Japs singing down there. From your last spot, no change, right five hundred; fire one star."

The ship's main battery roared, but the night remained dark.

"A dud, I guess. Give me another. . . . That's swell. Fire one salvo under the star."

Corrections followed. "Down six hundred, no change." *Salvo.* "Up two hundred, no change." *Salvo.*

Then the Charlie went off-line for a few minutes. There had been some excitement near his position. To be of the greatest value to their unit, the Charlies had to set up near the front lines, where talking into a radio at night was likely to get a man killed. At length he came back on the air to explain. "They're throwing grenades around here and we had to keep down and could not observe. Let's have another one in the same spot." And the Marine Corps team went back to work, coaching the ship onto its target.

"No change. Rapid fire ten salvos. We can hear them screaming."

"Excellent firing. Cease firing. Mission accomplished. For your own information, you have started two large fires, and for our own information, we would like to have your DD number as we have never had a ship that gave us such excellent firing."

The *Philip*'s skipper, James B. Rutter, Jr., said, "Them's mighty kind words, but I can't help feeling the credit is all yours. Our number is four-nine-eight." In the combat information center, Lieutenant Ben Bradlee listened, pleased, and his ship, duly acknowledged, kept the star shells coming.

The Marine spotter coached the warship's battery onto a new target. "We would like you to fire on a road which runs along the shore, just where it cuts back in. We have no map to give you coordinates. Do you think from information I have given you, you could put one there?"

"Affirmative, I think."

"Okay. I've got a lot of confidence in you now. Put five rapid-fire salvos in there."

"Coming up." The destroyer's battery did its thing.

"That was perfect, really beautiful. We have another bunch of singing Japs there. Let's give them ten rapid-fire salvos."

"Right in there. That star was excellent. Please fire one salvo up one hundred, no change."

"No change, no change. Rapid fire five salvos. We can hear them screaming again."

"Up two hundred, no change. Rapid fire five salvos. Think we tagged an ammo dump that time."

As he directed Rutter's fire farther north and toward the coast, the observer and his team pulled up stakes and walked down the road to keep a direct view.

"No change, right two hundred. Five salvos."

"No change, no change. The singing is over now. As is the screaming, for that matter."

After two hours of collaboration, the *Philip* exhausted her nightly allotment and retired. The Marine battalion was impressed. "You have been the best ship we have ever fired," the Charlie said, "and if I ever hit your port, I am going to pay you a visit and tell you again in person." With this, Rutter handed off the 1/25 to the light cruiser *Birmingham,* which had been listening in while firing in support of Colonel Jones's hard-charging 1/6. The *Birmingham* raised the 1/25's Charlie and resumed serving as his remote source of illumination and heavy artillery, coaching her six-inch guns onto three enemy tanks in the highlands inshore of the village. At sunrise, the *Birmingham* handed off the account to the destroyer *Wadleigh* and the persecution continued.

As the Second Marine Division pushed up the coast toward Tanapag Harbor, Holland Smith realized that the last phase of the Saipan campaign was at hand.

General Saito had come to that same realization.

* * *

It was eight miles from Donnay to Makunsha, and progress on foot was slow over terrain marked for unceasing naval bombardment. Every time a star shell burst overhead, Shizuko Miura dropped to hug the ground until the light faded away. Moving again in the darkness, passing through a forested area, she collided with something heavy but yielding: The corpse of a woman hung on a rope from a branch. Straining to see, she could make out that there were many of them. She regarded them numbly and kept walking. She knew the group wouldn't cover the entire distance overnight, so after making about half the distance, she bedded down in a wood. They hid for the entire next day and resumed moving the following night. In the hills on the downslope to Makunsha, she found a mountain stream, but she couldn't bring herself to drink out of respect for those left behind. The captain told her to abandon their memory. "Our friends left in Donnay cannot recover. It would have been crueler to let them live," he said.

For days now, General Saito had neither eaten nor slept, and his appearance suggested it. Haggard and bearded, he was pitiable in the eyes of his men. On July 4, an American unit appeared at the far end of the valley facing his cave and turned heavy automatic weapons on it. His new command post was about a mile up the coast from the rallying point at Makunsha. Like his HQ on the island's east side, this one, too, was vulnerable to naval bombardment. When some U.S. ships found the range, it shook the cave so violently that some feared they might be buried forever. Saito was among those wounded by shrapnel. He despaired that he was surrounded. The American advance across the highlands north of Mount Tapotchau had broken any hope he had of forming a firm defensive line. His men were scattered, able to defend strongpoints such as caves, cliffs, and hills but never able to anchor a line of resistance against the overwhelming enemy firepower. Everywhere he had men who had gone to ground in overrun areas. His communications had been disrupted so badly that it would have been impossible to move his reserves, even if he had known where they were.

Saito called his chief of staff and held a conference with his available commanders. Admiral Chuichi Nagumo had argued that a prolonged defensive action might yet win time for the Japanese navy to come to their rescue. Saito could only scoff. As far as he was concerned, the decimation at sea of several badly needed regiments had testified to the uselessness of the fleet. Like the top brass at the Imperial General Staff, he saw the navy as a bunch of "sampan sailors" who had done little to keep hundreds of the army's finest from becoming bait for sharks. Saito felt the time had come.

Nagumo's optimism—supported by orders from Tokyo or not—was roundly rejected and overruled. The argument about what to do next continued into the night before Saito forced a consensus.

The endgame at Saipan would have an aspect of ceremony.

There were rules and unwritten rules, and the brute reality of circumstance often determined which ones applied in the rare instances in which Japanese soldiers were captured. Roy H. Elrod, a captain with the First Battalion, Eighth Marines, said, "We didn't have any specific code. We just shot everybody we could get a bead on. We figured if they were dead they weren't a problem anymore, at least not much of a problem." It was not the first campaign in which Marines on the line had found prisoners too much of a burden to take under tow, and what happened in the tangle decayed in the tangle. On Saipan, brute pragmatism reigned anew. "Nobody wanted to dig the graves for them," Elrod said. "If there were bodies around, somebody decided to pour gasoline on one or two and burn them. That didn't work too well. It just sort of cooked them and it made an awful stink and lots of smoke. Finally somebody hit on a real solution. If there was a little house around, they would put all the bodies that were in the way in the house and burn the house down. That worked fine. I know in the areas where I was there were no efforts to take prisoners." Lewis J. Michelony, Jr., a corporal with the Eighth Marines, said, "Your life is at stake. You're fighting for your life, and anything goes."

The reliable treachery of those who did surrender, springing grenades on their captors after waving the white flag, explained part of this attitude. First Lieutenant Fred Stott's company from the 1/24 was advancing fast into Saipan's northern neck when a group of wounded Chamorros and their children emerged ahead of their lines. First Lieutenant Phil Wood, from the mortar section, led a patrol forward to bring the civilians to safety. As they advanced, Japanese soldiers who had sent the Chamorros forward opened fire from thirty yards. The entire patrol was hit, and five died instantly. Among the dead was Lieutenant Wood. His sergeant, Arthur B. Ervin, who had a Navy Cross from Kwajalein, rushed to his aid and was killed, too. The use of civilians as decoys and shields by Japanese forces was systemic on Saipan. The 25th Marines reported hundreds of civilians swarming their lines in droves, as many as a thousand all told, prodded forward by Japanese military personnel looking to get close to their enemy. Such were the horrors all along Saipan's northern front, a gray area where

Marines had to make reflexive judgments on the fly concerning life and death, mission and mercy. For the first time they confronted large numbers of innocents intermingled with enemy troops variously looking to fight, flee, surrender, or die, all on the same battlefield, with fronts both above- and belowground.

Bivouaced south of Garapan, Lieutenant Colonel Wood B. Kyle and his battalion from the Second Marines were nominally in reserve now, but every night they saw Japanese stragglers coming down from the hills, lost or looking for food. When they ran into Marine lines, most of them were shot. "We did try to capture them, but we couldn't do it," Kyle said.

He was walking his perimeter one night when he smelled the sweet stench of human decay. Looking around, he determined that it was coming from a deep ravine near B Company's sector. Maxie Williams and his men, he realized, had been shooting the infiltrators and tossing them into the ditch. Wood found Captain Williams and informed him that it was the company commander's job to bury all these bodies. It was a matter of hygiene, morale, and the law of war. "This kind of annoyed them," Wood said, "and Maxie thought it wasn't fair—that somebody else should do the burying." They argued for a while before Kyle pointed out that service troops weren't available and simply ordered Williams to take care of it. Marines in combat were supposed to bury those they shot in their sector. That was the rule, and the whole battalion was going to follow it.

But there was another rule, too. The other rule said you couldn't shoot your rifle inside your own perimeter. So Williams adjusted his approach, or so Kyle surmised. When Japanese ambled through, the Marines kept quiet, platoon by platoon, and did not fire. The second rule obtained. Duty bound, they let the enemy soldiers pass through. "All night long I had Japs coming by," Kyle said. "They were working their way out of the battalion to go up to the other side." It gave cover to those who wanted to spare their ammunition, save their shoulders a bout with a spade, and keep their nostrils free of the diverse aromas of burial. Once the wanderers had passed through the battalion area, the last company on the line shot them on the way out. "It didn't take me long to figure out what was happening," Kyle said. "Old Maxie had just told his boys to let them go. He didn't want to bury these people. This is what they did."

The next morning, Kyle tracked down his willful company commander and said to him, "Okay, you win." They cut a deal. Williams's company would shoot to kill, but grave-digging duty would rotate daily among all the companies. The bargain bucked up morale, and in one corner of the

Second Marines, some ruthlessly practical men found a way to square a different circle.

The narrow coastal corridor between Tanapag and Makunsha was hot. Two Army regiments, the 105th and 165th Infantry, were assigned to conquer it. The whole area had been dug out in order to accommodate defensive works never to be installed. The tradecraft required to pick through such positions—even when they were unmanned, as most of them were—slowed the Army's progress. On July 5, the 105th encountered the first large minefield it had yet seen, a stretch plagued with buried aerial bombs between the coast road and the railroad spur north of Tanapag. Eight tanks paid the price. When Japanese antitank guns and machine gunners hidden in the cliffs ahead and also in the coconut grove unlimbered on them, their progress ground to a halt.

Interrogation of POWs by U.S. intelligence pieced together what was happening in the north. As many as two thousand Japanese soldiers had gathered near Makunsha. That number had been suggested by reports from pilots as well as the growing volume of mortar fire falling on U.S. positions. Prisoners were unanimous in saying that their comrades were tired of the fighting, but some said they would nonetheless resist to the end. A soldier taken prisoner from the naval base force at Garapan said that the finale would take place on the night of the sixth and seventh. The tip was transmitted to all 27th Division headquarters and its intelligence unit. The analysts at G-2 believed most Japanese would fight to the end and not surrender. They thought a leaflet-dropping operation could be effective, as the enemy seemed to be concentrated in the north. But as night fell it was quiet along Saipan's tiny northern front.

On the morning of July 6, a master sergeant with the 135th Infantry, Toshio Kitani, noticed a crowd gathering near General Saito's new command post. Normally the sergeant major would not have entered without orders, but Japanese discipline wasn't what it once was and he was anxious to know the state of affairs. Inside he found Lieutenant General Yoshitsugu Saito and his chief of staff, Brigadier General Keichi Igeta, in the company of Vice Admiral Nagumo and his chief of staff, Rear Admiral Hideo Yano.

Saito was preparing to address the troops. Frail and gaunt, he appeared exhausted, his shirtsleeve torn and blood-soaked where a bandage had been wrapped around his shrapnel wound. A hush fell over the cave as

Saito stepped onto a small platform. Two candles mounted on the wall of the cave behind him cast the flickering light by which he read:

> For more than twenty days since the American devils attacked, the officers, men, and civilian employees of the Imperial Army and Navy on this island have fought well and bravely. Everywhere they have demonstrated the honor and glory of the Imperial forces. I expected that every man will do his duty. Heaven has not given us an opportunity. We have not been able to exploit the terrain. We have fought in unison up to the present time, but now we have no materials with which to fight, and our artillery for attack has been completely destroyed. Our comrades have fallen one after another. Though defeat is bitter, we pledge our lives to repay our country. The barbarous attack of the enemy continues. Even though the enemy has occupied only a corner of Saipan, we are dying without avail under the violent shelling and bombing. Whether we attack or whether we stay where we are, there is only death. However, in death there is life. We must utilize the opportunity to exalt true Japanese manhood. I will advance with those who remain to deliver still another blow to the American devils, and leave my bones on Saipan if that is how it must be.

Saito's solution was ceremonial: a *gyokusai* attack.* A colonel, Saito's aide, stood and announced that the attack would take place before dawn on July 7. At a stroke, they fancied, the assault would sever the Americans from their seaborne lines of supply, isolate them, and expose them to counterattack and destruction.

Stunned by the oration, Sergeant Major Kitani went to check on the platoon of thirty-two men that he had collected, a unit he called the First Platoon, Saipan Infantry. They were milling among the crowd outside Saito's cave, buzzing with the news of the *gyokusai*. When Kitani reentered the cave to learn more about the plans for the assault, he was surprised to find that the conference had adjourned and a feast was underway. By the candlelight he could see Saito and Nagumo and their chiefs of staff sitting

---

* The term means "smashing the jewel," a metaphor for a ritual suicidal attack by an overmatched or doomed force, the purpose of which was to preserve its eternal honor.

cross-legged at low tables, facing sixty or so men who sat cross-legged on the floor. The mood was solemn, but flashes of laughter—fraternal humor, old stories—enlivened their resignation to what was to come. The naval officers were unknown to Kitani, but he understood by the white bands the four top commanders were wearing that they would not long survive after finishing this feast of canned crabmeat, squid, and rice, washed down by liberal portions of sake.

When the meal was done, Saito nodded to one of his staff, and two soldiers came forward to spread four white sheets on the ground. The two commanders conferred privately, exchanging toasts. On each of the sheets was laid a white pillow, and on each of the pillows was a short sword wrapped in white cloth. At once all four men went to the sheets and knelt on the pillows, eyes closed, mouthing a silent prayer. Saito stood, bowed toward the Imperial Palace, then knelt again. Admiral Nagumo and the others did the same.

Saito was not going to advance with his men after all. A junior officer holding a pistol advanced to stand behind each of the four kneeling seniors while Saito, then Nagumo and the others, reached for their swords, unswaddled them, and held them to their abdomens. As one, the four men shouted *"Tenno Heika, banzai!"*—May his heavenly Majesty live ten thousand years!—and spitted themselves through the midsection. The junior officers then raised their pistols and fired single shots into their heads. They fell over, legs jerking, and it was done.

Shizuko Miura was still thinking the fleet might arrive when the captain assembled the remnants of the Donnay field hospital that night and said, "Tonight we execute a general attack on the enemy, combining all of our forces." He announced that the field hospital would take part, too. "Prepare to fight, anyone who can walk." The rest were to go to the top of the mountain and await orders. He stood among them—the worst of the wounded—and said, "The nurse, she will lead you all." He handed the woman a grenade and told her to use it should the worst come to pass.

As the throng of walking wounded started up the valley toward the mountains, Shizuko knew it was a fool's errand. She didn't know where she was going, and the wounded were laboring terribly with every step. *Please let me die with the field hospital,* she thought. As they reached terrain with a fuller view to the east, her heart raced. "To our surprise, the eastern coast was covered with enemy warships, too. They were shooting in the moonlight." She heard gunfire in the west and wondered if the attack had begun. She wondered about the fate of the others from the field hospital. Unable to bear the uncertainty, she soon ran, alone, back down in the direction she had come.

The captain was not pleased to see her return. "Why did you come? You don't know my heart. This position is surrounded by the enemy. But the western exit is safe yet, Go. Hurry up!" But Shizuko refused.

"I've come back here to die with you," she said. He and his lieutenant were already waiting to die. She would join them. At least she knew the patients were safe in the mountains.

It was about six o'clock in the morning when she awoke in the foxhole along with the captain and the lieutenant. High in the mountains, she saw movement. Soldiers—Americans, it seemed. Many of them. From the mountain, ten or twenty figures were advancing toward her. One of the oldest patients who remained called her over and said, "Thank you. You have kept me alive. But at last the end is coming for me. But you are not a soldier, and your life begins from now. You must live."

When the Americans were about two hundred yards away, she heard music of some sort echoing in the valley. Its rhythm was alien, its syncopation disturbing to her. As the soldiers came closer, the sound of jazz echoed in the valley, and the effect on Shizuko Miura and the soldiers was frightening. She thought it drained them of their fighting spirit. Its exotic rhythms and time signatures rang as the antithesis of her culture. The impulse to fight vanished as the men hid down in their foxholes. A gunshot came from the foxhole of the senior officer who had thanked her. From a different hole there came another sharp report. The captain again urged her to leave. "Return to the field hospital," he told her, but she no longer knew what such an order implied. Gripping the dirt at the edge of the foxhole, unsure what to do, she saw the Americans through the trees. They were close now. *Are they gorillas?* she wondered. "I supposed so, for I had been told the Americans were using gorillas on the front. I had never seen negro soldiers." She watched them, bewildered, as they began rushing toward her. It was an assault. Some of them rolled grenades into the holes; others knelt and fired, seeming to shoot everything that moved. "I could see their faces. Black faces in helmets, only eyes and teeth, shouting things." Thirty yards, twenty yards, then closer: ten. The captain turned his rifle on himself, barrel to the throat, and pulled the trigger. The lieutenant produced his combat knife and slashed his throat up and down, and again. He sagged down on Shizuko, blood running warm over her legs. She held a grenade and pulled its pin. She held the lever desperately, tears filling her eyes, before throwing it against a rock she had positioned for just this purpose, and fell down upon it.

23

Beyond All Boundaries

Before surging toward American lines around midnight on the morning of July 7, the Japanese Army killed all the seriously wounded patients and destroyed all of their food stores and supplies within reach. This left about fifteen hundred to two thousand men in the group, about a third of them equipped with rifles and grenades. The rest, service workers and personnel, hospital patients, and civilians seeking a glorious end, carried rudimentary weapons such as handmade spears. The entire group had just ten light machine guns. Colonel Suzuki ordered them to attack Garapan and push straight through, carrying all the way to Aslito Field. They found their way south by following the railroad that paralleled the coast road. Many of the labor units gradually disappeared into the night during the march. Suzuki and his men no doubt lamented that hundreds of Japanese soldiers were holed up in caves that were beyond the reach of General Saito's messengers.

Other soldiers had the job of shepherding the civilians north, away from the advancing enemy line. They used the time to continue telling horrific stories about what the Americans would do to them if they were caught. It was a constant drumbeat: They were brutal, hungry to divide families, shove children into pits, turn dogs on them, and crush their bodies with tanks. They would dismember the men and collect the women for the pleasure of Negro troops. "What else could be expected from U.S. Marines?" this cynical, racist line went. They were savages who had proved their dedication by murdering their own mothers before going off to war. A decision to surrender can be rational when one understands the practices of the conquering army. By the mechanism of baroque lies, the Japanese command ensured their countrymen would prefer death to capitulation.

As the soldiers dragged the civilians along the coast road and through the lowlands, heading north, they promised them that Japan's naval and air forces would yet be their salvation. In line with this optimism, Captain Sakae Oba had arrived in the tent camp near Makunsha with the eighty-odd survivors of his aid station. He had every intention of selling his life in a final suicide charge. He sent one of his sergeants to a naval headquarters in the village and instructed him to bring back any food the navy could spare. Then Oba rested. He was awakened by a shouting voice in midsentence: "—to act otherwise is not only cowardly, but evidence of a lack of faith in the ultimate and unquestioned victory of Japan over the barbarous enemy—"

The voice belonged to the sergeant he had sent looking for food.

"All imperial forces, whether navy or army, are therefore ordered, by the authority of Vice Admiral Chuichi Nagumo's headquarters, to continue fighting and to avoid participation in an obvious suicide attack. Only by continued resistance can we provide assurance to our naval forces that are even now en route to this area to drive out the invading American devils and to retake the island."

Oba raced to find the sergeant and confront him. *How dare you countermand the army commander on the island!* But the sergeant apologized, saying he was merely following orders. He handed Oba an order from Nagumo, signed by a Commander Onodera. Oba's mind raced: Could it be true? Could the Combined Fleet really be coming to save the garrison? His urge to rally to the banner of suicide faltered. What right did he have to end his own life when the act would only deny the emperor one more soldier to fight for Nippon? He went to his men and shared this view forcefully: To die in such a way was an act of betrayal. He said anyone who would join in the *gyokusai* was a coward.

> You would rather take the easy way out and think of yourself as an honorable soldier. But you won't be. You'll have weakened our ability to fight just as surely as if you were to kill one of your own men. Don't worry, we will attack, and we will attack tonight. But we will not expose our weakness to the enemy. We will hit him silently, and we will move to his rear from where we can strike again and again until he is unable to oppose our returning navy and landing forces. The jungles and hills of Tapotchau will become our stronghold. We know every ravine and hill. We have caches of food and ammunition hidden throughout the area. Regrouped, the forces in Makunsha can hold Tapotchau forever.

That might or might not be true, Oba thought, *but at least there is honor in it.* He would not attack like a fool, straight into the teeth of enemy lines. He would lead his men as a reconnaissance patrol into the mountains, where they would set up an observation post. He ordered a young officer to take a message to 135th Regiment headquarters at Makunsha, informing Colonel Suzuki that he would attack from the hills rather than join the *gyokusai*.

Late in the afternoon, hopeful that his message had reached Suzuki, Oba set out with two men to reconnoiter the area. He followed a dry creekbed into the hills, coming to a rocky cliff. The two men scaled it and found a ledge on which to set up the observation post. Through binoculars he surveyed three miles of heavily tangled coral faultlands between him and Mount Tapotchau. The valley near Makunsha, to his right, was under artillery fire and he wondered whether anyone would survive to join the attack. The rough terrain between the observation post and the coastal plain would make it hard for Americans to find him first. Oba and the sergeant descended the cliff and returned to their camp. He found Lieutenant Banno and ordered him to assemble the men, move out to the cliff, and conceal themselves until nightfall.

Having taken Tanapag, the Army held the line along the coastal plain, if somewhat awkwardly. The 106th and 105th Regiments had crossed the island abreast, left and right. When they reoriented to push north up the coast, the 105th, on the right, took the lead. The other regiment of the 27th Division, the 165th Infantry, held fast in the hills and hadn't yet turned, much less sewn its lines with the others. After the fast advance across the island, the 27th Division's commanding officer, Major General Griner, tried to adjust, but for three regiments comprising almost eight thousand men, pivoting could be difficult even on flat terrain. With Japanese troops putting up sharp resistance with machine gun and mortar fire from protected positions along ridges and in caves, it would take time to turn.

During the night of the sixth, Japanese scouts had probed the Army's perimeter looking for a weak spot. They found one. The Army troops, unlike the Marines, had done no patrolling in front of their lines. What followed was a nightmare.

Major Edward McCarthy saw it develop in the black void in front of him. Distant shouting sharpened into unintelligible commands. Shadows of movement resolved as human figures, soldiers, surging en masse toward him. Hundreds of Japanese troops assaulted the sector held by his battalion, the 2/105. "It reminded me of one of those old cattle-stampede scenes in the movies," McCarthy said. "The camera is in a hole in the ground and you see the herd coming and they leap up and over you and are gone. Only the Japs just kept coming and coming. I didn't think they'd ever stop."

They came on like madmen. Few were sober. Led by screaming officers waving swords, they flowed through the gap between the battalions. The idea of covering it with interlocking arcs of machine guns and field pieces was fanciful. Charging masses of soldiers eager to die could be stopped only by a physical barrier. The leading wave of the charge absorbed the enfilade and kept on running right through. Behind them, hundreds of Saito's "wounded reserve"—limping men with bandages on their heads, hobbling on crutches, poorly armed—followed. The 27th Division would estimate the assault as fifteen hundred strong, then three thousand, then more than four.

The Navy was helpless to intervene. The *Birmingham* had enough firepower to have disrupted the attack before it gathered steam, but once it developed, it was impossible to fire without risking American lives as well. The fast-moving regiments of the Fourth Marine Division, advancing across the island, had stepped into the ship's line of fire. As the melee developed in depth behind U.S. lines all across the Tanapag plain, Captain Inglis and the rest of the fire-support ships could do nothing but watch.

The commander of the 1/105, Lieutenant Colonel William J. O'Brien, was idolized by his men. He ran along the front waving his .45 pistol aloft and yelling at his men to hold. He seemed to be everywhere. They called him "one of the boys" that day. He took a rifle from a wounded soldier and fired until the magazine was dry. Wounded in the shoulder, he refused medical evacuation. He ran to a jeep, charged its .50-caliber machine gun, and hosed the oncoming swarm. Sergeant Thomas A. Baker, at his commander's side, was seriously wounded in close combat after breaking the butt stock of his rifle on enemy helmets. Quite against his will, Baker was lifted and carried to the rear by a soldier who was then shot in turn. He refused evacuation at that point, insisting he be left to die. Another soldier dragged him to a tree that the wounded sergeant had indicated, sat him down, propped him in place, and gave him a cigarette and a pistol, just as Baker had asked. When O'Brien was last seen alive, he was surrounded by saber-wielding Japanese soldiers and the bodies of many he had killed. According to a witness, his final words were "Don't give them a damned inch." But there was no way to hold. An overrun unit cannot stand against the tide. Scores of men from the 105th were in retreat, many running all the way to the Tanapag waterfront to make a last stand at the beach.

The 105th's two line battalions had essentially ceased to be. In short, horrible order there were nine hundred casualties from their combined rolls of twelve hundred men. Every officer but two in the First Battalion was killed or wounded. The Second Battalion had just seven officers left of its original twenty-four. Third Battalion, in the rear, begged its regimental HQ to saddle up and send forward every self-propelled mount that could move. In the confusion and surprise, neither of the 27th's other two regiments, the 106th or 165th, came forward to engage.

The assault was just minutes along when wounded began arriving at Captain Ben Salomon's battalion aid station. The surgeon for the 2/105, he occupied a small tent that was quickly filled beyond its capacity. Salomon, who had been trained as a dentist at the University of Southern California, was trying to manage the overload when he noticed a Japanese soldier at the tent, running a bayonet into one of his wounded. Salomon squatted to a firing position and killed him. Two more enemy who reached the tent entrance were shot dead by other soldiers. Seeing four more Japanese crawling under the flaps, Salomon ran at them. He kicked a knife from the grip of one of the soldiers, shot another, and bayoneted a third. He ordered his wounded to evacuate to regimental headquarters a thousand yards to the rear, then grabbed a rifle from one of his wards to cover their retreat.

The Marine artillery assigned to support the 105th was next in harm's way. Positioned southwest of Tanapag along the coastal railroad track, the gun pits of Third Battalion, Tenth Marines, had been arrayed by Major William L. Crouch in "echelon right" formation, on a diagonal facing the northeast, with the fire direction center in the rear. It was 5:30 A.M. when some five hundred Japanese, supported by tanks, fell upon his forwardmost unit. Captain Harold E. Nelson, commander of H Battery, hesitated to order his howitzers to fire, knowing American troops were to his north. But when the enemy broke through, he instructed his gunners to cut their fuzes short and drop their muzzles so as to ricochet their rounds off the ground. When the suicide wave overran Nelson's firing pits, his artillerymen grabbed their carbines and fought like infantry. The sudden concussion of heavy direct fire smashed into the artillerymen from their flank. A Japanese tank was concealed behind a house, firing through it to deadly effect. Nelson organized a group of twelve men to flank it. Machine gun fire lit into them, severely wounding Nelson, but he stayed on his feet. Forming a defensive perimeter, he kept firing until he fell. As Japanese troops broke through and attacked the fire direction center, Major Crouch tried to raise regimental headquarters and request support. Realizing his communications were dead, he broke cover and ran to deliver the request, while the clerks of his headquarters made their last stand. Crossing an open field under a withering barrage, Crouch was finally hit. The battalion commander died along with forty-five other men. More than three hundred dead Japanese lay around their positions.

The penetration did not run out of steam and dissipate before American lines were overrun—to a depth of nearly a mile in some places. As the Sixth Marines advanced through the lines of the 106th to take position at the front, they were shocked by the carnage. They estimated conservatively that fifteen hundred Japanese dead were in their area on July 8. Afterward, battalion intelligence confirmed the division's estimate that about three thousand Japanese had attacked the division front.

The body of Ben Salomon was found with nearly a hundred dead enemy soldiers piled in front of his position at a machine gun. Sergeant Baker lay dead by his tree with eight enemy soldiers on the ground around him. Lieutenant Colonel O'Brien lay where he fell with at least thirty dead Japanese soldiers near his body. A destroyer retrieved forty men from the 105th from a reef about a half mile into the lagoon from Tanapag. The beach was littered with American wounded—and more than three hundred Japanese dead. Some Japanese troops had waded into the lagoon to avoid participating in the charge. The reefs harbored them now. Embarked in amtracs, U.S. language teams motored out to them, shouting through bullhorns for them to surrender. Half of a group of twenty-four raised their arms to the sky and became POWs, but only after the rest had either taken their own lives or been killed by their officers. As the Americans approached, one Japanese officer turned on his own men, beheading four of them before the disgusted Marines shot him dead.

The driver of the jeep fishtailed in the mud, ascending a steep, narrow road to the island's heights, and it was there, near the top of Mount Tapotchau, that Raymond Spruance understood that he would have to kill them all. There were an estimated twenty thousand Japanese troops on Saipan. All twenty thousand would have to die.

The jeep stopped, and the Fifth Fleet commander got out with members of Holland Smith's staff to walk the final two hundred feet to the peak. It was his second visit ashore, and the wastage of total war lay all around him. Dead enemy soldiers were decaying where they had fallen. If Spruance was disturbed by the inattention of Marine burial parties, he didn't let on. Carl Moore described their indifference to the whiff of rotten death. "We didn't like the odor very much, but we made no particular point of it. . . . We had reached the stage of disregarding that sort of thing entirely. There they were, and most of them with the stern sticking up in the air, tight trousers, bodies expanding." It wasn't bravado. They had been seeing such gruesome sights since Tarawa.

From the mountaintop, looking to the west and south, Spruance scanned the towns, the beach, the harbor, and all his ships. He wrote Margaret, "We had a grandstand view of a modern land battle. With good glasses, we could see our tanks in action, troops on foot moving up in support, other troops coming in trucks from rear areas, could hear our shells passing overhead and see them exploding in enemy territory." By hammer and tongs, the Americans were drawing the last gasp from Saipan's garrison.

On the way down the mountain, Spruance stopped the jeep to observe Marines assaulting a hill, a last redoubt for some Japanese holdouts above Garapan. He admired the spectacle from above as he might a tabletop war game, a set piece with foxholes spread across the valley below, troops fanning out, leapfrogging forward, bright fingers of flame issuing from canisters of jellied gasoline.

On the Tanapag plain, where cleanup operations were in progress, Griner's men noted that many of the survivors they encountered were still defiant, if not eagerly suicidal. The "jewel" had been shattered, and what was left were mere shards. Disorganized groups offered a spectrum of behavior under extreme duress. There were volleys of spasmodic shouting, occasional gunfire and sniping, and a steady percussion of suicides. Fearing possum-players, U.S. troops advancing through the area of the great last assault put bullets into every Japanese body they found. While doing so, the men of the 106th were said to be "having a regular field day," a division report noted. The 23rd Marines helped root out the largely spent Japanese force holding the pocket at Makunsha and joined in the mop-up. The 24th and 25th Marines rolled across the island farther north, reaching the airstrip at Marpi Point and cutting across to the western shore. Isolating the northern tip of Saipan, they received reports of numberless holdouts in caves along the coast. Civilians caught in this madhouse had been told to expect no quarter from the Americans. Wherever they mingled with Japanese soldiery bound never to surrender, seldom was any given.

On the morning of July 8, the *Philip* closed within five hundred yards of the cliffs near Saipan's northern coast, strafing caves on the water's edge and the limestone ramparts above. After two passes, grass fires spread along the shoreline. When the destroyer hit what seemed to be a gasoline storage depot, the Marine spotter from the 1/25 radioed the ship, exultant. "That's what we want. They can't stay around that stuff very long." The destroyer's skipper, Captain Rutter, noted with satisfaction how vaporized limestone gusted from cave openings other than the one he had hit, suggesting his success in rooting out honeycombed positions underground. Cruising around Marpi Point, he warned the Marines of caves large enough to house submarines. He gave the whole area a sweep with his forties, then called it a day. In closer, amtanks and LCI gunboats prowled within a football field's distance of shore. Keeping contact with infantry battalions via backpack radios, they pounded cave openings and beach areas with time-delayed 75 mm rounds, killing hundreds.

Spruance viewed warfare as a puzzle to be solved. But Saipan could not be a puzzle if it had no intellectual solution. Since the start of the operation, corps intelligence analysts had put great effort into crafting psychological messages to induce surrender. Propaganda and counterintelligence had been a major part of Holland Smith's plan. These efforts had been informed by the efforts of Nimitz's headquarters to produce a concise cultural portrait of the Japanese for the benefit of propaganda writers and interrogators. "The Japanese is a sensitive person," it read,

> invested with all the emotions and affections that we associate
> with our own homes and families. He suffers the pangs of home-
> sickness; he has almost a passionate desire to return to his home-
> land, and he certainly longs for his hot baths, his good food, and
> his good wine. His entire training and tradition have made him
> particularly sensitive to suggestive modes of speech and writing.
> The indirect and the inferential has been instilled in him. He dis-
> likes syllogistic reasoning, and his mental reactions are intuitive
> and sharp. He is, even in lower intellectual groups, responsive to
> the artistic. He is readily impressed with calligraphy or fine hand-
> writing. Poetry is read by the most churlish Japanese and is at-
> tempted by many. The disposition of the Japanese is highly
> impressionistic. All Japanese aspire for aesthetic effect in every-
> thing—in floral arrangements, in pictorial representations of na-
> ture, and in ceremonies. But all this emotion and this love of the
> aesthetic is completely hidden behind an inscrutable mask that

occidentals can only with difficulty penetrate. From the day he is born the Japanese is trained to conceal his emotions and to wear his mask. In preparing these attached leaflets, therefore, all of these qualities have been noted. Pictorial and floral designs are used, and appeals are made to emotions, to homesickness, and to the frailty of body and spirit, although the Japanese will pretend to respond to none of these.

Fourteen separate leaflets had been crafted for use in the Marianas, each designed to overcome prideful Japanese resistance to the idea of surrender. A total of 175,000 pieces had been distributed by air through D Day plus two. Japanese language broadcasts were ongoing, and platoon leaders carried "patrol cards" printed with translated messages to use as necessary. And yet after twenty-five days of combat operations, only about half of the 1,734 military POWs taken on Saipan through July 27 would say they had seen and read the propaganda, and they offered mixed reviews of its effectiveness. Sometimes the messages were too sophisticated in content, the kanji too advanced for poorly educated enlisted men to understand. The messages sometimes failed to take hold because soldiers in groups feared lethal retribution from their officers if they showed any willingess to entertain them. Several Japanese prisoners volunteered to rewrite the texts, assist in broadcasts, or perform calligraphy, saying that they believed a humane dividend might result from educating their comrades as to the true nature of the Americans and their way of treating POWs. But successful persuasion sometimes depended on balls as much as on brains.

That was the forte of a remarkable private first class from the headquarters company of the Second Marines, whose flair for negotiating surrender was unparalleled. Guy Gabaldon was a Mexican American tough from East Los Angeles. His youth had nearly been devoured by gang life before he moved in with a Japanese American family whom he befriended in the neighborhood. He came to consider the Nakanos his own kin. Their children taught him to speak Japanese before their transfer to an internment camp left Gabaldon rootless again. He moved to Alaska at that point to work in a fish cannery, then enlisted in the Marine Corps when he turned seventeen. His wayward spirit survived the drill instructors at Camp Pendleton.

The first time Gabaldon left his post without permission, sneaking outside the perimeter for a long walk, he returned with a group of Japanese prisoners. He was warned sternly not to try such a stupid thing again, but he would. He felt called upon to use his rare language talents to persuade enemies who ostensibly valued death over surrender to give up without a fight. When he brought back fifty more prisoners one day, his commanding officer's attitude changed. "Let the little jerk go. He's getting results." From then on, Gabaldon freelanced as a POW negotiator whenever he sniffed a chance.

After the *gyokusai* attack of July 7, Gabaldon took two Japanese prisoners to the top of a coastal cliff. "Why die when you have a chance to surrender under honorable conditions?" he had told them. "You are taking civilians to their deaths. This is not part of your Bushido military code." To keep fighting, he told them, would mean certain death. "Our flamethrowers will roast you alive." Knowing they had survived in spite of receiving orders to commit suicide by banzai charge, he felt confident he knew what their reaction would be. And he was right. When he asked his prisoners to take his message to their comrades still in hiding, one of them said he wanted no part of posing provocative questions such as these to a cave full of *gyokusai* survivors. But the other man was more amenable. He volunteered to walk down to the caves at the bottom of the cliff.

At length his intermediary returned with twelve men—who were armed. Realizing he wouldn't stand a chance if they decided to shoot, Gabaldon gathered himself, summoning all the command presence he could muster. Offering each a cigarette, he invited them to sit. Then he said in Chicano-accented street Japanese, *"Heitai san!"*—Fellow soldiers!—"I am here to bring you a message from General Holland Smith, the shogun in charge of the Marianas operation. General Smith admires your valor and has ordered our troops to offer a safe haven to all the survivors of your intrepid *gyokusai* attack yesterday. Such a glorious and courageous military action will go down in history. The general assures you that you will be taken to Hawaii, where you will be kept together in comfortable quarters until the end of the war. The general's word is honorable. It is his desire that there be no more useless bloodshed."

That they declined to shoot him was encouraging. It suggested the possibility of a breakthrough. Gabaldon knew they didn't know who General Smith was. But he hoped the word *shogun* would be a bridge. He closed with a note of strength: *"Heitai san! America no Kaigun no Kampo de anata tachi minna korusu koto ga dekimas!"*—The American navy with all of its firepower can kill all of you! He gestured to Kelly Turner's fleet.

The Japanese whispered among themselves, then the senior officer, a first lieutenant, approached Gabaldon, accepted a cigarette, and asked whether his headquarters had a hospital. When the American answered in the affirmative, the lieutenant directed four men to stay and took the rest back to their cave. *Guy, you short-assed bastard, you did it!* the Marine thought.

Nimitz's social scientists had urged all hands to banish the words for surrender (*kosan* or *kofuku*) and prisoner of war (*horyo* or *furyo*) from their dialogue with Japanese prisoners. A Pacific Fleet psychological study concluded, "This is in conformity with the general conviction that everything must be done to help the captured ones save face." The surprise most Japanese felt upon discovering the true nature of their enemy was used to good effect. "Fear of torture is quite *widespread,* having been systematically implanted in all personnel—military and civilian—by the Japanese leaders. Indeed, one of the first reactions of the prisoners taken has been surprise that they were not tortured." In some cases it was enough to overcome the shame and compel them to urge others to lay down their arms.

And sure enough, in less than an hour, the Japanese lieutenant returned with fifty men. Gabaldon could tell they hadn't all made up their minds. Once again he steeled his posture to project maximum authority. When they demanded water and medicine, he showed them a sulfa powder packet and promised more would be forthcoming. He was still giving assurances when he saw a long file of humanity streaming up the trail from the cliffs. Surprised, then fearful, he was relieved when a nearby Marine patrol noticed the distant commotion and turned in his direction. By day's end he had done the unthinkable, corralling about eight hundred Japanese in the Second Marines stockade. That day on Saipan, Gabaldon said, "The good Lord had his hand on my shoulder."

Sometimes his surrender-with-honor-and-tell-all-your-friends spiel worked wonders. But sometimes it didn't. He was no saint, and no pacifist. "Sometimes I had to throw grenades and kill everybody," he said. So did the high commanders. It was a war of snap judgments and binary results— shoot or don't, live or die. Thus went the war. After Saipan, the judgments that American commanders made about the character of their enemy were severe indeed. The trials of July 7 cemented them at levels high and low.

24

Atop Suicide Cliffs

As far as U.S. troops cared, it was an unrivaled anticlimax when the announcement came that Saipan was secure. With untold numbers of stragglers holed up in caves and a breakdown of military order evident following the mass banzai attack, there was no telling what cost was left to be paid. Each knot of holdouts was a separate and distinct obstacle. No instrument of surrender would pull them from their caves, and no safe means existed to distinguish armed holdouts from cowering refugees. When every soldier had a grenade, and every civilian was a hostage to him, there was often no option but to kill them all.

On July 9, a flag-raising ceremony took place at the Marpi Point airfield. In the midst of it, an observation plane swooped low over Fred Stott's battalion in the field and dropped a message to them reporting enemy troops moving north along the beach. The island's northern end was generally too narrow for air, naval, or artillery to safely fire in support, so Stott's company was asked to handle the job root and branch. As the Marines of A Company saddled for movement to the east end of Marpi Airfield, he saw little meaning in the flag raising. Some twenty-five thousand civilians were known to live on the island, all but three thousand of them Japanese. Wasn't it curious, Marines wondered, that fewer than half had been detained at this late date, with the battle formally won? Where were the rest?

As Stott's patrol explored the cliffs fronting the sea, some Chamorro civilians emerged, faces alive with joy. Among them were two priests, some nuns, and many of their faithful. On the left, First Lieutenant Al Santilli was leading his machine gun section through an open cane field when he was confronted by about twenty people, women and children and men holding babies, emerging from the tree cover. He and his interpreter went forward and began directing them to safety. That was when Japanese troops hidden in the sugarcane opened up, scattering the squad.

According to Stott, the last officer in A Company to die on Saipan was Al "Saint" Santilli. The hero of Fordham University's 2–0 win in the 1942 Sugar Bowl was cut down with his platoon sergeant, among others, as the American flag flew over the airfield. *Secured* did not mean *conquered*. "It was very depressing to have suffered so heavily at a time when we thought the organized opposition practically ended," Stott wrote. "To us, securing would come when we boarded ship."

From the place where Al Santilli fell, the jagged coastline curved around the highest peak in the north, Mount Marpi, an eight-hundred-foot plateau that descended in overgrown limestone ridges and steep terraces to the surf below. A two-hundred-foot rampart of limestone fronted the sea at the island's northern tip. The cliffs at Laulauwan, the Japanese called it. Everybody else called it Marpi Point. Still shaken by his losses, Lieutenant Stott sent patrols down to explore this rough terrain, his last objective, following the few passable trails. At the bottom, in caves near the sea, his men continued to find signs of Japanese presence. Marksmen atop the cliffs dealt with armed enemy troops wherever they appeared—"a shooting gallery at four hundred yards," he called it. "Such targets were invariably military personnel, and the shooting ceased whenever the military and civilians intermingled."

Here, at the last extremity of the embattled island, the Americans learned why so few Japanese civilians had been taken. They had been herded here, convinced that death was inevitable, the only choice left to them being the choice of means. By early afternoon, a crowd had collected at the water's edge. "Imperceptibly a psychological reaction seemed to emerge and the people drew closer together into a compact mass," Stott said. "It was still predominantly civilian, but several in uniform could be distinguished circling about in the throng and using the civilians for protection.

"As they huddled closer, sounds of a weird singing chant carried up to us. Suddenly a waving flag of the Rising Sun was unfurled. Movement grew more agitated, men started leaping into the sea, and the chanting gave way to startled cries, and with them the popping sound of detonating grenades. It was the handful of soldiers, determined to prevent the surrender or escape of their kinfolk." At the sight of the approaching Americans, women took their children to the precipice and leaped. The cliffs echoed with muffled blasts.

"Saipan was filled with horror, but it was during these securing days

SB2C Helldivers from the *Hornet*'s VB-2 take wing. (USN)

Cdr. James D. Ramage of Bombing 10 got in some licks against Ozawa's carriers as they withdrew, before nursing his Dauntless back to the task force after dark, running on fumes. (USN)

Lt. (j.g.) Warren R. Omark from the *Belleau Wood*'s Torpedo Squadron 24 (at center) put a torpedo into the *Hiyo*. (USN)

A TBM Avenger prepares to "trap" on board a Task Force 58 carrier, while an *Iowa*-class battleship rides shotgun on her port quarter. (USN)

The Japanese carrier commander, Vice Adm. Jisaburo Ozawa, thought he could strike Task Force 58 from standoff range, using bases on Guam to land and refuel his planes.

The *Zuikaku* under attack by Task Force 58 planes on June 20. Though smothered in splashes, she survives. (USN)

The Japanese carrier *Junyo* finished the Battle of the Philippine Sea still afloat, her stack destroyed by a bomb and her air group largely shredded.

A pilot from the *Monterey*, Ens. Robert L. Peugh, tells Ens. Gerald R. Scholz (right) how their roommate was shot down during a strike against ground targets in the Marianas. (USN/Lt. Victor Jorgenson)

After sinking the IJN *Shokaku*, the crew of the submarine *Cavalla* received a rousing welcome in the Saipan anchorage on June 30. Her captain, Herman J. Kossler, wearing a T-shirt, is fourth from right. (USN)

Army aircraft, including this P-47 Thunderbolt from the 318th Fighter Group, were ferried to Saipan on board escort carriers and took over the job of softening up Tinian. (USAAF)

An armorer uses an aiming tube to boresight the eight .50-caliber guns of a P-47 at Isely Field. (USAAF)

Mechanics fill an auxiliary fuel tank with jellied gasoline, a mix of aviation fuel, diesel oil, and napalm. The terrible new firebombs were used for the first time against Japanese targets on Tinian. (USAAF)

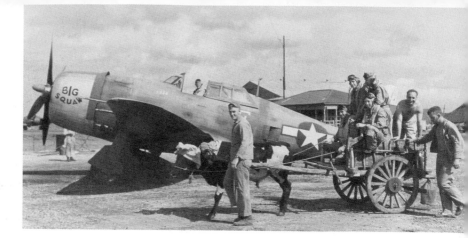

Army pilots commandeered a Japanese oxcart for transit to and from the flight line. (USAAF)

A tank crewman recovers after clearing Garapan. (U.S. Army/Sgt. Bill Young)

Marines descend the slopes of Mount Tapotchau in search of water after assaulting the enemy stronghold. (USMC)

When Marine commanders complained to Holland Smith (above, right) about the Army's progress on Saipan, Admiral Spruance (above, left) was forced to act, relieving the commander of the 27th Infantry Division, Maj. Gen. Ralph Smith (left).
(above: USN/Alfred J. Sedivi, courtesy of U.S. Naval Institute; left: U.S. Army Signal Corps)

Among Saipan's eastern ridges and valleys, U.S. troops saw some of the most challenging close-quarters combat of the war. For platoon, company, and battalion alike, it was difficult and sometimes impossible to maintain contact with neighboring units. Enemy infiltrators prospered. (USMC)

After Ralph Smith's relief, Lt. Gen. Robert C. Richardson, commander of Army forces in the Pacific (left), arrived unannounced on Saipan and complained vigorously to the Navy brass, whereupon Kelly Turner shouted him down for a breach of protocol. Maj. Gen. George Griner (right) replaced Smith as commander of the 27th Division. (U.S. Army Signal Corps)

Japanese dead, the remnants of the mass suicide attack of July 6–7, litter a beach on Saipan's northwest coast. (USMC)

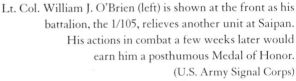

Lt. Col. William J. O'Brien (left) is shown at the front as his battalion, the 1/105, relieves another unit at Saipan. His actions in combat a few weeks later would earn him a posthumous Medal of Honor. (U.S. Army Signal Corps)

Medal of Honor recipients (left to right) Harold Christ Agerholm, Harold Glenn Epperson, and Grant Frederick Timmerman. (USMC)

Marine tanks and infantry advance through Saipan's northern slopes and canebrakes, July 7, 1944. (USMC)

Marines with Japanese children.
(U.S. Coast Guard)

The flag flies over Saipan, July 10, 1944. Admiral Spruance stands at center right, wearing a tan pith helmet. Holland Smith is to his left. (USMC)

Chamorro civilians on Saipan were removed from harm's way and interned at Charan Kanoa. (USN/Alfred J. Sedivi, courtesy of U.S. Naval Institute)

On July 17, Holland Smith (standing, holding carbine) shows
Adm. Ernest J. King (left) and Adm. Chester Nimitz around Saipan. (USMC)

Staff Sgt. Timerlate Kirven
and Cpl. Samuel J. Love were the
first black men to receive combat
decorations from the Second Marine
Division. Their Purple Hearts for
wounds suffered on Saipan hang
from their left breast. (USMC)

Rear Adm. Harry W. Hill, Kelly Turner's right hand at Saipan, took command of the Tinian landing force and executed a brilliantly conceived diversion. (USN)

Maj. Gen. Harry Schmidt (left) was elevated to corps commander at Tinian while Maj. Gen. Clifton B. Cates took over command of the Fourth Marine Division. (USMC)

July 24: Marines dismount from an amtrac at Tinian. The decision to land on the northern White beaches surprised the Japanese and saved many lives. (USMC)

Tanks and vehicles move off White Beach. (USMC)

From Saipan, Kelly Turner (left) watches the Tinian landings through
captured Japanese field glasses. Holland Smith is at right. (USMC)

A camouflaged Marine engages Japanese snipers on Tinian. (USMC)

Marine infantry in action on Tinian. (USMC)

Huddling over a relief map of Guam, Maj. Gen. Roy S. Geiger, the corps commander, confers with his chief of staff, Col. M. H. Silverthorn, and corps artillery commander, Maj. Gen. Pedro del Valle. (USMC)

Rear Adm. Richard L. Conolly earned the nickname "Close-in" for the manner in which his ships conducted fire support on Guam. (USN)

UDT swimmers paddle away from Guam after planting charges at the reef. (USN)

On board the cruiser *Honolulu,* journalist Frank N. Morris interviews Lt. William G. Carberry, commander of UDT 4 (center), and combat swimmer Sergei Aalto (shirtless). Wags from one of Carberry's platoons erected a sign on the beach welcoming the Marines to the island. (USN)

them to the safety of their lines. "The women were crazy over cigarettes," Charland said, but the smokes had to be demonstrated, lit and drawn deeply from, or the women were likely to suspect they were explosives.

Everyone wondered what level of fear made a woman holding a baby feel her best option was to jump. Slaughtered by warships gutting their caves from the sea, the Japanese civilians might have wondered, *What kind of enemy is this? The brutality that* heitai-san *speaks of is true!* After watching families fall upon the grinder of limestone and lava, or clasp hands and wade stoically into the swirls washing over the rocks, drowning by groups, Americans wondered the same thing. The horror of the Marpi Point suicides went on for two days before the innocents settled their fates. By the end of it, American forces had their first look at Japanese militaristic collectivism in action, and it hardened their hearts. They stood at the edge of a new combat front: a grotesquerie in which predatory propaganda, well rehearsed by the Japanese army all through the imperial realm, turned the citizens of the Greater East Asia Co-Prosperity Sphere into their fellow travelers in suicidal fanaticism. The grisly job of gathering and burying the dead fell to those who declined to participate.

As reports, formal and otherwise, circulated of this horror, the ice-water reality of it convinced those who had the most skin in the brutal game that in a war zone, a reflex of mercy and humanity offended Darwin's law. They had been witnessing suicidal atrocities for weeks now, though some were reluctant to believe their own eyes. What cultural puzzle required solving in order to induce a beaten army and their dependent populace to surrender as rational beings should?

The crews of Marine and Army amtanks, fresh from cave-clearing operations, moved among the rocks, turning their tracks against the flow of the current, looking to render aid. They retrieved and took to safety elderly men and women, small children who were wounded, and pregnant women. Unloading the refugees at Tanapag, the amtanks refueled and returned. "A nude young woman held a naked infant in her arms," said Winton W. Carter, an amtrac crewman. "*Stop!* I yelled. She didn't, and plunged down in front of us." A Japanese soldier at the base of the cliffs charged an amtrac with a hand grenade and was reaching back to throw when he was cut down by an alligator crewman. The surf washed the rocks clean, and the sea ran red.

Against uniformed regulars, Americans seldom hesitated to level their weapons and go cyclic, but the human heart still beat and the unpredictable presence of innocents stilled the warrior impulse to unlimber, unlock, and traverse broadly. A sailor on a patrol craft that bobbed and yawed amid this horror said:

> It's just the damnedest feeling deep in your stomach when you see somebody die like that, especially women and young kids, babies even. I was up on the bow already. I had no reason to be up there, and I probably shouldn't have been because that's when we'd see these big, bloated bodies, and the bow would just cut them right in two. The gas would come out, *speeeew,* like that. Of course, they'd go down, and then sharks would have really a ball with them. Yes, I was scared. It was a different kind of scared, though.

Fred Stott was numb to the emotions such a sight would have given him on another day.

> No pangs of conscience were felt over civilian death, for dead people and wrecked buildings had become commonplace. We felt no more tired on D plus 28 than on D plus 3, probably less so. For after the first four days we were in a constant state of fatigue, but becoming inured to it. Our sensitivities were gradually dulled—hence the lessening of sympathy. Even the death of close friends seldom affected men visibly. That might come later, when the physical pressure had relaxed. Our hatred for the enemy increased little if any. Substantially the same amount of satisfaction was felt upon killing an enemy soldier at all times throughout the operation. Essentially it was a period of prolonged physical exertion, spotted with moments of bravery, fear, anger, and cruelty.

Back home, reports of what happened at Marpi Point pushed editorialists to firmer conclusions. A staffer for *Collier's* wrote, "It was a ghastly business; but beyond that, what significance did it have for our war in the Pacific?"

> One guess is that it means the entire Japanese nation, with only a handful of exceptions, will choose to die rather than surrender; that we shall have virtually to exterminate the Japs before we can consider then really defeated.
>
> Another guess is that these civilian suicides were propaganda to make the extermination theory seem sound—that these civil-

ians killed themselves on instructions from their military rulers in the hope of persuading the white man that the conquest of Japan will entail horrors which he, with his ingrained compassion and sportsmanship, cannot stomach to the end.

The truth of the matter will probably unfold as our forces work closer to the heart of Japanese power.

Already, though, we know one truth about the Japs: that they are deadly and remorseless as enemies, and that they hate us with their instincts, their hearts and their blood. We'd be foolish to steam up a similar hate for them. But we'd be inviting our own destruction as a nation—making suicide gestures of our own—if we should ease up on these people before we are sure that their power to make war has been blown to bits.

As he slipped through the foothills of the mountain slopes by night, Captain Sakae Oba took advantage of the chaos of the immediate aftermath of Suzuki's final charge. He was eager to put as much distance as possible between his small band of survivors and the frontline American troops, who would soon regroup and recover from the *gyokusai* attack. The rear-area American troops seemed to belong to support units—they were not as vigilant as their comrades at the front. Oba, Lieutenant Banno, and their band kept high, near the ridges, for the Americans seemed to concentrate in the valleys. By the light of star shells that were concentrated in the north, to their rear, they were able to spot American encampments, vehicles, and even occasional sentries, which they were diligent to avoid.

By midmorning on July 8, on the jungle slopes of the mountain about two miles from Garapan, Oba was awakened by Lieutenant Banno, who reported voices in a valley below. He dispatched a scout, who returned reporting they were Japanese soldiers. When Oba descended to meet them, he found them thoroughly demoralized in spite of an impressive stock of food. They were survivors of a mountain artillery regiment that had been left behind as the Americans pushed north. Oba found a major with a bandage around his head, who explained that the unit had been standing by, awaiting orders. Oba asked if his small band could join them. The major directed him up the slope to a cave where the unit's colonel made his headquarters.

Oba, Banno, and their band hadn't gone far when Oba noticed a warrant officer kneeling over his meal, eating with a studied formality that seemed out of place. The man finished eating, rose, and walked into the woods. Moments later there came a single shot of a pistol. Oba thought for a time that he might like to follow the man's example, but he wondered what would happen to Banno and the others if he did. Concern for his men ultimately led Oba to decide not to join the group. Artillerymen could not fight without their big guns. Oba decided to make camp nearby but remain independent.

From among the ranks of the artillerymen, clustered in groups along the hillside, a sharp voice reached Oba's ears. "Hey!" The shout, directed at Oba, bordered on angry. It came from a black-bearded soldier who was short and stout but not quite obese. He approached Oba and demanded a cigarette. Oba assessed him as suffering from shell shock, judging by his neutral expression. The officer produced a pack of smokes, handed him one, and watched him as he walked away.

Banno asked Oba why he had tolerated such insolence. Oba asked Banno whether he had noticed the tattoos on the man's forearms. They announced to Oba that the soldier was more than a soldier. He was a *yakuza*, a gangster. His name was Horiuchi. Even in normal circumstances, such a man was unlikely to bow very deeply to rank. After everything the Americans had laid upon Saipan, circumstances encouraged a certain latitude, Oba thought. Horiuchi, with his pedigree in crime, might prove valuable.

As Oba and his men spent several days among the artillery regiment, it didn't bother the officer that his men grew lax in their company. Everyone needed a rest. And here, in this valley surrounded by swaths of high sugarcane, they seemed well protected from discovery. It was on their third day of rest that the illusion of security fell to pieces.

When Shizuko Miura became conscious again, her abdomen ached for reasons she could not remember. At first she was unable to see, but as the blinding light resolved, she heard alien voices and saw that she was among strangers in a quiet, comfortable room.

Then a voice said, in Japanese, "You are wounded. Do not try to move."

Two American officers were near her. She was surprised to hear her own tongue spoken by the enemy.

"You are wounded. You must not drink water." She asked for water again, insistently, and a young officer put a can to her lips. It was tomato juice. She spat it away, but her caretaker insisted, and her fear of him compelled her to comply.

She remembered the grenade, pulling the pin, leaning forward against the rock. It must have been a faulty one, a lifesaving low-order blast. He examined the wound in her abdomen. "You will stay here. We will heal you," he said. But the mystery of her own survival paled next to a larger question.

"What happened to the field hospital?"

The American said, "Everyone died except for you alone."

He told her there were other Japanese civilians in the camp. Skeptical that the Americans would allow any of her countrymen to survive, she asked to see for herself. When she mentioned that she was afraid of the African American troops, her captor could only laugh. "It was Negro soldiers who saved you. They found you and took you in."

What Shizuko really wanted to see was the field hospital at Donnay. Her interpreter was sympathetic and arranged for a truck to be summoned. She was injected with penicillin, then carried outside on a stretcher and loaded into the truck, fighting to hide her grief.

As the driver turned onto the coast road, night had begun to fall. One of the two soldiers who accompanied the driver, an African American, lifted her to a sitting position, allowing her to look out upon the ruination of Saipan. Barren ranks of blackened cane stalks stood dead in the moonlight. A right turn into the hills, a bumpy ride through the scrub, and then she recognized the site of the field hospital. Surveying the remains of her proudest duty station, near Donnay, she saw bodies. Children, mothers, fathers, soldiers, fields of them. Their extent seemed endless.

The officer said, "There are also many bodies in the sea. Do you wish to see them?"

"Yes, I do."

The driver turned onto the road to Marpi Point, then pulled over and stopped beside the cliffs. The officer directed the two soldiers to carry her stretcher and lay it at the edge of the drop. The sea glinted with moonlight. Two hundred meters below, floating in the surf zone among the rocks, were human figures, the bodies of women, she thought, but some children, too. She looked down vacantly at them and found the sight "too terrible for tears."

Putting a hand on her shoulder, the officer said, "Let's go now," and the soldiers carried her stretcher back to the truck. As the engine coughed to life and the truck started to move, she looked up at the moon, glowing down from above.

As his eyes glistened, the American officer asked her, "Why do Japanese kill themselves like this?"

A real answer, like real grief, was as yet unavailable to her.

On the afternoon of July 9, an American patrol found Oba and his men. The platoon of Marines advancing up a draw announced themselves with a volley of machine gun fire that shredded leaves from a bush mere inches from Oba's head as he napped. He awoke in an instant, rolled over, sprang up, and set off running as gunfire sounded behind him. His downhill route took him into a ravine that was bounded on one side by a rocky cliff. As foreign voices shouted some fifty yards to his right, he continued running. He had not run far when he realized he was trapped. He had the choice of running left or straight ahead. To the left was open terrain that he judged would be suicide to attempt to cross. Ahead of him the route was closed by the face of a cliff, but its base was a tangle of brush. He ran toward it. As he did so, he noticed two Japanese soldiers emerge from the brush and begin to climb. He shouted a warning that they would be shot dead, then realized that he had only one chance to escape. Two dead Japanese soldiers lay on the ground nearby. He tossed his sword, pistol, and some other gear into the brush. He then dropped to the ground between the two bodies and feigned death.

The American voices grew louder, and a volley of rifle fire popped. He heard more voices, nearer now, and the dragging of something heavy over the ground. A great weight slumped down on him, forcing his face into the earth. He felt the butt end of a rifle jam into his leg, and there was more talking. Trying to breathe shallowly so as to avoid attention, he calmed the panic welling inside him and remained in this fragile state for perhaps fifteen minutes. Then he sensed a distance opening between himself and the voices. Daring to open an eye and turn his head, he looked down the draw. The Americans were gone.

This is like rising from the dead, he thought as he rolled out from under the body of a Japanese soldier and got to his feet. He retrieved his weapons and looked up the hill he had come running down. Near his sleeping area, two dozen of his group lay dead on the ground. Among them, at the top of the hill, was Lieutenant Banno, shot through one eye. He arranged Banno's hands on his chest and, looking for a means of showing his grief, extracted a bayonet from a nearby body, walked back to Banno, and severed his thumb from his left hand. If he ever got off this island, Oba decided, he would deliver this small talisman and testament to Banno's family.

There was no sign of survivors. But that night, about an hour after sunset, Oba heard Japanese voices in the valley and advanced down the trail. He came upon four men and, cautiously revealing himself, found they belonged to the artillery regiment. More joined them as the night passed, a total of about twenty, including the gangster Horiuchi. The *yakuza* laconically described how he had survived the American attack by concealing himself in the eroded undercutting of a dirt bank while the enemy platoon went through. Oba had the impression he would not duck another fight. Sitting idly with a Nambu machine gun cradled in his lap, Horiuchi announced his intention to kill a hundred Americans before he died.

But the numbers were running with irresistible momentum the other way. On Saipan, the tentative count of Americans killed in action or died of wounds stood at 2,949. That number would climb to more than 3,400 once the counting was done. With the ranks of the wounded bringing total casualties to 13,438, it was to date the costliest U.S. operation of the war. Japanese losses were harder to measure. There was no counting those who had been bulldozed in place and left to dry, or burned out and left unrecovered in ravines and cave depths, but Holland Smith's staff collated the numbers based on a count of the units at Saito's disposal and figured that more than 23,000 Japanese had been killed on Saipan.

The number of captives was a small fraction of this total. Among prisoners taken after the mass suicide attack, one stood out as a prize. Mitsuharu Noda was the chief yeoman to Admiral Nagumo. In that role, the twenty-seven-year-old had been privy to just about every piece of paper that the senior Japanese officer on Saipan received. American interrogators found him a willing conversationalist.

As Spruance read him, Noda resented the fact that his conscription into the navy had interfered with his plan to pursue higher education. He told his captors he would talk freely so long as no report was made to Japan of his capture. "The prisoner has a bit of a dramatic flair," the interrogator's report said, "and will require considerate treatment or he may dry up as a further source of information. It is felt that careful treatment, even to the extent of catering to his prima donna complex, will prove profitable, as he has a wealth of knowledge that should prove of value to the Navy." Kelly Turner's intelligence staff was quick to agree to his terms, assuring him that his surrender would not be divulged and that his wounds would be treated aggressively. Three "devices" lubricated his willingness to talk, according to Turner: suggestions that he was a true samurai who had the power to help end his people's suffering by working to bring about a speedy end to the war; assurances that American forces bore no animosity toward the Japanese people, as demonstrated by the good treatment given to POWs; and statements that U.S. commanders saw how Japan's military and political leaders had betrayed the innocent.

Noda told his captors of Nagumo's despair at the reach and power of U.S. aircraft. Combined Fleet morale was low, he said, for its commander in chief, Soemu Toyoda, lacked fighting spirit. Fuel shortages were hampering operations; the battleship *Yamashiro* had been relegated to serve as a gunnery training ship at Yokusuka because she consumed so much oil.

The intelligence windfall pleased Spruance. But nothing seemed to satisfy him more than the report that in a cave outside Makunsha, the body of a certain Japanese admiral had been found. When Spruance, at Truk, took the *New Jersey* on that remarkable foray to hunt for cripples, he had revealed the hidden passion of his fighter's heart. His sentiments regarding the death of Chuichi Nagumo suggested it, too, a warrior instinct that was a match for that of his peer, Halsey, who never seemed to refrain from exulting publicly over the killing of an enemy. As Spruance confided to Margaret in a letter, "One thing that has appealed to me most in this operation was the end of the Commander, Central Pacific Fleet here, Vice Admiral Nagumo. He is the gentleman who commanded the Jap fleet on December 7, 1941, and again at Midway. After Midway he went ashore to Sasebo and then came here in May. Three strikes and out."

25

Regime Change

As planning began for the near-simultaneous landings on Guam and Tinian—Spruance had set the dates for July 21 and July 24, respectively—the question that consumed Harry Schmidt, the corps commander at Tinian, was, "How can we bring this fanatical enemy to heel without again paying such a heavy cost?"

Tinian was a valuable strategic objective, but launching another invasion while the experience of Saipan was still rattling in them was more than some Marines could understand. The arrival of replacement troops from Hawaii and San Diego underscored the change that had overtaken the Saipan veterans. "We survivors were intensely proud of having carried through the operation," Fred Stott would write. "So it was pleasant to enjoy the role of 'greatness' as they sweated their way up the hill and into camp."

As the line companies began a two-week rest and replenishment phase ahead of their jump across the sound, Stott noticed his numb sense of the world, the banality of his thinking, the lack of a sense of moment, and the absence of lessons clearly learned. "If we did not know what we were fighting for on June 15, on July 13 our minds were no clearer on the matter. Death and destruction came to be the natural order. Wounded comrades were given little sympathy unless the wound was critical. Mostly they were envied for being out of it."

A controversy was developing as to the choice of a landing beach on Tinian. As far as Kelly Turner was concerned, the island's most promising invasion site was the spread of beaches near the administrative center of Tinian Town, on the southwest coast. They were wide enough to accommodate battalion-strength landing teams and the seaborne train needed to sustain them. He liked the shallow rise to the bluff, the absence of an inshore tidal marsh like Susupe Swamp to complicate maneuvers ashore, and the protected harbor that would allow ships to unload in all but the heaviest weather.

But Harry Hill, who had been tapped to command amphibious operations, wasn't sure. Documents captured on Saipan revealed that the Japanese were expecting the Americans to land at Tinian Town. "The more we studied it," Hill said, "the worse it looked from the troops' point of view. Playing the game by Japanese rules would be very expensive in lives." Neither of the Harrys, Hill nor Schmidt, wanted Marines charging into a meat grinder when a less costly alternative existed.

On the northwest face of Tinian's northern point was a pair of narrow strands known as the White beaches. They were far too small for ordinary landing doctrine to recommend. An assault force was at its most vulnerable when passing from ship to shore; landing on a too-narrow front, it could be subjected to concentrated enemy fire and the rallying of reserves. That lesson had been learned at Tarawa, where the landing force attacked the narrow northern end of the island and had to advance down its length, facing stiff resistance on a restricted front. Ever since, amphibious doctrine required that a six-hundred-man battalion have five hundred yards of beachfront on which to operate. White Beach One was only about fifty yards wide, and White Two just a hundred. But surprise was always valuable. Holland Smith and his commanders, mindful that their legion was weary, thought that using the White beaches might give them a measure of surprise—an advantage that would be especially useful given that the Tinian operation was to be carried off without rehearsal.

Kelly Turner would dispute the claim that he tried to shut down the idea from the start, but when Harry Hill first broached it with Boss Alligator, "I literally got blasted out of the cabin," Hill said.

> He just would not accept the idea that White beaches were adequate and on at least three occasions gave me flat and positive orders to stop all planning for these beaches, and land at Tinian Town.
>
> He simply would not listen, and again ordered me in very positive terms to stop all White Beach planning and to issue my plan for the Tinian Town landing, which had already been prepared.

Turner had given Hill the job of taking Tinian with the idea of testing his mettle. When Hill asked Turner why he had been placed in command, "a twinkle came in his eye," Hill said, "and he told me how his father taught him to swim by throwing him overboard in deep water." That twinkle was nowhere to be seen now. "I never saw Kelly when he was so mean and cantankerous. It just wasn't like him. He must have been a bit under the weather"—by which Hill seemed to suggest Turner had been drinking.

But Hill was not alone in his view. Holland Smith and Harry Schmidt preferred the White beaches, too. Hill, feeling empowered by their support, dared to take his case directly to Spruance. Spruance liked the White beaches proposal, so long as he could be sure the weather would be clear. The narrowness of the beachhead meant that supply operations would have to be continuous in order to keep the troops moving. Hill couldn't afford delays from heavy weather. Typhoons spawned in the waters south of Guam, and their swells were sometimes large enough to be seen from low-flying aircraft. They tended to radiate to the north and west, covering sometimes as much as four hundred miles per day.

No aerographer was needed to forecast the disturbances that were possessing Kelly Turner. He had been on edge all along as Operation Forager unfolded. When he learned of Spruance's support for Hill's idea, Turner's temper flashed white hot. But he was out of options to stop the plan. Seeing that he faced a losing showdown with his willful tribe, Turner called in Draper Kauffman and ordered his UDT to carry out a night reconnaissance of the White beaches as a precaution. Always wary of Navy agendas, Holland Smith insisted that an "impartial" group join the frogmen. A Marine reconnaissance company under Jimmy Jones worked up the plan cooperatively with Kauffman, and they organized a pair of twelve-man teams, six UDT and six Marines in each, to do the job.

In the new-moon blackness of the night of July 10, the USS *Gilmer* ghosted through the sound toward Tinian. Two miles out, the recon teams embarked into landing craft, motored another mile, then transferred to rubber boats. Four hundred yards from shore, they slipped into the water and swam the rest of the way in. When Kauffman got close, he found that tides had pushed him to land on White Beach One instead of White Two, and that Jones's team had missed its objective completely. He reconnoitered the beach where the ocean had seen fit to put him. Some heavy coral blocked about twenty yards of White Beach One. Searching the bluff for exits, he discovered a brushy coral ledge that he thought might need a little tetratol in order to open an exit for wheeled or tracked vehicles. From the top of the bluff, a narrow dirt road ran west to Tinian's largest airfield, near Ushi Point.

The next night Kauffman repeated the swim, this time exploring White Two. Paddling through the surf, he heard voices. He was about to shout at his men to shut up when he realized the voices were speaking Japanese. He went ashore on the opposite end of the beach, removed his swim trunks, and rolled himself in sand for concealment. When the voices went away, he searched the beach and found a string of inoperable mines on the flank of the landing area. The teams finished their recon, then slipped back into the surf, wiping their footprints from the sand.

When Kauffman returned to the *Rocky Mount,* Kelly Turner called a conference of his commanders, inviting Admiral Spruance to observe. Spruance liked the surprise inherent in the White Beach plan. True, the tiny beaches were unsuited to the large-scale ship-to-shore operation carried out at Saipan. But as Holland Smith and Graves Erskine stressed, the Tinian landings would be essentially a *shore*-to-shore movement. The staging shore, Saipan, just six miles away, was like a supply convoy that never needed to refuel, an unsinkable aircraft carrier that never had to worry about turning into the wind. It also held General Harper's XXIV Corps Artillery, eleven battalions strong, all of which occupied positions on Saipan's southern plateau. The entire area south of Iseley Field was a firing pit that would put the entire northern half of Tinian to Harper's lash.

Impressed by these merits, Turner agreed to landings at White Beach. The operation plan was circulated to Clifton Cates's Fourth Marine Division, which was set to make the principal landings, as well as to Watson's Second Division, which would carry out an amphibious feint off Tinian Town before following Cates's men ashore.

Hill addressed his concerns about weather with Spruance afterward, and Spruance agreed to send seaplanes carrying a Pacific Fleet aerographer to patrol out to a thousand miles to the west. Spruance authorized Hill to postpone the landings at his discretion if the weather seemed threatening.

The plan to take Tinian would be an ongoing improvisation. The decision to land in a decidedly nonregulation fashion, using beaches that were a scant fraction of the size urged by the doctrine recently tested and proved at Saipan, reflected the concern over the toll taken on the two Marine divisions who were to handle the back-to-back operations. That trial had tested Kelly Turner as well. Harry Hill could see that something wasn't right with him. Hill didn't think he was bearing up physically. He had a back problem that required him to wear a heavy brace. Though Turner seldom talked about it, Hill had learned from members of Turner's staff how much it had been affecting him. Alcohol was a ready remedy for the pain and stress that threatened to pull him off the line. But Turner's stormy sea state was only going to get worse.

On July 12, the ugliness of the "Smith versus Smith" affair reared up again when the commander of Army forces in the Pacific Ocean Areas, Lieutenant General Robert C. Richardson, flew to Saipan without giving notice to either Turner or Holland Smith. Richardson compounded the breach of courtesy by proceeding immediately upon his arrival to 27th Division headquarters and taking it upon himself to award combat decorations to Smith's men.

Spruance knew about Richardson's visit and was eager to head off an explosion, for he knew how Richardson resented Holland Smith's serving as corps commander. Spruance warned Smith that Richardson had shown up and asked him to "suffer in silence" through the affront to his authority. But Spruance didn't anticipate the half of it. After handing out the valor awards, Richardson announced that he planned to investigate the decision to relieve Ralph Smith, and possibly even to refer disciplinary charges against Holland Smith. When Harry Schmidt and Holland Smith finally met Richardson at the Army general's temporary quarters, Holland Smith's temper was put to the test.

"You had no right to relieve Ralph Smith," Richardson began. "The Twenty-seventh is one of the best trained divisions in the Pacific. I trained it myself. You discriminated against the Army in favor of the Marines. I want you to know that you can't push the Army around the way you've been doing. You and your Marine Corps commanders aren't as well qualified to lead large bodies of troops as general officers in the Army. We've had more experience in handling troops than you've had and yet you dare remove one of my generals?"

It was a fair measure of Holland Smith's respect for Spruance that he managed to hold his tongue. Richardson continued, accusing Smith of wasting valuable lives with his overly aggressive tactics. His final salvo would resound in Holland Smith's report to Spruance: "You Marines are nothing but a bunch of beach runners, anyway. What do you know about land warfare?" It was only by some rare alignment of natural forces that Holland Smith had managed to restrain himself.

There was no way the phenomenon would occur twice. Kelly Turner wouldn't stand for Richardson's conduct. He called him to his cabin in the *Rocky Mount*. When Richardson was shown in, the amphibious force commander lit all boilers and opened his valves. He shouted and raved, telling Richardson that his failure to call on him or advise him of his plans was an unthinkable slight to him. The general whitened, firing back using words that have gone unrecorded, then turned on his heel and stormed aboard the boat for a ride back to the *Indianapolis*. Years later Carl Moore would remain appalled by Turner's conduct, saying, "I believe he had a hangover. Otherwise I can't explain it."

When Richardson complained to Spruance, the Fifth Fleet commander said, "Oh, well, that's just Kelly Turner. Nobody pays any attention to him." Spruance's deflection held a measure of hard truth. Turner's inner fires were most productively stoked when he was drawing up war plans and seeing them into action. In matters of personal relations, they were no asset to the war effort. When Turner gave Nimitz a taste of it, submitting an outraged report titled, "Reporting Unwarranted Assumption of Command Authority by Lt. Gen. R. C. Richardson, Jr., USA," CINCPAC was dismissive. Nimitz understood it was Turner's dark side talking.

Four days after the Richardson contretemps, an aircraft landed at Isely Field bearing Admirals Ernest King and Chester Nimitz. Spruance was on hand to greet his superiors when they touched down. King's first order of business was to reassure Spruance about the controversy over his decisions in the great carrier engagement off the Marianas of June 18–20. At Pearl Harbor and elsewhere, the air admirals were in a stir. They couldn't seem to grant this battleship sailor credit for a victory in their game. John Towers had long considered Spruance a dilettante and made his lack of respect for him obvious. "It was the chance of a century missed," Jocko Clark complained to Samuel Eliot Morison ten days after the Great Marianas Turkey Shoot. Clark never seemed to get over missing his "golden opportunity to be a Beatty." But chief among the complainants was Marc Mitscher. Though he had deflected his subordinates' protests, according to Chuck Barber the carrier boss later took their complaint directly to Admiral King.

King would be unmoved. "As I could," the Navy's top man wrote, "I told Spruance that I believed that he had done exactly the correct things with his own fleet in the Battle of the Philippine Sea, no matter what other people might say, especially since he had to remember that the Japanese had another fleet ready in the Inland Sea to pounce on the many transports which hadn't been entirely discharged of their troops, nor had the supply ships had enough time to discharge their cargoes."

King elsewhere wrote, "Spruance was rightly guided by the basic obligation. . . . Spruance accomplished more lasting results than he or anyone else realized at the time, for the great loss of Japanese naval aircraft in the Battle of the Philippine Sea crippled Japanese naval aviation for the remainder of the war."

The amphibious forces were grateful that Spruance stood by. "I think I should be classed as Raymond's number-one rooter for his decision at Philippine Sea," Harry Hill said. "I was sitting as a lone duck at Saipan, in tactical and unloading command. Our gunfire support ships were somewhere over the western horizon as an interposing force against a Jap end run. But had the Japs hit with full strength, Oldendorf probably couldn't have stopped them. With three divisions on the beach, we were very vulnerable. And Raymond knew it. His decision not to be drawn off was exactly right, and I'm positive will be adjudged so by all future historians."

King, Nimitz, and Spruance were taken by jeep from Isely Field to Charan Kanoa, where they met Holland Smith at his headquarters. After lunch, the general gave them a tour of the landing beaches. When the trio asked to be driven to the top of Mount Tapotchau, Smith refused, mentioning the threat of enemy snipers. But King and Nimitz insisted on it. And not only that, they wanted to make a circuit of the entire island. Summoning several additional jeeps to accommodate their combat escort, a picked squad of Marine riflemen, the luminaries began their tour. King clearly wanted to take the measure of the war at the sharp end ahead of Nimitz's strategy meeting with President Roosevelt, scheduled for July 26 on Oahu, and prior to his participation in a Combined Chiefs of Staff conference in Quebec in September.

What the top commanders saw at Marpi Point shocked them. Preserved on the rocks below the cliffs was "the crowning horror of Japanese lunacy," King would write: the bodies of hundreds of civilians, "egged on by the military, [who] had cast themselves from the cliffs . . . in an orgy of self-destruction." They drove south to Garapan, past the cliffs where Saito and Nagumo had taken their lives. Two realities were made clear to the U.S. Navy brain trust: A great victory was at hand in the Central Pacific, and far worse lay ahead.

That evening the three admirals boarded a landing craft and proceeded to the *Indianapolis.* Carl Moore met them at the gangway and showed them

to their quarters, then saw to the arrangements for the festivities that evening. Saipan's conquest was cause for celebration, and there were two more
invasions to discuss. On the night of July 17, Spruance hosted a lavish dinner in the cruiser's flag mess. The Fifth Fleet commander as host sat at the
head of the table, with King on his right and Nimitz on his left. The admirals and generals and their staffs, a glittering assembly of gold stars and
stripes, were arrayed by descending seniority down the flanks, seated at
long tables adorned with the accoutrements of a fleet flagship, its presentation silver service and fine china. But no sooner had the steward's mates
brought the food from the scullery than the evening's unbidden guests arrived. It was a cloud of black flies, swarming out from the island.

Nearly an inch long, they were "the kind of fly that you couldn't scare
off," Moore said. "They had to be pushed." They fixed their sticky legs into
linen-draped tables and buzzed noses and ears, landed on plates and sam-
pled the food, wriggled across cheeks and underneath eyeglass lenses. Outside, they landed on the guylines and rails, piling atop one another such
that quarter-inch lines grew to three inches in diameter. "It was a horror,"
Moore said. Saipan, rotten with corpses, was a buffet for these miniature
hellions, and he couldn't help but imagine what they had last touched upon
shore.

Harry Hill, swatting away, sent a bowl of ice cream skittering across the
table. Crystal glasses toppled over, soaking the white linen. All that could
be done about the destruction of decorum was to laugh about it. The flies
of Saipan, it was said, were the only foreign air force in the world that had
proved itself capable of overcoming the Fifth Fleet. "Nobody stayed there
any longer than they could help," Moore said.

In Tokyo that same day, the Japanese high command was in a far greater
state of agitation. Ever since the loss of the Marshalls, powerful voices had
been calling for the removal of Prime Minister Tojo. The original war-
monger, he headed the army clique whose racialist aggression had started
the war in the thirties. Tojo had raised the stakes in an "emergency declaration" issued in February, pledging the death of the entire nation as the cost
of failure in the war. An *ichioku gyokusai,* a hundred-million-person "shattering of the jewel," crystallized his conviction that the prestige of his army
outweighed the fate of his people. According to Matsuo Kato, an American-
educated journalist who worked for a Japanese news agency before the
war, "His experience in the small world of the army was his whole life and
he believed that the same principles he had learned there could be applied

to the entire nation." Partially realized on Saipan, Tojo's death fantasy was a madness that only a change in leadership could cure.

After Kwajalein and Eniwetok fell, a Navy Ministry analyst, Rear Admiral Sokichi Takagi, produced a study concluding that "Japan could not possibly win" and urging Japan's leaders to "seek a compromise peace immediately," to include withdrawal from China and relinquishment of Formosa and Korea. On June 29, nine days after the Battle of the Philippine Sea, the brother of Emperor Hirohito, Prince Takamatsu, met secretly with Foreign Minister Shigemitsu and explained that the Imperial Navy was "unfit for further engagements." The prince, a naval captain, had opposed going to war from the first, as had Takagi. Now he said, "When Saipan fell, as it very soon would, there would be no raison d'être for our fleet. The war was as good as lost." The prince urged Shigemitsu "to seek the termination of hostilities without delay, provided in the process the imperial house was left intact."

These conclusions were considered unspeakable. Naval officers were still spinning yarns about their great victory against the U.S. fleet, while a cabal of militarists, including Tojo, conspired to keep the true state of affairs from Emperor Hirohito. Though their public rhetoric was a shimmering web of lies, the truth did reach the palace. Marquis Koichi Kido, who served the emperor as Lord Keeper of the Privy Seal, got wind of reality through the whispers of his confidants. His awareness served to undermine Tojo's position and make him vulnerable to further bad news.

When word of Saipan's fall reached Tokyo, it upended the vulnerable prime minister. Tojo's wife began receiving anonymous phone calls asking whether her husband had killed himself yet. More than one party was planning to do the honor for him. Admiral Takagi was organizing a group to carry out a machine gun ambush. Another cabal—led by one Major Tsunoda, a midgrade army officer transferred to Imperial Headquarters from central China, and Tatsukuma Ushijima, the president of the Tokyo chapter of the East Asia Federation—was plotting to throw a hydrocyanic gas bomb at Tojo's car while he was en route to the Imperial Palace for a cabinet meeting.

Tojo tried to re-form his cabinet by having the Navy minister, Mitsumasa Yonai, join it. Yonai had been a voice of moderation, strongly opposed to the Tripartite Pact with Nazi Germany and Fascist Italy during his eight-month stint as prime minister in 1940. But on July 17, in spite of Tojo's lobbying, Yonai said he would not join his rival. With his refusal, wrote Takagi, "the pulse of the Tojo regime stopped completely." Desperate, Tojo went to the Imperial Palace to see his sponsor and ally, Kido. The imperial adviser was frosty, informing Tojo that the emperor was "extremely annoyed" at his manner of consolidating power within the cabinet. Distraught at the loss of confidence, the prime minister presented himself at the Imperial Palace the next morning to tender his resignation.

The president of the Privy Council, Kiichiro Hiranuma, an influential senior adviser to Emperor Hirohito, would claim after the war, "We were convinced that it would be useless to continue the war as soon as Saipan fell." But the ensuing change in leadership produced no change in war policy. The man who replaced Tojo as prime minister, Kuniaki Koiso, a retired army general who was serving as governor-general of Korea, had little support on either side of the moderate/militarist divide. The ascent of this mandarin all but ensured continuation of a dysfunctional war policy that was driven with a certain fervor to ignore what all knew to be the case: Japan was beaten; to resist further was hopeless.

The realists found no courage in their convictions at any time when it might have mattered. Hiranuma's posturing reflected the predominant prideful cowardice. He later declared in spite of his own convictions that "there is no way out but to fight to the end." Kido, who was Hirohito's most influential adviser, agreed. Tojo's resignation had two important consequences: It protected the throne by averting the political trauma that either of the active assassination plots against him would have caused, and it delivered an ineffectual timekeeper, Koiso, as head of state. A bloody status quo continued in spite of Japan's dramatic losses on the battlefield.

In Washington, even the least hawkish of commentators understood that any talk of peace would only serve the nihilist designs of the Japanese government. The editorial writers at the liberal *New Republic* discerned that Tokyo would "follow a strategy of making the cost of our victories as high as possible and at the same time seek to encourage new illusions that peace is possible with a Japan that has not been thoroughly defeated."

On July 21, fifty-six thousand Marine and Army troops were arrayed at sea off Guam, prepared for their assault on the first American ground seized by Japan during the war. Rear Admiral Richard L. Conolly's Southern Attack Force had been hitting the island with a vengeance.

Conolly was a favorite of many top Marines. Any admiral who insisted his fire-support ships work at point-blank range would have admirers in the Corps. "Close-in Conolly," they called him. Holland Smith's operations chief, Colonel Robert Hogaboom, considered Conolly "one of the great amphibious commanders that I have met" and said "he had all of the great features of Kelly Turner and none of his faults. He was a very splendid, strong, able man who would listen. He would send for Marines and listen to them talk about amphibious operations. He would send for me and sit at a table with me and talk with me by the hour, questioning me, and then he'd put on his field boots and go ashore and follow the Marines all through the operations. He studied and mastered the Marines' problems as well as the naval problems."

Spruance, fearing for the well-being of the Guamanians, so loyal to the Americans during the hard years of Japanese occupation, cautioned Conolly to avoid indiscriminate bombardments, so Conolly supervised the attack directly, knowing from intelligence reports where the local people were hiding. With three ammunition ships parked at Saipan, he ran cruisers and destroyers in and out of Guam. "We had a regular conveyor belt," he said. "We'd shoot all the ammunition out of a division of cruisers, then send them over to Saipan to refuel and load from these ammunition ships and they'd come back and start shooting again. They'd leave one evening, take all night to get over there, they'd fuel and load ammunition all day and come back the next night. They would be gone about thirty-six hours and be ready to start another round of shooting. This was, I think, the most prolonged directed bombardment of the war." Marc Mitscher backed him up, committing all four carrier groups to Guam for the first time in weeks. Bolstered by the squadrons of the escort carriers, his pilots had been pounding the island around the clock, putting up fourteen hundred combat sorties in the four days of the action.

The western coastline was inhospitable to invasion. Its natural ramparts of rocky cliffs offered less than ten miles of coast to amphibious assault. But that would have to suffice. Underwater Demolition Teams 3, 4, and 6 got the job of dealing with the extensive antiboat obstacles installed by the Japanese. Under close support from LCI gunboats, the frogmen maneuvered through the treacherous coral heads of the lagoon off Agat and Asan and made note of where wire was strung along the low-tide line, and where piles of coral were baled together inside wire mesh like cyclone fencing. They sounded the lagoon right up to the beach line, marking the safe approaches with buoys. That night they returned with tetratol packs to blast the obstacles. Their work done, they delivered a report to Conolly's staff, who forwarded copies via destroyer to the amphibious groups at sea.

For the benefit of the first wave of Marines that would land on Guam, some free spirits from UDT 4, Lieutenant Gordon Carberry commanding, posted a sign on Agat Beach: "WELCOME MARINES. AGAT USO—2 BLOCKS." Every team involved at Guam claimed this prank as their own, "but Murray Henry and Walt Hlebechuk claim they actually had a hand in this," Bob Baird wrote.

Aircraft flew over the amphibious force under the concussion of naval bombardment. General Geiger announced to his troops through shipboard loudspeakers, "You have been honored. The eyes of the nation watch you as you go into battle to liberate this former American bastion from the enemy. The honor which has been bestowed on you is a signal one. May the glorious traditions of the Marine Corps' esprit de corps spur you to victory. You have been honored."

With UDT frogmen serving as pilots for the landing craft, Conolly and Geiger put the first wave ashore on two beaches, widely separated on either side of Orote Peninsula, whose airfield complex was the island's major strategic asset along with its harbor at Apra. The leading echelon of the Third Marine Division, under the command of Major General Allen H. Turnage, landed just north of Asan Point. Nearly simultaneously, the First Provisional Marine Brigade, under Brigadier General Lemuel C. Shepherd, Jr., went ashore about seven miles down the coast, at Agat Village, south of Orote Peninsula.

Withering naval and air bombardment had knocked out virtually all the enemy defensive positions on the beaches, but the rise of the land behind them was much more pronounced than it was at Saipan. Enemy gunfire from the hills commanding the beaches near Agat destroyed twenty amtracs on approach. From its lodgment at Asan, Turnage's Third Division faced a tumult of hills in whose multitiered chaos General Takashina made his command post. They were met by mortar and artillery fire converging on the landing beach as well as fire from well-sited machine gun nests. From the higher ground, Japanese soldiers rolled grenades right into Marine positions. Major General Kiyoshi Shigematsu, commander of the 48th Independent Mixed Brigade, exhorted his troops: "The enemy, overconfident because of his successful landing on Saipan, is planning a reckless and insufficiently prepared landing on Guam. We have an excellent opportunity to annihilate him on the beaches." From the heights overlooking Turnage's left flank, Japanese artillery supported a counterattack down the beach from the town of Agana, inflicting heavy casualties and stalling the attempt to break out. The Third Regiment, on the division's far left, faced

ASSAULT ON GUAM, *July 21*

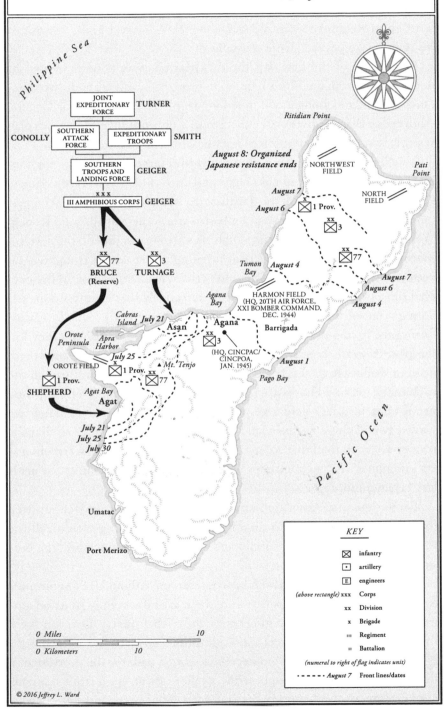

Philippine Sea

JOINT EXPEDITIONARY FORCE — **TURNER**

CONOLLY — SOUTHERN ATTACK FORCE

EXPEDITIONARY TROOPS — **SMITH**

SOUTHERN TROOPS AND LANDING FORCE — **GEIGER**

xxx III AMPHIBIOUS CORPS — **GEIGER**

August 8: Organized Japanese resistance ends

Ritidian Point

NORTHWEST FIELD

Pati Point

August 7
August 6

NORTH FIELD

xx 77 — **BRUCE** (Reserve)

xx 3 — **TURNAGE**

x 1 Prov.

xx 3

xx 77

August 7
August 6
August 4

Tumon Bay *August 4*

Agana Bay

HARMON FIELD (HQ, 20TH AIR FORCE, XXI BOMBER COMMAND, DEC. 1944)

Cabras Island *July 21*

Asan **Agana**

xx 3 (HQ, CINCPAC/ CINCPOA, JAN. 1945)

Barrigada

Orote Peninsula *Apra Harbor*

July 25

OROTE FIELD

x 1 Prov.

▲ *Mt. Tenjo*

xx 77

August 1

Pago Bay

x 1 Prov. — **SHEPHERD**

Agat Bay **Agat**

July 21
July 25
July 30

Pacific Ocean

Umatac

Port Merizo

0 Miles 10
0 Kilometers 10

© 2016 Jeffrey L. Ward

KEY

⊠	infantry
⊡	artillery
E	engineers
(above rectangle) xxx	Corps
xx	Division
x	Brigade
III	Regiment
II	Battalion

(numeral to right of flag indicates unit)

- - - - *August 7* Front lines/dates

direct assault as well as infiltration, losing 615 men killed, wounded, and missing in action. Marine tanks, which came ashore within thirty minutes of the first wave, helped hold off small but spirited infantry counterattacks. The Third Regiment's commander, Colonel W. Carvel Hall, committed his reserve to repel the Japanese assault.

By evening of the first day, the two Marine assault forces, joined by one regiment from the 77th Infantry Division, had pushed about two thousand yards inland along a two-mile-long front. The rest of Major General Andrew D. Bruce's division, held at sea in a dozen transports as the corps reserve, stood ready to reinforce either beachhead.

Conolly's fire-support ships found plentiful targets on Guam's high inland slopes, which were not as craggy and cave-ridden as those on Saipan. Cruiser fire alone forced the Japanese to abandon the island's highest mountain, Mount Tenjo. "We never had to attack them at all," said Donald Weller, commander of the Third Division's artillery regiment, the Twelfth Marines. Artillery air bursts were devastating where enemy troops had no overhead cover. In the Third Division's center, artillery and naval fire covered the advance of the 21st Marines so effectively that enemy troops seldom got out of their trenches. "The Japs had apparently leaned forward during the barrage to protect themselves. However, in so doing, they lost the protection of their steel helmets," Weller said. Marines found them dead in shallow foxholes, felled by fragments that took them through the back of the neck and in the back. "After this attack we habitually adjusted fire against Japanese defensive positions using ground bursts. Then we waited two or three minutes, and followed up with air bursts so that the frag could reach the Japanese in their shallow foxholes." Forward observers sometimes saw enemy troops break cover and run as soon as the artillery began thumping.

Those signature American advantages, lift and heavy power, ensured the landing force's ability to tilt any table. Admiral King would call the revolution in amphibious capacity and refinement of tradecraft "the outstanding development of the war."

On W plus 2, Geiger landed his corps reserve. Without UDT swimmers to guide them to channels penetrating the reef and woefully short on amtracs, the two remaining regiments of the 77th Infantry Division were forced to disembark at the reef and wade ashore at Agat. One of the shorter Navy lieutenants on hand volunteered to scout a path for the short men in the regiment to wade through, while a taller officer, six feet plus, broadened it to discover its limits, where tall men could keep their heads above water. After and forevermore, these two officers were known as "Low Water" and "High Water." Water, food, and ammunition followed a similar wet path, transferred from LSTs and other craft to rafts and rubber boats, then pushed, towed, and paddled across several hundred yards of lagoon to the beach. As the commander of a transport division observed: "Beach parties could more properly be called *reef* parties in this operation since the reef was where the beach parties were set up. They worked from life rafts, floats in the water, and generally all over the reef keeping things moving. . . . This was truly an amphibious operation, almost a submarine one in fact; officers and men of these parties became 'water rats' and half submerged stevedores."

When the handiwork of Lieutenant Carberry's demolition swimmers was discovered—a channel leading into the left flank of White Beach One—beach parties lashed together a causeway of life rafts linking the channel to the reef. On land, the routes of passage were little better. A single narrow road served each of the White beaches, running over the bluff and into an area of fields and coconut groves where Marines were hunkered down in thickly developed clusters of foxholes and supply dumps. A few days of heavy traffic under sporadic rain squalls turned the roads into quagmires. Congestion on the beach grew steadily worse as the reserve came ashore, reinforcing the pair of American lodgments straddling Orote Peninsula. On W plus 3, a pair of pontoon barges with cranes sped the flow of supplies into the jam. The churning of tires and tracks transformed the roads into ribbons of mud and eventually turned up the stinking gristle of a Japanese burial site, freshly installed after the days-long naval and air bombardment.

"This was not a gentleman's job," the transport commander wrote. "It took a combination of Simon Legree and a bucko mate to keep it moving. We produced that combination."

On July 22, the second day of operations on Guam and two days before landings on Tinian, the director of an experimental weapons development program, Lieutenant Commander Louis W. Mang, arrived on Saipan to exhibit a motion picture demonstrating the use of a terrible new weapon. He gained quick entrée to Fifth Fleet brass via his friendship with Harry Hill, who was a Naval Academy classmate. On board the *Cambria,* Mang showed a movie reel of a P-51 Mustang dropping a firebomb on a test range. The canisters carried by the fighter plane contained a hellish brew.

It was a mixture of a jelly compound used to waterproof vehicles and hundred-octane aviation fuel. Released in 165-gallon external fuel tanks at low altitude, the gelatinous compound ignited and flowed like a lethal plasma over everything in its path, burning dugouts and foxholes and whatever lay within.

Mang let on that he was having trouble selling the Pentagon on the na-palm bomb. If he could persuade field commanders in the Pacific to adopt it, he felt he could better make his case. Mang said the bombs could be readily fashioned from available airdrome inventory. He had brought with him several hundred fuzes and proposed to demonstrate them by equip-ping the Army fighter group at Isely Field with the new weapon. Oversee-ing assembly of the bombs, Mang instructed the P-47 Thunderbolt pilots of the 318th Fighter Group in their use.

When the test missions were flown over Tinian, Hill invited Spruance, Turner, and the Marine headquarters staff to board a destroyer and ob-serve. "The effect was awe-inspiring," Hill said. "A burst of flame rose a hundred feet or more into the air, and then the flame just seemed to flow along the ground." Measurements afterward showed the payload had burned out a strip a hundred yards long and more than thirty yards wide, nearly the size of a football field. The result was far better than anything that white phosphorus ordnance could do. When Hill found the compound did not burn long enough to suffocate enemy holed up in blockhouses, he recommended adding brown tar pitch to the mixture to enhance the vol-ume of noxious smoke. If any moral questions attended the innovations that made the horrible device even more horrible, they did not trouble Harry Hill. He considered death by napalm "probably an easier way to die than it is to get a piece of shrapnel tearing your insides out of you. War brings death, and many of the so-called horrible forms of death are really the quickest and easiest, when you come right down to it. It seems a hor-rible thing because we all dread fire and burning. But war is war, and as I pointed out several times, when you fight Japs, you either kill him or he kills you. I don't think you can be too particular about the means of de-stroying your enemy." After the test, Hill wrote the Navy Department rec-ommending the full development of napalm for naval use. When Holland Smith endorsed its utility on Tinian, Hill wrote Nimitz requesting air shipment of 8,500 pounds of the compound, which was duly dispatched.

The intramural Army-Navy feud had escalated after the Smith versus Smith controversy. It raged again after General Richardson's nose-thumbing tour of Saipan. When General Douglas MacArthur went to the press with charges that the Navy and its Marine Corps had been careless with life in the Central Pacific, it seemed the rift would never heal. Though Marine casualty rates on Saipan were the same as the Army's, MacArthur shouted to the rafters that the aggressive, fast-moving tactics of the Marine Corps were causing unnecessary losses. In reality, American forces were indeed growing careless with life—Japanese life, which had been cheapened first by the murderous eagerness of Tojo to actualize the militarists' race theories and join the worldwide Axis offensive, and then by the dizzying exhibition of suicide warfare perversely showcased at Saipan, from the military folly of Saito's last charge to the quasi-systemic killings of civilians at Marpi Point with calculated innuendo as well as other weapons. The novelty of the horror registered at all levels of the U.S. command. If there had been nothing racial or exterminationalist about America's impetus to go to war, the tactics of extermination arose as just that—as military tactics, developed in the field by necessity as the enemy's suicidal mind revealed itself at full scale. Napalm and diversions were both part of Nimitz's grim resolve to destroy Imperial Japan's death cult at the lowest possible cost.

Lines of military ethics had been crossed as the Rising Sun pushed east, and lines were crossed as the Americans surged west. It was the U.S. Navy that introduced napalm to the Pacific. But it would be the Army Air Forces that perfected the science of laying low the enemy's strongpoints and population centers with storms of fire. In Washington, Hap Arnold and his air strategists were preparing to change the rules of warfare, the new practices to be carried out from their airdromes in the Marianas.

Meanwhile, off Tinian, the old steel navy was getting ready to sell the Japanese once again on a seaborne invasion that would not come.

26

Steel Like Snowflakes

N apoleon thought God Himself fought on the side with the best artillery, and as a king of old Prussia saw it, "Artillery lent dignity to what would otherwise be a vulgar brawl." If these maxims were true, what could be said of the fires that converged upon Tinian in late July 1944? The bombardment it absorbed from the guns on its neighbor island, and from ships roaming offshore, might have been, acre for acre, the most "dignified" military operation in history. That the island did not crumble to pieces from the weight of it was the result of simple physics. Tinian's low silhouette made it a hard target for flat-trajectory naval gunfire. Destroyers fired white phosphorus to denude cane fields and overgrown ravines. Cruisers and battleships dealt with fortified targets. From three thousand yards, not much could withstand a sixteen-inch shell. Now, having replenished her magazines from an ammunition ship in the Garapan roadstead, the USS *Colorado* took station off Tinian Town.

Commissioned in 1923, the *Colorado* and her sister the *West Virginia* were the last battleships to join the fleet before international treaties stopped U.S. capital ship production for seventeen years. On the day Pearl Harbor was attacked, she sat safely in a West Coast dry dock. Thereafter, a lack of fuel and fuel transport kept her chained to the coast. When the *Colorado* at last reached the South Pacific, she remained parked at Fiji, standing guard against Japanese incursions farther east that never came. She never got up to Guadalcanal. Thereafter it seemed she was the ward of a shipyard supervisor every time battle offered. Technicians made her modern but would never make her fast. When Captain William Granat took command in late 1943, he and his men wondered whether they would ever catch up with the war. It seemed the last heavy ships of the post–Great War era would never enter the fight. The landings at Tarawa were their baptism. In the Marianas, the old battlewagons became ships of the line again. If the fire-support sector wasn't as romantic as the traditional battle line facing powerful opposite numbers, there was something to be said for the sheer volume of fire that bombardment duty required of a main battery. The *Colorado* served up call fire off Saipan in the first weeks after the invasion and spent three days hitting pillboxes and gun positions on Guam ahead of the landings that took place on July 21.

Now, before lunch, Admiral Hill gave the *Colorado* a special assignment at Tinian. Army intelligence had detected a serious threat to the White beaches: three 120 mm coastal defense guns whose hillside emplacement on the island's north end left them immune to artillery fire from Saipan. So the battleship turned to, assisted by an intelligence officer from General Harper's headquarters, who boarded a Piper L-4 Grasshopper to observe and correct the battleship's fire.

Installed at the foot of a small rise, the guns were hard to see until the first salvos had denuded them of their camouflage. After an hour and a half, during which she closed within just three thousand yards of shore, the *Colorado* had extracted this thorn from Harry Hill's side. Captain Granat then turned his main battery on the coral lip behind the White beaches, shattering it in hopes of improving access from strand up to bluff.

The steel necklace of naval power drew tight around Tinian on the day before J Day, so tightly that the links themselves were at some risk of damage from each other. As the *Colorado* fired point-blank into Japanese gun positions, one shell in six was a ricochet. Skipping off the rocks and hills, several of these landed in the sea on the far coast. One sixteen-incher raised a spout just eighty yards ahead of the *Montpelier* while another straddled her astern. Her captain noted, "Enemy fire had been expected, but nothing so large as this." He was compelled to move a bit farther out to sea.

The *Colorado* checked fire while a flight of P-47s plastered the table-lands above White Beach with napalm. As the flames spilled through the sugarcane, Granat delivered a fusillade of time-fuzed antiaircraft rounds, producing air bursts intended to cut down fleeing enemy troops. This brutal business finished, the *Colorado* hove back to the south after dark to take station off Tinian Town again. Joined by the light cruiser *Cleveland* and the destroyer *Norman Scott,* she awaited the dawn of J Day.

★ ★ ★

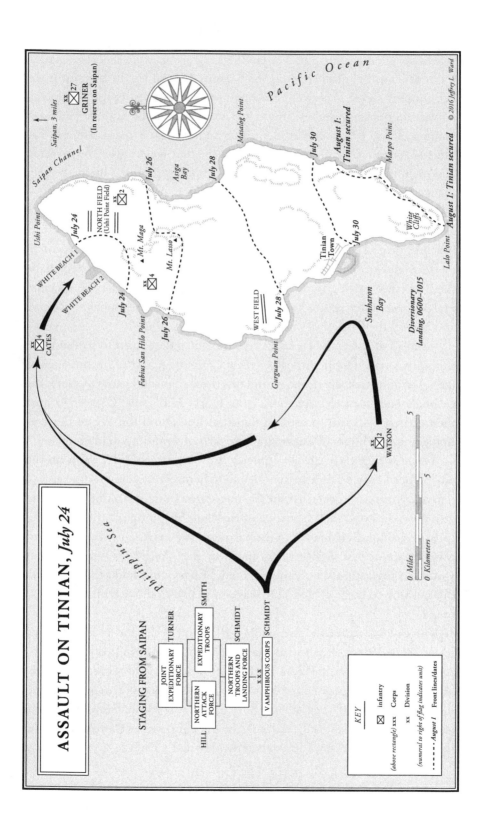

ASSAULT ON TINIAN, *July 24*

Pacific Ocean

Saipan Channel

Saipan, 3 miles

GRINER
27
(In reserve on Saipan)

Ushi Point

WHITE BEACH 1
July 24

NORTH FIELD
(Ushi Point Field)

July 24

CATES
4

WHITE BEACH 2

July 26

▲ Mt. Maga

July 24

July 26

Mt. Lasso ▲

4

Fabius San Hilo Point

July 26

2

July 28

Asiga
Bay

WEST FIELD

July 28

Gurguan Point

Philippine Sea

Masalog Point

July 30

July 30

Tinian
Town

August 1:
Tinian secured

White
Cliffs

Marpo Point

Lalo Point   *August 1: Tinian secured*

© 2016 Jeffrey L. Ward

Saipiaron
Bay

WATSON
2

*Diversionary
landing, 0600–1015*

0 Miles   5

0 Kilometers   5

STAGING FROM SAIPAN

JOINT
EXPEDITIONARY
FORCE | TURNER

NORTHERN
ATTACK FORCE | HILL

EXPEDITIONARY
TROOPS | SMITH

NORTHERN
TROOPS AND
LANDING FORCE | SCHMIDT

V AMPHIBIOUS CORPS | SCHMIDT
xxx

KEY

⊠ infantry

(above rectangle) xxx Corps

xx Division

(numeral to right of flag indicates unit)

------ August 1 Front lines/dates

Typhoon season was at hand. On the morning of July 24 off Tinian's White beaches, it was hard to tell where the sea ended and the land began. Persistent winds raised a heavy surf but did little to clear the smoke and dust that had been stirred up inland by the bombardment. At 5:15 A.M., Draper Kauffman radioed Admiral Hill to report that surf conditions had made it impossible for his UDT to carry out a night mission to clear some land mines found on White Beach Two. The job fell to the main battery of the USS *California* instead. With squalls cutting visibility to five hundred feet, neither ships nor spotting planes could see their targets, but the rough trade of mine clearing with high-capacity ordnance needed little in the way of precision.

At 7:00, all fires were checked to let an air strike rumble through, and then the bombardment resumed. Naval fire and artillery alike held the entire island in its grasp. The artillery on Saipan commenced firing before sunrise, rolling across the airfield at Ushi Point and its road junctions and rail line. When the *California* fired on an ammunition dump reported miles to the south, near Tinian Town, her gunnery officer found the irregular coastline easy to orient to via the PPI scope, and he used radar control to blanket the area.

As the transport group carrying the Second Marine Division showed itself off Tinian Town, beginning their diversion, the Fourth Marine Division embarked in amtracs from their LSTs, LCIs, LSDs, and pontoon barges and formed in waves, beginning the real thing off the White beaches. General Cates would land a regiment on each beach, a single battalion at a time. H Hour was 7:40.

Harry Hill marveled at the humble spectacle of two small groups of amtracs carrying the first battalion toward shore as relays of P-47s overflew them, buzzing the center of each beach on a perpendicular. "Never had such an insignificant first wave started a major offensive operation," he would say. "I can assure you that many a prayer was said and many fingers were kept crossed during that critical half hour." It concerned General Cates that each of his regiments was understrength, as casualties at Saipan had outpaced the influx of replacements. But Nimitz's Law assuredly held: "If things are bad for us, they must be at least equally so for the enemy." On the way in, some men from the 2/25 broke into song: "Oh, what a beautiful morning, oh what a beautiful day, I've got a terrible feeling, everything's coming my way."

With luck, the Japanese garrison, expecting landings at Tinian Town, would be frozen in place by the diversion. Once the Marines were ashore in the north, their opponents would have to move, and that movement would mean their death, for troops on the move could not hide, and the thunder set to fall down upon them would be murderous. It seemed unlikely that anyone could be alive in the area that had absorbed their neutralizing bombardment. The troops newly ashore were amazed, therefore, to find automatic weapons firing on their amtracs from the beach. But with the *Tennessee* standing to the east, the *California* to the west, and the *Louisville* in the center, enemy forces in northern Tinian were generally overwhelmed. Ultimately, resistance to the breakout from the beachhead was light and enemy crews, while valiant, did not long hold. The largest Japanese formation was left waiting in the bluffs behind Tinian Town to repel landings that never came.

On the destroyer *Norman Scott,* the morning watch had excitedly greeted the news that they would be joining two of the most proficient players in the bombardment business, the *Colorado* and the *Cleveland,* to support the feint. Destroyermen always wanted to be where the action was, but the *Norman Scott*'s tour off Saipan, while full of opportunities to shoot, ended in anticlimax with orders to escort the battleship *Maryland,* damaged by a torpedo, back to Eniwetok. The ten-day reprieve from combat had been a letdown. Now the ship named for a great naval hero of Guadalcanal was about to get back into the thick of it.

Screening the *Colorado* south of Tinian Town, the *Norman Scott* was moving lazily, just fourteen hundred yards off the beach. Captain Seymour D. Owens was running his main battery through the schedule of fires designed to keep Japanese troops from moving north. Shortly after 7:30, his lookouts saw flashes and gouts of smoke coming from the base of a cliff behind the town. Up to that time, no U.S. ships had taken fire from shore batteries in the area. Owens estimated there were six to eight guns concealed at the base of the cliff. The fire-support commander in the *Colorado,* Rear Admiral Theodore D. Ruddock, scanned the coastline through a thirty-two-power telescope but found no telltale signs. When the gallery of British-built six-inch guns at long last revealed themselves, swinging out from within heavy foliage that sheltered them, their fire was rapid and effective.

The *Colorado* had just put on sternway to stay clear of the boat lanes— the first wave of amtracs was passing just ahead—when she took her first hit. No report records the sequence of hits that the Japanese artillerists scored. They must have been elated to have this target of a lifetime. Twenty-two shells tore into the battleship, all along her starboard side. Her side plate was penetrated twice, and her bunkers were opened to the sea. She bled out forty-five thousand gallons of fuel oil, a black stain that rolled on the swells. Set afire, the oil-fed flames climbed from the waterline to the forecastle deck. Another shell struck below the bridge, smashing a five-inch gun and whipping shrapnel across the forward superstructure. Captain Granat was nicked in his right ear. His navigator was hit, too, and his communications officer and signal officer as well. Admiral Ruddock, an expert in naval ordnance, experienced life on the receiving end of his craft, taking shrapnel in the heel.

The shipfitter's machine shop, penetrated on a vertical, had its overhead nearly collapsed. The shell, igniting lower compartments, vented smoke that gave rise to a flash report that a magazine was cooking. Quickly investigated and proved false, this nearly averted calamity was followed by a hit to the forecastle deck that punched through the steward's mates' washroom, killing six and wounding four more. A hit to the superstructure caused 40 mm ammo in a clipping room to begin popping, whipping fragments through all bulkheads, overheads, and decks within reach, starting a fire, and leaving three dead and ten wounded. A direct hit on a 20 mm platform on the superstructure deck riddled the ship's stacks with shrapnel and disabled a 40 mm gun mount as well, killing nine and wounding thirty. Another shell exploded in the number five 40 mm gun tub, destroying both it and the after signal station and killing everyone in it, and starting electrical fires. A hit on the number one five-inch/25 battery destroyed the gun and ignited ready-service boxes full of ammunition, killing four. A man who was passing a shell had it explode in the cradle of his arms. The ship's brand-new combat information center was hit, killing two and wounding sixteen and starting fires that burned bedding, clothing, charts, and the life raft stowage.

Eleven fires around the ship were professionally brought under control, but had the manuals not been followed—had all gas lines not been filled with carbon dioxide at the outset of operations, for example—it would have been far worse. The Japanese shells exploded on contact but left the deep structure of the ship unscathed. The ship listed only slightly, did not founder, and suffered only in terms of the flesh that was torn or burned in unprotected spaces. The fleet firefighting schools paid handsome dividends in saved lives, but they did not save the boys in the 20 mm gun tubs in the forecastle, or the Marines in the boat deck amidships, from being cut to pieces by a razor storm of shrapnel. Of the twelve men on every gun, and sixty more in the ammunition train, nearly half were killed or wounded.

The chaplain and his volunteers handled the horror of collecting the dead and the parts of the dead, taking them out of sight. The task lasted ten hours, hampered by the fact that just eleven of the thirty-nine killed wore identification. Fingerprints were taken where it was physically possible. Bodies were wrapped in flashproof bunk covers and stored in the junior officers' head. The stretcher cases were taken below to the M Division berthing compartment, the biggest on the ship. Limbs gone, burns pervasive, the odors of sulfa powder and dumped bowels rich in the air, the number of casualties proved too great for the battleship's medical detachment. "They could have been saved if they had had help," Leon Shook said. "There were just too many guys for our medics to take care of, so they died."

The ferociously efficient shore battery mauled not only the *Colorado* but the *Norman Scott,* too, hitting her six times within half a minute. One of the shells punched through the splinter shield on the starboard side of the pilot house and exploded in the nerve center of the ship, the bridge, inflicting catastrophic losses. The medical and repair parties who entered the pilot house were horrified to find Captain Owens and his officer of the deck, Noyes David Farmer, among the dead.

The *Colorado*'s helm opened the range but the ship could still fight. Though all four guns in her two forward turrets were badly gouged, they were intact where it mattered—in the long avenues of their rifled liners. Captain Granat coached them onto the offending bluff and opened fire. The *Cleveland,* a witness to the carnage, opened rapid fire with her main battery on the enemy position while moving to interpose herself to protect the other ships. Carl Moore, watching the light cruiser from the *Indianapolis,* was spellbound. "She steamed in there, and she looked like she was on fire, with all twelve of the six-inch guns blazing at once in rapid fire." Moore thought she knocked out the shore guns completely. The fleet flagship relieved the *Colorado* on her fire-support station.

In the *Norman Scott,* command devolved to a junior-grade lieutenant while the exec was having his wounds treated in triage. Steering with engines, Will C. Jumper conned her ahead of the *Cleveland* to seaward, flying flags to indicate that she had lost steering and was suffering serious fires. Still the crews of her four undamaged guns returned fire in local control. The destroyer *McDermut* came alongside and loaned out her medical team. The *Cleveland* maintained rapid fire, countermarching suddenly to throw off enemy fire, then stopped her engines. The battery appeared to have been neutralized. The fires raging around it touched ammunition from time to time, producing impressive explosions through the rest of the day.

After her firefighters prevailed and her engineers restored power, Lieutenant Jumper got the *Norman Scott* moving, steering with her engines. Shortly after eight, Admiral Hill ordered her to clear the area and return to Saipan. Bearing nineteen dead and twenty-seven seriously wounded, she retired at her best speed.

A poet of considerable talent, Jumper would write more than once about the morning of July 24, 1944:

> Suppose I could create for you the horror of it, make you see,
> build with more than weakling words the structure of this agony:
> the deck inch-deep in clotted blood like cranberries jelled;
> the blinding stench of butchery-explosion-fire–salt water,
> like a stifling fusion (think with your nostrils) of the smells
> of ammonia, burning rags, an inland bay when the tide is out,
> and the quivering viscera of just-cleaned mountain trout.
>
> Solid steel, you thought, crumbling like snowflakes dropping
> into a bonfire; forty-millimeter shells madly popping
> beneath your feet in gargantuan Chinese New Years festival;
> the ominous "ching" from geysers that spout from the sea about you;
> the helm spinning wantonly like a reckless gaming wheel;
> the telephones, suddenly dumb, like interlopers on a private grief;
> the slow, implacable turning toward the waiting reef.
>
> The bubbling plea there from the midst of jagged growths like kelp
> of twisted steel: "Don't leave me here. For God's sake help
> me. Take me out of here!" You can't. That was your cabin mate;
> another there, the mouthpiece of the battle telephone plunged
> into the curve of the classic jaw, the forehead perforated
> like a pumpkin caught beneath a hayrake, a shapeless blue-clay pile
> where fat metallic flies explore the slate-gray of a shattered smile.
>
> Suppose I could explode all this before you—only a claim in part,
> even against *my* war—by some strange power could catch your heart
> in tentacles of terror, not with pale symbols, but the wrenching
> gauntness of reality. You, too, might sense the crouching madness.
> But would you be the wiser? Where the gain? I cannot change
> the part of you, or me, or all mankind, the atavistic self that solves
> all riddles with: "I am the center, and about me the universe revolves."

* * *

When the *Norman Scott* dropped anchor in Saipan's transport area, a hospital ship was on hand to take her stretcher casualties and convey the dead to the graves registration service ashore. The *Colorado* remained off Tinian through the day, fulfilling her schedule of fires with her gouged main battery, holding a long roster of dead. Her 244 casualties included 39 killed, 4 missing in action, and 98 seriously wounded. Seven legs and an arm were amputated aboard ship without general anesthesia. Sodium pentothal was available, but none was used. "Shock was so marked that morphine seemed to provide enough analgesic for the procedures," the medical officer wrote. In spite of his wounds, Admiral Ruddock kept a close watch on the cliffs and bluffs and directed the battleship's fire on two coastal guns whose barrels were barely visible at the lower edge of a steep tumble of woods. The *Colorado*'s task complete, Kelly Turner ordered the ship to proceed to Saipan, and she dropped anchor there in the evening. As the dead were taken off, the crew turned to the task of cleanup. "Some of the men, what remained of them, were shoveled into buckets and heaved over the side of the ship." It was a grim chore to wash down the boat deck. "It was of particular interest to recall the fact that during all of the excitement of being hit, firing at the enemy, seeing mangled bodies and wounded shipmates, no one exhibited any hysterical reactions or maniacal tendencies, nor was there unnecessary shouting at one another," the medical officer wrote.

The assault landings on Tinian's White beaches went unopposed in part because of the convincing exhibition staged by UDT 6, the transport divisions carrying the Second Marine Division, and their fire-support ships. As the amtracs bearing the Fourth Division rolled ashore in the north, the Japanese were for critical hours unaware, but even after the alarm sounded, Colonel Kiyochi Ogata was forced to hold a battalion from his 50th Infantry Regiment near Tinian Town, just in case. A total force of more than eight thousand Japanese troops were on Tinian when the campaign began, including a battalion of the 135th Regiment, stuck there on maneuvers when the Americans arrived. Vice Admiral Kakuji Kakuta, his air forces eviscerated after the Turkey Shoot, yielded command to his junior, Colonel Ogata, for the defense of the island.

In the north, the 24th and 25th Marines were fully ashore by midmorning. The amtracs that carried them in were piggybacking articulated ramps improvised from surplus I-beams, timber, and piping. They drove them up against the steep bluff behind the beach, then backed down, and as Marines affixed the ends of the ramps to the bluff tops, the amtrac drivers enjoyed a steep but manageable crawl straight up the ramps for a speedy exit inland.

Targets were plentiful for warships, artillery, and aircraft. Before noon the leading Marine companies were reaching the western edge of Ushi Point Airfield when a great blast jarred the earth. About a mile to the south, a column of brown smoke rose into the air, white streamers of phosphorus arcing in all directions. The expanding shock wave of it, which could be seen from the *Pennsylvania*, was powerful enough to roll destroyers, and men stationed topside on the battleship had to duck away. The great brown smoke plume, rising seven thousand feet, memorialized a feat of marksmanship that would become legendary in the fraternity of artillerymen. While registering their weapon for the first time across the strait, a pack howitzer crew had managed to drop a 75 mm shell right down the ventilation intake of an underground magazine. Its fires would burn for two days.

The wisdom of the decision to land in the north was reflected by the nearly hopeless prospects Ogata faced in swinging his companies north under fire from Saipan and ships offshore. On the nearly flat tabletop of Tinian, there was nowhere to hide. Ruddock and his fire-support ships cinched tight their steel ring. Neutralization fire, interdiction fire, destruction fire—the whole playbook was by now familiar and used to good effect, stopping the movement of troops and vehicles and dispersing their concentrations. Off Tinian Town, a trio of cruisers filled in for the departed *Colorado*. The *Indianapolis, New Orleans,* and *Cleveland* blasted all of the roads leaving the city, blanketing them, with an assist from Marine artillery that had landed behind the first waves. The *California* kept up a deliberate cadence of harassing fires all night long, supporting a Marine advance toward a ridge about three miles east of Fabius San Hilo Point. Fear of friendly incoming fire compelled U.S. ground commanders to deny the ship some lucrative opportunities to shoot, and the flat terrain was frustrating to the gunnery officer, who preferred the perpendiculars of targets set in cliffs. But the very flatness of that terrain, free of cover, seldom allowed a Japanese company to move without being detected by the Navy's eager eyes.

By late afternoon, four battalions of Marine artillery were ashore, along with forty-eight tanks. When the companies of the First Battalion, Eighth Marines landed after carrying out the diversion in the south, the guys hauling the long tubes gave them some good-natured ribbing about hiding behind the artillery. The weary veterans of Saipan were all smiles when

General Cates, from his station on an LST afloat, announced the first day's losses in the assault: just fifteen men killed and 255 wounded, with most of the fatalities arising from a pair of amtracs that struck submerged mines off White Beach Two. The Navy team had performed with astonishing efficiency.

Late on the first night, small groups of Japanese charged the 24th Marines' front, tossing grenades as artillery fell around the beachhead. Naval and air troops stationed at Ushi Point Airfield tried to infiltrate into the American rear by using the draws on the outer slopes of Mount Lasso, "but their power was that of a small wave against rocks, washing up against well-formed defensive lines," the correspondent Fletcher Pratt would note. Water metaphors might have been apt, for on J Day plus 2, the storm season was rolling and the rains never stopped.

By the end of their first night ashore, the Second and Eighth regiments of the Second Marine Division had advanced more than a mile. Tying in with the Fourth Division, they took over the left of the line and the two divisions held the entire northern half of the island. Their progress was so rapid that by day they walked fully upright, saving their energy, and they dug in every night. "We were covering the length of the island so fast that we overran pockets of Japs that formed into suicide squads and followed us, harassing us at night looking for food and ammo," said Robert L. George of the Tenth Marines, the artillery regiment attached to the Second Division.

The larger Japanese echelons were plagued by interdiction fires whenever they tried to move. Eviscerated on the march, they had little left to do but infiltrate north as best they could after dark and launch the inevitable midnight banzai charge. They needed most of the night to come up from Tinian Town. On the turn of the second day, supported by six tanks and some field artillery, the force of several thousand Japanese soldiers charged the beachhead, marking the beginning of a night of ferocious close-quarters fighting. More than twelve hundred bodies littered the beach area the next day. It was estimated that total Japanese losses were two thousand or more, almost a quarter of their entire force on Tinian.

The Second Division's advance the next day was a miserable one in the rain, and the Marines slept that night in slit trenches filled with water, but from that point forward their advance would meet only spotty resistance from small groups.

"As the troops moved south," Harry Hill said, "they overran many gun emplacements and defensive positions constructed in such a manner that they could only be used against attack from the southern sectors. They had to be abandoned without a fight as the Marines advanced from the north." The Americans were kept honest by bursts of enemy machine gun fire that stitched across open spaces, but Japanese resistance did not impress their hard-forged eyes.

For more than a month, the Japanese garrison on Tinian had had a front-row seat to the horror across the sound on Saipan. The abrupt disappearance of Admiral Kakuta's pilots from the airdrome at Ushi Point was a baleful sign of what Task Force 58 had done to Japanese airpower. Every day the message came home louder and clearer: The Imperial Japanese Navy would not save them, and without that, there was no hope that the Imperial Army would come, either.

Spruance could not understand why the enemy persisted. He described to his daughter how little he could see of the beach through the smoke, mist, and squalls and admitted that his sense of the enemy was as obscured as his vision. "I sometimes wonder what the state of mind of these Japs is when they know that they are just waiting to be killed off."

On the morning of July 26, off Saipan, Spruance attended funeral services on the *Colorado*. Two days later he called on the *Norman Scott* and joined in the same solemn ritual. The destroyer was soon underway for Mare Island by way of Eniwetok and Pearl Harbor. The last major element of Task Force 58, the *Essex* task group, had quit Tinian, too, leaving the day after the troops went ashore to support operations on Guam. Air support on Tinian was the domain of the Army now. The 318th Fighter Group, bolstered by a newly arrived squadron of B-25 Mitchell medium bombers and a faithful assembly of escort carriers, stood by as the Marines expanded their hold on Tinian and Guam and continued the cleanup on Saipan.

On Guam that same morning, General Geiger launched an assault on Orote Peninsula. The tip of the spear of the corps-level operation was the First Provisional Marine Brigade. Its two regiments jumped off after dawn behind a thunderous preparatory bombardment by seven artillery battalions along with naval fire support and air attacks. Supported by armor, the Fourth and 22nd Regiments confronted the network of pillboxes and dugouts that General Obata had erected to defend Guam's most valuable prize.

The Marines needed four days to reach the airstrip, and even then the mile-long strip was the site of some of the most difficult fighting of the campaign. The defenders fought stubbornly with small arms and mortars, generally choosing to die in their dugouts and pillboxes rather than surrender. The five-hour firefight on the morning of the twenty-ninth concluded with General Shepherd's First Provisional Marine Brigade overrunning Orote Field and pushing down jungle trails to the sea. In four days the two reinforced regiments killed between two and three thousand Japanese. In seizing Orote Peninsula, they gained not only its valuable airfield, but Apra Harbor as well. U.S. planes were staging in right away, while Marines supported by armored bulldozers cleared out snipers.

As the first week of operations on Guam was coming to a close, President Roosevelt arrived in Hawaii to meet with Admiral Nimitz and General MacArthur. Nimitz had been chagrined at MacArthur's refusal of his and King's invitations to attend the private session, which lasted from July 26 to 29. Nimitz was none too pleased, either, at the cavalier manner of the general's arrival: late, wearing a leather jacket, and bringing no notes, maps, or staff. In his defense, when Marshall finally ordered MacArthur to go to Hawaii, the Southwest Pacific Area commander had not even been informed whom he would be meeting with. When King realized that neither he nor Generals Marshall or Arnold were invited, he surmised that the president's purpose was political. With the Democratic National Convention in Chicago having just ended with Roosevelt's nomination for a fourth presidential term, King figured that FDR wanted to be seen taking charge of the war effort by meeting directly with his two top theater commanders. It might also have been an act of one-upmanship vis-à-vis King, whose use of the title "commander in chief" bothered the president. Through Secretary Leahy, FDR had made known his wish that King stop using it. King told Leahy he would desist if he received an order to do so. None came, and his use of the title continued. But of course an important matter of substance was at issue as the supremos of the Pacific arrived at a private mansion on the slope of Diamond Head, Oahu's landmark volcano, to confer with their commander in chief. The purpose of the meeting was to settle the direction of the Pacific war and determine the shape of its next phase.

The abundance of resources produced a superabundance of options. MacArthur had resolved to return to the Philippines since the day he was driven out in 1941. He considered it a moral obligation and asked the president if he would accept responsibility for breaking MacArthur's public vow to liberate eighteen million Christian Filipinos from a brutal occupation. He laid out his plan, driving first to Leyte, then Luzon. Nimitz outlined the scheme finalized by King: to bypass the Philippines and push to Formosa.

It was a measure of Roosevelt's talent as a politician, and of the capacity of the national industrial plant that he wielded, that both commanders left the meeting with their ambitions intact. Leahy would later tell the Joint Chiefs that "Nimitz and MacArthur said they had no disagreements at the moment and that they could work out their joint plans in harmony." Afterward, Roosevelt wrote to MacArthur citing "the splendid picture of the whole vast area" that he had gained and congratulating him on his successful campaigns. "You have been doing a really magnificent job against what were great difficulties, given us by climate and by certain human animals. As soon as I get back I will push on that plan for I am convinced that it is logical and can be done." The president's punishing rhetoric with regard to the Japanese would be echoed again soon.

27

The Will to Lose Hard

In the Marianas, Pacific Fleet aerologists were startled to find a major storm system building a few hundred miles west of the islands. Winds shifted from easterly to northwesterly and the ocean swells grew. Guam's western harbor was well protected by reefs, but Tinian was more exposed. Waves bashed the west coast violently enough to cause an LST to broach. Before going aground, she disgorged twenty-four trucks into the sea, much to the misery of the walking wounded who had come aboard for evacuation. After a salvage tug failed to haul her off the beach, her crew settled for hooking one of her anchors to shore to keep her from slipping off the reef and sinking. That night, the causeway at White Beach One was torn from its moorings and thrown broadside onto the beach, and the pier at White Two was smashed and piled onto the coral. Turner ordered the remnants of this valuable infrastructure hauled around for reassembly at Tinian Town. Harry Hill canceled ship-to-shore operations and ordered his transports and most smaller craft to depart for Eniwetok. With seaborne transport largely shut down, it was only by the canny seamanship of DUKW drivers braving the heavy surf that the flow of ammunition continued. A squadron of C-47 cargo planes was pressed into service as an air shuttle, flying in emergency supplies from Saipan and evacuating wounded.

On Tinian, the rapid push south continued under a steady rain, the Second Division on the left and the Fourth on the right. On the afternoon of July 30, the 24th Marines overran Tinian Town. Small pockets of Japanese resisted, but the town that Colonel Ogata had planned to make the anchor of his defense had been largely abandoned. Marine intelligence estimated that Ogata would make a last stand with his regiment in the south. Though the city was surrounded by rough country, the high escarpment on the southern end of the island was better suited to defense. Anchored by three hills that rose more than five hundred feet from sea level, it was a natural stronghold.

The following day, Hill summoned the *Tennessee, California, Louisville, Montpelier,* and *Birmingham* to blast the wooded ridge and high plateau with high explosives in preparation for a ground assault. The ships hit it with more than six hundred tons, checking fire when their aerial spotter could no longer see the island. The next morning, August 1, the 23rd and 24th Marines, well supported by tanks, began the final assault, advancing from the west toward the steep, rocky cliff, while two regiments from the Second Division attacked from the north. Clearing a minefield and over-running a series of machine gun positions situated at the base of the cliff, they got quickly to the top but had to leave their heavy weapons behind. As on Saipan, their playbook was sponsored by Ronson. They poured liquid fire liberally.

Along the way, a battalion from the Sixth Marines delivered to Colonel Louis R. Jones's headquarters an English-speaking Japanese national who had been the superintendent of Tinian's sugar refinery, along with his wife. From them Jones learned that the Japanese civilians on Tinian had been indoctrinated with a fear of Americans that was as profound as that of their countrymen on Saipan. Another ritual suicide was in the offing. The man was given a loudspeaker, loaded into a jeep, and sent along with an escort of tanks and half-tracks to address the hundreds of refugees who were hiding in caves along the cliff.

The sugar baron told them the battle was over, that the Americans could be trusted and would give them food, water, and medical care. His wife made a similar appeal, assuring them they would not be harmed. A handful of civilians edged into view, huddling on the plain a few hundred yards from the jeep. When a few of them began wandering toward U.S. lines, there was a commotion. Japanese soldiers were trying to keep them from surrendering. One of the soldiers ran to the cliff and flew. A volley of similar suicide leaps ensued. From the caves in the cliff, puffs of gray smoke told of grim rituals with grenades.

At length a group of about forty people emerged from some caves on the western slope of the plateau. When they got within a rifle shot of Jones's jeep, he could see that they were carrying bags with what he assumed were their possessions. They began waving flags back and forth in some sort of demonstration. Then he could see that the group was bound together with a long rope. All of a sudden the whole group was airborne. Their bags had held satchel charges. Robert Graf's company from the 23rd Marines was among those who watched the horrible demonstration. The big blast seemed to break the spell for civilians whose conviction was teetering, and hundreds of them made for American lines. In little more than a week, thirteen thousand civilians would be brought safely into American custody, saved from being slaughtered by their "protectors."

With this sad horror of orgiastic suicide the last organized resistance on Tinian collapsed. Few of the enemy soldiery heeded the broadcasts to surrender. Eager to die honorably for their emperor, they were accommodated by pack howitzers, which were rolled forward and trained into the mouths of the caves. Delayed-fuze rounds ricocheted into the stony depths and exploded. Marine sappers lowered TNT charges on ropes and swung them into cave openings.

Having watched some Japanese women and children emerge from a cave only to be shot down from behind by Japanese troops, Charles Pase, a machine gunner with the Tenth Marines, was pushed beyond his limits. "Believe me, we didn't have any mercy for the Japs left in those caves. We no longer felt sorry for the bastards when we saw what had happened. All of us who took part in that remembered it for the duration."

Just before seven P.M. on August 1, General Schmidt declared Tinian secure. But the mop-up phase was little less dangerous than the assault. The following morning, a company-sized element of Japanese that had been secreted in caves atop the escarpment launched an attack, falling upon the command post of Third Battalion, Sixth Marines. The engagement was brief and violent and one-sided in the usual way. By the time it was over, more than a hundred enemy lay dead around the command post. The handful of American casualties included the stalwart commander of the 3/6, Lieutenant Colonel John W. Easley, wounded a lifetime ago during the first day of combat on Saipan and now fatally shot just above the heart.

This same day was the end for Vice Admiral Kakuji Kakuta, steward of the remnants of Tinian's eviscerated land-based air force. The First Air Fleet commander reportedly made several attempts to leave the island in a raft, hoping to rendezvous with a Japanese submarine for evacuation. Foiled in that effort, he and his staff disappeared into the deep crevices of the island's eastern coast, never to be seen again. The officer who succeeded him as commander of the First Air Fleet, Vice Admiral Takijiro Onishi, arrived in Manila on that day to begin the process of transforming the mission of his unit. "There is only one way to assure that our meager strength will be effective," he said to one of his subordinates. He proposed a new tactic, the *tai-atari* (body-crash) attack. The so-called *tokko* units, or kamikaze, had roots in the collapse of the Marianas, and they would be just one of its reverberations.

Carl Moore joined Kelly Turner and Harry Hill for the flag-raising ceremony at Tinian Town. Touring the island in a jeep afterward, they inspected the remains of the shore batteries that had surprised the *Colorado* and *Norman Scott*. Farther down the waterfront, amid the plumeria, was a much older ruin: a pair of megalithic columns of moss-covered stone, each about four feet in diameter and fifteen to twenty feet high, capped by a massive bowl-shaped boulder. Moore thought they resembled Stonehenge or Easter Island, legacies of a vanished race. "What they were, and why they were there, on this strange little Chamorro island, nobody ever explained," he said. Local legend held that the immortal souls of the children of a Chamorro chief, Taga, were held within the columns. Trapped in lonely limbo, they could be released to the sky only upon toppling. Once standing in parallel rows of six, the stones had served as the foundation of a large structure in the village believed to have been an honorary crypt. Now in the archaeological site known as the House of Taga, only two columns remained. One stood tall but damaged, and the other lay fallen, victim of an American bombardment. It was as if the foundations of Tinian's prehistory, and the serenity of the natives' ancestral spirits, had been shaken from the earth.

Battered by war, the islands were set for a revival. Draper Kauffman had surveyed Tinian Town harbor to determine the scope of work needed to make it ready for large-scale unloading. Afterward, he flew back to Pearl Harbor. As he joined planning for landings at Ulithi, Peleliu, and Leyte—the first step into the Philippines—Kelly Turner told him that all UDT officers were to receive the Silver Star and his enlisted men the Bronze Star. Kauffman protested the class-based discrimination to no avail. He had better luck on the matter of pay. One day at Pearl Harbor an admiral arrived with news that hazardous-duty pay had been approved for all of Kauffman's men. Already struggling to keep egos in check and avoid peculiar appearances that might compromise secrecy, Kauffman thought the bonus might be counterproductive. Inflated pay stubs, he feared, risked inflating both egos and operational profiles. He asked for and got permission to put the idea to a vote among his men. The rank and file of UDTs 5 and 7 returned with a unanimous verdict:

"We want hazardous-duty pay when all Marine infantrymen get it," it read.

"You say this is unanimous?" the admiral asked.

"Yes, sir," Kauffman said.

"Well, the first person I'm going to make sure sees this is General Holland Smith."

"We had an intrepid group," Bob Marshall of UDT 5 said. "There is no question about it, but there were so many who went in on that beach who were far braver. In the early days of Saipan, when I was with the beachmaster watching those Marines going ashore and dying. . . . Every one of them should have had a Congressional Medal of Honor."

Many Marines settled for exploiting the eagerness of ships' companies to touch the spoils of their victory. Sailors were easy marks for counterfeit souvenirs. Marines shredded their mess kits with metal shears and sold them as parts from downed enemy planes, and they cut and stitched old parachutes into facsimile Japanese flags, using iodine and catsup to paint authentic-looking rising suns, carefully applying the strokes of kanji that they copied from captured pornographic materials. It was easy money, but they protected their gross margins by being careful to avoid flooding the market. "We were good at free enterprise," Robert Graf said.

The finish on Guam was a repetitive and familiar third act in the horror show that was the Japanese defense of the Marianas. Spruance spent the first days of August observing the progress of Geiger's men against the dead-end determination of its defenders to sell their lives dearly. The heaviest action was in the island's north. As the *Indianapolis* entered Apra Harbor, he stood out on the bridge wing, relishing the close vantage point on the battle ashore. Later, he took a boat to the beach. He wrote Margaret, "I spent the day amid mud and dust traveling around the accessible part of the area which we held. The hills on our left flank near Agana were recently taken and were still plentifully occupied by dead Japs. I have never seen a live Jap except those who have been taken prisoner. They are experts at concealment. There are probably about 10,000 Japs on Guam who have moved up to the northern end of the island, which makes our own job of rounding them up easier! What sort of resistance they will put up remains to be seen." The enemy garrison made its last organized stand on the slopes of Mount Santa Rosa in the north. Though they were hampered by jungle, Geiger's troops, supported by air strikes, overwhelmed them.

By now the pilots of the *Essex*, *Belleau Wood*, and *Langley*, the last task group left in theater, were thoroughly exhausted and demoralized. The grind was reflected in the reports of David McCampbell's Air Group 15, which began using identical boilerplate language from report to report. It was hard to tell success from failure from the air when targets were well hidden in woods and ravines. The performance of new replacement pilots left much to be desired, McCampbell thought. He wrote a withering review of them, deriding "Johnny Newcomer," who attacked Japanese planes without remembering to charge his guns, "Mr. Not-Interested," who ran low on fuel and signaled an emergency landing, forgetting that he carried a full belly tank, "Sleepy," who "while awaiting his turn on takeoff spot, allowed his plane to be blown back into the plane behind, causing three flight-deck duds, for which the strength of the strike was to suffer," and

> Johnny Eager, a numerous clan, [who] went at the Japs with pardonable enthusiasm and exuberance but without his "thinking cap"; made bombing runs with bomb bays closed or with his bomb-torpedo switch set on torpedo—he forgot to arm his rockets—he pressed his machine-gun firing switch instead of his rocket switch (they're only a good twenty inches apart), and in one case he sailed into formation over the rendezvous point, opened his bomb bay to inspect for release failures and promptly dumped three incendiary clusters which made a perfect straddle on a friendly plane below him.

"Did somebody say 'get busy and train them'?" McCampbell continued. "Sure, that's a great idea, but unfortunately the VF squadron lost one-fourth of its pilot complement and they needed these new people to help carry the load. CAP [combat air patrol] and ASP [antisubmarine patrol], yes, they can 'snoop' and 'chase tails' as well as the trained pilot when no opposition is expected, but that still doesn't teach them how to shoot, dive-bomb, fly formation, rendezvous (pre-dawn-like) and so forth." In other words, training and experience were the coin of the realm no matter how many legendary victories were in the books. It might also have been the case that one of these legends, David McCampbell himself, was sorely in need of a rest.

At the ruins of the old U.S. Marine barracks on Guam, Spruance was part of the ceremony marking the capture of Orote Peninsula. As garrison troops piled into the conquered parts of the island, the Third Marine Division performed the usual brutal extraction in the north, accommodating the general death wish at no small cost to themselves. Spruance got an armed tour of the wildly overgrown arena as Geiger's men carried on. "As you go north from Agana the cleared areas for small farms or planted in coconuts give way to dense tropical growth which looks almost impenetrable without cutting trails or bulldozing roads," he wrote to Margaret. "Our offense moved against the Japs along the few roads, while our air and naval gunfire support worked over concentrations of them that were seen from the air or encountered by the troops. How long it will take to eliminate the Jap remnants from the jungle and the caves in the cliffs I don't know."

Though the pacification of Guam would remain a work in progress, Japanese resistance was declared at an end on August 10. Returned to American hands, the island would finally fulfill its long-recognized potential as the strategic pivot of the Western Pacific. In the next month nearly five thousand Japanese would be rooted out of its canyons and caves. Few surrendered; mostly they fought to the end. Though U.S. casualties on Guam would be less than half of those on Saipan, they still exceeded seven thousand, including fifteen hundred killed or missing in action, after twenty-two days of fighting. The harmony and mutual respect that characterized the collaboration between the Army and Marine Corps there stood in marked contrast to what had taken place on Saipan, to the credit of Geiger and his division commanders.

On August 15, Kelly Turner's amphibious organization, Task Force 51, was dissolved and Turner transferred from the Fifth Fleet to Nimitz's direct command. Admiral Conolly, too, accepted his relief and departed for Pearl Harbor a few days later to join the planning effort for landings farther westward. Their amphibious team had delivered most of six divisions to the Marianas and fired some twenty-seven thousand tons of naval ordnance in their support, including more than sixteen thousand rounds from battleships, forty-three thousand from cruisers, and nearly a quarter million from shipboard five-inch batteries. But the byword in the Marianas now was construction, not destruction. Spruance remained in the forward area until August 23 to coordinate the development of the Marianas' bases and harbors, then embarked in the *Indianapolis* for the return to Pearl Harbor.

Hap Arnold and his globe-spanning strategic air forces would need all three islands to contain the fleets of B-29s rolling out of the Boeing, Bell, and Martin factories. Under the overall direction of Lieutenant General Millard F. Harmon, working through the respective island garrison commanders, consistent with directives from Rear Admiral John H. Hoover, the commander of the forward area, aviation engineers and Seabees would transform the islands utterly. That fall, the garrison and aviation cadre on Saipan was sixty-five thousand strong. Isely Field was home to a 6,000-foot fighter strip and an 8,500-foot B-29 runway with hardstands for more than 120 bombers. A quartet of five-thousand-gallon aviation fuel tanks supplemented the storage the Japanese had built. Tanapag Harbor received floating piers fashioned out of cubic pontoons linked with angle irons. On Tinian, a quarrying operation was working to improve the airfields, with plans to lay six B-29 strips on the island's expansive northern plain. Though Nimitz's decision to move his headquarters from Oahu to Guam delayed that island's development as an air base, in the coming months it, too, would become a hive, home to five airfields: one on Orote Peninsula, two near Agana, and two more on its northern limestone plateau. In the north, the diesel-driven landscaping carried on in spite of a continued threat of Japanese troops. The massive D8 bulldozers operated in pairs, plowing through the undergrowth escorted by infantry and half-tracks, their drivers secured in armored cabs and wielding submachine guns. Road construction went on twenty-four hours a day.

The islands' conquest in two short months was made possible by a record-breaking feat on the part of the combat fleet. With only brief visits to Eniwetok or Saipan to replenish, Task Force 58 set what Spruance believed was a record for sustained operations at sea, putting up more than twenty-one thousand combat sorties (almost half flown by Hellcats) and destroying an estimated 1,300 Japanese planes—including 909 in aerial combat, 51 by shipboard AA, and 276 on the ground. Carrier planes dropped nearly seven thousand tons of bombs. A total of 334 aircraft were lost, including 54 in aerial combat, 150 to antiaircraft batteries, 7 to friendly fire, and 19 more from unknown causes. The remaining 111 were lost because of combat exigencies, including 73 to fuel exhaustion and deck crashes on June 20.

Admiral Halsey, having relieved Spruance of operational control of the fleet, prepared to move on to the next combat front, staging a series of carrier raids into the western Carolines, the Palaus, and the Philippines. The tag team setup with Spruance would allow the Pacific Fleet to seize and retain the initiative, sustaining a rapid operational tempo as long as might be necessary. The fact that the name of the one and only fleet changed depending on who was in command fooled the Japanese, meanwhile, and some American journalists as well. The editors of *Newsweek* marveled that the Third Fleet "is probably as large as the vast Fifth Fleet commanded by Vice Admiral Raymond Spruance." However one counted it, its potential had been revealed for the first time in the Marianas.

As most of the assault units reembarked for rear areas, garrison troops arrived to replace them. The lessons returned to Hawaii with the veterans. Donald Weller, the Marine artillery commander, huddled with Admiral Kauffman to revise the fire-support curriculum at Kaho'olawe. Ships had to earn their places by their performance in the school. Failure could delay a ship's coveted assignment to a combat task force and was a black mark on a skipper's record. "The destroyers always did better than the cruisers, and the cruisers always did better than the battleships," Weller noted, "the reason being simply that the destroyers recognized this as a mission." When shore fire-control parties at Kaho'olawe flunked a cruiser with a "very, very hot reputation in the training cycle back on the coast," her captain lodged a protest, but Admiral Kauffman made the grade stick, backing Weller and his Marines all the way.

The kudos and valedictories that passed among Nimitz, Spruance, Turner, and their top ground commanders were a thin veneer on a terrible reality: After Operation Forager, it was clear that the Japanese meant to immolate themselves fully on the altar of war. Though Tinian had been taken artfully, and at a price in life that was relatively low—just 290 killed in action and about fifteen hundred wounded, as against 5,524 Japanese buried and 404 prisoners of war—the events of the endgame there, like those on Saipan less than a month earlier, were devastating in their confirmation of the Americans' worst fear: Defeating this cult of death would require bloodletting on a grand scale. As Nimitz wrote, "The enemy met the assault operations with pointless bravery, inhuman tenacity, infiltration, cave fighting, and the will to lose hard." Nimitz's observations made an impact at the highest level.

On September 13, 1944, at a series of strategy meetings with Winston Churchill and the Combined Chiefs of Staff in Quebec City, a conference that was code-named Octagon, President Franklin Roosevelt remarked on "the almost fanatic Japanese tenacity. In Saipan not only the soldiers but also the civilians had committed suicide rather than be taken." It was no doubt King who conveyed the horrific reality directly to his president. En route to visiting Saipan with Nimitz and Spruance in July, the top admiral had stopped over in Honolulu, where he spoke with every man who had been wounded in the Central Pacific.

Nimitz and MacArthur had both been dismayed by Roosevelt's physical condition when they saw him on the president's visit to Hawaii in late July. He was no better in September. Hap Arnold noted, after seeing him in Quebec, "I didn't think the president was up to par. He didn't seem to have the same pep or power of concentration; he didn't make his usual wisecracks, but always seemed to be thinking of something else. Also, he closed his eyes and rested more than usual." But his eyes had been opened to something else: the essential suicidal nature of Japanese forces in the combat zone, and the terrifying pliability of civilians in following their lead.

That realization resounded in the remarkable public statement that was issued after the conference. A full report on the conclusions reached was given to the two heads of state, with a summary issued to Josef Stalin. A communiqué went out to the press. Never before had this august body of Allied leaders referred to their enemies other than by ordinary proper nouns. The statement released on September 16, however, had a different tone: "In a very short space of time they reached decisions on all points, both with regard to the completion of the war in Europe, now approaching its final stages, and the destruction of the barbarians of the Pacific."

The barbarians of the Pacific. Such language had long been common in the press and at dinner tables from coast to coast. From the Bataan Death March onward, the Japanese military had been notorious for cruelty. But now, with this bracing declaration from the highest level of Allied command, it was as if the anguish of every rifleman, forward observer, and second lieutenant who witnessed what happened that summer in the Marianas traveled up the chain of command to activate a signal of sorts, from the top, that would have meaning to U.S. operating forces worldwide. There was no explaining away what thousands of Marines had observed with their own disbelieving eyes in the Marianas. The ritual suicides of the Japanese garrisons, and their predatory brainwashing and murder of the innocent unarmed, have been insufficiently considered as a turning point that shaped the war's final year. It was not old news. The first direct U.S. experience of total war occurred in the Marianas, and it renewed the will to win and to win totally, using all means available, without restraint. Unconditional surrender became the byword of this new resolve.

At Quebec City, the otherwise stately process of discussion, deliberation, recommendation, further study, negotiation, revision, and decision led to the formulation of "A New Strategic Concept for the Defeat of Japan." Based on a June 30 study by the U.S. Joint Staff Planners, it fused the strategic concepts preferred by the Army (invasion), Navy (blockade), and Army Air Forces (bombardment) into a strategy that was thoroughly maximalist in nature. Envisioning concurrent amphibious advances through the Ryukyus and Bonins and along the southeast China coast, a total naval blockade, and strategic air bombardment of the Japanese home islands, it would set up the climactic grand amphibious operation against Japan itself. Unconditional surrender would leave no room for talking.

The brutal convergence would be known as Operation Downfall, the climactic invasion of the home islands. Drawing deeply from ground and air forces released from duty in the European Theater of Operations, whose arrival in the Pacific would take place no earlier than September 1945, Operation Downfall would proceed in two stages. The first, Operation Olympic, would commence on November 1, with the fourteen divisions of the U.S. Sixth Army, staging in the Philippines, landing on the southernmost Japanese home island, Kyushu. On March 1, 1946, would come the knockout blow. Operation Coronet would land twenty-five divisions into the Japanese heartland, the Tokyo-Yokohama area. Though Admiral King fervently opposed landing in the home islands, preferring a strategy of blockade and bombardment, the plan would acquire an inexorable momentum that was reflected in a naval order of battle involving three thousand ships, including 22 battleships, 27 fast carriers, 36 escort carriers, 50 cruisers, and 458 destroyers.

The divided Pacific command structure, in spite of the bitter interservice schism that it encouraged, had been profoundly useful. The parallel offensives of MacArthur and Nimitz had confused the Japanese high command and enabled the Americans to seize a foothold in the Marianas unopposed initially by the Japanese fleet. Now U.S. control of the Marianas, a commanding central strongpoint, gave Tokyo a continuous waking nightmare: Allied forces threatened an arc of potential targets that were too widely dispersed for the Japanese to defend effectively. From the Marianas, an attack could be pressed to the southwest against the Palaus, to the west toward Formosa, or to the north toward Iwo Jima. Ernest King had long seen the Marianas as the key to the Pacific. Now that gateway had been thrown open.

At the same time, the geographic separation between the Southwest Pacific and Central Pacific theaters was narrowing by the season. Simultaneous landings in September at Peleliu in the Palau Islands and at Morotai (which was seen variously as the last objective in the New Guinea campaign or the first assault on the Philippines) brought Nimitz's and MacArthur's forces within five hundred miles of each other, setting up a common advance into the Philippines.

During the Octagon conference, a dinner gathering of the U.S. Joint Chiefs of Staff was interrupted by delivery of a dispatch from MacArthur: He proposed to accelerate his schedule, landing at Leyte in the Philippines on October 20, two months sooner than planned. Halsey's recent carrier raids had convinced him that Japanese air strength in the area wasn't what it was feared to be. So Nimitz went along, canceling plans to land at Yap and Mindanao and approving the assault on Leyte. He retained Peleliu as an objective because he believed its seizure would support MacArthur's advance and complete the isolation of the Carolines, a process that began with Spruance's February raid on Truk. The amphibious forces freed from the Yap order of battle were given to MacArthur. This impromptu deliberation and response made that dinner in Quebec one of the most consequential planning sessions of the war. When MacArthur sloshed ashore on schedule at Leyte, cameras were on the beach to capture the spectacle. But his counterparts in Army aviation were working steadily toward an even more spectacular end as they expanded into Saipan, Tinian, and Guam. Acre by acre, the three captured islands were being remade into the most strategically valuable pieces of military real estate in the world.

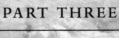

PART THREE

Air

Marianas-based B-29 Superfortresses, high in the substratosphere, head for the Japanese homeland. (USAAF)

28

Secrets of New Mexico

The voice on the other end of the line sounded panicked.

"Paul, are you in some kind of trouble?" Mr. Tibbets asked his son from Miami.

"Not that I know of. What makes you think so?"

The pilot's father said that family friends had called to tell him that federal investigators had visited them, asking questions. Paul Tibbets didn't attach any significance to this news until he arrived at Colorado Springs from Alamogordo, New Mexico, in mid-September, summoned there to meet with the commanding officer of the Second Air Force, Major General Uzal G. Ent.

Before going in, Tibbets was taken aside by a stranger to him, a lieutenant colonel who wore an unusual insignia, that of the Army Corps of Engineers. As he began questioning Tibbets in a particularly probing way, the man seemed to know everything about him: his personal history, his military record, his premilitary life. Tibbets was asked about critical comments he had made about America's European war strategy. He was made to explain how he had come to be in the backseat of his car with a girl one night, parked by the beach in Surfside, Florida, with the windows all steamed up, an indiscretion that had nearly gotten him arrested.

Tibbets answered Lieutenant Colonel Jack Lansdale's questions as honestly and transparently as he could. Persuaded that the pilot was no subversive, merely a straight shooter, an independent thinker, and perhaps a hard man to satisfy, the security officer took him in to see General Ent.

When he entered the general's office, he was seated alongside a naval officer and a civilian, who were introduced as Captain William S. "Deak"

Parsons, USN, and Dr. Norman F. Ramsey, a physicist. Tibbets understood then that his new assignment might well be important. And it was.

On cue from Ent, Dr. Ramsey turned to Tibbets and asked, "Did you ever hear of atomic energy?" The Manhattan Project, he explained, was a far-flung and pioneering scientific enterprise that was working on a new type of bomb so powerful that its potential had yet to be grasped. Ramsey, who worked at the government laboratory complex at Los Alamos, New Mexico, was one of Parsons's deputies in the Manhattan Project's Ordnance Division, which would oversee design and development of this fearsome new weapon.

The secret nature of the project accounted for why, on another Florida beach about a year earlier, Draper Kauffman had been stood up by the explosives expert who had been helping him start the Underwater Demolition Teams. George Kistiakowsky, "the Mad Russian," was a no-show that morning because his talents were required elsewhere. When his employer, the president of Harvard, James B. Conant, joined Robert Oppenheimer and Major General Leslie R. Groves, director of the U.S. Army Corps of Engineers' innocuously named Manhattan Engineer District, in pressuring him to sign on to their classified project to build an atomic bomb, Kistiakowsky gave in to the call of service. He disappeared into life as a cog in the wheel whose long axle turned in Los Alamos. That same powerful force had just reeled in Paul Tibbets to Colorado.

With the science and engineering challenges of producing an atomic bomb largely in hand, the remaining piece was delivery. Ent explained that Tibbets had been selected to lead a new aerial combat force, one whose mission would be unprecedented and highly secret. They would train for a single mission: to deliver the world's first atomic bomb. Ent offered him the job over two other men, one of whom had been Tibbets's own commanding officer in North Africa, because of his combat experience, deep knowledge of the B-29, and reputation as an independent operator. "Ours was not a nation with a kamikaze mentality," Tibbets would write. "When our bombers took off, the odds had to favor their safe return by at least ten to one."

He was forgiven his ugly run-in with Brigadier General Lauris Norstad, which had been duly recorded in his personnel file, because General Arnold understood Norstad's behavior to have been "a display of pettiness by an ambitious officer," as Tibbets would put it. More than that, Tibbets's talent urged forgiveness. The man whom he would choose as his bombardier, Dutch Van Kirk, would say, "It's hard to even explain to you just what an excellent pilot Paul was. He could do things with an airplane that I never saw anyone do in my life. . . . I think he just understands the dynamics of an airplane, how they fly, more than other people. I'm not even sure if *he* is aware of how far above other people's feel for airplanes his feel is."

Thus did Paul Tibbets ascend to command of a unit that was effectively his own air force. With a roster of eighteen hundred men and fifteen B-29s, the 509th Composite Group would be officially established by the end of 1944. The unit's name was chosen to sound unremarkable, but "composite" was a telling word. Suggestive of the "all-types-in-one" air squadrons that were assigned to escort carriers, it meant that the unit, unlike other bomber groups, would be completely self-contained, with its own maintenance, engineering, and technical units, an ordnance and troop transport squadron, military police, and a medical team that included specialists in radiology. Under this umbrella of secrecy, Tibbets would have broad discretion to solve problems in his own way, consistent with the needs of the Manhattan Project.

Those who were fluent in air-force-speak were instantly curious about the unit, so his first order of business was to ensure security. He was asked to choose one of three locales that Ent offered him as a training site— Wendover, Utah; Great Bend, Kansas; or Mountain Home, Idaho. Three squadrons of B-29 pilots and crews coming out of flight training in Nebraska were earmarked for him, but he would have the authority to recruit his own key people.

On his frequent visits to Los Alamos in early 1945, Tibbets came to know many of the scientists working there. "I was actually awed in their presence," Tibbets wrote, but he came to know many as friends.

Awe was replaced by admiration as friendships developed, and I found that people who were harnessing the atom had equal respect for my own special skills as a pilot and organizer of aerial attack strategy. . . . I was most impressed, as were all who met him, by the trigger-quick mind of J. Robert Oppenheimer. A pleasant man and unpretentious, he had a way of making a non-academic layman like myself feel at ease. In size, he was a wisp of a man, very slender and seemingly fragile. He was highly nervous, a chain smoker who talked so rapidly one had to concentrate to catch all the words. One had the feeling that, when he was talking to you, he was thinking of two other things at the same time. I felt that here was a man whose brain was divided into several remark-

able parts from which he could extract bits of knowledge, on demand, in the same way that a computer spits out stored-up
information.

Because he sometimes became so immersed in a problem that
he was oblivious to all that was going on around him, [his wife]
frequently had to remind him when it was time to eat or take a
drink of water, or even—I suspected—go to the bathroom.

The mental strain of his intense concentration created stomach
problems that required frequent medicine, administered dutifully
by Katherine, who was both maid and nurse to this frail genius.

The magnitude of his task was not lost on the twenty-nine-year-old
pilot. "My job, in brief, was to wage atomic war. It didn't matter that I was
not a scientist and had very little understanding of the strange world of
neutrons, protons, electrons, and gamma rays. The question that worried
Ent and others, and which now became my problem, was how to drop a
bomb of such magnitude without risking damage to or destruction of the
airplane that made the delivery."

The fate of the plane that carried such a weapon might have seemed
trivial when some scientists worried that its explosion might be powerful
enough to crack the earth's crust. But Tibbets's first concern was that of any
responsible pilot: the safety of his crew. Captain Parsons figured that a B-29
that dropped an atomic bomb would have to be eight miles away from
ground zero to survive the shock wave. The pilot's challenge was somehow
to create that distance.

There wasn't much Tibbets did not like about Wendover Army Air
Base, Utah. The base outside that village of a hundred souls was the only
one of the three options Ent gave him that he visited. From Denver to
Laramie to Salt Lake, then west toward Elko and Reno, he found it was
the very definition of remote. He appreciated the fact that such a back-
water, on a desert highway to nowhere, was no draw for rabble-rousers.
The casino in the Stateline Hotel had as many slot machines as the town
had people. The best restaurant in town was run by the mayor.

But mile after mile of salt flats offered plenty that mattered, mainly
space for huge runways with generous margins for error. And the austere
surroundings would make it easier to enforce security protocols. A single
railroad spur served the base directly, an ideal setup for protecting classified shipments. On base, his enlisted men would live in cement blockhouses
with cold, concrete floors and equipped with coal stoves for heat and cook-

ing. Junior officers shared one-story tar-paper shacks with bunk beds. Only the bachelor officers' quarters had the luxury of central heating. Tibbets arrived at Wendover to set up his headquarters in the second week of September 1944. A few days later, the B-29 unit assigned to Tibbets's group, the 393rd Heavy Bombardment Squadron, arrived with its fifteen planes, as well as flight and ground crews.

The potential of their project was mind-boggling. The horror of the war that Alex Vraciu and Fred Stott and Dave McCampbell and John Chapin knew, which fell upon Japanese and Chamorros out of the open blue sea, that enabled and then upended Tojo's ambitions, that ennobled and destroyed thousands in the line of duty, and that tested the fortitude of Holland and Ralph Smith, Kelly Turner, and Raymond Spruance, was generally unknown in its particulars to the scientists at Los Alamos and to most of the pilots, crew, and technicians at Wendover. They knew whom they were fighting and why. But they had not seen the dead stiffen and bloat. In the sort of warfare waged from thirty thousand feet, they were meant never to see it. The killing lacked a certain personal quality, was bled of a certain color.

Spruance had more than a passing acquaintance with war's results, if not its processes. He was not deeply run through by its wrenching realities. From Pearl Harbor he wrote to a friend who was marooned at the Pentagon, ribbing him for his remoteness from the action: "It is too bad, for we really have a most interesting war going on in the Pacific, and I know you would enjoy it." War's operational challenges remained an intellectual puzzle to him.

At Los Alamos the war was seen in much the same way. The scientific systems and engineering processes that occupied the likes of Robert Oppenheimer and George Kistiakowsky were abstract. But when the atomic bomb was finally tested and released upon the world, given to Deak Parsons and Paul Tibbets to carry over blood-soaked islands to its target, it would make Louis Mang's field tests of liquid fire at Tinian seem like a child's game. The gulf between theory and horrific practice had never been wider.

The alligator navy and its accompaniment of naval aviators stayed on the move in the Southwest Pacific through the fall. After the First Marine Division was done at Peleliu, a third of its roster were casualties, sixty-five hundred men. The 81st Infantry Division, arriving in the middle of the campaign, took thirty-three hundred more. The next objectives were the subject of constant study and discussion. At Pearl Harbor, Nimitz told Spruance that his next operation would be the capture of Formosa and offered him stateside leave to recharge. Spruance flew home to Monrovia and enjoyed a week with Margaret and the family. Shortly before he was due to return to Oahu, he received orders from CINCPAC to attend a conference between King and Nimitz and their staffs in San Francisco. The September 28 meeting settled the question of the Navy's direction in the first part of 1945.

In the headquarters of the commander of the Navy's Western Sea Frontier, Spruance was waiting for King to freshen up when Nimitz's war plans officer, Rear Admiral Forrest Sherman, handed him a paper to read. It was a recommendation that Iwo Jima and Okinawa be substituted for Formosa as the Fifth Fleet's next objectives.

Spruance, largely a structural thinker, viewed the map of the Pacific as a patchwork of circles and arcs. One very large circle, centered in the Marianas, corraled Tokyo, Kyushu, the Ryukyus, Formosa, the Philippines, and New Guinea. A smaller circle, centered on Iwo Jima, halfway between the Marianas and Japan, linked Tokyo, Kyushu, and the Ryukyus. Spruance also saw that ownership of Okinawa would allow U.S. forces to control an arc encompassing Kyushu, Korea, China's northern coast, and Formosa, thus taking control of the South China Sea—the key to blockading the home islands. Like Ernest King, Spruance wanted no part of the hell that would engulf U.S. troops in a landing on Japan proper. Naval power was at bottom about sea control. Without sea control, an island nation like Japan was bound to starve.

At the conference, King argued strongly for an invasion of Formosa, which he preferred to Okinawa as a base for conducting a blockade of Japan. He had no interest in invading Iwo Jima, saying it would be a "sink hole" for whomever held it. Spruance worried how the options seemed to narrow as the advance continued west. He had grown to appreciate the value of strategic surprise, attacking where the enemy did not expect to have to defend. But the farther west U.S. forces went, the harder it would be to fool the Japanese. Spruance pushed back against King, arguing that Iwo was needed as a base for land-based air support for fleet operations against the Japanese mainland and was, in turn, well within range of support aircraft based in the Marianas.

Okinawa would be a bolder venture. King had asked Spruance, on Saipan in July, whether he thought he could take Okinawa. Spruance said he could so long as a method were devised to transfer heavy ammunition between ships at sea. During operations in Japanese home waters, carriers and battleships would go long periods between replenishment as they ran interference between Japan and Okinawa. He wouldn't be able to apply the constant pressure on nearby enemy bases unless he could avoid frequent long journeys to the rear area. Nimitz brought in the commander of CINCPAC's service force, Vice Admiral William L. Calhoun, to discuss devising a special rig for his ammunition ships. With the advent of that new capability, together with improvements in underway replenishment, the fast carrier task force acquired what one of the air admirals called "seven-league boots"—the ability to operate almost continuously at sea.

After the naval conference in San Francisco on September 28, King formally recommended to the Joint Chiefs a timetable that provided for the seizure of Iwo Jima the following February and Okinawa in April. The chiefs promptly approved. All three service branches had separate interests that converged at Okinawa. Possession of that island would give Spruance a base from which land-based tactical aircraft could cover the fleet while it operated against the China coast and in the South China Sea. MacArthur could stage the invasion of Kyushu there. Hap Arnold would have a closer base from which to bomb Japan.

With an assist from George Marshall, Arnold had prevailed in his years-long battle to retain control of the B-29 progam. He fended off the efforts of King, MacArthur, and others to have bomber wings assigned to theater commands for use in support of local objectives. "The average military man accepts certain principles of war as fundamental," Arnold would write. "Yet, these principles were violated, or would have been violated, time and time again, had we of the Air Force not fought against dispersion."

The unusual centralized command structure of the Twentieth Air Force suggested the strategic importance of the new bomber. It also suggested Arnold's determination that his branch become a "balanced air force," with integrated autonomy over not only operations, but also such matters as aircraft procurement, crew training, maintenance, and basing. With this independence, the Twentieth Air Force was said to be organized more like a naval task force than a bomber command. Indeed, Arnold saw his big new aircraft, with triple the production cost of a B-17, more as a warship than an aircraft. "We must consider the B-29 more in terms of a naval vessel, and we do not lose naval vessels in threes or fours without a very thorough analysis of causes," he wrote to Major General Haywood Hansell, his theater commander in the Marianas, who considered this notion spurious.

Originally the Twentieth Air Force planned to stand up three separate commands: Curtis LeMay's XX Bomber Command in India and China, Hansell's XXI Bomber Command in the Marianas, and a prospective XXII Bomber Command to be based in the Philippines. LeMay's outfit failed for its inability to sustain a mission tempo owing to problems of supply. Each month through the fall of 1944, his groups based in China and India managed just five or fewer missions. The idea of stationing B-29s in the Philippines died after MacArthur could not promise that bases would be ready in time (and perhaps also to keep the prized new aircraft from falling under control of the ever-acquisitive chief of the Southwest Pacific theater). In the end, only Hansell's Marianas-based unit managed to plant roots and grow.

Following the trail of the Fifth Fleet's conquest, from Hawaii to Kwajalein and then Saipan, the first of the Superfortresses given to XXI Bomber Command touched down at Isely Field on October 12, 1944. The newcomers from the Kansas-based 73rd Bombardment Wing landed upon an island transformed. Saipan was a major crossroads for fleets, troops, and air forces. Johnny Hoover, Nimitz's forward-area commander, wrote to his friend Spruance of this freshly built beehive and its whirl of comings and goings. "You would be astounded to see the progress on Saipan, and to a considerable extent on Guam. On Saipan we have big, broad highways paved with asphalt, and on the landing fields many big airplanes, and coming in all the time. . . . The congestion is going to be pretty heavy around Isley [sic] Field for some time." The three islands in the Marianas would absorb nearly the entirety of the stateside production of B-29s in 1945. Though Saipan's hard terrain would defy the Seabees' ability to fulfill General Harmon's ambition to operate two major bomber strips there, limiting that island to basing only the four groups of the 73rd Wing, airfield construction on the other islands proceeded rapidly.

Spruance's reply to Hoover suggested the pride he felt in having had a hand in these developments. "I have always maintained that we were a great nation of builders, and, from what you say, I judge we continue to be that way in the Marianas."

Off the Philippines, America's character as a nation of fighters was at issue again shortly after MacArthur's Sixth Army went ashore.

Whenever the Navy's great Pacific stagecoach changed drivers—Spruance for Halsey, or vice versa—a difference in attitude was palpable among the ranks. An officer who commanded the *Yorktown* under both men would say, "When we worked for the Spruance/Mitscher combination we knew what we were going to do; the plans came out, and we knew what we were going to do. You could plan, you could give your crew some sleep, you could do some maintenance, you could spot your planes." But under Halsey, "you would get changes at two o'clock in the morning, and you would have to change everything around and it disrupted the schedules."

Impulse versus plan, wind-driven flames versus the steady roll of a stream. This was the difference between William F. Halsey, Jr., and Raymond A. Spruance. The two had been friends since their days in destroyers in the early twenties. Spruance came to admire Halsey's skill in seamanship, not to mention his daring. In downtime, on the beach, when the bonfire was roaring high, Spruance and Margaret relaxed, stone cold sober. Halsey was always in high spirits. "I can remember one evening he dropped in rather late," Margaret said. "It must have been about ten o'clock. We had a fire crackling in the fireplace. Raymond told Billy that the only liquor in the house was a little bit of cognac. Raymond offered Billy some cognac, and Billy replied, 'Not at this time of night, Spruance. You still haven't learned how to drink.'"

What happened off Leyte within a week of the October 20 landings underscored their differences and settled the debate over Spruance's caution in the Battle of the Philippine Sea. MacArthur's operation triggered the first large-scale sortie of the Combined Fleet since the Marianas campaign. The Sho Plan involved every remaining major fleet unit. Its hopes rested on surface combatants now. Two large battleship task forces were to pass through Philippine waters and strike the Sixth Army beachhead in a pincer attack from north and south. Though Japanese naval aviation had been virtually destroyed off the Marianas, U.S. intelligence estimates continued to point to a revival. The reported launching of several new carriers had impressed Halsey more than did any hint that their air groups had been wiped out (the full extent of which, to be fair, was not fully understood). But Halsey was more strongly animated by a determination to redeem what he saw as blown chances and failures, both his own and those of others. His health had betrayed him when battle offered at Midway. To his eternal chagrin, he sat it out. And Spruance's nerve had failed, he thought, when Ozawa showed up to confront the Fifth Fleet off Guam. While Alex Vraciu and others searched for a friendly flight deck after dark on June 20, all Halsey could do was join the air admirals' bitter chorus about a missed opportunity to win the war.

On the afternoon of October 24, operating east of Samar, aircraft from

Halsey's Third Fleet ravaged the powerful Japanese Center Force, under Vice Admiral Takeo Kurita, sinking the superbattleship *Musashi,* then abandoned that rich target in favor of attacking a squadron of carriers that, with a sparse complement of planes, presented little threat to the U.S. beachhead. Jisaburo Ozawa was the commander of this small force, which was a mere shadow of the one he had led to the Marianas. It was in fact little more than a decoy, deployed specifically to lure Halsey out of position. Task Force 38 administered to it thoroughly, but was thereafter out of position to participate in engagements farther to the south.

That night the Japanese Southern Force tried to transit Surigao Strait. The Seventh Fleet's fire-support group, with six old battleships, destroyed Vice Admiral Shoji Nishimura's force nearly to a ship, including the battleships *Fuso* and *Yamashiro*. Halsey's decision to run north left the way open for Kurita to reverse course to the east and transit San Bernardino Strait. As he turned south toward the Leyte beachhead, all that was left to resist him was a detachment of six escort carriers under Rear Admiral Clifton Sprague, the former captain of the *Wasp.* What took place in the Battle off Samar is a story for the ages. The two-and-a-half-hour daylight surface battle on the morning of October 25 was one of the most remarkable battles in naval warfare. Kurita's mighty squadron, astonishingly, was forced to turn and flee by the heroics of Sprague's small task unit. In the end, though, it was not Taffy 3's unlikely performance that most impressed U.S. naval high command. It was the near disaster whose proximate cause was Halsey's impulsiveness and carelessness with communications. Raymond Spruance, perhaps more than anyone else, understood the root sources of his counterpart's errors. The Japanese carrier force, shorn of its air groups by attrition, was dangerous only to the extent that it might tempt a fleet commander who was desperate to indulge himself. Ozawa's flattops symbolized power, but carried none of it, and the great irony is that their symbolism survived to induce an actual blunder from Halsey that was several orders of magnitude greater than even the worst that Spruance was accused of committing for his failure to sink them in the Marianas. The Japanese ploy masterfully exploited the psychology that was at work in the flag quarters of the Third Fleet flagship *New Jersey*.

It was now Spruance's turn to play the role of second-guesser. He did so quietly and privately. Recapping the drama of those twenty-four hours in a letter to Margaret, he wrote: "Why any of our CVEs escaped to tell the tale nobody knows. The Japs had them and then, after sinking two CVEs, two destroyers, and a DE, let them go." His eyes were clear about his colleague's ultimate failure: "What happened during the whole action [in the Philippines] was just what I was expecting off Saipan and trying to prevent—being drawn off to the westward while part of the Jap fleet came in around our flank and hit the amphibious force at Saipan." The air admirals were wrong. It was indeed possible for carriers to be end-run, if their commanders were determined to permit it. Halsey had proved Spruance's case.

Admiral Ozawa would be a discerning judge of his enemies. As E. B. Potter, an eminent naval historian, wrote to Spruance after the war:

> The Japanese frothed at the mouth because you always moved at just the right time (wrong time, for them) and they could never lay a finger on you. Casting about for a word to describe your baffling elusiveness, they came up with something that translates into English as "caution."
>
> In calling you cautious, Ozawa meant chiefly that you were a man almost impossible to trap. He used another adjective describing you that might be translated as "orthodox," by which he implied that you could be expected to think out each step carefully and arrive at a solution that was aggressive but involving no unnecessary risks—a solution in line with established principles of war. For that reason they believed that they could anticipate your actions more readily than they could anticipate Halsey's. . . . The adjective Ozawa used to describe [Halsey] is best translated as "impulsive."

If that was true, then it should not have been entirely predictable that Halsey would take the bait. But from Spruance's point of view, Ozawa's comments were an authoritative supporting brief.

The Battle off Samar had a shocking coda. Late on the morning of October 25, as Sprague's men pondered their impossible survival, a bomb-laden Zeke dived into the escort carrier *St. Lo* (which had been named the *Midway* while serving off Saipan) and sank her. It was the war's first successful kamikaze attack. The loss of this minor ship prefaced the horrendous suicide campaign the American fleet would face throughout the rest of the war. Admiral Onishi had transformed the First Air Fleet, lately of Tinian, into a fearsome new weapon.

The great air battles of the Leyte Gulf campaign would quickly be a thing of the past. Regular Japanese air groups faced their Waterloo in the Philippines. The same day as the Battle off Samar, David McCampbell and his wingman, Roy Rushing, intercepted sixty Japanese planes heading toward the *Essex*. In a single swirling action, McCampbell shot down nine planes and claimed two probables, vaulting him past Alex Vraciu as the Navy's top ace.

The exposure of his fleet as it pushed farther westward impressed Spruance powerfully. He wrote to Johnny Hoover in late November: "This suicide method of attack is very sound and economical war and a form especially suited to the Japanese temperament. Unless we can think up some tactical counter to it, perhaps we should stop fighting the products of the Jap aircraft factories on the perimeter, and take our carrier air in to the center to knock out the factories themselves."

Major General Haywood Hansell, who had commanded the Eighth Air Force's B-17 wings over Europe and had been a principal player at the Cairo Conference, where the Army Air Forces secured a primary role in the war against Japan, was a longtime advocate of daylight precision bombing. "Let us make it emphatically clear," he had written in the 1930s, "that [strategic bombing] does *not* mean the indiscriminate bombing of women and children." But on arrival in the Marianas, he found his strategy opposed by Air Force officers who had entirely different views of the B-29's role. The commander of the 73rd Wing, Brigadier General Emmett "Rosie" O'Donnell, was committed from day one to waging incendiary warfare against the Japanese mainland. He had support in high places. The man who held Hansell's former post as Twentieth Air Force chief of staff in Washington in August 1944 had been impressed by Tokyo's vulnerability to fire and was eager to exploit it. This was none other than Brigadier General Lauris Norstad, Paul Tibbets's old nemesis from North Africa.

Norstad oversaw all plans to bomb Japan, from target lists to ordnance loadouts, and he stood in position to filter all the information that reached the desk of the commanding general of the Army Air Forces. Hap Arnold was not a man of theory. He was a quantifier, a devotee of hard numbers, impressed by measurable inputs as a proxy for results. Arnold counted success in terms of tonnage of bombs dropped, not how many targets were destroyed. Hansell was candid with his boss, protesting the use of this "fallacious criterion." But Arnold pushed back: "Every bomb that is added to each airplane that takes off for Japan will directly affect the length of the war." This was a rather fuzzy theory, to be sure, but it had the virtue of being susceptible to capture in tables and spreadsheets. And so the XXI

Bomber Command stood up an office for just that purpose. The Office of Statistical Control was prolific, using punch-card sorting machines to measure aircraft on hand, sorties per ready aircraft, tonnage delivered, and the efficiency of death delivered wholesale. An officer who was assigned to the outfit, Lieutenant Colonel Robert S. McNamara (a future secretary of defense), embraced a single overriding mandate above all others: Maximize efficiency.

The first missions carried out by Saipan-based B-29s were teeth cutters, warm-ups, raids on smaller targets such as Iwo Jima and Truk. These milk runs were poor preparation for what would await them over Tokyo, in terms of both air defenses and weather phenomena. The first major raid on Tokyo since Doolittle's took place on November 24, 1944, as B-29s began rolling to the flight line from Isely Field's taxiways and hardstands.

Led by a newly arrived veteran of the European theater, Major Robert K. Morgan, who had flown twenty-five missions in the famed *Memphis Belle,* the mission sent one hundred and eleven planes to bomb an aircraft engine factory outside Tokyo. Morgan would recall the dreamlike quality of leading the first mission: taking off over the cliff rising up from Magicienne Bay; turning north to pass over Iwo Jima, soon to be washed with blood; making landfall over the "entry point" above Hamamatsu; then the final run northeast toward Tokyo, heralded by the cone of Mount Fuji sliding into view on the left.

This first mission, a test run of Hansell's high-altitude daylight precision bombing theory in a new theater, was doomed to failure. Not even the Irish luck and temper of Rosie O'Donnell, who flew with Morgan in the co-pilot's seat, could defeat the winds that roared like a hurricane at thirty thousand feet. O'Donnell didn't like any part of the mission's conception. Most of the eighty-eight planes that managed to reach Tokyo found themselves pushed along by a hurricane-force jet stream that boosted their ground speed to well over four hundred miles per hour. This tempest blew their payloads far off the mark.

The fact that only two B-29s failed to return led Hansell to feel that daylight missions could be conducted reasonably safely, but Arnold judged the mission a failure for the lamentable accuracy of the drop. Although they met with only meager to moderate antiaircraft fire and spirited but ineffective fighter opposition, fewer than one in ten of the bombs landed in the target area. Three days later another mission flew, with similar results. The Japanese, prompt to avenge it, sent twin-engine planes to strafe Isely Field, burning a number of B-29s.

For airplane commanders and their crews, the missions were adventures into a terrifying void. Soaring above the clouds, where the air was not breathable, they donned insulated suits to protect them from subzero temperatures and relied on their pressurized crew compartments to keep them alive. The jet stream winds, like some trailing afterbreeze of the original kamikaze, forced extreme accommodations. Crews shed unnecessary weight, stripping away guns, bunks, thick glass panels on the front windscreen, and miscellaneous hardware such as hot plates for warming food. Lightening the craft by seven thousand pounds increased airspeed by five miles an hour, and at thirty thousand feet, the B-29 could outrun many Japanese fighters. But the planes were burning out their engines fast, and the bombing remained inaccurate. The mission abort rate was about twenty percent. And aircraft losses were mounting. Every time a Superfortress went down, eleven men were typically lost. When four or more planes were lost, as they were on several missions, the effect was like an infantry company losing a whole platoon. The sudden vacancies that yawned in the sleeping quarters were hard on morale.

On his third mission out of Isely Field, First Lieutenant Norman Westervelt's plane was hit and began leaking fuel. The stream of gasoline, flowing from a wing tank along the bottom of the fuselage, reentered the plane through a camera hatch. The crew understood that their only chance to get home was to lighten ship, so they stripped the airplane, tossing the highly secret Norden bombsight. The flight engineer frantically calculated their fuel levels, transferring between tanks to keep all four engines working. The navigator, First Lieutenant David Braden, tried to establish a fix or a dead reckoning position so that they might know where they were when they crashed. The aircraft commander, Westervelt, alerted two other planes nearby to his plight. Then the engines sputtered and died. The plane descended until the fifteen-foot swells were visible. With his fuel gone, Westervelt didn't have the power to pull his nose over the next swell. He clipped that wall of water at nearly a hundred knots. It would have been easier on the crew to hit a concrete wall. The impact crumpled the greenhouse nose, launching Westervelt straight through it and decapitating him. The bombardier, Gordon Nedderson, was in the prescribed crash position—facing rearward, head tucked between his knees—but the impact was so violent that it killed him, too. Braden survived in his crash position in the tunnel linking the navigator's compartment to the rear of the plane. The gunner who controlled the central fire-control system, Bob Curtis, was found after impact sitting on the floor with his back broken.

They spent three hours in rafts, coddling Curtis as he screamed in pain, before a "Dumbo"—a Navy PBY on air-sea rescue duty—came in and saved them. Braden couldn't tell this story for six years after the war. The first time he smelled the sea, in Galveston, he started shaking.

The fear worked on you. The youngest airplane commander based on Guam, George Savage, recalled how one of his veteran crew, his first central fire-control gunner, lost his nerve. "He would take all the flak jackets in the back of the plane and arrange them into a little silo and sit in the middle of them. He would shoot at everything he thought he saw," Savage said. Afraid that his trigger-happy gunner was going to make Savage a "Jap ace," the pilot sent him to a maintenance crew after a few missions.

A waist gunner in one of the Saipan-based squadrons developed a tremendous phobia that his cabin would be depressurized. When a hole opened in a pressured fuselage at high altitude, everyone inside was at risk of being sucked right out into the void. Gunnery Sergeant James Krantz, stationed in front of a large Plexiglas bubble in the side of the plane, couldn't let go of the fear of being turned into a particle in that vacuum hose. So he did something about it. He tore strips from an old parachute and jury-rigged a safety line and always made sure to fasten it to his parachute harness.

On a mission over Nagoya at twenty-nine thousand feet, a Japanese fighter attacked his plane from the side, shattering the glass dome with cannon fire, and Krantz's nightmare came true. Yanked by air pressure through the side canopy and thrown into open air, he was saved only by his harness, which jerked tight and held him for about ten minutes, rustling like a dangling leaf in the slipstream. He lost consciousness, coming to only after the copilot, who raced back to investigate, and the other gunner hauled him back aboard and slapped an oxygen mask on his face while the pilot descended into breathable air.

It wasn't three days before the Japanese landed blows in return. Before dawn on November 27, a pair of G4M Betty bombers came roaring in from the sea and attacked Isely Field while construction lights shone. Finding the airfield vulnerable, they destroyed one B-29 and damaged eleven others. At noon on the same day, a formation of eleven Zekes appeared and began strafing Isely's hardstands. By the time the 318th Fighter Group rose to its defense, downing four of the attackers, five more B-29s were out of action. General Hansell, arriving at the airfield in a jeep while the attack played out, saw one of the Zekes lining up his vehicle for a strafing run. He dived to the ground and rolled under the vehicle, where he watched dumbstruck as the Japanese fighter touched down and rolled to a stop and the pilot jumped out, pistol drawn. He went down in a cross fire of rifle rounds.

Even when Isely Field wasn't hopping from such excitement and terror, managing tension was an ongoing process. Strange modes of recreation became popular. Pilots gathered at the officers' club, which had a fine view south, to watch B-29s taking off from Tinian across the strait. Engine failure was common enough that these waters saw more than their share of tragedies. "If an engine burped on takeoff, you were a dead man. That was all there was to it," one airman attested. The bomber strips on Guam and Saipan ended atop steep cliffs. Tinian offered no such "bonus altitude" to use as a margin for error. The spectators placed bets on which planes wouldn't make it. Watching the failures come to grief on the sea became a horrible spectator sport for those who played the unforgiving game themselves.

The pilots were in a league of their own, but Hap Arnold thought he still had much to prove. Arnold was always doubtful that precision bombing would work against Japan and its jet stream winds. He needed to show his president some results—and what result would impress more than a city afire? When Norstad wrote Arnold on November 29 suggesting a bombing raid against the Imperial Palace to mark the occasion of the third anniversary of the Pearl Harbor attack, Arnold returned the letter with a telling reply handwritten at the top:

"Not at this time—our position—bombing factories, docks, etc., is sound—later destroy the whole city."

Later destroy the whole city. Arnold seemed to be sold on the ambitions of his fire bombers, and biding time.

Three weeks was enough. On December 19, Hansell received a letter, written by Norstad above Arnold's signature, directing a full-scale incendiary attack against the city of Nagoya as soon as one hundred B-29s were ready to go. The mission, Norstad wrote, was "an urgent requirement for planning purposes." Hansell protested to Arnold that incendiaries were not meant to destroy precision targets. But that wasn't anything the Army's top airman did not already know. What Arnold seemed to understand was that his bombers were in a race against the ground forces and his strategic Air Force needed to make its case. On December 1, the Joint Chiefs approved Operation Olympic. With the Army's ambitious amphibians eager to end the war by direct assault, Arnold had little time to stir the world with the value of strategic airpower.

Raymond Spruance was in a hurry himself. With the fleet working in exposed waters, he needed a better and faster way to shut down the Japanese air attacks that were falling upon it. Marianas-based B-29s weren't getting it done. On December 27, they set out to hit the Nakajima aircraft engine plant complex at Musashino-Tama but whiffed badly, damaging only a hospital. Eyeing Iwo Jima and objectives farther west, Spruance knew the fleet could not wait for the B-29s to do the job.

At Wendover, Utah, in mid-December, Paul Tibbets stood before his entire outfit at the base auditorium. "I've looked at you. You have looked at me," he said. "I'm not going to get stuck with all of you, but those of you who remain are going to be stuck with me. You have been brought here to work on a very special mission. Those who stay will be going overseas. You are here to take part in an effort which could end the war. Don't ask what the job is. That's a surefire way to be transferred out. Do exactly what you are told, when you are told, and you will get along fine. Never mention this base to anybody. This means your wives, girls, sisters, family. It's not going to be easy for any of us but we will succeed by working together. However, all work and no play is no fun. So as of now, you can go on furlough. Enjoy yourself."

Noting their shock and delight, Tibbets hoped his people understood the strict security precautions that governed life in this one-bomb town. The base technical area, surrounded by security fencing, was off-limits. He told them flatly, "Stop being curious." Curiosity was hard to suppress with families about. As a concession to morale, he had allowed married men to bring their families to Wendover. His own wife, Lucy, and their two sons, Gene and Paul, lived right there on the base. But he kept them at a distance and had no choice but to lie about what was going on. Sometimes it took a comic turn. Once when Lucy asked him about some civilians who looked out of place on an air base, he told her they were sanitary engineers. He came back to the house one day to find that she had corralled one of these Ph.D.s from the Manhattan Project to unplug a bathroom drain. "He was a good sport," Tibbets wrote, "and took care of the problem, for which his advanced degree in physics did not necessarily qualify him. He and I laughed about it later."

On December 17, 1944, the forty-first anniversary of the first flight of the Wright brothers, the 509th Composite Group was officially activated by the United States Army Air Forces. The ten-day Christmas furlough began that same day. Major General Leslie Groves, the military director of the Manhattan Project, was "fit to be tied" when he heard about the plans, but then Tibbets explained his scheme. It was not the act of charity that it seemed. It was a ploy he had devised to test his people. He wanted to release them from the strictures of secrecy and see how they reacted. When the furloughers passed through one of the two transit hubs that served the base—the train and bus station in Salt Lake City and the bus station at Elko, Nevada—friendly civilians would happen by and strike up idle conversation.

Soon after his men got home, the reports started coming back to Tibbets. The reporters were these innocuous-seeming interlocutors—members of a thirty-man security detachment that Groves had installed at Wendover. Just as he expected, some of his people hadn't been able to resist the urge to talk. These individuals found their leaves cut short. Summoned back to base, they were hauled before Tibbets, and his tone was calibrated to scare the devil out of them.

"Why didn't you *keep your mouth shut*?" If there were denials or protests, he produced the report and went over it, reading off the time and place of the offense and the exact content of the conversation. He then put them under arrest. After a few days confined to quarters, they were called back in to see him. "Look, it will cause me a lot of trouble if we go through a court-martial now," Tibbets said. "I'm willing to forget this one, but it's going into your record. We've got one strike on you. If you talk too much again, it's going to be rough."

The security agents infiltrated every phase of his operations. They monitored phone calls and cut them off if any reference to classified information seemed imminent. If they happened to hear a man's wife whisper to a friend that she was pregnant, Tibbets found out and made sure someone approached the expectant father to quietly congratulate him. When the base librarian reported someone whose curiosity led him to check out a book on atomic science, he was promptly visited by agents. "Fiendish in some aspects, perhaps, but our methods were effective," Tibbets wrote. "Not one single leak was ever traced to a member of the 509th."

Because trust on every level was the currency of the realm, Tibbets was allowed to handpick his own close circle, including his copilot, Bob Lewis, and the aircrew who would fly his own plane. Many were veterans of his old B-17 squadron in Africa: Dutch Van Kirk, navigator; George Caron, tail gunner; Wyatt Duzenbury, flight engineer; Tom Ferebee, "the best bombardier who ever looked through the eyepiece of a Norden bomb-sight." In addition to serving as crew on Tibbets's personal plane, they oversaw the training of their counterparts in the other aircraft. Tibbets drove everybody hard. He expressed his style on the base handball court. "He took pity on no one," one member recalled. Certainly he did not pity those who breached his trust. He let rumors spread that offenders would be shipped to Alaska. Near the main gate of the base he hung a large sign: WHAT YOU HEAR HERE — WHAT YOU SEE HERE — WHEN YOU LEAVE HERE — LET IT STAY HERE.

It marked the credibility of Paul Tibbets's leadership style that he had very few instances of trouble. After three years of war, the confectioner's son had learned it didn't pay to be sweet.

29

Going Critical

About four thousand souls from the Second Marine Division remained in the Marianas after combat operations ended. Given that Erskine and company had concocted a phony plan in order to secure hulls to bring an additional battalion to Saipan in the first place, it was rich that not enough shipping was on hand to take them home. Other cargoes outranked them on the list of priority carriage as the great river of war-fighting assets streamed west. There would be no frolic in Auckland.

Nimitz decided to retain the Second Division in the Marianas in hopes that they could rest and rehabilitate in theater. Doing so where the foot trails still reverberated with terrible memories was a setback. On Saipan, where units of the Second and Sixth Marine Regiments were encamped, and on Tinian, where the Eighth Marines joined the garrison, tent camps proliferated and USO shows rolled through. Along the way, the veteran assaulters, their ranks filled out by replacements, were invariably pressed into service tracking down Japanese stragglers in the hills. The pace of cleanup operations had slowed since late July, when General Jarman reported the killing or capture of as many as a hundred Japanese a day.

South of the peak of Mount Tapotchau, a Marine platoon, while searching for Japanese souvenirs, came under fire from about thirty-five Japanese troops. The next day, elements of another company was shot at with automatic weapons in the same area. At the encampment near Charan Kanoa, a nurse mentioned to a doctor that one of her patients had told her of a Japanese captain holding out in the hills with several hundred people. This came as a revelation to Colonel Pollard, the intelligence officer of the Second Marine Division. He set in motion a plan to bring in the stubborn holdouts once and for all.

The biggest effort took place in November, with a skirmish line five thousand men long. It took several hours to assemble it, drawing men from three regiments. Assisted by dogs, the troops advanced elbow to elbow, sweeping up-island nearly across its entire width, westward across Saipan's rough interior terrain to the coastal plain. Pollard flew in an observation plane, watching as the operation proceeded. He couldn't see a thing through the jungle canopy. The view from the ground wasn't much better. The sweep produced no contact with the enemy.

Captain Sakae Oba had been duly warned of the operation ahead of time by one of his men who was in the Charan Kanoa compound, masquerading as a civilian. Having observed the skirmish line forming up, and having watched its progress through binoculars from a promontory atop the ridge, Oba came to an important realization: The Americans on patrol always kept their heads down. They looked ahead, but never up. His men could hide, he thought, by staying above them. They would climb higher on the ridge and cling to the sides of the cliffs. And so, as the sweep proceeded in his direction, he ordered his flock of three hundred to climb, find places on the ridge, and cling to the cliffs as the Americans approached. There wasn't room for everyone. Some climbed and hid in the tops of trees.

As Oba held on to the cliff, muscles cramping, he feared he might fall. *We'll die like the Christ of their religion,* he thought, *crucified to this cliff.* American troops were visible below, through the trees, just twenty yards away. They seemed to linger for some reason. Oba feared that the slightest twitch of a cramping muscle, or a droplet from his brow, would draw startled attention and a fusillade that would end him and his entire command. Then came the thumping sound of a Nambu machine gun. Horiuchi. The commotion drew the Americans away, enabling Oba and his people to get off the ridge, scurrying around out of sight from the ground below. As he gathered his entire force, he wondered if the tattooed *yakuza* would make it. The gunfire became distant, then stopped, as the Americans discovered and tossed his encampment in the ravine below.

The men of the U.S. patrol returned to camp with their haul: just seventeen scared civilians. Colonel Pollard's wrath fell hard upon the Marine who announced this paltry result.

The Japanese continued to pick their spots. Around Christmas, the Second Division operations officer, Lieutenant Colonel Samuel G. Taxis, attended a party at his officers' club. He had had a few drinks when a call came in that five sailors on shore leave had picked the wrong time to go souvenir hunting. That night outside the club they ran into an armed party of Japanese and were killed to a man. A Marine patrol arrived too late to catch the culprits, who vanished into the hills.

Oba's covert camp, in the lee of a high west-facing ridge, attracted a following of about one hundred fifty Japanese soldiers and some civilians who earned their privileges by providing medical aid. Supplies in the camp did not last long. Over time, American patrols discovered and cleared out nearly every food cache hidden in the scrub. After about a week, Oba and his men were left to subsist on the land, eating breadfruit, papaya, and large snails. From then on, their struggle was more to find food than to lead ambushes, though they did that when necessary and effectively enough to encourage most Marine patrols to keep to the main trails. Oba made sure his men never started firefights within three miles of camp.

It had been a sober, rational sense of what duty required of a soldier that had led Oba to decline General Saito's order to make a suicide rush from Makunsha that night in July. But he still found himself in a daily struggle with mysticism. One day a nurse came to him and confided that a lance corporal in his camp, Ikegami, had instructed her to stop treating the wounded. Claiming to be a former Shinto priest, he declared that he was taking over as camp healer. The nurse, outraged, whispered to Oba that the man had convinced half the camp that he could heal by touch.

One day Oba saw Ikegami huddling with some soldiers. He could just barely hear the priest, and was surprised to find him speaking in the tones that Shinto clerics used in the temple. "You will follow Captain Oba's words because through me, he will carry the word of God. Together we will defeat the barbarian heretics who surround and threaten us." That evening Oba summoned Ikegami to his cave and asked him what he had said. When the man repeated the details of his promise, Oba was convinced of his sincerity and made no issue of it. He dismissed Ikegami with his thanks. He decided he could tolerate the upstart, for anything that brought solidarity and confidence was useful, so long as the man did not challenge his authority or endanger his people.

Finally, though, the mystic's increasingly extravagant boasts of his supernatural abilities forced Oba's hand. The last straw came on the day Oba saw Ikegami tracing large Xs in the air, in the belief that such a symbol would block the Americans from entering the camp. Later Ikegami actually ventured down a mountain trail toward a U.S. position, tracing the same figure in the air as if it would confine the Americans. At this, Oba ordered him taken under guard. After a few weeks the deranged soldier seemed to be doing better, until one day he slipped free, stepped out of the jungle, approached an American patrol, and, bowing with a broad smile, permitted himself to be taken into custody.

The Susupe Swamp internment camp, just inland of Charan Kanoa, was run by naval civil affairs officers who had been trained at Columbia University's school for military governance. The camp would hold 189 civilian houses, a handicrafts building, fourteen workshops, thirteen new water wells, sewage, sanitation, and drainage infrastructure, and a bevy of latrines that were sprayed against flies. It would boast by the end of September a seven-hundred-bed field hospital staffed by U.S. medical personnel who had been diverted from serving their own military. More than 12,000 Japanese civilians and 4,300 Chamorros and Koreans would be the recipients of 129,000 medical treatments there.

In the camp Shizuko Miura had been pressed into service as a nurse, her white shoes now ragged and irretrievably darkened by bloodstains from her service to the garrison on Saipan. During her recovery, she had acquired something of a reputation: the nurse who had refused to save herself. Hospital orderlies said, in a vaguely sympathetic sort of mockery, "Hara-kiri, hara-kiri," making the gesture of sword to belly. Whenever extra food was given to her she passed it along to patients, but an American nurse gave her a new uniform and she accepted and wore it with pride. Her duties were menial and included carrying chamber pots.

Along the way, a patient brought her astonishing news. A Japanese man in a working party had identified her brother's tank, "the Swallow," south of Garapan. One night, after her shift was over, she found a Japanese-speaking officer she had come to trust and asked him to help her find a ride so she could investigate.

As she drove north in the jeep, she was stunned by the transformation of the road to Garapan. It had been made "splendid beyond recognition," and the city had, too. It was full of strange buildings with curved aluminum roofs, new roads. Almost overnight, miraculously, the administrative capital had risen again, an entirely alien place. Her driver asked some U.S. soldiers milling about if they had seen any ruins of Japanese tanks. They directed her down another road, and at length her jeep came upon a cluster of disabled armored vehicles. They looked as if a giant's hand had thrown them down from a height. One stood out to her. It lay on its side in the grass, wounds open and rusting red with tall green fronds growing through them. Its turret was emblazoned with Japanese kanji for "the Swallow." She leaped from the jeep and ran to it.

Retrieving a hammer from the jeep, she climbed onto the tank and pounded at the hatch, but it was rusted shut. She hammered and hammered, steel ringing on steel, until some American soldiers, curious, came along.

"This Japanese girl wants to look inside. Please help us open it."

"Why on earth . . . ?"

"She says her brother is inside."

They nodded gravely, then went to work with hammers. Half an hour later, with rust knocked away and metal bent, they wrenched open the steel burial mound. Looking in, she was overcome by a smell of decay so heavy it seemed liquid. Nose stinging, eyes squinting from the stench, she braced herself and looked down inside. There was a face, decayed and unrecognizable, but she knew it was her brother. His name was printed on his fatigues and the insignia of a corporal was on his collar. Behind him was another body, that of his commander, wearing an officer's uniform. A pistol lay on the deck of the vehicle between them. Her tears spattered it, and some dropped onto her brother's body.

"I was unwilling to leave my brother's side, but there was nothing for me to do, really," she wrote. So she managed some final words—"My brother, goodbye"—then went back to the jeep, got in, and was driven away.

Something about the experience changed her. She began to process the impressions she had gained from the Charan Kanoa encampment, and from her encounters with Americans and Japanese alike, in the season that had passed since the end came on Saipan. "What was clear to me was that the American enemy were not monsters at all," she wrote. And not just the Japanese-speaking American officer, whose eyes, she noticed, had welled up at the sight of her brother in the tank. It was men in the hospitals who said, "The Japanese are fools. Tojo is mad." None of the Americans showed even the slightest interest in killing her.

So why had we killed each other? she thought. The futility of it overwhelmed her.

On New Year's Day 1945, after a visit with Halsey on Guam, where the Pacific Fleet command was establishing its new headquarters, Chester Nimitz returned to Pearl Harbor and held a press conference. One of the reporters began with a declaration, not a question. "It seems to me some Nips are going to be very unhappy in 1945, in Japan. They are going to be bombed and shot up, and burned, turned out of their houses," the writer said.

Nimitz agreed heartily, though the Texan's answer fell short of Halsey-esque epigrammatism. "Oh, yes," he said,

> I can foresee—now, I am not a predictor—but I foresee an un-happy 1945 for the Japanese.
>
> I foresee their shipping continuing to dwindle, as the result of the attacks of our submarines, air forces, and surface vessels when we can get close enough to their merchant shipping.
>
> I foresee that Japanese combatant vessels, whenever they leave the safety of their harbors, will be increasingly endangered by our submarines that are constantly increasing in numbers.
>
> I foresee an increase in the tempo of the air war against Japan itself during the year. And from the standpoint of the Japanese high command, I see no cause whatsoever for any optimism.

"You don't believe we can starve or bomb the Japanese into submission?"

"I don't know. I have nothing to gauge their ability to withstand punishment."

"Admiral, would you welcome Russian participation in this Pacific war, on our side?"

"Yes. I am glad you put that last in."

"Excuse me, but the laughter drowned out your answer."

"I said we would welcome it and I am glad you put that last phrase, 'on our side,' in there."

"Admiral, was there any single accomplishment in the Pacific in 1944 that was outstanding, above others? Any single campaign?"

"Yes, I think the capture of the Marianas was a tremendous blow to Japanese prestige and to their ability to go back and forth freely between the Carolines and the homeland. . . . I can say that my own peace of mind today is somewhat different from what it was just three years ago, which was my first day in command of the Pacific Fleet, Pacific Ocean Area. Prospects then were dim and now we are full of optimism."

The optimism flourished as war heroes such as David McCampbell returned home to receive high decorations and barnstorm the country. Shipped home from Ulithi on board the carrier *Bunker Hill,* McCampbell flew from Bremerton to New York to speak to an industry group, then drew regular pay from Grumman for three weeks to make appearances on behalf of the aircraft manufacturer. He was summoned to Washington to receive the Medal of Honor for his exploits in a Hellcat. On January 10, Roosevelt, sunken-eyed and unable to rise from his wheelchair, draped McCampbell and submarine skipper Lawson P. "Red" Ramage with a star-spangled baby blue ribbon from which dangled a five-pointed, trefoil-tipped bronze star crowned with laurel and oak. The honorees bantered with Admiral King and Generals Marshall and Arnold. Then, for McCampbell, came the worst experience of the war: celebrity. He was roped into making promotional appearances for the feature documentary *The Fighting Lady* (shot on board the *Yorktown*), touring the country in a twin-engine Beechcraft Model 18. He hit naval training centers from Jacksonville to North Island, hobnobbing on the Gulf Oil radio broadcast with the legendary sole survivor of Torpedo Eight from the Battle of Midway, Ensign George Gay. McCampbell's war was over. The Navy's leading ace could hardly stand it.

It was around this time at Pearl Harbor that another kind of film was exhibited for the private consideration of Raymond Spruance. It was a short one, featuring three goats. One was fitted with a Japanese gas mask. A second was fitted with an American gas mask. And the third had no gas mask at all. When poison gas was released into their pen, the unprotected animal dropped dead nearly at once. The goat wearing the Japanese gas mask lingered for a while, then fell over dead. Only the goat wearing the American model remained unharmed. "After viewing the picture, I remarked that if we could be allowed to use this new gas mask at Iwo Jima, we would save a lot of American lives. The Japanese defenders of Iwo would die anyway, and there was no civilian population. Being killed quickly by gas was at least as merciful as being killed by flamethrowers, bullets, bombs, and shells," Spruance recollected to Savvy Forrestel.

Iwo Jima was a special case, Spruance noted, in that no civilians were on it, so he did not see the same moral strictures applying. "The same number of Japs would have died in possibly a more humane way, and many American lives would have been saved, but we would have been branded with the initiation of gas warfare and justified Jap retaliation with gas," Forrestel would write. Spruance decided against its use before boarding the *Indianapolis* again on January 14 and setting out for Ulithi to relieve Halsey after the Leyte operation. But this same view on the utility of poison gas was long the view of General Marshall himself. In the end it was President Roosevelt who shut down consideration of its use by the Joint Chiefs.

The Fifth Fleet was ready. Shipping was arrayed at Pearl Harbor to carry the veterans of the Fourth Marine Division to Tinian, where they would stage for Iwo Jima. Their arrival turned into a landing exercise as the assault troops climbed down rope ladders in full kit into landing boats that circled in waiting in Tinian Town harbor, then proceeded to the line of departure. Time devoured experience like rust. The returning troops scarcely recognized the place. "The entire north end of the island, where we had made our landing assault the previous July, had been turned into a giant airfield," said First Lieutenant Frank S. Craig of the 2/25. "It gave us a great feeling of accomplishment to see them taking off one after another, in a seemingly endless stream across the very area where we had beaten back the Japanese counterattack on J Day at Tinian."

Every week the roster of aircraft available to the XXI Bomber Command was growing. Before year's end, Tinian would be ready to take on the 313th Bombardment Wing at North Field (previously known as Ushi Point), and early in 1945 the 58th Wing, decamped from India, would take up at West Field near Gurguan Point. Two more wings, the 314th and 315th, were bound for Guam, where Haywood Hansell had his new headquarters. But the slow pace of progress, as measured by tonnage dropped, had been a persistent frustration to Hap Arnold. Lauris Norstad was in good position to ensure that his boss continued to feel that way as he filtered Hansell's communications back to Washington, making sure to emphasize Hansell's ineffectiveness.

All services had their squabbles. In the strategic air forces the debate pitted advocates of high-level precision bombing against those who preferred incendiaries. Hansell, an advocate of precision bombing, had little use for Colonel McNamara's Office of Statistical Control. He doubted the value of measuring tonnage dropped and sorties flown. Such numbers "are easily compiled, seem factual and specific, and are impressive," he wrote. But they said little about the war-making capacity that was destroyed. With Arnold doubting him, Hansell had little standing to block Norstad's overriding ambition: to burn down all of Japan. To carry out that program, the Army Air Forces had sent a new sheriff to town. On January 6, Curtis LeMay, who had commanded the B-29s in China and India, arrived on Guam, ostensibly for a tour of the forward area. But Norstad was on hand to inform Hansell that LeMay was his relief as commander of the XXI Bomber Command. Hansell's campaign had been inaccurate and ineffective. Hap Arnold was eager for his Marianas-based bombers to stage a show of force against Japan, by way of impressing both evangelists and

skeptics alike as to the value of an independent air force, and Hansell's results simply weren't photogenic enough to suit Arnold's needs.

Norstad was unimpressed with Hansell in any event. He disdained the
Marianas commander for his "utter absolute complete and irreversible lack
of competence." No agreement on means and ends could overcome that
impression, taken on its face. It didn't help that Hansell was having trouble
with a certain willful subordinate—General O'Donnell, who did not believe in high-altitude bombing and disliked him personally. In the end,
Norstad decided to relieve Hansell from command "before we lost the
goddamned war." Any vindication Hansell might have felt in the success
of the final mission he had authorized—a January 19 high-altitude precision raid against a Kawasaki aircraft factory near Kobe that shut down
most of its production—would be exclusively for his personal pride.

Curtis LeMay would continue the high-altitude precision raids for another forty-nine days, to no better result. At that point he resolved to
change dramatically the nature of the effort. A firebombing campaign just
might be the fix. LeMay was about to change the way the XXI Bomber
Command waged war.

The first thing LeMay did was see to morale. The Office of Statistical
Control, with its punch-card machines and fastidious combing of data,
learned through study of Eighth Air Force operations over Germany that
mission abort rates varied directly with loss rates. In other words, Robert S.
McNamara and his analysts concluded, pilots were aborting out of
fear. LeMay instituted a new personnel policy: thirty-five missions and
home. "Until General LeMay gave us a tour limit, most of us had experienced so many scrapes that we became fatalists," David Braden said. "We
really did not expect to live through it." The new policy gave pilots an
incentive to carry through. LeMay took that lesson to heart in the Marianas. "He was the finest combat commander of any service I came across
in the war, but extraordinarily belligerent, many thought brutal," McNamara remembered.

At the end of January, LeMay flew to Ulithi and called on Raymond
Spruance to express his support for the plan to invade Iwo Jima. Spruance
was glad to have his mind put at ease about the return on investment the
war effort would see after the Marines took the island. Heavily fortified in
the short six months since the fall of Guam, Iwo was closer to Japan than
any target the Fifth Amphibious Force had assaulted to date. Holland
Smith's dire casualty estimates haunted Spruance. He felt responsible for
the bloodletting that was to come, having lobbied for the island's capture.

When Spruance asked LeMay, "What do you think about the value of Iwo Jima?" the Air Force commander said, "Oh, but it's going to be of tremendous value to me. Without Iwo Jima, I couldn't bomb Japan effectively." The island was both a forward observation station and a hive for Japanese fighter aircraft. Coming and going, the B-29s took a shellacking. Its capture would remove it as a double threat and transform it into a haven for B-29 pilots whose planes or crews were in no shape to reach the Marianas.

"This took a load off my mind," Spruance wrote.

To prepare the way for Kelly Turner's alligator fleet and hold down Japanese airpower, Spruance directed Marc Mitscher and the fast carrier task force to strike the Tokyo area. Spruance wanted to hit enemy aviation at its source, attacking airfields and aircraft factories. "I am tired of fighting them all along the perimeter," he said to Mitscher. "We would use our accuracy in bombing to attack military targets and would leave attacks on the civilian population to the Army Air Forces." The carriers sortied from Ulithi on February 10.

That same day, the *Indianapolis* brought Spruance to Saipan to confer with Kelly Turner about the Iwo landings. Shown to Turner's quarters in his new flagship, the *Eldorado,* Spruance was told that Turner had turned in with a high fever. "He had been driving himself so hard for the past two years that he had lost weight and looked badly," said Turner's faithful number two, Harry Hill. The illness had plagued him for nearly a month and now threatened to keep him laid low during a critical operation. "I had never seen him so ill, and was deeply concerned," Hill wrote. "The Navy just couldn't afford to lose him." Spruance let him sleep.

Two days later, with Spruance on board, the *Indianapolis* departed Saipan to rejoin Mitscher and the carriers underway. The Fifth Fleet commander had managed a brief conference with Turner in which he explained how, as a prelude to the landings on "Sulfur Island," he would spring a simultaneous double surprise on the Japanese: three days of carrier strikes against mainland airfields and aircraft factories, along with the naval bombardment of Iwo. The Marines had wanted ten days of bombardment, but Spruance approved only three. He felt the naval gunfire had to be simultaneous with his Tokyo strikes in order for both to achieve surprise, and he was unwilling to expose the fleet any longer than that off the enemy's home coast—certainly not without the antiaircraft services of the battleships *Washington* and *North Carolina,* which Turner had yoked into bombardment duty on D Day. The rapid timetable for an Okinawa assault—the Joint Chiefs had approved April 1—would afford him little time to dally at Iwo Jima. Already he was feeling pressed about replenishing the fleet at Ulithi between the operations. Kelly Turner, for his part, was at loggerheads with his own staff over how efficiently warships could dismantle Iwo's network of new gun positions and blockhouses. Turner's optimistic estimates supported Spruance's decision to allow for just three days of bombardment.

On February 16, exactly one year since the great raid on Truk, the sixteen carriers of Task Force 58 pushed through strong winds and gathering squalls to within one hundred miles of the Japanese coast. The path of the task force had been scouted by submarines and also by a special flight of ten B-29s from Saipan, which flew in a 110-mile scouting line at three thousand feet, watching for picket boats. Undetected on approach, Mitscher began launching at daybreak, his air groups assigned to a broad schedule of airfields and aircraft engine factories and assembly plants near Tokyo. Japanese fighter defenses, scrambled locally without evident coordination, were robust but not up to the task of handling five carrier task groups. Good weather over the target area enabled the pilots to press home effective attacks against as many as ten different airfields near Tokyo as well as the aircraft engine plants at Tachikawa and Musashino-Tama, the latter of which was at one time thought to produce forty percent of Japan's fighter engines.

On the morning of the seventeenth, faced with worsening weather, Spruance ordered Mitscher to stop launching. As the carriers landed their strikes and turned south, Spruance announced results that were nearly equal to the Great Marianas Turkey Shoot: 332 Japanese planes destroyed in the air, 177 destroyed on the ground, a light aircraft carrier and numerous small craft sunk, and serious damage to several aircraft engine factories and assembly plants. U.S. losses were forty-nine planes and fifty-five pilots and aircrew, including the skippers of the *Lexington* and *Langley* air groups.

Before returning to base, some pilots from the *Cabot* carried out a special task on orders from Mitscher. Over Tokyo, they opened their bomb bay doors and began cutting loose bales of paper. Falling like leaves over the city, thousand by thousand, came the leaflets. They depicted Emperor Hirohito, sword drawn and held backward, leading a serpentine creature with a death's head that slithered over the bodies of the Japanese women and children, set upon by snakes and insects. The kanji scrawled around the grotesque cartoon read, "The companion to war is disease." And on the back, "Bombers are destroying water lines and electric lines. Food and supplies cannot be delivered. The people become weak and ill. You must rise up and face the *gunbatsu* [military industrial establishment] and put a stop to the senseless war." The pilots dropped twenty-seven thousand of these over Tokyo and four thousand more over the island of Chichi Jima. The shower of paper was meant as an entreaty, and also perhaps as a warning to a benumbed public. There were certain factions in the Japanese government that might have just as well produced the piece themselves.

The "strategic leaflet campaign" over the Japanese home islands began with Spruance's foray against Japan in February. Ultimately, one hundred million leaflets and newspapers would be dropped on Japan before the end of the war, the majority from B-29s of the XXI Bomber Command. The effect would be gradual but significant. Commentaries on Radio Tokyo indicated the Japanese government's grave concern over "thought warfare" that was waged with "paper bombs." The weekly newspaper *Mariana Jiho* (*Marianas Review*), prepared by the Psychological Warfare Branch of CINCPAC/CINCPOA and the Office of War Information and dropped weekly beginning in March 1945, would produce acute fears of subversive effect.

Doubts about the war were festering in the highest precincts of Japanese government. Prince Fumimaro Konoye, who as prime minister in 1941 had failed to stop the army militarists from starting war with the United States, issued a plaintive lament in a February 14 letter to the throne:

> Regrettable though it is, I believe Japan's defeat is now inevita-
> ble. . . . What should be the gravest concern to us, from the stand-
> point of maintenance of our national polity, is not the defeat itself
> but rather its subsequent Communist revolution. I really think the
> internal and external situation of our nation at present is rapidly
> heading for Bolshevization. . . . It appears to me that every condi-
> tion for the achievement of Communist revolution is being daily
> fulfilled. That is: poverty, an increased voice for laborers; a pro-
> Soviet sentiment in contrast to the rising hostility toward Britain
> and the United States, a reform movement by some elements
> within the Army, a movement of so-called new bureaucrats who
> are taking advantage of the movement within the Army, and also
> secret maneuvers by the leftist element behind the scenes, and so
> forth. . . .
>
> As the war situation is getting critical lately, there has been a
> loud cry for a hundred million people to die in honor. People who

advocate such an idea are so-called rightists, however, in my judgment, they are tools of the Communist element who are trying to
throw the country into chaos in order to revolutionize the country. . . . I think continuation of this futile war will play into the
hands of the Communists. Consequently, I am convinced that we
should take measures to end the war as soon as possible, in order
to maintain our national polity.

But such pleas did not impress the Imperial Army junta that held a veto
over war policy in Tokyo. The army, in its fanaticism, had been calling for
the entire Japanese public to perish as a penalty for defeat. Their resolve
was duly revealed in intercepts of Japanese military messages and conveyed
directly to Washington. General Korechika Anami, the army minister, believed that an American invasion would give Japan an opportunity to win
a decisive victory, and that even if the invasion were not repulsed entirely,
a vigorous defense could inflict losses great enough to force the Americans
into a favorable peace settlement. Emperor Hirohito himself confirmed to
Kido, his close adviser, his confidence that such a victory might yet be won.

In the early stages of planning Operation Olympic, U.S. Army planners used the experience of Saipan to estimate likely losses. There, for the
first time, U.S. troops had confronted a large enemy force on physical and
human terrain that resembled those of the home islands. Both Army and
Marine units suffered about twenty percent casualties in the Marianas
while exposed more or less equally to combat. American casualties on
Saipan—more than 3,400 dead and 10,000 wounded—relative to the size
of the Japanese garrison defending the island, suggested a ratio by which
to estimate the cost of operations in the home islands. One American
dead and several wounded for every seven Japanese defenders in place
was known as the "Saipan ratio." Facing a mobilization in the home islands that promised to make the garrisons in the Marianas seem threadbare and halfhearted, U.S. Sixth Army staff figured that battle casualties
in the first four months of fighting on Kyushu alone would reach 124,935,
including about 25,000 dead, with an additional 269,000 men lost to disease and nonbattle injury. They would be alarmed to discover that Japan
had grown its pool of manpower from 3.5 million to 5 million and was
mustering an air fleet of ten thousand planes, half of them to be assigned
to suicide units.

Each side's estimate of the other's combat power, and each side's sense of
the other's willingness to use it, were the crux of the politics of the war ef-

fort in the spring of 1945. Would Japan ever surrender without conditions? No nation surrenders until it is shown that there is no better option. What demonstration of Japanese martial spirit would force the Americans to the negotiating table? No power fights who cannot find marginal value in the next battle. Where and when would the breaking point come? These were the questions of the hour. Some answers would come in Admiral Spruance's two final campaigns of the war.

Iwo Jima, which means Volcano Island, had risen out of the deep and was still rising, uplifting by four and a half inches a year at the time Raymond Spruance, Kelly Turner, and the U.S. Marine Corps conspired to seize it. Day after day through the millennium since its emergence, the winds drove the sea to thrash Iwo Jima's shores, producing a strand of rust-black ash. On the morning of February 19, the same Navy team that had taken Saipan returned in force to seize the tiny two-by-four-mile speck in the Western Pacific.

Spruance had the Fifth Fleet, Kelly Turner the amphibians, and Marc Mitscher the fast carriers. Spike Blandy commanded the naval forces that carried Holland Smith's expeditionary troops and would stand by in support. Smith's corps commander, Harry Schmidt, was responsible for the three Marine divisions that would handle the dirtiest of the dirty work. The commanding generals of the Third and Fourth Marine Divisions, Graves Erskine and Clifton Cates, respectively, were veterans of Saipan and Tinian. Only the Fifth Division commander, Keller E. Rockey, was new to the Pacific.

After three days of bombardment from air and sea, the preassault reconnaissance by four Underwater Demolition Teams began. Their approach drew heavy fire that inflicted casualties on all the LCI gunboats that led them. On the night of the eighteenth, a Betty hit the APD *Blessman* with a bomb, killing thirty-seven men from her crew and UDT Fifteen. When the frogmen reported neither mines nor obstacles to complicate the landings, Turner issued the order to send in the landing force. The leading wave reached the beach at nine A.M., amtanks leading the way.

The naval and air bombardment had been a bust. No additional volume of ordnance would have made a difference against the defenses that Lieutenant General Tadamichi Kuribayashi had excavated in the island's solid basaltic rock. Subterranean hospitals, command posts, and artillery positions, interconnected by tunnels, were invulnerable to bombardment.

Japanese mortars and artillery, presighted on the beach, pulverized the assaulters as they struggled to climb the deep-ash bluff that seemed to yield only one step up and forward for every four taken. It took them four hours to reach the airfield, and four days to get to the top of Mount Suribachi, where a patrol from the 28th Marines planted a length of pipe flying an American flag that would snap forever in the vista of history.

At evening twilight on February 21, the carrier *Saratoga,* having returned to Iwo Jima's waters after striking Tokyo, was preparing to begin night air operations when she came under coordinated attack by six suicide planes northeast of the island. Four of these single-engine kamikazes hit her, as did several of their bombs. The ship's company was left to bury ninety-three men at sea and puzzle another sixty-one missing in action. The *Saratoga* was taken out of the war. In the half-light after sunset, just to the south, the escort carrier *Bismarck Sea* was attacked and sunk by a pair of twin-engine kamikazes, leaving a third of her crew as casualties.

Long foreseen and dreaded by U.S. planners, the casualty surge suffered in the climactic offensive year of the war was now in full swing. Between the summer of 1944, when the record-breaking exertions of amphibious forces fell on Normandy and the Marianas, and the summer of 1945, American forces suffered one million of their one and a quarter million battle casualties. What might the invasion of Japan cost? The projections tracked the latest intelligence as to the size of the Japanese garrison and the extent of its hardware. The Joint Chiefs would estimate the low-end range of U.S. ground and naval casualties, in a ninety-day campaign, at 156,000 to 175,000 men, with as many as 38,000 killed in action.

Paul Tibbets spent the first months of the new year drilling his crews intensively over the western deserts of Utah, Nevada, and California with their new modified airplanes. Though the power of the atomic bomb remained theoretical, the scientists at Los Alamos concurred with Captain Deak Parsons's estimate: A B-29 would have to be at least eight miles from ground zero to survive an atomic blast. With the release of the bomb, therefore, a countdown began, a race between the bomb's descent to explosion and the aircraft's flight to survival. It would take the bomb forty-three seconds to fall on a slant from thirty thousand feet to its detonation altitude of around two thousand feet. The only way to achieve an eight-mile standoff distance in the short period of time between release and explosion was to reverse course and make use of the fact that the bomb would continue following the vector of the aircraft, at a substantial ground speed, as it fell on a diagonal. Tibbets calculated that a 155-degree diving turn would be the key to the aircrew's survival. Doing so in a four-engine bomber would take a high degree of precision flying talent. And even then, no one knew if the B-29's flight surfaces would withstand the force of it.

Rigorous classroom work and lectures, followed by long training exercises, sharpened the crew's skills in the unusual maneuver, while bombardiers rehearsed dropping dummy Fat Man bombs (known as pumpkins) into a circle four hundred feet in diameter. The Norden bombsight's reputation for "pickle-barrel accuracy" was a myth, Tibbets said. Though superior to any other such device, it could not eliminate the factor of wind.

Overwater navigation was another challenging curriculum. Five at a time, his crews went to an airfield outside Havana, Cuba, to practice radar bombing and gunnery against small Caribbean islands. With the secrecy of the missions, crews enjoyed a freedom from scrutiny that enabled them to smuggle booze and cigars back to Wendover.

When Tibbets visited Los Alamos, he adopted a sort of disguise. Before entering the gate of the 45,000-acre base in the mountains beyond Santa Fe, he removed the Army Air Forces emblem from his uniform, substituting the gold castle insignia of the Corps of Engineers. As he would write, this was necessary to "keep from ruffling the sensitive feathers of a few scientists who didn't mind making a bomb but were appalled by the thought that it might actually be used. These touchy types knew they were working for the military, but only for a nonfighting branch of the service, the Manhattan Engineering District. They chose to ignore the fact that there were military people who were actually engaged in the ugly business of dropping bombs."

If his remark was a gratuitous shot at the patriotism and commitment of those who staffed the Manhattan Project, most of whom were keenly aware that a bomb would be the fruit of their labor, Tibbets could be excused for having some bile in his voice. Never before had he worked at such a pace, and never before had the nature of the work weighed more heavily on him. The constancy of it, and the extreme secrecy, too, was taking a toll on his marriage. "I'm afraid that I treated Lucy very badly," he would tell a journalist.

> If you were told not to say anything to anyone, that included your wife. You never knew who a guy's wife was going to talk to after she had talked to her husband. So I wouldn't talk to her. About

anything, I'm afraid. Especially when she was in Wendover. I found myself shutting down completely. I couldn't talk to her about the things that were most important to me, so I found myself not saying very much of anything to her about other things, either. It wasn't fair to her—it also probably wasn't fair to me, being put in that position, but I know it wasn't fair to Lucy.

I was not a good husband, and I was not a good father. I was so wrapped up in doing a good job in what I was entrusted to do in the war that I did not do a good job with the other things. I've told my boys: Your mother got a bum deal. I was distant from the boys. I didn't know how to show them any affection. . . . I didn't see them almost at all for years. I was flying those missions over Europe, and then there was Wendover—it's not like I had the chance to do well or not well with them. I wasn't there. I was in the war.

Ernest King had known about the Manhattan Project since late 1943, when George Marshall called on him and explained the nature of the secret multi-billion-dollar project based in the deserts of New Mexico. Marshall promised to pass updates to the CNO every three months, and he did, in exchange for a promise of strictest secrecy. It was not until mid-February 1945 that Admiral Nimitz was let in on the secret. Commander Frederick L. Ashworth, Deak Parsons's deputy, presented himself at the new CINCPAC headquarters on Guam carrying a top secret letter, which he insisted on handing personally to Nimitz. Admiral Nimitz dismissed his aide, then invited Ashworth into his office. The visitor opened his uniform jacket, unbuttoned his shirt, extracted a money belt, and, as Nimitz grinned in amusement, produced a sweat-stained letter that he handed to his commander in chief.

The letter, which Ashworth suspected had been written by General Groves though it bore Admiral King's signature, in effect told Nimitz just how prescient he had been at his New Year's Day press conference. It announced the nature of the atomic bomb, described its unprecedented explosive yield, and authorized CINCPAC to inform one officer on his staff. Tinian had been chosen to house the bomb because its air operation facilities were superior to what was available on Saipan, and Guam was considered too far south.

As coordinator of the delivery and assembly of the bombs to the combat theater, Ashworth asked Nimitz for his cooperation in selecting a site on

Tinian to house his advance echelon. This included a team known as Project Alberta, under Parsons, which was responsible for handling the weapons after delivery to the island and for training aircrews. Hap Arnold had established "Silverplate" as a code word for the 509th's secret program. The word's use signaled that its user should receive highest priority within the Army Air Forces. When Ashworth went to see the top AAF officer on Tinian, Brigadier General Kimble, it was recommended that he set up on North Field, where the 509th's B-29s would blend in among other bomber units. And so, on this island whose grid of streets had been named after the streets of Manhattan by a New Yorker in the Army Corps of Engineers, the 509th took up residence in the "Columbia University district."

Nimitz summoned his chief of staff, Vice Admiral Charles H. "Soc" McMorris, and handed him the letter to read. He then said that his operations officer, Tom Hill, would have to be read in to the secret, too, if his command was to fulfill the various requests made of it. Noting the rush schedule, Nimitz asked Ashworth, "Don't these people in Washington realize we have a lot of war to fight between now and August?" Nimitz wanted to know why he couldn't have the bomb right away. Ashworth explained the development process of the implosion weapon, indicating that August was, in General Groves's judgment, the most realistic timetable for completion. Nimitz walked to the window and looked out at the green slope rolling down past Agana to cliffs fronting the blue Pacific. He stayed there awhile as he considered what Ashworth had said. At last, he turned back to the Navy three-striper. "Well, thank you very much, Commander. I guess I was just born about twenty years too soon."

"I felt that he had then sensed the magnitude of the thing," Ashworth would say.

The future was coming early to the Marianas, whence the future would soon be sprung upon the world. The veterans of the XXI Bomber Command's conventional B-29 units, suffering high losses through the grind of conventional missions over Japan, felt they had earned their place in the present, entitled to the minimal comforts their bases offered. In a few months' time, they would be none too happy to discover the privileges enjoyed by the unusual group of aviators and nonregulation civilian types who kept a secret technical facility in a storm-fenced corner of Tinian's northern plateau.

But more immediate concerns faced them as the calendar turned to March. Their cigar-chomping leader, Curtis LeMay, was about to change all the rules of the conventional strategic air campaign.

30

Everybody's Business

All the same, there was seldom anything new under the nuclear-fired sun. Before Kelly Turner pushed onto Saipan, the Greeks had landed at Troy, and before Curtis LeMay visited damnation upon Tokyo, the Axis had led the way in killing civilians from the air. In 1940, over dinner in the Reich Chancellery, Adolf Hitler turned to Albert Speer and asked, "Have you ever seen a map of London?" He was pondering the British capital as a target for his planes. "It is so densely built that one fire alone would be enough to destroy the whole city, just as it did over two hundred years ago. Goering will start fires all over London, fires everywhere, with countless incendiary bombs of an entirely new type."

The assessment of possible targets was the business of any air force. The U.S. Army's air war theorists had taken notice of Tokyo in 1923, when an 8.3 magnitude earthquake, abetted by a tsunami, killed a hundred forty thousand people and awakened planners to the Japanese capital's vulnerability to fire. Billy Mitchell, the influential aviation evangelist, wrote in 1928 that "an air offensive against Japan itself would be decisive because all Japanese cities are congested and easily located. In general, their structure is of paper or wood or other inflammable substances. It makes their country especially vulnerable to aircraft attack." In 1939, officers at the Air Corps Tactical School lectured on bombing Japan with that insight in mind. By 1942, the OSS was publishing maps of Tokyo with its districts variously shaded to indicate their susceptibility to fire. At the Dugway Proving Ground in Utah, the Standard Oil Development Company was commissioned to research how to destroy by fire "small dwellings and tenement type construction which represent the largest portion of roof area in industrial Japan." At Eglin Field on the Florida panhandle, models of

Tokyo were constructed on which to test new incendiary munitions. Replicas of German villages were also put to the test.

In 1943, Walt Disney produced an animated film promoting the war-winning potential of aerial bombardment. With a triumphal symphonic sound track, *Victory Through Air Power* presented to the American public the ideas of Major Alexander P. de Seversky, a former Russian naval aviator who as a naturalized American became an influential airpower theorist. He explained how planes could carry munitions over the heads of armies and navies to destroy an enemy's war industries directly. This revolution, he claimed, made civilians legitimate targets in war. "The science of aviation," he explained in his heavy Russian accent, promised to "transform the entire surface of our planet into a battlefield. The distinctions between soldiers and civilians will be erased. And I believe that it is only a matter of time before we here in America will suffer our share of civilian casualties. And so warfare becomes everybody's business."

It certainly would become the Japanese people's business. Three weeks prior to the Thanksgiving Day 1944 strike on Tokyo, B-29s equipped with new cameras flew over and took thousands of aerial images. These were used in the manufacture of studio-sized scale models of the city, which planners studied closely. Their war industries were dispersed among residential communities. Homes that fabricated parts for factories were said to constitute a "shadow industry." Estimates by the Joint Target Group in Washington indicated that the entire military and economic capacity of the Japanese nation could be destroyed by 1.6 million tons of bombs, a number that narrowly exceeded the grand total of what the Army Air Forces had dropped on Germany. Hap Arnold estimated that two-thirds of that, delivered in 1945, "would make possible the complete destruction of interior Japan."

When Curtis LeMay had visited Grand Island, Nebraska, in 1944 to have his first look at the B-29, Paul Tibbets, the director of operations there, took him aside and offered a suggestion. Based on tests he had seen of incendiary devices at Eglin, Tibbets suggested that LeMay hit Japan as Britain had bombed Germany: with firebombs, at low altitude, at night. "He didn't seem impressed," Tibbets wrote. But less than a year later, LeMay had come around. He calculated that nighttime incendiary raids conducted at six thousand feet or lower would justify the Army's investment in strategic airpower by ending the war.

At low altitude, heavier loads could be carried, with less strain on the B-29's tetchy engines. Flying at night, bombers would be less vulnerable to fighters—so much less, LeMay believed, that his planes need not even carry machine gun ammunition. The weight savings on eight thousand rounds, about thirty-two hundred pounds, could be made up in the bomb bays. Three hundred planes, each carrying twenty-four five-hundred-pound cluster munitions, with intervalometers set to release a bomb every fifty feet, could spread twenty-four tons of incendiaries (more than eight thousand M-69 incendiary bomblets, six pounds apiece) over every square mile of the city.

On March 8, LeMay cut field orders that would marshal three hundred B-29s from all three islands against Tokyo the next night. That same day, Norstad alerted the Twentieth Air Force public relations office in Washington to get ready for "what may be an outstanding show." It would be carried out by bombers flying low, at five thousand feet.

Paul Tibbets knew well the feeling of the line aviators from his days in North Africa. "We thought it was stark raving mad, and we did not want to go on that mission," said Fiske Hanley, a flight engineer with a group stationed at North Field on Tinian. George J. Savage, a pilot with a Guam-based squadron, heard the mission parameters and thought, *Boy, somebody's awfully dumb.* Some men wrote goodbye letters to their families. "We really thought we were dead men," Braden said. "But that was our job, so there was no other way. You're going to be dead men anyway, so, yeah, we'll go." Savage got practical. He told his crew to fill buckets with aviation fuel, grab bundles of rags, and wash down their airplanes. A smoother finish would coax more speed and range out of their birds and improve their chances of getting home. The pilots and crews of the three hundred B-29s that rose from the bomber strips on Saipan, Tinian, and Guam on the afternoon of March 9 were convinced that LeMay's orders would lead to their ruin. The innovation of portable bottled fire, which Raymond Spruance had introduced in a trickle for tactical use at Tinian, was coming to the Japanese home islands on a mass-industrial scale. Spruance had declined to authorize the use of poison gas against enemy troops at Iwo Jima. But now jellied fire was going to rain down on the home islands, from planes washed slick by gasoline.

An hour ahead of the main strike, pathfinder planes made their runs over Tokyo, dropping firebombs at low altitude to start blazes marking the aiming points for the host that would follow. The main body of LeMay's force, a single-file stream four hundred miles long, approached on a path perpendicular to the route taken by the pathfinders. They needed only two and a half hours to rewrite the annals of air warfare.

Incendiary bombs were wicked things. Time-detonated at an altitude of about two thousand feet, each five-hundred-pound cluster scattered thirty-eight bomblets, metal tubes twenty inches long, each containing a cheese-cloth sack filled with jellied gasoline. These M-69 bomblets contained an ejection-ignition charge that lit on impact, shooting the jellied gasoline into the air. The thousand-degree fires burned white-hot for six to ten minutes and were impossible to extinguish. As the falling speed of incendiary munitions was less than that of conventional iron bombs, the wind carried them around more. As a result, pilots and crews rarely saw their own effects. But those following in the rear of the bomber stream were in for exactly what Lauris Norstad had promised his PR people: an outstanding—and horrible—show.

When David Braden's plane arrived over Tokyo, fires had been burning for a while. Smoke filled the sky, an ill mist, and coming closer, he felt the aircraft lurch as updrafts from ground fires seemed to push his B-29 away from the earth. Flying this low, there was no need of pressurized cabins. But the smell of the city on fire, of burning humanity, was carried to him on the infernal updrafts. Permeating the aircraft, it nauseated some of the men. Here and there the updrafts were so strong they could throw a plane all over the sky. Strapped in tight, wearing protective goggles, Braden could see through his red lenses the searchlights probing the night. Amid the smoke, two aircraft lost their bearings and collided, pancaking and falling apart, twenty-two men down.

Fuel shortages had compelled Tokyo's central air headquarters to cease scrambling fighters to intercept U.S. bombers, according to Sadao Mogami, a captain on the staff. But the city bristled with heavy antiaircraft guns, and George Savage was among the many who experienced the terror of having their planes fixed like pinned insects atop a cone of powerful searchlights. Illuminated and taken under barrage, Savage found his left wing shredded and his number one engine knocked out. He had no sooner feathered the propeller and raised his left aileron to hold his wings level when word came that the number four engine was on fire. As he watched the oil pressure drop, he ordered that propeller feathered, too, but amid many diversions he forgot to take up the right aileron. This was the only reason he could think of that his underpowered plane suddenly rolled onto its back. Upside down, he thought it might be the end. Two further thoughts flashed through Savage's mind: *So this is how an aircraft gets shot down,* and then, *Since we aren't dead yet, surely something can be done.*

This second realization saved him that night. "I would bet that at least half of the airplanes that were shot down in combat were shot down because the pilot gave up, because he said, 'Oh, what a terrible predicament I'm in! What will I do?' And he cries instead of thinks." In training he had learned hundreds of emergency procedures for every situation. "There must be thirty different ways to put out an engine fire," Savage said, "the first being to cut off the fuel. You have fire extinguishers. Pull the fire bottle handle. Be sure you pull the right one. Feather the propeller. Sideslip so that the fire burns away from the aircraft. I've had a lot of engine fires in airplanes, and I'm still around." After rolling back over to a normal flight attitude and dealing with his engine fire, Savage was glad to find that his wild gyrations had taken him out of the cone of searchlights. Savage and his crew did see several Japanese fighters in the air that night, but they flew conservatively and attacked singly and ineffectively.

His navigator needed thirty minutes to fix their position and find a bearing to Iwo Jima. Five and a half hours later, their big silver bird was crash-landing on Central Field, coming to rest after prevailing in a collision with a truck and a jeep. No one was hurt. At least not yet. The five-week struggle for the island was still on. Artillery was roaring all around the island, and fighters were taking off every few minutes to fly close-support missions. That afternoon, a transport plane returned them to Saipan, then to Guam.

Lieutenant Colonel Robert J. McNamara took part in the interrogation of the crews that returned to Guam after the Tokyo incendiary raid. General LeMay was on hand for some of them. In a room full of aircrews and intelligence people, the atmosphere got heated. A young airplane commander shouted, "God damn it, I'd like to know who's the SOB who took a magnificent airplane designed to bomb from twenty-three thousand feet and took it down to five thousand feet. I lost my wingman last night."

LeMay was not one to return overheated emotion in kind. Unlike the voluble Hap Arnold, whose nickname came from the smile that was a deceiving tic of his facial expression, LeMay spoke in monosyllables, enunciating them around a cigar that was as much a fixture to him as Arnold's faux grin. McNamara said, "I never heard him say more than two words in sequence. It was basically, 'Yes, no, yup'—that was all he said." But now, according to McNamara, the bomber chief of the Marianas complex stood and confronted the young captain. Staring darkly, his face like a furnace, he displayed his complete disregard for anything unrelated to the metrics of the mission. "Why are we here?" he barked. "You lost your wingman. It hurts me as much as it does you. I sent him there. And I've been there. But you lost one wingman, and we destroyed Tokyo."

Japanese police records would count more than 267,000 buildings destroyed—about a quarter of the structures in the city—and a million people homeless. The official death toll would stand at 83,793. An American military psychologist, having talked with survivors of a German city that was firebombed just a month after the Tokyo fire raid, observed that "the population, although obviously showing an innate wish to tell its own story, lost the psychic power of accurate memory. . . . The accounts of those who escaped with nothing but their lives do generally have something discontinuous about them, a curiously erratic quality so much at variance with authentic recollection that it easily suggests rumor-mongering and invention." And so writing about it tended to employ clichés—"a prey to the flames," "all hell was let loose"—which served to "cover up and neutralize experiences beyond our ability to comprehend," the writer W. G. Sebald wrote. The flimsiness and pallor of such formulations impressed the bombers as well as the bombed. Fiske Hanley called the sight of Tokyo burning "awesome" in its dictionary sense, but said, "That's a meager term to describe it." B-29 crews tried not to let their imaginations stir as they picked blackened plywood and newspapers and parts of houses from their engine nacelles back at base. "I didn't have any feelings about that," David Braden said, "except that I was glad to get away from it. I think maybe that's the reason young men fight wars."

For some, a question of means and ends arose, hanging in the air but seldom articulated. "We were pretty uptight about what we had just done," Hanley said, "but we finished our mission. Our postmission reconnaissance showed machine tools all over those burned-out areas where these people were making parts, so they were in the war." The need to justify the horrific results by military necessity seemed to come from the soul.

Expression of emotion was not often helpful in the B-29 aviator's unforgiving line of work, where death often struck within the glide path, engines quitting on the base leg, planes crashing within view of the Quonset hut. "There's one thing you learn," Savage said.

> You never wring your hands when somebody gets killed in an airplane. What you do is you keep doing what you're doing until it's done. And then you say, "What happened?" "What caused it?" "How can we keep it from happening again?"

The chaplain didn't come over to you and say, "Okay, fellows, we're all going to sit around and cry about this crew that didn't come back." What happened was that the operations officer said, "Here's what he did that got him killed! Don't do it!" Maybe that sounds terrible, but that's how you survive in an airplane, particularly in combat.

Life on an island still inhabited by enemy troops could be harrowing. Blowing off steam watching movies and hunting souvenirs was darkened by the reality that Captain Oba and his like were watching from the hills. When people told George Savage that off-hours wayfaring might get him killed, he found that a simple attitude adjustment banished the stress of it: "If I see any Japs, I'm gonna kill them. They better look out for me. I don't have to look out for them. And that's what you did."

After the raid, Tokyo's central air headquarters reconsidered the ban on sending fighters to intercept bomber raids. "The fighter units couldn't bear just sitting on the ground while the Americans attacked us," Sadao Mogami said.

> They wanted at least to feel they had launched some planes and perhaps disrupted the plan of the American raid, and after the terrible damage done to Tokyo on March 10, 1945, we at the air headquarters didn't feel we could prohibit intercepting any longer. At the very least we had to defend the area where airplane parts were manufactured. In those days, I was commuting from my home. Even my own father berated me, demanding to know what we were doing.

Shortage of fuel was a reason to skimp on fighter sorties. But there was another reason as well, one that headquarters did not wish to articulate: "I couldn't say we had to preserve our fuel for the special-attack-force planes that would be used against the huge American invasion fleets about to descend on the homeland," Mogami said.

When Emperor Hirohito toured the burned-out districts of Tokyo about a week after the raid, the aide in the car that followed him noted the Japanese people's vacant expressions and how they "became reproachful as the imperial motorcade went by. Although we did not make the usual prior announcement, I felt they should have known that his was a 'blessed visitation' [gyoko] just the same, for after all, three to four automobiles bearing the chrysanthemum crest were passing." The aide's attitude reflected the political culture of the Empire. Unquestioning duty to the emperor was expected. No amount of suffering should compromise it.

Two days later, on March 20, a retired foreign minister who was widely seen as a moderate, Kijuro Shidehara, wrote to a friend that Japan might secure a better peace deal "if we continue to fight back bravely, even if hundreds of thousands of noncombatants are killed, injured, or starved, even if millions of buildings are destroyed or burned." As disaster loomed for the people of Yamato, "Shidehara still saw advantages in turning all of Japan into a battlefield. . . . This was the mindset of the moderate Shidehara; it was probably shared by Hirohito," the historian Herbert P. Bix wrote. The former prime minister, Prince Fumimaro Konoye, confided to his secretary, "When I think of the madmen leading the present situation, I can't help but feel weary of life."

Norstad's and LeMay's blitz of fire continued on March 19, with major raids against Nagoya, Osaka, Kobe, and again Nagoya, using an average of three hundred eighty bombers per mission. They did not invent the destruction of cities from the air. But they practiced it on a scale that was unprecedented.

In all the writing on the U.S. Army's strategic bombing campaign against Japan, no senior commanders can be found specifically espousing the slaughter of civilians. It is more accurate to say they regarded it clinically and somewhat indifferently, as an unavoidable reality. It was brute business, and no air force ever won a war wringing its hands over morality. Euphemisms prevailed.

But in March 1942, the U.S. Naval Institute's influential journal, *Proceedings,* had reprinted a chilling essay by a British aviator and air war theorist making the case for the targeting of people:

> It may be said that if you destroy a man you do less than if you destroy a machine, because the machine represents the work of many men during much time. But our own bombing experiences have demonstrated that the destruction of a human being does not end there; it has far-reaching repercussions. Thus, if a workman is killed it may well be that his brother will find it necessary to absent himself from his work and possibly also his father or son. There is a chain in the human family which is in the last analysis

far longer than that of the largest and most complicated machine. I know, of course, that there are ethical objections to the attack on civilians, but I am not here concerned with them. I am concerned merely with pointing out that the selection of bomb targets should, first of all, be based on measurement and calculation of the effects that can be achieved. If it be shown by convincing survey that the killing of a child does, in fact, do more harm to the enemy's war effort than the destruction of a machine tool, then the fact should be noted, and one can proceed to other and ethical aspects of the matter.

The burning of Japan's major cities was a national trauma for Japan that would reverberate through decades of war and peace. The production of this effect was not the reason the Marianas were invaded in the first place. Haywood Hansell, an advocate of precision bombing of military targets, had been perhaps the deciding voice in sending Kelly Turner to take them. Hansell was in the end summarily cast out and replaced, but only after securing for LeMay his stage. And Fiske Hanley was presumably not alone in the ranks of XXI Bomber Command aviators who, on lazy weekends years hence, never managed to enjoy the smell of barbecue.

31

Divine Winds

"I understand some of the sob fraternity back home have been raising the devil about our casualties on Iwo," Spruance wrote to Margaret. "I would have thought that by this time they would have learned that you can't make war on a tough, fanatical enemy like the Japs without our people getting hurt and killed." Fresh from touring a base hospital and later a hospital ship, Spruance found the sight of wounded men sapping his satisfaction over a successfully completed operation. Thus embittered, he considered Joe Rosenthal's shot of six of his warriors raising the flag atop Mount Suribachi "the finest photograph this war has given us up-to-date." It deserved pride of place in their home after the war, he wrote his wife, for he owned his part in the decision to take the island, and he wanted to remember it the right way. "When we settle down, I want to have this picture framed. Some first-class sculptor should do this in bronze, it is so perfect." The photo stood as a heartening aesthetic in a war that was shaking his faith in humanity. He rolled up a copy of it and sent it to Margaret in a tube.

Much as he liked the press photo, Spruance continued to be displeased with what his friend Halsey was saying in the presence of war correspondents. "In the first place," he wrote to his wife, "I do not think we should call our enemies a lot of names the way Bill does. In the second place, to belittle their resistance and fighting qualities is no way in which to prepare the country for the hard and perhaps long war that still lies ahead of us. There is still a sizable portion of the Jap fleet left, and I have every expectation that they will come out to sink or be sunk when they consider that the time is most propitious for them. . . . Bill's attitude seems to be—the Japs are low rats, whom I have already licked, and there is not much more to be done to finish them off. Our Marines on Iwo certainly do not feel that way about them."

Spruance thought highly of his Marine leadership. Iwo Jima would be Holland Smith's last turn in a major command, and he had no trouble with the Army in this all–Marine Corps operation. But the pressure of a high-casualty environment worked on people. While it was still ongoing, Smith paid a visit to Harry Hill. The admiral yielded his cabin to his corps commander, and pity might have been behind it. Hill was worried about Smith:

> He was a different man—bitter, dejected, and morose. In fact, his condition worried me, and I spoke to the doctor about it. He stuck close to his cabin, and whenever I could find a few free minutes I would go down and play cribbage with him, which was one of his favorite recreations. His bitterness was outspoken. I don't know what discussions he had with Nimitz after Saipan, but he seemed to be mad at everyone: General Richardson, the senior Army man at Oahu, Nimitz, Spruance, Turner, and many others. He was so depressed I feared he might try to harm himself, and the doctor and I took several steps to try to keep him under frequent observation.

Thousands of Japanese troops who had once been earmarked to reinforce the Marianas, only to be thwarted by submarines in the summer of 1944, were routed to Iwo Jima, where General Kuribayashi employed them well. The casualties suffered by U.S. forces on Iwo Jima exceeded twenty-six thousand, surpassing combined U.S. losses in all three Mariana Islands campaigns. Yet the invasion of Okinawa, far larger than Iwo and closer to Japan, figured to be worse.

In preparation for the Okinawa landings, set for April 1, Task Force 58 was to hit Kyushu's airfields, many of which were within range to threaten the operation. Japan's home waters were a risky place for U.S. aircraft carriers, but Spruance was eager to support a major campaign that he had recommended.

On March 18, Mitscher's carriers sent antishipping and fighter sweeps against the Kobe and Osaka areas, Okinawa, Ie Shima and Kerama Retto, Kanoya, and the naval base at Kure. More leaflets were in the strike package as well. Over Kanoya the carrier planes dropped ten thousand more comic portrayals of Hirohito leading his people to slaughter, with the message: "The companion to war is disease."

The next morning Spruance was sitting on the bridge of the *Indianapolis* after the planes took off when he saw a column of smoke rising from a nearby task group. It was the aircraft carrier *Franklin*. It had been stalked by an incoming bogie, which had hidden from the all-seeing radar among the throngs of outbound U.S. strike planes.

Shortly after seven, the Judy fell suddenly out of the two-thousand-foot cloud ceiling dead ahead and hit the carrier with its bomb. The 250-kilogram weapon pierced the flight deck just a hundred feet ahead of the next plane up for launch, detonating in the hangar and blasting upward, shredding the flight deck from below. The thirty-one planes on deck were a feast for the flames. Spinning up for launch, spotted aft, they were carrying a maximum ordnance load. The explosions of the wing-mounted bombs and rockets started at the head of the gaggle and walked aft. Bombs kicked loose from wing mounts and fell through the flight deck to explode below. Big twelve-inch antishipping rockets—Tiny Tims, aviators called them—ignited on the hard points of Corsairs and rushed down the flight deck, some tumbling, some sprinting ahead on a line to ricochet off the sea. The hangar deck was fully engulfed by flames, which ventured as deeply as the fourth deck below.

Joe Taylor, the executive officer, marveled at the courage of his firefighters as the rockets continued to ignite. "Each time one went off, the firefighting crews forward would instinctively hit the deck. I wish there was some way to record the name of every one of these men. Their heroism was the greatest thing I have ever seen."

It was a dilemma for a time whether to abandon her or salvage her. The skipper of the *Santa Fe* doubted the *Franklin* would stay afloat. Rear Admiral Ralph E. Davison, the task group commander, shared this view, instructing Captain Leslie E. Gehres to stand by to abandon the carrier. Gehres was suffering badly at the time, having been nearly overcome by smoke. Davison asked Taylor to signal a destroyer to come alongside and directed his staff to leave the ship. Gehres, bent nearly to his knees and coughing with a small rag to his face, managed to recover. Staggering to his feet, he found his resolve to save his ship hardening. As the *Franklin* began to list, flaming rivers of fuel cascaded from a ruptured gasoline riser and into the catwalks. At noon, Raymond Spruance committed all of Task Force 58 to stand by until the carrier could be saved and gotten underway.

As the *Santa Fe* came alongside to fight fires, the listing carrier leaned over into her, battering the cruiser's superstructure with the imposing overhang of her flight deck. But as the carrier went dead in the water, Captain Harold C. Fritz kept his smaller ship close aboard, laying her slender shoulder into the carrier's starboard beam. As wave action clapped the warships together, there was the terrible sound of gun sponsons crushing and antennae snapping. Crewmen standing on the flight deck were in a shattering panic. "I want off this fuckin' thing! It's gonna blow! It's gonna roll over!" On the destroyer *Hunt,* more than a thousand yards away, a signalman was monitoring the *Franklin*'s flag hoist through his forty-power scope when he found himself a close spectator to a hangar deck explosion that was so powerful it shattered parked planes and sent their engines flying through the air. Sailors ran around the flight deck on fire. One large group, fleeing the explosions, poured off the bow "just like a huge herd of cattle being shoved over a cliff," the signalman said.

The *Franklin*'s chaplain, Joseph T. Callaghan, was a prolific reader of last rites. Joe Taylor, the exec, called him "a soul-stirring sight. He seemed to be everywhere, giving Extreme Unction to the dead and dying, urging the men on and himself handling hoses, jettisoning ammunition, and doing everything he could to help save our ship. He was so conspicuous not only because of the cross dabbed with paint across his helmet but because of his seemingly detached air as he went from place to place with head slightly bowed as if in meditation or prayer."

Davison ordered the *Santa Fe* to maintain the direction of the combat air patrol provided by carrier *Hancock,* and to handle the transfer of the wounded and the fight against the fire. Survivors climbed across radio antennae and slid down lines from the flight deck to the forecastle. When the exodus had finished and the fires were under control, the *Pittsburgh* was ordered to take the *Franklin* under tow. As gasoline leaks continued to spill flaming pools into the sea and magazines continued to ignite, the deck force pulled on board a tow line from the *Pittsburgh* and attached it to the carrier's starboard anchor chain. The large carrier's hull was like a sail to the easterly winds, but by two P.M. the *Pittsburgh* had her making a southerly course at two knots. By morning on March 20, her engineers had restored steering and power, and she was making cruising speed on two engines with an entourage that included the battle cruisers *Guam* and *Alaska* and a dozen destroyers.

The *Wasp,* too, took a hit from an opportunistic Judy that morning. It dropped a bomb that exploded in the crew's galley and laundry, causing structural damage on four decks, killing ninety-one, and leaving fourteen missing in action. The *Enterprise* suffered a hit and a near miss, earning her two weeks at Ulithi. But the *Franklin*'s losses—more than eight hundred dead—were the worst sustained by any U.S. carrier in the war. She and the two other damaged carriers arrived four days later at Ulithi, where they joined the *Randolph,* which had been hit by a kamikaze while at anchor there. Including the *Saratoga,* under repairs at Puget Sound after being hit off Iwo Jima, five large flattops were out of action. Their deployment in Japanese home waters had come at an intolerable cost. Such losses certainly would not be sustainable off Okinawa, that much closer to the home islands. A week later, it was Spruance's turn to stand personally in these crosshairs.

Task Force 58 returned to the waters off Okinawa in advance of the landings there, code-named Operation Iceberg. The Fifth Amphibious Force brought more than twelve hundred ships under Kelly Turner's flag, including 179 attack transports and cargo ships and 187 LSTs that carried and supplied the assault echelons, eight divisions with more than a hundred eighty thousand men. Turner's LSTs and LCI gunboats had a rough passage from Ulithi, pushing ahead in spite of typhoon forecasts. As March 31 arrived, Spruance was satisfied with the progress of the preliminaries. Landings on an island group just west of Okinawa—the jagged and unwelcoming Kerama Retto—had secured a sheltered anchorage in the forward area. This would be useful in providing, among other things, ammunition replenishment, which had been Spruance's foundational question when King asked him whether the operation could be carried out at all. Based on a study of Iwo Jima, Kelly Turner had determined that ammunition usage by fire-support vessels at Okinawa would be triple that of Saipan. As for the landings themselves, the assault on the west-coast Hagushi beaches would use a plan that closely resembled the scheme at Saipan, but on a larger scale.

Spruance's arrival at Okinawa was met with sudden thunder. The *Indianapolis* was standing by in her fire-support sector on L Day minus one when Japanese planes were seen attacking some ships just three miles ahead. Within minutes an Oscar appeared from the clouds, winged over, and dived on the ship's starboard quarter. The 20 mm guns opened up, but there was no time for the larger weapons to train and elevate. As tracers whipped into the plane in its terminal descent, it seemed to falter, as if the pilot had lost control. Down it plunged, finally hitting the port side of the main deck aft. The plane's bomb, separating before impact, crashed through the deck into the mess hall below.

Ripping through a table around which several men were seated at breakfast, it crashed on through the crew living quarters, breached a fuel tank, and exited the bottom of the hull before exploding underwater. Oil blended with seawater and gasoline shot like a geyser back up through the hole in the main deck, showering the after turret with gray water. An OS2U Kingfisher floatplane, on standby to launch, was thrown from its catapult car and came to rest upside down on the deck, injuring two sailors. The ship settled slightly aft and listed to port, but damage control teams localized the flooding and soon the flagship began covering the thirty miles to Kerama Retto under her own power. Though her wounds were manageable, the *Indianapolis* needed the attention of the yard, and so Spruance lost his flagship, for which he had developed a certain utilitarian affection. With nine men killed and twenty wounded in the attack, her mission to Okinawa was over.

The landings, carried out the next day by Lieutenant General Simon Bolivar Buckner's Tenth Army, were largely unopposed. By sunset, more than seventy-five thousand troops of Buckner's main elements—Major General Roy Geiger's Third Amphibious Corps (with the First and Sixth Marine divisions) and Major General John R. Hodge's XXIV Corps (with the Army's 7th, 77th, and 96th Infantry divisions)—were ashore. Spruance stood by at Kerama Retto as a salvage ship tended to the *Indianapolis*. While divers were removing a battered propeller, Spruance paced the fantail, watching them work. Late in the day, a chief from the salvage unit approached him sheepishly. "I'm sorry to report, sir, that my men have dropped the propeller and it is at the bottom of the harbor."

"That's too bad," Spruance said, and resumed a brisk walk.

Being moored and under repair, and now stuck, did not faze Spruance, not on such a landmark day. He would transfer to a new flagship and carry on. His choice of the *New Mexico,* an old battlewagon assigned to the fire-support group, signaled his need to remain close to the combat area, where he could monitor directly the progress of his forces. Mitscher's own commitment was no less complete. Task Force 58 remained at sea for ninety-two straight days to protect the U.S. foothold in the Ryukyus.

On request from Admiral Nimitz, MacArthur's Fifth Air Force on Luzon struck airfields on Formosa, while from the Marianas, Curtis Le-May's B-29s attacked air bases on Kyushu in an effort to keep Japanese land-based airpower at bay during the battle for the island. LeMay also directed the Tinian-based 313th Wing to begin dropping aerial mines via parachutes into Japanese waters, targeting first Shimonoseki Strait, an important shipping artery, and later other waterways and harbors chosen by the Navy. The Japanese were powerless to sweep these advanced devices, which included pressure mines (detonated by the slightest pressure from a ship passing above), magnetic mines, and acoustic mines, triggered by the sound of a propeller. LeMay chose a code name for these operations with a level of nuance that seemed suitable to him: Operation Starvation I and II.

As Spruance and his staff were settling in on board the *New Mexico,* Hirohito forced the resignation of Prime Minister Kuniaki Koiso, on whose watch Iwo Jima and Leyte were lost, and installed Kantaro Suzuki, seventy-eight, a close adviser to the emperor who was said to be an "unwilling statesman." As prime minister, however, he resubscribed his nation and people to the mission of national suicide. His war policy, known as Ketsu-Go, envisioned a mass summoning of the death-wishers, a sending forth of kamikaze aircraft, human torpedoes, small boats packed with explosives, human-guided rockets delivered by planes, and wave after wave of the "bamboo lancer brigade" (*takayari butai*)—young men, women, and the elderly, equipped with long wooden spears and specially though hastily trained by the *gyokusai* artists. In a land where fragments of enemy bombs were being harvested and melted down for the production of shovels, tools for killing would be easy to come by so long as a certain spirit prevailed.

That spirit manifested itself in the dramatic final sortie of the superbattleship *Yamato* from Kure. She got underway on April 6 to attack U.S. forces massed off Okinawa. Often pursued but seldom seen, the beloved pride of the IJN became the latest offering on Hirohito's gruesome altar. The largest battleship ever built could manage only symbolic acts. But none of the aviators of Task Force 58 would ever forget the moment.

Alerted by code breakers, U.S. submarines spotted the *Yamato* that night. When Spruance's chief of staff, Rear Admiral Arthur C. Davis— who had replaced Carl Moore in September because of a new Navy policy that required a surface officer have a right hand from the aviation ranks, and vice versa—went to his boss and handed him a detailed plan to strike this landmark target, Spruance gave the plan the courtesy of a glance, then, saying nothing, tore it to pieces. He grabbed a piece of paper and scribbled four words, *Mitsch, you get 'em,* and with a glint in his eye handed that order back to Davis. "Art," Spruance said, "Mitsch would never forgive me and would think that I was surely slipping if we gave him such a detailed order. He knows what to do." Mitscher sent three hundred eighty planes to do the job. By midafternoon, the *Yamato,* after taking her eleventh torpedo, exploded and went to the bottom with more than ninety percent of her thirty-three-hundred-man crew, including Kosaku Aruga, her well-seasoned captain.

Spruance's light touch with his leadership sustained their partnership through the worst part of the war. On Okinawa, General Geiger, commander of Third Amphibious Corps, Spruance's "shipmate" from the Guam operation, summoned the Fifth Fleet medical officer to his headquarters complaining of fever, a sore jaw, and a swollen right cheek. "You are in for a siege," Dr. David Willcutts said. "Mumps do not agree with old folks."

Geiger, who was all of sixty, begged him to be discreet. "I would be the laughingstock of the outfit. And Willcutts, please don't tell Spruance. Get me well quick. I'll behave." The general said he had the means to keep his own physician away for a few days in order to keep his condition secret. So, would the Fifth Fleet's top doctor cooperate? Willcutts made no promises.

Taking his leave, he ran into Spruance on the *New Mexico*'s quarterdeck. "What's wrong with Geiger?" Spruance asked. "I do hope nothing serious."

Willcutts shared the diagnosis with his boss. "He is frantic that you and his staff may kid him and begs confidential management of his case."

Spruance replied, "Very well, you carry on and see him often. Get him well."

Nothing else was said of it until the end of the week, when Geiger made it back to his desk. A package had been delivered for him. It contained a piece of cloth, oddly folded. When Geiger spread it on a table he beheld a diaper fastened together with a safety pin. Spruance had fashioned it himself.

"The old sea devil!" Geiger roared. "But I must not fight him. That is what he wants. Please tell him, I repeat, *the old sea devil,* that I will keep this in my private archive along with my most treasured battle flags and trophies."

On May 11, behind a host of mortar- and rocket-firing amphibious craft, Buckner's Tenth Army launched an assault along the entire Okinawa front, aiming to envelop the Japanese stronghold of Shuri Castle. The middle stage of the campaign produced some of the deadliest infantry combat of the war.

Sunset gave way to a new-moon night in the Kerama Retto as the *New Mexico* returned to the anchorage, the men of her deck force exhausted after a day of hauling stores and ammunition on board. After dinner, Spruance and Dr. Willcutts walked out to the quarterdeck to enjoy the calm, cool air. "Indiana springtime weather," the physician said.

"Good kamikaze weather," replied Spruance. In spite of his tone, he was deeply upset by the day's events, which saw burial services held on Marc Mitscher's flagship, the *Bunker Hill,* for 352 men killed when kamikaze planes struck her off Okinawa the previous morning.

Then, abruptly, the *New Mexico*'s klaxon began honking. A destroyer had reported radar contact with two bogies thirty-five miles out. A pair of F4U Corsair pilots had spied them closing with the anchorage and set out in pursuit. It was just after seven when the two Japanese planes came within sight, bearing down on the Fifth Fleet flagship while chased in vain by the duo of gull-winged fighters.

As the first plane, a Kawanishi N1K2 George, entered its terminal descent, a five-inch round from the ship exploded under it, lifting the fighter so that it passed, burning, over the foremast of the anchored ship and crashed close off the port quarter. A second Japanese plane, a Nakajima Ki-84 Frank, made a wide orbit and attacked on the starboard beam. The Frank was too speedy for the antiaircraft gun director to bring around his five-inch/25s in time. The gunners on twenties and forties did what little they could in the eight to ten seconds they had to save their shipmates' lives. Squinting through smoke from other batteries and from the battlewagon's voluminous exhaust, they could neither destroy nor divert the suicider. As volleys from nearby ships tore into the *New Mexico*'s superstructure, wounding at least six, the aircraft crashed her amidships. Willcutts recalled a thunderous impact, loud cries, and the sound of bodies falling to the deck. Then another explosion as a second kamikaze struck amidships. A bomb from the second plane exploded in the "Jap trap" cluster of 20 mm guns, while the plane plowed forward into the number two stack, tearing a thirty-foot hole and disintegrating as it went.

Fed by ready-service ammunition, flames rushed upward through the stack, causing it briefly to roar like a blowtorch, the overpressure producing a Venturi effect that might actually have served to draw some of the inferno away from the gun deck. The two Corsair pilots, peeling away, took fire from the flagship and several other vessels for their trouble.

Willcutts feared he might be the only medical man topside. With the

ship at battle stations, her entire medical department, he thought, was belowdecks. "Sir," he said to Spruance, gesturing amidships, "I'm needed
there."

The admiral appraised the situation at a glance and said, "Yes. You stay
with the men. I'm going to the bridge. I know a quick way." Then Spruance disappeared into the wreckage.

For several harrowing moments the Fifth Fleet staff had no idea where
their commander had gone. His flag lieutenant, Cy Huie, had last seen him
in his cabin aft. Frantically searching, Huie and Chuck Barber finally
found the four-star admiral manning a hose with the crew, fighting the fire
amidships. He ordered the two officers to assess the damage to the ship and
check for any codebooks that the enemy planes might have left on deck.
Then he proceeded to the bridge.

It was around midnight when Willcutts finished administering triage
care to the wounded and supervising the collection of the dead. Spruance
paced as Willcutts, bloody and disheveled, gave his report. "I'm glad you
were there, Surg," the admiral said, blue eyes hard as ice. "The ship is hard
hit. Even the engine rooms are exposed. But I believe that we can remain
on station, complete repairs, and carry on." Forty-four badly wounded
men were evacuated to transports in the anchorage. Identifying the fifty-
one dead had been difficult, especially in cases where only dental charts or
fingerprints would do, and others where not even those could be found.
Kamikazes killed hard.

The assault forces on Okinawa would suffer unprecedented casualties:
more than 7,600 killed and 31,800 wounded, including General Buckner,
killed by an artillery round just three days before the campaign ended. The
Navy paid its steepest price there since Guadalcanal—nineteen Fifth Fleet
ships sunk and another 181 damaged, nearly all of it from suicide planes.
The blitz of kamikazes peaked in early April, just as America was mourning the loss of President Franklin D. Roosevelt, and continued through the
surrender of Germany and most of June. The destroyers assigned by Kelly
Turner to serve as radar pickets around Okinawa, warning of inbound
kamikazes, were especially vulnerable. In one astounding case, the destroyer *Laffey* faced twenty-two suiciders in less than ninety minutes. Six of
them hit, and yet the ship survived. By the end of the campaign, nearly five
thousand naval personnel would be killed in action and more than ten
thousand wounded. "It was one of our toughest experiences of the war,"
Spruance said.

Willcutts stood in awe of Raymond Spruance's all-conquering luck against the ubiquitious and reliably deadly kamikaze. For the second time now he had survived a direct suicide hit on his flagship, manning a fire hose along the way for good measure. Physical bravery was seldom required of admirals, but the physician considered Spruance "a true Spartan in every sense. In combat he was calmly brave and heroic, thus easing those about him into some degree of fortitude and comfort. . . . His composure was inspiring. I thought of Forrestal and his reference to Nelson. I felt great pride, great comfort, and assurance that the Fifth Fleet under Spruance was unbeatable, that Okinawa and Japan must fall as had Germany, that this tragic war would be won."

As the war came to a crescendo in the Western Pacific, the Suzuki government left high national policy to a self-selected group of officials known as the Supreme War Direction Council. Composed of the prime minister, Foreign Minister Togo, Navy Minister Mitsumasa Yonai, Army Minister Korechika Anami, Chief of the Army General Staff Yoshijiro Umezu, and Combined Fleet commander Admiral Soemu Toyoda, it was also known as the Big Six.

In a series of meetings in the first half of May, the Big Six broached the idea of persuading the Soviet Union to broker an end to the war. The very idea was richly fanciful, as Moscow had already informed Tokyo that it would not renew the Russo-Japanese Neutrality Pact. As a result, the key questions—what to offer Moscow in exchange for its assistance, and what terms of surrender should be offered to the Allies—were never seriously raised.

The Japanese leadership's unwillingness or inability to govern responsibly in the face of major setbacks repeated itself in a meeting of the Big Six on May 22. As the Shuri line on Okinawa reeled under assault and with at least fifty thousand of his soldiers dead, Umezu said, "We are not yet beaten on the Okinawa front. We are fifty-fifty. Why should we take the attitude of a defeated country? Should we not negotiate on a 'give and take' basis? It is useless to begin from a position of weakness." According to Sokichi Takagi, "He put it in so strong a manner that the meeting hardly got underway." In a land such as Japan, with its rich tradition of political assassination, it was dangerous for an official to diverge too boldly.

Consensus among the three dead-enders, Anami, Umezu, and Toyoda, and their more pragmatic colleagues was impossible in any case. The politics was so poisonous as to shut down any suggestion of diplomatic outreach to neutral states at a time when it might have mattered.

Never more than on Okinawa did the perversity of Japanese war policy harm the ordinary people caught up in it.

On May 27, the battleship *Missouri* arrived at Hagushi Anchorage, Okinawa, and Admiral William F. Halsey relieved Spruance, who had become thoroughly exhausted in spite of his habitual efforts to maintain his mental discipline. When Halsey asked Spruance what MacArthur's Army Air Forces were doing to support naval operations, the departing commander icily recapped the Fifth Air Force's performance against Formosa, a campaign in which General George C. Kenney's fliers eliminated an estimated eighty percent of the island's industrial capacity. "They've destroyed a great many sugar mills, railroad trains, and other equipment," he said, but they had done little to hold down Japanese airpower. Spruance had had a run-in with Hap Arnold when he learned the AAF primo had instructed the general in charge of Okinawa airfield construction to slow-walk new fighter strips in favor of building new facilities for bombers. At a time when Curtis LeMay was protesting any use of B-29s for tactical missions such as hitting kamikaze airfields, Spruance urgently needed the Army Air Forces to stand up somewhere and give the fleet a break.

Nimitz understood the psychological and physical strain of this rain of blood. Spruance's staff was exhausted. The grind had worn down Kelly Turner, Holland Smith, and the others. As the command turned over, with Harry Hill replacing Turner as boss of Fifth Phib and John McCain relieving Mitscher as top carrier commander, a Halsey staffer, having noted the wholesale depletion, was startled by Spruance's evident serenity.

Spruance's last night on a Pacific battlefront was sleepless. The air defense alert sounded after dinner, summoning him to the bridge of his wounded battleship at anchor in Hagushi Anchorage. By ten P.M., planes were still coming in. As the moon glowed eerily through the haze, the report of heavy antiaircraft guns rolled over the sound from shore, then from ships nearby. Enshrouded by the nightly smoke screen, the *New Mexico* kept her batteries quiet, but the drone of motors filled the grayness overhead. "I stepped outside—and as I searched the sky it was as though I were looking for witches riding their broomsticks across the harvest moon," Barber would recall. Spruance somehow found he could sleep through the

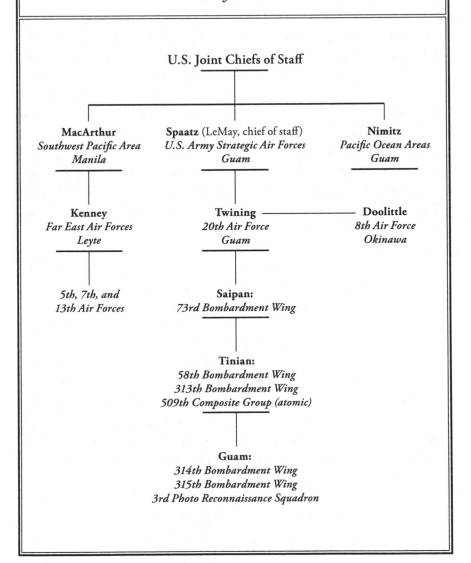

U.S. ARMY AIR FORCES IN THE PACIFIC
May 1945

U.S. Joint Chiefs of Staff

MacArthur
Southwest Pacific Area
Manila

Spaatz (LeMay, chief of staff)
U.S. Army Strategic Air Forces
Guam

Nimitz
Pacific Ocean Areas
Guam

Kenney
Far East Air Forces
Leyte

Twining ——————— **Doolittle**
20th Air Force   *8th Air Force*
Guam   *Okinawa*

5th, 7th, and
13th Air Forces

Saipan:
73rd Bombardment Wing

Tinian:
58th Bombardment Wing
313th Bombardment Wing
509th Composite Group (atomic)

Guam:
314th Bombardment Wing
315th Bombardment Wing
3rd Photo Reconnaissance Squadron

percussion of main battery and five-inch gunfire, so long as it kept up a certain cadence. Any break or lull followed by a resumption of salvos tended to disturb him. But there was no getting used to the horror of Okinawa.

Spruance was no supporter of Operations Olympic or Coronet. He had backed the invasion of Okinawa because he considered the island ideally located for enforcing a blockade of Japan. The risks of carrying out landings in the home islands were extreme, he thought, and not only for U.S. forces. He had seen what had become of the civilians who survived Okinawa. Most were old men and middle-aged mothers with children. He had seen no young men there, and scant few women of working age. "In all of these islands the poor natives are generally innocent bystanders who have no interest in the quarrel and who suffer most from it," Spruance informed Margaret. But in spite of all he had seen, Spruance still could have had no idea, at the time he wrote these words, of the true and unfathomable monstrosity of what had actually unfolded on Okinawa.

Masahide Ota, an Okinawan youth who had been dragooned just before the landings into an auxiliary known as the Blood and Iron Student Corps, would say that the Japanese regarded Okinawans as "third-class Japanese" who "were supposed to lack in loyalty and patriotism." The local residents were thus ripe targets for scapegoating and brainwashing by the birds of prey who filled out Okinawa's garrison. Some of its officers had presided over the atrocities at Nanking. After Okinawa was lost, Ota said, they turned on the locals. "Japanese soldiers spread the story that the defeat was the result of Okinawans spying for the enemy. Children from Okinawa, who were evacuated to Kyushu and other areas, were told the battle was lost because Okinawans had betrayed their country. There were lots of dark incidents."

The latter had included a ghastly ritual known as "group suicide," which was ordered by the Japanese Army and enacted locally through elders in the community. According to Shigeaki Kinjo, who had grown up in the Kerama Retto, the term for it, *shudan jiketsu,* was not coined until after the war ended. "It's a term easily subject to misinterpretation," she said. "The state now wants to say these deaths were 'voluntary deaths.' But that isn't the way it was. The people of Okinawa never killed themselves on their own initiative." But there remained in every precinct of the Co-Prosperity Sphere the sacred tradition of *gyokusai.*

According to Harumi Miyagi, "Everyone knew intuitively what they were supposed to do. In a great hurry they began to 'dress for death.' They dressed their children in their best clothes. They ate all their remaining food. They left the caves in the midst of a late-night naval bombardment and made their way to the monument." This was a shrine to the war dead, built in 1940 to mark the twenty-six hundredth anniversary of the Japanese nation's founding. It was an important gathering place, a center of community. "There, on the eighth day of every month, they prayed for success in war and sang the national anthem as the flag was raised. Gathering there meant a lot. The villagers assembled in small clusters that night. But the severity of the naval bombardment soon scattered everyone. Although everyone went there with the intention to die, they were unable to carry out the act. The next morning the Americans landed."

And this was the spark to the powder. When American soldiers arrived on Zamami, an island in the Kerama Retto, "It was like a hair trigger—one touch and it exploded," Miyagi said.

> The villagers had received an education in not disgracing themselves as Japanese. That education centered on the emperor and was pounded into them. "Don't use your own local dialect! Don't value Okinawan culture! Try to stand shoulder to shoulder with the Japanese!" This penetrated to the depths of their hearts. . . . And what were they told would happen if they were caught by American soldiers? The veterans, those who'd been to China, taught the villagers what would happen if you were captured. They used things like the Nanking massacre as examples. "Japanese did things like this," they'd say. "The Americans naturally will do the same things." It's better to kill your children first and die by your own hand than be shamed and abused, disgraced and raped.

"My memory tells me the first one we laid hands on was Mother," Shigeaki Kinjo said. "Those who had blades, or scythes, cut their wrists or severed arteries in their necks. But we didn't do it that way. We might have used a string. When we raised our hands against the mother who bore us, we waited in our grief. I remember that. In the end we must have used stones. To the head. We took care of Mother that way. Then my brother and I turned against our younger brother and younger sister. Hell engulfed us there."

Harumi Miyagi's grandmother panicked and asked to be killed quickly. Her husband tried to strangle her with a rope, but he wasn't strong enough to do it. He then tried a barber's straight razor but only made a mess. Miyagi's aunt, whom he thought dead with a slash to her throat, opened her eyes to find an American soldier looking down at her. "Their eyes accidentally met," Miyagi said. "She was shocked and closed hers in a hurry. But the soldiers poked at her eyes to get her to open them. She tried not to breathe, but it was impossible, as you can imagine. He carried her out of the cave. She was eighteen, old enough to remember most of the things that had taken place in the cave. She said she didn't feel any pain when her throat was slashed. The blood just gushed out and her body got warm. Then she grew sleepy. It was a sea of blood. Everyone was bathed in the blood of others."

If first contact with the enemy had resulted in such outcomes for ordinary Okinawans, who were hardly affectionate toward their overlords, could it be said that an invasion of the home islands would not provoke a proportionally larger catastrophe for Japanese civilians who were on the wrong side of the predominant standard of racial purity? It would breed horrors so diverse, numerous, protracted, and novel as to dwarf even the Tokyo fire raid. The loosely documented roster of forces defending Okinawa made any final calculation of Japanese losses difficult. But an authoritative tally put it at more than 65,000 Japanese soldiers, 28,000 Okinawans in uniform, and 94,000 civilians.

The act of drawing moral boundaries around the multitude of styles and manners of death in total war became quickly arbitrary and absurd. Those who struggled to draw distinctions in this land of brutal abstractions, to define the acceptable methods by which five- and six-digit sums of casualties were permitted to amass, bothered Spruance. "The sob fraternity," he had called them. There was a war to be won, and it had long since crossed beyond all ethical and moral boundaries heretofore known.

No campaign prior to Okinawa could reasonably reflect what now lay ahead. And so planners no longer spoke of the Saipan ratio. U.S. losses at Okinawa foretold a far higher cost in Operations Olympic and Coronet. MacArthur's staff, reckoning with the alarming Japanese buildup, began to revise their estimates based not on the Saipan ratio, which was suggesting a half million dead, but on a new metric, the "sinister ratio." Derived from the experience of Okinawa, it revised the forecast of one American soldier killed in action for every seven defenders in place to one for every two.

The achievements of the Imperial Japanese death cult on and around

Okinawa were not missed at CINCPAC headquarters on Guam or in the American press. "The whole nation," Herbert Bix wrote, "had become enveloped in the imagery of national salvation through mass suicide." Le-May's fliers upped the ante in the propaganda war, releasing millions of leaflets encouraging a revolt against the militarists. The message had the unique moral power of being perfectly true to fact.

32

Methods of Death on the Wing

The air war that raged in the Western Pacific in 1945 juxtaposed the two nations' preferred methods of serving up death on the wing. Kamikazes were tactically effective, strategically useless but personal in a way, diving down, closer, closer, on you, then *boom,* a pilot in control the whole way. Remnants of both plane and pilot left the survivors with souvenirs to ponder, sometimes even revealing the pilot's name. Having faced suiciders twice, Spruance saw their handiwork as "the opposite extreme" from what the USAAF practiced as it dropped bombs "safely and ineffectively from the upper atmosphere." LeMay's missions were tactically inconsequential in the sense that they failed to hit particular targets that turned battles in the immediate term. But in their effect on heavy industry they were strategically lethal, and as purely impersonal as the tradecraft of warfare could ever be.

On May 29, the cargo ship SS *Cape Victory* arrived at Tinian, from Seattle by way of Honolulu and Eniwetok, carrying twelve hundred passengers—the ground echelon of the 509th Composite Group. A week later, transport planes delivered the outfit's air echelon, five hundred twenty officers and enlisted aviators assigned to the 509th's transport and support aircraft. In June, the combat aircrews of the eighteen B-29s assigned to the 393rd Heavy Bombardment Squadron, who flew the 509th's Superfortresses, began arriving at North Field. The "Silverplate" B-29s were specially modified with upgraded engines, reversible-pitch propellers, pneumatically operated bomb-bay doors, no guns except the tail stinger, and cockpit space for an additional crew member, a "weaponeer" who would arm and monitor the atomic bomb in flight.

According to Tibbets, until the arrival of the *Cape Victory,* the overseas movement of his classified outfit had been a rogue act of a sort. Without asking anyone's advice or consent, not even General Groves's, Tibbets had transmitted to Washington the code word that set the whole process in motion. "Knowing the interminable discussions that would result if I went through the routine channels," he wrote, "I had deliberately avoided mentioning my plans to the higher ups. Then all kinds of things began to hit the fan, as I had anticipated. General Groves summoned me to Washington. When I walked into his office, he gave me a thorough chewing out, complete with profanity. He said my unilateral decision bordered on insubordination. Before he was through, I began to see myself as the oldest second lieutenant in the Air Corps, ferrying worn-out airplanes back from war zones. As he finished, I noticed a twinkle in his eye.... He disliked surprises. Nevertheless, he was privately pleased.

"'Damn it, you've got us moving,' Groves said.

"By leaving for the Pacific, I would be putting pressure on the scientists to quit quibbling over the odds and finish the job."

On the northwest corner of the island, just three hundred yards from Tinian's White beaches, the world's first atomic airmen prepared their nest. Groves's special assistant, Colonel Elmer E. Kirkpatrick, supervised the construction of the area reserved for the 509th and the Project Alberta weapons technicians. Secrecy was so complete that Vice Admiral John Hoover, the Navy's area chief, believed the compound was "some kind of torpedo shop."

Housed in a vacant area reserved for the 18th Naval Construction Battalion, Tibbets's pilots and aircrews were thrown into an orientation curriculum covering the history of the combat theater, the culture of Japan, methods of air/sea rescue, radar bombing, emergency procedures, camera operations, and so on. Having personally overseen the training of his secretive unit, Tibbets was not keen on the idea of submitting to even this much administrative authority of the 313th Wing commander. Brigadier General John Davies knew nothing of the 509th's special mission, and Tibbets thought he seemed to resent Tibbets's refusal to answer his questions. But Tibbets had to chuckle when the wing commander called him to his office and asked, "Are all of your crews like the ones you sent here this morning?"

"Yes, sir, they are."

"Well, goddamn it, they're demoralizing my whole school. They know more about airplanes and navigation and everything else than my instructors know."

Tibbets clashed later with LeMay's staff over their insistence on centralizing maintenance of his B-29s. Tibbets "didn't want anyone but my own mechanics fooling around with my airplanes." He eventually prevailed upon LeMay to order his staff to leave the 509th alone.

In their scant downtime the newcomers toured the remains of Tinian Town, surveyed destroyed tanks and planes, and pondered the stoneworks of the House of Taga. There were USO shows and exhibition baseball games on fields where camouflage netting served as an outfield fence. Enos Slaughter of the St. Louis Cardinals showed up, playing one game in stocking feet. For the price of two quarts of Early Times, a bombardier hired some Seabees to build a private tent quarters with a shower for his crew and commandeer a jeep for them from Saipan. "We didn't let them know we kept the good stuff, Jack Daniel's, for ourselves," he said. It was a release from the gravely serious business that Tibbets directed on Tinian in the summer of 1945.

He would call those months "among the most frenzied of my military career." From Wendover it was seventy hours of air time to Tinian, and the crews of the so-called Green Hornet line, run by the 320th Troop Carrier Squadron, made a round-trip every fifteen days, flying key personnel to Tinian. The pilots who kept up this air bridge for the atomic program included a pair of women whom Tibbets called "two of the most competent multiengine pilots I ever hope to meet: Dora Dougherty and Helen Gosnell."

Conferring on Guam with LeMay and Nimitz, who briefed him on plans for an invasion of Japan, Tibbets understood what was at stake with his mission. "Only a few of us knew that these elaborate invasion plans would probably not be carried out," he wrote. "Our small force of 1,800 men and eighteen planes would do the work of two million soldiers! We were confident we would end the war and save hundreds of thousands of lives, both American and Japanese." After lunch at his headquarters, LeMay showed Tibbets to a briefing room where a spread of photographs was displayed on a table. They were aerial shots of burned-out Japanese cities, the result of the incendiary area bombing strategy that Tibbets, at a barbecue in Grand Island, had urged LeMay to use. "You were right, Paul," LeMay said. The irony could not have been lost on Tibbets, who had been sent to the Pacific for his refusal to fly at low altitude. Waves of fire would ensue.

Tibbets had flown to Washington twice in the spring and early summer to discuss targets for the atomic bombs. Leslie Groves had presided over the first meeting of the Manhattan Project's Target Committee, held in late April in Larry Norstad's conference room at the Pentagon. The next two meetings, in Los Alamos, brought in Captain Deak Parsons, Tibbets's "weaponeer," and Norman Ramsey as advisers. On May 31, the Target Committee ended discussion with Kyoto, Hiroshima, Yokohama, and Kokura, in that order, as targets of the bomb, owing to their as yet undamaged condition and their status as centers of war industry and military administration. Two weeks later, Secretary of War Henry L. Stimson removed Kyoto from the list because of its status as a treasure house of Japanese culture. After further study, Nagasaki would be added to the list, and Niigata replaced Kokura. A proposal to stage a demonstration of the bomb, which some thought might bring the Japanese to the table, was quickly shot down. Robert Oppenheimer said there could be no substitute for the impression of an actual atomic ruin in an urban area. Secretary of State James F. Byrnes wondered what would happen if the bomb failed to detonate. And if it did, what proof would convince the Japanese that the spectacle was the product of a single weapon? What if the Japanese delivered Allied prisoners to the demonstration site?

On the afternoon of May 31, three weeks before Okinawa was declared secure, the *New Mexico* arrived at Guam. Going ashore, Spruance moved into a spacious house on a high hillside with four bedrooms (each with a bath), a kitchen, a servants' room, a combined living and dining room, and a big screened porch. He shared this accommodation near CINCPAC headquarters with his chief of staff, Art Davis; his personal physician, Dr. Willcutts; and his operations officer, Savvy Forrestel. On the third anniversary of the victory at Midway, Lieutenant Commander Edward Spruance, twenty-nine, crossed paths with his father again on Guam. Spruance the younger had just been relieved of command of the submarine *Lionfish*.

They had never been especially close. They took a long walk, Edward wrote, during which the Fifth Fleet commander "expressed much concern over the casualties to ships and crews off Okinawa being inflicted by the kamikaze. He seemed more worried than I had ever seen him before."

Halsey was trying to do something about it. From Okinawa he led the fast carriers to strike targets on Kyushu. His air strikes on June 2 and 3 cost sixteen planes and a dozen pilots. Two days later, Halsey and his task force failed to avoid a major typhoon, costing the cruiser *Pittsburgh* one hundred feet of her bow, the carriers *Hornet* and *Bennington* twenty-five feet of forward flight deck, and serious damage to three other ships, with six killed. Spruance would have preferred to finish what he had started in the Ryukyus. That Nimitz didn't let him do so suggested the high value CINCPAC placed on Spruance as a planner. Halsey's impulsiveness had cost lives at Leyte Gulf and again in the typhoons of November 1944 and June 1945. That was the price Nimitz had to pay to have his best campaign planner on hand to help scheme Operation Olympic. The timetable was urgent and CINCPAC was eager to get on with it.

At a meeting of the Supreme War Direction Council on June 6, the Japanese high command first formally addressed the question of ending the war. The Big Six seemed to fall under the spell of the "psychological blitzkrieg" launched by Anami and Umezu, the torchbearers for army militarism. So powerful were their voices that even Prime Minister Suzuki, who was widely considered indecisive by temperament and a moderate in his politics, roused himself to an impassioned speech on the urgency of an honorable national death. The final policy statement that issued from this fateful meeting declared that the people of Japan were well united, had the advantage geographically, and must pursue the war to the bitter end.

The Big Six reconvened on June 8 in the presence of Emperor Hirohito, and after reciting their findings in the imperial presence, Japan was formally committed to a decisive battle on home soil, a national *gyokusai*.

Marquis Kido, the Lord Keeper of the Privy Seal, was said to be stunned by the result, and afterward he began drawing up potential terms under which to end the war. But all along both he and the emperor "viewed a military victory as a prerequisite to any peace move," and on the same day his highly conditional terms for peace were presented to the prime minister and others for discussion, the emperor issued an Imperial Rescript calling for Japan to "smash the inordinate ambitions of the enemy nations" to "achieve the goals of the war." As the historian Richard B. Frank noted, "The rescript gave no hint of any policy beyond a fight to the finish, and thus in no way enlisted public understanding, much less support, of the covert and halting moves for peace."

The gestures of Japanese diplomats no longer impressed Americans at home. Those who had paid attention in 1941 recalled the photos of the imperial emissaries in Washington, earnestly proposing terms on the day before Pearl Harbor exploded. In a June 1, 1945, opinion poll, Gallup asked, "Japan may offer to surrender and call her soldiers home provided we agree not to send an army of occupation to her home islands. Do you think we should accept such a peace offer if we get the chance, or fight until we have completely beaten her on the battlefield?" Responses to the hypothetical offer ran nine to one against accepting a peace offer.

And no such offer would come. After the war, the president of the Privy Council, Hiranuma, explained to American interrogators the circular thinking that paralyzed Tokyo from doing what most knew had to be done. "Those who were in the know, particularly those who had long service with the army and navy, naturally were of the opinion that under the prevailing circumstances the war would not end favorably," he said.

> Consequently what it amounted to was that the war must be terminated immediately. Suzuki was also of that belief. It may sound somewhat strange that he made some very warlike statements when he became the prime minister. I nevertheless assume that it was motivated by his belief that a prime minister should abstain from making pacifistic statements amidst a war. It would be a grave error to hastily conclude that his apparently warlike statements meant that he would, by no means, seek peace. I assume that his real intention was that the war must be halted, and efforts to halt it must be adequately made, but that his real intention must not be shown to the people.

Hiranuma himself felt the same way. "I came to the conclusion that the war could not be continued, so that peace must be made as soon as possible. But at the same time I actually felt that crying for peace would defeat its own purpose. . . . Even though we could not possibly continue the war, it was not a good policy to cry for peace in order to end the war." As dangerous to Japan as any American combat unit was the implacable task force of its own pride.

33

Opportunity and Madness

The American forces being assembled to carry out Operation Olympic and Operation Coronet were to be unprecedented in size. For Olympic, Spruance's Fifth Fleet would land General Walter Krueger's Sixth Army on Kyushu on November 1, with Halsey's Third Fleet (at last there were enough ships to manifest both fleets at once) in support. Coronet, bringing Major General Robert L. Eichelberger's Eighth Army to the Tokyo plain on March 1, 1946, would be the crowning blow. After three and a half years of waging war on resources that paled next to what was made available in Europe, the U.S Army in the Pacific was soon to swell with ground divisions and air wings no longer needed on the Continent. The Eighth Air Force, equipped with B-29s, was setting up on Okinawa under Lieutenant General Jimmy Doolittle. Operation Starvation lay in place, with vast fields of magnetic, acoustic, and pressure devices moored beneath Empire waters. Submarines lurked, carriers roamed, and Marianas airdromes hummed. The multidimensional U.S. assault on the enemy homeland seemed an irresistible force.

But the object of the assault promised to be less movable by the day. U.S. radio intelligence units, monitoring Japanese military frequencies, were discovering a startling buildup on Kyushu. On June 18, General Marshall had briefed President Truman that a maximum of three hundred fifty thousand troops would defend Japan's southern island, and Admiral King backed Marshall's claim that U.S. naval and air forces could block Japanese reinforcements from getting through. MacArthur's headquarters forecast that Japan had twenty-five hundred to three thousand aircraft in the home islands. Six weeks later, decrypts of intercepted Japanese military radio communications by code breakers under MacArthur's Southwest Pacific command—part of the important worldwide Allied crypto intelligence project known as Ultra—revealed that nearly twice Marshall's top estimate of troops were ready to oppose the Americans on Kyushu—680,000 men—producing a dangerous one-to-one ratio between forces. And after witnessing what kamikazes had wrought off Okinawa, CINCPAC was gravely disturbed in mid-July to count 8,750 planes in the Japan-Korea region. Less than a month later, the USAAF estimated Japan could marshal a total of more than ten thousand aircraft, half of them belonging to suicide squadrons. That summer would bring a startling development in the kamikaze campaign and a frightening marker of the fleet's vulnerability to even completely obsolete airplanes. Just a few days after Vice Admiral Aubrey Fitch appeared on NBC to boast, "The kamikaze boys carried the pitcher to the well once too often, now they are shocked to find the divine wind blowing in the wrong direction," the destroyer *Callaghan* was struck by a single-engine biplane carrying a small bomb. The flimsy construct of the obsolete aircraft—wood, plywood, and lacquered fabric—defeated two of the staples of U.S. naval air defense: search radar and radar-emitting projectiles. And when its bomb penetrated an upper handling room, it produced a secondary blast that sank the ship. The success of this retrograde stealth bomber in sinking a fast, well-armed warship suggested to the Navy the grave danger that even antique planes (often discounted in intelligence estimates) posed to shipping, and especially to the slower, lightly armed transports packed with troops, which would be the primary target of the kamikazes off Japan. A mark of the seriousness with which the Navy viewed the threat ahead of Operation Olympic is the fact that Rear Admiral Willis Lee, one of its leading gunnery specialists, had left the Pacific to head a special group stationed at Casco Bay, Maine, to improve radar detection of kamikazes and the fire-control techniques that targeted them.

The prospects for the landings in Kyushu were grim. In late August, the JCS Joint Strategic Survey Committee* calculated a steep price for Olympic: as many as half a million American casualties, assuming a ninety-day timetable. Even the most cautious projections of U.S. losses exceeded one hundred thousand, a number that was said to have caused General Marshall to "recoil sharply" at the revelation that the invasion of Japan would be as costly as the conquest of Hitler's Germany. After reviewing the num-

---

* Carl Moore referred to the JSSC as "the wise old men who reviewed everything that the Chiefs were in doubt about": General Embick, U.S., General Fairchild, USAAF, and Vice Admiral Russell Willson.

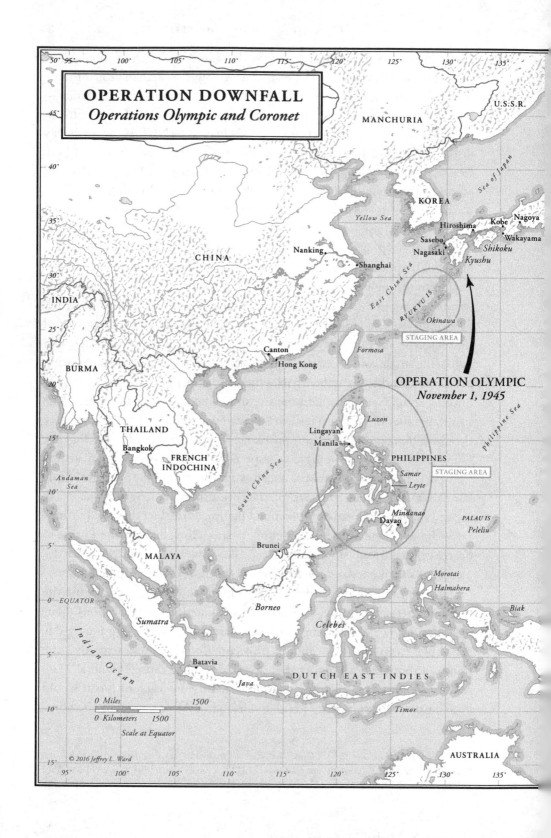

OPERATION DOWNFALL
Operations Olympic and Coronet

U.S.S.R.

MANCHURIA

Sea of Japan

KOREA

Yellow Sea Hiroshima Kobe Nagoya

Sasebo Wakayama

Nagasaki *Shikoku*

Kyushu

CHINA Nanking

•Shanghai

East China Sea

RYUKYU IS.

INDIA Okinawa

STAGING AREA

OPERATION OLYMPIC
November 1, 1945

Canton *Formosa*

BURMA Hong Kong

Philippine Sea

Luzon

THAILAND Lingayan

Manila

Bangkok PHILIPPINES

FRENCH *Samar* STAGING AREA

INDOCHINA — *Leyte*

*Andaman
Sea*

South China Sea *Mindanao* *PALAU IS*

Davao *Peleliu*

Brunei

MALAYA

Morotai

Halmahera

EQUATOR *Biak*

Borneo

Sumatra *Celebes*

Java *Timor*

DUTCH EAST INDIES

Batavia

Indian Ocean

0 Miles 1500

0 Kilometers 1500

Scale at Equator

AUSTRALIA

© 2016 Jeffrey L. Ward

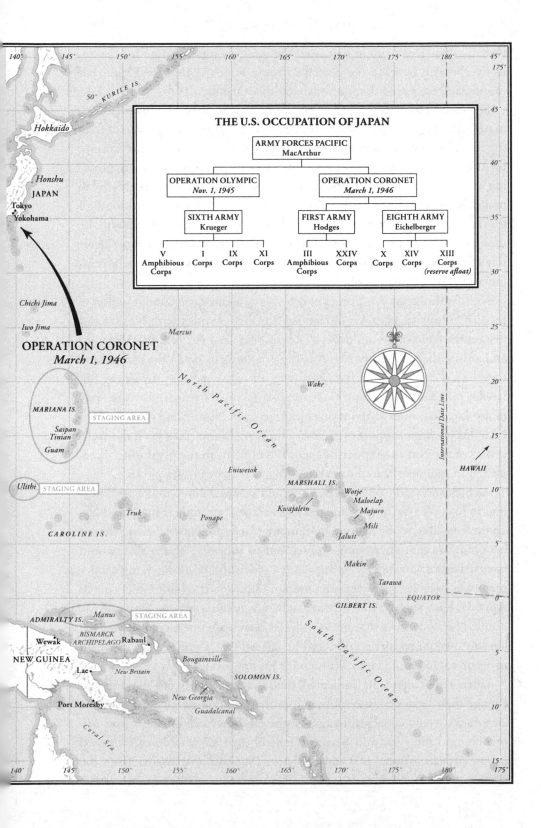

THE U.S. OCCUPATION OF JAPAN

ARMY FORCES PACIFIC
MacArthur

OPERATION OLYMPIC
Nov. 1, 1945

OPERATION CORONET
March 1, 1946

SIXTH ARMY
Krueger

FIRST ARMY
Hodges

EIGHTH ARMY
Eichelberger

V
Amphibious
Corps

I
Corps

IX
Corps

XI
Corps

III
Amphibious
Corps

XXIV
Corps

X
Corps

XIV
Corps

XIII
Corps
(reserve afloat)

50° KURILE IS.

Hokkaido

Honshu

JAPAN

Tokyo
Yokohama

Chichi Jima

Iwo Jima

OPERATION CORONET
March 1, 1946

Marcus

Wake

North Pacific Ocean

MARIANA IS.

STAGING AREA

Saipan
Tinian

Guam

Ulithi STAGING AREA

Eniwetok

MARSHALL IS.

HAWAII

Wotje
Maloelap
Majuro
Mili

Truk

Ponape

Kwajalein

CAROLINE IS.

Jaluit

Makin

Tarawa

GILBERT IS.

EQUATOR

ADMIRALTY IS. Manus STAGING AREA

BISMARCK
ARCHIPELAGO Rabaul

Wewak

NEW GUINEA

Lae New Britain

Bougainville

SOLOMON IS.

Port Moresby

New Georgia

Guadalcanal

South Pacific Ocean

International Date Line

Coral Sea

bers, the War Department increased the monthly intake quota for the Selective Service by sixty-six percent, to one hundred thousand men per
month, and estimated that the war would last through 1946.

Spruance was deeply concerned about the updated intelligence estimates that suggested Japanese forces in Kyushu were more powerful than
the first projections. Data on the number of planes available to the Empire
for suicide attacks, and the number of divisions and brigades, were growing with every study. After Iwo Jima and Okinawa, Spruance preferred to
make the next landings on the China coast, north of Formosa and south of
the Yangtze River. With an excellent fleet anchorage on the mainland, he
thought, "we could inflict a lot of damage at relatively little expense. Their
line of supply to the south, because of MacArthur's presence in the Philippines, was practically cut off."

Neither the Army Air Forces nor the Navy wanted a ground invasion of
Japan. On June 13, Hap Arnold landed on Guam to meet with Nimitz and
inspect the fruits of his ambition to stage a thousand B-29s in the Marianas
and ensure that the Army Air Forces were doing to Japan the same thing
they had done to Germany: destroying all of its industry from the air.
LeMay told Arnold he could "take care of" (Arnold's words) thirty to sixty
major Japanese cities in about one hundred days. Nimitz had disavowed to
King his previous support of an invasion. King himself had been the wellspring of the Navy's skepticism about Olympic from the beginning. It reflected "a complete lack of understanding of sea power," he wrote.

As Spruance had told Nimitz, "It would be wiser not to make any landings in Japan for the time being and let the Japs 'stew in their juice' and 'die
on the vine' like we have done in so many places previously." King shared
his optimism that after being starved out of supplies, "the enemy would
have to beg for surrender." As a specimen of wishful thinking, King's statement was notable. However, in a memorandum to the Joint Chiefs dated
April 30, King showed that he knew which way the wind was blowing. He
notified his colleagues that he considered it an open question whether the
landings would be carried out, and he agreed that a proposal to make an
invasion should be given to Truman for his approval.

Ultra radio intercepts indicated that the Japanese were planning to
change their tactics considerably in a campaign to resist invasion. Suicide
air attacks would concentrate against the landing force during its sea approach, and the First and Second General Armies would stage massed
counterattacks as soon as it came ashore. This was a departure from the

tactics the Japanese had used in every island campaign since Tarawa, where the phibs were allowed to land before counterattacks commenced.

Suicide teams were instructed to carry their explosives into the tracks of tanks and armored amphibians. Imperial Army Headquarters had deployed fourteen divisions, five independent mixed brigades, and three armored brigades to defend Kyushu, and work was feverishly underway to train new units. The Japanese were in fact eager to see the invasion come as soon as possible in the fall, for resources were in place and if an invasion were delayed they would fear running low on rations, among other problems.

But MacArthur, who prided himself on his thrift with the lives of his men, wanted the landings to proceed. After all the invective he had thrown at the naval services concerning the bloodletting that they had ostensibly blundered into at Saipan and elsewhere, when faced with the bloodiest invasion of the war, the Army chieftain was hell-bent on an amphibious frontal assault. It was the Navy that was looking to take things slowly.

Though bombardment and blockade were no doubt weakening Japan ahead of the planned November 1 landings, there was still no precedent in military annals for the successful invasion of a major industrial nation from the sea. MacArthur's headquarters was estimating that the successive operations on Kyushu and Honshu would inflict a total of 720,000 American casualties. Quietly, MacArthur also confirmed to Marshall in June that the training of chemical weapons specialists was accelerating and that stocks of cyanogen chloride and mustard gas were being moved from chemical weapons arsenals in Australia to Luzon for possible use during Operation Olympic.

A pipeline for another perishable commodity was under construction as well. A system for the transport of whole blood to the Western Pacific had been in development since 1944 and had acquired monumental proportions by the time of Okinawa. Collected from donors all over America, the blood was packed in dry ice and flown to Oakland for transshipment to a refrigerated storage facility on Guam. The blood supply architecture to sustain Operation Olympic would be a life-or-death question of logistics. Good for just after twenty-one days, the blood needed to reach floating distribution centers installed on LST hospital ships rapidly in order to be of any use. Failure of delivery, or any loss among the vulnerable LST(H)s in the transport area, could doom hundreds of wounded to a slow death.

On shriveled fortress islands from Rabaul to Truk to Yap, where the

Americans had not seen fit to land, the principal problem facing Japanese garrisons was starvation. In rear areas from the Marianas to the Ryukus, where the alligator navy had struck, holdouts were rooted out by Ronsons. On the Asian mainland, more than eight thousand innocent noncombatants died every day. In Japan, home to thousands of American prisoners of war, water and food supplies dwindled. And Hap Arnold, Lauris Norstad, and Curtis LeMay saw to it that the major cities continued to burn, the penultimate blow to Hirohito's decades-long ambition to consolidate power in league with the militarists who had encouraged their nation to derangement. Yet Japan's will to fight endured. Intercepted radio traffic between the Japanese Foreign Office and its diplomats worldwide—a U.S. cryptographic initiative known as Magic—had revealed, to the dismay of Marshall and others, that the Tokyo fire raid had "seemingly had no effect whatsoever" on morale. Perceptions of national psychology were highly subjective and never measurable. But trends could be detected if one knew where to listen. After Okinawa fell, Sokichi Takagi wrote, "The people felt as if they had awakened from a great surgical operation, feeling a chill all over and pain in every bone. The army, in contrast, was madly proclaiming that the time had come to stage a great decisive battle on the homeland that would defeat the enemy. A heaven-sent opportunity."

If it seemed the very definition of madness for the Big Six to see opportunity in continuing the war, then both madness and opportunity were relative. The two nations did not define victory the same way. Spruance and other rationalists wondered: What methods of warfare does an existential struggle against a cult of death allow, and what restraints might apply? Should an air force deny itself metric efficiency? Was negotiation to be opened at all cost, driven by idealistic sentiment? What credence might Tokyo's diplomats command, three years after the Oahu surprise, a perfidy that had been enabled by a certain laxity and a willingness to trust?

Philosophers would think themselves in circles writing doctrines requiring "proportionality" between lethal means and morbid ends when neither was subject to measurement, and when final determination of right and wrong came down to gut determinations of what conduct is "appropriate." In a sense, the war had overthrown civilization. In the growing part of the world governed by the practices of capitalism, time was money. Now, on a scale not seen before, time was death. "When you are making war, Time is sometimes fighting for the enemy," Spruance said. "But it is also sometimes fighting for you. If Time is fighting for the enemy, it is better to push the war. When you reach the stage where Time is on your side, you can slow down and let it assist you." During the casualty surge of 1944, American forces worldwide had been averaging sixty-five thousand casualties a month. During the first several weeks at Okinawa alone, losses ran to seven thousand killed and wounded per week. The Japanese could run their own numbers. The imponderable question was whether it was right and moral to let loose a sudden atomic blitz and thereby stop the tick-tock of death, or whether the Japanese would come to see time as the Americans did and hasten to stop the clock themselves. In the end, only Japan had the power to decide when it would quit.

The bomb known as Little Boy was based on a design that everyone knew would work. Its ballistic casing contained a simple gun barrel that fired a slug of uranium-235 into a hollow uranium cylinder. The engineers at Los Alamos had calculated its failure rate as one in ten thousand. When purists complained that odds should be further reduced to a million to one, Tibbets retorted, "Hell, nothing is certain. I'll take ten thousand to one any day," pointing out that odds for survival on a bombing mission over Europe had been one thousand times worse. The design was sound, but because production of the fissionable uranium element at Oak Ridge, Tennessee, was a slow process, the capacity to produce bombs was limited, and so an alternative device was needed.

The bomb known as Fat Man yielded a more efficient reaction and used a radioactive isotope, plutonium-239, that could be produced in volume. In December, General Groves had promised General Marshall that the DuPont Company production reactor in Hanford, Washington, would turn out enough of it to make eighteen bombs by the second half of 1945—if only the rest of the weapon could be engineered to work. The Fat Man weapon was massively complex.

The trick to be mastered by Dr. Luis Alvarez and his explosives team, led by George Kistiakowsky, was to get thirty-two initiating charges fitted into a four-foot-diameter sphere to detonate with such perfect simultaneity—within a microsecond, or one-millionth of a second—that the implosive wave crashing into the five-inch plutonium core would compress it so uniformly that it went "supercritical," starting an atomic chain reaction. When Kistiakowsky first came to Los Alamos, he had found the physicists easy marks in poker—maybe some frogman cunning had rubbed off on him during his exposure to Kauffman and the underwater demolition crowd. After a while, though, the theoretical brilliance of the physicists began to tell. It was Alvarez who steered Kistiakowsky away from using that favored tool of the UDT, primacord, to trigger the detonators. He realized that electronic detonators, when hit with high voltage, produced more predictably simultaneous explosions.

The task of building and testing the sphere fell to a technician who worked for Kistiakowsky, Lawrence H. Johnston. He set to work in a generator-powered portable building two miles from the main technical area. The principal tools were a five-thousand-volt direct current power supply, an assortment of capacitors, a large roll of primacord, a gasoline blowtorch, some chemical glassware, matches, and a box of electric blasting caps. In a weeklong series of dangerous, concussive tests that cost him his hearing, Johnston perfected a device that produced the thirty-two explosions within the given tolerance, forming a perfectly spherical implosion wave. Kistiakowsky's team hired Native American women from neighboring pueblos to assemble these "exploding bridgewire" devices. If it all came together in a test at Alamogordo in the New Mexico desert on July 16, Tibbets would at last know whether the mission he and the 509th Composite Group had been training for would take place.

On the evening of July 12, the Japanese government went ahead with its attempt to enlist the Soviet Union to broker an end to the war. Foreign Minister Togo cabled Tokyo's ambassador to Moscow, Sato: "It is His Majesty's heart's desire to see the swift termination of the war. In the Greater East Asia War, however, as long as America and England insist on unconditional surrender, our country has no alternative but to see it through in an all-out effort for the sake of survival and the honor of the homeland."

Sato replied: "I believe it no exaggeration to say that the possibility of getting the Soviet Union to join our side and go along with our reasoning is next to nothing." Sato well understood that Stalin was not about to forgo the fruits of victory that hung low before him in Northeast Asia. An opportunity to control Manchuria beckoned, and also to gain a measure of revenge for Russia's defeat in the 1905 Russo-Japanese War.

The Japanese overture was a dead letter from the start, and the Americans knew it. Through the Magic intercepts, the U.S. discerned from nearly the first moment that the initiative was going nowhere. Truman and his administration knew the Supreme War Direction Council was in a state of dysfunctional paralysis. A split between the dead-enders and the peace seekers blocked any possibility of formulating peace terms to present to the Allies.

Togo pressed his case, instructing the ambassador on July 13 to inform the Kremlin that the emperor wished to dispatch Prince Konoye as a "special envoy" to Moscow "carrying with him the personal letter of His Majesty stating the Imperial wish to end the war." However, Soviet Foreign Minister Molotov immediately replied that he was "simply not able to accommodate" the request. The Magic intercepts of Japanese diplomatic cables, which were sent directly to the White House, dismantled any argument that the Japanese were seriously discussing peace, much less on the verge of surrender in mid-July 1945.

Sato had done his best to warn his superiors of the futility of their Soviet gambit. His view did not register in Tokyo, but it did so, and powerfully, in Washington. The Americans understood all too well what Sato had revealed. If it came as news that the idea of surrender was actually on the lips of some Japanese leaders, any hope to be derived from it was negated by the vicious resistance the dead-enders were putting up. As Secretary of War Stimson wrote with neither sadness nor spite, "It was not the American responsibility to throw in the sponge for the Japanese; that was one thing they must do for themselves."

"As late as July 21," Secretary of State Byrnes would write, "the Japanese militarists caused their government to wire the Ambassador [to Moscow], 'We cannot consent to unconditional surrender under any circumstances. Even if the war drags on, so long as the enemy demands unconditional surrender we will fight as one man against the enemy in accordance with the Emperor's command.' That cable, which we intercepted, depressed me terribly. It meant using the atomic bomb; it probably meant Russia's entry into the war."

Preparing to return to the Central Pacific from Washington in mid-July, Tibbets had planned to stop over in New Mexico to observe the test at Alamogordo. The static trial of the complex plutonium implosion weapon known as Fat Man would determine the feasibility of the Air Forces' ambition to drop three bombs a month on Japan. He never got to Alamogordo. On the eve of the test, he received a dispatch from Tom Ferebee, his bombardier, urging him to return straightaway to Tinian.

Landing on North Field on the same day as the test, Tibbets discovered that an administrative coup d'état was underway within the Army Air Forces. It seemed that Curtis LeMay had leaked what little information he had on the atomic bomb to his operations officer, who, seeing an opportunity, lobbied LeMay to take over what promised to be a historic mission.

With a slow burn in his gut, Tibbets flew to Guam. By temperament he was better equipped now to deal with an important disagreement than he had been in 1942, when his blowup with Lauris Norstad nearly ended his career. Having formed a sort of friendship with LeMay, Tibbets had no wish to go over his head to Arnold. He settled on dealing directly with his friend. When they met, the cigar chomper asked the pipe smoker why a veteran crew from the 313th should not handle the job. Tibbets offered not a reason but a declaration. "I answered politely but firmly that I intended to fly the mission myself and that the 509th must be allowed to operate, as intended when it was formed, without outside interference." The merits, he seemed to believe, spoke for themselves. If LeMay's operations officer needed proof of the unit's skill, he should strap-hang on one of their practice flights and see for himself.

Tibbets understood the loneliness of command, having had plenty of time to experience it in the context of all-encompassing secrecy. He would say,

> A lot of times I felt this real need to talk to someone about what I was going through—and there was no one I could talk to. Because of the orders I had, I really was alone with the knowledge of what we were doing and why. . . .
>
> When a man is in command, he sits in a position where he cannot have friend or foe. Regular human relationships do not figure into it. So you can't worry about what people think of you, and you can't lie awake and have sleepless nights. The job of being in command is lonely by definition. This one was just a little lonelier than most. . . . Twenty-nine didn't seem so young that year.
>
> It had been told to me quite directly: If we were successful, we were going to hasten the end of the war. That was worth the loneliness.

On July 16, the *Indianapolis* completed repairs at San Francisco and was made available to Spruance again as his flagship. As she weighed anchor from San Francisco and headed west, unbeknownst to any of her officers she carried a top secret crate marked for delivery to the Army Air Forces at a forward Pacific base. That night, the War Department's report of the success of the Alamogordo test reached Secretary Stimson, who was in

Potsdam, Germany, outside Berlin, helping President Truman prepare for a conference with Churchill and Stalin. The military commander of the Manhattan Project, Major General Leslie Groves, sent a coded dispatch to Tibbets announcing that the test of the Fat Man device had been successful.

The following morning, Tibbets ensured that his group would be the one to deliver it. He took his would-be usurper, LeMay's ops officer, Colonel Robert Blanchard, on the training flight of his life. Arriving over their aiming point at the precise time calculated by Tibbets's navigator, Dutch Van Kirk, Ferebee dropped the inert "pumpkin," a replica of the Fat Man, dead on target. Then Tibbets executed the maneuver he had devised to get his plane clear of atomic ground zero, pushing over and pouring through the course-reversing 155-degree turn that they had been practicing. Pressed into his seat, Blanchard blanched, looking ill. Returning to base, Tibbets touched down within fifteen seconds of Van Kirk's terminal estimate. "Blanchard was so glad to scramble out of that airplane that I heard no more from him or LeMay or anyone else about our qualifications to carry the bomb to Japan."

On Guam, a film of the Alamogordo test was brought to Nimitz for viewing. At the Joint Intelligence Center, Pacific Ocean Areas, Edwin Layton hinted to his staff that there was going to be a major event but he couldn't talk about it. On orders from Washington, Nimitz directed Halsey in mid-July to lay off launching carrier strikes against certain Japanese cities, among them Hiroshima and Nagasaki. "No explanation was given," Halsey wrote, "and I was puzzled until Rear Admiral William R. Purnell[*] came aboard on July 22nd, under CINCPAC's instructions, and gave me my first word of the bomb."

On the morning of July 21, in Potsdam, a special courier delivered Groves's technical report of the test to Stimson. He saw General Marshall about it that afternoon, then the two men were received by Truman. After reviewing Groves's report, Stimson would record, the president felt "tremendously pepped up." Two atomic bombs would be ready for combat use by August 1. The record would remain unclear for all time exactly

---

[*] Purnell, a close adviser to General Groves, was the Navy representative on the War Department's Military Policy Committee. Headed by FDR's top scientific adviser, Vannevar Bush, the committee governed military research and development and had ultimate authority over the Manhattan Project. It was the unsung Purnell whom Groves credited for the insight that it would take two bombs to end the war: the first to prove the existence of an atomic bomb and the second dropped as quickly as possible so as to imply that the United States had an arsenal of such weapons. See Norris, *Racing for the Bomb*, 381.

when, or even whether, Truman specifically ordered their use against Japan. According to General Groves, "As far as I was concerned, his decision was one of noninterference—basically a decision not to upset the existing plans."

The war after the war to end all wars was finally set to end.

34

Prompt and Utter Destruction

In the days leading up to the U.S. landings on Guam, a man emerged from hiding in the hills, ran toward the island's northwestern cliffs, and began signaling an American destroyer with a mirror and semaphore. During the long Japanese occupation, the Guamanians had come to admire and even lionize George Ray Tweed. With salvaged radio receivers, he intercepted news broadcasts and published an underground newspaper for the people of Guam. After more than two years of evasion, the Navy radioman who had served at the U.S. naval station on Guam prior to its fall in 1941 became a symbol of hope to them, for as long as he lived they had confidence that the Americans would return. When Tweed climbed aboard a whaleboat sent by the USS *McCall* for transit to Jocko Clark's carrier group on the evening of July 10, news of his recovery energized the fleet. He was a symbol of the overrun but undefeated, the type of man who would not stop resisting no matter the odds.

On the same day that Tweed was delivered to the fleet, Saipan was declared secure. In the year that followed, on that island, Sakae Oba held out stubbornly with his men. In his extended tour of duty, he had no other mission except to forage and evade. A year from the day that Tweed resumed his life as a Navy radioman, and eventually an officer, Captain Oba had to decide what kind of soldier he would be. The culture of the Japanese Army surely offered him a powerful example. There was Tojo, whose unbounded aggression had inspired Oba to serve as the war began; Umezu, the head of the Army General Staff; and the fierce Army minister, Anami, who carried the idea of resistance to absurd, quixotic lengths. But Oba had not seen utility in martyrdom. He had refused to sacrifice himself as Colonel Suzuki and his men had. His duty to his nation was to defend it, and that required more than shattering himself like a jewel in a foolish rush, no matter how glorious the spectacle. Others of like mind had joined Oba's band; some had only the vaguest memories of how it had all come to pass. Closer to his station, there was the example of Lance Corporal Ikegami. His hallucinations were akin to what animated the most determined of the Japanese dead-enders now. Oba placed little faith in illusion. But if it was fruitless to hope to win, it was certainly not unrealistic to believe that one could maintain one's dignity as a soldier, regardless of the outcome. This very same message had been raining down by the millions from the bomb bays of American planes, alighting all across the Empire.

One such message nearly knocked Oba off his feet when one of his men brought it to him. It included a photograph depicting Tokyo razed to its blackened roots. When the leaflet was shown around the camp, many of his men said they thought it was fake. Oba was not sure. He had seen the huge silver bombers returning to Saipan from missions unknown. He showed the photo to a soldier who hailed from the Japanese capital. He recognized several railway lines, marveling that whole districts had burned away.

"Do you think they really are bombing Japan, Captain?" he asked.

"I don't know. But if they are, we're lost. The navy will never return."

And then there was Horiuchi, the *yakuza,* who was still working on his body count, having pledged to take a hundred of the enemy with him. He had saved Oba's life during the November sweep, staging a diversion to draw the Americans away from the cliffs. Valuable though he was, however, the gangster had never actually consented to Oba's control. Joined by two comrades armed with captured American BARs, he preferred to play the role of the freelance killer. Oba settled for merely managing him. Though Horiuchi seemed to scoff at military rank, refusing to acknowledge anyone addressing him as "Private" Horiuchi, he did essentially comply when he was instructed to stand down from freelance hunting at a time when it risked betraying the group's location. Horiuchi said, "Tell Captain Oba I understand," but he never stated outright that he would obey.

As a rogue element operating on his own idea of honor, Horiuchi resembled in microcosm the army leadership that he only grudgingly served. Anami, Umezu, and others on the Supreme War Direction Council were gangsters of a certain stripe, beholden to a darker purpose, standing beyond any higher officer's command, and threatening to bring everyone else down with them. From the Marianas, their will to fight would have to be broken. That ferocious resolve hardened as the summer solstice of 1945 reached its peak.

If it can be said the sun went down for the Japanese navy after its losses at Leyte Gulf, the second half of July 1945 saw the last traces of its twilight fade to black. Admiral Halsey had made sure of this, taking all of the Third Fleet's combat elements from Leyte Gulf, where it had replenished in June, toward Japan with the mission of completing the annihilation of the enemy fleet in its harbors and targeting the nation's very will to fight.

Halsey's task groups roamed freely within a hundred fifty miles of the Japanese coast, unmolested by air attacks thanks to "continuous blanket operations" that smothered airfields with fighter sweeps and liberal use of a new 260-pound fragmentation bomb equipped with a VT fuze. Its ground-sensing radar automatically triggered air bursts that were lethal against targets protected in foxholes and revetments. The scouring power of the new bomb was so great that whenever intact enemy aircraft were visible on the ground, they were suspected of being dummies, bait for a flak trap. The Japanese hid their working planes far from the flight line, under tree canopies, between buildings in villages, and under haystacks in fields.

On July 14 and 15, strikes targeted transportation infrastructure, sinking or damaging nine railroad ferries that delivered the fruit of Hokkaido's extensive coal mines to Honshu. On the seventeenth, Halsey and McCain welcomed a carrier group from the British Pacific Fleet to their order of battle. They released their battleships to bombard industrial facilities northeast of Tokyo. The next day the task force loosed its air groups against Yokosuka Navy Yard, with orders to find and sink the battleship *Nagato*. These strikes were hampered by bad weather, heavy antiaircraft fire, and an aircraft arming plan that did not allow use of armor-piercing bombs. The flagship of Admiral Yamamoto during the Pearl Harbor attack almost four years earlier got off with cosmetic damage to her superstructure.

On July 24 and 25, Halsey hit Kure Harbor on the Inland Sea. Though Spruance wanted more to be done against enemy airfields, and Halsey's own carrier task force chief, John McCain, opposed the antishipping strikes, Halsey saw good reasons to target the fuel-starved enemy fleet at anchor: national morale—revenge for Pearl Harbor; protection of convoy routes to Russia; and preventing any chance that Japan might rebuild its fleet after the war. And there was a fourth reason, which Halsey considered "sufficient alone": "CINCPAC had ordered the fleet destroyed." Even when other, arguably more important missions were in play, Halsey was always a ship killer. His returns were handsome, and well captured by aerial photographers: the battleship *Ise,* keel in the mud; her sister ship, the *Hyuga,* shattered, decks awash; the storied *Haruna, Tone,* and *Aoba* beached, as if dead from exhaustion; the new *Katsuragi,* flight deck torn and buckled; the *Amagi,* whose flat top "could have been used as a ski slide," Halsey wrote. "The commander in chief of the Combined Japanese Fleet could reach his cabin in his flagship, the light cruiser *Oyodo,* only in a diving suit." Of Japan's twelve battleships, only one was left afloat, and five of her twenty-five carriers, two of eighteen heavy cruisers, two of twenty-two light cruisers, and five of 177 destroyers. And as had been the case all along, Japanese airpower managed not a scratch against the carriers. The Third Fleet raids put twenty-four hundred planes out of action, most destroyed or damaged on the ground, as well as 173 locomotives, 40 hangars and barracks, 41 tank and freight cars, 4 bridges, a power station, and a lighthouse.

Halsey's triumphalist flourish reached the public through the Associated Press. "What's left of the Japanese navy is helpless, but just for good luck we will hunt them out of their holes. My only regret is that the ships do not have wheels—so we could chase them inland after we drive them from the coast."

On July 24, in Potsdam, Marshall received and promptly approved a draft directive from Leslie Groves ordering the use of the atomic bomb. The next morning, Marshall secured Secretary of War Stimson's approval and discussed the plan with President Truman. Word of this development went by cable to the headquarters of U.S. Army Strategic Air Forces on Guam. The directive, now effective, read, "The 509 Composite Group, 20th Air Force, will deliver its first special bomb as soon as weather will permit visual bombing after about 3 August 1945 on one of these targets: Hiroshima, Kokura, Niigata, and Nagasaki."

The headlines that Halsey had made after the Kure strikes were quickly overshadowed by news from the outskirts of Berlin. On July 26, Harry Truman and Prime Minister Winston Churchill, with the concurrence of the head of China's nationalist government, Chiang Kai-shek, issued a declaration that read in part:

Japan shall be given an opportunity to end this war.

The might that now converges on Japan is immeasurably greater than that which, when applied to the resisting Nazis, necessarily laid waste to the lands, the industry, and the method of life of the whole German people. The full application of our military power, backed by our resolve, will mean the inevitable and complete destruction of the Japanese armed forces and just as inevitably the utter devastation of the Japanese homeland.

Following are our terms. We will not deviate from them. There are no alternatives. We shall brook no delay.

We call upon the government of Japan to proclaim now the unconditional surrender of all Japanese armed forces, and to provide proper and adequate assurances of their good faith in such action. The alternative for Japan is prompt and utter destruction.

The requirement of unconditional surrender was nothing new. President Roosevelt had made it the basis of surrender demands since the Casablanca Conference in January 1943. And there was good reason for it. Far from being rhetorical coinage, the phrase was specifically important as a legal term of art. As State Department attorneys stressed, unconditional surrender would empower an occupier to enact political reform to a degree beyond what international law otherwise permitted. At a press conference in mid-1944, FDR had vowed not to repeat what he had seen as the mistakes of the Versailles Treaty. "Practically all Germans deny the fact that they surrendered during the last war, but this time they are going to know it. So are the Japs."

But the terms demanded at Potsdam were far from unconditional. They actually did limit the extent of Japan's submission. It was suggested in the declaration that the American occupation would be temporary, and that the home islands would become sovereign again. The most debated provision had to do with the position of the emperor. Disagreement over how to handle his office was rife within the U.S. Department of State. While Acting Secretary of State Joseph Grew, a Japan expert, had wanted to assure Hirohito's position, the "China crowd" at Foggy Bottom saw no justice in treating imperial militarists any differently than those of National Socialist Germany. The Potsdam Declaration ultimately pulled up short of guaranteeing Hirohito's status. In blaming "self-willed militaristic advisers" for the ignition of war, it suggested that Hirohito himself would not be held responsible and thus that the United States might be inclined to preserve his throne. But it did not promise to do so.

In spite of the declaration's various conditions limiting the extent of a Japanese surrender, Tokyo was unsatisfied. Upon receiving the product of the Potsdam Conference, Prime Minister Kantaro Suzuki took it to the Big Six. The old schism held. Accordingly, the Japanese response to the Allies was broadly ambiguous. Suzuki issued a short statement to the press in which he belittled the declaration as a repeat of previous demands. "The government does not think that it has serious value. We can only ignore [*mokusatsu*] it. We will do our utmost to complete the war to the bitter end."

The word *mokusatsu* had several meanings—"to let the other party's case die in a vacuum of silence," or "to wait in silence until we can speak with wisdom," or "to wait in silence until we can speak about something wise," or "to disregard as unworthy of a response." Whether the word was meant to suggest contempt or a need for further deliberation was a matter of context. In context with the rest of Suzuki's statement as reported— including the promise to "do our utmost to complete the war to the bitter end"—Allied leaders read the response as an official rejection. *Mokusatsu* was an evasive term used advisedly by an indecisive man in an impossible circumstance in order to buy time that his nation, it turned out, did not have. Less than a fortnight earlier, the imperial Japanese government had asked Russia's help in brokering a peace. Hirohito sent a personal message to Stalin, opening top-level channels. But the effort was doomed so long as Russia had an appetite to seize Manchuria and take a measure of revenge for defeat in the Russo-Japanese War, while the Big Six had nothing to offer. The determined wishful thinking of the Japanese manifested itself in the views of the "moderate" Navy minister, Admiral Yonai, who managed to read the Potsdam Declaration as evidence that America's will to fight was faltering and regarded *"mokusatsu"* as a savvy response.

The declaration had made no specific reference to an atomic bomb, but that weapon's components were en route to Tinian even as it was being transmitted. On July 26, Spruance's old flagship, the *Indianapolis,* dropped anchor inside the antisubmarine netting of Tinian Town's harbor. When an LCT drew alongside, the deck force quickly turned to, attaching a fifteen-foot wooden crate stored on the hangar deck amidships to the hook of the ship's aviation crane and hoisting it into the landing craft. The crate contained the firing mechanism for the Little Boy device. A bucket of lead in the close custody of two men who did not appear on the cruiser's personnel roster was carried off the ship, too. The men were Colonel James F. Nolan, MD, a radiologist from the Manhattan Project, and Major Robert R. Furman, the Manhattan Project's chief of foreign intelligence. The bucket contained a single slug of uranium-235. Truman had no intention of announcing the bomb's existence to a hostile power when secrecy had kept him from informing his own Congress about the two-billion-dollar project.

On July 25, General George Marshall, with the approval of Secretary of War Stimson, brought to President Truman the directive prepared by General Groves ordering use of the atomic bombs.

Three days later, a flight of B-29s from Kirtland Field, near Albuquerque, landed at North Field, one of them carrying the bulbous assembly of Fat Man in its front bomb bay. A pair of C-54s from the Air Transport Command delivered the bomb's plutonium core in custody of Dr. Luis Alvarez and Lawrence Johnston, civilians from Project Alberta who were freshly commissioned as Army Air Forces officers.

On July 29, General Carl A. Spaatz, the commander of the deactivated U.S. strategic air force command in Europe, arrived at Harmon Field to take command of all strategic air forces in the Pacific. He named Curtis LeMay his chief of staff but allowed him to retain effective control over all Marianas-based B-29s. The XXI Bomber Command, relabeled the Twentieth Air Force, was placed under the command of Lieutenant General Nathan Farragut Twining, a veteran of the South Pacific who had headed Allied strategic air forces in the Mediterranean.

When Spaatz landed at Guam from Washington, he carried the draft directive from Groves authorizing use of the first "special bomb."

Delivering an atomic weapon to the Marianas was the final service of the war for the USS *Indianapolis*. Having taken on her secret cargo at Hunters Point Naval Shipyard in San Francisco and carried it to Tinian, she was en route from Guam to Leyte when she steamed into the periscope crosshairs of a Japanese submarine.

Spruance had feared for her vulnerability. She was top-heavy after extensive modernization. A single torpedo, he thought, might cause the cruiser to turn turtle and sink. After midnight on July 30, two torpedoes slammed into the *Indianapolis* on the starboard side.

The explosions destroyed her electrical generating capacity as well as her outdated firefighting system. With the loss of power, Captain Charles B.

McVay's emergency dispatch and SOS radio call did not seem to transmit, and destruction of the engine order telegraph kept the officer of the deck's order to stop engines from reaching the ship's engineers. Fires raged forward until they were quenched by the flood scooped up by the speeding ship. The old heavy cruiser listed hard, finally rolling all the way over and sinking by the head. Her survivors were left to drift on a slow southwesterly current, three hundred miles from the nearest shore. On the morning of the fourth day, by which time sharks and exposure had savaged the surviving company, a search aircraft reported them to a naval headquarters in the Philippines that had not even known they were missing. The following noon, the 318 survivors from the 1,196-man crew were picked up by ships and taken to hospitals on Peleliu and Samar. It was a sad loss for Spruance.

As the survivors from the *Indianapolis* languished adrift, on the other side of the world Harry S. Truman prepared for his own oceanic passage. At 11:20 on the morning of August 2, the president and a party that included his chief of staff, Fleet Admiral William D. Leahy, and Secretary of State James F. Byrnes, boarded the cruiser USS *Augusta* for transit to Virginia, weighing anchor in the late afternoon.

On Guam, Spruance called his staff into his office and read from a top secret dispatch: Within the next several days the Army Air Forces would drop an atomic bomb on a Japanese city. "I don't recall his words," Chuck Barber would write, "but the mood was one of satisfaction that the step might shock the Japanese into terminating the war. I sensed no feeling of moral crises either in Spruance or in myself."

When the time came for Paul Tibbets to take a Silverplate B-29, he traveled to Omaha and selected it off the line of the Glenn L. Martin Company plant. With the help of a couple of production foremen, he chose a plane that seemed to have come together well. Tibbets had also handpicked the men he considered best qualified in the outfit to serve with him in that plane: Tom Ferebee, bombardier; Dutch Van Kirk, navigator; and Bob Lewis, copilot. Once the aircraft had received its final touches, Tibbets sent Lewis to the factory to pick it up for him.

After the bomber was delivered to Tinian and painted with its circle-R group designation and the numeral 82, Lewis flew a number of missions in it and came to regard the plane as his. Tibbets, however, took over when the time came to fly the historic mission. He felt that the plane that carried out such a momentous task needed a more meaningful name. "My thoughts turned at this moment," Tibbets wrote in his memoir, "to my courageous red-haired mother, whose quiet confidence had been a source of strength in me since boyhood, and particularly during the soul-searching period when I decided to give up a medical career to become a military pilot. At a time when Dad thought I had lost my marbles, she had taken my side and said, 'I know you will be all right, son.' I remembered the excitement she displayed on our rough flight through the thunderstorms from Wendover to Miami. From that flight, she had come to understand and even share some of the thrills of flying that had led me into my present career. Her name, Enola Gay, was pleasing to the ear."

Having completed practice runs with inert replicas of both bomb types, the 509th, its demanding commander thought, was ready. On August 3, LeMay issued the order to execute Special Bombing Mission No. 13, with Hiroshima as the primary target. Secondary, pending weather, was Kokura. Tertiary was Nagasaki.

On the morning of the fifth, Tibbets convened the Tinian "joint chiefs," his top officers and scientists in the 509th Composite Group. They included Major General Thomas F. Farrell, Groves's deputy and the ranking officer from Los Alamos on Tinian; Rear Admiral William R. Purnell, the Navy representative on the Military Policy Committee; Captain Deak Parsons, the officer in charge of Project Alberta and Tibbets's weaponeer on the Hiroshima flight; Commander Frederick L. Ashworth, Parsons's number two; and Norman F. Ramsey, the physicist.

Parsons got everyone's attention by describing a nightmare scenario that kept him up at night: an accident on takeoff. Four planes had crashed just the previous night, igniting incendiary payloads that lit up the nightscape. He worried that such a mishap with a live atomic bomb on board could destroy half of the island. Farrell suggested prayer as a solution, but Parsons had another in mind. He recommended an idea he had rejected when his own deputy offered it some months before: performing the final assembly of the bomb while in flight. By inserting the uranium slug and the explosive charge into the "gun" of the Little Boy after takeoff, they would ensure that no one beyond the plane's crew would need fear for their lives if the worst came to pass. The idea was approved by general acclamation, and Parsons as weaponeer began drawing up his work process.

After the meeting, Tibbets went to the hardstand on North Field where his aircraft was parked, his mother's name newly painted in black on the left side below the cockpit. Then he went to watch as Little Boy was rolled on a trailer to the bomb loading pit and the *Enola Gay* was towed into position to take it on board. Tibbets thought the bomb, a tapered cylinder twelve feet long and weighing more than nine thousand pounds, painted gunmetal gray, was "an ugly monster." Some members of the unit stopped by to scrawl messages on it. Lawrence Johnston wrote, "To the people of Japan, from my friends in China." Another message was addressed to Emperor Hirohito, signed, "From the boys of the *Indianapolis.*"

After the Marianas, the remaining operations of the war, from Iwo Jima to Okinawa to the plans for Operations Olympic and Coronet, were in a sense merely insurance against the eventuality that the air theorists were wrong, that George Kistiakowsky didn't time his charges properly, that Paul Tibbets hadn't been able to maintain secrecy within his pioneering command, that Deak Parsons couldn't arm a bomb in flight, that the atomic calculations of the brilliant minds of Robert Oppenheimer, Leo Szilard, and Enrico Fermi were wrong, and that Emperor Hirohito, as his cities smoldered, would not find the courage to see the urgency of powering down the militarists' death frenzy, managing the nation's pride, and throwing in the towel.

Ever since he had seen the aerial photos of the four cities on the Target Committee's "reserved list," Tibbets had favored Hiroshima as his primary target. It had been spared from previous attack because it lacked aircraft factories. A pristine, intact target such as this would ensure that it registered the most powerful impression possible of the new bomb's effect. For the impact of the bombs was always meant to be psychological, not military. Truman's remark that Hiroshima was a miiltary target was simple dissembling. The target of the bomb was not actually Second General Army headquarters, or its training and marshaling centers, or even Hiroshima itself. As plans went forward, the understanding developed that the real target was the mind and conscience of the occupant of an imperial palace that had been kept off-limits to B-29s prior to August 6.

The last mission briefing started at eleven P.M. on August 5, as the crews of the three B-29s that were to fly the mission, plus a fourth which was to fly with them as an emergency alternate as far as Iwo Jima, gathered in the base auditorium. Tibbets presided, with Deak Parsons and Professor Ramsey joining him on a platform. "Tonight is the night we have all been waiting for," Tibbets said. "Our long months of training are to be put to the test. We will soon know if we have been successful or failed. Upon our efforts tonight it is possible that history will be made. We are going on a mission to drop a bomb different from any you have ever seen or heard about. This bomb contains a destructive force equivalent to twenty thousand tons of TNT." Tibbets did not say the words "atom" or "atomic," but the explosive yield offered enough of a challenge to their imagination. They had seen still photos from Alamogordo, but this number was off the grid.

Parsons announced that he had brought a motion picture of the New Mexico test to illustrate what they should expect, but the projector malfunctioned and the film could not be shown. The weaponeer settled for offering a lecture, drawing pictures of the expected mushroom cloud and describing the color display that would come with the blast.

Tibbets closed the briefing, running through the plan one more time: three weather planes scouting the primary, secondary, and tertiary targets an hour and a half ahead; rendezvous of the *Enola Gay* with the instrument plane and photographic plane over Iwo Jima; the flight over Shikoku and overland west to the target; detection of the aiming point; the release of the weapon, followed by the oft-rehearsed course-reversing dive to the right; the release of a parachute-rigged bale of sensors by the instrument plane, a B-29 named *The Great Artiste,* then a diving turn to the left; the photographic plane, aircraft number 91, lagging safely behind to film the historic and terrible event. The session ended at about one in the morning with a prayer by the bomb group chaplain, Captain William B. Downey: "Almighty Father, Who wilt hear the prayer of them that love Thee, we pray Thee to be with those who brave the heights of Thy Heaven and who carry the battle to our enemies. . . . We pray Thee that the end of the war may come soon, and that once more we may know peace on earth."

Afterward, the flight surgeon, Don Young, approached Tibbets and the other pilots, handing each a small cardboard box. In the event of a crash over Japan, this supplemental payload was to be dropped on their crews. The boxes contained capsules of cyanide, one suicide pill for every man.

35

Clear-cut Results

E nola Gay Tibbets would have thought it unbecoming to mug for the cameras. At the flight line at North Field, the B-29 emblazoned with her name was bathed in floodlights, glinting silver as motion picture cameras rolled. When he first laid eyes on the production, Colonel Tibbets feared for the security of his mission. "Any Japanese lurking in the surrounding hills had to know something special was going on," he wrote. "I had known, of course, that there would be routine picture taking, but I was unprepared for this." The setup by Army public affairs struck him as a distraction in the midst of preparations for history's most consequential air mission. The weather planes had already taxied away and the *Enola Gay* was set for an 0245 takeoff. Tibbets and his crew forced themselves to smile through this command performance, enduring a strobe light assault for twenty minutes before he tired of it and ordered the photographers away shortly before two A.M.

After inspecting his plane, Tibbets and eleven other men climbed into the bomber: the copilot, Captain Robert A. Lewis, of Ridgefield Park, New Jersey; the bombardier, Major Thomas W. Ferebee, of Mocksville, North Carolina; the navigator, Captain Theodore J. Van Kirk, of Northumberland, Pennsylvania; the radar countermeasures officer, First Lieutenant Jacob Beser, of Baltimore; the weaponeer, Captain William S. Parsons, USN, of Fort Sumner, New Mexico; the electronics assistant, Second Lieutenant Morris R. Jeppson, of Carson City, Nevada; the flight engineer, Staff Sergeant Wyatt E. Duzenbury, of Lansing, Michigan; the assistant flight engineer, Sergeant Robert H. Shumard, of Detroit; the radar operator, Sergeant Joseph A. Stiborik, of Taylor, Texas; the tail gunner, Staff Sergeant

George R. Caron, of Lynbrook, New York; and the radio operator, Private First Class Richard H. Nelson, of Los Angeles.

Tibbets settled into the left seat of the cockpit and ran through the preflight checklist with Lewis. When the airplane commander signaled engine start, the ground crew pulled each of the four huge propellers through three revolutions to distribute oil through the radially aligned cylinders. Then Duzenbury pulled the starter. Each engine coughed and spat flames, and as Tibbets throttled up, he was satisfied with the smooth basso roar and the oil pressure gauges, rising and holding steady. He made sure the brakes were set, then showed two thumbs up, signaling the ground crew to remove the chocks from his wheels. Waving to the crowd of almost a hundred well-wishers, Tibbets gunned the engines and started the mile-long run to the southwest end of the runway, mindful of the burned wreckage of the four crashed Superfortresses, which had not yet been cleared away.

"Dimples eight-two to North Tinian Tower. Ready for takeoff on Runway Able," he said.

"Dimples eight-two. Dimples eight-two. Cleared for takeoff."

The *Enola Gay* rolled.

They were just eight minutes airborne, turning and passing Saipan, climbing in tandem with a just-risen crescent moon, when Deak Parsons and Morris Jeppson lowered themselves into the bomb bay. Jeppson held a flashlight while Parsons inserted the cordite charge into the explosive gun that would fire one block of U-235 into another. He kept Tibbets apprised during the twenty-five minutes it took to arm the weapon. Jeppson replaced the electrical safety plugs with live plugs. After the men had bolted up the access plates and checked the circuits, Tibbets relayed news of each step in code to General Farrell on Tinian, until the stretching distance defeated his low-frequency transmitter.

Tibbets made contact with the three other planes, then left the cockpit and went to see about his crew in the back of the *Enola Gay*. Crawling through the sealed tunnel that connected the front and rear pressurized crew spaces, he huddled with Stiborik, Shumard, and Caron, who had left his cold and lonely post in the tail gun position. "Have you figured out what we're doing?" he asked Caron.

"Hell, Colonel, I'd probably get in trouble with the security around here. I don't want to think."

"We're on our way now—you can guess anything you want," Tibbets said.

"Is it a chemist's nightmare?"

"Not exactly, but you're warm." The men talked some more, and as Tibbets was squeezing into the tunnel to return to the cockpit, Caron grabbed him by the boot.

"Are we splitting atoms today, Colonel?"

"That's about it."

Returning to the airplane commander's seat, Tibbets made himself comfortable with his life jacket and parachute pack, reclined as best he could, then knocked off for a bit. Less than an hour later, Lewis awoke him. It was time to begin climbing. Iwo Jima lay ahead, their rendezvous point. Tibbets called the instrument plane, *The Great Artiste,* flown by Major Chuck Sweeney, and aircraft number 91, flown by Captain George Marquardt, and as he finished circling the island, the two other planes slid into formation with him at ninety-three hundred feet. The backup plane, *Top Secret,* flown by Chuck McKnight, left their company and landed at Iwo Jima. It was shortly after six A.M. The first light of dawn had warmed and turned bright, the sun flaming red in the east.

The weather plane over Hiroshima, the *Straight Flush,* flown by Claude Eatherley, sent a coded message indicating good weather over the primary target, two-tenths cloud cover at 15,000 feet. As the *Enola Gay* neared the coast, Lieutenant Beser tuned his radio to eavesdrop on some known Japanese fighter control frequencies. As Tibbets began the long climb to bombing altitude, 30,700 feet, Beser's receivers returned an audio tone indicating that air defense radars had touched the plane. In the days prior to the mission, the 509th had sent B-29s in twos and threes over Japan, only to turn around again. Thus lulled, the Japanese now seemed to show no interest in the arriving trio of planes. The fighter control frequencies were quiet. Beser intercepted some radio traffic from Task Force 38, which was beginning a day of refueling and gunnery exercises in waters three hundred miles east of Tokyo. He found the radio chatter between the Navy pilots fascinating.

The intercom was quiet as the *Enola Gay* flew over Shikoku and crossed the coast to Honshu. Ahead, over the wakening target city, clouds were sparse. There was no flak and no interceptors. Deak Parsons came forward and looked over Tibbets's shoulder as they reached the initial point, where the bombardier took over control of the plane from the pilot. Ninety seconds from release, Tibbets gave control of the plane to his twenty-six-year-old bombardier, Tom Ferebee.

"It's all yours," Tibbets said, taking his hands from the yoke.

Ferebee entered the eight-knot southerly wind speed into the Norden bombsight. Peering through it, he said, "Okay, I've got the bridge." The Aioi Bridge spanning the Ota River had been chosen as the aiming point for its recognizable T shape. The airmen in all three planes pulled on their polarized goggles. All but Ferebee. He found that the eyewear impaired his use of the bombsight. There came the whine of pneumatic motors opening the bomb bay doors; the *oooh* of a continuous radio tone activated by Robert Nelson, signaling the fifteen-second warning; a motion picture camera whirring as Dr. Alvarez and Lawrence Johnston in *The Great Artiste* began taking readings from three oscilloscopes that would receive signals from the package of telemetric sensors, swinging down on parachutes. At 0815:15 the radio tone stopped. The *Enola Gay* flinched upward. Tibbets's seat slapped him hard on the rear as the nine-thousand-pound Little Boy fell from the bomb bay. *Now it's in the lap of the gods,* Deak Parsons thought.

He turned the yoke sharply right and pushed over into the long-rehearsed dive, pouring through 155 degrees. As the bomb traced its parabola toward Aioi Bridge, the instrument package drifted downward, listening. Aircraft number 91 lagged behind, cameras rolling.

A flash of light drained all color from the world. As the interior of his plane brightened, Tibbets tasted lead on his tongue. From the navigator's seat just forward of the tunnel, Dutch Van Kirk saw a flash like that of a photographer's bulb and heard a hard snapping sound, like the sound of sheet metal flexing, or shrapnel against a fuselage, a lifetime ago over Europe.

The only man in the *Enola Gay* to see the blast was the tail gunner, George Caron, who watched the storm of inward-curling gases whirl upward through the stratocumulus, followed by the angry shimmer of the shock wave. Each plane took a hard double jolt, one from the shock wave, the other from its rebound off the ground. Tibbets gripped the yoke tightly to keep his attitude level. Deak Parsons shouted, "It's flak!" Bob Lewis thought it felt as if a giant had swung a telephone pole into the plane.

The city below reverberated with supernatural sensations. Michiko Yamaoka, fifteen, an operator at a telephone exchange five hundred meters from the hypocenter, recalled, "There was no sound. I felt something strong. It was terribly intense. I felt colors. It wasn't heat. You can't really say it was yellow, and it wasn't blue." She fainted and felt the sensation of floating through the air.

When the girl regained consciousness, she found herself buried beneath a pile of stones. Her mother got some soldiers to help uncover her. She emerged into an alien world. A photographer who was attached to a Japanese Army press unit, Yoshito Matsushige, noticed how showers of sparks leaped from the power lines entering his house. Then he heard a great cracking noise and saw a flash, magnesium-bright, and he felt "an explosive wind like needles." As he ran outside with his wife, the world seemed totally black.

"Nobody looked human. Everyone was stupefied," Yamaoka said. "Humans had lost the ability to speak. People couldn't scream 'It hurts!' even when they were on fire. People didn't say 'It's hot!' They just sat catching fire." The flattened area around the hypocenter was cast in dull brown hues, the shade of unfired pottery. "Nothing was standing, no gates, pillars, walls, or fences," a survivor recalled. "You just walked in a straight line to where you wanted to go."

In the midst of the great diving turn, Tom Ferebee could not see the blast cloud, but coming around, he saw its cargo. "Parts of buildings were coming up the stem of the bomb—you could tell that something strange was going on, because you could see parts of the city, pieces of the buildings, like they were being sucked up toward us," Tibbets would recall. Finishing his evasive diving turn, the mission commander decided to circle the city once before going home.

"The city we had seen so clearly in the sunlight a few minutes before was now an ugly smudge," Tibbets wrote.

> It had completely disappeared under this awful blanket of smoke and fire. A feeling of shock and horror swept over all of us....
>
> Whatever exclamations may have passed our lips at this historic moment, I cannot accurately remember. We were all appalled and what we said was certain to have reflected our emotions and our disbelief.
>
> It is unfortunate that there is no way to reconstruct, with complete accuracy, the excitement that seized all of us aboard the *Enola Gay.*

Bob Lewis wrote in his flight log, "My God!" But he elaborated on this later, for he had agreed to maintain the log for the benefit of a *New York*

Times reporter on Tinian. Robert Oppenheimer had invoked Hindu scripture to express the power that he had helped summon into being. Tibbets understood his cadre as heralds: "My eleven companions and I were improbable choices to become the messengers of a war god more terrible than any who had walked this earth in all the centuries past. We were no Genghis Khans, no Tamerlanes, no Julius Caesars or Napoleons. Yet any of these ruthless warriors, whose deeds are written in blood across the pages of human history, would have trembled at what we had done."

On the return flight the intercom was largely quiet. George Caron had a full hour and a half to stare at the mushroom cloud from the tail gunner's compartment, commenting occasionally on the fires that twinkled through its base and finally noting when it vanished in the haze beyond the northern horizon.

Silence, stunning for its depth and totality, was the byword of the bomb in Tokyo, too. The first sign of Hiroshima's destruction came when a technician at the Japanese Broadcasting Corporation noticed that the Hiroshima radio station had gone off the air. Telegraph communications fell suddenly, unaccountably mute, and a puzzling silence was all the operators at Imperial General Staff headquarters could raise from the burning city. Several railway stations near Hiroshima issued reports of a terrible explosion. It was generally thought at headquarters that nothing serious had occurred, that it was just a rumor starting from a few sparks of truth. To ascertain this, a young officer from the General Staff was ordered to fly there, land, survey the situation himself, and make a report.

On board the *Enola Gay* there was no celebration. "We certainly were trained not to be that way on our missions," Van Kirk said. "Think about the era we grew up in. Babe Ruth would hit a home run and he would run around the bases and that would be it. You didn't show much. You took pride in being disciplined."

Paul Tibbets, in the moment, believed that the horror they had unleashed might serve to abolish the contagion of war from the earth. "I reflected on the wonders of science and rejoiced that the new weapon had surely made future war unthinkable. Just as the spear had been more deadly than the club, the bow and arrow a more formidable weapon than the spear, gunpowder had made the bow and arrow obsolete. Each technological advance in weaponry had made war more hideous but so far had not persuaded mankind to abandon this means of settling quarrels between peoples. Now certainly we had developed the ultimate argument for keeping the peace."

Lawrence Johnston would say, "Many people have asked me if I was praying for the Japanese people who were dying at that time. No, I was not. I had done all that praying before starting on the mission, including the prayer for guidance whether I should be part of it. I was all prayed up and convinced that God was having mercy on the Japanese and on us in getting the wartime killing and waste stopped. I was thanking God that I could be and had been part of the process."

Yoshito Matsushige ran to his house to fetch his camera, then returned to his office at Hiroshima Castle. The horrors he saw along the way were so profound that he could not bring himself to depress the shutter. Bodies roasted in molten asphalt, a woman holding her baby in the crook of an arm, shouting "Please open your eyes!" It was twenty minutes before he could expose his first frame, only to realize there was nowhere to go with his work, for no newspaper office remained to publish it.

Deak Parsons sent an encoded message back to Norman Ramsey on Tinian: "CLEAR-CUT RESULTS, IN ALL RESPECTS SUCCESSFUL. EXCEEDED TRINITY TEST IN VISIBLE RESULTS. NORMAL CONDITIONS OBTAINED IN AIRCRAFT AFTER DELIVERY. VISUAL ATTACK ON HIROSHIMA AT 05/2315Z WITH ONLY ONE-TENTH CLOUD COVER. FLAK AND FIGHTERS ABSENT." General Farrell passed a summary of this message to the Pentagon. It was promptly relayed to President Truman on board the cruiser *Augusta,* en route from Plymouth, England, to Newport News, Virginia, after the Potsdam Conference.

At lunch in the wardroom with Leahy and Byrnes, Truman was elated over the savings in human life. He said, "This is the greatest thing in history. It's time for us to get home." Afterward, the joyful president moved through the ship, spreading word to everyone he met. Raucous cheering greeted him in every case. "Send some more of 'em over Japan and we'll all go home" was the predominant feeling from the crew, according to the ship's newsletter. "The president afterward said he had never been happier about any announcement he had ever made."

On Tinian, Parsons's prompt report left plenty of time for "the End of the War Picnic" to start before the planes returned in midafternoon. Those who had not witnessed in awe the destruction of a city with a single shot had enough cushioning distance to celebrate. On a flatbed truck with a band, ground crews danced the jitterbug with each other because there were no women around. There were pie-eating and egg-tossing contests, and a three-legged race.

All eyes turned westward as the planes returned. When the *Enola Gay* came to a stop at its hardstand, Tibbets emerged, smoking his pipe, and official ceremonies began. General Spaatz pinned him with a Distinguished Service Cross. Tibbets offered brief remarks that continued to maintain operational security: "We sighted a Japanese city and destroyed it; further details will be released from Washington."

Tokyo news broadcasts that evening were opaque. One of them announced, "A few B-29s hit Hiroshima at 8:20 A.M. August 6 and fled after dropping incendiaries and bombs. The extent of the damage is now under survey." By midafternoon of the next day a broadcast reported, "It seems that the enemy used a new type bomb."

When Foreign Minister Togo learned of the atomic bombing from the Domei News Agency, he saw the plain meaning of the stunning development and urged the cabinet that the occasion was at hand to surrender on the basis of the Potsdam Declaration, but honorably. The cabinet did not agree, and from the Imperial Army came word that it wished to postpone any decisions until it learned what had happened to the city.

The staff officer who had flown to Hiroshima from Tokyo at the behest of Imperial General Staff headquarters was struck dumb by the great cloud of smoke hanging in the bright afternoon sky a hundred miles away. His plane circled the flattened city, now a great scar on their land, and landed south of it. The officer wasted no time trying to help organize civil relief. By the time he reported back to Tokyo, the White House had already issued its public announcement.

Tibbets believed the manner in which the Japanese seemed to minimize the destruction of the city "no doubt influenced Washington's decision to authorize the use of a second atomic bomb," though that discretion now belonged to General Spaatz. In Washington, the Ultra intercepts of Japanese military radio communications were of special interest to Truman and the Pentagon. As Admiral Purnell had predicted, two bombs would be needed to force Japan to yield, but just in case, the components for a third would be delivered to Tinian by August 21. General Farrell and Deak Parsons recommended that a third bomb, if it were ordered, be dropped on the Tokyo area.

Because the size of Hiroshima's population was difficult to document amid the outflow of refugees and inflow of helping hands from adjacent towns, an accurate death count would be impossible to fix. The prefectural police counted the toll at 78,150, with another 13,983 missing. Measurement and analysis of the varied effects of the million-degree flash of heat against granite and its component minerals led to the conclusion that the bomb exploded forty-five meters south of Shima Hospital, just southeast of Aioi Bridge. The death tally would climb to 140,000, and within five years the count of fatalities traceable to the event would reach two hundred thousand, according to Richard Rhodes, though at the time no one believed that the danger of fallout from the air bursts—"persistent radiation"—could even exist.

Numbers on such a scale became abstractions, falsely precise in their ability to measure the destruction of civic, industrial, or economic capacity or to suggest its existential horror. But no group in Japan was more committed to its own inviolable illusions than Japan's military leaders. To encourage the rational move—immediate cessation of hostilities—Hap Arnold ordered his Marianas bomber command to renew leaflet-dropping operations. Radio Saipan issued broadcasts to the same effect, encouraging its Japanese audience to "make inquiry as to what happened to Hiroshima" and to "petition the emperor to end the war."

On Tinian, a bomb assembly technician named Bernard O'Keefe was well aware of the value of every day, for his command was pushing to have the second bomb ready as soon as possible:

> With the success of the Hiroshima weapon, the pressure to be ready with the much more complex implosion device became excruciating. We sliced off another day, scheduling it for August 10. Everyone felt that the sooner we could get off another mission, the more likely it was that the Japanese would feel that we had large quantities of the device and would surrender sooner. We were certain that one day saved would mean that the war would be over one day sooner. Living on that island, with planes going out every night and people dying not only in B-29s shot down, but in naval engagements all over the Pacific, we knew the importance of one day; the *Indianapolis* sinking also had a strong effect on us.

On August 9, the Fat Man implosion bomb went to war. The B-29 named *Bockscar,* piloted by Major Chuck Sweeney, took off from Tinian's North Field and flew toward its primary target, Kokura, carrying Fat Man. When heavy cloud cover forced Sweeney to reroute to the secondary target, Nagasaki, the bombardier, Kermit Beahan, narrowly managed to make the required visual drop through a heavy cloud layer. Low on fuel after these dramatic contingencies, the plane did not have legs to fly all the way back to base. Sweeney made an emergency landing on Okinawa.

The stunning double blow of fission weapons was a seismic jolt to the Japanese government. And a third blow was soon to fall. That same day, the news arrived after midnight on the ninth that Soviet forces were attacking along the entire eastern Manchurian border. War Minister Anami ordered imperial forces to "fight to the last" in this "holy war" for the "divine nation."

But at an imperial conference that started before midnight on August 9 in an underground air raid shelter next to the palace library, peace was the topic of the day. In this session, which lasted until dawn on the tenth, the usual divisions held. After Hirohito had seated himself on a chair atop a dais that stood before the two long parallel tables, Prime Minister Kantaro Suzuki ordered a reading of the Potsdam Declaration. Proceeding to review the arguments pro and con, he then asked each member of the Big Six to state his opinion.

Suzuki, Navy Minister Yonai, and Foreign Minister Shigenori Togo urged acceptance, with the one condition of preserving the imperial throne. Generals Anami and Umezu, joined by Admiral Toyoda, angrily rejected the Allied terms, insisting that any peace carry three additional caveats: Japan must endure no Allied occupation, must control its own war crimes trials, and must manage the disarmament process. Without these conditions, they said, field officers could not be counted upon to comply with a surrender order. "We still have fighting power left and cannot be said to be defeated," said Anami, the most stubborn of the dead-enders. "If the enemy lands here, it will give us a favorable chance to crush them. We are making the preparations. We must resolve to find life in death and fight the decisive battle. But if it is possible to terminate war by plan B, conditional acceptance, we shall be ready to accept it."

Umezu railed, "We cannot promise victory, but we are not yet defeated. We are aware that the war situation is difficult, but with the determination of one hundred million people and with further preparations, it might be possible to find life in death." He declared again that the Potsdam Declaration could not be accepted without the several conditions. Baron Hiranauma talked in circles, at once recounting the nation's hopeless position, crediting "above all" the impact of the atomic bombs, before suggesting that the four conditions should be pressed upon Washington.

The dissonance left Prime Minister Suzuki entirely at a loss. Faced with an irreconcilable deadlock, he did something that had never been done before. He asked the deific Japanese head of state to express his personal opinion. "Your Imperial Majesty's decision is requested as to which proposal should be adopted—the one stated by the Foreign Minister or the one containing the four conditions."

Such a direct question was a political revolution of sorts, for the personal view of the emperor held no legal force. Only by action of the cabinet could his wish become policy. As Hirohito would put it himself in January 1946, "I was given the opportunity to express my own free will for the first time without violating anybody else's authority." But there was no course left except to have Hirohito do what he and others knew should have been done months ago.

"I have given serious thought to the situation prevailing at home and abroad and have concluded that continuing the war means destruction for the nation and a prolongation of bloodshed and cruelty in the world. Those who argue for continuing the war once assured me that new battalions and supplies would be ready at Kujukurihama by June. I realize now that this cannot be fulfilled even by September. As for those who wish for one last battle here on our own soil, let me remind them of the disparity between their previous plans and what has actually taken place. I cannot bear to see my innocent people suffer any longer. Ending the war is the only way to restore world peace and to relieve the nation from the terrible distress with which it is burdened."

Many of the conferees wept openly. The emperor paused. Regaining his own composure, he continued:

> It pains me to think of those who served me so faithfully, the soldiers and sailors who have been killed or wounded in far-off battles, the families who have lost all their worldly goods—and often their lives as well—in the air raids at home. It goes without saying that it is unbearable for me to see the brave and loyal fighting men of Japan disarmed. It is equally unbearable that others who have rendered me devoted service should now be punished as instigators of the war. Nevertheless, the time has come when we must bear the unbearable. When I recall the feeling of my Imperial Grandsire, the Emperor Meiji, at the time of the Triple Intervention, I swallow my own tears and give my sanction to the proposal

to accept the Allied proclamation on the bases outlined by the Foreign Minister.

Prime Minister Suzuki announced, "His Majesty's decision should be made the decision of this conference as well." It was between three and four A.M. in Tokyo when the cabinet, in the presence of the Big Six, voted to enact Hirohito's will.

At Guam, CINCPAC communications staff were listening attentively to Radio Tokyo among other broadcasts, mindful of what the strategic air headquarters on their island had wrought upon Japan. "The effects of this avalanche of disasters was quickly apparent," the Pacific command would write. "In the succeeding hours, announcement by Radio Tokyo indicated that some extraordinary action was under consideration by the Japanese government. Domei, the official Japanese agency, announced at 0015 on 10 August that its transmitters would remain open throughout the night for 'an important announcement.'"

The announcement, when it came, was not as clear as Hirohito intended. Continuing opposition by Anami, as representative of his die-hard army, colored the surrender proposal that was beamed toward the U.S. in English by Radio Tokyo late on the tenth. Eleven hours and fifteen minutes elapsed before it reached the Allied capitals. Switzerland acted as intermediary in the transmission of the message to the United States and China, and Sweden did so for the UK.

That same night, which was August 9 in Washington, President Truman issued a radio broadcast announcing the use of the atomic bombs. "The world will note that the first atomic bomb was dropped on Hiroshima, a military base," he said.

> That was because we wished in this first attack to avoid, insofar as possible, the killing of civilians. But that attack is only a warning of things to come. If Japan does not surrender, bombs will have to be dropped on her war industries and, unfortunately, thousands of civilian lives will be lost.
>
> Having found the bomb we have used it. We have used it against those who attacked us without warning at Pearl Harbor, against those who have starved and beaten and executed American prisoners of war, against those who have abandoned all pretense of obeying international laws of warfare. We have used it in

order to shorten the agony of war, in order to save the lives of thousands and thousands of young Americans.

We shall continue to use it until we completely destroy Japan's power to make war. Only a Japanese surrender will stop us.

Thus began a five-day drama in which it was far from clear whether Japan's military commanders would cooperate or revolt against the throne. The B-29s resumed their strikes from the Marianas on the tenth, hitting the Nakajima Aircraft factory outside Tokyo. Then, concerned that the bombing would be taken as a sign that peace talks had broken down, Truman ordered the B-29s to rest.

Ironically, the Japanese government was equally determined to maintain appearances: It wished to avoid giving the public more information than it felt it could handle. The "compromise" statement written by the Information Board, as published in Japanese newspapers on August 11, contained no clear statement of capitulation. To the contrary, in fact, it exalted victories that did not occur, lamented the barbarity of America and its new bomb, and called on the people to "rise to the occasion and overcome all manner of difficulties in order to protect the national essence of their Empire."

As a refusal to obey the will of the emperor and a lawful act of the cabinet, it was a reckless act, perhaps even treasonous; no doubt such rhetoric exposed the Japanese public to the risk of another visit by the 509th Composite Group. A third atomic bomb would be ready at Tinian by around August 21. The official notice that the Japanese finally transmitted to Allied capitals did actually announce acceptance of the Potsdam Declaration, but it contained a qualifier. Acceptance was given "with the understanding that the said declaration does not comprise any demand which prejudices the prerogatives of His Majesty as a sovereign ruler."

This, of course, would not do. At 10:30 A.M. on August 11, Secretary of State James F. Byrnes saved the Japanese people from another atomic horror, drafting and pushing through channels a reply stating affirmatively that the emperor would be subservient to the Supreme Commander for the Allied Powers, who was to be General Douglas MacArthur. This proposal was transmitted to Tokyo via Berne at 1715 Washington time that same day.

On August 13 in Tokyo, the Japanese cabinet met throughout the day

Marines advance on Guam. (USMC)

War dogs supported the push into heavily defended
Orote Peninsula. (U.S. Army Signal Corps)

The U.S. conquest of the Marianas was the death knell for Japan. Before Saipan was even secure, Army aviation engineers were blasting and bulldozing coral, transforming the island into a base for the XXI Bomber Command's B-29s. They shortly did the same on Tinian and Guam. (U.S. Army Signal Corps)

After the Marianas fell, Prime Minister Hideki Tojo, architect of the Japanese war of aggression, was forced to resign.

A Navy corpsman tends to a wounded Marine. (USN)

Brig. Gen. Haywood S. Hansell, the first commander of the XXI Bomber Command, based in the Marianas, led the way to Tokyo. (USAAF)

The bomb groups tended to make the war personal. (USAAF)

Gen. Henry H. "Hap" Arnold, Army Air Forces chief of staff, exercised direct control over the new Twentieth Air Force from Washington. His ambition to strike directly at Japan helped steer the Navy to the Marianas. (USAAF)

Stepping carefully in the bomb bay of a Superfortress, an armorer sets fuzes into the tails of 500-pound bombs. (USAAF)

An airman's work was always grim, but the public relations staff tried to capture the lighter moments. Waddy's Wagon was the first B-29 back to Saipan after the inaugural strike against Tokyo from the Marianas in November 1944. The mission was a failure. (USAAF)

Japanese aircraft from Iwo Jima managed several raids against Isely Field. Here, aviation engineers brave burning fuel and exploding ammunition, using a bulldozer to save other planes on the tarmac. (USAAF)

Isely Field, circa November 1944. (USAAF)

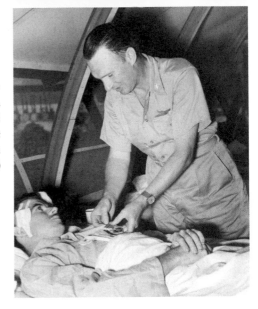

General Hansell consoles the first casualty of his command, Lt. Carl W. McKinney, a bombardier, who suffered a head wound and a broken leg during Japanese fighter attacks against his formation during the strike. (USAAF)

The view of the cockpit from the navigator's seat. Over Tokyo, a bombardier (left) takes control of the plane before release of the bombs. (USAAF)

The fast carrier task force under
Admiral Halsey completed the
destruction of the Imperial
Japanese Navy with a series
of strikes on Kure Harbor.
The battleship *Hyuga,*
the aircraft carrier *Amagi,* and
a dry-dock load of Type D midget
submarines were among the losses.
(U.S. Strategic Bombing Survey)

Maj. Gen. Curtis LeMay took over from Hansell and unleashed his bombers at low altitude, using incendiary bombs. (USAAF)

Incendiary cluster munitions fall on Yokohama, June 1945. (USAAF)

This CINCPAC propaganda leaflet depicts the destruction of a "Japanese imperial munitions factory." Written in Chinese, it warns residents of Formosa (Taiwan) about the bombing of Japanese military installations there and urges them to stay away. (USAAF)

This leaflet, dropped by Navy planes, warns: "The companion to war is disease." On the back, it tells Japanese civilians: "You must rise up and face the *gunbatsu* [military-industrial establishment] and put a stop to the senseless war." (USN)

29

Col. Paul W. Tibbets, founding commander of the 509th Composite Group, the Twentieth Air Force's atomic striking force, shown here on Tinian wearing the Distinguished Service Cross after the mission to Hiroshima. (USAAF)

The first atomic weapon, nicknamed Little Boy, destroyed Hiroshima on August 6 via a fission reaction of uranium-235. (Los Alamos National Laboratory)

The second atomic weapon, nicknamed Fat Man, destroyed Nagasaki three days later. This bomb produced a fission chain reaction using a highly complex implosive detonation of conventional charges, compressing a plutonium-239 core. (Los Alamos National Laboratory)

The flight crew of the *Enola Gay.* Bottom, left to right: Staff Sgt. George R. Caron, tail gunner; Sgt. Joseph A. Stiborik, radar operator; Staff Sgt. Wyatt E. Duzenbury, flight engineer; Pfc. Richard H. Nelson, radio operator; and Sgt. Robert H. Shumard, assistant flight engineer. Top, left to right: Maj. Thomas W. Ferebee, group bombardier; Capt. Theodore J. Van Kirk, navigator; Col. Paul W. Tibbets, group commanding officer and pilot; and Capt. Robert A. Lewis, airplane commander and copilot. (USAAF)

The atomic attack on Hiroshima. (USAAF)

Captain William S. "Deak" Parsons was the weaponeer on Tibbets's plane, the *Enola Gay,* during the Hiroshima mission. (USAAF)

The ruins of Hiroshima. At right is the Agricultural Exposition Hall, at left the remains of Shima Hospital. (U.S. Strategic Bombing Survey)

The Nagasaki blast. Before Japan surrendered, the Twentieth Air Force had plans to drop three or four atomic bombs a month on Japan. (USAAF)

Nagasaki, before and after August 9, 1945.
(U.S. Strategic Bombing Survey)

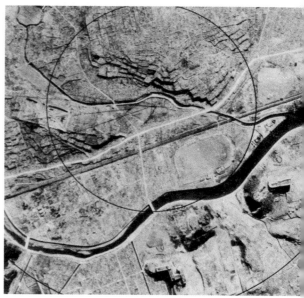

Survivors set up shanties in the shadow of the ruins of
Urakami Roman Catholic Cathedral.
(U.S. Strategic Bombing Survey)

Gen. Korechika Anami and the other hardliners on the Supreme War Direction Council preferred the destruction of their people to the shame of surrender. Even after the two atomic bombings, the Council could not agree upon acceptable terms to communicate to the United States or Russia.

Japanese prisoners of war on Guam listen to Hirohito's broadcast. (USN)

Only Emperor Hirohito, who was regarded by his people as a living god, had the power to break the deadlock. He did so on August 15, issuing an Imperial Rescript that announced his decision to surrender. He broadcast it personally over the radio to the Japanese people.

Under the guns of the battleship *Nagato,* which is powerless to stop them, U.S. Marines in assault gear land in the Tokyo area, August 30, 1945. (USN)

Pride: On December 1, 1945, assured by a Japanese flag officer on a neighboring island that the war was really over, Captain Sakae Oba surrenders his sword on Saipan.
(Time Life Pictures/Getty Images)

Shame: If the Japanese abhorrence of surrender had not been so profound, the realization that the war was lost with the fall of the Marianas— widespread within the Japanese military even in 1944—might have carried the day and saved tens of thousands of lives. (USN)

and Foreign Minister Togo conferred with the emperor. Hirohito's confidant, Kido, realized that the time had come. That morning an attendant had brought him an American propaganda leaflet that recapped the requirements of the Potsdam Declaration and urged Japanese civilians to make their voice heard once and for all. Reading it "caused me to be stricken with consternation," Kido said. "Here, such leaflets were being distributed at this juncture! If they should fall into the hands of the troops and enrage them, a military coup d'état would become inevitable." And he was right.

He urged the emperor to meet with his cabinet; only he could turn the intransigent militarists. Hirohito at once summoned Foreign Minister Togo and received him, saying, "Now that a weapon of this devastating power has been used against us, we should not let slip the opportunity. . . . Tell Prime Minister Suzuki that it is my wish that the war be ended as soon as possible on the basis of the Potsdam Declaration." Gathering his cabinet, Hirohito said, "I have listened carefully to the various views expressed in opposition, but my decision, as given previously, remains unchanged. After careful study of the world situations and conditions at home, I have arrived at the conclusion that it is pointless to continue the war any longer." He sensed, from the language of Potsdam, that the Allies were "quite sympathetic" to the importance of his throne. Kido's chief secretary actually remarked that the emperor "trusted the Allied powers and knew that they would not do away with either the nation or the people." Hirohito's decision was momentous enough to compel Anami, his onetime aide, to cast his lot with the capitulators. With this reversal by the willful army general, all opposition to surrender ended among those present, and the fifteen cabinet members signed a memorandum of decision to accept the Potsdam terms.

As American leaders and commanders endured a tense period of waiting through the night of August 13 and 14, B-29s showered major cities on all four home islands with five and a half million leaflets containing the text of the exchange of proposals and of the Potsdam Declaration and the usual urgings for the people to pressure the imperial government to capitulate. Would an invasion still be necessary in spite of the use of the bombs?

The mystifying silence persuaded Truman to lift his momentary standdown on air strikes. On the morning of the fourteenth, the B-29 campaign resumed at full strength, with more than eight hundred planes launching from the Marianas in day and night strikes against Honshu. Including the 186 fighters that escorted them, Hap Arnold could say he achieved his ambition to stage a thousand-plane raid against the Japanese capital. General

Jimmy Doolittle, newly installed on Okinawa as the Eighth Air Force transitioned to a new theater with a new airplane, was less charmed by gestures and symbols. Pushed by a subordinate to stage at least one B-29 mission against Japan before the war ended, Doolittle replied that if the war really was over, there was no need to risk a single airman's life simply to gild the record of his storied command.

At 2:49 P.M. on August 14 in Tokyo—1:49 A.M. the same day in Washington—Radio Tokyo announced that an Imperial Rescript accepting the Potsdam Declaration would be "forthcoming soon." The emperor and his cabinet anguished over the wording, but really the words used were moot. Late on the fourteenth, it came. Japan's surrender in World War II was effective, and the war in the Pacific terminated when the rescript was published that evening in the Japanese government's official gazette. Acceptance of the U.S. terms was relayed in a message to the United States via the Swiss government. Retransmitted to the U.S. State Department, it reached Foggy Bottom at 6:10 P.M. Eastern War Time in Washington. Within the hour, Truman gathered in the Oval Office with his cabinet, joined by former secretary of state Cordell Hull, to make the announcement and read the text of Japan's acceptance. The White House press corps erupted in cheers and rushed to pass the news to their employers. Truman repaired with Mrs. Truman to the fountain on the North Lawn and flashed a V sign to the large crowd, "in the manner of Churchill," the president would write. He took to a microphone and said a few words. In his memoirs he would note, "The United States, as I had stated at Berlin, wanted no territory, no reparations. Peace and happiness for all countries were the goals toward which we would work and for which we had fought. No nation in the history of the world had taken such a position in complete victory. No nation with the military power of the United States of America had been so generous to its enemies and so helpful to its friends. Maybe the teachings of the Sermon on the Mount could be put into effect."

The commander of the Pacific Fleet did not wish to risk turning the other cheek. Although Nimitz ordered all stations in his theater to stand down, his dispatch, ALPOA 579, read: "Cease offensive operations against Japanese forces. Continue search and patrols. Maintain defensive and internal security measures at highest level and beware treachery or last moment attacks by enemy forces or individuals." When this order reached Halsey, Task Force 38's five groups were at sea a hundred fifty miles southeast of Tokyo. Halsey notified his commanders of the end of hostilities, and seventy-three pilots en route to strike Honshu targets jettisoned their bombs and returned to base. The *Missouri* sounded her whistle and siren for a full minute, while all ships broke their personal and battle flags.

On August 15 in Tokyo, the air was sultry as the rains of the season lashed at the coast. People's movements were lethargic. They no longer hurried to shelters at the sound of air raid sirens. As word leaked that the Potsdam Declaration had been accepted, a small group of army officers launched an assault on the Imperial Palace, aiming to seize the recording of the Imperial Rescript, which was set to be broadcast nationwide later in the day. The palace guard successfully suppressed the revolt, however, leaving the conspirators to commit *seppuku* at the palace gate. Army Minister Anami retreated to his home, drank himself dizzy, then opened his belly and his throat with his sword. His last testament was handwritten on a scroll: "Believing firmly that our sacred land shall never perish, I—with my death—humbly apologize to the Emperor for the great crime."

All this high drama was unknown to the Japanese people. It caused no stir. Nor did the rumble of Soviet artillery and armor moving into eastern Manchuria, nor the threats that had come from the United States—most recently from a captured fighter pilot—that more atomic bombs were coming and that Tokyo would be next. What did get people's attention was news that an important radio broadcast would follow at noon.

It was the first time they had heard the divine voice of the emperor. In the Imperial Rescript that he had recorded the previous night, Hirohito professed the noblest of intentions.

He said, "We declared war on America and Britain out of Our sincere desire to ensure Japan's self-preservation and the stabilization of East Asia, it being far from Our thought either to infringe upon the sovereignty of other nations or to embark upon territorial aggrandizement."

He went on, "But now the war has lasted for nearly four years. Despite the best that has been done by everyone—the gallant fighting of military and naval forces, the diligence and assiduity of Our servants of the State and the devoted service of Our one hundred million people—the war situation has developed not necessarily to Japan's advantage, while the general trends of the world have all turned against her interest. Moreover, the enemy has begun to employ a new and most cruel bomb, the power of which to do damage is indeed incalculable, taking the toll of many innocent lives."

He asked, "Should we continue to fight, it would not only result in an ultimate collapse and obliteration of the Japanese nation, but also it would lead to the total extinction of human civilization. Such being the case, how are we to save the millions of our subjects; or to atone ourselves before the hallowed spirits of our Imperial Ancestors?"

He said, "This is the reason why We have ordered the acceptance of the provisions of the Joint Declaration of the Powers."

He concluded, "Let the entire nation continue as one family from generation to generation, ever firm in its faith of the imperishableness of its divine land, and mindful of its heavy burden of responsibilities, and the long road before it. Unite your total strength to be devoted to the construction for the future. Cultivate the ways of rectitude; foster nobility of spirit; and work with resolution so as ye may enhance the innate glory of the Imperial State and keep pace with the progress of the world."

As Tojo's enabler, Hirohito had made it possible for the Imperial Army to claim status as a sacred institution; and they had run far with that exalted status. His station and spirit had empowered their zeal. He who had endorsed and catalyzed the hemisphere-spanning race war had now risen to spare not only his country but "human civilization," he said, saving innocent lives and averting the perils of "a new and most cruel bomb." The conceit was spectacular, the pose of victimhood audacious. If even some American commanders would harbor doubts about the military necessity of the bombs, there was no questioning their practical psychological and political effect. It was by this latter score that they registered most powerfully.

The best evidence suggests that the special bombs that Tibbets's planes had delivered from Tinian were the specific causes of the emperor's change of heart. The Imperial Rescript of August 15 stated as much, and Prince Konoye, the former prime minister, confirmed it when he wrote in his diary, "In the unforeseen and unanswerable bomb, Hirohito saw a face-saving excuse for Japan's fighting men, one which could be used to ease the humiliation of defeat and smooth the pathway to surrender."

The same day that the Imperial Rescript went out from Tokyo, Brigadier General Thomas F. Farrell from Manhattan Project headquarters arrived in the Marianas to assemble a special investigating group to travel to Japan's two atomic hypocenters and assess the novel effects of the weapons. But no gamma ray detector or photo reconnaissance unit would record their impact on their hidden target. There would be no denying the sudden change of heart that gripped the intransigent war emperor as a result of the two bombs.

* * *

Planning Operation Olympic's initial landings in southeastern Kyushu with General Eichelberger's staff in Manila, Draper Kauffman had been worn thin by the strain. From sheer fatigue, the lean 175-pounder had lost fifty pounds. Handed a spot promotion to captain, he faced the burden of commanding waterborne reconnaissance operations ahead of the largest amphibious landing in history. Casualties suffered by the UDT in Normandy had been especially severe. Worse lay ahead. "It seemed to me that the best we could hope for was to lose only two-thirds of our people," he said. Planning to send thirty UDT teams into harm's way, his entire command was in the grip of profound pessimism. Kelly Turner, too, had held grave doubts. He was privy to the estimates of burgeoning Japanese defenses—nine hundred thousand troops on Kyushu, ten thousand aircraft, more than half of which were kamikazes that would strike not cruisers and battleships but troop transports while their essential cargoes were most vulnerable, at sea with their supporting vessels.

Turner had been so alarmed by Kauffman's deterioration that he decided to send him home for two weeks. Kauffman was in Washington when the bombs were dropped. "The first reaction Peggy and I had was to hightail it down to the cathedral and say just a few words of thanks." One of Kauffman's platoon leaders from Saipan, Bob Marshall, now had command of UDT 3, which was earmarked to spearhead the invasion of Kyushu. He was afloat in his APD off Oceanside, California, rehearsing the rigors of Operation Olympic, when a blitz of fireworks exploded from the Marine base ashore. When news of Japan's capitulation reached Los Alamos, all work stopped. A siren sounded and car horns blared. George Kistiakowsky returned from an impromptu booze fest at a colleague's house and celebrated as only he would: lighting off a thousand pounds of surplus charges in a field.

Across the ocean he had conquered, Spruance and his son were taking a walk on Guam. As they passed some Quonset huts, a great shout went up. Edward Spruance wrote eighteen years later to a friend, "On our inquiry, we were told that the radio had just announced the Japanese surrender. RAS expressed satisfaction, and we continued our walk with no visible signs of emotion from RAS." The Fifth Fleet commander was "thankfully elated but spoke gravely of unfinished work ahead."

PART FOUR
_____
Earth

Downtown Tokyo, August 27, 1945. (USAAF)

36

Eight Bells for an Empire

The shock wave of the war's end rolled through days and weeks, then faded. With the cessation of hostilities, the grandest invasion plan ever designed by the U.S. military underwent a transformation in character and purpose. Operation Downfall, the culminating stroke, was returned to the scabbard. Its unprecedented scheme of seaborne lift and amphibious heavy power, of bombardment by tactical aircraft and warships, of logistical sustenance, ammunition resupply, medevac and blockade, of burgeoning strategic airpower employing atomic weapons tactically to support corps-level operations by units reassigned across oceans and continents, would never be tested. But no one lamented this outcome, for the most difficult feat of all had been performed successfully from Tinian: to force upon one mortal man a fateful change of heart. With that mission accomplished, the unrivaled engine of battle known as the U.S. Pacific Fleet found that its final campaign would be a mission of mercy. After more than a year of total war, the conquerors would be occupiers.

Operation Blacklist was the code name of the vast humanitarian project that was derived from the unnecessary final reckoning. Douglas MacArthur, designated by President Truman as Supreme Commander for Allied Powers (SCAP), would preside over its complex military, logistical, and psychological mission: to bring Imperial Japan to heel for all time.

Since Saratoga and Yorktown, the American style of accepting an enemy's surrender had departed from historical practice. When Genghis Khan conquered swaths of Asia, he slaughtered the vanquished and left as a warning a mountain of skulls. Charlemagne, conquering Muslim and pagan alike, staged the beheading of thousands of prisoners in a single day. Rome, whose soldiers preferred death to surrender as fervently as did the

Japanese, were famous for ravaging conquered territory. Defeat at the hands of the people of Cicero and Seneca meant, simply, extinction. An opponent of Rome warned his countrymen on the eve of battle: "They create a desert and call it peace." Afterward the victorious Legionnaires were notorious for inflicting violent humiliation and shame. Livy described the popular ritual whereby enemy captives were lined up in order of rank and made to pass under the yoke. Taunted and mocked under brandished swords, they risked summary execution if their facial expression showed anything less than full subservience.

Japan had been made a desert of sorts, but the rebuilding began almost as soon as its militarists had capitulated. MacArthur turned to that task with a passion that could never have possessed a man of greater humility. That the project succeeded would redeem the errors that had plagued his stewardship of the war in its earliest days. Carried out by three major ground echelons, Operation Blacklist would begin in the Tokyo area and spread from there. Admiral Halsey would go in first, his Third Fleet partnered with General Eichelberger's Eighth Army (247,000 strong) in occupying the Tokyo Bay area, central Honshu, and Hokkaido. Spruance and the Fifth Fleet would shepherd the second echelon, General Krueger's Sixth Army (with 279,000 men, including three Marine divisions embarked with Vice Admiral Harry Hill's Fifth Amphibious Force), which would take western and southern Honshu, Shikoku, Kyushu, and the southern half of the Sea of Japan, in conjunction with a British Commonwealth occupation force. Vice Admiral Thomas Kinkaid's Seventh Fleet and the Army's XXIV Corps, 92,000 strong under Lieutenant General John R. Hodge, would handle Korea and China's neighboring coasts. Vice Admiral Frank Jack Fletcher, Commander, Northern Pacific, had minesweeping duties off northern Honshu and Hokkaido and would stand by to take charge of local areas ashore. The cargo planes of the Army's Far East Air Forces, assisted by the Pacific Air Transport Command, with 89,000 men, would establish an air bridge to the Japanese home islands from Okinawa. Nimitz's Pacific Fleet command on Guam would prepare to create a naval government in the Mariana, Bonin, Volcano, Izu, and Kurile islands.

The initial objective of the 707,000 men of MacArthur's combined command was to carry out the surrender, occupation, and disarmament of Japan. That mission was as sweepingly transforming as it was revolutionary: to develop in this demilitarized land a desire for liberty, representative democracy, and respect for human rights. MacArthur's ultimate purpose was to bring the character of the imperial nation into harmony with the

Charter of the United Nations, "with the authority of the militarists and the influence of militarism to be totally eliminated from her political, economic, and social life," as CINCPAC would put it.

The Navy always used the feminine: Japan in defeat was a new ship to be run. An illustration gracing the cover page of Task Force 38's final combat report depicted its last air operations against the home islands as "a clean sweepdown, fore and aft." The metaphor would apply to the larger political task as well. MacArthur's genius was to find a way to exert total control over Japan as Supreme Commander without actually administering the conquered country. The trick was to place Emperor Hirohito under his direct command, but to use the existing system of local governance to carry out his directives.

The preliminaries began late on the afternoon of August 19, when a C-54 transport plane landed at Nichols Field near Manila carrying a Japanese surrender delegation consisting of sixteen officers under Lieutenant General Torashiro Kawabe, the vice chief of the Army General Staff. At MacArthur's emphatic insistence, this aircraft was given the call letters B-A-T-A-A-N.

When the plane landed, MacArthur made sure to be elsewhere. He was "too shrewd an Orientalist to show himself," a biographer would write. MacArthur's intelligence chief, Charles Willoughby, ushered the Japanese into cars for the drive from the airfield to the general's Manila headquarters. Willoughby and Kawabe did not need an interpreter. Both spoke German.

MacArthur's chief of staff, Lieutenant General R. K. Sutherland, presented to Kawabe's delegation documents that stipulated the time and manner of the first U.S. entry into the conquered nation, guaranteed safe passage for the advance echelons, and required Japanese forces to withdraw, to immobilize and disarm all ships, planes, and tanks, and to set up communications facilities for American commanders to use. Admiral Nimitz's requirements were given to the Japanese as well: that all Japanese ships remain in harbor pending further orders; that ships at sea report their positions in plain language to the nearest Allied radio station, remove breech blocks from guns, secure main batteries pointing fore and aft, empty all torpedo tubes, and proceed to the nearest Allied port, displaying searchlights held vertically at night. Submarines were to remain surfaced, flying a black flag or pennant and showing their lights, and present themselves at Guam, Midway, or Subic Bay for boarding. Minesweepers, once disarmed, would refuel and report to CINCPAC for duty under a U.S. flag. All Japanese aircraft would be grounded, and all harbors would have their boom defenses opened, demolition charges and minefields removed, navigational lights lit, and harbor pilots ready for service, providing charts that showed all obstructions.

Two days later, Raymond Spruance arrived in Manila Harbor, flying his flag in the battleship *New Jersey* for the first time in sixteen months. At SCAP headquarters on August 21, he sat down with MacArthur, Krueger, Kelly Turner, and Harry Hill to plan landings in the Sixth Army zone of control and the evacuation of POWs from western and southern Honshu. One of Krueger's three corps was composed of the Second, Third, and Fifth Marine divisions under Harry Schmidt.

Spruance and Hill reviewed the demands they would make of Japanese harbormasters: that they vacate all shipping and prohibit movement near landing areas, reestablish aids to navigation, clear docks and piers, remove debris from all seaways, hoist out of the water and disarm the innumerable arsenals of one-man suicide torpedoes, secure large naval guns to ship decks, provide corrected charts and terrain maps, assign harbor pilots and translators, decamouflage gun positions and paint all barrels white, set up voice radio circuits for communications with commands afloat, and report on local compliance with the terms of surrender. In all of these details, the Japanese fully obeyed.

Given that U.S. aircraft had seeded home waters with more than seventeen thousand mines during Operation Starvation, it would be tricky for the box-hulled saviors of Harry Hill's alligator navy to deliver occupation troops to the beach. During the last four months of the war, U.S. mines had accounted for more than half of all Japanese shipping tonnage sunk or damaged, virtually closing major ports such as Kobe, Osaka, Shimonoseki, Fukuoka, Kure, and Nagoya. Old-fashioned mines that were moored to the sea floor were relatively easy to detect and clear, requiring two or three sweeps by a minesweeper. But clearing a waterway of the new "influence" mines, which were detonated by water pressure, magnetic fields, and acoustic signatures, required seven or eight passes in order to exhaust their "ship counters," which were used to delay the triggering of an explosion. Only American minesweepers were equipped to do the job. The one hundred surviving vessels of Japan's minesweeping force were unable to handle it.

Halsey and Eichelberger were the first into Japan with their Third Fleet / Eighth Army occupation team. On August 26, a detachment from the Eleventh Airborne Division landed at Atsugi Airfield, twenty-five miles southwest of Tokyo, to reconnoiter the area, install communications equipment, and prepare for the arrival of the rest of the division four days later. Japanese soldiers who observed their former enemy were stunned by their efficiency. "The Japanese made no attempt to conceal the degree to which they were impressed by the speed with which the Americans motorized themselves and invested the entire field area," MacArthur wrote. Within forty-five minutes, portable radio transmitters were on the air with Okinawa.

On August 27, the weather mostly fair with haze on the shore, the *Missouri,* accompanied by the destroyers *Nicholas, O'Bannon, Taylor, Stockham,* and *Waldron,* entered Sagami Wan, south of Tokyo Bay. A Royal Navy squadron led by HMS *Duke of York* followed behind. Battle colors flew and all crew stood at attention topside, which made for a spectacle and also ensured their safety against unswept mines. The passage of the Anglo-American fleet into Japan's heartland waters was announced via radio broadcast by the Task Force 38 public affairs officer, Lieutenant Commander Don Thorburn, observing from an aircraft. The *Nicholas* met a Japanese destroyer, took aboard some harbor pilots and interpreters, and delivered them as needed. A high-priority parcel was piped aboard the *Missouri.* The chamber of commerce in Reno, Nevada, had arranged delivery to Admiral Halsey, for use in a long-promised personal project, a saddle to mount on Emperor Hirohito's white horse. (Halsey never carried out the gesture.)

The next morning, the first U.S. warships entered Tokyo Bay proper. Halsey took pains to record for history the order of their passage: the destroyer-minesweepers *Ellyson, Hambleton,* and *Thomas E. Fraser,* the destroyers *Southerland* and *Twining,* the light cruiser *San Diego,* flagship of the occupation task force commander, Rear Admiral Oscar C. Badger, the destroyer transport *Gosselin,* the destroyer *Wedderburn,* and the seaplane tenders *Cumberland Sound* and *Suisun.* These ships anchored in the stream while the evacuation force, under Commodore Rodger W. Simpson, prepared to go ashore. As a seaplane from Guam landed in Tokyo Bay bearing Admiral Nimitz, who hoisted his flag in the *South Dakota,* the *Missouri* entered the anchorage to prepare for the surrender ceremony.

On the afternoon of August 29, the fleet built for conquest began its work as an engine of mercy. The cruiser *San Juan,* followed by the *Gosselin,* the destroyer *Lansdowne,* and the hospital ship *Benevolence,* entered the bay and anchored about four miles offshore. On a man-made island housing Tokyo's main prisoner of war camp, known as Omori, the appearance of landing craft provoked joyful bedlam. As landing craft neared shore, hundreds of Allied POWs streamed out of the perimeter and swarmed the pier. Some leaped into the water and tried to swim out to meet the landing craft. The camp's senior Allied officer, Commander Arthur L. Maher, USN, of the heavy cruiser *Houston,* was asked to return his men to the compound and prepare a more orderly effort. Maher informed the Third Fleet medical officer, Commodore Joel Boone, of the existence of a "hellhole of filth, disease, and death" known as Shinagawa Hospital and its satellite camp. Simpson's medical teams, aided by Third Fleet pilots, pursued the reconnaissance mission with urgency. What was known as Plan Jail Break freed fifteen hundred men from camps around the Japanese capital by the end of the following day.

As the two-hundred-fifty-ship procession into Tokyo Bay continued, a storied landing force hit the beach at Yokosuka, about thirty miles to the south. This was the reconstituted Fourth Marine Regiment, the old China Marines, which had been destroyed in 1942 on Corregidor. Simultaneously, the deep drone of aircraft engines filled southern Honshu as a large flight of Skytrains, escorted by Seventh Fleet F6Fs, delivered Major General Joseph M. Swing's Eleventh Airborne Division into Atsugi Airfield, twenty miles northwest of Yokosuka. Two weeks earlier, this facility, a major training base for kamikaze pilots, had been stirring with violent rebellion at the idea of surrender. At noon, the Eighth Army took control with the full cooperation of imperial forces. The Americans, in full combat kit, were greeted by Japanese officers and officials who looked more ready to stage a garden party than last-man resistance.

For the U.S. Navy bluejackets charged with occupying Yokosuka Naval Base, there was no greater honor than seizing as a war prize the battleship *Nagato.* The 43,000-ton behemoth had been the Combined Fleet flagship during the Pearl Harbor attack. Now she was the sole survivor of what had once been the most commanding battleship force in the world. The APD *Horace A. Bass* moored alongside her, disembarking a prize crew of ninety-one sailors from the *South Dakota* and forty-nine bomb disposal technicians. Under Captain Thomas J. Flynn, the boarding party was cordially received by the Japanese sailors, who were decidedly "salute-conscious." As Flynn noted, "It seemed almost incredible that these bowing, scraping and scared men were the same brutal, sadistic enemies who had tortured our prisoners, reports of whose plight were being received the same day." The *Nagato*'s Japanese ensign was promptly struck and the U.S. flag hoisted in its place.

The men of Underwater Demolition Teams 18 and 21 went ashore at Yokosuka to disarm shore batteries and coastal forts, evaluate piers, and demilitarize naval vessels. Alert for booby traps but finding none, they neutralized all gun batteries, removing and tossing overboard gun slides and other removable parts, burring all gear teeth, and inspecting magazines to confirm they were empty. A British landing party tended to island forts located in the channel while a battalion from the Fourth Marines handled two forts at Futtsu Saki, across the sound.

The flagship of the landing forces, the *San Diego,* docked at Yokosuka at ten thirty, delivering Admiral Badger and Halsey's chief of staff, Rear Admiral Robert B. Carney, to accept the surrender of the naval base and make it their headquarters. Brigadier General William T. Clement, who had been one of the few China Marines to escape Corregidor, was given the honor of leading the reconstituted regiment during its occupation landings. At the Japanese headquarters building, he presided over the raising of the American flag, the same one the Marines had raised after the conquest of Guam and Okinawa. Early in the afternoon, General Eichelberger arrived to take command of all area forces. A few hours later, a plane embarking MacArthur set down at Atsugi and he was taken to Yokohama to set up a temporary headquarters in the Hotel New Grand.

With the discovery of so many POW camps in the Tokyo area, the mustering of naval medical parties became an emergency operation. Working on the Yokohama waterfront, the 42nd General Hospital would handle the processing of three men a minute. In all, more than twenty-four thousand prisoners would be evacuated by the Eighth Army from central and northern Honshu. Marianas-based B-29s flew nine hundred sorties, dropping more than four thousand tons of food, clothing, and medical supplies over 158 camps. When the stock of parachutes ran low, some supplies were released in free fall, giving rise to a few tragic reports of prisoners killed by the packs.

MacArthur's tour of the Tokyo Bay area revealed a nation "near economic and industrial collapse," he observed. "Manpower alone was the only warlike resource available or potential." He inferred from the "submissiveness and apparent sincerity" of the Japanese high officials he met that the government and its highest commanders were "completely through with this war." The impulse to triumphalism, which positively filled almost every soldier's and sailor's heart, was not indulged in by MacArthur. The Supreme Commander's sense of Japanese morale was well tuned. Prime Minister Kantaro Suzuki recalled:

Calm and serene was my feeling at the time of making the surrender. People about me were much worried. Some insisted that
we should negotiate to get a definite guarantee from the Allies
regarding the preservation of our national structure. But such a
proposition seemed essentially illogical, and I did not care to go to
the trouble of taking it up. My position was this: we were defeated,
and as long as we admitted our defeat, the only manly thing to do
was to leave everything to the victor. Such had been the military
tradition from ancient times. Only I had one absolute conviction
as to what to do. That was to trust the enemy commander. The
Bushido is not a Japanese monopoly. It is a universal code. To protect your adversary who has surrendered as one enlisted on your
side is the way of the warrior. . . . As is well known, His Majesty
never inclined to suspect others. He even commanded me to con-
fide in the enemy and to place everything at his disposal.

The formal ceremony of surrender took place on the USS *Missouri* on September 2. The destroyer *Buchanan* delivered Nimitz and other Allied rep-
resentatives at 8:05 A.M. With MacArthur insisting on absolute punctuality,
the ship's company had rehearsed the transit time of the peg-legged Japanese foreign minister, Mamoru Shigemitsu, from the bottom of the forward gangway to the veranda deck, where the ceremony would take place.
Sailors took turns stuffing a broom handle down their dungarees, then
walking stiff-legged along the route while a stopwatch ticked.

At 8:56, the destroyer *Lansdowne* came alongside, delivering the eleven-
man Japanese delegation headed by Shigemitsu and General Umezu.
When he learned what his role was to be that day, Umezu, the most extreme of the militarist dead-enders, had threatened to commit hara-kiri.
"It required the emperor's personal persuasion to make him execute the
duties with good grace," said Toshikazu Kase, the secretary to the foreign
minister. Umezu survived to carry out his stunning act of acquiescence.

The Americans were dressed in their informal khakis or "suntans," col-
lars open, no neckties, ribbons, or sidearms, wearing overseas caps or regular caps at personal discretion. Having lobbied hard for a role in the
endgame, the British, serenely victorious, wore open-necked white shirts,
white shorts, no decorations, and appropriate headgear. The thirty-one-
star U.S. flag that Commodore Matthew Perry had flown on his arrival in

Tokyo Bay in 1853 hung over the door of Captain Murray's sea cabin, facing forward so as to be visible to all on the veranda deck.

At an ordinary mess table, Shigemitsu signed the surrender document for the emperor and the government, and Umezu did the same for Imperial General Staff headquarters. MacArthur and Nimitz then led ten Allied signatories in turn. "The atmosphere was frigid," Morison would write.

MacArthur knew he was smaller than this moment. "Trying to recall my emotions and impressions as I prepared to receive the surrender of the mighty warlords of the Far East," he would write,

> I wish that my pen were wielded by one on such intimate terms with words—those immortal heralds of thought which at the touch of genius become radiant—that at my call they would convey my feelings in terms that would satisfy the ultimate sources of reason, history and interpretation. For I have a consciousness that in the events culminating at this immortal moment lie those truths which at last are transplanted into epics and lyrics, and those exalted terms which we find on the lips of the great seers and prophets.

The Navy brain trust of Task Force 38 was joyous. John McCain grabbed Halsey by the arm and they danced a quick little jig, "grinning like schoolchildren."

When the short ceremony was over at 9:25, MacArthur offered a brief benediction. "Let us pray that peace be now restored to the world and that God will preserve it always. These proceedings are now closed." As the morning sun bathed the bay, the Twentieth Air Force mustered a victory flight, sending six hundred of its silver gleaming death machines over Tokyo Bay, joined by 349 carrier planes.

It seemed a fitting coda to four years of war that Raymond Spruance was not part of the proceedings. As the *Missouri* played host to the formalities of capitulation, the Fifth Fleet commander was in Okinawa. Inoculated with two shots of cholera serum, courtesy of Dr. Willcutts, he had arrived on August 30 in the *New Jersey* and remained there by Nimitz's direction. Who would be left to command the fleet, CINCPAC wondered, if the Japanese carried out a terrible new perfidy, somehow eliminating the gathering of U.S. high commanders? No doubt Spruance preferred the anonymous Spartan bustle of Buckner Bay to the festivities taking place nine hundred sixty miles to the northeast.

The ease of the initial entry into Honshu enabled MacArthur to accelerate the timetable to occupy the rest of Japan. Spruance would deliver three divisions of the Sixth Army's First Corps to Wakayama on September 25, with General Krueger to establish his area headquarters at Kyoto, the "city of ten thousand shrines." Spruance's task included deploying Japanese and American minesweepers to make possible the landings, and evacuating Allied prisoners of war from the hundreds of Japanese camps in his area. Spruance chose Sasebo-Nagasaki and Hiro Wan as the Sixth Army's other two landing sites.

To ensure safe passage through waters that had only recently been mineswept, Spruance had the idea of using "guinea pig" vessels. A brave band of sailors stepped forward to man these battle-damaged Liberty and Victory ships. Ballasted with drums of asphalt to absorb underwater blasts and reinforced below the waterline with internal bracing and plates, the guinea pigs were operated by remote control from upper decks, their skeleton crews wearing crash helmets and life jackets and further protected from blast by mattresses fastened to decks, overheads, and bulkheads. No ships from these "special sweep squadrons" were lost, but their use provided comfort to the vessels that followed.

Margaret disliked her husband's talk of "an interesting war." Well acquainted with its terrible details, she asked, "Raymond, how can you say that?"

"It was my profession and it *was* an interesting war," he always replied.

He never chased credit. It got in the way of the work. He relished the work on its own terms, tailoring a plan to a challenge. For four years there had been no shortage of challenges, and meeting them was Spruance's pleasure. Tarawa, the Marshalls, Saipan, Tinian, Guam, Iwo Jima, Okinawa, and now this, the last wartime project of the Navy's most influential technocrat.

Though they had suffered defeat after defeat through 1945, the Japanese had never confronted the Allies with the main body of their army. On scattered islands of the Pacific, through New Guinea and into the Philippines, the Allies had engaged it piecemeal. After the surrender, it retained colossal combat potential. As the chief of the Imperial General Staff informed MacArthur, two and a quarter million men remained under arms in the home islands, with millions more deployed on the Asian mainland

and in garrisons scattered across the hemisphere. The first U.S. forces to land in Japan did so "prepared equally to fight or favor," MacArthur would write. For if the madness that had enveloped Saipan or Okinawa had been activated among that massive, obedient host, what might have resulted? In the words of a leading contemporary historian, "A conventional invasion of Japan would have been no D Day; it might have been more like Stalingrad by the sea." This concern dominated the thinking of every American who had had a place in Operation Downfall.

Imagining the terror of assaulting the mountainous terrain of Kyushu or the wide Kanto Plain, given the inadequacy of roads and railways, they marveled at and thanked heaven for the impact of the bomb on Emperor Hirohito's state of mind, and for the nation's thoroughgoing subservience to MacArthur.

The horrors of the great land battle averted on Kyushu were suggested everywhere, from the sharp terrain features and terrible roads to the stockpiles of chemical gas weapons that reconnaissance parties found in hidden storage. Spruance arranged their transport to the open sea, where they were neutralized and dumped. The Japanese had produced seven million chemical munitions between 1937 and 1945 and would have had no compunctions about using them in the final battle.

On September 4, the emperor called an emergency session of the Diet. Though Hirohito did not use the Japanese word for "surrender," he confirmed that he had ordered "capitulation" and instructed the Japanese people, in MacArthur's words, "to abide by the terms of surrender and to work toward regaining the trust and faith of the world." That is exactly what they did as U.S. troops filled their defeated nation. Against all hope the Japanese populace fell in line, and nearly at once, like some kind of superorganism obeying a pheromonal cue to go dormant. The emperor's status, protected with dignity by MacArthur, made possible in turn an orderly, all-consuming surrender.

Contrary to Tojo's lies, inflicted by brute calculation upon innocents in the Marianas and elsewhere, the United States occupied Japan with its law, its organization, and its culture of accountability as surely as with its uniformed numbers. Almost everywhere the occupiers were surprised by the extent of cooperation shown by the Japanese—who were equally surprised in turn. According to MacArthur, "Japanese ideas of how their conquerors would react once Japan was occupied were based on former Japanese Army policy in the conquered Asiatic and Pacific Ocean areas. In those areas, the native populations, regardless of their own food shortage, were always expected to feed Japanese troops." And so, as the Americans arrived, prefectural authorities offered up the community's precious reserve of onions, potatoes, fruits, and meat. In every case these offers were refused. U.S. commanders explained that their own rations were adequate. On September 4, twenty truckloads of flour, oats, canned goods, and rice arrived at the municipal office in Yokosuka, relief supplies for the local people. The next day eleven more trucks brought medical supplies, blankets, tea, and other needed items. The mayor was "completely overwhelmed by this unexpected generosity," MacArthur wrote.

MacArthur understood that conquerors throughout history had erred as occupiers by succumbing to "the disease of power." As a division commander in Germany at the end of World War I, he had seen firsthand the pitfalls of an occupation that was animated by hubris and the conspicuous flashing of foreign bayonets. Emphasizing that all American soldiers were to exhibit proper dress, conduct, and courtesy and ordering his commanders to respect and protect shrines, objects of art, and historic and religious monuments, MacArthur secured almost total cooperation. The Imperial General Staff promised that its entire army would be demobilized by early October. Holland Smith's scapegoat at Saipan, the 27th Infantry Division, landed at Atsugi on September 6, followed forty-eight hours later by the Americal and First Cavalry divisions. The latter's advance echelon had the honor of being the first U.S. Army force to reach Japan's capital city.

At the American embassy, MacArthur, Halsey, and Eichelberger presided over the raising of the same flag that had flown over the U.S. Capitol on the day of the Pearl Harbor attack, over Rome on July 4, 1944, and over Berlin on July 20, 1945. On September 10, MacArthur directed Hirohito to dissolve Imperial General Staff headquarters, to be effective three days later. This broke the hold of the militarists once and for all, for many viewed the headquarters as "the hands governing the movements of the puppet emperor."

The next afternoon, in a suburb outside Tokyo, a U.S. counterintelligence team led by Major Paul Kraus knocked on the front door of a fine home situated on farmland opening in the back to an expansive view of Mount Fuji. The front yard had become an encampment for the American press.

Inside, a Kempeitai secret policeman was on duty to guard the home's occupant from Japanese assassins. Through Kraus's interpreter, the occupant said he would speak only to the man in charge. After Kraus declared himself as such, the occupant opened a window, leaned out, and said, "I am General Tojo."

The pop of a newsman's flashbulb startled and angered him, and he disappeared inside. When he appeared again, a journalist remarked, "This is beginning to look like a balcony scene from *Romeo and Juliet.*" Finally Kraus was asked to state his business. He said he was there to arrest the former prime minister. At this, Tojo vanished again. A few minutes later, from inside the house, there came a single gunshot.

Bursting in, Major Kraus, his team of five, and a surge of reporters found Tojo lying on the floor with a sucking wound in his chest. Still conscious, he pointed his .32-caliber pistol at Kraus, who said, "Drop it." Tojo moaned and his pistol fell. A reporter said, "Look at that yellow bastard. He didn't even have the guts to use a knife." One of the American soldiers, John Wilpers, secured the pistol and called for a Japanese doctor.

The collection of souvenirs began. A reporter took a cigarette case from Tojo. Another cut a piece of fabric from his riding breeches. Another, searching the room, plucked from an armchair the bullet that had torn through his chest. A few of them produced handkerchiefs and dipped them in Tojo's blood. As the former prime minister blanched, holding on to life, his wife, who had been watching from a neighbor's lawn across the street, was on her knees in grief.

As doctors were summoned to tend to him, a quick-on-his-feet reporter used the house phone to file the first dispatch about the incident. After Tojo was stabilized, he was evacuated by stretcher to a medical station in Yokohama, where General Eichelberger visited him.

"I am dying," Tojo said to Eichelberger, who had served long and well in New Guinea and in the Philippines. "I'm sorry to have given you so much trouble."

"Do you mean tonight or for the last few years?"

Tojo said, "Tonight." He went to offer Eichelberger his sword but found that the American had already taken it.

Saving Tojo's life for trial and the gallows would require a series of transfusions of type B whole blood from American GIs. Sergeant John A. Archinal of Allentown, Pennsylvania, spoke for this collective contribution to justice when he said, "I'd like to see him live so he gets his just due. It would be too easy for him to come in here and pass out comfortably." As Tojo recuperated, against his wishes, in Yokohama, his countrymen mocked him for his failure in suicide. How could he have missed his heart with the pistol shot? Before the Japanese surrender was even effective, he had gone to see his own doctor, who had marked his chest, center mass, with a pen.

Nagasaki, in spite of its hazards, had such a fine harbor that Spruance had chosen it as the evacuation port for all POWs on Kyushu. On September 12, the hospital ship *Haven* arrived in company with the cruiser *Wichita* and moored at Dejima Pier. The medical department of the two ships, under Commander Joseph Timmes, took on their primary task of rescuing thousands of Allied POWs from the surrounding area. More than nine thousand of them, mostly Dutch and British, would pass through the dockside triage center in the coming days for delousing, examination, issuance of clean clothes, and evacuation.

The hospital ship's staff did not miss the historic opportunity to study the human impact of atomic weapons. They took a keen professional and personal interest in the more than three hundred Japanese refugees who were found sheltered in a damaged schoolhouse nearby. The dying sat cross-legged against scorched walls, "holding sad little court with their families, answering their tender questions with the mild, consenting indifference of those whose future is canceled," a journalist, George Weller, wrote. "I felt pity but no remorse. The Japanese military had cured me of that."

Nagasaki had been "frizzled like a baked apple, crusted black at the open core," observed Weller, who became the first westerner to enter the city by impersonating a colonel. He eluded MacArthur's public relations staff and military police long enough to file the first dispatches, many of which would go unpublished for more than sixty years after being intercepted by censors.

Weller was struck by the stubborn manner in which life endured. "Nagasaki cannot be described as a city of the dead," he wrote. "The unquenchable Japanese will to live has asserted itself. Though the smashed streets are as barren of production or commerce as Pompeii's, yet a living stream of humanity pours along them, looking with alert, shoe-button eyes for today's main chance."

The Navy medical team had been at work for two days by the time a special detachment from the Manhattan Project arrived, led by General Farrell, to evaluate the radioactive danger. The risks of exposure were not deemed high, and neither MacArthur nor the Allies or their censors were about to allow the nature of the bomb's effects to become public in any event. What the Japanese were calling *"atombomben* disease" encompassed the diverse results of catastrophically irradiated bone marrow, including anemia, nausea, bleeding gums, anorexia, pancreatitis, and general lassitude. The effects of generalized exposure to gamma rays of this magnitude were horrific but novel and were considered important to document and understand if not publicly announce. In the first few weeks, mortality was one hundred percent, the doctors found, but it dropped to fifty in the fifth and sixth weeks. While "a comprehensive survey of the state of health of the Japanese was neither possible nor justifiable," the *Haven*'s war diary claimed, the medical team treated the *hibakusha,* as they would be known, for their symptoms, studied X-rays, collected pathological specimens, and conducted biopsies and necropsies. They noted that the mortality rate in the city would have been far lower if those who suffered from the radiation sickness had received minimally adequate care afterward. Weight loss was severe. A large-scale intervention was beyond the means of a small naval task unit and its improvisations, but the *Haven* staff made sure to provide penicillin to the infected, as well as a limited quantity of a bone-marrow-building drug, pentnucleotide, a yeast extract, which had been tested in the United States.

On the morning of September 15, the *New Jersey* brought Spruance to Wakayama. Areas struck by incendiary attacks were alien landscapes whose remaining strands of civilization produced scenes worthy of a Charles Dickens novel. Homeless people lived in streetside shanties, and bands of hungry children, known as *charinko* after the sound of clinking coins, begged, picked pockets, and bartered for subsistence. The Japanese minister of finance announced that without an urgently pursued food relief effort, ten million Japanese might starve in the coming winter. The acute need for food and clothing prompted MacArthur to allocate the entire Japanese merchant fleet—211 freighters, 21 tankers, and 101 troop transports—to serve the home islands. Basic supplies were so badly needed that the Japanese were forbidden to convert naval ships for passenger use until further notice.

Spruance joined a survey party for a tour of the countryside, still picturesque, searching the bays and hilly coasts for landing sites for his occupation troops. The beauty of the rolling green landscape impressed him, as did the people, farmers, and fishermen who appeared "stolid and emotionless," he wrote Margaret.

On September 17, as a typhoon made landfall at Wakayama, driving ships and seaplanes aground and causing several fatalities with its ninety-knot winds, MacArthur summoned Spruance to his new headquarters in the capital city. The complex encompassed the U.S. embassy, the lavish Dai-Ichi Hotel, and an office building facing the Imperial Palace. It also enjoyed a view of the Imperial Plaza, where Tokyo Rose had once pledged MacArthur would be hanged. Here now instead MacArthur discussed the repatriation of Allied prisoners of war. Spruance also caught up with his old partners in arms, Bill Halsey and Frank Jack Fletcher. The trio called on General Eichelberger, then visited Yokohama Prison. Spruance came face-to-face with several dozen potential war crimes defendants. They included Japanese cabinet officials who had overseen the start of the war, Filipino collaborators, and Lieutenant General Masaharu Homma, who was responsible for the Bataan Death March. One man in particular appalled Spruance: Josef Albert Meisinger, the Gestapo's liaison to the Japanese secret police. Known as "the butcher of Warsaw" before his transfer to Tokyo, he had tried to persuade the Japanese to exterminate twenty thousand Jews living in Shanghai. "He was a fat slob and bully," Spruance wrote Margaret, "whose morale was completely shattered and whose execution will rid the earth of vermin."

In January 1946, consistent with the Potsdam Declaration, MacArthur would establish the International Military Tribunal for the Far East to deal with Meisinger and his like. Spruance relished the idea of justice and had confidence in MacArthur to deliver it.

> When he gets Japan thoroughly under control, I think those responsible for the maltreatment of our POWs will get what is coming to them. That cleanup should start with those involved in the prison camps, and go back up through the chain of command until we have gotten all those in responsible positions who, at least, condoned, if they did not order, what went on. By this means we should be able to eliminate a lot of the worst Japanese militarists. I believe a lot of the common people in Japan will view such a cleanup with no great sorrow or anger.

Sickened though he was by his encounter with the Nazi, Spruance was enough of a realist to wonder what his or any American officer's fate might have been if the war had gone the other way. But the cause had been just; the enemy had been exorbitant.

Spruance's temper would never become stoked hotter than this. He "never hated them," his daughter said. "He admired them. I think that's why he fought them so well." Having run a heavy squadron around his enemy's greatest base, he restrained himself off Saipan when an even greater bid for glory was offered, keeping the combat fleet near the landing force. Having poured fire on Tinian, he refrained from spreading poison gas at Iwo Jima, rounded up the enemy's stockpiles on Kyushu, and sent doctors to save the sick and irradiated at ground zero. His beloved *Indianapolis,* hit by a kamikaze, then hit again by torpedoes and sunk, drowning most of a crew whom he had come to know—even this did not turn him. When the madness had come diving on him again, tearing up the *New Mexico* at Okinawa, he did what duty required, manning a hose. He was not immune to flashes of vindictive relish. The death of Admiral Chuichi Nagumo, his Midway foe, pleased him, but as his daughter saw it, "He tried to think as they would think, and he tried to understand them." That irrational beast, hatred, had no hold on Spruance, not ever.

Having seen the prisoners at Yokohama, Spruance seemed to allow his puritanism to soften, for vices are relative. While in Yokosuka, he and his staff met with the mayor to discuss the issue of prostitution. As far as the Japanese and even MacArthur were concerned, it was not a terrible problem. The Japanese Home Ministry had ordered local police in Tokyo to set up "comfort facilities" in order to contain the urges of the occupiers and reduce the risk of rape. Many of the young women who entered that line of work had lost their homes in firebombing raids and engaged in this highly personal entrepreneurship out of a sense of duty to provide for the well-being of their families. Some would see these women, by their enterprise and initiative, as having delivered a rebuke to the overthrown old order, whose strictures had kept them in a socioeconomic straitjacket. Outside Tokyo, at a brothel known as the International Palace, they worked on such an efficient, quasi-industrial scale that U.S. servicemen took to calling it Willow Run, after the giant Ford aircraft factory in Michigan.

Through an interpreter, Dr. Willcutts spoke to some of the workers there, explaining the benefits of contraceptives and medications to prevent disease. "Everything was working according to plan," Cy Huie, Spruance's flag secretary, wrote. "The rate of venereal infection was low, reports of drunkenness and rape at a minimum, the shore patrol having no difficulty, and the men were happy." That is, until a chaplain complained to his congressman that prostitution was being sanctioned by the U.S. Navy. Under pressure, Admiral King shut it all down in the two areas that were under permanent naval jurisdiction, Yokohama and Sasebo. "The house closed, crime and V.D. rates climbed, and that was the end of that," Huie wrote. But everywhere else, MacArthur let the good times roll. "They keep trying to get me to stop all this Madame Butterflying around," he said. "I won't do it. . . . I wouldn't issue a nonfraternization order for all the tea in China."

The incipient social revolution was the byproduct of a teeming, traumatized society adjusting to dizzying change, from the nihilism of total war to a merciful, rehabilitative peace. As imperial thinking was extracted root and branch, black markets opened for all things urgently wanted and consumable. Political prisoners were freed, the secret police dissolved, Shintoism separated from the state. The emperor renounced his divinity. Women were given the vote. Trade unions were legalized. And so a liberalized future began to rise from the ruins, within mere weeks of the finale of Japan's Ragnarök and the Greater East Asia Co-Prosperity Sphere's catastrophic end of days.

On the night of September 17, the commander of the Royal Navy's Pacific carrier task group, Vice Admiral Sir Bernard Rawlings, hosted a boisterous party for Spruance and Halsey on board HMS *King George V*. "It was quite a celebration," Spruance recalled, "and, as Bill was having a thoroughly good time and feeling no pain whatever, it was 1:30 A.M. before we got back to our ships." The therapy for Halsey's hangover in the morning was a visit with MacArthur in Tokyo. It was mercifully brief. With his part in the occupation done, Halsey got orders to return stateside. "Mrs. MacArthur was arriving by plane from Manila shortly, so we had a few minutes of interesting conversation before the general had to leave to meet her," Spruance wrote.

The next night, a farewell celebration for Halsey and his departing staff, held at Yokosuka Navy Yard, ran long past the midnight hour. Spruance turned in early. "I judge that the party lasted well into the night, with Bill the life of the party and again feeling no pain." The next afternoon, Halsey boarded a plane to begin the long series of hops back to Hawaii, and Spruance toured the antiquated battleship *Mikasa*. It was a touchstone to his career. As a young officer in 1908, Spruance had visited the ship while the officer whom he would so admire, Admiral Togo, was still in command. With Halsey's departure, Nimitz gave Spruance command of all U.S. naval forces in Empire waters. He was in the end responsible for the repatriation of more than eleven thousand Allied POWs from Japanese camps in the Sixth Army area.

After the Fifth Marine Division landed at Sasebo, Kyushu, the commander of the amphibious task force, Rear Admiral Morton L. Deyo, went ashore and examined the disorderly, congested facility, littered with scrap and junk. "The question which was uppermost in the minds of our officers after inspecting Sasebo Naval Base," he noted,

> was how it had been possible for the Japanese to do as well as they did with the primitive and meager tools and equipment available. They have no conception of quantity production methods nor up-to-date production. They are indeed very efficient in doing things with their hands, and they contrive astonishing results with handwork performed in long hours of toil. They are years behind in industrial organization, equipment, and methods. . . .
>
> Here as well as in all other areas of Japan, their characteristic of hiding material in dispersed caves and dugouts was apparent. Countless man-hours of labor were expended in hiding away all manner of equipment. This was often badly done with perishable material in wet caves, which appeared to indicate the state of mind of the Japanese in the latter part of the war.
>
> While there were some exceptions, the general impression was that we had considerably overrated the Japanese ability to produce up-to-date war equipment, and that we should have had less trouble with them than we did. It would appear that only their great personal bravery and willingness to sacrifice everything for their emperor, plus the vast distances our forces had to come, made it possible for them to carry on as long and as effectively as they did.

The next day, two regiments of the Second Marine Division landed at Nagasaki, while the APD *Ira Jeffrey* delivered the frogmen of Underwater Demolition Team 3 to the shoreline of Wakayama, leading the way for the 33rd Infantry Division. Sidestroking toward the beach in preassault fashion, Bob Marshall, the unit's commander and a veteran of Saipan, conducted string reconnaissance ahead of the landings. Going ashore, Marshall encountered a party of several dozen people dressed up in formal finery, top hats and suits. These were the mayor and his entourage. The Navy frogmen didn't have to paint the welcome signs this time around. "Welcome to Wakayama," their hosts declared, and invited them to a garden party.

The Japanese home army, two and a quarter million strong on August 15, disbanded at a rate of fifty thousand men a day until October 15, when all of the Imperial Japanese Army's combat units were declared formally dissolved. Some eighty thousand men would remain in uniform to serve as "liaison personnel for demobilization," but none of them would carry a gun. As CINCPAC wrote, "The Japanese Army as such had ceased to exist. This marked the culmination of one of the greatest mass surrenders in history, involving the laying down of their arms by some seven million Japanese troops, including those in outlying theaters of the Pacific and Indian oceans, within a period of only six weeks."

The demilitarization went so well that MacArthur would announce a reduction of the size of the occupation force from four hundred thousand to two hundred thousand Army troops within six months. After Japan's War and Naval ministries were abolished on October 16, General Umezu, the last Army Chief of Staff, testified directly to the extent of the effort. He reported to the Imperial Diet that there had been not only a disarmament of troops but "a disarming of the fighting spirit." When asked about possible secret designs of the members of his ousted clique, Umezu answered that the Japanese Army would not be kept alive by "any clandestine organization" and that the people would "attempt to regain the respect for Japan in a new peaceful world."

MacArthur's proposal to send half the occupation force home had met with a negative reaction stateside, with some of the press suggesting it was more about public relations than public safety. The War Department, already struggling with the task of repatriating its victorious armies amid public clamor to do so as quickly as possible, did not relish the additional burden of people to bring home. The political pressure could be heard in the speech MacArthur gave in Tokyo on October 16. In his characterization of a trembling Japanese populace and the "retribution" that was delivered by Allied forces, he distorted the nature of his achievement. The Supreme Commander was playing to critics back home who felt the occupation was taking too long, and that his manner with the former enemy was too soft.

MacArthur said,

> I know of no demobilization in history, either in war or in peace, by our own or by any other country, that has been accomplished so rapidly or so frictionlessly. Everything military, naval, or air is forbidden in Japan.
>
> This ends its military might and its military influence in inter-

national affairs. It no longer reckons as a world power either large or small. Its path in the future, if it is to survive, must be confined to the ways of peace.... In the accomplishment of the extraordinarily difficult and dangerous surrender in Japan, unique in the annals of history, not a shot was necessary, not even a drop of Allied blood was shed. The vindication of the great decision of Potsdam is complete.

Nothing could exceed the abjectness, the humiliation and finality of this surrender. It is not only physically thorough, but has been equally destructive on Japanese spirit. From swagger and arrogance, the former Japanese military have passed to servility and fear. They are thoroughly beaten and cowed and tremble before the terrible retribution the surrender terms impose upon their country in punishment for its great sins....

Again, I wish to pay tribute to the magnificent conduct of our troops. With few exceptions, they could well be taken as a model for all time as a conquering army. Historians in later years, when passions cool, can arraign their conduct. They could so easily—and understandably—have emulated the ruthlessness which their enemy have freely practiced when conditions were reversed, but their perfect balance between their implacable firmness of duty on the one hand and resolute restraint from cruelness and brutality on the other, has taught a lesson to the Japanese civil population that is startling in its impact.

Nothing has tended to impress Japanese thought—not even the catastrophic fact of military defeat itself. They have for the first time seen the free man's way of life in actual action and it has stunned them into new thoughts and ideas.

37

The War Wearies

The great Asian war, like a whirlwind, had scattered a polyglot diaspora of refugees all across the hemisphere. In Japan proper, more than a million foreign nationals, predominantly Koreans, Chinese, Formosans, and Ryukyuans, had languished as prisoners and slaves. Flocking to ports seeking to return home, they posed a serious public health challenge to the occupiers, whose duty it was to maintain their safety while waiting for the chance to repatriate them.

After freeing starving Allied POWs from captivity in Japan and tending to the broader crisis of Japan itself, the engine of American humanitarianism turned to the problems of refugees farther afield. There were 6.7 million Japanese nationals—combatants and civilians alike—to bring home from the Pacific area, more than half of these in China and Manchuria, plus another 936,000 from Soviet-controlled areas. Hundreds of thousands more languished in garrisons all across the Pacific. Priority was given to repatriating experienced Japanese coal miners, for a shortage of skilled labor foretold another crisis with the approach of the bitter winter. Potsdam had been a contract, and America turned to its duty, delivering mercy on a mass scale to its enemies of the season just past.

At the end of September, Admiral Spruance stood up the Japanese Repatriation Group under Rear Admiral Donald B. Beary. The commander of an underway replenishment group, Service Squadron Six, Beary was a master logistician. He controlled not only more than a hundred fifty LSTs and Liberty ships, but the entire Japanese merchant marine as well. Armed detachments traveled from island to island in destroyer escorts, bringing in Japanese and conducting spot interrogations with an eye toward locating Allied personnel held prisoner. If evidence of war crimes was found, the

Japanese in question would be detained for interrogation by higher authority, their names and ranks referred to MacArthur's headquarters for possible arrest. At its peak, the repatriation campaign returned 193,000 people a week to the home islands.

The surrender of Japan's major bases took place in some instances simultaneously with the surrender ceremony in Tokyo Bay. Truk was one such case. The naval commander of the Marianas area, Rear Admiral George D. Murray, received the stronghold's surrender delegation on board his flagship, the heavy cruiser *Portland*. With the capitulation of the Japanese on all of the islands within Truk's administrative sphere, more than 130,000 personnel in the Carolines, including 49,000 troops on Truk itself, had to be taken home. Malnutrition was rife. Bugs and worms had ravaged the sweet potato crop. "Rank upon rank of living scarecrows lined up along the route of the inspecting party—men with ankles as thin as skinny wrists, with sunken cheeks, and with every rib showing sharply," CINCPAC reported.

Grim stories emerged from the emperor's far-flung bastions. On Mille Island in the Marshalls, the first Central Pacific base to capitulate after issuance of the Imperial Rescript, the garrison of five thousand was down fifty percent, winnowed by air attack and illness, but mostly by starvation. On Woleai in the Carolines, two-thirds of the 6,500-man garrison were dead of starvation, and another five hundred had been killed during air raids. On Rota in the Marianas, 2,600 Japanese troops and fully double that number of civilians were found subsisting by fishing and farming, sheltering in caves under the overhanging cliffs. A landing force of Marines and Seabees rebuilt the airfield and set up an airlink to Guam to send them home.

It was in December that Captain Sakae Oba at last understood that his time had come. Having narrowly evaded capture in November, he had led a fifty-one-man platoon through a harrowing stretch of escape, evasion, and selective raiding. In the end, he got more than he bargained for against a platoon from K Company, Third Battalion, Second Marines. When Oba's group was ambushed by the Americans, not even Horiuchi could save them. In a sharp firefight along a trail leading to their hidden hilltop encampment in a place Oba called Gakeyama, a dozen of Oba's group fell. Horiuchi led seven other Japanese soldiers in a direct assault on an American heavy weapons position, but the K/3/2 responded as a veteran unit of the tangle would. Horiuchi, charging into the open, was killed in crossfire from some twenty Marines.

Captain Oba and his survivors retreated into the hills. His pride had never tempted him to court a symbolic death, but led him to hang on and endure, humbly praying for deliverance. The death of the *yakuza* shook him. *It was over. He had lost. Japan had lost. Even the seemingly invincible Horiuchi had lost.* One of his officers jerked him back to his senses and led him up the slope to Gakeyama. Oba turned the last page in the chronicle of his war when a single-engine plane flew over his position, showering leaflets that settled in trees and fell to the blood-rich earth.

"The war is over!" they read in Japanese.

He had seen no American patrols for a week but still considered it a trick. Rumors had come of the fall of Iwo Jima, of a terrible new bomb, and even of a surrender. But Oba needed proof.

Through civilian friends in the encampment at Charan Kanoa, he exchanged communications with the American headquarters. It was arranged for a garrison commander on a small bypassed island in the Marianas, Pakanto, to write him a letter. Signed by Brigadier General Ano Umahachi, it was delivered to Oba with ceremonial formality by the civilians. Confirming all the rumors, the letter buckled the castaway officer to his knees.

On December 1, 1945, Sakae Oba and and his band marched down from the ridges of Mount Tapotchau. In two ranks, singing lustily, they stopped in front of a thunderstruck assembly of American troops and laid down their arms. Major Herman Lewis of the Second Marine Division walked forward and stopped one stride from the Japanese leader. Oba drew his sword from its scabbard with his left hand and pulled the hilt to his forehead in salute. Then he handed the sword to Lewis, who accepted it with both hands.

The Japanese aircraft carrier *Hosho* evacuated two thousand Japanese from Wotje, Maloelap, and Jaluit in the Marshalls. With the removal of twelve thousand Japanese military and civilians from Ponape two days before Christmas, the repatriation effort in the Marshalls-Gilberts area was complete, and the area merged with Admiral Murray's Marianas command. By January 10, 1946, the process of shipping home the eighty thousand Japanese nationals in the Marianas began.

In every case, the departure of the Empire left a void to be filled by native hands and hearts. The temporary U.S. naval government tried to "inspire the natives with interest and initiative in their own welfare and administration," handing power to local native councils and police, opening schools, and even preparing textbooks written in the local vernacular. On Majuro and Roi, schools were established to train native citizens as medics and nurses. Naval officers collaborated with them in distributing food, rebuilding cisterns, and salvaging lumber, canoes, cement, canvas, cooking utensils, and clothing.

Shizuko Miura was among the last of the Japanese to make the homeward passage from Saipan. Nursed back to health, she nursed everyone else in turn. She had been so zealous about her duties that she ended up facing charges of petty thievery for stealing supplies. The happy consequence of her appearance before the U.S. Summary Provost Court had been meeting her Japanese interpreter, Isami Sugano, whom she fell in love with and married.

When the radio had carried the emperor's rescript, she could not hear his words. But they reverberated all through camp. A Japanese man she knew, a Mr. Kuwano, had declared in a workshop the next day that yes, Japan had been defeated. For his candor he was set upon and beaten to death by loyalist dead-enders, murdered for having the courage to speak those words. According to Shizuko, "It was whispered by the people in the camp that it was only natural for him to be killed." Feeling this way, she was none too pleased when her husband was pressed into service to join an American reconnaissance party that traveled to neighboring islands to pass word of the surrender. She said nothing of his mission out of fear for his life. When he returned, he talked of it to no one but her. A purge had begun: of ideas, of history, of people, of spurious claims of the powerful. On New Year's Day 1946, Emperor Hirohito renounced his divinity.

Shizuko was instructed to write to relatives back home and make arrangements for a place to live in Japan. Were her parents and sisters, who had been living on Tinian, even alive? The family had been in the Marianas so long, who would even remember her? Her best bet was to contact a Buddhist temple in a town in Yamagata Prefecture, where her uncle was a member of the clergy. She decided to return there.

Taken to Garapan harbor and shown to an American ship, she was struck by the town's utterly alien appearance. It was swollen with new buildings and buzzing with activity. She was quickly underway as part of a convoy. As her ship cleared the harbor, an escorting Japanese destroyer sounded its horn and the American freighters answered in unison. Turning to look at the island for one last time, she beheld Mount Tapotchau and said farewell to her patients, the soldiers, and the honorable dead, including her brother, who had come there to stay.

The next mountain she saw was Fujiyama. The sight of the sacred peak, draped in white snow, took her breath away. She returned to experience a series of miracles. Her uncle's Buddhist temple in Yamagata was now a refugee camp for schoolchildren displaced by the war. On March 21, she arrived there to discover, among the evacuees in residence, her very own sister, Toeko. Shizuko knew Toeko had left the Marianas on board a freighter, and that subsequently several freighters had been reported sunk. Her spirits swelling, they embraced. Her sister had a story to tell. Her freighter had indeed been sunk, but the attack occurred close enough to Japan that rescue was possible. Another ship pulled her from the sea. Afterward, she had the same impulse Shizuko had, and sought out her uncle's temple.

While her husband went to see his family in Fukushima, north of Tokyo, Shizuko visited the capital with Toeko, who was active in the black market. She and Toeko stayed in Tokyo for a few days, talking about the things they had seen in the war, the people they had known. Along the way Shizuko went to the head office of her former employer, the South Seas Trading Company, where she was given a check for her retirement allowance, one thousand yen, which nicely supplemented the four hundred yen she had saved from her earnings in camp on Saipan. That very day, however, street criminals mugged her, taking all the money.

But for Shizuko, the return home did not end up being about loss. It was after she returned to her uncle's temple in Yamagata that she learned, to her astonishment, that she was pregnant. As she awaited the return of her husband from Fukushima, she took up a peaceful residence among the monks. In a room with a fire burning in the hearth, she was cared for by her aunt and uncle, who fed her generously with rice porridge flavored with miso and slices of radish. In time her aunt learned that Toeko was working on the black market. Deeply displeased and suspecting Shizuko of doing the same, her aunt threatened to cast them out.

On May 4, 1946, Toeko and Shizuko experienced the greatest miracle of all. The yearly pilgrimage to the three sacred mountains was under way in Yamagata and the two sisters were enjoying the cherry blossoms when they noticed, walking across a bridge ahead of them, two other girls about their age. Shizuko was accommodating her pregnancy by wearing oversized clothing, U.S. Army trousers courtesy of MacArthur's occupiers. These other girls were similarly dressed and carrying American military-issue rucksacks. On the back of the rucks, strips of white cloth had been sewn. Drawing closer, Shizuko saw the name on the strips: Miura. These were her sisters. Her parents were with them. Their reunion was joyous, and the story they told profound.

Of course, their ordeal on Tinian had been an all too familiar one, though it lacked the typically calamitous ending. Fleeing bombardment, her parents and three sisters had taken refuge in a cave. It wasn't long before the cave came under assault. A series of detonations left them concussed and badly wounded. Shizuko's parents were carrying the bloodied bodies of their daughters out of the cave, determined to take their own lives in a final leap into the sea, when they were confronted by an American tank. Shizuko's mother shouted at the steel monster to kill them. Then a man, a Nisei interpreter, came forward speaking soothing words. Taking her by the hand, he led her to a jeep. Two of her three girls were still alive, but Toshiko might not make it. Her stomach had been opened by the blast. Her mother stripped herself naked and tied her loincloth around Toshiko's belly to hold her entrails in place. American combat medics took her in and kept her alive. And in the end, the repatriation effort delivered them home, among the last of those to return from their island. It was on the day after this reunion that Shizuko went into labor, giving birth to a daughter.

The scars of such a war would never fade from the earth. A survivor of the group suicides on Okinawa, Shigeaki Kinjo, who had been compelled to turn against her mother, brother, and sister, said,

> The coming of peace meant a return to a normal mentality from an abnormal psychological state. But the more I recovered my normal mind, the more strongly the abnormal came back to me. I began to experience indescribable internal torment. I was still a child, remember. I didn't have the mental strength to criticize the state ideology or really think about what group suicide was. All I had were doubts about why my family—my mother, my brother, my sister—had to meet such violent deaths. . . . It took me more than twenty years before I could speak in public about group suicide. Most of the islands still would prefer to forget. I understand their pain.

But after all that Shizuko Miura had gone through on Saipan, it was a sublime deliverance to return bearing life from the island of death.

* * *

By the end of 1946, the U.S. Navy had completed the mass repatriation of Japanese from the Pacific Ocean Areas, about 5.1 million souls in all. Some 1.3 million more, however, remained in Soviet custody. MacArthur would respond in fury when Stalin indicated he would renege on promises to send all of them home. The Soviets would finally hold 469,000 Japanese as slave laborers. The commissars favored keeping the young, for they tended to be more receptive to political indoctrination. According to MacArthur, the Soviets made no attempt to justify these actions in the eyes of the world. He wrote, "Their repatriation policies should have demonstrated to the peoples of the Far East what international communism really holds for them."

On Tinian, the agents of the A-bomb stood down only after it was clear there was no need to use a third weapon against Japan. Norman Ramsey and his technical group left two weeks and a day after the surrender ceremony on the *Missouri,* boxing up and shipping home key components of plutonium bombs and dumping leftover electronics and parts into the sea. The bomb laboratory was ordered to be kept intact for six months, but it was not that long before the vines began to reclaim it.

A large contingent from the 509th Composite Group returned to the States on board the attack transport USS *Deuel* after seeing to the completion of Operation Magic Carpet, the project to repatriate U.S. combat veterans worldwide. Arriving in San Francisco on November 4, Tibbets's men felt a surge of excitement as they passed under the Golden Gate Bridge. People waving from the railing could not guess at whom they waved, or at the magnitude of their accomplishment. A troop train carried them to a week of idleness and recreation at the Army Air Forces base at Roswell, New Mexico, where they awaited discharge.

To ferry its people home from the Marianas, the Army Air Forces tended to assign B-29s that were no longer fit for the flight line. Known as "war wearies," these planes had engines that had run well beyond their service lives. The war weary that brought David Braden home pushed the luck of its crew and passengers, losing an engine between Saipan and Kwajalein, another between Kwajalein and Oahu, and a third between Oahu and San Francisco.

"My bombardier on my second crew was a superstitious guy," Braden said.

We had a mission where we were carrying someone from group or wing headquarters with us, making thirteen on the plane. He wouldn't fly! He just refused to fly because there were thirteen people on the plane. So they said, "Okay, that's all right." He flew all of the rest, but he was one mission behind us. We had thirty-five, and he had thirty-four. He had to fly another mission before he was sent home on a war weary.

That plane crashed five hundred miles off San Francisco, and he died.

Flying over the Grand Canyon, Braden wondered, "What am I going to do with the rest of my life now that I know I'm going to have one?" By the time they landed at Tinker Field in Oklahoma, their own plane was three-quarters powered by brand-new Wright R-3350s.

The wear and tear on the airmen was less easily serviceable. After the war, "Our aircraft commander decided not to live long," Hap Halloran said.

"He took his own life?" an interviewer asked.

"He did not live long after he came home."

It seemed appropriate, given the range of his accomplishments, that Raymond Spruance stood as the supreme Allied naval commander in Japanese territorial waters after the war was over. By the end of 1945, he had yielded his flag as commander of the Fifth Fleet to his longtime detractor and rival, Vice Admiral John H. Towers. A few weeks later came the reward. When Nimitz went to Washington to become Chief of Naval Operations, he saw to it that Spruance was elevated to commander in chief of the Pacific Fleet and of Pacific Ocean Areas. Towers had wanted that job. Spruance would have been content to let him have it, but Nimitz would not hear of that. "He wanted Raymond to be his relief," Margaret said. He considered no candidate but one, and so Spruance relieved Nimitz as CINCPAC/CINCPOA on Thanksgiving weekend 1945. One of Spruance's first acts as Nimitz's successor was to permit the Japanese to resume hunting whales and seals in the Bonin Islands, in order to help alleviate the winter food shortage.

That Spruance never got a fifth star, thereby finishing his wartime career inferior in rank to his inferior in merit, William F. Halsey, is just as he would have had it, for Spruance's ego would have drawn nothing essential from the honorific "Fleet Admiral Spruance," or from the pomp and circumstance and lens-shoving photographers it would have attracted. Though Nimitz would lobby the House Armed Services Committee through the 1950s to grant him a fifth star, Spruance did not act on his own behalf, content, it seemed, for a quorum of the well-informed to consider him the most acutely competent operational naval commander of the war. In June 1948, Spruance wrote King, "The fourth five-star promotion went where it belonged when Bill Halsey got it, and I never had any illusions about Congress ever creating a fifth vacancy. I have always felt that I was most fortunate in being entrusted with the command of the operations that I had during the war, and their successful outcome was ample reward in itself." But King's evaluation of Spruance as the most intelligent officer in the Navy survived, unrebutted by events.

America's future in the Pacific continued to take shape on Spruance's watch. On the fourth anniversary of the Pearl Harbor attack, the Army Air Forces stood up the Pacific Air Command, with General George Churchill Kenney commanding. Strategic airpower in the theater henceforth had one name. Into its fold, headquartered at Hickam Field, came Kenney's Far East Air Forces, including the Fifth, Seventh, and Thirteenth air forces as well as the Twentieth and Eighth. Two days later, the Fifth Amphibious Corps was released for reembarkation to the States, given to the control of Spruance as CINCPAC. On December 15, Chester Nimitz relieved Ernest King as Chief of Naval Operations, at King's request. On New Year's Day, the U.S. Treasury Department resumed control of the Coast Guard, which had been on loan to the Navy Department since the war began.

At Pearl Harbor, Dr. Willcutts continued his service to Spruance as CINCPAC fleet surgeon. "We again enjoyed daily walks, usually early morning before breakfast. The admiral conversed freely. Time and again he spoke of the Navy's great war effort in the Pacific. He was proud of his Fifth Fleet. He expressed no regrets except for the loss of so many gallant men. He acknowledged with great respect the desperate and courageous fighting caliber of the Japanese. And again he would repeat his great desire to be assigned to the Naval War College at Newport."

Assignments to professional schools ashore were typically boxes to be checked en route to higher sea commands and better pay grades. But Spruance's interest in returning to Newport was intrinsic to the station itself. He was looking to recapture something, to finish turning a circle far larger than the one he had inscribed around Truk. It would be a return to the good old days when he and Kelly Turner were coming of age, ambitious senior instructors rewriting manuals and running war games, applying fire and ice to students who vied with them and challenged them, when they and their wives were young and the two men could carry on like brothers and uncles. Named president of that institution in March 1946, Spruance would devise to improve its focus on strategy, operations, and logistics. He cherished it as a place where the study of naval affairs was more than the vocational or technical trade that he had been offered at the Naval Academy. "There," Spruance said quietly to his physician, "I can review and study the great battles of the entire war. Let history record the victories, the defeats and mistakes." It had been, indeed, an interesting war.

Postwar, Holland Smith continued to be an embittered man. He wrote three articles for *The Saturday Evening Post,* airing complaints large and small. "I'm sorry he saw fit to cut loose like that," Spruance wrote to Carl Moore, his former chief of staff, in 1948. "However, I am not going to engage in any controversies with him." Media accounts of Ralph Smith's relief at Saipan fed the old controversy. Battle lines formed, with the correspondent Robert Sherrod carrying water for the Marine Corps in *Time* and General Griner rebutting him in the Army publication *Infantry Journal.* In his tendentious memoir, Holland Smith threw gasoline on the fire and sullied his own reputation as an honest broker in the process. As the controversy stretched into 1949, General Marshall himself ordered his principals to stand down.

Draper Kauffman headed the UDT training command at the amphibious training base at Coronado after the war's end. Some leaders in the Marine Corps felt strongly that the frogmen should be folded into the Corps. That argument was settled in favor of leaving the frogmen in the Navy. But one Marine made history along the way. Gordon Leslie, who served with Team Five at Saipan and Tinian, stayed with the team through Leyte and ended the war as its executive officer. Somewhere the Marine Corps lost track of him. Leslie never drew a dime of pay for the better part of 1944 and was unaware that he had been promoted twice. When Kauffman learned this, he realized he had to get his man back into good standing with the Marines at a proper pay grade. But people at headquarters seemed horrified by the slipup, fearing the consequences of processing the return of their lost man. "Then Gordon made it even worse," Kauffman said. "He put in a request for transfer from the USMC reserve to the regular Navy, and he was informed very positively that no Marine had ever requested transfer to the regular Navy. It was absolutely unbelievable that any Marine would think of doing such a thing." Kauffman went to Holland Smith, who handed the case to several colonels in turn, each with instructions to deprogram the poor Marine of his brainwashing at the hands of the UDT. But Leslie did not relent, and the transfer went through.

When Gordon Leslie finally got his back pay, he went to the manager of the Hotel del Coronado, the finest hotel on the Silver Strand, and offered him the money, and said, "I want to give a party, and it's up to you to end the party before the four thousand dollars is spent, because that's all I'm going to give you." He rented a whole floor of suites and invited all his teammates. As far as Kauffman could tell, the revelers subsisted for thirteen days on nothing more than brandy milk punch. At that point, his earnings from the liberation of the Western Pacific were presumably gone, and the story ended well, as the hotel did not burn down.

The Navy's accidental bombsmith soon got into the business of the atomic bomb. Idling in Coronado, Draper Kauffman saw a newspaper article indicating that Admiral Blandy, his father's old friend, was standing up a joint task force to test atomic weapons at Bikini. The project was known as Operation Crossroads, the first major scientific and battlefield test of a fission bomb. Kauffman wrote to Blandy and secured an assignment as radiation safety officer for the test. After a fission weapon went off, how close was too close? Scientific minds differed. Some were extremely cautious. Others were just as extremely blasé. Kauffman turned to his old teams to fill out his crews. Blandy stressed that it was a joint scientific-military enterprise, not a military operation with scientific advisers. The world had been made new; war and the risks it posed for nations had mushroomed to new heights. Like the doctors and corpsmen of the hospital ship *Haven* who had examined victims of *atombomben* disease at Dejima Pier, Kauffman arrived at the frontier of war science, which had moved from the London Blitz to the Saipan reefs to the blast site where relics of the last world war were lit up in gamma rays in order to perfect the craft of Armageddon as safely as possible.

The captured Japanese battleship *Nagato* made her final voyage to Bikini to take part in the test. Surviving the initial air burst and an underwater blast, the *Nagato* stayed afloat for five days before succumbing to the concussion and sinking. The final service of Admiral Nagumo's old flagship was to serve as a guinea pig ship, measuring the implications of the atomic age.

Working with Dr. Stafford Warren, who later started the medical school at UCLA, Kauffman and his teams puttered into the atoll in their landing craft to take measurements. They could go anywhere within three days of an air burst, and six of an underwater test. Collecting water samples as close as fifty yards from ground zero, they even went aboard the ships to determine whether conditions were safe for people to come on board. He had to fend off the ship repair people, who were all wired to keep the irradiated ships from sinking. On August 27, Kauffman returned to Washington to start a school for radiological safety monitors, setting up a permanent schoolhouse at the naval shipyard in San Francisco formerly known as Hunters Point, under the aegis of the Navy's nuclear defense division, headed by Rear Admiral Deak Parsons. In the end, Kauffman's high valor awards did his career little good. As his father pointed out, the Navy had little use for an admiral who could disassemble a bomb or sneak onto an enemy beach, even if he had a fistful of Navy Crosses to show for it. On the other hand, his mundane commendation awards for establishing a bomb disposal school, a demolition cadre, and an experimental testing board were a foundation for an organization man to build upon. He retired with the three stars of a vice admiral after serving in a variety of commands and as superintendent of the Naval Academy.

The scientists who had worked on the Manhattan Project were "all of them self-conscious" about their involvement, Kauffman said. "They all seemed to have somewhat of a guilt complex, varying in size and amount." Guilt was not the stock in trade of the military men who had served on the atomic bomb project. Paul Tibbets seemed frequently to disappoint interlocutors who expected him to be racked by remorse. He was not. Tibbets considered his flight to Hiroshima on August 6 to have been a necessary mission, efficiently carried out.

Writers who instinctively related to the moral ambivalence of the scientists struggled to comprehend Tibbets, whose brute pragmatism left him at peace with the idea of total war as a menu of terrible but compulsory choices. He slept well with a clear conscience—*how*? And imagine: After everything Tibbets had seen and done, he came home and drove a Toyota. But what would have suited such an expert in systems and organization better than the rational economics that governed his choice of a ride?

Small points that Tibbets deemed trivial became subjects of journalistic inquiry. There were juxtapositions and manufactured profundities: Had he touched the bomb after it had been loaded into his plane? He had not. And this irony was considered amazing: The pilot smoked while delivering the weapon to its target, and that act, of smoking, has killed millions more than atomic bombs have ever since. This, a writer noted, was "a twist the most inventive author could never have devised."

In 1948, President Truman invited Tibbets to the White House with three other prominent Air Force men. The meeting was quick. In the Oval Office, Truman addressed each man in turn: Carl Spaatz, the first chief of the new U.S. Air Force; Jimmy Doolittle, the architect of the mission bearing his name; and Colonel David Shillen, the inventor of aerial refueling. When the president turned to Tibbets, he just stared at him for perhaps ten seconds.

"What do you think?" Truman asked.

"Mr. President, I think I did what I was told."

Truman slapped his hand on the table. "You're damn right you did, and I'm the guy who sent you. If anybody gives you a hard time about it, refer them to me." But there were questions. Questions about the bomb's necessity, its effect, and its consequence, and about the role of conscience in the military chain of command.

What, critics asked, had been Truman's final reason for ordering the use of the bombs? In a January 12, 1953, letter to an Air Force historian, Truman explained that he had conferred at Potsdam with Byrnes, Stimson, Leahy, Marshall, Eisenhower, King, and others "to discuss what should be done with this awful weapon. . . . I asked General Marshall what it would cost in lives to land on the Tokyo plain and other places in Japan. It was his opinion that such an invasion would cost at a minimum one quarter of a million casualties, and might cost as much as a million, on the American side alone, with an equal number of the enemy." The higher number, which had no basis in military estimates, became Exhibit A for those who claimed that the United States needed to rationalize the gratuitous use of the atomic weapon in service to an ulterior motive. The implication of most of this commentary has been that lower-end casualty estimate, the mere quarter million, which was a considerable fraction of the total number of American combat deaths worldwide during the war, would not have justified the bomb. Should the expectation of losing "just" two hundred fifty thousand (not even to mention Japanese losses, which were likely to be a multiple of that figure) have taken the bomb off the table? Such was the view of Robert S. McNamara, the future Secretary of Defense who would be responsible for his own terrible war, who had served LeMay in the Office of Statistical Control. "Killing 50 to 90 percent of the people of sixty-seven Japanese cities and then bombing them with two nuclear bombs is not proportional, in the minds of some people, to the objectives we were trying to achieve," he wrote. But that line of argument seemed only to beg definitions.

Some began to argue, as they do to this day, that Truman's decision was only secondarily—or perhaps not at all—motivated by a desire to avoid bloodshed, and that it was principally designed to impress or intimidate the Soviets, or to end the war quickly to keep them from joining in the occupation of Japan. But few historians having deep acquaintance with the diplomatic record are unconvinced of Truman's sincerity in wishing to minimize U.S. losses in an invasion.

U.S. motivations would be scrutinized with gimlet eyes throughout the ensuing decades. Stalin's good faith as a broker of peace has often been assumed. A number of top American commanders did not accept the military necessity of the atomic missions. Admiral Nimitz would say that the bombs were militarily unnecessary, and in his 1950 memoir, Fleet Admiral Leahy wrote, "The use of this barbarous weapon at Hiroshima and Nagasaki was of not material assistance in our war against Japan." Both of these statements were truisms and largely beside the point. Neither "purely military" effects nor "material assistance" was the purpose of the weapons. The Navy had the material mission well in hand: By its preferred strategy of blockade and bombardment, it was prepared to inflict a pandemic and wholesale famine that would likely have killed millions of Japanese, and slowly, in the name of humane battle ethics.

Leahy also made the remarkable claim that Japan was ready to surrender, though the evidence for such a conclusion is murky at best, given that the individuals Leahy and others might consider as constituting "Japan" were not only numerous but also locked in a paralyzing disagreement—as Truman himself knew, thanks to the Magic and Ultra intercepts. The bombs were surgical weapons in that they and only they managed to target and break the imperial war council's tragic deadlock.

Was it the bombs, exactly, that had forced Japan to surrender? Historians over the years have offered new "interpretations of events" as well as restatements of a priori moral conclusions. But no one has produced new data that weigh on the only question that really mattered: What was actually in Emperor Hirohito's mind when he decided to issue the Imperial Rescript on August 14? "Japan" did not surrender. Faced with a hopelessly divided war council, Hirohito himself did. While his calculus was no doubt complex, the emperor's own words credited the significance of the atomic bombs: "The enemy has begun to employ a new and most cruel bomb," he had said,

> the power of which to do damage is indeed incalculable, taking the toll of many innocent lives. Should we continue to fight, it would not only result in the ultimate collapse and obliteration of

the Japanese nation, but also it would lead to the total extinction of human civilization. Such being the case, how are we to save the millions of our subjects; or to atone ourselves before the hallowed spirits of our Imperial Ancestors? This is the reason why We have ordered the acceptance of the provisions of the Joint Declaration of the Powers.

To dismiss such a direct and contemporaneous expression of motivation in the absence of better evidence is curious practice for a historian, and yet it still goes on today. The moral argument against the use of the atomic bombs against a civilian population cannot be refuted any more than the moral argument against the use of any weapons against a civilian population can be refuted. All we can do is discuss circumstances.

Challenged by the leadership of the Federal Council of Churches on the morality of targeting cities, Truman offered revenge as a motive, replying famously, "Nobody is more disturbed over the use of atomic bombs than I am, but I was greatly disturbed over the unwarranted attack by the Japanese on Pearl Harbor and their murder of our prisoners of war. The only language they seem to understand is the one we have been using to bombard them. When you have to deal with a beast you have to treat him as a beast. It is most regrettable but nevertheless true." This contemporaneous expression, so heated, so binary—and salted with its own flavor of moral equivalence—would be fodder for revisionists and counterfactualists for a long time to come.

But it remains telling that none of Truman's vindictiveness ever found its way into U.S. policy during the occupation of Japan. A government whose passion for retribution survived the surrender might have been expected, at the least, to have insisted on a peace that installed such draconian punishments as were imposed on Germany after World War I—a policy that Roosevelt had specifically promised as early as 1943. Though the second Quebec Conference produced a remarkable public statement referring to the Japanese as "the barbarians of the Pacific," such a sentiment was notably absent when the messianic life force that was Douglas MacArthur turned to the task of carrying out Washington's plan to disarm, demilitarize, and reconstruct Japanese society. In the end, the United States departed from the heritage of war-making handed down to it by the great centurion-states of the West. Unlike Sparta and Rome, America ministered to its enemy with surpassing mercy after it had thrown him to his knees with pitiless brutality.

Those whose lives depended on whether an invasion of Japan would take place had worried little over the philosophical aspects of the decision. They knew what had to be done. And yet Draper Kauffman was not alone among U.S. warriors in expressing concern for the Other. "I am convinced to this day that the losses on the part of the Japanese in defending their own homeland against an invader would have been many times more than the losses they suffered from the bombs, and of course, our losses would have been comparable. I listen to the discussions of the morality of dropping the bomb and I am never able to concentrate on the theory. My mind immediately goes to the more practical aspects, particularly as I was one of the people who were going to be involved." What controversy would have arisen after disclosure of the news that a war-winning weapon sat unused while tens of thousands of Americans died? Secretary of War Henry Stimson was to observe, "In war, as in a boxing match, it is seldom sound for the stronger combatant to moderate his blows whenever his opponent shows signs of weakening. The only road to early victory was to exert maximum force with maximum speed."

And then there was the matter of Japanese lives. Karl T. Compton, president of the Massachusetts Institute of Technology, was situated to observe the relevant deliberations, serving on the Interim Committee, created by Stimson to advise President Truman on the use of the atomic bomb, and also under MacArthur during the planning for Operation Downfall. Having also spent a month in Japan after the surrender, he wrote in the *Atlantic* in 1946:

> I believe, with complete conviction, that the use of the atomic bomb saved hundreds of thousands—perhaps several millions—of lives, both American and Japanese; that without its use the war would have continued for many months; that no one of good conscience knowing, as Secretary Stimson and the Chiefs of Staff did, what was probably ahead and what the atomic bomb might accomplish could have made any different decision. . . .
>
> If the atomic bomb had not been used, evidence like that I have cited points to the practical certainty that there would have been many more months of death and destruction on an enormous scale. Also the early timing of its use was fortunate for a reason which could not have been anticipated. If the invasion plans had proceeded as scheduled, October 1945 would have seen Okinawa covered with airplanes and its harbors crowded with landing craft

poised for the attack. The typhoon which struck Okinawa in that month would have wrecked the invasion plans with a military disaster comparable to Pearl Harbor.

These are some of the facts which lead those who know them, and especially those who had to base decisions on them, to feel that there is much delusion and wishful thinking among those after-the-event strategists who now deplore the use of the atomic bomb on the ground that its use was inhuman or that it was unnecessary because Japan was already beaten. And it was not one atomic bomb, or two, which brought surrender; it was the experience of what an atomic bomb will actually do to a community, *plus the dread of many more,* that was effective.

Spruance retired from the Navy on July 1, 1948. With Margaret he drove west to California, buying a house on the Monterey Peninsula in which to live out the rest of his days. No such contentment offered itself to Kelly Turner. For the Boss Alligator, the last years of his life were "an absolute nightmare," Margaret Spruance said. After his wife, Harriet, passed away in January 1961, "he began drinking terribly. He went to the dogs. Shortly after Harriet's death, Raymond called up Kelly and said, 'What is the best time to call you? I intend to call you every day.' Raymond would call him every morning about about seven A.M. We were so very worried that something tragic was going to happen to him." It was no more tragic than the fate assigned to every human on earth. On Sunday morning, February 12, the Spruances received the call letting them know that Kelly Turner had passed on. He had survived his wife by just six weeks.

Carl Moore visited Spruance frequently in Pebble Beach in the years after that. Moore had always appreciated Spruance for his expertise in devising solutions to engineering, supply, and maintenance problems. Visiting for five days in April 1963, Moore recalled, "His technical knowledge seemed at that time to be something of a social drawback. He insisted that his rather old automobile be warmed up by running the engine for fifteen minutes before being driven. He would be extremely indignant if Mrs. Spruance's plans failed to allow for this warming up period." The planner, having no more plans to write, settled for authority over a shrunken command.

Of his Navy, Ambassador Joseph L. Grew had said this on the occasion of Navy Day in 1944: "No dream castle ever erected could have surpassed the construction in these three years of the greatest, most powerful, and certainly the most efficient and effective navy that the world has ever seen." Though the Navy, Marine Corps, and Coast Guard had lost more than fifty-six thousand dead, more than eighty thousand wounded, and another nine thousand missing in action, Ernest King relished victory as a vindication of everything he had fought for in Washington and in fractious planning sessions with the Allies.

> Never before in the history of war had there been a more convincing example of the effectiveness of sea power than when a well-armed, highly efficient and undefeated army of over a million men surrendered their homeland unconditionally to the invader, without even token resistance. True, the devastation already wrought by past bombing, as well as the terrible demonstration of power by the first atomic bombs, augured nothing less for the Japanese than total extinction, yet without sea power there would have been no possession of Saipan, Iwo Jima, and Okinawa from which to launch these bombings. True, the Japanese homeland might have been taken by assault in one final amphibious operation of tremendous magnitude, yet without sea power such an assault could not have been attempted.

With its worldwide reach, the fleet would drive a fractious but unmistakably American century, so dominant everywhere that its mission would reach beyond ambitions that were merely nationalistic. Six decades later, its advertising message would become expressly moralistic: "A global force for good."

Eighteen Japanese scrap metal firms participated in the disposal of the capital assets of the Imperial Japanese Navy. That once-peerless force finally ceased to be on January 15, 1949, with the rending to pieces of the heavy cruiser *Tone,* the last of four hundred fifteen vessels so handled, including thirty-five major warships. Japan, remade, had no use for them. A new morality arose in their place, an appreciation of the atomic age's heightened stakes and a call for world community. Silent during the war years, Japanese liberals gave voice to the problem of love versus power, a problem older than Christendom or Rome. Influential voices urged a turning back of the clock. "I contemplated the human destiny, the prospect of civilization, and searched for any new direction for Man to live," wrote Ichiro Moritaki, a professor of ethics at Hiroshima University. "I was led, in my speculation, to designate modern civilization as a 'civilization of power' and to conclude that the 'civilization of love' alone should inherit the earth."

What were the prospects for humanity amid the yearly ravages of *atom-bomben* disease, daily funerals, schools turned orphanages, the desires of man, the consequences of power, and the ruin of ambition, whose effects were now so evident? Francis Bacon, in the seventeenth century, had urged upon England and the world a vision of science as both a tool and an everlasting challenge. "Making is knowing and knowing is making," he believed. Los Alamos could be seen as a landmark waypoint of Bacon's ideal of practical science pushed along by the state. But what of the weapons that were thereby produced? A sword had no morality, said even Ichiro Moritaki. Weapons were neither *mala in se* nor good in themselves, but were given life by the spiritual essence of their user. But the notion that nations, leaders—someone—should, for instance, "reorient the common mind of humanity toward spiritual-ethical principles and righteousness" neglected the fact that it had been just such a communal mind—Tojo's government—whose idea of righteousness had led the way to ruin, enabled by an emperor's divine right.

Perhaps it was the genius of the American way of war that questions of morality and national destiny were the province of politicians, not of warmakers, no matter how brilliant or visionary those practitioners of war's lethal technics might be. The failures of such men could be small and technical—confined to the manner of use of aircraft carriers during an amphibious operation. Or they could be small and personal.

Edward Spruance always thought his father "austere, remote, and inflexible. He expected obedience and appeared intolerant of childish foibles." But there were boundaries around the consequences of such failures. "Except for walks and an occasional sail when I owned a boat, we rarely did things together. I did not feel the urge to take him into my confidence with my problems. He was a 'father presence' as I imagine it to be in some German families, always in control, always unruffled, busy with his career. I cannot remember a harsh word ever being exchanged between him and my mother. Neither can I remember any display of affection toward me. I hope my father never sees these words."

The death in a car accident of the man who spoke them basically killed the commander of the Fifth Fleet, his wife would say. He knew he had missed an opportunity there, had failed to write an operation plan to deploy the father-son force effectively, and regrets dragged on him like an anchor. Call it the fault of the war. It had drawn them both in and consumed their best energies. This was a cost that no statistical control office could measure.

It had been a war of second lieutenants pushing their men into the next ravine, of sergeants telling privates to clear a cave and the privates complying, of the determination of an airplane commander to pull his crew together for yet another cruise on Honshu's jet stream. From the Marianas they had launched themselves on the world, forcing an end to the madness by using methods whose moral problems would be problematic. The concept of *jus in bello,* justice in war, required an acute sense of the neverending total war between good and evil. Its principles included proportionality, injunctions against weapons deemed evil in themselves, and avoidance of weapons whose effects cannot be controlled, such as biological agents. To be just, a war must have a future state of peace as its goal, and the ultimate settlement must be "measured and reasonable" lest weapons become instruments of revenge. Even unconditional surrender was held as unreasonable under the doctrine of *jus in bello,* if not under the law of physics, which dictates that every action brings an equal and opposite reaction. What if the surrender that was achieved by use of monstrous devices ended even bloodier predations perpetrated by a militarist regime bent upon race conquest?

In the thirties, Franklin Roosevelt had pleaded that civilians not become targets of industrial militaries. But there would be no stopping what the historian Barton J. Bernstein called "the great moral transformation of World War II . . . a redefinition of what constitutes a legitimate target, and who legitimately can or cannot be killed."

Thomas Aquinas had introduced the idea of the Doctrine of Double Effect. He envisioned a nation, X, contemplating war in response to an attack by an aggressor. Nation X foresees that, should it wage war to defend itself, civilian casualties will result, probably in both countries. The Doctrine of Double Effect permits such a war only if (1) X does not intend to inflict civilian casualties but only to protect itself and its people; (2) such civilian casualties are not in themselves the means whereby X's goal will be achieved; and (3) the importance of X's defending itself from aggression is proportionately greater than the harm of the civilian casualties. But all of this is a fog of words, for what device exists to measure the "importance" of any nation's effort to defend itself?

Pure realism counseled that war was organic and elemental to the anarchical world, the will to power being immutable, irresistible, and primary, and that in the free market of national interests, the strong deserved to prevail. The strong who had a sense of justice would always struggle with that thesis. Chester Nimitz and Raymond Spruance anguished over the loss of life, both within their own command and under the flag of their enemy, while authorizing perfectly ferocious and efficient killing methods that were aimed, they would always say, at ending the war quickly in order to minimize the total loss of life. It was a gentler rendition of "the end justifies the means."

On October 5, 1945, Admiral Nimitz gave a major address on the war at the Washington Monument. The subtext was the drawdown of the Navy. In the atomic age, Army generals doubted the need for a fleet.

Nimitz had mentioned the Navy's role in developing the bomb, and he promised to study its use "as a major component of your national sea power." He added, "Let us go forth in all friendliness, and with a desire to live in full amity with our neighbor, the world. But let us make certain that our olive branch is planted firmly in a rich soil with a high content of uranium-235. This I maintain is not cynicism, but what we in Texas and in the Navy call *savvy*."

A fly-by of a thousand Navy aircraft followed his remarks. Some of the planes arranged themselves in flight to spell the admiral's surname in block letters. Then came a parade of jeeps carrying veterans of Coral Sea, Midway, Guadalcanal, Tarawa, Saipan, the Marianas Turkey Shoot, Iwo Jima, and Okinawa, and flatbed trucks carrying artillery, landing craft, and planes. The last vehicle in the procession bore a pair of unusual items: an unexploded Japanese bomb that had been recovered from a battleship at Pearl Harbor, and a yellow pagoda from which dangled the samurai sword of a Japanese admiral, surrendered a month earlier on the USS *Missouri*. It was a day for conventional weapons on parade, but atomic weapons loomed over all of it, just as they had done in the Marianas.

With Truman flying top cover for him, Paul Tibbets slept well at night, mostly. If he ever dreamed again of dropping candy over Hialeah, he never mentioned it. The Air Force brigadier general who had thrilled, as all children do, to the rush of flight, and who had used that innocent ambition to wreak mass destruction from the air, bristled at the idea that it had all been unnecessary because, as some people will always want to say, "The Japanese were ready to surrender."

When he was confronted with this idea in the year he turned eighty-four, Tibbets was beyond any interest in discussing Thomas Aquinas, or considering the failed politics of Imperial Japan, or questioning the invincible logic of the cruelties that Mars had visited upon Earth in the hour of his derangement. No one except by the luck of advantageous geography had been spared targeting in this war. Was it the job of a combat pilot to educate a free people who were too lazy to read for themselves?

When Tibbets responded, he indulged the same pulverizing attitude toward nuance that had gotten him sent to the Pacific in the first place, to serve as the courier of a novel and paradoxical proposition: that in 1945, atomic war had been the antidote to total war.

Some could accept such a paradox and support it. Others seemed unequipped even to entertain it. Tibbets spoke for his generation in defending what had been sprung from his last battle station on Tinian. He knew that some people would never understand. They lacked, he felt, a certain kind of experience.

"Those people never had their balls on that cold, hard anvil," the war ender said. Shizuko Miura and Sakae Oba would have understood.

Acknowledgments

For her work diving deep, planting charges in narrative boulder fields, marking hazards to navigation, clearing man-made obstacles, and otherwise helping the reader land on this distant shore, Tracy Devine, my editor at Random House, once again deserves my gratitude. She is the publishing equivalent of an underwater demolition swimmer. Thanks also to Sarah Murphy, Carlos Beltran, Emily DeHuff, Kim Hovey, Greg Kubie, Shona McCarthy, Virginia Norey, Maggie Oberrender, and the rest of the Random House team headed by Jennifer Hershey and Kara Welsh. Jeffrey L. Ward did his usual superlative work on the book's suite of maps and line diagrams.

I am grateful to the members of a certain unofficial, unregulated guild of historians and authors who share helpful information with one another without expectation of return: John Bruning, Richard B. Frank, George Friedman, Chuck Haberlein, Meredith Hindley, Annie Jacobsen, Jonathan W. Jordan, Donald M. Kehn, Jr., Alex Kershaw, James Kunetka, John B. Lundstrom, Terry McKnight, Benjamin Milligan, Jonathan Parshall, David A. Rosenberg, James M. Scott, Barrett Tillman, Anthony Tully, and John Wukovits. Thank you all for your collegiality and generosity.

Special thanks to Richard B. Frank, Barrett Tillman, Adam Ward, and Gerhard L. Weinberg for reading early drafts of this manuscript and offering helpful comments. Of course, any remaining errors of fact or interpretation belong to me alone.

I am appreciative of anyone who has taken the trouble to prepare an oral history with a veteran, transcribe it well, and keep it in an accessible place. Among this large cast of history's intermediaries, lifetime achievement awards should go to Ronald E. Marcello, John T. Mason, and Paul Stillwell.

The archivists and staff at the following facilities around the country have been most helpful: Evelyn Cherpak at the United States Naval War College; Vice Admiral Pete Daly, Janis Jorgensen, and William Miller at the U.S. Naval Institute; Fred Allison, Annette Amerman, Colonel Peter Ferraro, Jim Ginther, John Lyles, and Lieutenant Colonel Charles Neimeyer at the Alfred M. Gray Marine Corps Research Center, Quantico; Joe Cavanaugh, Reagan Grau, and General Michael Hagee at the National Museum of the Pacific War; and Jeremy Collins at the National World War II Museum. I am grateful, too, to the professional staffs at the National Archives and Records Administration, the Franklin D. Roosevelt Presidential Library, the Naval History and Heritage Command, and the archival website fold3.com. For their good advice and counsel, thanks to Ike Williams and Hope Denekamp at Sennott and Williams in Boston.

My wife, Sharon, and our children, David, Grace Ann, and Hutch, have been patient with a husband and father who tends to distraction and over-generosity with fun facts about such things as combat air patrol doctrine or string reconnaissance technique. My parents, Elsa and Dave Hornfischer, have always been there with love and support, giving me the liberty to light my way and cheering me along in anything I tried to do. My deepest thanks and love to you all.

Notes

Prologue: Cashiered in Algiers *(pp. xxiii–xxviii)*

Young Tibbets in Florida: Tibbets, *Flight of the Enola Gay*, 14–21. **In North Africa:** Ibid., 92–96, 130–33. **B-29 program:** "Wrath of Giants," *Newsweek*, June 26, 1944, 35; Floyd Lemley in Krauss, *The 509th Remembered*, 127; Tibbets, 140, 144.

1. Engine of Siege *(pp. 3–18)*

Ship construction: Elliott, "Escort Ship Production in WWII," 193, 195; Lane, *Ships for Victory*, 35; Starr, *Embattled Dreams*, 13–14. **Taking Kwajalein and Eniwetok:** Spruance to Jeter A. Iseley, Jan. 14, 1949. Though some sources credit Nimitz, Ernest King said it was Spruance's idea to leap ahead to Eniwetok. Insofar as that leap created the need for a strike on Truk, which Spruance carried out, the "deliberate" Spruance can be credited for accelerating the drive to the Marianas by two and a half months. King, *Flight Log Book*, 1944, 1. **Truk attack:** U.S. Chiefs of Staff, Report M-120, July 25, 1943, 6; CINCPAC to COMINCH, "Operations in Pacific Ocean Areas," June 3, 1944, 30–31; Air Group 17, aircraft action reports, Feb. 16, 1944, 4–8. **Vraciu at Truk:** Vraciu interview, 16, 54. **"There were dogfights everywhere":** Jensen, *Carrier War*, 99. **VF-5 at Truk:** Ibid., 100–1; VF-5, aircraft action report, Feb. 17, 1944, 51. **Bullard in Truk lagoon:** USS *Intrepid*, action report, March 7, 1944, 3–4. **Sinking of *Naka*:** USS *Bunker Hill*, Air Group 17, aircraft action report, Feb. 27, 1944, 23–25. **Donald Dean crashes:** www.cv6.org/1944/truk. **Death of James E. Bridges:** Vraciu, 56–57; USS *Intrepid*, 4. **Spruance detaches battleships:** USS *Iowa* action report, Feb. 26, 1944, 2; USS *Bradford*, action report, Feb. 24, 1944, 2. **Expansion of carrier force:** Lundstrom, *Black Shoe Carrier Admiral*, 498; Hone, "Replacing Battleships with Aircraft Carriers in the Pacific in World War II," 58–70. **Spruance's personality, "I remember being told once":** Arthur C. Davis to T. B. Buell, Aug. 18, 1964. **"Everyone should have a family but":** Margaret Spruance, interview, Nov. 29, 1971, 2. **Spruance at Annapolis:** Ibid. **Moore on Spruance:** Forrestel interview, Dec. 1, 1971, 41. **Spruance at Truk:** Moore interview, 896, 908. **Spruance as battleship man:** Margaret (Spruance) Bogart interview, Sept. 27, 1971; Moore interview, Nov. 28, 1966, 4–5. ***Maikaze* hit:** USS *Essex*, action report, March 3, 1944, 14–15; USS *Yorktown*, action report, Feb. 18, 1944, 135–37, 141–45; USS *New Jersey*, action report, 3, 14–15; USS *Iowa*, 5. **"We're not out here fighting aircraft":** Moore interview, 896. **"Any strike leader": Ramage narrative. **"That would have been embarrassing"**: Barber interview, 57–58. **Sinking of Katori and Maikaze:** USS New Jersey, 6; USS Iowa, 7–8; COMDESRON 46, action report, 7–8; USS Izard, action report, 7. **"I'm getting rather hardened to seeing"**: Moore, 922–23. **"A ship is a fool to fight a fort"**: Hughes, Fleet Tactics, 36. **"Friendly plane"**: USS Iowa, 9, 17–19. **Deaths of Tepas and Leach:** USS Intrepid, 5. **"Shall I bring back some souvenirs?"** and **"In view of the probable rescue of survivors"**: USS Burns, action report, 5–6, 8. **Spruance's victory flags:** Jensen, 105. **Truk raid:** CINCPAC to COMINCH, "Operations in Pacific Ocean Areas," June 3, 1944, 40; "Field Survey," 139; Chihaya, "Account of the Fiasco at Truk," in Goldstein, Pacific War Papers, 282; Rems, "Two Birds," 20. **"King was well pleased"**: Forrestel, 118. **"What lesson then"**: USS Minneapolis, action report, Feb. 24, 1944, 5.

2. On the Western Warpath *(pp. 20–35)*

"Could almost be counted": Hill interview, 336–37. **"The actual invasion of Japan"**: U.S. Chiefs of Staff, "Specific Operations in the Pacific and Far East," 65–66, enclosure to Combined Chiefs of Staff, "Final Report to the President and Prime Minister," May 25, 1943, CCS 242/6. **Central Pacific strategy and timetable:** Morton, War in the Pacific: Strategy and Command, 454–72, Moore interview, 910, 919; Spruance to E. M. Eller, June 29, 1964; Miller, War Plan Orange, 344. **"An effective bomber offensive"**: CCS 323, Aug. 20, 1943, 289. **Bypassing Truk:** Moore interview, 910, 919; Spruance to E. M. Eller, June 29, 1964, 4; Hoffman, Saipan, 19. **"I was just thinking"**: Busch, "Task Force 58," 19. **"The difference between a good officer"**: Potter, Admiral Arleigh Burke, 73. **Towers coveted Spruance's job:** Forrestel interview, 37. **Spruance's sympathy for Pownall:** Spruance to E. M. Eller, June 29, 1964. **"Their personalities were completely different"**: Burke to T. B. Buell, Feb. 11, 1972, 1. **"Queer types of craft"**: Turner, press conference, Jan. 11, 1945, 5. **"Turner is here"**: Moore, 815–16. **"Kelly Turner was a strange individual"**: Hogaboom interview, 180–81. **"He was intolerant of mistakes"**: Hill, 204. **"On first meeting"**: Smith, Coral and Brass, 109–10. **Spruance and Turner as friends:** Margaret Spruance interview, 16–17; Spruance notes on ms. by E. B. Potter, Jan. 4, 1959. **Turner as bureaucrat:** Moore, 659, 760–61; Morison, Rising Sun in the Pacific, 134–35. **Orange and Rainbow Five plans:** Miller, War Plan Orange, 118; see also 2, 10–11, 245–46. **"The general result"**: Moore, 760–61. **"Whether or not Turner was entirely responsible"**: Conolly interview, 230–31. **"Both found themselves in awkward positions"**: King to Stark, Sept. 14, 1943, 2. **"I could talk to him"**: Moore interview, 926. **"Kelly was operating"**: Dyer, Amphibians Came to Conquer, 853. **Turner's alcoholism:** Margaret Spruance interview. **"Nine out of ten people"**: J. H. Doyle to Turner, Feb. 24, 1944, 4. **"He is able to handle"**: Spruance to Margaret, Aug. 3, 1944, 2. **Technical equipment, heavy power, and bombardment:** Turner, press conference, Jan. 11, 1945, 5. **"Very definitely B squad material"**: USS Yorktown, action report, Feb. 23, 1944, 8. **First strikes on Marianas:** Spruance to Jeter A. Iseley, Feb. 3, 1950; CNO, "U.S. Naval Aviation in the Pacific," 31; CINCPAC to COMINCH, "Operations in Pacific

Ocean Areas," June 3, 1944, 44–45. See also USS *Bunker Hill*, war diary, Feb. 1944, 16–17; USS *Yorktown*, 5, 23–24; USS *Essex*, action report, Feb. 22, 1944, 46–47; USS *Monterey*, action report, Feb. 26, 1944, 14. **Loss of McVay and Davis:** USS *Yorktown*, 5–6, 18, 21. **USS *Sunfish* on lifeguard duty:** USS *Sunfish*, "Report of Sixth War Patrol," 17, 26–27, 38; USS *Bunker Hill*, 40; USS *Yorktown*, 10. See also www.pacificwrecks.com/aircraft/f6f/40671.html. **Establishing JICPOA:** Showers interview, 52–56; Biard interview, 148; Ramsbottom interview, 11, 47–49. **Photo-reconnaissance technique:** Turner report, 85, 90–92, 229. **Velvalee Dickinson's spy ring:** Flanner, "The Doll Spy," 44. See also www.eyespymag.com/espionage%20cases/dickinson.htm. **Carrier strikes on Palaus/Carolines:** CTG 58.3, action report, April 8, 1944, 5–13. **"Almost miraculous":** Nimitz to King, April 2, 1944. **"West of Tokyo Missionary Society":** *Life*, "*Life* Goes to an Aircraft Carrier Party," 83–85. **Vraciu shot down/"GET ME OFF THIS DANGED ROLLER COASTER":** Vraciu interview, 57, 64–65.

3. In Turner's Train *(pp. 37–62)*

"I cannot describe the exultation": Smith, *Coral and Brass,* 153. **"There was a conviction":** Hogaboom interview, 188. **Parker Ranch drills:** Chapin, "Memoir," 45–46. **"They taught us in training":** Boots interview, 26–27. **"As we all settled down":** Hill interview, 453. **Amphibious training:** COMPHIBPAC to Amphibious Force, Pacific Fleet, "Amphibious Force Landing Exercises," April 19, 1943, 1–10; Morehouse; "Amphibious Training," *Marine Corps Gazette*, Aug. 1944, 35. U.S. Army, *Engineer Amphibian Troops*, 2–3. **"We must never make":** Kauffman interview, 175. **Deployment of UDT:** Robbins, "Narrative History," 2; Baird, "The Journeys of Underwater Demolition Teams," 8. **Kauffman in England:** Kauffman, 69–71, 93–116. **"If you think":** Ibid., 125. **"Have you ever seen pictures":** Ibid., 158. **"He was a great salesman":** Marshall interview, 11–12. **UDT at Fort Pierce:** Kauffman, 161; Robbins, 1. **Kistiakowsky's UDT work:** Kauffman, 164–65; Rhodes, *Making of the Atomic Bomb,* 542. **"Now just calm down":** Kauffman, 164–65. **"We were the despair"** and **"I will do everything":** Ibid., 173. **UDT training curriculum:** U.S. Navy, "Weekly Report of Training Activities" (NCDU), July 17, 1943, 1–2; Robbins, 1. **"At that time we didn't expect":** Marshall, 12–13. **"All we had":** Ibid., 21–22. **Japanese divers:** Yokoi, "The Japanese Version of the Black Chamber," 19. **"We wanted to use":** Kauffman, 183. **"We must think in terms"** and other UDT innovations: Gulbranson to King, "Criticisms, Suggestions and Opinions of Demolition Tools, Expressed by Observers During Critique of Demonstration 11 Feb. 1944," March 3, 1944, 1–2; COMFIFTHPHIB (R. K. Turner) to Com Group Three, FIFTHPHIBPAC, "UDT No. 2, organization, assignment, movement and equipment of," Dec. 23, 1943, 2. **"To lead the way":** COMFIFTHPHIB to CINCPAC, "Establishment of Underwater Demolition Experimental Station in Hawaii," Dec. 29, 1943, 1. **"Now, the first and most important thing":** Kauffman, 186–87. **UDT at Maui:** Robbins, 2–3; Kauffman, 188, 193–94; Baird, "The Journeys of Underwater Demolition Teams," 10. **"The idea that the Navy":** Spruance to J. A. Iseley, July 3, 1949. **"A few plain words":** Krulak, *First to Fight*, 103–4. **Roebling's swamp buggy:** Fawell, Second Armored Amphibian Battalion, 2ndarmoredamphibianbattalion.com/saipan; Roan, *Roebling's Amphibian*, 18. **Fifth Phib's military carriage:** CTF 51, "Report of Amphibious Operations," 278–82, 300; Northern Troops & Landing Force, Transport Quartermaster, "TQM Report, Phase I (Saipan)," Aug. 10, 1944, 1; Hill, 453–54; Chief of Staff, U.S. Army, "Operations Division Information Bulletin," Feb. 1, 1944, 4. **"From a fixed and steady gun platform":** R. C. Parker to Spruance, Dec. 15, 1943, 1–2. **"Sir, I'd like to borrow":** Kauffman, 189–90. **Kaho'olawe exercise:** LST-485, war diary, May 1944, 2–3; LST-390, war diary, May 1944, 2; Hoffman, *Saipan*, 32–33; Heinl, "Naval Gunfire Support in Landings," 2. CTF 51, 165; Com Gen Fifth Phib Corps, "Report of Marianas Operation, Phase I (Saipan)," G-2 Report, 127; Kauffman, USNI 190; Robbins, "Narrative," 4. **"So called 'doping off' ":** USS *Arthur Middleton* (APA-25), Operation Order 7-44, June 12, 1944, Annex H, 1–2, Amphibious Training Base, Coronado, *Skill in the Surf,* Feb. 1945. **Maui rehearsals:** USS *Clay* (APA-39), transcript of captain's briefing, June 11, 1944, 8; ATB Coronado, *Skill in the Surf;* USS *Arthur Middleton*, 3; CTF 51, "Report of Amphibious Operations," 139–40. **"I wanted to go ashore":** Erskine interview, 335–36. **West Loch disaster:** Graf, "Easy Company," 178, 180–85; Hoffman, *Saipan*, 33, Hill, 463; Dyer, *Amphibians Came to Conquer*, 893–95. **"When you appear up there":** Margaret Spruance interview; Buell, *Quiet Warrior*, 275–76. **"Let me handle him":** Ibid., 278. **"The cautious tactics of the Japanese":** CINCPAC, memorandum, "Tactical foresight," May 29, 1944, 1–2. **Estimates of Saipan defenses:** Craven and Cate, *The Pacific: Guadalcanal to Saipan*, 686; CTF 51, G-2 Report, 4–5.

4. A Charge for Ozawa *(pp. 65–70)*

Lt. Chihaya's flight: Kusaka, *Combined Fleet*, 160; Prange, *God's Samurai*, 123–24. **"The exploits of these scout planes":** Kusaka, 161–62. **Japanese cryptography:** Yokoi, "The Japanese Version of the Black Chamber," Yokoi, Toshiyuki, "The Japanese Version of the Black Chamber," Far East Command, Military Intelligence Section, No. 64718, Jan. 31, 1951, 20–21. **Ozawa at Tawi Tawi:** Morison, *New Guinea and the Marianas*, 214–17; Potter and Nimitz, *Great Sea War*, 353; Kusaka, 150–55. According to Sadao Mogami, an army captain at central air headquarters in Tokyo, "We calculated total national domestic production of aviation fuel, combined with fuel made from pine roots, was only ten thousand kiloliters a month (2.6 million U.S. gallons). If we used our reserve every month exclusively for training, we'd have had no reserve at all in just four months." Cook, *Japan at War*, 454. **Destroy it "with one blow":** Morison, *New Guinea and the Marianas*, 213. **Deployment of IJN land-based planes:** Fuchida, USSBS interrogation, 429; Morison, *New Guinea and the Marianas*, 219; Nomura, "Ozawa in the Pacific," in Evans, *Japanese Navy in World War II*, 310. **"The air battles over Saipan":** King, *Last Zero Fighter*, 247–51. **"Surprise operations will be carried out":** Morison, *New Guinea and the Marianas*, 214. **Capture of Plan Z:** McCollum interview, 617–18; Bradsher, "The 'Z

Plan' Story," part 2. **Deployments of First Air Fleet:** Matsuura, USSBS interrogation, 3; Morison, 219. **"In a very short time":** Buell, *Quiet Warrior*, 281. **"We have learned how to pulverize":** Pratt, "The Marines in the Pacific War," Aug. 1947, 43–44.

5. The Outer Colony *(pp. 71–79)*

Sakae Oba's arrival: Jones, *Oba*, 6, 17. **Emplacing defenses:** CTF 51, G-2, "Interrogation report of 1st Lt. Ando, Shigesaburo," 2; Jones, 19. **"Unless the units are supplied":** Yoshida interrogation, 6; Denfeld, *Hold the Marianas*, 15–17. **Chamorros on Saipan:** Ibid., 3–7. **"The streets belonged to the drunkards":** Sugano, "The End at Saipan," 67. **Manuel Sablan at Garapan:** Petty, *Saipan*, 34–35; Ada, "World War II—Saipan," 1–2. **"Garapan seems to die":** Sugano, 21. **"They were white":** Petty, 36–37. **"When I gazed at the sky":** Sugano, 69–73, 81. **Air raid on Saipan:** Air Group 15, aircraft action report, June 11, 1944, 2–8; Y'Blood, *Red Sun Setting*, 35; Air Group 15, aircraft action report, June 12, 1944, 26; Burke interview, Aug. 20, 1945, 11–12. **Death of Kenney:** Air Group 15, air action report, June 11, 1944, 3, 5. **Loss of Burckholter:** Air Group 16, "Reports of Attacks in Marianas, June 11–19," 6. **"When there was no raid":** Kusaka, *Combined Fleet*, 131–32. **"It was noted that the enemy fighters":** COMAIRPAC, "Analysis of Pacific Air Operations," 7–8. **"For eighteen years since my birth":** Sugano, 24–25, 56, 78, 83, 86.

6. A Rumor of Fleets *(pp. 81–87)*

McCampbell versus the *marus*: Air Group 15, air action report, June 12, 1944, 9–14. **Survivors on Anatahan:** Kalischer, "Dark Angel," 20–21. **Difficulty of air-field strikes:** CNO, "U.S. Naval Aviation in the Pacific," 49; ComAirPac, "Analysis of Pacific Air Operations, 11–30 June 1944," 22. **Death of Commander Isely:** Air Group 16, air action report, June 13, 1944, 22–24, 29–30. **Amphibious force sortie and approach to Saipan:** COMFIFTHPHIB, "Report of Amphibious Operations for the Capture of the Mariana Islands," Aug. 25, 1944, 8–14. **"This one morning I came up":** Boots interview, 86–87; CTG 52.17, Sortie Plan 4-44, 1–2. **Bombardment of Saipan, D minus 2:** CTU 58.7.3, action report, July 31, 1944, 6. **"A Navy-sponsored farm project":** Morison, *New Guinea and the Marianas*, 180. **"When we came out of the cave":** Petty, *Saipan*, 37. **Execution of Lt. McVay:** COMGEN, U.S. Army Forces, Middle Pacific, to JAG; "War Crimes," Aug. 30, 1945; "Witness statement of Neratus," 1–4. The Japanese regarded the June 11 fighter sweep on Saipan as "a routine attack," according to Major Kiyoshi Yoshida, a 43rd Division intelligence officer. The intensity of the subsequent air attacks convinced the garrison that Saipan would be invaded. Headquarters, Northern Troops and Landing Force, "Major Yoshida, Kiyoshi, intelligence officer of the former 43rd Division Headquarters, special interrogation of," 2. **"If the First Mobile Fleet sortied":** Kusaka, *Combined Fleet*, 113. **U.S. subs off Marianas:** COMFIFTHFLEET, "Initial

Report," 2–6; Lockwood, *Sink 'Em All*, 187. **"They were going to do something"**: Burke interview, 15.

7. OBB and UDT (pp. 88–98)

Fire-support mission at Saipan: COMFIFTHPHIB, "Report of Amphibious Operations for the Capture of the Mariana Islands," Aug. 25, 1944, 42–43; ComCruDiv 12, action report, July 31, 1944, 3; USS *Cleveland*, action report, July 20, 1944, 4–5; Morison, *New Guinea and the Marianas*, 183n; USS *California*, action report, June 30, 1944, 2–6; USS *Tennessee*, action report, June 30, 1944, 2; ComBatDiv Two, action report, July 3, 1944, 3–4. Commander, USS *Salt Lake City*, "Improvement of Naval Fire Support," May 14, 1945, 4. **"If everything was really moving"**: Vrana interview, 28–30. **Erskine's scheme/"This was the song and dance I gave"**: Erskine interview, 342–43. **UDT operations:** COMFIFTHPHIB, 43; Robbins, "Good to Be Alive," 56, 63–64; Robbins, "Narrative," 7; Kauffman interview, 197, 208; USS *California*, 3–4; USS *Indianapolis*, action report, July 1, 1944, 10–11. **"The dumbest idea"**: Kauffman, 195–96. **"Blow Pistol, this is Blow Gun"**: Kauffman, 207. **Captain Inglis and** *Birmingham***:** Inglis narrative, 8; USS *Birmingham*, action report, July 11, 1944, 11–12, 27. **"This was all close under the gunfire"**: Inglis, 8. See also Robbins, "Narrative," 4, 7, and COMFIFTHPHIB, 168–69. **"Due to faulty communications"**: USS *California*, 6–7. **"We anchored it there"**: Kauffman, 197. See also Robbins, "Narrative," 6–8. **Absence of fighter sweep for UDT ops:** Kauffman, 209; Commander, Support Aircraft, "Report of Support Aircraft," Sept. 11, 1944, 1. **UDT casualties:** Navy UDT–SEAL Museum, "A History of UDT 5, WWII," 25; UDT 7, action report 1; Robbins, "Narrative," 29; Fane, *Naked Warriors*, 101; Kauffman, 197–98. **"He had none of the rough"**: Hogaboom interview, 214. **UDT reports to fire-support group:** UDT 7, action report, 1; Bob Marshall interview, 36; Robbins, "Narrative," 7–8; CTG 52.2, "Report of Saipan Operation," Aug. 23, 1944, 31–35; Morison, *New Guinea and the Marianas*, 197. **"General, they'll never get through"**: Kauffman interview, 200.

8. Heavy Weather (pp. 99–107)

Cavalla's patrol: USS *Cavalla*, "Report of First War Patrol," Aug. 3, 1944, 4–5. **Spruance vs. Mitscher:** Arleigh Burke to T. B. Buell, Feb. 11, 1972. **"As we talked, I realized"**: Edwin T. Layton to T. B. Buell, May 3, 1972. **Midway contretemps:** Spruance to Savvy Forrestel, undated, ca. Nov. 1962; Spruance to E. M. Eller, June 29, 1964. **Third Fleet/Fifth Fleet:** Gilbert, *A Leader Born*, 121. **"Instead of the stagecoach system"**: Halsey, *Admiral Halsey's Story*, 197. **"If carriers are properly utilized"**: Clark, *Carrier Admiral*, 168–69. **"Leadership comprises a number of moral qualities"**: Spruance, "Command Thesis," date unknown, transcription by Thomas B. Buell. **Shizuko Miura on Saipan:** Sugano, "The End at Saipan," 69–73, 87–90. **"There arose suddenly a terrible sound"**: Ibid., 91. **Japanese defenses:** Denfeld, *Hold the Marianas*, 22–26. **"More than once I was told"**: Kase, *Journey to* the *Missouri,* quoted in Walter Muir Whitehill to Ernest King, September 1, 1950. **"The firehouse bell":** Sugano, 92–94.

9. Heavier, Higher, Faster *(pp. 111–115)*

B-29 problems: Floyd Lemley in Krauss, *The 509th Remembered,* 127. **"It was just another flying machine":** Tibbets, *Flight,* 146–48. **Logistical hurdles for China-based B-29s:** Craven and Cate, *The Pacific: Matterhorn to Nagasaki,* 58–91; Tillman, *Whirlwind,* 48–56. **USAAF calculations:** The figure of twenty-eight groups was based on 50 percent operational readiness. **Monthly maintenance tonnage:** Supplying the B-24 air bridge to Calcutta would have been more than 75 percent of the burden. Combined Chiefs of Staff, "Air Plan for the Defeat of Japan," 296–97. **"Give a wholly new impulse":** Nimitz, "Tactical Foresight," 2. See also King and Whitehill, *Fleet Admiral King,* 539–41. **"I was furious":** Moore interview, 788. **"An aerial battle fleet":** *Newsweek,* "Wrath of Giants," 34. **"That silhouette is made to order":** Zurlinden, "Prelude to Saipan," in Second Marine Division Association, *Heritage Years,* 91. **"TAKE CHARGE. GOOD LUCK":** CTG 52.2, "Report of Saipan Operation," Aug. 23, 1944, 31; Hill interview, 502.

10. D Day *(pp. 116–143)*

Bill "Killer" Kane at Saipan: CTG 52.2, "Report of Saipan Operation," Aug. 23, 1944, 31–35; Ramage, personal narrative. **"He carried it in his own mind":** Hogaboom interview, 181–82. **"Land the landing force":** Turner report, 43; Morison, *New Guinea and the Marianas,* 190. G. D. Morison, transcript, "Briefing of Forager Operation," June 12, 1944, 5; USS *Clay* (APA-39), transcript of captain's briefing, June 11, 1944, 4. **"Now our group was standing":** Graf, "Easy Company," 199. See also COMGEN, FIFTHPHIBCORPS, "Report of Marianas Operation, Phase I (Saipan)," 1109–10; CTG 52.2, 31–35; and USS *Arthur Middleton* (APA-25), Operation Order 7-44, June 12, 1944, 7–8. **"Being low in the water":** Graf, 200. **CVE air support:** CTF 52, Attack Order A11-44, Annex C, Appendix 6A, 1; CTG 52.2, 31–35; USS *Midway,* action report, Aug. 31, 1944, 2. **LCI gunboats:** Harig, "My Memories of World War II," 20; Rawn, "LCI(G)-459 at Saipan and Peleliu," 1–2. **"God bless you all!":** Graf, 200. **A "$6.60 orchestra seat":** Inglis narrative, 10. **"As the troops came abreast":** Harig, 20. **"Lock and load your pieces":** Graf, 200. **"The beaches were a mass of smoke":** USS *Tennessee,* action report, June 30, 1944, 3, 66. **"These bursting projectiles":** Hill interview, 304–5. **"Flames boiled out":** Harris, in Fawell, "Second Armored Amphibian Battalion website," unpaginated. **"There was a loud explosion":** Graf, 201. **Afetna Point:** TransDiv 28, "Report of Control Operations," July 11, 1944, 1; Hoffman, *Saipan,* 50–51; Hill, 503–4. **"It was really tragic":** Inglis, 11–12. **"The mobilization":** Hill, 520. **"I never will forget the concussion"** and **"Let's get the hell out of here":** R. J. Lee to Brooks, 1–2. **"On us like flies":** Barriger, "Second Armored Amphibian Battalion," unpaginated; S. A. Balsano, ibid. **Exploits of Livesey and Dickens:** Livesey and Shirley in "Barriger," unpaginated. **Battalion commanders wounded:** Jones, *Brief History of the Sixth Marines*, 89. **Jones "the best damn battalion commander":** Sherrod, "Battalion on Saipan," 10. **Casualties at Saipan:** COMGEN, FIFTHPHIBCORPS, G-1 Report, Phase I (Saipan). Aug. 10, 1944, 6; Hoffman, 68–69, n. 63. **"So you're just gonna drop us off":** Fontenot interview. **"I was so caught up":** Boots interview, 101–2. **Problems of battleship fire support:** COMBATDIV Two, action report, July 3, 1944, 10. **"A rare treat":** USS *California*, action report, June 30, 1944, 6. **Damage to USS *Tennessee*:** USS *Tennessee*, 10–11, 71–72, 89. **Fire support, daily battalion assignments:** Turner report, 183–99. See also Commander, Seventh Amphibious Force, "Tentative Standing Operating Procedure for Naval Gunfire Support in Landing Operations," Oct. 22, 1943, 22–23; USS *California*, 8; Heinl, "Naval Gunfire Support in Landings," 2; Inglis, 11. **Kauffman goes ashore:** USS *California*, action report, radio log for 1111/15 June. **"Get those planes out of the way":** USS *California*, action report, radio log for 1257/15 June. **"It was unfortunate":** Ibid., 6–8, and gunnery officer's report, 3. **"Beyond a certain point":** Turner, comments on USMC historical monograph on Guam, Jan. 27, 1953, 9. **"Whenever we reached":** Moore interview, 1040–41. **"He was the essence of ice water":** Slonim to Forrestel, Jan. 29, 1963. **"We don't even have the *beachhead* yet"** and **"I want it very, very badly":** Kauffman interview, 202–3. **"Casualties are piling up":** USS *California*, action report, radio log for 1404/15 June. **Casualty evacuation:** Turner report, 252–54; COMTRANSDIV 28, "Report of Control Operations on Dog Day and Succeeding Days," July 11, 1944, 1. **"On one of these LSTs":** NTLF (Corps), Surgeon, "Medical Report, Phase I (Saipan)," Aug. 6, 1944, 6. **"To me it looked awfully serious":** Sylvester narrative, 8. **"He was a real man":** Hill, 402. **"He walked up and down the beach":** Kauffman, 206. **"Anderson was everywhere":** Hill, 506. **"It was vital":** Chapin, "Memoir," 56–57. **"Several of the most gruesome things"** and **"The damned artillery fire":** Graf, 204–5. **Watson ashore:** COMTRANSDIV 28, 2. **"The distant night was alive with fires":** Hoffman, 66. **Sentry passwords:** Second Marine Division, Operation Order 18, Annex G, May 9, 1944, 1–2. **"The army this evening":** Crowl, *Campaign in the Marianas*, 95. **"Task Force 52 vanished again after dark":** CTG 52.2, 31–35.

11. Trail, Attack, Report *(pp. 144–152)*

"On the morning of the fifteenth": Morison, *New Guinea and the Marianas*, 221. **"The fate of our Empire":** Kusaka, *Combined Fleet*, 18. **"Everywhere in Japan":** Sakai, *Samurai!*, 258–59. **"In the vast reaches":** Ibid., 261. **First Air Fleet strikes:** COMAIRPAC, "Analysis of Pacific Air Operations, 11–30 June 1944," 11–12; Morison, 178–79. **"A lively bonfire":** Busch, "Task Force 58," 78. **Navy intelligence assessments:** Task Group 58.1, Operation Plan 7-44, June 1944, Annex I. **"Before leaving Pearl Harbor":** Turner, "Major Aspects of the Marianas Campaign," undated speech, Turner Papers, NHHC. **"This trick was possible":** Burke interview, 14. **"We didn't know":** Moore interview, 1000–1001. **Sighting by USS *Flying Fish*:** Risser lost contact at 1820H/2020K and at 1925H/2125K transmitted his report. USS *Flying Fish*, "Report of War Patrol Number Ten," July 5, 1944, 18–19. **"Very**

persistent jamming": USS *Seahorse,* "Report of Fifth War Patrol," undated, 1–2, 38. *Cavalla's* activities: USS *Cavalla,* "Report of First War Patrol," Aug. 3, 1944, 4–7, 34; Lockwood, *Sink 'Em All,* 189. "It appeared most important": Zimmerman, "Operation Forager," 85. "He spoke only": Robert L. Savage to T. B. Buell, May 16, 1972, 1. "Materially altered the situation": COMFIFTHFLEET, "Initial Report on the Operation to Capture the Marianas Islands," 3. Spruance's report misstates the time of the *Seahorse's* sighting report, which was sent at 2300(I), or midnight in Saipan's "Kilo" time zone, where Spruance was operating. "I thought that my estimate": Spruance to Nimitz, July 4, 1944, 3. Juggling the fleet to defend Saipan: COMFIFTHFLEET, "Initial Report," 3; CTG 51.1, action report, July 21, 1944, 2; Harry Hill interview, 509. "Do you think the Japs": Smith, *Coral and Brass,* 165. "An opportunity was presented" and "Harrill's refusal": Clark, *Carrier Admiral,* 166. "We would have had a glorious": Clark interview, 474. "After debating the pros": Clark, *Carrier Admiral,* 167. Spruance as admirer of Togo: Moore interview, 1034; Morison, *New Guinea and the Marianas,* 315.

12. Tank Attack *(pp. 153–162)*

The Battle of Marpi Point: CTG 51.1, action report, July 21, 1944, 1; USS *Gilmer,* action report, 1–5, 8. "You could move": Pase interview, 29. "One of the great experiences": Robert E. Wolin, quoted in Fawell, "Second Armored Amphibian Battalion website," unpaginated. "Working up courage": Jones, *Brief History of the Sixth Marines,* 90–91. "The attack will be made": Hoffman, *Saipan,* 87. Some accounts of the tank attack suggest it descended from the north, via the coast road, but a hand-drawn map by the 1/6 exec, Major J. A. Donovan, shows it hitting the 1/6 along a road from the west. Tank battle: Donovan, "Saipan Tank Battle," 27; USS *Halsey Powell,* action report, Aug. 10, 1944, 5–6; USS *Louisville,* "Report of Operations," Aug. 19, 1944, 7–8. "I hollered, 'Hit the deck!' ": Michelony interview, 52–53. "The battle evolved into a madhouse": Donovan, 26. "Impossible to sort claims": Ibid., 27. "The tank erupted": Jones, 92. "The incident was typical": Pratt, "The Marines in the Pacific War," 20. "Held onto the shoulders" and "As their guides": Donovan, 27. "Took the wrong road": COMGEN, FIFTHPHIBCORPS, "Report of Marianas Operation, Phase I (Saipan)," G-2 Report, 712. "Robbed the attack": Denfield, *Hold the Marianas,* 58. Protocol for handling enemy KIA: CTF 53, "Operation Order for Guam," May 4, 1944, Appendix 3, 6; Hays narrative, 16. "At all medical installations": Hoffman, 124–25. "They made our last hour": Kauffman interview, 203–4. "We were not skilled artists": Ibid., 266–67. Six hundred high-capacity battleship projectiles: 105,000 lbs. of tetratol divided by a 153-pound bursting charge of Explosive D (ammonium picrate). See U.S. Navy, Bureau of Ordnance, "U.S. Explosive Ordnance," May 28, 1947, www .hnsa.org/doc/ordnance. "A wall of absolutely black water": Kauffman interview, 205. "It is hard to realize": Hill interview, 459. The supply bottleneck: COMTRANSDIV 26, "Observations, Comments and Recommendations—Saipan Operations," June 28, 1944, 4–6. "Tens of thousands of these": Hill, 458–59. "We discussed the advisability": Kauffman, 205. "His own all-American football team": Marshall interview, 36; U.S. Naval Special Warfare Command (Roger Clapp, ed.), "A History of Underwater Demolition Team Five," 32. **"I was sixty-two":** Smith, *Coral and Brass*, 184–85. **Taking Aslito:** 27th Division, Journal of Forager Operation, G-3, 10. **"I was determined to take Saipan":** Smith, 184–85.

13. The View from the Mountain *(pp. 164–169)*

"As if they had no souls": Sugano, "The End at Saipan," 99. **"Woman! What are you doing?":** Ibid., 100. **"Then, suddenly":** Ibid., 104. **Air attack on Saipan anchorage:** USS *Midway*, action report, Aug. 21, 1944, 5–6; Morison, *New Guinea and the Marianas*, 207. **"I was excited":** Freer, "The Promise Aloft," 37. See also VC-65, air action report, June 17, 1944, 6–8. The position of this LST group was 15-10 N/ 145-40 E, per the LST-84 war diary. **Sunset attack on CVEs:** USS *Fanshaw Bay*, action report, 2; COMAIRPAC, "Analysis of Pacific Air Operations, 11–30 June 1944," 18. The CVEs were operating at 15-09 N / 146-25 E per USS *Coral Sea*, action report, 4. *Fanshaw Bay* **hit:** USS *Fanshaw Bay*, 12. **"It was apparent":** USS *Cavalla*, "Report of First War Patrol," Aug. 3, 1944, 9. **"On receipt of his message":** Ibid.; Lockwood, *Sink 'Em All*, 189–90. **"The above list of enemy ships does not frighten our varsity":** CINCPAC June 17/1856 CTF 17 to all subs, and June 18/0016 to individual subs, cited in Y'Blood, *Red Sun Setting*, 77. **PBMs at Saipan:** VP-16, war diary, June 1944, 4; USS *Ballard*, war diary, June 1944, 11–12; CTF 52.2, action report, 39; Hill interview, 511.

14. First Contact *(pp. 170–177)*

"If I were the Japanese admiral": Barber, interviewed by T. B. Buell, 63–64. **"The enemy, his strength, dispositions":** Spruance to E. B. Potter, Feb. 21, 1959, 1. *Cavalla's* **June 17–18 sighting of Combined Fleet:** COMFIFTHFLEET, "Initial Report," 6. Spruance received *Cavalla's* 2029(I)/17 June report at 0321(K), a delay of almost six hours. *Cavalla's* position at the time was 12-19 N/134-30 E. **"If we closed during the afternoon":** Burke interview; 21, Hone, "U.S. Navy Surface Battle Doctrine and Victory in the Pacific," 85. **"DO NOT—REPEAT NOT—BELIEVE":** CTF 58, action report, Sept. 11, 1944, 46. See also COMBATDIV 8 (Lee), "Report of Night Action, Task Force 64, Nov. 14–15, 1942," undated, 8; Hornfischer, *Neptune's Inferno*, 367; Hone, "U.S. Navy Surface Battle Doctrine and Victory in the Pacific," 85. **"Task Force 58 must cover Saipan":** COMFIFTHFLEET, Initial Report, 6; see also Moore interview, 1002–3. **"We would be lucky":** Burke interview, 21. **"WE WILL PROCEED":** Barber, interviewed by T. B. Buell, May 6, 1972, 62–64. See also Burke, "Spruance, Mitscher and Task Force 58," in Wooldridge, *Carrier Warfare in the Pacific*, 160–63. **Spruance suspects radio transmission is a trap:** COMFIFTHFLEET, war diary, June 1944, 19–20; CTF 58, action report, Sept. 11, 1944, 48. **"This is the first time":** Worden, "There Was a Man," 118. **"We so firmly believed":** Kusaka, *Combined Fleet*, 127. **"If the old man pulls it off":** Worden, 119. **"PROPOSE COMING TO COURSE 270":** CTF 58, 49. **"Here we are looking": USS *Stingray*, "Report of Eleventh War Patrol," 15–16. See also COMFIFTHFLEET, "Initial Report," 7. **Burns vs. flares:** CTG 58.1, action report, July 14, 1944, 8. **"CHANGE PROPOSED IN YOUR TBS MESSAGE":** CTF 58, 49. **"We wrote dozens of them":** Thach interview, 325. **"Junior officers began to talk":** Worden, 119; see also Toll, *Conquering Tide*, 477. **Nagumo's report:** Kusaka, 121. **"We were indeed orphans":** Smith, *Coral and Brass*, 166. **"Marines die for their country":** Ibid. **Lieutenant Arle and the delayed dispatch:** COMFIFTHFLEET, war diary, June 1944, 23. See also CTF 58, 50, and VP-16, war diary, June 1944, 4–5. **"Had the report arrived sooner":** Moore interview, 1007.

15. War of the Wind Machines *(pp. 178–193)*

Lt. Oveland over Guam: USS *Belleau Wood*, action report, June 26, 1944, 12, 77; Moore interview, 1006; Tillman, *Clash of the Carriers*, 130–31. **"We were certainly due":** Burke, personal statement, Aug. 20, 1945, 1. **"The plane made no report?":** Worden, "There Was a Man," 119–20. **"Are you excited?":** Busch, "Task Force 58," 79–80. **"Get out of the road":** USS *Lexington*, action report, June 30, 1944, 27; Burke, personal statement, Aug. 20, 1945, 2. **F6F interception of attack:** Winston narrative, 1; VF-15 ACA #29, 44–45. **"Any gunner":** Mustin interview, 13. See also USS *Indiana*, aircraft action report, July 10, 1944, 7; USS *South Dakota*, action report, June 26, 1944, 5, 23; Tillman, *Clash of the Carriers*, 145; Vraciu interview, 25; USS *Lexington*, 27. **Helena and the VT fuze:** W. S. Parsons to Raymond E. Lois, Jr., Feb. 5, 1949. **"No one kicked the tires":** Vraciu, 70–71. **"We weren't doing any striking":** Thach interview, 376. **"There was something in his voice":** Vraciu interview, 71–73. **"Every time we launched":** Burke, 3. **McCampbell's air action:** VF-15, air action report, June 19, 1944, 52–57; McCampbell, "Doctrine for a Fighter Pilot," in Wooldridge, *Carrier Warfare in the Pacific*, 196–97; McCampbell interview, 149–54, 157, 162–63, 179–80. McCampbell's plane handlers were E. E. Carroll and Chester Owens. McCampbell, 316. **Attack on TG 58.7:** USS *Alabama*, action report, July 8, 1944, 5–7; USS *South Dakota*, action report, June 26, 1944, 7, 21–23; USS *Indiana*, air action report, July 10, 1944, 12; USS *Minneapolis*, action report, Aug. 5 1944, 7. **"F6Fs risking friendly fire":** USS *Indiana*, air action report, July 10, 1944, 24, 55, 58. *There are enough cookies:* Vraciu interview, 73–74; Air Group 16, air action report, June 20, 1944, 71. **"The enemy planes had been pretty well chopped"** and **Vraciu's six kills:** Vraciu, 74–77. **"From their attitude":** Busch, "Task Force 58," 81. See also USS *Essex*, action report, July 6, 1944, 4; USS *Bunker Hill*, war diary, June 1944, 24–25.

16. Fast Carriers Down *(pp. 194–202)*

"The picture was too good": USS *Cavalla*, "Report of First War Patrol," Aug. 3, 1944, 11. **Shokaku in extremis:** Yuusuke Edo, *Marianas oki no shichimenchouchi* (The Tragic Marianas Turkey Shoot), 252–61, in Parshall, Tully, and Wolff, "The Sinking of Shokaku." **"Survivors remaining in the water":** Ibid. "The translator

518 NOTES

made grave expression as he read this, saying that the translation is describing *exactly* the effect of the movie *Titanic,* which he had seen—just as horrible as the end. This made clear many otherwise vague words." *Shokaku's* last reported position was 12-00 N, 137-46 E. Another source indicated 11-50 N, 137-57 E. **Loss of Taiho:** Ozawa USSBS; Kusaka, *Combined Fleet,* 128. *Taiho* sank at 12-05 N, 138-12 E. **McCampbell over Guam:** Air Group 15, air action report #31, 61–66; McCampbell interview, 180–81. **"Is this all the planes I get":** McCampbell interview, 181; Tillman, *Hellcats,* 82. **"He was supposed to stay":** McCampbell, 181; Air Group 16, action report, 76; Olynyk, "USN Aerial Victory Credits," 59; Tillman, *Clash of the Carriers,* 321. **"Congratulations. You're grounded":** Tillman to the author, July 30, 2015. **"Regrettable, but could not be avoided":** USS *Indiana,* air action report, July 10, 1944, 55–56. **TG 58.7 claimed sixteen kills:** *South Dakota* 4 plus 1 assist; *Indiana* 5 assists; *Alabama* 1 assist; *Fullam* 2 plus 2 assists; *Iowa* 2 plus 1 assist; *Minneapolis* 2; *New Orleans* 1 plus 3 assists; *Wichita* 2 assists; *New Jersey* 1 assist; *San Francisco* 1 assist. **"His torpedo went one way":** Moore, letter home, June 23, 1944. **"DESIRE TO ATTACK ENEMY TOMORROW":** Moore interview, 1010. **"You could sense":** Slonim, "A Flagship View of Command Decisions," 87–88.

17. To Build a Better Airfield (pp. 205–210)

"His presence there": Chapin, "Memoir," 73. **"Saipan possessed large numbers":** Stott, "Saipan Under Fire," 21–22. **"The whole panorama":** Chapin, 74. **Developing Aslito Field:** CINCPAC/CINCPOA, "Base Development Plan, Tearaway (Saipan)," May 6, 1944; Dod, *Technical Services,* 500. **"I knew the primary job":** Jarman, quoted by Green, "Our B-29 Base," 8. **"It is very difficult":** Kusaka, *Combined Fleet,* 129. See also Toland, *Rising Sun,* 627. **"The task force without planes":** Kusaka, 128. **"Our officers were desperate":** Sakai, *Samurai!,* 261. **"Only flea bites":** Ibid., 264. **"Through the whole of yesterday's fight":** Busch, "Task Force 58," 82.

18. Beyond Darkness (pp. 212–231)

"Every commander must be a gambler": Spruance, notes for E. B. Potter, Jan. 1959. **"The two fleets":** Burke, oral history, 1. **"We did everything we could":** Burke, personal statement, Aug. 20, 1945, 4; Burke, oral history, 1. **"We hoped against hope":** Burke, personal statement, 4–5. See also Air Group 16, air action report for June 20, 1944, 91–92; Moore interview, 1011. **"Someone had sighted something":** Burke, personal statement, 5. **"If the Japanese ships":** Ibid., 7. **"Mitscher warned the pilots":** Burke, personal statement, 5. **"The flight was so long":** Vraciu interview, 80–81. **"TELL TOKYO ROSE":** Clark interview, 528. **"Take a bath":** Ramage, narrative, 2. **Attacks on Ozawa:** USS *Belleau Wood,* action report, 15, 108–9; Air Group 16, 92. **"Unknown Strike Leader from 41 Sniper":** Ramage, "Turn on the Lights," in Wooldridge, 171–86. **"From 41 Sniper to all bombers":**

Ibid. **"I was scared"**: Lewis, in Wooldridge, 176. **"Skipper, look back"**: Ramage, personal narrative, 3. **"I heard Japs talking"**: Lewis, in Wooldridge, 177–78. **"I couldn't seem to go"**: Ibid., 178; VB-10, action report, 89. All three of these pilots carried 1,000-pound general-purpose bombs, not armor-piercing bombs. See also Tully and Casse, "IJN *Hiyo*: Tabular Record of Movement." **McLellan shot down:** Air Group 16, air action report, June 20, 1944, 92–94; "The Warren McLellan Story," 3. **"I'm hit"**: Vraciu interview, 83–84; Air Group 16, 83. **"Things were popping and cracking"**: Ibid., 84. **"Instead of the usual"**: Bronn, "The Tom Bronn Story." **Shields shot down:** Air Group 16, 86. **"My only hope"**: McLellan, 3. **"It was a botched-up hop"**: Vraciu, 83. See also COMAIRPAC, "Analysis of Pacific Air Operations, 11–30 June 1944," 31. **"I've got only twenty-five gallons"**: Vraciu, 83–85. **"If you want us to bail out"**: Bronn. **"Some of the guys were breaking down"**: Vraciu, 88. **"The most miserable case of radio and air discipline"**: Ramage, personal narrative, 3. **"Fatigue is a peculiar thing"**: Burke, personal statement, Aug. 21, 1945, 1. **Tate, Omark, and Brown:** USS *Belleau Wood* action report, June 24, 1944, 109–11. **"Mitscher sat on his windy bridge"**: Busch, "Task Force 58," 85. **"I kept thinking"**: Vraciu, 86. *"Bald Eagle, this is Blue Jacket himself"*: Joslin interview, 6; Burke, oral history, 2. Jocko Clark claimed credit for the dramatic decision, but J. D. Ramage testifies: "In spite of what a certain admiral has to say, the operation was planned in the afternoon by Arleigh Burke. . . . It wasn't a spur of the moment operation. It was a well-considered plan." Ramage, in Wooldridge, 184. "Lighted-ship was standard operating procedure for night recovery," wrote Clark Reynolds in *The Fast Carriers,* 201. Spruance confirmed that the dramatic gesture had been planned all along. "A carrier without its air group is a disarmed ship, a liability and not an asset," he would write. "The time to consider the risk in turning on the lights for a night recovery is before launching the attack. If the planes are to be launched so late in the day that a night recovery is probable, and if the tactical situation is such that you are not willing to do what is required to get the planes back safely, then you have no business launching the attack in the first place." Spruance to E. B. Potter, Jan. 2, 1960. "My recollection is that Admiral Spruance got a message from Admiral Mitscher recommending this procedure and he promptly authorized turning the lights on," Chuck Barber would say. Barber interview, 64. Burke's comment that pilots were not told in advance about what was standard operating procedure is curious in this light. *"Land at nearest base"*: Vraciu, 86. **"Their desperation to pull that trick"**: Burke oral history, 2. **"We stood open-mouthed"**: Winston, "How Our Navy Outfoxed the Japs at Saipan," 89. **"The planes were instructed"**: Barber interview, 64. **"Up ahead and to my port"**: Bronn. **"Because he was wounded"**: Busch, 85. **"Not a huge one"**: McLellan, 4. See also McLellan's personal account in Air Group 16, air action report, June 20, 1944, 93. **"Pilots were picked up right and left"**: Winston, 89. **Pilot rescues:** Operational losses of SB2C Helldivers on this day were 43 out of 51, or 84 percent. The venerable SBD, with less range, had losses of just 4 out of 26, or 15 percent. COMAIRPAC, 49–50. **"They lost a lot of their aircraft"**: Ramage, in Wooldridge, 185. **"I doubt if any other"**: Winston, personal narrative, 5.

19. Smith versus Smith (pp. 234–245)

"To me this callous disregard": Smith, *Coral and Brass*, 125–26. Fourth Marine Division, "Reports for Marianas-Saipan Operation," 22; Love, "Smith versus Smith," 4–6; Sherrod, "The Saipan Controversy," 19. **U.S. casualties on Saipan:** As of June 22, the two Marine divisions had taken more than 6,100 casualties, as against 320 for the 27th Infantry Division. Turner report, 256 (Joint Expeditionary Force, "Medical Report for Saipan Operation," Enclosure K, 5). **"Any objective examination":** Hogaboom interview, 186–87. **The 3/106 in Death Valley:** Hall-den, "The Operations of Company L, 3rd Battalion, 106th Infantry in the Battle of Death Valley, Saipan, 23–28 June 1944," 7–9, 25–28, 33–35; Headquarters, Northern Troops and Landing Force, "Special interrogation of Major Kiyoshi Yoshida, intelligence officer of the former 43rd Division headquarters," 2; Allen, *Sacked at Saipan,* unpaginated. **The 318th Fighter Group on Saipan:** Edward E. Gray interview. **"As one Army man to another":** Sherrod, "The Saipan Controversy," 19. **"I don't think I am really a combat commander":** Erskine interview, 319. **"I went out and met the regimental commander":** Hogaboom, 208–9. **Assault on Mount Tapotchau:** Shaw et al., *Central Pacific Drive,* 320–21. **Holland Smith to Ralph Smith:** CTF 56 to CG, 27th Infantry Division, 0836/24 June 1944. **"Your failure to maintain contact":** 27th Division, Journal of Forager Operation, G-3, 57. **"Bill, I hate to do it":** Hallden, 15. **"One of the most disagreeable tasks":** Smith, 173. Holland Smith's mistrust of the Army had roots. With some justification, he feared Big Army's machinations against his authority and command. (See Erskine interview, 317–19.) Smith would write after Tarawa that the Army's top man in the Pacific Ocean Areas, Lt. Gen. Robert C. Richardson, "reported in a secret 'eyes-only' memo to Nimitz that Marines were not competent to command amphibious operations and that my veteran V Amphibious Corps headquarters should be replaced by an Army Corps command over all the Central Pacific. Nimitz kept me in ignorance of this, but my old teammate, Admiral King (seconded by Vandegrift), made short work of the suggestion when it reached Washington." This is true. As recently as June 22, Richardson and Lt. Gen. Millard F. Harmon, the commanding general, Army Air Forces, Pacific Ocean Areas, had met with Nimitz (on instructions from General Marshall) to urge that Nimitz place all Army air and ground forces under Army operational command. See Marshall to Richardson, info CINCPOA; Harmon, 1944 June 24/2030Z, CINCPAC, *Grey Book,* 2320; also Richardson to WDCSA, info CINCPOA, 1944 June 23/0950, in CINCPAC, *Grey Book,* 2328–29. Smith continued: "Hostility to my initial endeavors from high Army sources was never demonstrated openly. Subtle influences were set in motion and permitted to flow unchecked through receptive channels. In combat it was disquieting to feel that my actions were being observed, not with the idea of constructive analysis but with the sole purpose of finding fault. Richardson seemed to be waiting for me to make a mistake that could be magnified to promote the grand plan of an Army-controlled offensive, well supplied with Marine troops to do the fighting." Smith, 115–16. **"Bid fair to be rather endless":** Moore interview, 1043–44. **"It smacked of infantry attachment":** XXIV Corps Artillery, "Final Report of

Marianas Operation," 1–2; Turner report, 17. **"When the record sums up":** War Department, *Small Unit Actions*. **Private Costanzo:** XXIV Corps Artillery, 31. **Experimental rocket detachment:** Second Provisional Rocket Detachment, action report, Aug. 21, 1944, 2–3. **"We had no place to go":** Mort Hamilton, in Everett, "World War II, Battle of Saipan," 40. **"If you want me to move":** Donald R. Lienesch, in Everett, 42. **"It was frustrating":** Hamilton quoted in Everett, 45. **"Having apparently finished":** Stott, "Saipan Under Fire," 25–26. **"From the heights":** Ibid., 26–29.

20. Satan's Breath *(pp. 247–261)*

Nafutan Point breakout: NTLF, G-2 report, 34, quoted in Shaw et al., *Central Pacific Drive*, 325–26; Hoffman, *Saipan*, 156; Smith, *Coral and Brass*, 170–71. **USMC battle drill:** Fourth Marine Division, "Reports of Canadian Officers Attached to 27th Infantry Division, USA, for the Saipan Operation," in Fourth Marine Division, "Reports for Marianas-Saipan Operation," 939. **"We got a hell of an education":** Charland interview, 40. **"How many of their lives":** Bollard, "First Corps Medium Tank Battalion," undated, 53; Shaw et al., 325–26. **"We sat and sat and watched":** Stott, "Saipan Under Fire," 30. **"They were in the Army's zone":** Chapin, "Memoir," 105. **"Stand by to move!":** Ibid., 106–8. See also Fourth Marine Division, "Reports for Marianas-Saipan Operation," 28. **"We're supposed to be":** Jones, *Oba*, 36–37. **"Orders from regimental headquarters":** Ibid., 38. **Oba under bombardment:** Ibid., 40–44. "Front lines were so irregular due to type of terrain that it was impossible in many cases to even attempt to coordinate an air mission," a Joint Assault Signal Company officer attached to the 27th Infantry wrote. Commander, Support Aircraft, Pacific Fleet, "Reports of Support Aircraft Operation, Marianas," Sept. 11, 1944, 4–5, 13–14. **"This seems logical":** Ibid., 29. **K/3/24 in the tangle:** Chapin, 110–27. **Cavalla arrives at Saipan:** USS *Cavalla*, "Report of First War Patrol," Aug. 3, 1944, 19–21. **"A scene which we":** Ibid., 21–23. **"This campaign is a stiff one":** Moore, letter home, July 2, 1944, quoted in Moore interview, 1047. **"The difficulties of the mountainous backbone":** Spruance to Nimitz, July 4, 1944, 1. **"If their views as to military forces":** Spruance to Nimitz, 1425/05 July 1944, in CINCPAC, *Grey Book*, 2332. **Setting W Day on Guam:** Spruance to Nimitz, July 4, 1944, 1; CTF 51, "Report of Amphibious Operations for the Capture of the Marianas Islands," Aug. 25, 1944 ("Turner report"), 23–24; Conolly interview, 243.

21. The Dying Game *(pp. 263–267)*

"The commander in chief is giving an order": Sugano, "The End at Saipan," 132–33. **Miura under fire:** Sugano, "Fate of the Donni Field Hospital," 1–2; USS *Louisville*, action report, Aug. 19, 1944, 22–24. **"I had confidence":** Sugano, "The End at Saipan," 158. **"By order of the high commander":** Sugano, "Fate of the Donni Field Hospital," 3. **Saito's new headquarters:** COMGEN, Fifth Phib Corps, "Report of Marianas Operation, Phase I (Saipan)," G-2 Report, 709, 714. See also

NTLF, "Captured Japanese officer's personal account of 'The Last Days of General Saito,'" 1. **"You must chew the American force to pieces!":** Ibid., 1. **"We felt this was":** Ibid., 2. **Assessments of Japanese strength:** COMFIFTHPHIB, Intelligence Section, "Special NTLF G-2 Interrogation of Shimizo, Masaaki," July 3, 1944, 1–3; 27th Division, G-2 Periodic Report, July 4, 1944, 2, included in 27th Division, "Report of Intelligence Activities, Saipan Operation," Sept. 15, 1944. **"I didn't feel they were a terrible enemy":** Sugano, "The End at Saipan," 109. **"Thank you, Miss Nurse":** Sugano, "The Fate of Donni Field Hospital," 9–10.

22. Sniper Ship on a Cave Shoot *(pp. 268–277)*

"It was our way of celebrating": Williams, *Measure of a Man*, 130. **"They appeared near exhaustion":** USS *Montpelier,* war diary, July 4, 1944, 4–5. See also USS *Birmingham,* action report, July 22, 1944, 22n; COMGEN, Fleet Marine Force, Pacific, "Naval Gunfire Support in the Forager Operation," Oct. 7, 1944, 17, 27. **"We are going to spot you"** and **"No change, no change":** USS *Philip,* "Report of Gunfire Support, Forager Operation," July 23, 1944, voice radio log, 7–10. Admiral Oldendorf praised the *Louisville* for setting "an all-time gunnery record by firing or standing by to fire night and day during the first eleven days of the Saipan operation, except for time out to fuel or to replenish ammunition." First endorsement, Aug. 26, 1944, to USS *Louisville,* action report, Aug. 19, 1944, 55. **"You have been the best ship":** USS *Philip,* "Report of Gunfire Support, Forager Operation," July 23, 1944, voice radio log, 7–10. See also USS *Birmingham,* 16–18. **"Our friends left in Donnay":** Sugano, "The Fate of Donni Field Hospital," 11–13. **IJN as "sampan sailors":** Takagi, "Memoirs of the War's End," 8. "Given the navy's mistakes, the General Staff headquarters was not committed to recovering Saipan," Sokichi Takagi would write. **General Saito's decision:** NTLF, "Captured Japanese officer's personal account of 'The Last Days of General Saito,'" 3. **"We didn't have any specific code":** Elrod interview, June 7, 2013, 2. **"Your life is at stake":** Hegi, "Extermination Warfare," 71. **Japanese civilians as shields:** 27th Infantry Division, "Journal of Forager Operation," G-2, entry 68, July 6, 1944. **"We did try to capture them, but":** Kyle interview, 93–94. **Kyle and Maxie Williams:** Ibid. **U.S. Army on Tanapag Plain:** 27th Division, G-2 Periodic Report, No. 20, July 6, 1944, 2, in 27th Division, "Report of Intelligence Activities, Saipan Operation," Sept. 15, 1944; see also "The Fight on the Tanapag Plain," in War Department, *Small Unit Actions,* 68–70; Jones, *Oba,* 51–53. **"For more than twenty days since the American devils attacked":** COMGEN, Fleet Marine Force, Pacific, "Naval Gunfire Support in the Forager Operation," Oct. 7, 1944, 38. Note: Saito's speech is attributed to an unidentified Japanese POW. This exact language also appears in Jones, 54–55. See also NTLF, "Captured Japanese officer's personal account of 'The Last Days of General Saito,'" 3–4. **Deaths of Saito, Nagumo, and their aides:** Jones, 63–65. **"Prepare to fight":** Sugano, "The Fate of Donni Field Hospital," 21. *"Please let me die with the field hospital"* and **"To our surprise":** Ibid., 23. **"Return to the field hospital":** Ibid., 28–29.

23. Beyond All Boundaries *(pp. 279–289)*

Accounts of the size of the *gyokusai* attack force conflict: The U.S. Army claimed Suzuki had 4,100 troops. See 27th Division, G-2 Periodic Report, No. 22, July 8, 1944, 2, in 27th Division, "Report of Intelligence Activities, Saipan Operation," Sept. 15, 1944; 27th Division, Journal of Forager Operation, G-2, entries 41, 82, and 89, for July 7, 1944, 120, 124. A Korean POW who had helped organize assault units in the far north said the suicide force consisted of about three thousand men, mainly of SNLF; eight hundred to a thousand army troops; and fewer than a thousand labor troops. COMGEN, FIFTHPHIBCORPS, "Report of Marianas Operation, Phase I (Saipan)," G-2 Report, 96. See also NTLF, "Captured Japanese officer's personal account of 'The Last Days of General Saito,'" 3–4. **American brutality:** Okuyama, "Surviving on the Island of Suicide," 2–9; Ada, "World War II—Saipan," 4. See also COMGEN, FIFTHPHIBCORPS, 90–93. **"To act otherwise":** Jones, *Oba*, 57–58. **"You would rather take the easy way":** Ibid., 60–61. **"It reminded me of":** Hoffman, *Saipan*, 223. **Naval support during *gyokusai* attack:** USS *Birmingham,* action report, July 22, 1944, 24–25; COMFIFTHFLEET, "Report on Japanese Counterattack at Saipan on morning of 7 July 1944," July 19, 1944, 2. **"Don't give them a damned inch":** Sergeant John G. Breen quoted in O'Brien, *Battling for Saipan,* 239, 27th Division, Journal of Forager Operation, G-2, 118; see also 27th Infantry Division, G-1 Report, 77. "The 3/105 never moved from its preattack position," reported Spruance. COMFIFTHFLEET, "Report on Japanese Counterattack," 2. Though General Griner would claim his units had killed more than 4,300 Japanese, that tally included many who as evidenced by their state of decomposition were killed in action well before the July 7 attack. See H. M. Smith to Griner, "Japanese Killed and Buried on 7 July 1944 in Zone of action of 27th Infantry Division," July 15, 1944, 2; COMFIFTHFLEET, 3. **"We didn't like the odor":** Moore interview, 1052–53. **"We had a grandstand view":** Spruance to Margaret, July 8, 1944, 1. **"Having a regular field day":** 27th Division, Journal of Forager Operation, G-3, 165–66, entry 15, July 8, 1944. See also 163, entry 100, and 167, entry 28, July 8, 1944; Jones, *Brief History of the Sixth Marines,* 100. **"That's what we want":** USS *Philip,* "Report of Gunfire Support, Forager Operation," July 23, 1944, voice radio log, 14–15. **"The Japanese is a sensitive person":** U.S. Pacific Fleet, "Psychological Warfare: Part 1," Aug. 1944, 5–6. See also Hegi, "Extermination Warfare: The Conduct of the Second Marine Division at Saipan," 64; COMGEN, FIFTHPHIBCORPS, "Report of Marianas Operation, Phase I (Saipan)," G-2 Report, 121–22. **"Let the little jerk go"** and **Gabaldon on Saipan:** Gabaldon, *Saipan: Suicide Island,* 105–6. **"This is in conformity"** and **"Fear of torture is quite widespread":** U.S. Pacific Fleet, "Psychological Warfare," 10. **"Sometimes I had to throw grenades":** Gabaldon interview.

24. Atop Suicide Cliffs *(pp. 290–300)*

Japanese fanaticism in northern Saipan: Commandant of the Marine Corps, "Extracts from Observations of Saipan Operation, dated July 11, 1944," July 21,

1944, 1; Sherrod, "Saipan: Eyewitness Tells of Island Fight," 78–79. **"It was very depressing to have suffered":** Stott, "Saipan Under Fire," 44. **"A shooting gallery at four hundred yards"** and **"Imperceptibly a psychological reaction":** Ibid., 45–46. **"Saipan was filled with horror":** Graf, "Easy Company," 228. **"Mothers and fathers stabbed":** Fourth Marine Division history quoted by Graf, 228. **"Every darn one of them":** Kyle interview, 92. **"There was no leaving anybody in there":** Boots interview, 110–11. **"Sometimes in fighting":** Ibid., 115–16. **"There was no stopping them":** Charland interview, 36–38. **"A nude young woman":** Winton W. Carter, quoted in Fawell, Second Armored Amphibian Battalion website; see also Bock interview, 50–51. **"It's just the damnedest feeling":** Bock interview, 54. **"No pangs of conscience":** Stott, 51–52. **"It was a ghastly business":** *Collier's,* "Suicides on Saipan," 94. **Oba after the *gyokusai* attack:** Jones, *Oba,* 81–86. **"You are wounded. Do not try to move":** Sugano, "Fate of the Donni Field Hospital," 30–31. **Miura's recovery:** Ibid., 30–36. *This is like rising from the dead:* Jones, 90. **Casualties:** Hoffman, *Saipan,* 268–69; NTLF, G-1 Report, Phase I (Saipan). Aug. 10, 1944, 6. **"The prisoner has a bit of a dramatic flair":** COMFIFTHFLEET, "Preliminary POW Interrogation Report, Noda, Mitsuharu," 4; COPHIBPAC to CINCPAC. "Observation on Noda, Mitsuharu, Chief Yeoman to Vice Admiral Nagumo Chuichi," July 19, 1944, 1–3. **"One thing that has appealed to me":** Spruance to Margaret, July 16, 1944, 1–2.

25. Regime Change *(pp. 301–316)*

"We survivors": Stott, "Saipan Under Fire," 47. **"If we did not know":** Ibid, 51. **Plans for Tinian landings:** Dyer, *Amphibians Came to Conquer,* 951–52. **"The more we studied it":** Hill interview, 528. **"I literally got blasted":** Ibid., 571. **"He just would not accept":** Hill, notes for T. B. Buell, 5–6. **"He simply would not listen":** Dyer, 955–57. **"A twinkle came in his eye":** Hill, 291. **White Beach recon by UDT/Marines:** Kauffman interview, 216–20; Hogaboom interview, 213–14; Robbins, "Good to Be Alive," 69; Hill, 527; CTF 52, action report, Aug. 24, 1944, 1–2. **General Richardson's visit:** Smith, *Coral and Brass,* 176–77; Erskine interview, 317–18, 327. **"I believe he had a hangover":** Moore interview, 1060–61. **"Oh, well, that's just Kelly Turner":** Ibid., 1062. **Nimitz was dismissive:** Dyer, 929. **"It was the chance of a century":** Clark interview, 482–83. **"As I could, I told Spruance":** King, *Flight Log Book,* 1944, 16. **Mitscher's complaint to King:** Barber interview, 34. **"Spruance was rightly guided":** King and Whitehill, *Fleet Admiral King,* 557, 563. Regarding the Battle of the Philippine Sea, a leading contemporary naval analyst praised Spruance for his "comprehensive thinking and clarity of purpose. For example, doctrine said you win command of the sea before exploiting it with an amphibious operation, but Spruance would have seen this as a trap of theory, because in his experience a practical enemy would not come and fight until the landing had taken place and the opposing fleet was tied to a beachhead." Hughes, "Clear Purpose, Comprehensive Execution: Raymond Ames Spruance," 14. **"I think I should be classed as Raymond's number-one rooter":** Hill, notes for T. B. Buell, 7. **King and Nimitz on Saipan:** Ibid., 563 65. **"His experi-**

ence in the small world of the army": Kato, *Lost War,* 21–22. **"Japan could not possibly win"**: Vogel, "Japan's Secret War Within," 30–31. See also Arahara, *History of the Great Rightists,* 1–2. **IJN "unfit for further engagements"**: Kase, *Journey to the* Missouri, quoted in Whitehill to King, Sept. 1, 1950. **"The pulse of the Tojo regime stopped"**: Takagi, "Memoirs," 12. See also Toland, *Rising Sun,* 655–56. **"We were convinced that it would be useless"**: Hiranuma interrogation, 7. **"There is no way out but to fight to the end"**: Hiranuma, quoted in *Kido's Diary,* 5. **"Follow a strategy of making the cost"**: *The New Republic,* "What Is Japanese Strategy Today?," 71. **"One of the great amphibious commanders"**: Hogaboom, 196–97. **"We had a regular conveyor belt"**: Conolly interview, 240. **UDT at Guam**: UDT 4, action report, Aug. 15, 1944, 5; UDT 3, action report, Aug. 18, 1944, 6; UDT 6, action report, Sept. 7, 1944, 2. **"WELCOME MARINES"**: Bush, *America's First Frogman,* 147. **"Murray Henry and Walt Hlebechuk claim they actually had a hand in this"**: Baird, "The Journeys of Underwater Demolition Teams," 22. **"You have been honored"**: O'Brien, *Liberation,* 1. **W Day at Guam**: War Department, "Guam: Operations of the 77th Division," 37–38. **"The enemy, overconfident"**: O'Brien, 8–9. **"We never had to attack"**: Weller interview, 82. **"The Japs had apparently leaned forward"**: Ibid., 81. **"The outstanding development of the war"**: COMINCI I, "Third Official Report to the Secretary of the Navy," in King, *War Reports,* vol. 3, 658. **"Low Water," "High Water,"** and **"Beach parties could more properly be called *reef* parties"**: COMTRANSDIV 18, "General Narrative Report of Guam Operation, 22–29 July 1944," 27. **"This was not a gentleman's job"**: Ibid., 26. **Lt. Cdr. Mang and napalm**: COMAIRPAC, "Analysis of Carrier Operations, July–Aug. 1944," 2–3, 39. **"The effect was awe-inspiring"**: Hill interview, 536–38, 575; Turner report, 56, 173. CTF 52, action report, Aug. 24, 1944, 96. **"Probably an easier way to die"**: Hill, 574.

26. Steel Like Snowflakes *(pp. 318–331)*

"Artillery lent dignity": Frequently attributed to Frederick the Great; see Weller interview, 79. **Fire support off Tinian**: COMGEN, Fleet Marine Force Pacific, "Naval Gunfire Support in the Forager Operation," Oct. 7, 1944, 105–6, 118. ComGen, XXIV Corps Artillery, Final Report on Marianas Operation, S-3 Report, 13. **"Enemy fire had been expected"**: The action report of the USS *Colorado* (p. 48) misstates that this was the *Birmingham;* see USS *Montpelier,* action report, Aug. 5, 1944, 5; CTU 52.17.3, action report, Aug. 10, 1944, 2. **"Never had such an insignificant first wave"**: Hill interview, 541–42. **"Oh, what a beautiful morning"**: Craig, "Recollections," 186. *Colorado* **hit**: COMBATDIV Four, action report, July 26, 1944, 1; USS *Colorado,* "Report to Bureau of Ships, War Damage Sustained," Aug. 4, 1944, 6–17; Leon J. Shook interview, 32–35; Patrick Walton diary, quoted in USS *Colorado* Association, "USS *Colorado,* WW2: Remembering Those Who Died in Battle," 4. **"They could have been saved"**: Shook, 33. *Norman Scott* **hit**: USS *Norman Scott,* action report, Aug. 7, 1944, 2–5, 9. **"She steamed in there"**: Moore interview, 1070; USS *Cleveland,* "Report of Bombardment of Tinian, July 23–29, 1944," Aug. 11, 1944, encl. C, 2, 7–8; CTU 52.17.3, A-4. **Will Jumper's verse:**

Jumper, "Since You Ask," in *From Time Remembered*. Jumper was professor emeritus of English at Iowa State University. This volume also contains a powerful tribute to a shipmate titled "For Noyes D. Farmer, who died but once, July 1944." **"Shock was so marked":** USS *Colorado*, action report, 110. **"It was of particular interest":** Ibid., 110–11. **Miracle pack howitzer hit on Tinian:** Cooper, "Jeff Cooper's Commentaries," 42. **"But their power was that of a small wave":** Pratt, "The Marines in the Pacific War," chapter 17, 44. **"We were covering the length":** George, "Too Young to Vote," unpaginated. **"As the troops moved south":** Hill, 548. **"I sometimes wonder":** Spruance to Margaret (Spruance) Bogart, July 25, 1944, 2. **FDR, Nimitz, and MacArthur in Hawaii:** King and Whitehill, *Fleet Admiral King*, 567–68; Hoyt, *Nimitz and His Admirals*, 412; MacArthur, *Reminiscences*, 196–98. **"Certain human animals":** FDR to MacArthur, Aug. 9, 1944, quoted in MacArthur, 199.

27. The Will to Lose Hard *(pp. 332–342)*

"Believe me": Pase interview, 36. **Securing Tinian:** CTF 52, action report, Aug. 24, 1944, 78; Turner report, 21; Jones, *Brief History of the Sixth Marines*, 104–5; Hill interview, 550. **Japanese suicides on Tinian:** Louis R. Jones interview, 121–22; Graf, "Easy Company," 250–51; Pase interview, 35–36. **Death of Kakuta:** Fuller, *Shokan*, 259. **First Air Fleet as kamikaze unit** and **"There is only one way":** King, *Last Zero Fighter*, 261; Sheftall, *Blossoms in the Wind*, 136. **"I spent the day":** Spruance to Margaret Spruance, Aug. 3, 1944, 1. **"Johnny Newcomer":** Commander, Air Group 15, "Comments and Recommendations on Air Operations for Period 18 July to 8 Aug. 1944," Aug. 16, 1944, 3–4. **"Did somebody say 'get busy and train them'?":** Ibid., 5. **"As you go north from Agana":** Spruance to Margaret, Aug. 15, 1944, 1–2. **Guam casualties:** Turner report 78, 260; Dyer, *Amphibians Came to Conquer*, 945. **"What they were, and why they were there":** Moore, 1074–75. **"We want hazardous-duty pay when":** Kauffman interview, 230–31. **"We had an intrepid group":** Marshall interview, 41. **"We were good at free enterprise":** Graf, 257. **Spruance-Halsey rotation:** Spruance to Potter, Dec. 1, 1964, 2–3. **Operation Forager summation:** COMFIFTHFLEET, final report, 4; COMAIRPAC, "Analysis of Carrier Operations, July–Aug. 1944," 45–48; CTF 52, action report, Aug. 24, 1944, 3, 45, 48. **"The destroyers always did better":** Weller, 86–88. **"The enemy met the assault":** CINCPAC-CINCPOA, Monthly Operations Report, July 1944, 37, in Dyer, 945. **"The almost fanatic Japanese tenacity":** Combined Chiefs of Staff, Second Quebec Conference, Proceedings, 317. **"I didn't think the president":** Arnold, *Global Mission*, 529. **"In a very short space . . . the destruction of the barbarians of the Pacific":** U.S. Department of State, *Foreign Relations of the United States: Conference at Quebec, 1944*, 477; Hayes, *History of the Joint Chiefs of Staff in World War II*, 643–44. **"A New Strategic Concept for the Defeat of Japan":** Ibid., 454–55, 627, 655. **Operation Downfall:** *Reports of General MacArthur*, vol. 1, 395–96. **Casualties:** Giangreco, *Hell to Pay*, 104, 316, n. 7. None of the Army's casualty projections included expected deaths among

POWs. **Dinner during the Octagon Conference:** Arnold, 527. **Twentieth Air Force in the Marianas:** U.S. Department of State, 340–41; Craven and Cate, *The Pacific: Matterhorn to Nagasaki,* 515–18; Dod, *Technical Services,* 503–5, 517.

28. Secrets of New Mexico *(pp. 347–365)*

"Paul, are you in some kind of trouble?": Tibbets, *Flight,* 152–53. **Kistiakowsky to Los Alamos:** Rhodes, *Making of the Atomic Bomb,* 452–453. **"Ours was not a nation with a kamikaze mentality":** Tibbets, 155. **"A display of pettiness":** Ibid., 159. **"It's hard to even explain":** Greene, *Duty,* 273. **"I was actually awed":** Tibbets, 177. **"My job, in brief":** Ibid., 155–56. **"It is too bad":** Spruance to W. W. Smith, Aug. 29, 1944, 1. **Spruance's view of strategy:** Spruance to Philip A. Crowl, Jan. 6, 1950, 1–2. **Iwo and Okinawa approved:** Spruance, "Notes for Possible Future Use," April 17, 1964, 1–2. **"The average military man":** Arnold, *Global Mission,* 541. **"We must consider the B-29":** Craven and Cate, *The Pacific: Matterhorn to Nagasaki,* 601. **"You would be astounded":** Hoover to Spruance, Nov. 5, 1944, 1. **"I have always maintained":** Spruance to Hoover, Nov. 30, 1944, 1. **"When we worked for the Spruance/Mitscher combination":** Walter F. Boone, recollected by E. P. Forrestel, Forrestel interview, 14. **"I can remember one evening":** Margaret Spruance interview, Dec. 6, 1971, 3–7. **Sinking of *Musashi*:** Fletcher, *Intrepid Aviators,* 275–77. **The Battle off Samar:** See Hornfischer, *Last Stand of the Tin Can Sailors,* 159–356. **"Why any of our CVEs escaped":** Spruance to Margaret, Oct. 31, 1944, 1–2. **"The Japanese frothed at the mouth":** E. B. Potter to Spruance, Feb. 13, 1959, 7. **"In calling you cautious":** Potter to Spruance, Feb. 20, 1959, 1. **"This suicide method of attack":** Spruance to J. H. Hoover, Nov. 30, 1944, 2. **"Let us make it emphatically clear":** Griffith, *The Quest,* 169. **"Every bomb that is added":** Ibid. **"He would take all the flak jackets":** Savage interview, 52. **First B-29 mission from Saipan:** Morgan, *Man Who Flew the Memphis Belle,* 285–89; Arnold, 540–41; Griffith, 177–78. **Krantz:** Braden interview, 61. **Japanese attacks on Isely Field:** Craven and Cate, 581; Tillman, *Whirlwind,* 86. **"If an engine burped":** Cooper interview, 31. See also Savage, 39, and Braden, 46–47. **"Not at this time":** Griffith, 180–81. **"An urgent requirement":** Ibid., 182. **"I've looked at you":** Tibbets, quoted in Krauss, *The 509th Remembered,* 214. **"Stop being curious":** Tibbets, 167. **"Why didn't you *keep your mouth shut*?":** Ibid., 165; Harlow Russ in Krauss, 170; Maurice C. Sullivan, in Krauss, 184. **"Fiendish in some aspects":** Tibbets, 166. **"The best bombardier":** Ibid., 162–63. **"He took pity on no one":** Charles D. Albury, in Krauss, 13. **"WHAT YOU HEAR HERE":** Russell E. Gackenback, in Krauss, 81.

29. Going Critical *(pp. 366–383)*

The pace of cleanup operations: Jarman to Turner, July 28, 1944, 2. Jones, *Oba,* 154–59, 164–65. **"We used every ruse":** Taxis interview, 174. **"You will follow Captain Oba's words":** Jones, 131. **"Splendid beyond recognition":** Sugano,

"The Fate of Donni Field Hospital," 218–20. *So why had we killed each other?*: Ibid., 237. **"It seems to me"** and **Nimitz presser:** Nimitz, transcript of press conference, Pearl Harbor, Jan. 1, 1945, 4–13. **McCampbell's celebrity:** McCampbell interview, 221–24. **"After viewing the picture":** Spruance to Forrestel, July 12, 1964, 1–2. **"The same number of Japs":** Forrestel to E. M. Eller, July 17, 1964, 1. See also Giangreco, *Hell to Pay,* 112; Morison, *Victory in the Pacific,* 74. **"The entire north end":** Craig, "Recollections," 194. **"Are easily compiled":** Hansell, *Strategic Air War Against Germany and Japan: A Memoir,* 48, as quoted in Griffith, *The Quest,* 201. See also Crane, *Bombs, Cities, and Civilians,* 141; Fedman and Karacas, "A Cartographic Fade to Black," 306. **"Utter absolute complete and irreversible":** Ibid., 193. **"Until General LeMay gave us":** Braden interview, 63. **"He was the finest combat commander":** McNamara, in Morris, *Fog of War,* at 30:00. **"What do you think about the value of Iwo Jima?":** Spruance to Forrestel, March 2, 1963, 1–2; Raymond Spruance interview, *Paris Match,* 22–23. **"I am tired of fighting them all along":** Ibid., 23. **"He had been driving himself":** Hill quoted in Dyer, *Amphibians Came to Conquer,* 1008–9. **Iwo preparations and Tokyo strikes:** Spruance to Jeter A. Iseley, Jan. 1950, 10; Dyer, 1045–46; Forrestel interview; 29. COMFIFTH-FLEET, war diary, Feb. 1945; COMFIFTHFLEET, action report, June 4, 1945, 3, 9; USS *Cabot,* action report, Feb. 28, 1945, 8; USS *Langley,* action report, March 4, 1945, 9; USS *Lexington,* action report, March 4, 1945, 9. **"The companion to war is disease":** Pamphlet reproduced in USS *Cabot,* 23. Translation by Dan King. **"Leaflets and their effect":** CINCPAC, "Report of Surrender and Occupation," 85. **"Regrettable though it is":** Prince Konoye, draft letter to the throne, Feb. 14, 1945, quoted in *Hosokawa Diary,* March 4, 1945, 349. **Anami and Umezu as dead-enders:** Frank, *Downfall,* 309; Drea, *In Service to the Emperor,* 204. **Magic and Ultra intercepts:** Frank, 99. According to the historian J. Samuel Walker, Frank's book "drives a stake into the heart of the most cherished revisionist contention—that Japan was seeking peace and the United States prolonged the war by refusing to soften its demand for unconditional surrender. Frank shows beyond reasonable doubt that neither Emperor Hirohito nor most of his top military advisers had concluded that the war must end." Walker, "Bomb! Unbomb!" (book review), *New York Times,* Dec. 12, 1999. **Iwo Jima flag raising:** A patrol led by 1st Lt. Harold G. Schrier, USMC, raised the first flag. The larger and more famous one photographed by Joe Rosenthal was a replacement put up by a patrol under Sgt. Michael Strank. See Hansen, "New Mystery Arises from Iconic Iwo Jima Image," and Bradley and Powers, *Flags of Our Fathers.* **Air attacks on *Saratoga* and *Bismarck Sea*:** CTG 52.2, action report, April 21, 1945, 16–17; USS *Saratoga,* action report, Feb. 26, 1945, 52–67; USS *Bismarck Sea,* action report, Feb. 25, 1945, 1–5. **Tibbets calculated:** Tibbets, *Flight,* 170. **509th Composite Group training:** Krauss, *The 509th Remembered,* 234; Robert J. Petrocelli, in Krauss, 161. **"Keep from ruffling the sensitive feathers":** Tibbets, 175–76. **"I'm afraid that I treated Lucy very badly":** Greene, *Duty,* 103–5. **Ashworth meets Nimitz:** Ashworth interview, 154–55; see also Krauss, 19; Jones, *Manhattan,* 524; Kunetka, *General and the Genius,* 257. **"Don't these people in Washington realize?":** Ashworth, 155; Kelly, *Manhattan Project,* 322. **"I felt that he had then sensed":** Ashworth, 155.

30. Everybody's Business (pp. 384–391)

"Have you ever seen a map of London?": Sebald, *On the Natural History of Destruction*, 103–4. "An air offensive against Japan itself": Fedman and Karacas, "A Cartographic Fade to Black," 306–28. Models of Tokyo at Eglin AFB: Craven and Cate, *The Pacific: Matterhorn to Nagasaki*, 610. "The science of aviation": *Victory Through Air Power*, TV program, at 26:03. Joint Target Group estimates to "make possible the complete destruction": Arnold, *Global Mission*, 596. "He didn't seem impressed": Tibbets, *Flight*, 188–89. "What may be an outstanding show": Craven and Cate, 614. "We thought it was stark raving mad": Hanley interview, 103. "Boy, somebody's awfully dumb": Braden interview, Feb. 4, 2005, 14. "We really thought we were dead men": Braden interview, Sept. 30, 2000, 39. M-69 incendiary bomblets: Department of Defense, "M-69 Incendiary Bomb" (training video). Tokyo fire raid: Hanley, 108–10; Braden interview, Feb. 4, 2005, 15, 40–42; Savage interview, 24–25. See also Dorr, *Mission to Tokyo*, 177–84. "I would bet that at least half": Savage, 11. "God damn it, I'd like to know" and "Why are we here?": McNamara, in Morris, *Fog of War*, at 36:27. Tokyo deaths: Craven and Cate, 617. "The population, although obviously showing": Sebald, 24–25. "That's a meager term": Hanley, 111. "I didn't have any feelings": Braden interview, Sept. 30, 2000, 43. "We were pretty uptight": Hanley, 109. "There's one thing you learn": Savage, 11. "If I see any Japs": Ibid., 21. "The fighter units couldn't bear": Sadao Mogami, in Cook, *Japan at War*, 454. "Became reproachful as the imperial motorcade went by": Bix, *Hirohito and the Making of Modern Japan*, 491. "If we continue to fight back": Ibid., 492. "It may be said that if you destroy a man": Major Oliver Stewart, "Scientific Approach to Air Tactics," *The Aeroplane*, Dec. 26, 1941, in *Naval Institute Proceedings*, March 1942, 434–35.

31. Divine Winds (pp. 393–409)

"I understand some of the sob fraternity" and "The finest photograph": Spruance to Margaret, March 13, 1945, 2. "In the first place, I do not think": Spruance to Margaret, March 6, 1945, 4. "He was a different man": Hill interview, 335. Naval operations off Okinawa: USS *Franklin*, action report, April 11, 1945, 12; USS *Hornet*, action report, May 3, 1945, 9–11; USS *Wasp*, action report, March 27, 1945, 103. USS *Franklin* hit: USS *Franklin*, action report, April 11, 1945, 45. Evidence suggests that only one bomb hit the carrier, contrary to her action report, which claims two hits. See also Spruance interview, *Paris Match*, 25; Springer, *Inferno*, 328–30. The *Santa Fe*'s war diary claims that two or more bombs hit the carrier. USS *Santa Fe*, war diary, March 1945, 15. "Each time one went off": USS *Franklin*, 46. "I want off this fuckin' thing!": Al Bullock, in Springer, 259. "Just like a huge herd of cattle": Ralph Packard, in Springer, 224. Father Callaghan, "a soul-stirring sight": USS *Franklin*, 46. "I'm sorry to report, sir": Buell, 379. Suzuki as "unwilling statesman": Takagi, "Memoirs," 21–22. "Art," Spruance said, "Mitsch would never forgive me": Willcutts, "Admiral Spruance," 8. "The old sea devil!": Ibid., 10–11. "Good kamikaze weather": Ibid., 7. *New Mexico* hit by kamikaze: USS *New Mexico*, action report, May 28, 1945, 138, 142, 145. "Sir, "I'm needed there": Willcutts,

7–8. **Spruance manning fire hose:** C. R. Huie to T. B. Buell, Aug. 17, 1972, 5. **"I'm glad you were there, Surg":** Willcutts, 7–8. **Fifth Fleet losses off Okinawa:** COMFIFTHFLEET, action report, June 21, 1945, 22. Buckner's death elevated Roy Geiger, who had been the amphibious force commander at Guam, to overall command of the Tenth Army on Okinawa, making him the only Marine Corps officer ever to command a U.S. field army. **Ordeal of the *Laffey*:** Wukovits, *Hell from the Heavens*, 146–205. **"It was one of our toughest":** Spruance interview, *Paris Match*, 27. **"A true Spartan in every sense":** Ibid., 4. **Peace overtures by Suzuki government:** Sigal, *Fighting to a Finish*, 49–64. The central role of Korechika Anami and Yoshijiro Umezu in preventing a Japanese surrender prior to August 9 is an inconvenient fact for atomic bomb revisionists. Gar Alperovitz scarcely even mentions the two important hard-liners on the Supreme War Direction Council. See Alperovitz, *Decision to Use the Atomic Bomb*, 821, 842. See also Maddox, "Gar Alperovitz: Godfather of Hiroshima Revisionism," in Maddox (ed.), *Hiroshima in History*, 7. **"We are not yet beaten"** and **"He put it in so strong a manner":** Takagi, "Memoirs," 43. See also Hasegawa, *Racing the Enemy*, 345, n. 70, which establishes that according to the diaries of Takagi and Hosakawa, the Supreme War Direction Council insisted on four conditions for surrender, not merely the preservation of the imperial throne. **"They've destroyed a great many sugar mills":** Halsey, *Admiral Halsey's Story*, 253. **Spruance versus Hap Arnold:** Reynolds, *Fast Carriers*, 343. **"I stepped outside":** Barber, quoted in Buell, 392. **"In all of these islands":** Ibid., 389. **"Third-class Japanese":** Ota, in Cook, *Japan at War*, 367, 461. **Group suicide** and **"It's a term easily subject":** Kinjo, in Cook, 364. **"Everyone knew intuitively":** Miyagi, in Cook, 474–75. **"My memory tells me":** Kinjo, in Cook, 365. **"Their eyes accidentally met":** Miyagi, in Cook, 473–74. **The "sinister ratio":** D. M. Giangreco, "Casualty Projections," 549, 574–77. **"The whole nation":** Bix, *Hirohito and the Making of Modern Japan*, 493–96.

32. Methods of Death on the Wing (pp. 410–415)

509th to Tinian: Krauss, *The 509th Remembered*, 245–47. **"Knowing the interminable discussions":** Tibbets, *Flight*, 180. **"Some kind of torpedo shop":** Hoover interview, 381. **"Are all of your crews":** Tibbets, 184. **Downtime on Tinian:** Paul Metro, in Krauss, 143. **"We didn't let them know":** Franklin K. Wey, in Krauss, 202. **"Among the most frenzied":** Tibbets, 183. **"Only a few of us knew":** Ibid., 183. **"You were right, Paul":** Ibid., 188–89. **Target Committee:** Rhodes, *Making of the Atomic Bomb*, 626, 630, 640–41. See also Tibbets, 184. Though it was the headquarters for the Second General Army, Hiroshima had escaped the B-29 raids for its lack of aircraft factories, a priority target of the XXI Bomber Command. Nagasaki, predominantly a shipbuilding town, was left unmolested because its main asset, its harbor, had been neutralized by aerial mining. See Frank, 263n. **Demonstration of bomb rejected:** Rhodes, 647–48; Kunetka, *General and the Genius*, 350; Hasegawa, *Racing the Enemy*, 90. **Spruance and son on Guam:** Edward D. Spruance to T. B. Buell, July 16, 1963, 12. **Halsey in the typhoon:** Halsey's failure to keep his fleet clear of this and another damaging typhoon landed him in front of two boards of inquiry. He survived the first. The second recommended his relief of command. King discussed this with Forrestal, and the Navy secretary took it to the White House. Though King had wanted to bring Halsey before a court-martial, Truman finally said, "You'd better not do it. The publicity would be terrible." Lamar interview, 26. Even after Leyte, Halsey couldn't let go of his chagrin at Spruance's decisions in the Marianas. "My talks with the Navy and Army at Okinawa had shown me that once again the fleet was being held in static defense instead of being sent to hit the enemy where it would hurt. This strategy was worse than unprofitable; it was expensive." In his characterization of Fifth Fleet operations—knowing full well that Mitscher had carried out a long slate of risky strikes within fifty miles of the Japanese homeland—Halsey was worse than incorrect; he was dissembling on behalf of obsolete arguments. Halsey, *Admiral Halsey's Story*, 253. "For almost three months the fast carrier task force operated in the Okinawa area under almost constant enemy aerial reconnaissance," a CINCPAC report stated. "In spite of this, not a single ship of the task force was sunk, a truly remarkable record." CINCPAC, Report of Operations, May 1945, 39. **"Psychological blitzkrieg":** Frank, *Downfall*, 96. **Big Six and Emperor Hirohito on June 8:** Hiranuma interrogation, 9. See also Frank, 93–96, and Sigal, *Fighting to a Finish*, 71–73. **"Viewed a military victory as a prerequisite":** Frank, 96. **"Smash the inordinate ambitions"** and **"The rescript gave no hint":** Ibid., 98. **Skepticism over Japanese peace overtures:** "Ambassador Sato validated this skepticism," Richard Frank noted. "The Magic Diplomatic Summary establishes that both Ambassador Sato in Moscow and American analysts asked for whom Togo spoke. With his customary bluntness, Sato on July 15 had demanded to know whether diplomatic efforts to end the war carried any legal sanction in the face of the Imperial decision on June 8 to battle to the end. In his waffling response of July 17, Togo made no claim of support from the Imperial Army and Navy, nor did he report any legal warrant behind the move. Without such sanction, could Togo's cables be deemed evidence that the Japanese government had embarked on a serious effort to end the war?" Frank, 239. **"Japan may offer to surrender":** Sigal, 95. **"Those who were in the know":** Hiranuma interrogation, 7. **"I came to the conclusion that the war could not be continued":** Ibid., 9–10.

33. Opportunity and Madness *(pp. 416–428)*

Estimates of Japanese strength: Frank, *Downfall*, 197–98, 210–12. See also Drea, Nimitz Museum lecture, at 1:56:00. **"The kamikaze boys carried":** Fitch on "Navy Hour," cited in Associated Press, "Record Blows Near for Japs," 3. **Loss of USS *Callaghan*:** USS *Callaghan*, action report, Aug. 8, 1945, 1–3. **Willis Lee at Casco Bay:** Lloyd Mustin, USNI interview, 879–910. Mustin explained how the Bureau of Ordnance, attemping to upgrade the battery that powered the VT proximity fuze, drastically degraded its performance by increasing its arming distance from three hundred yards to nine hundred. "This really hit us in the fleet with an impact that is hard to convey, because we had had our men standing to their guns in the face of these incoming planes that we knew were doing their very best to crash right on us with a load of explosives and a load of aviation fuel. The only defense was to tear them to pieces in the sky before they could do this, and the only real chance of success in this job of tearing them to pieces began at astonishingly short range. . . . Admiral Lee made this known [to BuOrd] in some of the more abrupt official exchanges that perhaps occurred during the war. . . . This was a real shocker, and it led to desperate efforts to keep the ships supplied with the old-fashioned VT fuze and the short arming range. Of course, this was hopeless. They were being expended by the thousands every moment. . . . I have a feeling that will never be erased of the stunned reaction to this incredible blunder on the part of the bureaucrats back home." Mustin interview, 859–61. **Joint Chiefs** and **JSSC esti-mate of casualties:** Giangreco, "A Score of Bloody Okinawas and Iwo Jimas," in Maddox, 82–83; see also Giangreco, *Hell to Pay*, 50. **Marshall "recoils sharply":** Giangreco, in Maddox, 83–84. **"We could inflict a lot of damage":** Spruance, in-terview by *Paris Match*, 27–28. **LeMay could "take care of" thirty to sixty cities:** Arnold, *Global Mission*, 563–64. **"A complete lack of understanding":** King, *Flight Log Book*, 1945, 31. **"It would be wiser":** Spruance interview, *Paris Match*, 28–29. **"The enemy would have to beg for surrender":** King to Hanson Baldwin, June 12, 1950, 1. **Japanese eager for invasion by fall 1945:** Ed Drea, Nimitz Museum lecture. **MacArthur's casualty estimates:** Kort, *Columbia Guide to Hiroshima and the Bomb*, 104. **Chemical weapons prepared:** Giangreco, *Hell to Pay*, 112. **Whole blood:** Ibid., 138–39. **Tokyo fire raid "seemingly had no effect whatsoever":** Ibid., 188; Frank, 108. **"The people felt":** Takagi, "Memoirs," 26. **"When you are making war":** Spruance interview, *Paris Match*, 28. **U.S. averaging 65,000 casual-ties a month:** Giangreco, 56, 95. **"Hell, nothing is certain":** Tibbets, 179–80. **Fat Man device:** Lawrence H. Johnston in Krauss, 108; Rhodes, 575–80; Institute of Electrical and Electronics Engineers, Global History Network, ethw.org/First-Hand:Adventures_at_Wartime_Los_Alamos. **"It is His Majesty's heart's desire"** and **"I believe it no exaggeration":** Rose, *Dubious Victory*, 323. **Konoye as special envoy:** Ibid.; see also Weinberg, *World at Arms*, 886–87. **"It was not the American responsibility":** Stimson and Bundy, *On Active Service in Peace and War*, 629. **"As late as July 21":** Byrnes, *All in One Lifetime*, 308. Japan's inability to decide what peace terms were acceptable to it was revealed to American leaders in "Magic"— Diplomatic Summary, War Department, Office of Assistant Chief of Staff, G-2, No. 1225, Aug. 2, 1945. **"I answered politely but firmly":** Tibbets, 186–87. **"A lot of times"** and **"When a man is in command":** Greene, *Duty*, 88–89. **"Blanchard was so glad to scramble":** Tibbets, 188. **Nimitz views Alamogordo film:** Show-ers interview, 74–75. **"No explanation was given":** Halsey, *Admiral Halsey's Story*, 266. **Stimson "tremendously pepped up":** http://marshallfoundation.org/library/digital-archive/editorial-note-on-the-atomic-bomb; Jones, *Manhattan*, 234, 236. **"As far as I was concerned":** Groves, *Now It Can Be Told*, 265.

34. Prompt and Utter Destruction *(pp. 429–439)*

Rescue of Tweed: USS *McCall*, war diary, July 1944, 20; Turner report, 53; Clark interview, 524. **"Do you think they really are bombing":** Jones, *Oba*, 171. **Horiu-**

chi's plan: Ibid., 159–60. **Third Fleet strikes against Japan:** CTF 38, action report, Aug. 31, 1945, 34–36; Commander, Air Group 1, war history, 5–7; USS *Bennington*, action report, Aug. 31, 1945, 15; King and Whitehill, *Fleet Admiral King*, 620. Radar-triggered airbursts, used here for the first time, gave U.S. Navy planes a devastating capability to suppress flak. See CTF 38, action report, 7. In 1944, the likelihood of a dive-bomber hitting an antiaircraft gun position had been figured at 300 to 1. But with VT-fuzed bombs, it was nearly automatic. See CNO, "U.S. Naval Aviation in the Pacific," 49. The commander of USS *Bennington*'s Air Group 1 lamented the unavailability of a new 1,600-pound AP bomb specifically designed to sink battleships. See USS *Bennington*, 104. **"CINCPAC had ordered the fleet destroyed":** Halsey, *Admiral Halsey's Story*, 264–65. **"What's left of the Japanese navy is helpless":** *Southeast Missourian*, July 25, 1945, 1. **"The 509 Composite Group, 20th Air Force, will deliver its first special bomb":** Bland, and Stevens, *Finest Soldier*, 248–51. **"Japan shall be given an opportunity" (Potsdam Declaration text):** www.nato.int/ebookshop/video/declassified/doc_files/Potsdam%20 Agreement.pdf. **Legal meaning of "unconditional surrender":** U.S. Department of State, "Memorandum Prepared by the Committee on Post War Programs, Japan: Terms of Surrender: Underlying Principles," PWC-284a, Nov. 13, 1944; *Foreign Relations of the United States: Diplomatic Papers, 1944*, vol. 5, 1275–85. **"Practically all Germans deny":** Kort, *Columbia Guide to Hiroshima and the Bomb*, 92. FDR's view of Versailles was out of step with the widespread view that the Allies had been too harsh on Germany in 1918, not too easy. **"The government does not think":** "Magic"—Diplomatic Summary, War Department, Office of Assistant Chief of Staff, G-2, No. 1221, July 29, 1945. *Mokusatsu:* See http://thisjapaneselife .org/2013/03/06/mokusatsu-hiroshima-japan. See also Hasegawa, *Racing the Enemy*, 167–68. In 1950, Kazuo Kawai, who had been editor of the *Nippon Times* in 1944, wrote, "The Japanese government never intended to reject the Potsdam Declaration. . . . The subsequent course of events predicated on the assumption that Japan had rejected the Potsdam Declaration represents a tragedy of errors for which the major responsibility must be attributed to the inexcusable bungling of the Japanese officials." Kawai, "Mokusatsu, Japan's Response to the Potsdam Declaration," 409. **The *Indianapolis* at Tinian:** Harlow Russ, in Krauss, *The 509th Remembered*, 172; James F. Nolan, in Krauss, 153; Tibbets, *Flight*, 194–95. Newcomb, *Abandon Ship!*, 33–35. **Delivery of plutonium device:** Lawrence H. Johnston, in Krauss, 110–11; James F. Nolan in Krauss, 153; www.laggindragon.com/History .html. **Spaatz carries directive:** Tibbets, *Flight*, 195. **Sinking of the *Indianapolis*:** USS *Indianapolis*, action report, Aug. 26, 1945, 1–2. Morison, *New Guinea and the Marianas*, 319. **Truman's actual order to use the atomic bomb:** A written order from the president to drop the atomic bomb has eluded historians. Truman wrote to James L. Cate in 1953, "I ordered atomic bombs dropped on the two cities named on the way back from Potsdam, when we were in the middle of the Atlantic Ocean." Craven and Cate, *The Pacific: Matterhorn to Nagasaki*, 712–14. But the *Augusta*'s return voyage from Plymouth to Newport News did not begin until Aug. 2, and the order was already effective then. See USS *Augusta*, war diary, Aug. 1945, 1–2; *Papers of George C. Marshall*, http://marshallfoundation.org/library/digital

-archive / editorial-note-on-the-atomic-bomb. Lisle Rose argued that Truman, in his letter to Cate, "honestly confused the timing of the final atomic decision," having made it en route to Potsdam, not while returning. Rose, *Dubious Victory*, 329–30. On July 22, General George Marshall, as Army chief of staff, asked his deputy, Thomas Handy, to draft the order. General Groves produced it for Marshall's approval. On July 25, from Potsdam, Marshall informed Handy that Secretary of War Henry Stimson had approved the order. According to Ernest King, "Truman gave Secretary Stimson the go-ahead signal for the use of the atomic bomb, and the Secretary approved detailed plans." King and Whitehill, 621. Gerhard Weinberg notes that prior to authorizing use of the bomb, Truman wanted to be sure Japan had no "second thoughts" about continuing the war. The content of Japanese Army communications intercepted by Ultra satisfied him that they did not. Weinberg, *World at Arms*, 888, 1122, n. 130. On July 25, it was Handy who executed a directive for the use of atomic weapons against Japan. See also Hayes, *History of the Joint Chiefs of Staff in World War II*, 723–24. The idea that the atomic bomb was meant primarily to intimidate the Soviet Union—"the first major operation of the cold diplomatic war with Russia now in progress," P.M.S. Blackett called the Hiroshima attack in 1949—commingles the principal purposes of the decision with its third-order effects. According to Barton J. Bernstein, "The anti-Soviet function was not propelling [as a motive for dropping the bomb], it was not primary, it was not even secondary, but it was present, it was confirming, and it helped make an already inevitable decision that was easy for [Truman] even easier. But he would have made it regardless. After the war, we can ask plausibly, but cannot answer systematically, what would have happened if. I think it's quite likely that a combination of Soviet entry, the continuing blockade, and heavy conventional bombing would very probably, far more probably than not, have ended the war before Nov. 1 [1945]. But to say this after the fact should not be confused with what was believed or known or deemed plausible before the fact. . . . For American leaders before the fact, any gamble was outrageous, unnecessary, and there was no desire. The gap between 'probably' and 'definitely' is a chasm in which Americans could have died and massively. No American president, and nobody in 1945 who plausibly could have been president—Henry Wall, Jimmy Byrnes, or others—would have not used the bombs in 1945." Bernstein, Nimitz Museum Symposium, March 19, 1995, www.c-span.org/ video/?66945-1/atomic-bomb-decision-preparations. **"I don't recall his words":** C. F. Barber to T. B. Buell, March 19, 1973, 1. **"My thoughts turned":** Tibbets, 196–97. **The Tinian "joint chiefs":** Ashworth, in Krauss, 19. **"An ugly monster":** Tibbets, 201. **"To the people of Japan, from my friends in China":** Lawrence H. Johnston, in Krauss, 112. **"From the boys of the *Indianapolis*":** Tibbets, 201. **"Tonight is the night":** Ibid., 202–3; Beser, quoted in Krauss, 35. **Manhattan Project history:** The Manhattan Project Heritage Preservation Association, www.mphpa.org/ classic/ HISTORY/ H-07L.htm; Krauss, 83. **"Almighty Father":** Manhattan Project Heritage Preservation Association, www.mphpa.org/ classic/ COLLECTIONS/ CG-JPAP/ Pages/ CGP-JPAP-054.htm. **One suicide pill for every man:** Tibbets, 204.

35. Clear-cut Results *(pp. 440–459)*

"Any Japanese lurking": Tibbets, *Flight*, 205–6. **"Dimples eight-two to North Tinian Tower"**: Ibid., 210. **Takeoff and arming**: Rhodes, *Making of the Atomic Bomb*, 706; Franklin K. Wey, in Krauss, *509th Remembered*, 202; Beser, ibid., 35. **"Hell, colonel"**: Tibbets, 213. **"Okay, I've got the bridge"**: Ibid., 223. **Ferebee did not wear polarized glasses**: Ferebee to Gerald M. Holland, Feb. 3, 1969, 1. **Release of Little Boy**: Johnston in Krauss, 113. **"Now it's in the lap of the gods"**: Parsons to Raymond E. Lois, Jr., Feb. 5, 1949, 3. **Detonation**: Tibbets, 225–26; Beser, in Krauss, 35; Greene, *Duty*, 271. **"There was no sound"**: Yamaoka, in Cook, *Japan at War*, 384–85. **"An explosive wind like needles"**: Matsushige, in ibid., 392–94. **"Nobody looked human"**: Michiko Yamaoka, in ibid., 384–85. **"Nothing was standing"**: Yasuko Kimura, in ibid., 396. **"Parts of buildings"**: Greene, 262. **"The city we had seen"**: Tibbets, 227. **"My God!"** Tibbets, 227–28. **"My eleven companions and I"**: Ibid., 5. **The first sign of Hiroshima's destruction**: Manhattan Engineer District, "The Atomic Bombings of Hiroshima and Nagasaki," 8–9. **Return flight**: Russell E. Gackenbach, in Krauss, 83. **"We certainly were trained not to be that way"**: Greene, 272. **"There had been in my mind"**: Tibbets, 230. **"Many people have asked me if I was praying"**: Lawrence H. Johnston, in Krauss, 114. **"Please open your eyes!"** Cook, 392–94. **"CLEAR-CUT RESULTS"**: Johnston, in Krauss, 113. **"This is the greatest thing in history"**: Rhodes, 734. **"Send some more of 'em"**: USS Augusta *Evening Press*, Aug. 6, 1945, quoted in Rose, *Dubious Victory*, 359. **"The End of the War Picnic"**: Armen Shamlian, in Krauss, 178; Paul Metro, in Krauss., 143. **"We sighted a Japanese city"**: Tibbets's comments "are permanently etched in my memory," said Wesley P. Peterson of the 390th Air Service Group. Krauss, 160. **"A few B-29s hit Hiroshima"**: Tibbets, 232–33. **Hiroshima bomb burst point and casualties**: Arakawa and Nagaoka, "Determination of the Burst Point of the Hiroshima Atomic Bomb," 9; Rhodes, 734; Frank, *Downfall*, 285–86. **Existence of "persistent radiation"**: Manhattan Engineer District, 32–33. **"Make inquiry as to what happened"**: Rhodes, 737. **"With the success of the Hiroshima weapon"**: O'Keefe quoted in Rhodes, 738. **Anami's order: "Fight to the last" in this "holy war"**: Quoted in CINCPAC, "Report of Surrender and Occupation of Japan," 84–85. It seems curious that any high official of Imperial Japan would have assumed the good faith of Joseph Stalin as a "neutral" broker of peace when Moscow had so much to gain by taking Manchuria. As Tsuyoshi Hasegawa wrote, "The Japanese would have to travel a long road from willingness to terminate the war to actual acceptance of surrender. The crucial question is, On what terms was Japan prepared to surrender?" Hasegawa, *Racing the Enemy*, 127. **Imperial Conference of Aug. 9–10**: Toland, *Rising Sun*, 1002–7; Frank, 292–96. **"We still have fighting power left"**: Takagi, "Memoirs," 56–57. **"We cannot promise victory, but we are not yet defeated"**: Ibid. **"Your Imperial Majesty's decision is requested"**: Frank, 295. **"I was given the opportunity"**: Toland, 1006n. **"I have given serious thought"**: Craig, *Fall of Japan*, 118–19. According to Rear Admiral Takagi, the influential Navy Ministry research analyst, Hirohito also lamented in this oration that "the enemy now uses a new type of atomic bomb, inflicting disaster beyond our forecasts. If the war is continued, it might lead finally not only to the destruction of the Japanese race but also to the ruins of civilization of mankind." Takagi, "Memoirs," 57–58; **"The effects of this avalanche"**: CINCPAC, 86. **"The world will note"**: Radio Report to the American People on the Potsdam Conference, Aug. 9, 1945, in Truman Library, *Public Papers of the Presidents,* 212. **"Rise to the occasion"**: Toland, 1008–9. **Third atomic bomb**: Frank, 303. In an August 10 memo to Marshall, Groves reviewed plans to use a third atomic weapon, weather permitting, after August 17 or 18. In his annotations to this memo, Marshall indicated, "It is not to be released over Japan without express authority from the President." Groves to Marshall, Aug. 10, 1945. http://nsarchive.gwu.edu/nukevault/ebb525-The-Atomic-Bomb-and-the-End-of-World-War-II/documents/082.pdf. Groves's command had developed the capacity to produce three atomic bombs a month by September 1945, but since Marshall believed that a third bomb, used against another city, would have had little marginal utility in encouraging the Japanese to surrender, the discussion turned to using them tactically, during Operation Downfall, to destroy Japanese troop concentrations several days ahead of amphibious landings. Ten bombs of the Fat Man type would have been available for such employment by November. Transcript of telephone conversation between Lt. Gen. John Hull and Col. L. E. Seeman, Aug. 13, 1945, http://nsarchive.gwu.edu/NSAEBB/NSAEBB162/72.pdf. See also Gallicchio, *"After Nagasaki,"* 396. **"Caused me to be stricken"**: Sigal, *Fighting to a Finish,* 268. **"Now that a weapon of this devastating power has been used"**: *Konoye's Diary,* quoted in Bergamini, *Japan's Imperial Conspiracy,* 82, 1116. **"I have listened"**: Sigal, 269. **Arnold's thousand-plane raid**: Craven and Cate, 732–33; CINCPAC, *Grey Book,* 3300; CINCPAC, "Report," 10. **No need to risk a single airman's life**: Thomas and Jablonski, *Doolittle,* 308–9. **Imperial Rescript "forthcoming soon"**: CINCPAC, "Report," 89; Sigal, 271. **"The United States, as I had stated at Berlin, wanted no territory"**: Truman, *Memoirs,* vol. 1, *Year of Decisions,* 436–37. **"Cease offensive operations"**: CINCPAC, *Grey Book,* 2304/14 August 1945; see also CINCPAC, "Report," 11, and ComThirdFleet, war diary, August 1945, 31–32. **"Believing firmly that our sacred land"**: Frank, 319. **"We declared war on America"** and **"Let the entire nation continue as one family"**: Imperial Rescript, Aug. 15, 1945, www.ibiblio.org/hyperwar/PTO/Dip/Crane.html. **"In the unforeseen and unanswerable bomb"**: Ibid., 82, 1116. See also Takagi, 60–62. **"It seemed to me that the best we could hope"**: Kauffman interview, 271–74. **"The first reaction Peggy and I had"**: Ibid., 274, 233, 265. **Kistiakowsky celebrates**: Kunetka, *General and the Genius,* 369. **"On our inquiry"**: Edward D. Spruance to T. B. Buell, July 16, 1963, 13.

36. Eight Bells for an Empire *(pp. 462–480)*

"They create a desert and call it peace": Tacitus, regarding the warning given by Calgacus to the people of Caledonia (Scotland), quoted in Loretana de Libero, "Surrender in Ancient Rome," in Afflerbach and Strachan (eds.), *How Fighting Ends*, 37. **Operation Blacklist:** MacArthur, *Reports of General MacArthur*, vol. 1, "The Campaigns of MacArthur in the Pacific," 450–51; MacArthur, *Reports of General MacArthur*, vol. 1, suppl., "MacArthur in Japan: The Occupation: Military Phase," 10, 16–27; CINCPAC, "Report of Surrender and Occupation of Japan," Feb. 11, 1946, 9. **"to bring about the establishment":** CINCPAC, 109–10. A Japanese historian has argued that Japan's establishment of the Greater East Asia Co-Prosperity Sphere as an answer to the Atlantic Charter foretold Tokyo's willingness to accept internationalism after the war and facilitated rapprochement with the United States. Iriye, *Power and Culture*, 119–20. **"a clean sweepdown":** CTF 38, action report, Aug. 31, 1945, cover page. **Kawabe delegation in Manila:** Kenney, *General Kenney Reports*, 572. **"too shrewd an Orientalist":** Manchester, *American Caesar*, 516. **Nimitz's requirements:** CINCPAC, 91–93. **"The Japanese made no attempt":** MacArthur, *Reports*, vol. 1, suppl., 25. **U.S. fleet enters Sagami Wan:** Commander, Carrier Task Force Two, war diary, Aug. 1945, 13; Associated Press, "Airborne Troops Land in Japan, Fleet Units Enter Tokyo," *The Saratogian*, Aug. 28, 1945, 1; USS *Missouri*, action report, 7; USS *O'Bannon*, war diary, Aug. 1945, 9; USS *Waldron*, war diary, Aug. 1945, 11; USS *Iowa*, war diary, Aug. 1945, 15. **A high-priority parcel:** ComThirdFleet, war diary, Aug. 1945, 56. **Order of entry into Tokyo Bay:** Ibid., 61. **Liberation of Omori:** CTG 30.6, action report, Sept. 22, 1945, 6–7; CINCPAC, 26–27. **11th Airborne at Atsugi:** MacArthur, *Reminiscences*, 269; ComThirdFleet, war diary, Aug. 1945, 65–66; CINCPAC, 20. *Nagato* **as war prize:** CTU 31.3.3, action report, 8. USS *Horace A. Bass*, action report, Sept. 8, 1945, 2–3; ComThirdFleet, 66–67; CTG 31.8, action report, Sept. 5, 1945, 3; UDT 18, war diary, Aug. 1945, 5. **"It seemed almost incredible":** Smith, *Securing the Surrender*, 10. **"near economic and industrial collapse":** CINCPAC, 37. **"Calm and serene was my feeling":** Suzuki, quoted in MacArthur, *Reminiscences*, 279. Of course, Suzuki's idea that Bushido required victors to treat surrendered enemies with grace and comfort materialized only after the surrender. Prior to it, Japanese soldiers almost everywhere saw "the way of the warrior" as mandating unbridled savagery against Allied POWs. **Sailors took turns stuffing brooms:** Murray, "Reminiscences of the Surrender of Japan and the end of World War II," https://ussmissouri.org/learn-the-history/surrender/admiral-murrays-account. **"It required the emperor's personal persuasion":** Kase, quoted in MacArthur, *Reminiscences*, 273. **"The atmosphere was frigid":** Morison, *Victory in the Pacific*, 363. **"Trying to recall my emotions":** MacArthur, 277–78. **McCain and Halsey "grinning like schoolchildren":** Frank Tremaine interview, 35–36. **"Let us pray that peace":** Morison, 366. **Spruance in the occupation:** COMFIFTHFLEET, war diaries, Aug. and Sept. 1945; COMFIFTHPHIBFOR, action report, Oct. 3, 1945, 5. **Surrender:** Tremaine interview, 35–36. **"Raymond, how can you say that?":** Margaret Spruance interview, Dec. 9, 1971, 5–14. **Minesweeping and guinea pig vessels:** COMFIFTHPHIBFOR, 5; CINCPAC, 51–52, 77–79; ComMineDiv 8, action report, Oct. 8, 1945, 2–8. **"prepared equally to fight or favor":** MacArthur, *Reports*, vol. 1, suppl., 57. **"A conventional invasion of Japan would have been no D-Day":** Ferguson, *War of the World*, 572. **Chemical weapons:** Forrestel, *Admiral Raymond A. Spruance*, 225; Vilensky, *Dew of Death*, 139. **"to abide by the terms of surrender":**

MacArthur, *Reports,* vol. 1, suppl., 38. **"Japanese ideas":** Ibid., 49. **"Completely overwhelmed by this unexpected generosity":** Ibid. **"The disease of power":** MacArthur, *Reminiscences,* 282. **U.S. flag over Tokyo embassy:** CINCPAC, 34. The CINCPAC report states that this same flag had flown from the foremast of the *Missouri* on September 2, a claim that was picked up by Morison. (Morison, *Victory in the Pacific,* 363.) But according to the best source on this question, Captain Stuart S. Murray of the *Missouri,* "The only thing I can say is they were hard up for baloney, because it was nothing like that. It was just a plain, ordinary GI-issue flag and a Union Jack." https://ussmissouri.org/learn-the-history/surrender/admiral-murrays -account. **"the hands governing the movements":** CINCPAC, 105. **Tojo's arrest and suicide attempt:** Craig, *Fall of Japan,* 316–21. **Nagasaki "frizzled like a baked apple":** Weller, *First into Nagasaki,* 3–4. **Evacuation of Nagasaki:** Manhattan Engineer District, "The Atomic Bombings of Hiroshima and Nagasaki," 1–2; USS *Haven,* war diary, Sept. 1945, 39–40, 50–51; CINCPAC, 57–58; Shaw, *United States Marines in the Occupation of Japan,* 11–15. **Censorship regarding radiation:** Weller, 253. **"Nagasaki cannot be described":** Ibid., 25. **"Atombomben disease":** USS *Haven,* 39–40, 50–51. **"a comprehensive survey":** CINCPAC, 58. For more on the human experience of the Nagasaki bombing, see Susan Southard's *Nagasaki: Life After Nuclear War.* **Naval medicine at Nagasaki:** Weller, 133–35; USS *Haven,* 19. **Charinko:** Dower, *Embracing Defeat,* 63. **"stolid and emotionless":** Spruance to Margaret Spruance, Sept. 16, 1945, 3. **"the butcher of Warsaw":** Spruance to Margaret, Sept. 23, 1945, 1. **Spruance "never hated them":** Margaret (Spruance) Bogart interview, Sept. 27, 1971, 7–8. **Prostitution:** Tanaka, "Japan's Comfort Women," 153; Buruma, *Year Zero,* 34–38; Dower, 131–33. **"Everything was working according to plan":** C. R. Huie to T. B. Buell, Aug. 17, 1972, 7. **"They keep trying to get me to stop":** MacArthur, quoted in Cohen, *Remaking Japan,* 123, and Buruma, 35. **"It was quite a celebration":** Spruance to Margaret, Sept. 23, 1945, 2. **"I judge that the party"** and **touring the *Mikasa:*** Ibid., 3. COMFIFTHFLEET, action report, Nov. 8, 1945, 9. **UDT "The question which was uppermost":** CTF 55, action report, Nov. 23, 1945, 31–32. **"Welcome to Wakayama":** Robert P. Marshall interview, 38–40. **"It was quite a celebration":** Spruance to Margaret, Sept. 16, 1945. **"I judge that the party lasted":** Spruance to Margaret, Sept. 16, 1945. **"The Japanese Army as such":** CINCPAC, 105. **"A disarming of the fighting spirit":** Ibid., 106–7. **"I know of no demobilization in history":** MacArthur, *Reports,* vol. 1, suppl., 131. The Navy's final report misattributes MacArthur's words to President Truman. See CINCPAC report, 106.

37. The War Wearies *(pp. 482–503)*

Scope of repatriation effort: CINCPAC, "Report of Surrender and Occupation of Japan," Feb. 11, 1946, 40–43, 185–87; MacArthur, *Reports of General MacArthur,* vol. 1, suppl., 149. **Surrender of Truk:** USS *Portland,* war diary, September 1945, 1. **"Rank upon rank":** CINCPAC, 187–88. **Death of Horiuchi:** Jones, *Oba,* 201–9. **Captain Oba's surrender:** Ibid., 219, 236–41. **"Inspire the natives":** CINCPAC, 200. **"It was whispered by the people in the camp"** and **Shizuko's repatriation:**

Sugano, "Fate of the Donni Field Hospital," 241–67. **Hirohito's renunciation of his divinity:** National Diet Library, "The Birth of the Constitution of Japan," documents with commentaries, 3-1, "Imperial Rescript Denying His Divinity (Professing His Humanity)." **"The coming of peace meant":** Shigeaki Kinjo, in Cook, *Japan at War,* 366. **"Their repatriation policies":** MacArthur, 161, 187. **Return of Norman Ramsey and the technical group:** Kunetka, *General and the Genius,* 372. **509th Composite Group returns:** Paul Metro, in Krauss, *The 509th Remembered,* 143. **"My bombardier"** and **"What am I going to do":** Braden interview, Feb. 4, 2005, 20–21. **"Our aircraft commander decided":** Halloran interview, 135. **"He wanted Raymond":** Margaret Spruance interview, Dec. 16, 1971, 6. **"The fourth five-star promotion":** Raymond Spruance to King, June 24, 1948. **"We again enjoyed daily walks"** and **"There I can review":** David Willcutts, "Reminiscences," 18. **"I'm sorry he saw fit":** Spruance to Carl Moore, Nov. 29, 1948, in Moore interview, 1133–35. **Saipan controversy:** Sherrod, "The Saipan Controversy," 17; Love, "Smith versus Smith," 12–13. **Gordon Leslie, USN:** Kauffman interview, 282–84. **IJN *Nagato*'s end:** GlobalSecurity.org, "IJN *Nagato* Class Battleships," www.global security.org/military/world/japan/nagato-bb.htm. **Draper Kauffman at the Bikini test:** Kauffman, 296–312. **"They all seemed to have somewhat of a guilt complex":** Ibid., 314. **Tibbets postwar:** Greene, *Duty,* 50, 144. **Tibbets with Truman** and **"What do you think?":** Tibbets, interviewed by Studs Terkel; Greene, 21. **"To discuss what should be done":** Truman to Cate, Jan. 12, 1953, reproduced in Craven and Cate, *The Pacific: Matterhorn to Nagasaki,* 712. See also www .atomicarchive.com/Docs/Hiroshima/Truman.shtml. **"Killing 50 to 90 percent":** McNamara, in *Fog of War.* **"Nimitz on the bomb's necessity":** "Admiral Nimitz Addresses in Congress and at Monument," *New York Times,* Oct. 6, 1945, 6. Given that the rest of this speech was principally a brief in support of full funding for the Navy Department, Nimitz's remark about the bomb's insignificance as a "purely military" factor in the defeat of Japan must be seen in the light of appropriations politics. *"The Navy had the task of defeating Japan's military forces well in hand, thank you,"* was what he meant to say. **"The use of this barbarous weapon":** Leahy, *I Was There,* 441. As Richard B. Frank noted, Leahy lacked either the clarity or the courage to make his view known before the fact. Frank, *Downfall,* 333n. **"This is the reason why we have ordered the acceptance of the provisions of the Joint Declaration of the Powers":** Paul Ham, an Australian author, is the latest to protest the barbarity of the atomic bomb, complaining that its principal purpose was to "shock Japan into submission by annihilating a city." Ham, *Hiroshima Nagasaki,* 472. Like most who object on moral grounds, he does not credit either that project's sad necessity or its specific success. Confronting a deadlocked enemy high command, Stimson and others had sought exactly this result. See Stimson and Bundy, *On Active Service in Peace and War,* 625; Weinberg, *World at Arms,* 885. After writing, "Not a shred of evidence supports the contention that the Japanese leadership surrendered *in direct response to* the atomic bombs" (emphasis in original), Ham describes that direct response: "The two atomic strikes did, however, furnish Tokyo's leaders with a face-saving expedient. . . . Imperial forces were able to capitulate with military honour intact. Little Boy and Fat Man saved the faces of a people for whom 'saving face' meant more than saving their lives." Ham, 473, 486. While Ham is correctly skeptical that Japanese war leaders actually cared about civilian lives, it is possible that Hirohito's fears were sincere in the end. Whether the emperor's thinking was genuine (shock) or cynical (expedience), the rescript of August 15, by its plain language, points directly to the importance of the bombs, as do the statements by Konoye and Takagi. Ham repeats the common misapprehension that Japan's "sole condition" of surrender all along was the preservation of the emperor's position. The record is clear regarding the three additional requirements that Anami, Umezu, and Toyoda insisted upon to the end. Their intractability paralyzed the government and prevented the formulation of terms that could have been proposed for the consideration of the Allies. **"Nobody is more disturbed"**: Truman, quoted in Rose, *Dubious Victory,* 363. **"I am convinced to this day"**: Kauffman, 274–75. **"In war, as in a boxing match"**: Stimson and Bundy, 629. **"I believe, with complete conviction"**: Compton, "If the Atomic Bomb Had Not Been Used," 54. **"An absolute nightmare"**: Margaret Spruance interview, Dec. 6, 1971, 17. **"His technical knowledge seemed"**: Moore interview, 1160. **"No dream castle ever erected"**: Grew, NBC Radio Navy Day address, Oct. 27, 1944, in Grew, *Turbulent Era,* 1402. **USN casualty figures:** King, *Report of Admiral King,* 723. **"Never before in the history of war"**: King and Whitehill, *Fleet Admiral King,* 623. **Scrapping of the IJN:** MacArthur, *Reports,* vol. 1, suppl., 147, 281, n. 28. **"I contemplated the human destiny"**: Moritaki, "New Morals for the Atomic Age," 2. **"Making is knowing"**: *Stanford Encyclopedia of Philosophy,* http://plato .stanford.edu/entries/francis-bacon/#SciMetNovOrgTheInd. **"Reorient the common mind"**: Moritaki, 6. **"Austere, remote, and inflexible"**: Edward Spruance to T. B. Buell, July 16, 1963, 2–3. *Jus in bello, mala in se,* and **the Doctrine of Double Effect:** *Stanford Encyclopedia of Philosophy.* **"The great moral transformation"**: Bernstein, Nimitz Museum Symposium, March 19, 1995. **Nimitz in Washington:** "Admiral Nimitz Addresses in Congress and at Monument," *New York Times,* Oct. 6, 1945, 6. **"Those people never"**: Greene, 269.

Bibliography

Primary Sources

Principal Archives

Columbia University Center for Oral History, New York (CCOH)

Cushing Library, Naval War College, Newport, Rhode Island (NWC)

Franklin D. Roosevelt Library, Hyde Park, New York (FDRL)

National Archives and Records Administration II, College Park, Maryland (NARA)

National Museum of the Pacific War, Fredericksburg, Texas (NMPW)

University of North Texas Oral History Collection, Denton, Texas (UNT)

United States Marine Corps Archives and Special Collections, Gray Research Center, Marine Corps University, Quantico, Virginia (USMCU)

United States Navy, Naval History and Heritage Command, Washington Navy Yard, Washington, DC (NHHC)

Collections

Papers of Chester W. Nimitz, Operational Archives, NHHC

Papers of Ernest J. King, Library of Congress

Papers of John Toland, FDRL

Papers of Raymond A. Spruance, NWC

Papers of Richmond Kelly Turner, Operational Archives, NHHC

Papers of Thomas B. Buell, NWC

Record Group 38, Chief of Naval Operations Files, NARA

Record Group 313, Records of Naval Operating Forces ("Flag Files"), NARA

Amphibious Forces, Atlantic Fleet (PHIBFORLANT), miscellaneous files (Blue 148)

Amphibious Forces, Pacific Fleet (PHIBPAC), general administrative files (Blue 160 and 168); miscellaneous files (Blue 170)

Documents

Note: After-action reports issued by commands smaller than a naval task force are too numerous to itemize here. References to them as they bear on the text appear in the Source Notes.

Amphibious Training Base, Coronado. *Skill in the Surf: A Landing Boat Manual.* February 1945.

Army Air Forces, Historical Office (Maj. James L. Cate). *History of the Twentieth Air Force: Genesis.* U.S. Air Force Historical Study no. 112., October 1945.

Atomic Bomb Casualty Commission. "Determination of the Burst Point and Hypocenter of the Atomic Bomb in Hiroshima," Technical Report 12–59, 1959.

Chief of Staff, U.S. Army. "Operations Division Information Bulletin." Feb. 1, 1944.

Combined Chiefs of Staff. "Air Plan for the Defeat of Japan" (CCS 323). Aug. 20, 1943.

Commander, Air Forces, Pacific (COMAIRPAC). "Analysis of Pacific Air Operations, 11–30 June 1944."

Commander, Fifth Amphibious Force (COMFIFTHPHIB). "Interrogation report of 1st Lt. Ando, Shigesaburo." July 7, 1944.

———. "Observation on Noda, Mitsuharu, Chief Yeoman to Vice Admiral Nagumo Chuichi." July 19, 1944.

———. "G-2 Report, Phase I." August 12, 1944.

———. "Report of Amphibious Operations for the Capture of the Mariana Islands." Aug. 25, 1944 ("COMFIFTHPHIB report").

Commander, Fifth Fleet (COMFIFTHFLEET). "Initial Report on the Operation to Capture the Marianas Islands." July 13, 1944.

———. "Preliminary POW Interrogation Report, Noda, Mitsuharu, Chief Yeoman, IJN, Writer to Vice Admiral Nagumo." July 13, 1944.

———. "Final Report on the Operation to Capture the Marianas Islands." Aug. 30, 1944.

———. "Action Report—The Occupation of Japan, 15 August 1945 to 8 November 1945." Nov. 8, 1945.

Commander in Chief, Pacific Fleet and Pacific Ocean Areas (CINCPAC/CINCPOA). "Tactical Foresight," memorandum to commanders. May 29, 1944.

———. "Report of Surrender and Occupation of Japan." Feb. 11, 1946.

———. "Field Survey of Japanese Defenses on Truk." CINCPAC/CINCPOA, bulletin no. 3-46, part 1. March 15, 1946.

Commander in Chief, United States Fleet (COMINCH). *Official Reports to the Secretary of the Navy.* Dec. 8, 1945.

Commander, Second Carrier Task Force, Pacific. "Action Report-Operations Against Japan, 15 August–2 September 1945." Sept. 7, 1945.

Commander, Support Aircraft. "Report of Support Aircraft, Operations, Forager." Aug. 24, 1944.

Commander Task Force 51. "Report of Amphibious Operations for the Capture of the Marianas Islands," Aug. 25, 1944 ("Turner Report").

Commander Task Force 52. "Report of Capture of Timian." Aug. 24, 1944.

Commander, Third Fleet. "Report on Operations of the Third Fleet, 16 August 1945 to 19 September 1945." Oct. 6, 1945.

Commanding General, Fifth Amphibious Corps. "Report of Marianas Operation, Phase I (Saipan)." Aug. 12, 1944.

Commanding General, U.S. Army Forces Middle Pacific, to Judge Advocate General, Western Pacific Base Command. "War Crimes." Aug. 30, 1945.

Department of Defense, Army Pictorial Service. "M-69 Incendiary Bomb" (training video). Combat Bulletin No. 48. 1945. www.youtube.com/watch?v =uPteVZyF4U0. Last viewed by the author on Sept. 7, 2015.

National Diet Library. "The Birth of the Constitution of Japan," documents with commentaries, 3-1, "Imperial Rescript Denying His Divinity (Professing His Humanity)," http://www.ndl.go.jp/constitution/e/shiryo/03/056shoshi .html.

Northern Troops and Landing Force (NTLF), Intelligence Section (G-2). "Special Interrogation of Major Yoshida Kiyoshi, intelligence officer of the former 43rd Division Headquarters." July 11, 1944.

———. "Captured Japanese Officers' Personal Account of the Last Days of Lieutenant General Saito." July 14, 1944.

Office of Naval Intelligence, Air Branch. *Naval Aviation Combat Statistics, World War II*. Washington, D.C.: Office of the Chief of Naval Operations, June 17, 1946.

Reports of General MacArthur. 2 vols., 2 parts. Washington, D.C.: U.S. Government Printing Office, 1966.

U.S. Army, Manhattan Engineer District. "The Atomic Bombings of Hiroshima and Nagasaki." Doc. no. N-13910.2-A. Fort Leavenworth, Kansas, 1945.

U.S. Department of State, *Foreign Relations of the United States: Conference at Quebec, 1944*. Washington, D.C.: U.S. Government Printing Office, 1944.

———. *Foreign Relations of the United States: Diplomatic Papers, 1944*. Vol. 5: *The Near East; South Asia and Africa; The Far East*. Washington, D.C.: U.S. Government Printing Office, 1965.

War Department. *Landing Operations On Hostile Shores* (Basic Field Manual 31-5). Washington, D.C.: U.S. Government Printing Office, June 2, 1941.

———. *Guam: Operations of the 77th Division, 21 July–10 August 1944*. Center of Military History, publ. 100-5. Washington, D.C.: Center of Military History, U.S. Army, 1946.

———. *Small Unit Actions*. Washington, D.C.: U.S. Government Printing Office.

April 4, 1946. www.history.army.mil/books/wwii/smallunit/smallunit-fm .htm. Last viewed by the author on Nov. 12, 2014.

War History Office, Ministry of Defense (Japan). *Boeicho Boeikenshujo Senshibu.* War history series, 102 volumes. (Also known as *Senshi Sosho.*) Tokyo: Asagumo Shimbunsha, various dates, 1960s and 1970s.

The War Reports of General Marshall, General Arnold, Admiral King. Philadelphia: Lippincott, 1947.

Yokoi, Toshiyuki. "The Japanese Version of the Black Chamber," Far East Command, Military Intelligence Section, General Staff Allied Translator and Interpreter Section, no. 64718. Jan. 31, 1951.

Personal Narratives (Unpublished)

Ada, Francisco C. "World War II—Saipan." John Toland Papers, FDRL.

Baird, Robert R. "The Journeys of Underwater Demolition Team Six," undated. NMPW.

Barriger, Glenville D. "Second Armored Amphibian Battalion," undated. USMCU.

Bollard, Ed. "First Corps Medium Tank Battalion," undated. http://2ndarmored amphibianbattalion.com/saipan. USMCU.

Chapin, John C. "Memoir," undated. USMCU.

Craig, Frank S., Jr. "Recollections," 1993. USMCU.

Davis, J. W. "Recollections of a Tin Can Sailor," May 12, 1994. NMPW.

Depner, Sidney G. Unpublished manuscript, undated. NMPW.

Duane, Lawrence A. Diary, undated. USMCU.

Everett, Robert E. "World War II, Battle of Saipan," undated. USMCU.

Freer, Charles H. "The Promise Aloft," undated. NMPW.

Gabaldon, Guy. *Saipan: Suicide Island.* Self-published, 1990.

George, Robert L. "Too Young to Vote." Draft manuscript, undated, circa 2001. USMCU.

Goerner, Fred. "Silent Thunder." Oral history, undated. NMPW.

Graf, Robert F. "Easy Company," 1986. USMCU.

Harig, Paul. "My Memories of World War II," undated, circa 2000. NMPW.

Harris, Marshall E. "Second Armored Amphibious Battalion—Saipan," undated. 2ndarmoredamphibianbattalion.com/saipan. USMCU.

Hays, Loyal B. "Combat Recordings of the Saipan Operation," recorded July 21, 1944, Office of Naval Records and Library. NARA.

Hosokawa, Morisada. *Hosokawa Diary.* Draft manuscript. John Toland Papers, FDRL.

Inglis, Thomas B. "Narrative by Captain Thomas B. Inglis," recorded January 10, 1945, Office of Naval Records and Library. NARA.

Kato, Masuo. *The Lost War: The Japanese Reporter's Inside Story.* Draft manuscript, ca. 1946. Toland Papers, FDRL.

Keeler, William E. "Report of LCI Duty from 1944 to 1947," undated. NMPW.

Kido, Koichi. *Kido's Diary* (corrected), International Prosecution Section, Document Processing Unit. Exhibit no. 1277, Doc. No. 1632W. Toland Papers, FDRL.

King, Ernest J. *Flight Log Book, 1944–1945.* King Papers, LOC.

Kusaka, Ryonosuke. *The Combined Fleet: Memoirs of Former Chief of Staff Kusaka.* Draft manuscript. Toland Papers, FDRL.

Lee, R. J. Letter to Jerry D. Brooks, Second Armored Amphibious Battalion, Aug. 3, 1989. USMCU.

Lewis, Jack R. "Jack's War, 19 March 1943–21 December 1945," undated. NMPW.

Livesey, Benjamin R. "Second Armored Amphibious Battalion—Saipan," undated. http://2ndarmoredamphibianbattalion.com/saipan. USMCU.

McLellan, Warren. "The Warren McLellan Story." School presentation, Fort Smith, Ark., November 11, 2002. www.rb-29.net/html/81lexingtonstys/05.01mclellan.htm. Last viewed by author on Sept. 5, 2015.

Metz, Elmer Robert. Untitled narrative of LCI(G)-81, undated. NMPW.

Okuyama, Ryoko. "Surviving on the Island of Suicide," undated. Toland Papers, FDRL.

Prime, Jimmie Allen. "Because I Cannot Forget," 2001. NMPW.

Ramage, James D. Personal narrative, USS *Enterprise* (CV-6) website. www.cv6.org/1944/marianas. Last viewed by the author on Sept. 5, 2015.

Rawn, John R. "LCI(G)-459 at Saipan and Peleliu," recorded November 29, 1944, Office of Naval Records and Library, NARA.

Robbins, Sidney. *Good to Be Alive: The Memoirs of Sidney Robbins.* Self-published. Cortez, Florida, 2000. Courtesy of Victoria Robbins.

———. "Narrative History of Underwater Demolition Team #7," undated. Courtesy of Victoria Robbins.

Shirley, Milton G. "Second Armored Amphibious Battalion—Saipan," undated. http://2ndarmoredamphibianbattalion.com/saipan. USMCU.

Smith, Stuart G. "World War II as I Saw It on the LCI(G)-372," undated. NMPW.

Stott, Frederic A. "Saipan Under Fire." Draft manuscript, ca. 1945. USMCU.

Sugano (nee Miura), Shizuko. "The End at Saipan." Translator uncredited. Draft manuscript. ca. November 1959. Toland Papers, FDRL.

———. "The Fate of Donni Field Hospital." Translator uncredited. Draft manuscript, undated. Toland Papers, FDRL.

Sylvester, E. W. Untitled narrative. Recorded July 18, 1944, remarks at the U.S. Navy's Bureau of Ships. Office of Naval Records and Library. NARA.

Takagi, Sokichi. "Memoirs of the War's End" (*Shusen Oboye Gaki*). Translator uncredited. Draft manuscript. January 22, 1948. Toland Papers, FDRL.

Webb, Wilbur. Untitled narrative, ca. 1995. Collection of Barrett Tillman.

Wedding, James H. "My Notes of World War II (1943–1945)," undated. Collection of Barrett Tillman.

Willcutts, David. "Admiral Spruance: Reminiscences of David Willcutts, Fleet Medical Officer, 1945–1946," undated. NWC.

Winston, Robert A. Untitled narrative, recorded Aug. 7, 1944, Office of Naval Records and Library. NARA.

Interviews and Oral Histories

Ashworth, Frederick L. Interviewed by Paul Stillwell, 1990. Transcript courtesy of Frederick L. Ashworth, Jr.

Barber, Charles F. Interviewed by T. B. Buell, May 6, 1972. Buell Papers, NWC.

———. Interviewed by Evelyn M. Cherpak, March 1, 1996. NWC.

Bock, Leonard. Interviewed by Ronald E. Marcello, Aug. 7, 1997. UNT.

Bogart, Margaret (Spruance). Interviewed by T. B. Buell, Sept. 17, 1971. NWC.

Boots, Donald. Interviewed by Ronald E. Marcello, May 17, 2001. UNT.

Braden, David. Interviewed by Kep Johnson, Sept. 30, 2000. NMPW.

———. Interviewed by Alfred F. Hurley, Feb. 4, 2005. UNT.

Brown, Joseph B. Interviewed by William G. Cox, March 23, 2001. NMPW.

Burke, Arleigh A. Personal statements, Aug. 20–21, 1945. Office of Naval Records and Library.

———. Oral history, undated, OH00168, NMPW.

Charland, George. Interviewed by William J. Alexander, Dec. 7, 1998. UNT.

Clark, J. J. Interviewed by John T. Mason, October 1962 (various dates). CCOH.

Conolly, Richard L. Interviewed by Donald F. Shaughnessy, 1958–1959. CCOH.

Cooper, William E. Interviewed by Ronald E. Marcello, Sept. 7, 1999. UNT.

Craig, Earle M. Interviewed by Chuck Nichols, Sept. 30, 2000. NMPW.

Crowe, Henry P. Interviewed by Benis M. Frank, April 4–5, 1979. USMCU.

Delisle, Norman. Interviewed by Chuck Nichols, March 15, 2001. NMPW.

Dillon, C. Douglas. Interviewed by Peter. B. Weed, June 11, 1998. NHF.

Elrod, Roy H. Interviewed by Fred H. Allison, Allyson Stanton and Mike Miller, May 24, 2013, and June 7, 2013. USMCU.

Erskine, Graves B. Interviewed by Benis M. Frank, Feb. 11, 1970. USMCU.

Fontenot, Merlin. Interviewed by the author, Jan. 18, 2014.

Forrestel, E. P. Interviewed by T. B. Buell, Dec. 1, 1971. Buell Papers, NWC.

Fuchida, Mitsuo. Interrogated by Ralph A. Ofstie, November 25, 1945. United States Strategic Bombing Survey, Interrogation No. 448 (Nav. No. 99).

Gabaldon, Guy. Interviewed by Ralph Edwards, *This Is Your Life*, June 19, 1957. NBC.

———. Interviewed by Alfredo Lugo, Sept. 25, 2013. KOCE/PBS SoCal.

Gould, Horace Chester. Interviewed Jul. 9, 2003. NMPW.

Graves, John. Interviewed by Kep Johnson, Dec. 14, 2003. NMPW.

Gray, Edward E. Interviewed by William J. Shinneman, Feb. 2, 1993. NMPW.

Groves, Robert L. Interviewed by Eddie Graham, April 30, 2004. NMPW.

Halloran, Raymond F. Interviewed by Bill Alexander, March 15, 1998. UNT.

———. Interviewed by John Garvey, March 12, 2004. Center for Military History and Strategic Analysis, Virginia Military Institute.

Hanley, Fiske. Interviewed by Ronald E. Marcello, Oct. 13, 1999. UNT.

Harper, R. Marlow. Interviewed by Justin R. Smith, February 17, 2009. Center for Military History and Strategic Analysis, Virginia Military Institute.

Hill, Harry W. Interviewed by John T. Mason and Richard West, 1966 (various dates). CCOH.

Hiranuma, Kiichiro. Interrogated by U.S. Army Far East Command, January 28, 1950. Doc. No. 55127 Interrogations of Japanese Officials on World War II. Military Intelligence Section, Historical Division. FDRL.

Hogaboom, Robert E. Interviewed by Benis M. Frank, 1972. USMCU.

Hoover, John H. Interviewed by John T. Mason, ca. 1963–64. CCOH.

Hustvedt, Olaf M. Interviewed by Colonel Wright, November 17, 1944. Office of Naval Records and Library.

Johnson, Hubert. Interviewed by Ken Lightfoot, Sept. 12, 2002. NHF.

Jones, Louis R. Interviewed by Thomas E. Donnelly, 1973. USMCU.

Joslin, Royal K. Interviewed by T. B. Buell, February 5, 1972. NWC.

Kauffman, Draper L. Interviewed by John T. Mason, May 1978. 2 vols. U.S. Naval Institute, 1982.

Kawabe, Ija. Interrogated by Ralph A. Ofstie and T. J. Hedding, November 26, 1945. United States Strategic Bombing Survey, Interrogation No. 447 (Nav. No. 98).

Kerr, Baine P. Interviewed by John Daniels, May 4, 1993. NMPW/UNT.

Krauss, Robert. Interviewed by Barry Cauchon, Dec. 16, 2008.

Kyle, Wood B. Interviewed by Benis M. Frank, 1969 (various dates). USMCU.

Lacey, Jon R. Interviewed by Larry Rabelais, Oct. 19, 2002. NMPW.

Lamar, Hal. Interviewed by Calvin Christman, Oct. 9, 1994. UNT.

Laux, James A. Interviewed by Ted Conerly, March 23, 2001. NMPW.

Lee, Kent L. Interviewed by Paul Stillwell, 1987–1988. USNI.

Marshall, Bob. Interviewed by Floyd Cox, Sept. 22, 2001. NMPW.

Matsuura, Goro. Interrogated for USSBS interrogation, USSBS No. 123 (Nav No. 30), Oct. 20, 1945.

McCampbell, David, with Wayne Morris. Press conference, USS *Bunker Hill*, Nov. 19, 1944. NARA.

————. Interviewed by Paul Stillwell, July 13–18, 1987, released 2010, USNI.

McCollum, Arthur H. Interviewed by John T. Mason, 1970–71. USNI.

McNamara, Robert S. Interviewed by Errol Morris. *The Fog of War* (documentary). Sony Classics, 2003.

Michelony, Lewis J. Interviewed by John Daniels, May 2, 1993. UNT.

Moore, Charles J. Interviewed by John T. Mason, 1965–66 (various dates), Columbia Center for Oral History. Spruance Papers, NWC.

Mumme, Floyd C. Interviewed by Richard Misenhimer, April 12, 2002. NMPW.

Mustin, Lloyd M. Interviewed by Lieutenant Porter, June 3, 1943. Office of Naval Records and Library, RG 38. NARA.

————. Interviewed by John T. Mason, 1972–1975. USNI.

Nagano, Osami. Interrogated by Ralph A. Ofstie and Capt. T. J. Hedding, Nov. 29, 1945. United States Strategic Bombing Survey, Interrogation No. 392 (Nav. No. 80).

Norwood, James A. Interviewed by Richard Misenhimer, Nov. 14, 2008. NMPW.

Ohmae, Toshikazu. Interrogated by Cdr. T. H. Moorer, Nov. 23, 1945. United States Strategic Bombing Survey, Interrogation No. 441 (Nav. No. 95).

Ozawa, Jisaburo. Interrogated by Ralph A. Ofstie, Oct. 16, 1945. United States Strategic Bombing Survey, Interrogation No. 32 (Nav. No. 3).

Pase, Charles. Interviewed by Floyd Cox, April 12, 2001. NMPW.

Peltier, Carl. Interviewed by Chuck Nichols, March 24, 2001. NMPW.

Prendergast, George. Oral history, March 8, 2007. NMPW.

Price, James Norman. Interviewed by Floyd Cox, May 2, 2001. NMPW.

Radford, Arthur W. Interviewed by T. B. Buell, Feb. 8, 1972. Buell Papers, NWC.

Rainey, Dewie H. Oral history, Dec. 6, 2002. NMPW.

Ramage, James D. National World War II Museum, Digital Collections. www .ww2online.org/view/james-d-ramage/segment-5/2013. Last accessed Nov. 7, 2014.

Ramsbottom, I. J. Interviewed by Bonnie A. Lovell, July 1, 2003. UNT.

Reif, George. Interviewed by Ken Lightfoot, Sept. 14, 2002. NHF.

Robertson, Stanley. Interviewed by Richard Misenhimer, Nov. 30, 2001. NMPW.

Sasaki, Akira. Interrogated by Ralph A. Ofstie, Nov. 23, 1945. United States Strategic Bombing Survey, Interrogation No. 434 (Nav. No. 91).

Savage, George J. Interviewed by Jason Snow, Oct. 21, 1996. UNT.

Shook, Leon J. Interviewed by Richard Misenhimer, Nov. 18, 2008. NMPW.

Showers, Donald Mac. Interviewed by Bill Alexander, March 13, 1998. UNT.

Spruance, Margaret. Interviewed by T. B. Buell, 1971 (various dates). Buell Papers, NWC.

Spruance, Raymond A. Interviewed by *Paris Match* magazine (France), July 6, 1965. Spruance Papers, NWC.

Taxis, Samuel G. Interviewed by Benis M. Frank, 1984. USMCU.

Taylor, Jack. Interviewed by David Winkler, July 9, 2001. NHF.

Thomassen, Edmund T. Interviewed by Richard W. Byrd, May 4, 1993. UNT.

Tibbets, Paul. Interviewed by Studs Terkel, ca. 2002. NMPW.

Titus, Jay. Interviewed by Richard W. Byrd, Nov. 9, 1996. UNT.

Toyoda, Soemu. Interrogated by Ralph A. Ofstie, Maj. Gen. O. A. Anderson, and Lt. Cdr. W. Wilds, Nov. 13–14, 1945. United States Strategic Bombing Survey, Interrogation No. 378 (Nav. No. 75).

Tremaine, Frank. Interviewed by Richard W. Byrd, March 18, 1995. UNT.

Twohig, Tom. Interviewed by Ned A. Smith, Oct. 21, 2000. NMPW.

Vraciu, Alex. Interviewed by Ronald E. Marcello, Oct. 9, 1994. UNT.

———. Interviewed by Bruce Petty, July 11, 2000. NMPW.

Vrana, Leo. Interviewed by Richard Misenheimer, March 20, 1993. NMPW.

Weller, Donald M. Interviewed by Benis M. Frank, 1989. USMCU.

Wilshusen, Richard C. Interviewed by Richard Misenhimer, March 11, 2004. NMPW.

Yoshida, Kiyoshi. Interrogated by G-2 staff, Northern Troops and Landing Force, Aug. 12, 1944.

Secondary Sources

Books

509th Composite Group. *509th Pictorial Album,* 1945. Columbus, Ohio: Mid Coast Marketing, 2002.

Afflerbach, Holger, and Hew Strachan (eds.). *How Fighting Ends: A History of Surrender.* Oxford: Oxford University Press, 2012.

Agawa, Hiroyuki. *The Reluctant Admiral: Yamamoto and the Imperial Navy.* New York: Kodansha, 1982 (Japanese edition 1969).

Albion, Robert Greenhalgh, and Robert Howe Connery, with Jennie Barnes Pope. *Forrestal and the Navy.* New York: Columbia, 1962.

Alexander, Joseph A. *Closing In: Marines in the Seizure of Iwo Jima.* Washington, D.C.: Marine Corps Historical Center, 1994.

———. *Storm Landings: Epic Amphibious Battles in the Central Pacific.* Annapolis, Md.: Naval Institute Press, 1997.

Allen, Thomas B., and Norman Polmar. *Code-Name Downfall: The Secret Plan to Invade Japan—and Why Truman Dropped the Bomb.* New York: Simon and Schuster, 1995.

Alperovitz, Gar. *Atomic Diplomacy: Hiroshima and Potsdam.* New York: Simon and Schuster, 1965.

———. *The Decision to Use the Atomic Bomb: And the Architecture of an American Myth.* New York: Alfred A. Knopf, 1995.

Anderson, Charles R. *Western Pacific: The U.S. Army Campaigns of World War II.* www .history.army.mil/html/books/072/72-29/CMH_Pub_72-29.pdf. Last viewed by author May 2, 2015.

Appleman, Roy E., James M. Burns, Russell A. Gugeler, and John Stevens. *Okinawa: The Last Battle.* Washington: Center of Military History, U.S. Army, 1948.

Arahara, Bokusui. *History of the Great Right Wing.* Draft manuscript, English translation of *Dai Uyoku-shi.* Tokyo: Dai Nippon Kokumin To, 1966. Toland Papers, FDRL.

Arnold, H. H. *Global Mission.* New York: Harper, 1949.

Asada, Sadao. *Japan and the World, 1853–1952.* New York: Columbia University Press, 1989.

Asahi Shimbun, staff of. *The Pacific Rivals: A Japanese View of Japanese-American Relations.* New York: John Weatherhill, 1972.

Astor, Gerald. *Wings of Gold: The U.S. Naval Air Campaign of World War II.* New York: Presidio Press, 2004.

Barlow, Jeffrey G. *From Hot War to Cold: The U.S. Navy and National Security Affairs, 1945–1955.* Stanford, Calif.: Stanford University Press, 2009.

Bath, Alan Harris. *Tracking the Axis Enemy: The Triumph of Anglo-American Naval Intelligence.* Lawrence: University Press of Kansas, 1998.

Beach, Edward L. *Scapegoats: A Defense of Kimmel and Short at Pearl Harbor.* Annapolis, Md.: Naval Institute Press, 1995.

Becton, F. Julian, with Joseph Morschauser III. *The Ship That Would Not Die.* Englewood Cliffs, N.J.: Prentice-Hall, 1980.

Bergamini, David. *Japan's Imperial Conspiracy: How Emperor Hirohito Led Japan into War Against the West.* New York: William Morrow, 1971.

Bird, Kai, and Lawrence Lifschultz (eds). *Hiroshima's Shadow: Writings on the Denial of History and the Smithsonian Controversy.* Stony Creek, Conn.: Pamphleteer's Press, 1998.

Bird, Kai, and Martin J. Sherwin. *American Prometheus: The Triumph and Tragedy of J. Robert Oppenheimer.* New York: Alfred A. Knopf, 2005.

Bix, Herbert P. *Hirohito and the Making of Modern Japan.* New York: HarperCollins, 2000.

Blackett, P. M. S. *Fear, War, and the Bomb.* New York: Whittlesey House, 1949.

Bland, Larry I., and Sharon Ritenour Stevens. *The Finest Soldier: January 1, 1945–January 7, 1947,* vol. 5, *The Papers of George Catlett Marshall.* Baltimore: Johns Hopkins University Press, 2003. http://marshallfoundation.org/library/digital-archive/editorial-note-on-the-atomic-bomb. Last viewed by the author on Sept. 7. 2015.

Borneman, Walter R. *The Admirals: Nimitz, Halsey, Leahy and King—the Five-Star Admirals Who Won the War at Sea.* New York: Little, Brown, 2012.

———. *MacArthur at War: World War II in the Pacific.* New York: Little, Brown, 2016.

Bradley, James, with Ron Powers. *Flags of Our Fathers.* New York: Bantam, 2000.

Braisted, William Reynolds. *The United States Navy in the Pacific, 1909–1922.* Austin: University of Texas Press, 1971.

Brodie, Bernard. *A Guide to Naval Strategy* (3rd ed.). Princeton, N.J.: Princeton University Press, 1944.

Brooks, Victor. *Hell Is Upon Us: D Day in the Pacific, June–August 1944.* Philadephia: Da Capo, 2005.

Buell, Thomas B. *Master of Sea Power: A Biography of Fleet Admiral Ernest J. King.* New York: Little, Brown, 1980.

———. *The Quiet Warrior: A Biography of Admiral Raymond A. Spruance.* Annapolis, Md.: Naval Institute Press, 1974.

Buruma, Ian. *Year Zero: A History of 1945.* New York: Penguin Press, 2013.

Bush, Elizabeth Kauffman. *America's First Frogman: The Draper Kauffman Story.* Annapolis, Md.: Naval Institute Press, 2004.

Butow, Robert J. C. *Japan's Decision to Surrender.* Stanford, Calif.: Stanford University Press, 1954.

Byrnes, James F. *All in One Lifetime.* New York: Harper and Bros., 1958.

Calvocoressi, Peter, Guy Wint, and John Pritchard. *Total War: The Greater East Asia and Pacific Conflict.* Rev. 2nd ed. New York: Pantheon, 1972.

Carlson, Elliot. *Joe Rochefort's War: The Odyssey of the Codebreaker Who Outwitted Yamamoto at Midway.* Annapolis, Md.: Naval Institute Press, 2011.

Carter, Worrall Reed. *Beans, Bullets, and Black Oil: The Story of Fleet Logistics Afloat in the Pacific during World War II.* Washington: Government Printing Office, 1953.

Chisholm, Donald. "Right Man, Right Place, Right Time—Richmond Kelly Turner." In Hattendorf and Elleman (eds.), *Nineteen-Gun Salute,* pp. 35–50.

Christman, Al. *Target Hiroshima: Deak Parsons and the Creation of the Atomic Bomb.* Annapolis, Md.: Naval Institute Press, 1998.

Clapp, Roger (ed.). *A History of Underwater Demolition Team Five.* Coronado, Calif.: U.S. Naval Special Warfare Command.

Clark, J. J., with Clark G. Reynolds. *Carrier Admiral.* New York: David McKay, 1967.

Cleaver, Thomas McKelvey. *Fabled Fifteen: The Pacific War Saga of Carrier Air Group 15.* Havertown, Pa.: Casemate, 2014.

Cohen, Theodore. *Remaking Japan: The American Occupation as New Deal.* New York: Free Press, 1987.

Conant, Jennet. *109 East Palace: Robert Oppenheimer and the Secret City of Los Alamos.* New York: Simon and Schuster, 2005.

Cook, Haruko Taya, and Theodore F. Cook. *Japan at War: An Oral History.* New York: New Press, 1992.

Cooper, Jeff. "Jeff Cooper's Commentaries," newsletter of the American Pistol Institute, vol. 1, no. 9, October 1993. myweb.cebridge.net/mkeithr/Jeff/jeff1.pdf.

Craig, William. *The Fall of Japan.* New York: Dial Press, 1967.

Crane, Conrad C. *The Bomb, Cities and Civilians: American Airpower Strategy in World War II.* Lawrence: University Press of Kansas, 1993.

Craven, Wesley Frank, and James Lea Cate (eds.). *The Pacific: Guadalcanal to Saipan, August 1942–July 1944.* The Army Air Forces in World War II, vol. 4. Washington, D.C.: Office of Air Force History, 1950. www.ibiblio.org/hyperwar/AAF/IV/AAF-IV-20.html.

———. *The Pacific: Matterhorn to Nagasaki, June 1944 to August 1945.* The Army Air Forces in World War II, vol. 5. Washington, D.C.: Office of Air Force History, 1953.

Cresswell, John. *Sea Warfare, 1939–1945.* Berkeley: University of California Press, 1967.

Cunningham, Chet. *The Frogmen of World War II: An Oral History of the U.S. Navy's Underwater Demolition Units.* New York: Pocket Books, 2005.

Daso, Dik Alan. *Hap Arnold and the Evolution of American Airpower.* Washington, D.C.: Smithsonian, 2000.

De Chant, John A. *Devilbirds: The Story of Marine Corps Aviation in World War II.* New York: Harper and Bros., 1947.

Denfeld, D. Colt. *Hold the Marianas: The Japanese Defense of the Mariana Islands.* Shippensburg, Pa.: White Mane, 1997.

de Seversky, Alexander P. *Victory Through Air Power.* New York: Simon and Schuster, 1942.

Dingman, Roger. *Deciphering the Rising Sun: Navy and Marine Corps Codebreakers, Translators and Interpreters in the Pacific War.* Annapolis, Md.: Naval Institute Press, 2009.

Dobbs, Michael. *Six Months in 1945: FDR, Stalin, Churchill and Truman.* New York: Alfred A. Knopf, 2012.

Dod, Karl C. *Technical Services, Corps of Engineers: The War Against Japan.* Washington, D.C.: U.S. Government Printing Office, 1966.

Dorr, Robert F. *Mission to Tokyo: The American Airmen Who Took the War to the Heart of Japan.* Minneapolis: Zenith, 2012.

Dower, John W. *Embracing Defeat: Japan in the Wake of World War II.* New York: Norton, 1999.

———. *War Without Mercy: Race and Power in the Pacific War.* New York: Pantheon, 1986.

Drea, Edward J. *In the Service of the Emperor: Essays on the Imperial Japanese Army.* Lincoln: University of Nebraska Press, 2003.

———. *MacArthur's ULTRA: Codebreaking and the War against Japan, 1942–1945.* Lawrence: University Press of Kansas, 1992.

Dull, Paul S. *A Battle History of the Imperial Japanese Navy (1941–1945).* Annapolis, Md.: Naval Institute Press, 1978.

Edo, Yuusuke. *Marianas oki no shichimenchouchi* (The Tragic Marianas Turkey Shoot). Trans. by Hiro Inoue. Tokyo: Kojinsha, 1992.

Eichelberger, Robert L. *Our Jungle Road to Tokyo.* New York: Viking Press, 1950.

Evans, David C. (ed. and trans.). *The Japanese Navy in World War II: In the Words of Former Japanese Naval Officers.* 2nd ed. Annapolis, Md.: Naval Institute Press, 1986.

Ewing, Steve. *Thach Weave: The Life of Jimmie Thach.* Annapolis, Md.: Naval Institute Press, 2004.

Fane, Francis Douglas. *The Naked Warriors.* New York: Appleton Century Crofts, 1956.

Ferguson, Niall. *The War of the World: Twentieth-Century Conflict and the Descent of the West.* New York: Penguin Press, 2006.

Ferrell, Robert H. (ed.). *Harry S. Truman and the Bomb: A Documentary History*. Worland, Wy.: High Plains, 1996.

————. *Off the Record: The Private Papers of Harry S. Truman*. New York: Harper and Row, 1980.

Fletcher, Gregory G. *Intrepid Aviators: The American Flyers Who Sank Japan's Greatest Battleship*. New York: NAL Caliber, 2012.

Forrestel, E. P. *Admiral Raymond A. Spruance: A Study in Command*. Washington, D.C.: Department of the Navy, 1966.

Frank, Richard B. *Downfall: The End of the Imperial Japanese Empire*. New York: Random House, 1999.

————. *MacArthur: A Biography*. New York: Palgrave, 2007.

Friedman, Norman. *U.S. Amphibious Ships and Craft: An Illustrated Design History*. Annapolis, Md.: Naval Institute Press, 2002.

————. *U.S. Battleships: An Illustrated Design History*. Annapolis, Md.: Naval Institute Press, 1985.

————. *U.S. Cruisers: An Illustrated Design History*. Annapolis, Md.: Naval Institute Press, 1984.

Fuller, Richard. *Shokan: Hirohito's Samurai: Leaders of the Japanese Armed Forces, 1926–1945*. London: Arms and Armour, 1992.

Gailey, Harry A. *Howlin' Mad vs. the Army: Conflict in Command, Saipan 1944*. Novato, Calif.: Presidio, 1986.

Giangreco, D. M. *Hell to Pay: Operation Downfall and the Invasion of Japan, 1945–1947*. Annapolis, Md.: Naval Institute Press, 2009.

Gilbert, Alton Keith. *A Leader Born: The Life of Admiral John Sidney McCain, Pacific Carrier Commander*. Havertown, Pa.: Casemate, 2006.

Gluck, Carol, and Stephen R. Graubard (eds.). *Showa: The Japan of Hirohito*. New York: Norton, 1992.

Goe, W. Charles. *Is War Hell?* Self-published, 1947.

Goldberg, Harold J. *D Day in the Pacific: The Battle of Saipan*. Bloomington: Indiana University Press, 2007.

Goldstein, Donald M., and Katherine V. Dillon (eds.). *The Pacific War Papers: Japanese Documents of World War II*. Washington, D.C.: Potomac Books, 2004.

Greene, Bob. *Duty: A Father, His Son, and the Man Who Won the War*. New York: William Morrow, 2000.

Grew, Joseph C. *Turbulent Era: A Diplomatic Record of Forty Years*. Boston: Houghton Mifflin, 1952.

Griffith, Charles. *The Quest: Haywood Hansell and American Strategic Bombing in World War II*. Maxwell Air Force Base, Ala.: Air University Press, 1999.

Groves, Leslie M. *Now It Can Be Told: The Story of the Manhattan Project*. New York: Harper and Row, 1962.

Halsey, William F., and J. Bryan III. *Admiral Halsey's Story*. New York: McGraw-Hill, 1947.

Ham, Paul. *Hiroshima Nagasaki: The Real Story of the Atomic Bombs and Their Aftermath*. New York: St. Martin's Press, 2014.

Hammel, Eric M. *War in the Western Pacific: The U.S. Marines in the Marianas, Peleliu, Iwo Jima, and Okinawa, 1944–1945*. Minneapolis: Zenith, 2010.

Hanson, Victor Davis. *Ripples of Battle: How the Wars of the Past Still Determine How We Fight, How We Live, and How We Think*. New York: Doubleday, 2003.

Harding, Stephen. *The Last to Die: A Defeated Empire, a Forgotten Mission, and the Last American Killed in World War II*. Philadelphia: Da Capo, 2015.

Hasegawa, Tsuyoshi. *Racing the Enemy: Stalin, Truman, and the Surrender of Japan*. Cambridge, Mass.: Harvard University Press, 2009.

Hastings, Max. *Inferno: The World at War, 1939–1945*. New York: Alfred A. Knopf, 2011.

———. *Nemesis: The Battle for Japan, 1944–45*. London: HarperCollins, 2007. (Published in the U.S. under the title *Retribution*.)

Hata, Ikuhiko, Yasuho Izawa, and Christopher Shores. *Japanese Naval Fighter Aces: 1932–45*. Mechanicsburg, Pa.: Stackpole, 2011.

Hattendorf, John B., and Bruce A. Elleman (eds.). *Nineteen-Gun Salute: Case Studies of Operational, Strategic, and Diplomatic Naval Leadership During the 20th and Early 21st Centuries*. Newport R.I.: Naval War College Press/Government Printing Office, 2010.

Hayes, Grace Person. *The History of the Joint Chiefs of Staff in World War II: The War Against Japan*. Annapolis, Md.: Naval Institute Press, 1982.

Henebry, John P. *The Grim Reapers: At Work in the Pacific Theater*. Missoula, Mont.: Pictorial Histories, 2002.

Herman, Arthur. *Douglas MacArthur: American Warrior*. New York: Random House, 2016.

Hersey, John. *Hiroshima*. New York: Alfred A. Knopf, 1973.

Higuchi, Wakako. *The Japanese Adminstration of Guam, 1941–1944*. Jefferson, N.C.: McFarland and Co., 2013.

Hoffman, Carl W. *Saipan: The Beginning of the End*. Historical Branch, U.S. Marine Corps, 1950. http://ibiblio.org/hyperwar/USMC/USMC-M-Saipan/index.html.

———. *The Seizure of Tinian*. Historical Branch, U.S. Marine Corps, 1951. www.ibiblio.org/hyperwar/USMC/USMC-M-Tinian/USMC-M-Tinian-1.html#cn32.

Holmes, W. J. *Double-Edged Secrets: U.S. Naval Intelligence Operations in the Pacific During World War II*. Annapolis, Md.: Naval Institute Press, 1979.

Holwitt, Joel Ira. *"Execute Against Japan": The U.S. Decision to Conduct Unrestricted Submarine Warfare.* College Station: Texas A&M University Press, 2009.

Hornfischer, James D. *The Last Stand of the Tin Can Sailors: The Extraordinary World War II Story of the U.S. Navy's Finest Hour.* New York: Bantam, 2004.

———. *Neptune's Inferno: The U.S. Navy at Guadalcanal.* New York: Bantam, 2011.

———. *To the Marianas: War in the Central Pacific, 1944.* New York: Van Nostrand Reinhold, 1980.

———. *McCampbell's Heroes: The Story of the U.S. Navy's Most Celebrated Carrier Fighters of the Pacific War.* New York: Van Nostrand Reinhold, 1983.

Hoyt, Edwin P. *How They Won the War in the Pacific: Nimitz and His Admirals.* Guilford, Conn.: Lyons Press, 2000.

Hughes, Thomas Alexander. *Admiral Bill Halsey: A Naval Life.* Cambridge, Mass.: Harvard University Press, 2016.

Hughes, Wayne P., Jr. "Clear Purpose, Comprehensive Execution—Raymond Ames Spruance." In Hattendorf and Elleman (eds.), *Nineteen-Gun Salute*, pp. 51–64.

Huie, William Bradford. *The Hiroshima Pilot.* New York: Putnam, 1964.

Hutchinson, John A. *Bluejacket: In Harm's Way from Guadalcanal to Tokyo.* New York: Vantage, 1995.

Ickes, Harold L. *Fightin' Oil.* New York: Alfred A. Knopf, 1943.

Ienaga, Saburo. *The Pacific War, 1931–1945.* Trans. Frank Baldwin. New York: Pantheon, 1978.

Iriye, Akira. *Power and Culture: The Japanese-American War, 1941–1945.* Cambridge, Mass.: Harvard University Press, 1981.

Iseley, Jeter A., and Philip A. Crowl. *The U.S. Marines and Amphibious War: Its Theory and Its Practice in the Pacific.* Princeton, N.J.: Princeton University Press, 1951.

Ito, Masanori. *The End of the Imperial Japanese Navy.* Trans. Andrew Y. Kuroda and Roger Pineau. New York: Norton, 1962.

Jensen, Oliver. *Carrier War.* New York: Simon and Schuster, 1945.

Jones, Don. *Oba: The Last Samurai.* Novato, Calif.: Presidio Press, 1986.

Jones, William K. *A Brief History of the Sixth Marines.* Washington, D.C.: History and Headquarters Division, U.S. Marine Corps, 1987.

Jones, Vincent C. *Manhattan: The Army and the Atomic Bomb.* Washington, D.C.: Center of Military History, 1985.

Jordan, Jonathan W. *American Warlords: How Roosevelt's High Command Led America to Victory in World War II.* New York: NAL Caliber, 2015.

Jumper, Will C. *From Time Remembered,* El Dorado, Calif.: Foothills Press, 1977.

Kaiser, David. *No End Save Victory: How FDR Led the Nation into War.* New York: Basic Books, 2014.

Kase, Toshikazu. *Journey to the* Missouri. New Haven, Conn.: Yale University Press, 1950.

Kelly, Cynthia C. (ed.). *The Manhattan Project: The Birth of the Atomic Bomb in the Words of Its Creators, Eyewitnesses and Historians.* New York: Tess Press, 2010.

Kennedy, Paul. *Engineers of Victory: The Problem Solvers Who Turned the Tide in the Second World War.* New York: Random House, 2013.

Kenney, George C. *General Kenney Reports: A Personal History of the Pacific War.* Washington, D.C.: Office of Air Force History, 1949.

King, Dan. *The Last Zero Fighter: Firsthand Accounts from WWII Japanese Naval Pilots.* Irvine, Calif.: Pacific Press, 2012.

King, Ernest J., and Walter Muir Whitehill. *Fleet Admiral King: A Naval Record.* New York: Norton, 1952.

Kort, Michael. *The Columbia Guide to Hiroshima and the Bomb.* New York: Columbia University Press, 2007.

Kotani, Ken. *Japanese Intelligence in World War II.* Trans. Chiharu Kotani. New York: Osprey, 2009.

Koyanagi, Tomiji (ed.). *The Koyanagi File.* Tokyo: Suiko-kai, 2010.

Krauss, Robert, and Amelia Krauss (eds.). *The 509th Remembered: A History of the 509th Composite Group as Told by the Veterans That Dropped the Atomic Bombs on Japan.* Buchanan, Mich.: Self-published, 2007. Rev. 2008.

Kuehn, John T. *Agents of Innovation: The General Board and the Design of the Fleet That Defeated the Japanese Navy.* Annapolis, Md.: Naval Institute Press, 2008.

Kunetka, James. *City of Fire: Los Alamos and the Atomic Age, 1943–1945.* Rev. ed. Albuquerque: University of New Mexico Press, 1979.

———. *The General and the Genius: Groves and Oppenheimer, the Unlikely Partnership That Built the Atom Bomb.* Washington, D.C.: Regnery, 2015.

Lacey, Sharon Tosi. *Pacific Blitzkrieg: World War II in the Central Pacific.* Denton, Tex.: University of North Texas Press, 2013.

Lacroix, Eric, and Linton Wells II. *Japanese Cruisers of the Pacific War.* Annapolis, Md.: Naval Institute Press, 1997.

Lamar, Hal. *I Saw Stars: Some Memories of Commander Hal Lamar, Fleet Admiral Nimitz's Flag Lieutenant, 1941–1945.* Fredericksburg, Tex.: Admiral Nimitz Foundation, 1985.

Lane, Frederic Chapin. *Ships for Victory: A History of Shipbuilding Under the U.S. Maritime Commission.* Baltimore, Md.: Johns Hopkins University Press, 1951.

Larrabee, Eric. *Commander in Chief: Franklin Delano Roosevelt, His Lieutenants, and Their War.* New York: Harper, 1987.

Layton, Edwin T., with Roger Pineau and John Costello. *"And I Was There": Pearl Harbor and Midway—Breaking the Secrets.* Old Saybrook, Conn.: Konecky and Konecky, 1985.

Leahy, William D. *I Was There*. New York: Whittlesey House, 1950.

Lockwood, Charles A. *Sink 'Em All*. New York: Dutton, 1951.

Lodge, O. R. *The Recapture of Guam*. Washington, D.C.: U.S. Marine Corps, Historical Branch, 1954.

Lundstrom, John. *Black Shoe Carrier Admiral: A Biography of Frank Jack Fletcher*. Annapolis, Md.: Naval Institute Press, 2006.

MacArthur, Douglas. *Reminiscences*. New York: McGraw-Hill, 1964.

Maddox, Robert James. *Hiroshima in History: The Myths of Revisionism*. Columbia, Mo.: University of Missouri Press, 2007.

Manchester, William. *American Caesar: Douglas MacArthur, 1880–1964*. New York: Little, Brown, 1978.

Mansell, Roger. *Captured: The Forgotten Men of Guam*. Annapolis, Md.: Naval Institute Press, 2012.

Marshall, George C. *General Marshall's Report: The Winning of the War in Europe and the Pacific. Biennial report of the Chief of Staff of the United States Army, July 1, 1943, to June 30, 1945, to the Secretary of War*. New York: Simon and Schuster, 1945.

McGee, William T. *The Amphibians Are Coming! Emergence of the 'Gator Navy and Its Revolutionary Landing Craft*, vol. 1, *Amphibious Operations in the South Pacific in WWII*. Santa Barbara, Ca.: BMC, 2000.

Mee, Charles L. *Meeting at Potsdam*. New York: M. Evans, 1975.

Meehl, Gerald A. *One Marine's War: A Combat Interpreter's Quest for Humanity in the Pacific*. Annapolis, Md.: Naval Institute Press, 2012.

Mets, David R. *Master of Airpower General Carl A. Spaatz*. Novato, Calif.: Presidio, 1988.

Miller, Donald L. *D-Days in the Pacific*. New York: Simon and Schuster, 2005.

Miller, Edward S. *War Plan Orange: The U.S. Strategy to Defeat Japan, 1897–1945*. Annapolis, Md.: Naval Institute Press, 1991.

Miller, Francis Trevelyan. *History of World War II*. Iowa Falls, Iowa: Riverside, 1945.

Millis, Walter (ed.), with E. S. Duffield. *The Forrestal Diaries*. New York: Viking, 1951.

Moore, Stephen L., with William J. Shinneman and Robert Gruebel. *The Buzzard Brigade: Torpedo Squadron Ten at War*. Missoula, Mont.: Pictorial Histories, 1996.

Morgan, Robert, with Ron Powers. *The Man Who Flew the Memphis Belle: Memoir of a WWII Bomber Pilot*. New York: Dutton, 2001.

Morison, Samuel Eliot. *Aleutians, Gilberts and Marshalls, June 1942–April 1944*, vol. 7, *History of United States Naval Operations in World War II*. New York: Little, Brown, 1951.

———. *New Guinea and the Marianas, March 1944–August 1944*, vol. 8, *History of United States Naval Operations in World War II*. New York: Little, Brown, 1953.

———. *The Two-Ocean War: A Short History of the United States Navy in the Second World War.* New York: Little, Brown, 1963.

———. *Victory in the Pacific, 1945,* vol. 14, *History of United States Naval Operations in World War II.* New York: Little, Brown, 1960.

Morris, Seymour. *Supreme Commander: MacArthur's Triumph in Japan.* New York: HarperCollins, 2014.

Morrison, Wilbur H. *Point of No Return: The Story of the 20th Air Force.* New York: Times Books, 1979.

Morton, Louis. *The War in the Pacific: Strategy and Command; The First Two Years.* Washington, D.C.: Office of the Chief of Military History, Department of the Army, 1962.

Mosley, Leonard. *Hirohito: Emperor of Japan.* Englewood Cliffs, N.J.: Prentice Hall, 1966.

Murray, Williamson, and Allan R. Millett. *A War to Be Won: Fighting the Second World War.* Cambridge, Mass.: Harvard University Press, 2000.

Neer, Robert M. *Napalm: A Biography.* Cambridge, Mass.: Harvard University Press, 2013.

Neiberg. Michael. *Potsdam: The End of World War II and the Remaking of Europe.* New York: Basic Books, 2015.

Newcomb, Richard F. *Abandon Ship!: The Saga of the USS* Indianapolis, *the Navy's Greatest Sea Disaster.* New York: HarperCollins, 2000.

Norris, Robert S. *Racing for the Bomb: General Leslie R. Groves, the Manhattan Project's Indispensable Man.* New York: Steerforth Press, 2002.

O'Brien, Cyril J. *Liberation: Marines in the Recapture of Guam.* Washington, D.C.: Marine Corps Historical Center, 1994.

O'Brien, Francis A. *Battling for Saipan.* New York: Presidio, 2003.

O'Dell, James Douglas. *The Water Is Never Cold: The Origins of the U.S. Navy's Combat Demolition Units, UDTs, and SEALs.* Dulles, Va.: Brassey's, 2000.

Pacific Star Center for Young Writers. *"We Drank Our Tears": Memories of the Battles for Saipan and Tinian as Told by Our Elders.* Saipan, Commonwealth of Northern Mariana Islands, 2004.

Petty, Bruce M. *Saipan: Oral Histories of the Pacific War.* Jefferson, N.C.: McFarland, 2002.

Peyton, Green. *5,000 Miles Towards Tokyo: How the United States Won the Naval Struggle in the Pacific.* Norman: University of Oklahoma Press, 1945.

Pike, Francis. *Hirohito's War: The Pacific War, 1941–1945.* New York: Bloomsbury, 2015.

Pogue, Forrest C. *George C. Marshall,* vol. 2, *Ordeal and Hope, 1939–1942.* New York: Viking, 1966.

————. *George C. Marshall,* vol. 3, *Engineer of Victory, 1943–1945.* New York: Viking, 1973.

Polmar, Norman. *The Enola Gay: The B-29 That Dropped the Atomic Bomb on Hiroshima.* Lincoln: University of Nebraska Press, 2004.

Potter, E. B. *Admiral Arleigh Burke.* Annapolis, Md.: Naval Institute Press, 1990.

————. *Nimitz.* Annapolis, Md.: Naval Institute Press, 1976.

Potter, E. B., and Chester W. Nimitz (eds.). *Great Sea War: The Story of Naval Action in World War II.* Englewood Cliffs, N.J.: Prentice Hall, 1960.

————. *Triumph in the Pacific: The Navy's Struggle Against Japan.* Englewood Cliffs, N.J.: Prentice Hall, 1963.

Prados, John. *Combined Fleet Decoded.* New York: Random House, 1995.

Prange, Gordon W., with Donald M. Goldstein and Katherine V. Dillon. *God's Samurai: Lead Pilot at Pearl Harbor.* Washington, D.C.: Brassey's, 1990.

Pratt, Fletcher. *The Fleet Against Japan.* New York: Harper, 1946.

————. *The Navy's War.* New York: Harper, 1944.

Prefer, Nathan N. *The Battle for Tinian: Vital Stepping Stone in America's War Against Japan.* Havertown, Pa.: Casemate, 2012.

Reynolds, Clark G. *The Fast Carriers: The Forging of an Air Navy.* New York: McGraw-Hill, 1968.

Rhodes, Richard. *The Making of the Atomic Bomb.* New York: Simon and Schuster, 1986.

Richler, Mordecai (ed.). *Writers on World War II: An Anthology.* New York: Alfred A. Knopf, 1991.

Rigdon, William M., with James Derieux. *White House Sailor.* New York: Doubleday, 1962.

Robinson, C. Snelling. *200,000 Miles Aboard the Destroyer* Cotten. Kent, Ohio: Kent State University Press, 2000.

Rose, Lisle A. *Dubious Victory: The United States and the End of World War II.* Kent, Ohio: Kent State University Press, 1973.

Rottman, Gordon L. *Saipan and Tinian, 1944.* Oxford: Osprey, 2004.

Sakai, Saburo, with Martin Caidin and Fred Saito. *Samurai!* New York: Dutton, 1957.

Scott, James. *The War Below: The Story of Three Submarines That Battled Japan.* New York: Simon and Schuster, 2013.

Sears, David. *Pacific Air: How Fearless Flyboys, Peerless Aircraft, and Fast Flattops Conquered the Skies in the War with Japan.* Philadelphia: Da Capo, 2011.

Sebald, W. G. *On the Natural History of Destruction.* New York: Random House, 2003.

Second Marine Division Association (William Benning, ed.). *Heritage Years: Second Marine Division Commemorative Anthology: 1940–1949*. Paducah, Ky.: Turner, 1988.

Shaw, Henry I. *The United States Marines in the Occupation of Japan*. Washington, D.C.: U.S. Marine Corps, Historical Branch, 1961. Rev. 1962.

Shaw, Henry I., Bernard C. Nalty, and Edwin T. Turnbladh, *Central Pacific Drive*, vol. 3, *History of U.S. Marine Corps Operations in World War II*. Washington, D.C.: U.S. Marine Corps, Historical Branch, 1958.

Sheftall, M. G. *Blossoms in the Wind: Human Legacies of the Kamikaze*. New York: New American Library, 2005.

Sherman, Frederick C. *Combat Command: The American Aircraft Carriers in the Pacific War*. New York: Dutton, 1950.

Sherrod, Robert. *On to Westward: War in the Central Pacific*. New York: Duell, Sloan and Pearce, 1945.

Sigal, Leon V. *Fighting to a Finish: The Politics of War Termination in the United States and Japan, 1945*. Ithaca, N.Y.: Cornell University Press, 1988.

Simpson, B. Mitchell, III. *Admiral Harold R. Stark: Architect of Victory, 1939–1945*. Columbia, SC: University of South Carolina Press, 1989.

Sister Joan of Arc. *My Name Is Nimitz*. San Antonio, Tex.: Standard Printing Co., 1948.

Skates, John Ray. *The Invasion of Japan: The Alternative to the Bomb*. Columbia, SC: University of South Carolina Press, 1994.

Smith, Holland M., and Percy Finch. *Coral and Brass*, New York: Scribner, 1949.

Smith, Michael. *The Emperor's Codes: The Thrilling Story of the Allied Code Breakers Who Turned the Tide of World War II*. New York: Arcade, 2001.

Smith, S. E. (ed.). *The United States Marine Corps in World War II*. New York: Morrow, 1969.

———. *The United States Navy in World War II*. New York: Morrow, 1966.

Southard, Susan. *Nagasaki: Life After Nuclear War*. New York: Viking, 2015.

Spector, Ronald H. *Eagle Against the Sun: The American War with Japan*. New York: Free Press, 1984.

———. *In the Ruins of Empire: The Japanese Surrender and the Battle for Postwar Asia*. New York: Random House, 2007.

Springer, Joseph A. *Inferno: The Epic Life and Death Struggle of the USS* Franklin *in World War II*. Minneapolis: Zenith Press, 2007.

Stafford, Edward P. *The Big E: The Story of the USS* Enterprise. Annapolis, Md.: Naval Institute Press, 1962.

Starr, Kevin. *Embattled Dreams: California in War and Peace, 1940–1950*. New York: Oxford University Press, 2003.

Stillwell, Paul (ed.). *Submarine Stories: Recollections from the Diesel Boats.* Annapolis, Md.: Naval Institute Press, 2007.

Stimson, Henry L., and McGeorge Bundy. *On Active Service in Peace and War.* New York: Harper and Bros., 1948.

Stoler, Mark A. *Allies and Adversaries: The Joint Chiefs of Staff, the Grand Alliance, and U.S. Strategy in World War II.* Chapel Hill: University of North Carolina Press, 2000.

———. *Allies in War: Britain and America against the Axis Powers, 1940–1945.* London: Hodder Arnold, 2005.

Stone, I. F. *The War Years, 1939–1945.* New York: Little, Brown, 1988.

Tanaka, Yuki. *Japan's Comfort Women: Sexual Slavery and Prostitution During World War II and the U.S. Occupation.* New York: Routledge, 2002.

Taylor, Theodore. *The Magnificent Mitscher.* Annapolis, Md.: Naval Institute Press, 1991.

Thomas, Gordon, and Max Morgan Witts. *Enola Gay: The Bombing of Hiroshima.* Old Saybrook, Conn.: Konecky and Konecky, 1977.

Thomas, Lowell, and Edward Jablonski. *Doolittle: A Biography.* New York: Doubleday, 1976.

Tibbets, Paul W. *Flight of the Enola Gay.* Reynoldsburg, Ohio: Buckeye Aviation Book Co., 1989.

Tillman, Barrett. *Clash of the Carriers: The True Story of the Marianas Turkey Shoot of World War II.* New York: NAL/Caliber, 2005.

———. *Enterprise: America's Fightingest Ship and the Men Who Helped Win World War II.* New York: Simon and Schuster, 2012.

———. *LeMay: A Biography.* New York: Palgrave, 2007.

———. *Whirlwind: The Air War Against Japan.* New York: Simon and Schuster, 2010.

Toland, John. *The Rising Sun: The Decline and Fall of the Japanese Empire, 1936–1945* (2 vols.). New York: Random House, 1970.

Toll, Ian W. *The Conquering Tide: War in the Pacific Islands, 1942–1944.* New York: Norton, 2015.

Truman, Harry S. *Memoirs* (2 vols.). New York: Doubleday, 1955.

Tully, Anthony P., "IJN *Shokaku*: Tabular Record of Movement." www.combinedfleet.com/shokaku.htm, 1998. Rev. July 30, 2010. Last accessed November 8, 2014.

Tully, Anthony P., and Gilbert Casse. "IJN *Hiyo*: Tabular Record of Movement," 1998. Rev. ed., 2013. www.combinedfleet.com/hiyo.htm. Last accessed by the author on November 7, 2014.

Ugaki, Matome. *Fading Victory: The Diary of Admiral Matome Ugaki, 1941–1945.*

Trans. Masataka Chihaya. Donald M. Goldstein and Katherine V. Dillon, eds. Pittsburgh, Pa.: University of Pittsburgh Press, 1991.

Vilensky, Joel A. *Dew of Death: The Story of Lewisite, America's World War I Weapon of Mass Destruction*. Bloomington: Indiana University Press, 2005.

Walker, J. Samuel. *Prompt and Utter Destruction: Truman and the Use of Atomic Bombs Against Japan*. Chapel Hill: University of North Carolina Press, 1997.

Walker, Stephen. *Shockwave: Countdown to Hiroshima*. New York: HarperCollins, 2005.

Weinberg, Gerhard L. *A World at Arms: A Global History of World War II*. Cambridge, U.K.: Cambridge University Press, 1994.

Weintraub, Stanley. *The Last Great Victory: The End of World War II, July/August 1945*. New York: Dutton, 1995.

Weller, George. *First into Nagasaki. The Censored Eyewitness Dispatches on Post-Atomic Japan and Its Prisoners of War*. New York: Crown, 2006.

Wheeler, Gerald E. *Kinkaid of the Seventh Fleet*. Annapolis, Md.: Naval Institute Press, 1996.

Wilcox, Robert K. *Japan's Secret War: Japan's Race Against Time to Build Its Own Atomic Bomb*. New York: Marlowe, 1995.

Williams, Kathleen Broome. *The Measure of a Man: My Father, the Marine Corps, and Saipan*. Annapolis, Md.: Naval Institute Press, 2013.

Winchester, Simon. *Pacific: Silicon Chips and Surfboards, Coral Reefs and Atom Bombs, Brutal Dictators, Fading Empires, and the Coming Collision of the World's Superpowers*. New York: HarperCollins, 2015.

Wolters, Timothy S. *Information at Sea; Shipboard Command and Control in the U.S. Navy, from Mobile Bay to Okinawa*. Baltimore: Johns Hopkins University Press, 2013.

Wooldridge, E. T. (ed.). *Carrier Warfare in the Pacific: An Oral History Collection*. Washington, D.C.: Smithsonian Institution Press, 1993.

Wukovits, John. *Admiral Bull Halsey: The Life and Wars of the Navy's Most Controversial Commander*. New York: Palgrave, 2010.

———. *Hell from the Heavens: The Epic Story of the USS Laffey and World War II's Greatest Kamikaze Attack*. Philadelphia: Da Capo, 2015.

Y'Blood, William T. *The Little Giants: U.S. Escort Carriers against Japan*. Annapolis, Md.: Naval Institute Press, 1987.

———. *Red Sun Setting: The Battle of the Philippine Sea*. Annapolis, Md.: Naval Institute Press, 1981.

Zalta, Edward N., Uri Nodelman, and Colin Allen (eds.). *Stanford Encyclopedia of Philosophy*. Stanford, Calif.: Metaphysics Research Lab, Center for the Study of Language and Information, 2015. http://plato.stanford.edu. Last viewed by the author on Sept. 9, 2015.

Articles

Allen, Thomas B., with Norman Polmar. "How Many Will Die?" *Naval History,* August 2015, p. 36.

Associated Press. "Record Blows Near for Japs." *Milwaukee Journal,* July 25, 1945, p. 3.

Bernstein, Barton J. "The Atomic Bombings Reconsidered." *Foreign Affairs,* Jan./ Feb. 1995. www.foreignaffairs.com/articles/asia/1995-01-01/atomic-bombings -reconsidered. Last viewed by the author on Sept. 7, 2015.

———. Lecture, Nimitz Museum Symposium (National Museum of the Pacific War), March 19, 1995. www.c-span.org/video/?66945-1/atomic-bomb-decision -preparations.

Bradsher, Greg. "The 'Z Plan' Story," *Prologue,* Fall 2005, vol. 37, no. 3. www .archives.gov/publications/prologue/2005/fall/z-plan-1.html. Last viewed by the author on Oct. 17, 2015.

Brady, Tim. "Spies and Dolls." History Channel Club, June 19, 2009. http://www .thehistorychannelclub.com/articles/articletype/articleview/articleid/68/spies -amp-dolls.

Busch, Noel F. "Admiral Chester Nimitz." *Life,* July 10, 1944, p. 82.

———. "Task Force 58." *Life,* July 17, 1944, p. 17.

Compton, Karl T. "If the Atomic Bomb Had Not Been Used." *Atlantic,* December 1946, p. 54.

Creel, George. "The Guilty." *Collier's,* Sept. 2, 1944, 29.

DeVore, Robert. "B-29—Rush! Destination—Japan!" *Collier's,* July 22, 1944, p. 20.

———. "Truk." *Collier's,* March 11, 1944, 18.

Donovan, James A. "Saipan Tank Battle." *Marine Corps Gazette,* October 1944, p. 25.

Drea, Edward J. Lecture, Nimitz Museum Symposium, San Antonio. March 19, 1995. www.c-span.org/video/?66945-1/atomic-bomb-decision-preparations. Last viewed by the author March 20, 2016.

Elliott, Peter. "Escort Ship Production in WWII." *Warship,* vol. 2, 1978, p. 193.

Fedman, David, and Cary Karacas. "A Cartographic Fade to Black: Mapping the Destruction of Urban Japan During World War II." *Journal of Historical Geography,* July 2012, p. 306. www.sciencedirect.com/science/article/pii/ S0305748812000266. Last viewed by the author Sept. 5, 2015.

Flanner, Janet. "The Doll Spy." *Harper's Bazaar,* July 1944, p. 44.

"Fortress Pacific" (editorial). *Collier's,* Sept. 23, 1944, p. 94.

Frank, Richard B. "The Moral Abacus" (lecture). National World War II Museum, New Orleans, La., Nov. 22, 2013.

Gallicchio, Marc. "After Nagasaki: General Marshall's Plan for Tactical Nuclear Weapons in Japan." *Prologue,* Winter 1991, p. 396.

Genda, Minoru. "Tactical Planning in the Imperial Japanese Navy." *Naval War College Review,* October 1969, p. 45.

Giroux, Robert. "Rescue from Truk." *Collier's,* May 13, 1944, p. 18.

Green, Clinton. "Our B-29 Base: An Epic Job." *New York Times Magazine,* Dec. 10, 1944, p. 8.

Hailey, Foster. "With a Task Force in the Pacific." *New York Times,* Nov. 5, 1944, p. SM8.

Hansen, Matthew. "New Mystery Arises from Iconic Iwo Jima Image." *Omaha World-Herald,* Nov. 23, 2014. http://dataomaha.com/media/news/2014/iwo-jima.

Heinl, R. D. "Naval Gunfire: Scourge of the Beaches." *Naval Institute Proceedings,* November 1945, p. 1309.

———. "Naval Gunfire Support in Landings." *Marine Corps Gazette,* September 1945, p. 2.

Hemingway, Ernest. "Voyage to Victory." *Collier's,* July 22, 1944, p. 11.

Hirama, Yoichi. "Japanese Naval Preparations for World War II," *Naval War College Review,* Spring 1991, p. 63.

Hoffman, Jon T. "Fighting Far from Home." *Naval History,* February 2013, p. 16.

Hone, Thomas C. "Replacing Battleships with Aircraft Carriers in the Pacific in World War II." *Naval War College Review,* vol. 66, no. 1 (Winter 2013), p. 56.

Hone, Trent. "U.S. Navy Surface Battle Doctrine and Victory in the Pacific." *Naval War College Review,* vol. 62, no. 1 (Winter 2009), p. 67.

Hughes, Wayne P., Jr. "Clear Purpose, Comprehensive Execution: Raymond Ames Spruance" (unpublished manuscript). Nov. 2007.

Kalischer, Peter and Gloria. "Dark Angel," *Collier's,* Jan. 26, 1952, p. 20.

Kawai, Kazuo. "*Mokusatsu,* Japan's Response to the Potsdam Declaration." *Pacific Historical Review,* vol. 19, no. 4, Nov. 1950, p. 409.

Lee, Clark. "How Japan Plans to Win." *Collier's,* May 22, 1943, p. 15.

"*Life* Goes to an Aircraft Carrier Party." *Life,* July 3, 1944, p. 83.

Love, Edmund G. "Smith versus Smith." *Infantry Journal,* November 1948, p. 3.

McCormick, Robert. "King of the Navy." *Collier's,* January 16, 1943, p. 18.

Morehouse, Clifford P. "Amphibious Training." *Marine Corps Gazette,* August 1944, p. 35.

O'Brien, Francis, A. "The Battle of Saipan." *World War II,* May 1997.

Parshall, Jonathan, Anthony Tully, and Richard Wolff. "The Sinking of *Shokaku*: An Analysis." www.combinedfleet.com/shoksink.htm. Accessed by the author on Sept. 14, 2014.

Pratt, Fletcher. "The Marines in the Pacific War." *Marine Corps Gazette*, serialized monthly July–Nov. 1947.

Rems, Alan P. "Two Birds with One Hailstone." *Naval History*, February 2014, p. 16.

Reynolds, Clark G. "Admiral John H. Towers and the Origins of Strategic Flexibility in the Central Pacific Offensive, 1943." *Naval War College Review*, Spring 1987.

Reynolds, Quentin. "He Built Our Navy," *Collier's*, July 15, 1944, p. 72.

Sainz, Adrian. "Campaign Aims to Get Dead Hispanic Marine the Medal of Honor" (Guy Gabaldon). Associated Press, May 4, 2008.

Say, Harold Bradley. "They Hit the Beach in Swim Trunks." *Saturday Evening Post*, Oct. 13, 1945, p. 14.

Sherrod, Robert. "Battalion on Saipan." *Marine Corps Gazette*, October 1944, p. 10.

———. "Saipan: Eyewitness Tells of Island Fight." *Life*, Aug. 28, 1944, p. 78.

———. "The Saipan Controversy." *Infantry Journal*, January 1949, p. 14.

Slonim, Gilven M. "A Flagship View of Command Decisions." *U.S. Naval Institute Proceedings*, April 1958, p. 87.

"Suicides on Saipan" (editorial). *Collier's*, Sept. 30, 1944, p. 94.

Trumbull, Robert. "Japanese Debacle Disclosed on Truk." *New York Times*, March 1, 1946, p. 14.

Vogel, Bertram. "Japan's Secret War Within." *Marine Corps Gazette*, February 1948, p. 30.

"What Is Japanese Strategy Today?" (editorial). *The New Republic*, July 17, 1944, p. 71.

Winston, Robert A. "How Our Navy Outfoxed the Japs at Saipan." *Saturday Evening Post*, Sept. 23, 1944, p. 89.

Worden, William L. "There Was a Man." *Reader's Digest*, April 1957, p. 117.

Zimmerman, Sherwood R. "Operation Forager." *Naval Institute Proceedings*, August 1964, p. 79.

Zurlinden, Pete. "Prelude to Saipan." *Naval Institute Proceedings*, May 1947, p. 581.

Monographs

Allen, William Bland IV. *Sacked at Saipan*. Fort Leavenworth, Kan.: U.S. Marine Corps, School of Advanced Military Studies, 2012.

Arakawa, Edward T., and Shogo Nagaoka. "Determination of the Burst Point of the Hiroshima Atomic Bomb," Atomic Bomb Casualty Commission, Technical Report 12-59, 1959." FDRL.

Campbell, Douglas. "USN Overseas Aircraft Loss Lists." Phoenix, Ariz.: Aviation Archaeological Investigation and Research, www.aviationarchaeology.com/src/USN/losslist.htm. Undated. Last viewed by author on Sept. 5, 2015.

Hallden, Charles H. "The Operations of Company L, 3rd Battalion, 106th Infantry in the Battle of Death Valley, Saipan, 23–28 June 1944: Personal Experience of a Company Commander," Fort Benning, Ga.: Infantry School, 1947–48.

Hegi, Benjamin P. "Extermination Warfare? The Conduct of the Second Marine Division at Saipan." Department of History, University of North Texas, May 2008.

Hooker, Howard C. "Amphibian Tank Battalion on Saipan," Fort Knox, Ky.: Armored School, May 1, 1948.

Moritaki, Ichiro. "New Morals for the Atomic Age," Hiroshima University, October 1958.

Olynyk, Frank. "USN Aerial Victory Credits of World War II," undated. Courtesy of Frank Olynyk.

Roan, Richard W. "Roebling's Amphibian: The Origin of the Assault Amphibian." Quantico, Va.: Marine Corps Development and Education Command, 1987.

Smith, Charles R. *Securing the Surrender: Marines in the Occupation of Japan.* Pamphlet, World War II Commemorative Series. Washington, D.C.: Marine Corps Historical Center, 1997.

U.S. Army, Engineer Amphibian Command (Camp Edwards, Mass.). *Engineer Amphibian Troops: A Manual for Boat Crews.* April 1943.

War Department, Historical Division. *Small Unit Actions.* American Forces in Action Series. Center of Military History Publication 100-14. Washington, D.C.: Government Printing Office, 1948.

Websites

Budge, Kent G. *The Pacific War Online Encyclopedia.* pwencycl.kgbudge.com. Last viewed by the author on August 29, 2015.

Fawell, Reed M. (ed). 2nd Armored Amphibian Battalion Association. 2ndarmored amphibianbattalion.com. Last viewed by the author on August 29, 2015.

HyperWar: "Strategic Victory in the Marianas: Liberation of Guam; Capture of Saipan and Tinian." ibiblio.org/hyperwar/PTO/Marianas.html. Last viewed by the author on August 30, 2015.

Parshall, Jonathan, and Anthony Tully (eds.). "Imperial Japanese Navy Page." combined fleet.com/kaigun.htm. Last viewed by the author on August 30, 2015.

Roecker, Geoffrey W. (ed.). "First Battalion, 24th Marines: A History of the Men of the 1/24 in World War II and Beyond." 1stbattalion24thmarines.com/the-battles/saipan. Last viewed by the author on August 30, 2015.

Tully, Anthony. "Tully's Port: WWII Naval Discussion of the Pacific Theater." propnturret.com/tully.

Truman Library and Museum. Public Papers of the Presidents, Harry S. Truman, 1945–1953. www.trumanlibrary.org/publicpapers/?pid=104.

U.S. Army, Center of Military History. "The U.S. Army in World War II: The War in the Pacific." www.history.army.mil/html/bookshelves/collect/ww2-ap .html.

———. Combined Arms Research Library. Digital Library, Fort Leavenworth, Kans., cgsc.cdmhost.com/cdm.

Index

A

A Force (Imperial Japanese Navy), 216
A6M Model Zero. *See* "Zeke"
A6M3 fighter. *See* "Hamp"
aerial reconnaissance, 39
    Japanese reconnaissance, 65
    Marianas campaign, 30, 31
    Nimitz and, 32–33
Afetna Point (Saipan), 89, 93, 106, 124, 125, 131, 239
African American troops, 140
Agana (Guam), 173, 312, 336, 383
Agat Beach (Guam), 312
Agingan Point (Saipan), 72, 123, 132, 133
Ainsworth, Walden L., 88
Aioi Bridge (Hiroshima), 443
Air Group 15, 77, 82
Air Group 16, 35, 214
Air Group 24, 216
aircraft carriers, 6, 18, 22
    mobility of, 15, 34, 68, 101, 175
    See also fast carrier task force
AKA. *See* attack cargo ship
Akagi Maru (armed merchant cruiser), 11, 13, 14
Alabama (BB-60), 85, 189, 190, 201
Alamogordo (New Mexico), 424, 425, 426–27
Alaska (CB-1), 396
Albacore (SS-218), 149, 179, 182, 196
Aleutian Islands, 3
Algiers, xxiii
Allen, Edmund T., xxvi
"alligator." *See* Landing Vehicle Tracked
Alperovitz, Gar, 530
ALPOA 579, 454
Alvarez, Luis, 423, 424, 435, 443
Amagi (aircraft carrier), 432
America (passenger ship), 75
amphibious warfare
    amphibious craft, 55, 117, 125
    development of U.S. doctrine, 29–30
    See also Landing Ship Tank; Landing Vehicle Tracked
amphibious exercises, 38–40
amphibious forces, 39–40
    offensive firepower added, 54–55
amphibious landings, 50, 51
amtanks, 60
amtracs. *See* Landing Vehicle Tracked
AN/APS-15 air-to-surface radar, 174
Anami, Korechika, 378, 403–4, 414, 429, 430, 449, 451, 453, 455, 540
Anatahan Island, 82
Anderson, Charles E. "Squeaky," 139, 155, 161
anemology, 20
antiaircraft guns, as targets of air attack, 83
"anvil" attack, 215
Aoba (heavy cruiser), 432

APA. *See* attack transport
APD. *See* auxiliary
     personnel destroyer
Apra Harbor (Guam),
     199, 330, 338
Aquinas, Thomas, 501,
     502
Archinal, John A., 473
Arle, H.F., 177
Armstrong, Frank, 112
Arnold, Henry "Hap,"
     xviii, xxv, 21, 22, 35,
     113, 114, 317, 330,
     338, 341, 353, 358,
     362, 372, 373, 385,
     404, 420, 422, 426,
     448, 453
Aruga, Kosaku, 400
Asan (Guam), 312
Ashworth, Frederick L.,
     382, 437
Aslito/Isely Field
     (Saipan), 31, 32, 77,
     78, 83, 84, 96, 105,
     142, 162, 206, 208,
     233, 236, 257, 339,
     354, 361, 362
     Gardiner Conroy
       Field, 206, 236, 240,
       248, 254
     Japanese ground
       assault on, 247–51
     Japanese air attack on,
       361–62
     renamed as Isely
       Field, 254
Atlantic Wall, 43–44
atombomben disease, 475,
     492
atomic bomb, xx, 428*n*
     509th Composite
       Group, 349, 363–64,
       410, 426, 432, 437

arming the bomb in
     flight, 437, 441
B-29 for, 380–81
Bockscar (B-29), 448
building and testing,
     424, 426–27
Compton on, 497–98
cyanide pills for B-29
     pilots, 439
development of,
     348–51, 363–65
dispute over who
     would deliver
     bomb, 426–27
"End of the War
     Picnic," 446
Enola Gay (B-29),
     437–38, 440–46
"Fat Man," 447,
     448–49, 536
guilt of Manhattan
     Project scientists
     over, 493
Hirohito and, 536
Hiroshima bomb
     dropped, 440–48
casualties, 447–48
mission briefing,
     438–39
informing military
     leaders, 427
informing President
     Truman, 427–28
injuries from, 475
Japanese reaction to,
     446, 447
Manhattan Project,
     348, 364, 381–83,
     427, 427*n*, 435, 474
mortality after
     exposure, 475
mushroom cloud,
     439, 445

Nagasaki bomb
     dropped, 448–49
order to use, 430, 432,
     437, 534
practice runs in B-29,
     437
preparing for
     deployment,
     410–13
production of,
     423–24, 536
Project Alberta, 383,
     411, 435, 437
reactions of *Enola Gay*
     crew, 444–46
security precautions,
     363, 364
Soviet Union
     intimidated by, 534
surrender of Japan
     and, 456, 536
tactical use of, 536
targets for, 413, 437,
     438
third atomic bomb,
     447, 452, 536
Tinian as base for,
     382–83, 410
training flight, 427
transport to Tinian,
     426, 434
Truman
     announcement to
     the world, 451–53
See also 509th
     Composite Group;
     Manhattan Project
atomic weapons, human
     impact of, 474
Atsugi Airfield, 464–65,
     466, 467, 472
attack cargo ship
     (AKA), 52

attack transport
   (APA), 52
Augusta (CA-31), 436, 446
auxiliary personnel
   destroyer (APD),
   49, 84, 91
Avenger (Grumman
   TBF/TBM)
   (torpedo bomber),
   6, 9, 10, 11, 13, 30,
   77, 81, 83, 84, 95–
   96, 116, 121, 202,
   212, 214, 219, 221,
   223, 226, 254–55
Ayres, Russell G., 241

B

B-A-T-A-A-N (aircraft
   call sign), 463
B-17 Flying Fortress
   (bomber), 111
B-24 Liberator
   (bomber), 114
B-25 Mitchell (medium
   bomber), 329
B-29 Superfortress
   (heavy bomber),
   xviii, 20, 21, 63,
   345, 346, 353, 354
   for atomic bomb
   delivery, 349, 351,
   380–81, 410
   Bockscar, 448
   China as base for, 21,
   113, 114, 144
   crash of XB-29
   experimental
   model, xxvi, 111
   development of,
   xxvi–xxviii, 111–13
   Enola Gay, 437–38,
   440–46

at extreme
   altitudes, 13
The Great Artiste, 439,
   442
   Japan air raids, 359,
   360, 361, 363, 376,
   377, 385–92, 398,
   404
   Operation
   Matterhorn, 113
   Saipan airfield, 207
   "Silverplate" B-29,
   410, 436
   Tibbets and, xxvi,
   111–13
   Top Secret, 442
   "war wearies,"
   488–89
B Force (Imperial
   Japanese Navy),
   215, 216
B6N Tenzan. *See* "Jill"
Bacon, Francis, 500
Badger, Oscar C., 465,
   467
Bainbridge (DD-1)
   (destroyer), 12
Baird, Bob, 312
Baker, Thomas A., 282,
   284
"balanced air force," 353
Balsano, S. A., 128
"bamboo lancer
   brigade," 399
Banazak (gunner), 227
Bancroft (DD-598), 247
Bang (SS-385), 149
Bangs, Louis L., 216,
   218, 230
Banno, Lieutenant, 71,
   253–54, 281, 295,
   296, 298–99
BAR team, 249, 255

Barber, Charles F., 14,
   306, 402, 436
"bat team," 9
Bataan Death March, 476
Bates, Richard W., 18
battleships, 13, 88–90
bazookas, 248–49
beachfront assault,
   offensive firepower
   for amphibious
   forces, 55
Beahan, Kermit, 448–49
Beary, Donald B., 482
Beatty, David, 152
Belleau Wood (CVL-24)
   (light carrier), 6,
   178, 215, 326, 336
Benevolence (AH-13), 465
Bennett, Carl J., 178
Bennington (CV-20),
   413–14
Bernstein, Barton J., 501,
   534
Beser, Jacob, 440, 442
"Betty" (Mitsubishi G4M
   medium bomber),
   31, 361, 379
Biak, 34, 69, 86, 149
"Big Six" (Japan), *See*
   Supreme War
   Direction Council
Birmingham (CL-62),
   93–94, 96, 107, 122,
   125, 135, 172, 270,
   282, 333
Bismarck Sea (CVE-95),
   380
Bito, Sergeant, 253
Bix, Herbert P., 391, 409
Bizerte, bombing of,
   xxiii–xxiv
Blanchard, J. W., 179
Blanchard, Robert, 427

Blandy, William H. P. "Spike," 42, 43, 153, 379, 492
Blessman (APD-48), 379
Blood and Iron Student Corps, 406
blood supply, U.S., 421
Blue Beach (Saipan), 93, 95, 97, 120, 121, 124, 125, 131, 133, 134, 142, 155, 161, 167, 241, 243
Bockscar (B-29), 448
Boeing B-29 Superfortress. *See* B-29 Superfortress
Bogan, Gerald F., 166, 167
Bogart, Margaret Spruance (daughter), 62, 329, 477
Bollard, Ed, 249
bomb disposal, 41–42, 493
bombers, high altitude and, 112
Bombing Squadron Sixteen (VB-16), 221
Bombing Squadron Ten (VB-10), 116
Bonin Islands, 86, 151, 462, 489
Boone, Joel, 466
Boots, Donald, 85, 126, 133, 292
Bougainville (Solomon Islands), 4
Braden, David, 360, 374, 387, 488–89
Bradford (DD-545), 14
Bradlee, Ben, 269

Brenden, Lieutenant, 249
Brewer, Charles W., 77, 82, 102, 183, 184, 199, 200, 210
British Pacific Fleet. *See* Royal Navy
Brockmeyer, Homer W., 214, 220
Bronn, Tom, 220, 221, 223, 226, 227, 230
Brooks (APD-10), 84, 91, 95, 96
Brown, George P., 215, 222, 224, 229
Bruce, Andrew D., 314
Buchanan (DD-484), 468
Buckner, Simon Bolivar, 398, 402
Buie, Paul, 185, 186, 201
Bullard, G. C., 9, 10
Bunker Hill (CV-17), 6, 7, 11, 13, 17, 19, 77, 178, 193, 202, 228, 230, 371, 401
Burckholter, Bill, 78
burial of the dead, 159, 272, 273, 285
Burke, Arleigh, 22, 87, 100, 147, 171, 172, 175, 178, 182, 212, 213, 224, 225, 226
Burke, Jack, 49
Burke, Richard F., 92, 96
Burnett, Henry Poynter, 95, 134
Burns (DD-588), 14, 16, 174
Bush, Vannevar, 427n
Byrnes, James F., 413, 425, 436, 446, 452, 494

C

Cabot (CVL-28), 6, 17, 79, 183, 226, 227, 231
Cabras Island, 198
Cabrera, Antonio, 75
Cairo Conference, 21, 358
Calhoun, William L., 353
California, amphibious exercises, 39
California (BB-44), 84, 88, 89, 93, 94, 95, 96, 107, 121, 124, 134, 135, 154, 322, 327, 333
Callaghan (DD-972), 417
Callaghan, Joseph T., 396
Cambria (APA-36), 137, 141, 160, 315
Camp Bradford (Virginia), 39
Camp Elliott (California), 39
Camp Maui, 37
Camp Peary, 43
Camp Tarawa (Hawaii), 37
Cape Victory (cargo ship), 410–11
Carberry, Gordon, 312, 315
cargo shipping, in 1943, 3–4
Carlson, Evans, 61, 205
Carney, Robert B., 467
Caroline Islands, 5, 34, 66, 67, 70, 74, 339, 343, 483
Caron, George R., 364, 441, 442, 443

Carr, George R., 184
Carter, Winton W., 293
cartography, JICPOA, 32–33
Casablanca Conference, 433
Casco Bay (Maine), 417
casualties
  average number per month for U.S., 423
  burial of the dead, 159, 272, 273, 285
  civilian deaths, daily, in Asia, 422
  Guam, battle of, 338
  Hiroshima atomic bomb, 447–48
  invasion of Japan, U.S. Army projections, 380, 421
  Iwo Jima, battle of, 380, 394
  Japanese raids on carriers (1944), 396–97, 401
  kamikaze attacks, 401, 402
  Marianas, battle of, 378
  Nagasaki atomic bomb, 475
  Okinawa, battle of, 402
  Peleliu, battle of, 351, 352
  Philippine Sea, battle of, 189–90
  Saipan, battle of, 138, 140, 141, 143, 159, 283, 299
  Tinian, battle of, 326, 328, 340
  Tokyo fire raid, 389

Cates, Clifton B., 262, 304, 321, 328, 379
Cavalla (SS-244), 100, 148–49, 168, 170–71, 194, 195, 196, 202, 258, 259
caves, 39, 70, 72, 104, 105–7, 154, 159, 163–65, 176, 204, 206, 237, 239, 243, 244, 246, 248–50, 252, 253, 267, 269, 271, 274–75, 279, 281, 285–86, 288, 289–93, 295, 299, 300, 314, 333, 334, 338, 340, 368, 408, 449, 479, 483, 487, 501
Cawley, David J., 217
Central Pacific Force, 6, 12, 18, 35
  chain of command, 24
  See also Fifth Fleet
Central Pacific theater, 342
Chacha Village (Saipan), 156, 204
Chamberlin, William, 239
Chamorro people, 73–75, 290
Chapin, John C., 140, 205, 206, 250, 251, 255, 256, 257
Charan Kanoa (Saipan), 32, 50, 73, 77, 85, 94, 105, 120, 132, 135, 140, 141, 142, 154, 155, 159, 161, 204, 255, 366, 367, 369, 484
Charette (DD-581), 14

charinko, 473
Charland, George, 249, 292, 293
"Charlies," 134, 269–70
chemical munitions, Japanese, 471
chemical weapons, U.S., 421
Chiang Kai-shek, 21, 432
Chichi Jima, 151, 377
Chihaya, Takehiko, 65, 70
China
  as B-29 base, 21, 113, 114, 144, 268
  Jews in Shanghai, 476
  Nimitz on, 114
  possible site for U.S. landings, 420
Chitose (light carrier), 66, 179
Chiyoda (light carrier), 66, 179
Christensen, Robert, 96
Christie, Ralph W., 87
Churchill, Winston, 340, 427, 432
CINCPAC, 36, 173, 262, 352, 353, 377, 382, 414, 417, 427, 432, 451, 463, 469, 480, 483, 489
civilians
  as targets of strategic bombing, 362, 384, 385–86, 391–92
civilians, Japanese
  brainwashed by Japanese army, 75, 159, 279, 341, 406
  group suicides on Okinawa, 406–08

civilians, Japanese (*cont.*)
   in war zones, 159,
      292–94, 368, 372
   murdered by Japanese
      army, 290–92, 334
   used as human
      shields, 272
   Spruance and, 406
   U.S. troops and,
      290–3, 334
"civilization of love,"
   500–501
Clark, John J. "Jocko,"
   102, 147, 151, 152,
   172, 178, 215, 268,
   306, 429
Clement, William T., 467
Clemson (APD-31), 84
Cleveland (CL-55), 89, 90,
   172, 319, 322, 324,
   327
Clobes, Leroy, 128
coastal fortifications,
   Atlantic Wall,
   43–44
Colorado (BB-45), 57, 84,
   88, 232, 318, 319,
   322–24, 326, 327,
   329, 335
"Columbia University
   district," 383
combat fatigue, 224
Combined Chiefs of
   Staff, 20–21, 340
Compton, Karl T., 497
Conant, James B., 348
concrete polyhedrons,
   Atlantic Wall,
   43, 45
Conolly, Richard L., 27,
   28, 50, 150, 168,
   261, 310–11, 312,
   314, 338

Coral Sea (CVE-57), 167
Coral Sea, battle of, 195
Coronado
   (California), 39
Corregidor, 466, 467
Costanzo, Private, 243
counterintelligence,
   286–87
courage, 133
Coward, Jesse, 84
Cowpens (CVL-25), 6, 77
Craig, Frank S., 373
Crommelin, John,
   230–31
Crouch, William L., 283,
   284
Crowe, Henry P., 130
Crutchley, Victor, 28
"cult of death," 340,
   422
Cumberland Sound
   (AV-17), 465
Curtis, Bob, 360, 361
Cushing, James M., 69
Cutter, Slade, 148
cyanide pills, for *Enola
   Gay* pilots, 439

D

D Day (Saipan), 116–43
   air strikes, 121
   Green Beach One,
      128–29
   H Hour, 116
   landing the landing
      force, 115–17,
      122–23
   map of landings and
      positions, 119
   O-1 line, 124, 131,
      135
D4Y Suisei. *See* "Judy"

"daisy cutter" air-burst
   fuzes, 43
Dale, Roland H.
   "Brute," 7, 8, 11, 13
Dauntless (SBD-5
   Dauntless), 6, 10,
   15–16, 202, 215,
   216, 221
Davao City, 34
Davies, John, 411
Davis, A.F., 31
Davis, Arthur C., 399,
   413
Davis, Doug, xxi
Davison, Ralph E., 395
de Seversky, Alexander
   P., 385
Death Valley (Saipan),
   205, 238, 241, 255
DeBold, Johnny, 93
Dejima Pier (Japan),
   474, 492
del Valle, Pedro, 260
Delgado, Frank M., 83
detonators, for nuclear
   weapons, 424
Deuel (APA-160), 488
Deyo, Morton L., 479
Diamond Head (Oahu),
   330
Dickens, Onel W., 129,
   130
Dickinson, Velvalee, 33
Dillon, Edward J., 134
Disney, Walt, 385
Doctrine of Double
   Effect, 501
Domei (Japanese
   agency), 451
Donnay (Saipan), 252,
   262, 271, 297
Donovan, James A., Jr.,
   157, 158

Doolittle, James, xxiii, xxv, 19, 34–35, 343, 416, 454, 494

Double Effect, Doctrine of, 501

Dougherty, Dora, 412

Downey, William B., 439

Dublon Atoll, 5, 7

Dugway Proving Ground (Utah), 384

Duke of York (battleship), 465

DUKWs, 137, 332

"Dumbo," 361

Duncan, George, 198

DuPont Company, 423

Durand, Paul, 128

Duzenbury, Wyatt E., 364, 440, 441

Dyson, Howard J., 33

E

Easley, John W., 130, 131, 334

Eason, Van V., 216

Easy Company, 140, 141

Eatherley, Claude, 442

Edson, Merritt A., 141

Eglin Field (Florida), 384, 385

Eichelberger, Robert L., 416, 462, 464, 467, 473

Eighth Air Force, 416, 435, 454

Eighth Army, 416, 462, 464, 466

Eighth Marines, 131, 155, 244, 327, 366

81st Infantry Division, 351

Eisenhower, Dwight D., 494

Elden (DE-264), 247

Eldorado (AGC-11), 375

electronic detonators, for nuclear weapons, 424

Eleventh Airborne Division, 464, 466

Eller, D.T., 16

Ellyson (DMS-19), 465

Elrod, Roy H., 272

"Emily" (Kawanishi H8K flying boat), 77

"End of the War Picnic," 446

engine failure, as spectator sport, 362

engineer-amphibians, 39

Eniwetok Atoll, 4, 17, 18, 20, 85, 101, 150, 167, 329, 507

Enola Gay (B-29), 437–38, 440–46

Ent, Uzal G., 347

Enterprise (CV-6), 1–2, 5, 6, 7, 14, 17, 77, 121, 145, 146, 199, 212, 215, 216, 217, 226, 228, 230, 254, 396

Erskine, Graves B., 60, 91, 154, 236, 238, 379

Ervin, Arthur B., 282

espionage, Japanese, 33

Essex (CV-9), 6, 7, 13, 40, 77, 81, 82, 151, 172, 183, 184, 198, 231, 254, 329, 336

Essex-class carriers, 3, 6

Eten Island, 5, 10

ethics of killing and warfare, xviii–xix, 316, 317, 496

Eubank, Eugene, xxvi

Evans, Gus, 127–28

"exploding bridgewire" devices, 424

explosives, 45
    bomb disposal, 41–42
    tetratol, 45, 138
    Underwater Demolition Teams (UDTs), xix, 41, 44–47, 49

F

F6F Hellcat. *See* Hellcat

Fabius San Hilo Point (Tinian), 327

Fanshaw Bay (CVE-70) 167

Far East Air Forces, 462

Farrell, Thomas F., 437, 441, 446, 447, 456, 474

fast carrier task force
    Japanese assessment of, 66
    use of, 6, 18, 22, 23, 100–103

"Fat Man" bomb, 381, 423, 425, 427, 435

fatigue, 224

Fefan Island, 5

Ferebee, Tom, 364, 425, 427, 436, 440, 443, 444

Fifth Amphibious Force (Fifth Phib), 25, 52, 84, 115, 150, 236, 397, 404, 462

Fifth Fleet, xviii, xix, xx, 12, 23, 30, 35, 70, 102, 308, 355, 462, 469, 489
chain of command, 24
Fifth Marine Division, 464, 479
58th Bombardment Wing, 113
fighter pilots, training of, 8–9
Fighter Squadron One ("Tophatters"), 183
Fighter Squadron Three (VF-3), 9
Fighter Squadron Five (VF-5), 10
Fighter Squadron Six (VF-6), 7, 8, 9
Fighter Squadron Fifteen (VF-15) ("Fighting Aces"), 77, 183, 187, 193, 198, 201
Fighter Squadron Sixteen (VF-16), 78, 185, 201
Fighter Squadron Thirty-One (VF-31) ("Meataxers"), 183
The Fighting Lady (documentary), 372
Filipino guerrillas, 69
Finback (SS-230), 149
fire hose explosives, 45, 46
firebombing, 315–16, 362, 374, 385
First Air Fleet (Imperial Japanese Navy), 30, 31, 68, 70, 145, 197, 334

First Battalion of the Second Regiment (1/2), 91
First Marines, 398
First Mobile Fleet (Imperial Japanese Navy), 55, 67, 86, 102, 203, 216
First Provisional Marine Brigade, 261, 329, 330
First Yokosuka Special Naval Landing Force, 266
fission weapons. See atomic bomb; nuclear weapons
509th Composite Group, 349, 363–64, 410, 426, 432, 437, 488
flak trap, 189
flamethrower tank, 248–49
flamethrowers, 249, 256
Flatley, Jimmy, 8
Fletcher, Frank Jack, 462, 476
Flores Point (Saipan), 105
Flying Fish (SS-229), 100, 147, 148, 170
Flying Fortress (Boeing B-17) (bomber), 111
Flynn, Thomas J., 466
FM-2 Wildcat. See Wildcat
Fontenot, Merlin, 133
Ford Island, 40
Formosa, 352, 398
Forrestel, Emmet P. ("Savvy"), 214, 372, 413

Fort Pierce, 40, 44, 45, 47
Fort Schofield, 43
Fort Shafter, 32
42nd General Hospital, 467
Fothergill, Sam, 255
Fourth Marine Division, 4, 18–19, 54, 55, 304, 466
Army help, 236
Hawaii training, 49, 50, 51
Iwo Jima, 373, 379
Saipan battle, 91, 117, 120, 123, 125, 132, 135, 142, 204–5, 233, 245, 250, 261, 263, 282
Tinian, 321, 326, 328
training at Camp Maui, 37
Fowler, Richard E., 183, 184
fragmentation bomb, 431
"Frances" (Nakajima PIY twin-engine bomber), 68
"Frances" (Yokosuka PIY), 146
"Frank" (Nakajima Ki–84 Frank), 401
Frank, Richard B., 414
Franklin (CV-13), 395, 396
Freer, Charles, 166, 167–68
Fritz, Harold C., 396
frogmen, 40, 49, 92, 96, 160, 379, 479, 491
Fukudome, Shigeru, 69
Fukuoka (Japan), 464
Fukushima (Japan), 486

Furman, Robert R., 435

Fuso (battleship), 356

G

G4M medium bomber. *See* "Betty"

Gabaldon, Guy, 287–89

Gabbert, Gordon A., 166

Gakeyama (Japan), 483, 484

Gallipoli peninsula, 59

Gambier Bay (CVE-73), 84, 167

Garapan (Saipan), 32, 71, 75, 86, 94, 120, 134, 153, 233, 251, 255, 258, 266, 279, 307

destruction of, 104–7, 109, 110

Gardiner Conroy Field, 206, 236, 240, 248, 254

gas, poison, film about, 372

Gay, George, 372

Gehres, Leslie E., 395

Geiger, Roy S., 50, 150, 260, 261, 312, 314, 329, 338, 398, 530

Genghis Khan, 461

"George" (Kawanishi N1K2 George), 401

George, Robert L., 328

Giffen, Robert C., 14

Gilbert Islands, xvii, 4, 234

Gilmer (APD-11), 84, 91, 96, 153, 154, 303

Glenn L. Martin Co., 436

Gosnell, Helen, 412

Gosselin (APD-126), 465

Goto, Takishi, 106, 156, 158, 159

Graf, Robert, 18, 60, 61, 120–21, 122, 123, 124, 133, 140, 141, 292, 334, 336

Granat, William, 318, 319, 324

Grasshopper (Piper L–4 Grasshopper), 319

grave-digging duty, 273

grease, rationing of, 4

The Great Artiste (B-29), 439, 443

Great Marianas Turkey Shoot, 229, 306, 376

Greater East Asia Co-Prosperity Scheme, 74

Green, Virgil, 166, 167

Green Beach (Saipan), 13, 92, 95, 120, 122, 125, 128–29, 131, 132, 135, 155, 156

Green Hornet line, 412

Greenhalgh, Selbie, 222

Grew, Joseph L., xx, 433, 498–99

Griner, George W., 250, 281, 285, 491

"group suicide," 406–9

Groves, Leslie R., 348, 364, 382, 383, 411, 412–13, 423, 427, 427n, 428, 432

Grumman F6F Hellcat. *See* Hellcat

Grumman FM-2 Wildcat. *See* Wildcat

Grumman TBF/TBM Avenger. *See* Avenger

Guadalcanal invasion, 3, 4, 20, 27, 28, 51, 171

Guam, 146, 150, 173, 178, 199, 206, 210, 261, 310, 311, 355, 362, 462

Japanese garrison on, 260, 336

map (1944), 313

pacification of, 338

post-battle construction, 339, 354

Guam (CB-2), 396

Guam, battle of, xviii, 30, 50, 77, 178, 182, 197, 310–14, 319, 329–30

beach landings, 315

casualties, 338

end of, 336–38, 429

W Day, 261

guilt, over atomic bomb, 493

Gulbranson, Clarence, 47–48

"gunner's delight," 184

Gurguan Point (Tinian), 373

gyokusai, 280, 281, 288, 399, 406, 414

H

H8K flying boat *See* "Emily"

Haguro (heavy cruiser), 197

Hagushi Anchorage (Okinawa), 404

Haha Jima, 151
Haleakala, 51
Hall, W. Carvel, 314
Hallden, Charles H., 238
Halloran, Hap, 489
Halsey, William F., Jr., 4, 23, 43, 102, 103n, 172n, 175, 339, 354–55, 356, 372, 393, 404, 414, 427, 431, 432, 454, 462, 464, 465, 467, 476, 478, 489, 490, 530
Halsey Powell (DD-686), 157
Ham, Paul, 540
Hambleton (DMS-20), 465
Hamilton, Mort, 244
"Hamp" (Nakajima A6M3 fighter), 183, 192, 219, 222
Hanai, Major, 252
Hancock (CV-19), 396
Hanley, Fiske, 389, 392
Hansell, Haywood, 21, 353, 354, 358, 359, 361, 362, 373, 374, 392
Harder (SS-257), 87
Harding, Warren G., 239
Harmon, Millard F., 338
Harmon Field, 435
Harper, Arthur M., 242
Harrill, William K., 151, 152, 172, 183, 202, 231
Harris, Marshall E., 123, 124
Haruna (battleship), 66, 432
Haven (AH-12), 474, 475

Hawaii, amphibious exercises, 38, 39, 51
Hellcat (Grumman F6F), 21–23, 77, 81, 82, 83, 96, 116, 145, 175, 177, 178, 182, 185, 188, 191, 192, 197, 200, 210, 212, 213, 214, 215, 220, 230
Helldiver (SB2C–1 Helldiver), 6, 10, 11, 81, 82, 96, 202, 217, 228
Heminway, William T., 241
Henry, Murray, 312
Hermin, David, 159
hibakusha, 475
Hill, Harry W., 20, 25, 39, 50–51, 55, 96, 97, 98, 115, 116, 121, 135, 137, 139, 143, 153, 160, 161, 176, 302, 304–5, 307, 315, 316, 319, 321, 328, 332, 333, 335, 375, 394, 404, 462, 464
Hill, Tom, 383
Hilo, 52, 54
Hiranauma, Baron, 449
Hiranuma, Kiichiro, 310, 415
Hiro Wan (Japan), 470
Hirohito (emperor), 309, 378, 390, 399, 422, 433–34, 438, 449, 452, 453, 455–56, 463, 465, 471, 495
breaks deadlock of Supreme War

Direction Council, 450–51
impact of atomic bomb on, 536
inspects Tokyo after fire raid, 390–91
Hiroshima (Japan), 413, 427, 432, 437, 438, 443–45
atomic bombing of, 440–48, 535
casualties, 447–48
Hiss, Annie Ames, 12
Hitler, Adolf, 384
Hiyo (aircraft carrier), 66, 215–19, 221, 222, 224, 229
Hlebechuk, Walt, 312
Hodge, John R., 398, 462
Hodges, Herbert J., 158
Hogaboom, Robert E., 25, 38, 97, 117, 237, 238, 311
Hokkaido (Japan), 462
Hollandia (New Guinea), 34
Homma, Masaharu, 476
Honolulu (CL-48), 89
"honorable national death," 414
Honshu (Japan), 421, 431, 462, 464, 466, 470
Hoover, John H., 152, 338–39, 354, 358, 411
Horace A. Bass (APD-124), 466
Horiuchi, 296, 299, 367, 430, 483
Horner, Jack S., 153

Hornet (CV-12), 5, 22, 77, 151, 178, 212, 215, 217, 227, 232, 413–14

hose explosives, 45, 46

"hose pipe method," 184

Hosho (aircraft carrier), 484

House of Taga (Tinian), 335, 412

Houston (CA-30) (heavy cruiser), 466 "Howling Mad." *See* Smith, Holland M.

Hudson (DD-475), 201

Huie, Cy, 402, 477, 478

Hull, Cordell, 454

"humiliation squad," 8

Hunt (DD-674), 396

Hunt, LeRoy P., Jr., 155

Hutchinson, John S., 222

hydrographic reconnaissance, 40

Hyuga (battleship), 432

I

ICPOA. *See* Intelligence Center, Pacific Ocean Areas

Idaho (BB-42), 88

Ie Shima, 394

Igeta, Keichi, 274

Ikegami, Corporal, 368–69, 430

Imperial General Headquarters, 472

Imperial General Staff, demobilization, 472

Imperial Japanese Army 135th Infantry Regiment, 106, 154, 251, 265, 281, 326

136th Infantry Regiment, 106, 156, 265

Imperial Japanese Navy A Force, 216

B Force, 215, 216

aviation fuel, shortages of, 67, 510

destruction of, 431–32

disposal of capital assets, 499

First Air Fleet, 30, 31, 68, 70, 145, 197, 334

First Mobile Fleet, 55, 67, 86, 102, 203, 216

Plan Z activated, 66–69

Second Carrier Squadron, 215

Special Naval Landing Force, 106, 156, 266

Truk strike, 7–18

Imperial Palace, 455

Imperial Rescript, 454, 455, 456

incendiary bombs, 362, 386–87, 391

Independence (CVL-22), 23

Indiana (BB-58), 85, 123, 184, 190, 201

Indianapolis (CA-35), 34, 89, 93, 96, 103, 107, 125, 137, 149, 170, 173, 174, 202, 231, 259, 260, 264, 307, 324, 327, 336, 338, 372, 375, 397, 398,

426, 434, 435–36, 477

"influence" mines, 464

Inglis, Thomas B., 94, 122, 126, 135, 282

intelligence, Japanese strength, 39

Intelligence Center, Pacific Ocean Areas (ICPOA), 32

International Military Tribunal for the Far East, 476

International Palace (brothel), 477

interrogation of POWs, 274

Intrepid (CV-11), 6, 7, 17–18, 31, 35

invasion beaches, scouting, 40

"invasion crawl," 92

Iowa (BB-61), 1–2, 11, 13, 14, 15, 16, 85

Iowa-class battleships, 3

Ira Jeffrey (APD-44), 479

"Irving" nightfighter, 68

Ise (battleship), 432

Isely, Robert H., 84, 254

Isely Field. *See* Aslito/ Isely Field

Ishikawa, Kenji, 251, 252

islands, importance of, 20, 21

Iwo Jima, 145, 151, 152, 210, 268, 352, 374–75, 379, 484

Iwo Jima, battle of, 379–80, 394, 399

Izard (DD-589), 14, 16,
177
Izu Island, 462

J

J Day (Tinian), 261
"Jack" (Mitsubishi J2M
Raiden), 146
Jaluit Atoll, 20, 484
JANET. *See* Joint
Army and Navy
Experimental and
Testing Board
Japan
1944 assessment of
war, 308–9
air offensive against,
384, 385–92
colonial
administration of
Saipan, 73–76
compromise
statement
regarding
surrender, 452
"honorable national
death," 414
imperial conference
after atomic
bombs, 449–51
Imperial Palace, 455
meetings and decision
to surrender,
448–52
national psychology,
286–87, 422, 429
possibility of
surrender, 379, 403,
425
possible ground
invasion of Japan,
420–22

Potsdam Declaration
calling for
unconditional
surrender, 433, 434,
446, 453, 455
rebuilding, 462
starvation in, 422
Supreme War
Direction Council,
403, 414, 422, 424,
430, 434
terms of surrender,
403–04, 414, 425
U.S. attack plans, 342,
345, 346, 358, 384,
394
victory defined, 422
will to fight on, 422
See also Imperial
Japanese Navy;
Japan, occupation;
Japanese war
effort; surrender
of Japan
Japan, occupation,
462–81
conditions of, 463
demilitarization, 480
Eleventh Airborne
Division lands,
464–65
food relief, 475
holdouts, 470–71
Honshu, 462, 464,
466, 470
Nagasaki, U.S.
landings, 479–80
minesweeping, 464,
470
Operation Blacklist,
461, 462
prostitution, 477–78
rebuilding, 462

repatriation, 482–83,
488
social revolution, 478
U.S. Third Fleet enters
Tokyo Bay, 465, 466
Japanese Combined
Fleet, 23, 144
Japanese holdouts,
286–89, 291–300,
366–68, 422, 470–71
Japanese people
as barbarians of the
Pacific, 341
calls for suicide of
Japanese residents,
378
character of the
people, 286–87, 422
repatriating refugees,
482–83
Japanese Repatriation
Group, 482
Japanese Southern
Force, 356
Japanese troops
disbanding of after
surrender, 479–80
murder of civilians,
341
suicides, 275–78, 280,
284, 285, 317, 340,
341, 358, 473
Japanese war effort
1944 self-assessment,
38–309
antique planes, 417
"bamboo lancer
brigade," 399
Big Six, 403, 414, 422,
434
carrier doctrine, 147
chemical munitions,
471

civilians as decoys and shields, 272
Combined Fleet, 23, 144
D Day, 126
fanaticism of, 340–41
gyokusai, 280, 281, 288, 399, 414
Harper on, 242
Japanese POWs, 82
kamikaze attacks, 335, 357, 380, 401, 402, 410, 413, 417, 420–21
Ketsu-Go (war policy), 399
killing of wounded patients, 279, 284
"Leopards" (263rd Air Group), 68
loss of pilots, 68
Ozawa's motivation and, 208
Plan Z (Operation A-Go), 66, 67, 69, 86, 144
possibility of surrender, 379, 403, 425
propaganda leaflets used by U.S., 374–77, 394, 409, 430, 448, 453, 484
Saipan defenses, 106, 126, 127, 128, 129, 132
scarcity of fuel, 67, 68, 86, 174, 387, 390
Soviet Union as broker for ending the war, 403, 424–25
spies for, 33
starvation and, 422
Supreme War Direction Council, 403, 414, 424, 430
"Tigers" (261st Air Group), 68
underwater teams, 47
victory defined, 422
See also Imperial Japanese Navy; surrender of Japan; war planning (Japan)
Jarman, Sanderford, 207, 237, 241, 250, 366
Jeppson, Morris R., 440, 441
jet stream winds, 359, 360
Jews, Chinese, 476
JICPOA. See Joint Intelligence Center, Pacific Ocean Areas
"Jill" (Nakajima B6N Tenzan), 67, 179, 188, 190, 191, 192, 202
J1N "Irving" nightfighters. See "Irving" nightfighters
Johnson, E.R., 93
Johnston, Lawrence H., 424, 435, 438, 443, 446
Joint Army and Navy Experimental and Testing Board (JANET), 47
Joint Chiefs of Staff, 113, 114, 353
Joint Expeditionary Force, 50
Joint Intelligence Center, Pacific Ocean Areas, 32–33, 69, 101
Joint Planning Committee, 26
Joint Strategic Survey Committee (JSSC), 417, 417n
Joint Target Group, 385
Jones, Jimmy, 303
Jones, Louis R., 333
Jones, William K., 130, 131, 140, 141, 155, 156, 157, 158, 270
Joshima, Takaji, 215
"Judy" (Yokosuka D4Y Suisei), 67, 166, 167, 173, 179, 183, 188, 191, 192, 193, 395, 396
Jumper, Will C., 324, 325, 526
Junyo (aircraft carrier), 66, 215, 216, 217, 221
justice in war, 501
Jutland, Royal Navy at, 152

K

Kagman Peninsula (Saipan), 90, 236, 238, 240, 245
Kahn, Lauren H., 158
Kaho'olawe (Hawaii), 56–57, 85, 93, 340
Kahului (Hawaii), 52
Kakuta, Kakuji, 67, 68, 145, 179, 197, 326, 329, 334

kamikaze attacks, 335, 357, 380, 401, 402, 410, 413, 417, 420–21

Kane, William R. "Killer," 116, 217, 230

Kanoya (Japan), 394

Kanto Plain, 471

Kasai, Tomokazu, 68

Kase, Toshikazu, 106, 468

"Kate" bombers, 67, 166

Kato, Matsuo, 308

Katori (light cruiser), 11, 13, 14, 15, 74

Katsuragi (aircraft carrier), 432

Kauffman, Draper, xix, 41
  Atlantic Wall, 43–44
  bomb disposal school, 42–43
  exhaustion and deterioration, 457
  fire-support curriculum at Kaho'olawe, 340
  fuze design, 43
  hazardous-duty pay for troops, 335–36
  on Hill, 139
  humility of, 160
  Joint Army and Navy Experimental and Testing Board (JANET), 47
  Kistiakowsky and, 43–44, 348
  personality, 97
  physical conditioning "Hell Week", 44

post-war bomb radiation studies, 492–93

public speaking club at Naval Academy, 44

retirement, 493

Saipan airfield construction, 207

service in British armed forces, 41–42

shore bombardment, 57

Tinian, 321, 335

UDT command, 56

UDT reconnaissance of Tinian White beaches, 303–4

UDT training, 44, 46–50, 491

UDTs in Saipan invasion, 92, 95, 96, 115, 137, 160, 267

on warfare, 497

Kauffman, James L. "Reggie," 41

Kavieng (New Guinea), 36

Kawabe, Torashiro, 463

Kawai, Kazuo, 533

Kawanishi H8K flying boat. *See* "Emily"

Kawanishi N1K2 George. *See* "George"

Kenney, George C., 404, 490

Kenney, L.T., 77

Kerama Retto (island group), 394, 397, 398, 401, 406

Ketsu-Go (war policy), 399

Ki-21, Type 97. *See* "Sally"

Ki-84 Frank. *See* "Frank"

Kido, Koichi, 309, 310, 378, 414, 453

Kido Butai (Japanese carrier fleet), 71

Kimble, Frederick V. H., 383

King George V (battleship), 478

King, Ernest J., 4, 18, 21, 28, 29, 34, 39, 43, 52, 101, 102, 306–7, 330, 331, 340–41, 342, 352–53, 372, 382, 416, 420, 490, 494, 499

Kingfisher floatplane, 398

Kingman, Howard F., 89

Kinjo, Shigeaki, 406, 407, 487

Kinkaid, Thomas, 462

Kirkpatrick, Elmer F., 411

Kiska Task Force, 3

Kistiakowsky, George ("Mad Russian"), 43–44, 348, 351, 423, 424, 438, 458

Kitani, Toshio, 274, 275

Kitkun Bay (CVE-71), 84

Klein, Max, 140

Knox, Frank, 27

Kobayashi, Masami, 7

Kobe (Japan), 391, 394, 464

Koehler, John T., 49

Koga, Mineichi, 11, 33–34, 69

Koiso, Kuniaki, 310, 399
Kokura (Japan), 413, 432, 437, 448
Kongo (battleship), 66
Konoye, Fumimaro, 377, 391, 425, 456
Kossler, Herman J., 99, 100, 168–69, 194, 195, 258
Krantz, James, 361
Kraus, Paul, 472–73
Krueger, Walter, 416, 462, 464, 470
Krulak, Victor, 52
Kure (Japan), 394, 399, 431, 432, 464
Kuribayashi, Tadamichi, 379, 394
Kurile Islands, 462
Kurita, Takeo, 356
Kusaka, Ryonosuke, 65, 67, 69, 79, 86, 173, 208
Kuwano, Mr., 485
Kwajalein Atoll, 4, 19, 20, 48, 49, 51, 84, 101
Kyle, Wood B., 91, 154, 292
Kyoto (Japan), 413
Kyushu (Japan), 113–14, 342, 353, 378, 394, 398, 413, 416, 417, 421, 457, 462

L

Laffey (DD-724), 402
land warfare, protocols of, 159
landing craft, LCPRs, 92, 95
Landing Craft Infantry (LCI), 55, 122, 123, 143, 379, 397
Landing Craft Medium (LCM), 52, 54, 117
Landing Craft Personnel Ramp (LCPR), 92, 95
Landing Craft Tank (LCT), 55, 56–57
Landing Craft Vehicle Personnel (LCVP), 117, 125
Landing Ship Dock (LSD), 29, 52, 58, 117
Landing Ship Tank (LST), 39, 54, 55–56, 58, 161, 167, 397
    D Day, 117–18
    hospital-equipped, 138, 143, 421
    LST-84, 118
    West Loch explosion, 60–61
Landing Vehicle Tracked (LVT) (amtracs; alligators), 51, 52
    D Day, 122–26, 127
    LVT(A) variant, 55, 142
    steering, 59–60
    "upgunned" model, 55
Langley (CVL-27), 77, 336, 376
Lansdowne (DD-486), 465, 468
Laulau Point (Saipan), 72, 89, 90, 91, 106, 159, 235
Laulauwan cliffs, 291
Layton, Edwin T., 101, 427
LCI. *See* Landing Craft Infantry
LCM. *See* Landing Craft Medium
LCPR. *See* Landing Craft Personnel Ramp
LCT. *See* Landing Craft Tank
LCVP. *See* Landing Craft Vehicle Personnel
Leach, Harold F., 16
leadership, Spruance on, 103
leaflet campaigns, 377, 394, 409, 430, 448, 453, 484
Leahy, William D., 330, 331, 436, 446, 494, 495
Lee, R. J., 127, 128
Lee, Willis A., 85, 171–72, 171–72n, 182, 183, 184, 189, 190, 193, 213–14, 231, 417
LeMay, Curtis, xix, 221, 354, 373, 374, 383, 385, 388–89, 391, 398, 399, 404, 412, 422, 425–26, 427, 435, 437, 494
"Leopards" (263rd Air Group), 68
Leslie, Gordon, 137, 491, 492
Lewis, Don "Hound Dog," 217–19, 230
Lewis, Herman, 484

Lewis, Robert A., 123, 124, 364, 436, 440, 443, 444–45

Lexington (CV-16), 1–2, 34, 35, 78, 83, 145, 146, 172, 175, 182, 185, 186, 192, 193, 212, 213, 214, 221, 223–27, 230, 231, 232, 254, 376

Leyte Gulf, battle of, 103*n*, 172*n*, 343, 355, 357, 399, 431

Liberator (Consolidated B-24) (bomber), 114

Liberty ships, 470

Lightning (Lockheed P-38), 23

Linson (radioman), 223, 227

Lionfish (SS-298), 413

Lipsky, John, xxii

Little, Lou, 8, 9

"Little Boy" (bomb), 423, 434, 437

Little Creek (Virginia), 39

Livesey, Benjamin R., 129–30

Livy, 462

Lockhart, Gene, xxii

Lockwood, Charles A., 33, 86, 99, 148, 149, 169, 174

Loomis, Samuel C., Jr., 174

Los Alamos (New Mexico), 348, 349, 351, 381, 423, 457

Louisville (CA-28), 88, 157, 264, 322, 333, 522

LSD. *See* Landing Ship Dock

LST. *See* Landing Ship Tank

LST-485, 56

LVT. *See* Landing Vehicle Tracked

M

M-69 bomblets, 387

M3A1 light tank, 248

Ma'alaea Bay (Hawaii), 51, 58

MacArthur, Douglas, xviii, xix, 21, 33, 34, 35–36, 87, 149, 316–17, 330–31, 341, 342, 343, 353, 398, 404, 416, 421, 452, 461, 462–63, 464, 465, 467, 468, 469, 471, 472, 474, 476, 478, 480–81, 488, 496

Magellan, Ferdinand, 74

Magicienne Bay (Saipan), 72, 73, 90, 91, 106, 205, 206, 237, 245, 266

Maher, Arthur L., 466

Maikaze (destroyer), 11, 13, 14, 15

Majuro Atoll, 5, 19, 34, 70, 485

Makalapa Hill, 33

Makin Island, 234

Makunsha (Saipan), 72, 263–67, 271, 274, 281, 285

Maloelap Atoll, 20, 484

Manchuria, 434, 455

Mang, Louis W., 315–16, 351

Manhattan Engineer District, 348

Manhattan Project, 348, 364, 381–83, 427, 427*n*, 435, 474

Manila Bay (CVE-61), 236

Mare Island, 329

Mariana Islands, 352, 462

civilian population, 73

history of, 74

post-battle construction, 338

U.S. control of, 342

U.S. strategy and, 4, 21–22

Mariana Islands campaign (Operation Forager), xvii–xx, 4, 19, 20, 29–36, 85, 101, 114, 149, 268, 319, 340

aerial photo-reconnaissance, 30, 31

casualties, 378

explosives, 49

Fifth Amphibious Force (Fifth Phib), 25, 52, 84

final exercises for, 54

Japanese preparation for, 65–70

objective of, 173

old battleships (OBBs), 88–90

ordnance for, 54

"Plan Johnny," 76–80

preparation for, 48–64

preparatory air strikes, 76–84

strategic importance of, 20, 21

submarines, 33, 71, 72, 86
supply shipping for, 52, 54
underwater demolition teams in, 48–50, 303–04, 312, 315
Marianas Review (newspaper), 377
Mariner (Martin PBM patrol plane), 168, 169, 171, 174, 177
Marines. *See* U.S. Marine Corps
Marpi Point (Saipan), 77, 88, 89, 285, 286, 290, 291–94, 297, 307
Marquardt, George, 442
Marshall, George C., 21, 268, 330, 353, 372, 382, 416, 417, 423, 427, 435, 491, 494, 534
Marshall, Robert P., 44, 47, 336, 457
Marshall Islands, 20, 483, 484
Marshall Islands campaign, 4, 5, 19
Maryland (BB-46), 84, 88, 322
mass suicide, 406–9
Matsubara, Hiroshi, 195, 196
Matsushige, Yoshito, 444, 446
Mayer, A. D., 123
McCain, John, 102, 212, 404, 431, 469
McCall (DD-400), 429
McCampbell, David, xix, 77, 78, 81, 82–83,

102, 186–89, 193, 197–201, 210–11, 231, 351, 357–58
aerial gunnery, 187
as celebrity, 372
exhaustion of, 337
focus on mission, 1865–87
replacement pilots, frustration with, 337
as smoker, 187
stateside decorations and honors, 371–72
McCarthy, Edward, 281, 282
McCrea, John L., 16
McDermut (DD-677), 57, 324
McKnight, Chuck, 442
McLellan, Warren, 219–20, 221, 222, 229–30
McMorris, Charles H. "Soc," 383
McNamara, Robert S., 359, 373, 374, 388, 494
McVay, Charles B., 435–36
McVay, Woodie, 31, 104
medical supplies, for POW camps in occupied Japan, 467
Meisinger, Josef Albert ("Butcher of Warsaw"), 476
Mellon, Glenn, 199, 200
Mellu Pass (Saipan), 84
Memphis Belle (B-17), 359
Merritt, Charlie, 158
Mester, Cecil R., 218
Metzel, Jeffrey, 43
Michael, Lieutenant, 124

Michelony, Lewis J., Jr., 157, 272
Midway, Battle of, xvii, 5, 22, 100, 101, 102
Midway (CVE-63), 166, 167, 357. *See also* St. Lo
Mili Atoll, 20
military ethics, xviii–xix, 316, 317
Mille Island, 483
Miller, John C., 130
Mindanao, 343
mines, 42, 464
minesweepers, 463, 464, 470
Minneapolis (CA-36), 11, 14–15, 18, 190
Minnick, Mike, 250
Mississippi (BB-41), 13
Missouri (BB-63), 404, 455, 465, 468, 469, 488
Mitchell (Consolidated B-25) (medium bomber), 329
Mitchell, Billy, 384
Mitscher, Marc A., 306
air strike planning, 10
biography, 22, 28
Carolines attack, 34
flak trap, 189
Great Marianas Turkey Shoot, 224
on Guam, 182, 311
Iwo Jima, 379
Japan attacks, 375, 376, 394, 399–400
Marianas, preparatory strikes on, 30–31, 34
Midway, battle of, poor performance in, 22, 23

Mitscher, Marc A. (*cont.*)
and Ozawa, 178, 186,
189, 212
Palau attack, 34
Philippine Sea, 182,
189, 202, 203, 224,
229, 230
"Plan Johnny," 76–80
Saipan battle, 80, 100,
102, 146, 147, 150,
171–77, 210
Spruance and, 23,
150–51, 172–75,
203, 229
Truk strike
(Operation
Hailstone), xviii, 5,
6, 10, 11, 14, 17, 18,
22, 23
"West of Tokyo
Missionary
Society," 35
Mitsubishi A6M Model
Zero. *See* "Zeke"
Mitsubishi G4M
medium bomber.
See "Betty"
Mitsubishi J2M Raiden.
See "Jack"
Mitsubishi Ki–21, Type
97. *See* "Sally"
Miura, Shinichi, 79,
369–70
Miura, Shizuko, 75,
76, 79, 80, 104–7,
163–65, 167, 263–
67, 271, 276–78,
296–98, 369–70,
485–87, 503
Miura, Toeko, 75, 486
Miura, Toshiko, 487
Miyagi, Karumi, 407,
408

Mizony, Harold I., 237,
241
Moen Island, 5, 8
Mogami, Sadao, 387, 390
mokusatsu, 434, 533
Molotov, Vyacheslav, 425
Monssen (DD-436), 124,
138, 155
Monterey (CVL-26), 6,
31, 79
Montgomery, Alfred
E., 17
Montpelier (CL-57), 89,
172, 268, 319, 333
Moore, Charles J. "Carl,"
12–13, 14, 15, 25,
26, 27, 28, 31, 70,
114, 147, 177, 237,
241–42, 259, 285,
306, 307–8, 324,
335, 399, 417*n*, 491,
498
morality in warfare,
xviii–xix, 316, 317,
496, 497, 499
Morgan, Robert K., 359
Morison, Samuel Eliot,
89, 306
Moritaki, Ichiro, 499,
500
Morotai, 343
Morris, Bert, 210
Mount Lasso (Tinian),
328
Mount Marpi (Saipan),
291
Mount Santa Rosa
(Guam), 336
Mount Suribachi (Iwo
Jima), 393
Mount Tapotchau
(Saipan), 72, 91,
107, 115, 120, 142,

154, 159, 162, 204,
233, 237, 240, 241,
247, 250, 252, 260,
271, 284, 307, 484
Mount Tenjo (Guam),
314
Murray, George D., 483
Murray, Raymond L.,
130, 469
Musashi
(superbattleship),
11, 66, 87, 356
Musashino-Tama
(Japan), 363
mushroom cloud, 439,
445
Mustain, Hollis, 133,
135, 269
Mustang (P–51
Mustang), 315
Mustin, Lloyd, 184

N

N1K2 George. *See*
"George"
Nafutan Point (Saipan),
72, 78, 88, 89, 96,
105, 233, 234, 236,
237, 247, 248
Nagasaki (Japan), 413,
427, 432, 437,
448–49, 470, 474,
479
Nagato (battleship), 66,
215, 216, 431, 466,
492
Nagoya (Japan), 362,
391, 464
Nagumo, Chuichi, 66,
71, 72, 105, 176,
271, 272, 280, 299
death of, 274–76

reaction of Spruance to death of, 300, 477

Naka (cruiser), 11

Nakajima, Yoshitaka, 69

Nakajima A6M3 fighter. *See* "Hamp"

Nakajima aircraft engine plant complex, 363, 452

Nakajima B6N Tenzan. *See* "Jill"

Nakajima Ki-84 Frank. *See* "Frank"

Nakajima P1Y twin-engine bomber. *See* "Frances"

Nakano family (U.S.), 287

Nalder, Lewis M., 158

Nall, Raymond L., 198

"Nambo" (South Seas Trading Company), 74, 75, 486

napalm, 315–16, 317, 319, 333, 351

Napoleon Bonaparte, 318

native populations, 73–75, 290, 471–72

Natoma Bay (CVE-62), 236

Naval Combat Demolition Units (NCDUs), 40, 46

Naval Construction Battalions. *See* Seabees

Naval War College at Newport, 490, 491

Navy. *See* U.S. Navy

Navy SEALs, xix

Nazi war crimes, International Military Tribunal for the Far East, 476

NCDUs. *See* Naval Combat Demolition Units

Neal, Harry, 244

Nedderson, Gordon, 360

Nelson, Harold E., 283

Nelson, Horatio, 15

Nelson, Richard H., 441

Nelson, Robert, 443

Nelson, Robert S. "Stu," 213

Neratus, 104

Neshanic (AO-71), 172

New Guinea, 3

New Jersey (BB-62), 6, 13, 14, 15, 17, 19, 34, 85, 356, 464, 469, 475

New Mexico (BB-40), 88, 398, 399, 401, 404, 413, 477

New Orleans (CA-32), 11, 14, 15, 327

"A New Strategic Concept for the Defeat of Japan," 342

Newton, Sir Isaac, 11

Nicholas (DD-449), 465

Niigata (Japan), 413, 432

Nimitz, Chester W., 62, 101, 307, 342, 343, 398, 462, 463, 465, 495, 502

aerial reconnaissance, 32–33

ALPOA 579, 454

atomic bomb, 382, 427, 502

on China's importance, 114

copy of Japanese Plan Z, 69

"cult of death," 340, 422

ground invasion of Japan, 420

intelligence, use of, 32–33

Marianas operation, 34, 35

meeting with Roosevelt and MacArthur, 330–31

Mitscher and, 23

occupied Japan, 468, 469

order to cease offensive operations against Japan, 454

press conference, 370–71

promoted to Chief of Naval Operations, 489

Roosevelt's condition, 341

Saipan airfield construction, 206–7

Saipan scheme of command, 102

San Francisco conference, 352

Smith and, 177

Spruance and, 4, 5, 11, 12, 13, 148, 150, 171, 232, 352, 478

surrender of Japan, 454

Nimitz, Chester W. (*cont.*)
  "Tactical Foresight" (memorandum), 62–23
  tactical philosophy, xix–xx, 4, 19
  Truk strike, 4, 13
  Turner and, 28, 62, 306
  understanding of effects of war on soldiers, 404
  W Day, 261
  on war, 502
Nimitz's Law, 321
96th Infantry Division, 398
Nobuhito, Prince Takamatsu, 309
Noda, Mitsuharu, 299–300
Nolan, James F., 435
Norden bombsight, 360, 381, 443
Norman Scott (DD-690), 122, 124, 319, 322, 324, 325, 326, 329, 335
Normandy invasion, 40, 85, 268
Norstad, Lauris, xxiii–xxv, 348, 358, 362, 373, 374, 386, 387, 391, 413, 422, 426
North Carolina (BB-55), 1–2, 85, 190, 375
North Field (Tinian) (Ushi Point), 373, 435, 448
North Pass (Truk), 10, 11

Northern Attack Force, 50, 56
Nowaki (destroyer), 11, 15
nuclear weapons
  detonators, 424
  "Fat Man" bombs, 381, 423, 425, 427, 435
  "Little Boy," 423, 434, 437
  Operation Crossroads, 492
  See also atomic bomb

O
Oak Ridge (Tennessee), 423
Oakland (CL-95), 214
Oba, Sakae, 71, 251, 252–54, 260, 264, 280, 281, 295–96, 298, 367, 368, 390, 429–30, 483–84, 503
O'Bannon (DD-450), 465
Obata, Hideyoshi, 69, 260, 329
OBBs. *See* old battleships
O'Brien, William J., 282, 284
Occupied Japan. *See* Japan, occupation
Octagon conference. *See* Quebec Conference
O'Donnell, Emmett "Rosie," 358, 359, 374
Office of Statistical Control, 359, 373, 374, 494, 501
Ogata, Kiyochi, 326, 327, 332

Ogawa, Yukimatsu, 106, 156, 266
O'Hare, Butch, 8, 9
Ohmae, Toshikazu, 69
Oka, Yoshiro, 106
O'Kane, Richard H., 33
O'Keefe, Bernard, 448
Okinawa, 86, 352, 353, 394, 397–401, 403, 404, 408–09, 465
old battleships (OBBs), 88–90
Oldendorf, Jesse, 88, 95, 176
Omark, Warren R., 215, 216, 224, 226
Omori (prisoner of war camp), 465
Onishi, Takijiro, 334–35, 357
Onodera, Commander, 280
Operation A-Go. *See* Plan Z
Operation Blacklist, 461, 462
Operation Coronet, 342, 406, 408, 416, 438
  map, 418–19
Operation Crossroads, 492
Operation Downfall, 342, 461, 471, 497
  map, 418–19
Operation Forager. *See* Mariana Islands campaign
Operation Hailstone. *See* Truk strike
Operation Iceberg, 397
Operation Magic Carpet, 488

Operation Matterhorn, 113

Operation Olympic, 342, 362, 378, 406, 408, 414, 416, 417, 421, 438, 457

map, 418–19

Operation Starvation, 399, 464

Oppenheimer, J. Robert, 348, 349–50, 351, 413, 438, 445

Orange Plan, 27

Orote Peninsula (Guam), 173, 197, 260, 312, 315, 329, 330, 337, 339

OS2U Kingfisher floatplane. *See* Kingfisher floatplane

Osaka (Japan), 391, 394, 464

Ota, Masahide, 406

Ota River (Japan), 443

Oveland, C. I., 178

Overton, Edward W., 199–200

Owens, Seymour D., 124, 322, 324

oxcarts, to haul aircraft ordnance, 205–6

OY-2 Stinson Sentinels, 240

Oyodo (light cruiser), 208, 432

Ozawa, Jisaburo, 66, 69, 70, 71, 145, 146, 171, 173, 174, 177, 178, 179, 189, 195, 197, 202, 208, 208n, 212, 213–14, 215, 231, 355, 356, 357

P

P-38 Lightning, *See* Lightning

P-47D Thunderbolt. *See* Thunderbolt

P-51 Mustang. *See* Mustang

Pacific Air Transport Command, 462

Pacific Fleet, 462

Pacific islands, importance of, 20, 21–22

"Pacific problem," 4

Pakanto Island, 484

Palau attack, 34, 339, 342

Palau Island, 11, 67, 74, 86

parachute mines, 42

Param Island, 5

Parker, R. C., 55

Parker Ranch, 38

Parsons, E. J., 107

Parsons, William S. "Deak," 347–48, 350, 351, 381, 382, 413, 437–43, 446, 447, 493

Pase, Charles, 154, 334

Patrol Squadron Sixteen (VP-16), 168

PBM Mariner. *See* Mariner

Pearl Harbor, 48, 54, 329, 352

Pearl Harbor attack, 27, 466

Pease, Philo, 128

Peleliu, battle of, 68, 342, 343, 351

Pennsylvania (BB-38), 26, 88

pentnucleotide, 475

Perry, Matthew, 468–69

Philip (DD-498), 258, 269, 270, 285–86

Philippine Sea, 87, 174, 343

Philippine Sea, battle of, 178–211, 339, 355

aircraft lost, 232

casualties, 190

Great Marianas Turkey Shoot, 229, 306, 386

kills claimed by U.S pilots, 201

map, 180–81

recovery of U.S. strike, 224–29, 519

Task Force 58 strikes Combined Fleet, 212–24

torpedoes, 195, 202

U.S. victory in, 231–32

Philippines, U.S. liberation of, 330, 343

Phillips, Sol, 214

photoelectric booby traps, 42

Pintado (SS-387), 72

Piper L-4 Grasshopper. *See* Grasshopper

Pittsburgh (CA-72), 396, 413

P1Y twin-engine bomber. *See* "Frances"

Plan Jail Break, 466

"Plan Johnny," 76–80

Plan Z (Operation A-Go), 66, 67, 69, 86, 144, 176

Plant, Claude, 189

Pletcher, Leo, 130

plutonium, "Fat Man"
    bomb, 381, 423,
    425, 427, 435
poison gas, film about,
    372
Pollard, Colonel, 366,
    367
Ponape Island, 19, 484
Portland (CA-33), 483
Potsdam Conference,
    427, 432–33, 446,
    494
Potsdam Declaration,
    432–34, 447, 449,
    453, 455
Potter, E. B., 357
POW camps, near
    Tokyo, 465–67
POW negotiator, 288
Pownall, Charles A., 23
POWs, 82, 274, 284, 287,
    474, 478, 482
Pratt, Fletcher, 158
primacord, 424
Prince, J. E., 216
Prince of Wales
    (battleship), 47
Project Alberta, 383,
    411, 435, 437
propaganda
    leaflets over Japan,
        374–77, 394, 409,
        430, 448, 453, 484
    design of, 286, 289
    in the Marianas, 287
"proportionality in
    killing," 16, 422
prostitution, in occupied
    Japan, 477–78
protocols of land
    warfare, 159
proximity-detonated
    fuze. *See* VT fuze

"pumpkins" (bombs),
    381, 427
Purnell, William R., 427,
    427n, 437, 447
Purple Heart Ridge
    (Saipan), 237

Q

Quebec Conference,
    340–42, 343, 496

R

Rabaul (New Guinea),
    36, 421
Radio Saipan, 448
Radio Tokyo, 377, 451,
    454
radiological safety
    monitors, 493
Rainbow Five (war
    plan), 27
Ramage, James D. "Jig
    Dog," 118, 121,
    215–16, 217, 224,
    230, 231
Ramage, Lawson P.
    "Red," 372
Ramsey, Norman F., 348,
    413, 437, 438, 446,
    488
Randolph (CV-15), 397
Ranes, R. E, 216
Rawlings, Sir Bernard,
    478
realism, war and, 501–2
reconnaissance, 152
    aerial reconnaissance,
        30–33, 39
    hydrographic
        reconnaissance, 40
    of Iwo Jima, 379

by Japanese, 65
for Saipan battle,
    48–50
string reconnaissance,
    49–50, 92, 479
swimming
    reconnaissance, 40,
    92–93, 96, 98
underwater
    reconnaissance, 47
Red Beach (Saipan), 93,
    97, 121, 122, 124,
    127, 130, 135, 138,
    141, 159, 160
Redfin (SS-272), 87, 99
Reed, Robert S., 158
reef-bound waterways, 49
Reeves, J. W., 78, 231
Reno (CL-96), 230
repatriation, 482–83, 488
Repulse (battlecruiser), 47
Reuben James
    (DD-245), 42
Rhodes, Richard, 448
Richardson, Robert C.,
    305–6, 316, 520–21
Rigg, James F., 77, 102,
    187, 199, 200
Riseley, James P., 130,
    132, 156, 158
Risser, Robert D., 147,
    148
ritual suicides, 333, 334,
    341
Robbins, Sidney, 92, 95
Rochefort, Joseph J., 32
rockets, 55, 84
Rockey, Keller E., 379
Rocky Mount (AGC-3),
    51, 70, 84, 96, 97,
    150, 161, 304, 306
Roebling, Donald, 51
Roi Island, 20, 84, 485

Rollen, Claude B.,
 156–57
Rome, 461–62
Roosevelt, Franklin D.,
 xviii, 3, 27, 35, 307,
 330–31, 372, 402,
 433, 496, 501
 attitude toward
  Japanese, 340–42
Rosenthal, Joe, 393
Rota, 146, 210, 483
Rota, battle of, 77, 254
rotary mower drill, 81
Roth, Carl, 118, 123,
 124, 141
Royal Navy, 431, 465, 478
rough-water
 operations, 59
Ruddock, Theodore D.,
 322, 323, 327
Running, Bill, 96
Rushing, Roy, 188, 358
Russo-Japanese
 Neutrality Pact, 403
Russo-Japanese War, 434
Rutter, James B., Jr., 269,
 270, 286
Ryuho (aircraft carrier),
 66, 215, 216, 217
Ryukyu Islands, 414

S

Sablan, Manuel, 73, 74,
 75, 104
Sagami Wan (Japan), 465
Saipan, 31–32, 362
 black flies, 308
 captive American
  aviators, 75–76
 Chamorro people,
  73–75
 civilian population, 73

D Day on, 34, 50,
 115–143
Death Valley, 205, 238,
 241, 255
Gardiner Conroy
 Field, 206, 236, 240,
 248, 254
Japanese colonial
 administration,
 73–76
map: June 16 to 22
 (1944), 209
map: June 23 to July 7
 (1944), 235
post-battle recovery,
 339, 354
Purple Heart Ridge,
 237
roads on, 255, 369
Saipan, battle of, xviii,
 5, 30, 34, 36, 115,
 204, 268
 African American
  troops, 140
 aircraft losses,
  U.S., 84
 antiaircraft fire,
  Japanese, 84
 Aslito/Isely Field,
  Japanese assault on,
  247–51
 Blue Beach, 93, 95, 97,
  120, 121, 124, 125,
  131, 133, 134, 142,
  155, 161, 167, 241,
  243
 bombardment, 85,
  88–90
 burial of Japanese
  dead, 159, 272, 273,
  285
 carrier raids, 72
 casualties, 138, 140,

 141, 143, 159, 283,
  299
 caves, 39, 70, 72, 104,
  105–7, 154, 159,
  163–65, 176, 204,
  206, 237, 239, 243,
  244, 246, 248–50,
  252, 253, 267, 269,
  271, 274–75, 279,
  281, 285–86, 288,
  289–93, 295, 299,
  300, 314, 333, 334,
  338, 340, 368, 408,
  449, 479, 483, 487,
  501
 convoy strikes (June
  12th), 81–83
 D Day, 50–51, 116–43
 final Japanese assault,
  281–84
 flag-raising
  occupation
  ceremony, 290
 Garapan, 32;
  destruction of,
  104–7, 109, 110
 Green Beach, 13, 92,
  95, 120, 122, 125,
  128–29, 131, 132,
  135, 155, 156
 holdouts, 286–89,
  291–300, 366–68
 interrogation of
  POWs, 274
 "invasion crawl," 92
 Japanese combat
  strength, 63, 68
 Japanese defenses,
  106, 126, 127, 128,
  129, 132
 Japanese troops on
  Saipan at end of
  war, 284

Saipan, battle of (cont.)
last phase of, 268–78
medical care for
victims, 159–60
medical evacuations,
138
"motorized
mattresses," 92,
93, 95
OL-5 line, 233
operations plan,
50–51
oxcarts to haul
ordnance, 205–6
pontoon causeway,
161
POW negotiator, 288
POWs, 82, 274, 284,
287
reconnaissance for,
48–50, 92–94, 98
Red Beach, 93, 97,
121, 122, 124, 127,
130, 135, 138, 141,
159, 160
rehearsals, 58–59
resupply for troops,
160–61
Satan flame-thrower
tank, 248–49
securing, 429
spotting the enemy,
170–77
suicides, xvii–xviii,
275–78, 280, 284,
285, 291, 317
supply shipping for,
52, 54
swimmers, 92–93, 96,
160
tank attack, 153–62
torpedoes, 146, 168
typhoon, 99

Underwater
Demolition Teams
(UDTs), 90–97, 115
Yellow Beach, 95, 120,
124, 125, 135, 139,
142
Saipan ratio, 378
Saito, Yoshitsugu, 2, 23,
72, 73, 105, 121,
125, 137, 156, 159,
204, 242, 243, 246,
250, 265, 266, 268,
270, 271, 274–75,
276, 282, 317
Sakai, Saburo, 144, 145,
210, 268
Sakito Maru (transport),
71
Sallada, Henry B., 166
"Sally" (Mitsubishi
Ki-21, Type 97), 166
Salomon, Ben, 283, 284
Samar, battle off,
355–56, 357
San Bernardino Strait,
86, 100, 147, 356
San Diego (CL-53), 465,
467
San Francisco (CA-38),
17, 201
San Francisco
Conference, 352,
353–54
San Jacinto (CVL-30),
145, 213
San Juan (CL-54), 465
Santa Cruz, 195
Santa Fe (CL-60),
395–96
Santilla, Al "Saint," 290,
291
Santos (cargo ship), 75
Saranac (AO-74) 172

Saratoga (CV-3), 18, 380,
397
Sasaki, Captain, 247
Sasebo Naval Base, 479
Satan flame-thrower
tank, 248–49
Sato, Naotake, 424, 425,
531
Savage, George, 361,
387, 388, 390
Savo Island, battle
of, 27
SB2C-1 Helldiver. See
Helldiver
SBD-5 Dauntless. See
Dauntless
Schaal (pilot), 218
Schmidt, Harry, 60, 117,
132, 141, 142, 161,
162, 245, 254, 261,
301, 303, 334, 379,
464
Schofield, Teddy, 10
Seabees (Naval
Construction
Battalions), 44, 206,
207, 339
Seahorse (SS-304), 148
seal hunting, 489
Sebald, W. G., 389
Second Armored
Amphibian
Battalion, 127
Second Carrier
Squadron (Imperial
Japanese Navy),
215
Second Marine Division,
4, 37, 38, 50, 51, 54,
304, 366, 479
Saipan battle, 91, 97,
98, 117, 118, 120,
125, 130, 132, 142,

154, 159, 233, 243, 266, 268, 270, 273
Tinian, battle of, 326, 328
Second Marines, 464, 483
segregated companies of African American troops, 140
Service Squadron Six, 482
Seventh Fleet, 462
Seventh Infantry Division (Army), 4, 18–19, 63, 155, 398
77th Infantry Division (U.S. Army), 314, 398
73rd Bombardment Wing, 354
708th Amphibian Tank Battalion, 55, 118, 135
shaped charges, 46
Shark (SS-174), 72
Shaw (DD-373) 153
shell shock, 296
Shepherd, Lemuel C., Jr., 312, 330
Sherman, Forrest, 352
Sherrod, Robert, 491
Shidehara, Kikuko, 391
Shields, J. A., 221
Shigemitsu, Kiyoshi, 312
Shigemitsu, Mamoru, 309, 468, 469
Shikoku (Japan), 439, 442, 462
Shillen, David, 494
Shimonoseki (Japan), 464

Shimonoseki Strait, 398–99
Shinagawa Hospital, 466
ship-to-shore movement, 51
shipbuilding (1942–1943), 3–4
Sho Plan, 355
Shokaku (aircraft carrier), 66, 179, 194, 195–96, 197, 202, 216, 258
Shonan Maru (minesweeper-trawler), 11, 14
Shook, Leon, 324
shore bombardment, 29–30, 56
shore fire-control party. See "Charlies"
shore landing, offensive firepower for amphibious forces, 55
Shumard, Robert H., 440, 441
"shuttle bombing," 173
"Silverplate" B-29, 410, 436
Simpson, Rodger W., 465
"sinister ratio," 408
Sixth Army, 342, 378, 416, 462, 470
Sixth Marines, 127, 130, 134, 155, 158, 266, 334, 366, 398
64th Engineer Base Topographic Battalion (Fort Shafter), 32
Skytrain, Douglas C-47, 332, 466

Solnit, Gil, 137, 202
Smith, Holland M. ("Howling Mad"), xix, 25–26, 29, 37, 176, 232, 233, 336, 374
Aslito Field, surprise assault, 248
conflict with U.S. Army, 237, 520
exhaustion of, 404
Hill and, 394
Iwo Jima, 379
on Marines, 177
on napalm, 316
postwar, 491
Ralph C. Smith and, 234–42, 247, 305, 316
Saipan battle, 51, 52, 70, 91, 96, 97, 142, 150, 161, 162, 176, 204, 206, 254, 260, 270
on Saito, 254
Tinian landing beach, 302, 303
Smith, Ralph C., 161, 234–42, 247, 305, 316
Smoky Hill Army Airfield, 112
snoopers, 17, 174
Snowden, Ernest M., "West of Tokyo Missionary Society," 35
"sob fraternity," 408
South China Sea, 352
South Dakota (BB-57), 85, 171, 189, 190, 191, 193, 201, 465, 466

South Seas Trading
Company. *See*
"Nambo"
Southerland (DD-743),
465
Southern Attack Force,
50, 261, 310
Southwest Pacific
command, 87
Southwest Pacific
theater, 342, 354
Soviet Union
as broker to end the
war, 403, 424–25
declaration of war
against Japan, 534
intimidated by atomic
bomb, 534
Japanese as slave
laborers to, 488
Spaatz, Carl A., 435, 447,
494
Spanish-American War,
treaty, 74
special sweep squadrons,
470
Speer, Albert, 384
Sprague, Clifton, 193,
356, 357
Sprague, Thomas L., 17
Spruance, Edward (son),
413, 458, 500
Spruance, Margaret
(wife), 62, 285, 300,
336, 352, 355, 356,
393, 406, 470, 476,
489, 500
Spruance, Raymond A.,
89, 285, 307, 339,
340, 363, 395, 397,
470
aircraft carrier use,
100–103

on the Army, 237
on the atomic bomb,
436
bravery of, 137, 403
career, xviii, xix, xx,
5–6, 15, 19, 51, 70
casualties, attitude
toward U.S., 393
Central Pacific
Force, 26
childhood, 12
commander as
gambler, 212
criticized by the air
admirals, 23, 102–3,
175–76, 306–7, 355,
357–58
denied a fifth star,
489–90
Formosa, 352
on Guam, 311, 336,
338
Halsey and, 355–56,
393–94, 414
and invasion of Japan,
406, 420
Iwo Jima and, 372,
374–75, 379
Japanese forces in
Kyushu, 420
Japanese occupation,
462, 464, 469, 470,
476, 478, 482
King and, 352–53,
490
Layton and, 101
on leadership, 103
LeMay and, 374
letters to Margaret,
336, 356, 393, 406,
476
management style,
354–55

Marianas battle,
30–31, 34, 36, 114
Midway battle and,
5–6, 15, 100–02, 300
mission, 173
Mitscher and, 23,
150–51, 172–77, 376
on Nagumo's death,
300, 477
napalm development,
316
Naval War College at
Newport, 490, 491
Nimitz and, 4, 5, 11,
12, 13, 148, 150,
171, 232, 352, 478
on Noda, 299
poison gas, refuses
use of, 372
in the occupation of
Japan, 475–78
offensive firepower
added to
amphibious
force, 55
Okinawa, 406
Operations Olympic
and Coronet, views
on, 406
Ozawa's location, 178,
212, 213–14
Palau attack, 34
personal
characteristics, 12,
149, 357, 500
Philippine Sea, battle
of, 175–76, 192,
202, 231, 232
promoted to
CINCPAC/
CINCPOA, 489
Saipan battle, 50, 55,
76, 91, 93, 100, 102,

137, 146–52, 241, 259–60, 284
Saipan preparatory air strikes, 76–80
Saipan strategy, 100–102, 170, 174
as Saipan task force commander, 102
Smith and, 26, 52
stateside leave before Operation Forager, 61–62
submarines, 148, 149
surrender of Japan, 457
temper, 476–77
Tinian, battle of, 329
Tinian landing, 304
Towers on, 23
Truk strike, 4, 6, 11–12, 13, 15, 17–18, 231
Turner and, 26, 28, 29, 375
on war, 286, 351, 422, 436, 470, 502
St. Lo (CVE-63), 357. See also Midway
Stalin, Josef, 341, 427, 434, 488, 495
Standard Oil Development Co., 384
Stane, John R., 199
Stark, Harold R., 28
starvation, 475, 483
Sterrie, Norman A., 219, 220, 223, 225, 226, 230
Stiborik, Joseph A., 440, 441

Stimson, Henry L., 413, 425, 426–27, 432, 435, 494, 497, 534
Stingray (SS-186), 149, 174
Stockham (DD-683), 465
Stott, Frederic, 205, 240, 242, 245, 246, 249, 250, 290, 294, 301, 351
Straight Flush (weather plane), 442
"The Strategic Plan for the Defeat of Japan," 20–21
string reconnaissance, 49–50, 92, 479
Suamico (AO-49), 259
submarines, 149, 194
Marianas campaign, 33, 71, 72, 86
Philippine Sea, 194, 202–3
Saipan battle, 99–100, 147, 258, 259
Sugano, Isami, 485
suicide
of civilians, xvii–xviii, 278, 285, 291, 307, 317, 333
"group suicide," 406–9
gyokusai, 280, 281, 288, 399, 406, 414
of Japanese government officials, 473–75
of Japanese public, 378
of Japanese troops, 275–78, 280, 284, 285, 317, 340, 341, 358

ritual suicides, 333, 334, 341
Tinian, battle of, 333, 334
"voluntary deaths," 406
Suisun (AVP-53), 465
"Sulfur Island," 375
Sullivan, Sergeant, 256
Sulu Archipelago, 66
Sulu Sea, 87
Sunfish (SS-281), 31, 33
Sunharon Harbor (Tinian), 247
Superfortress (Boeing B-29). See B-29 Superfortress
Supreme Commander for Allied Powers, 461
Supreme War Direction Council (Japan) (Big Six), 403, 414, 424, 430
conditions of surrender, 449, 530
deadlock of, 449–50, 451–53, 495, 530
unconditional surrender rejected by, 425, 433
Surigao Strait, 86, 356
surrender, style of accepting, 461–62
surrender of Japan, 452–56
conditions demanded by Japanese, 449, 463
Emperor Hirohito and, 453, 456
Imperial Rescript, 454, 455, 456

surrender of Japan
(*cont.*)
  meetings and decision
    to surrender,
    448–52
  motivation to
    surrender, 495
  possibility of, 379,
    403, 425
  Potsdam Declaration
    and, 432–34, 447,
    449, 453, 455
  signing paperwork,
    463
  unconditional
    surrender rejected,
    425, 433
  See also Japan,
    occupation
Susupe Swamp (Saipan),
  140, 142, 155, 156,
  208, 239, 369
Sutherland, R. K., 462
Suzuki, Eisuke, 106, 251,
  252, 279, 281, 295,
  429
Suzuki, Kantaro, 399,
  414, 415, 434, 449,
  450, 451, 453,
  467–68
"swamp buggies," 51,
  91, 98
Sweeney, Charles J., 442,
  448
swimming
  reconnaissance, 40,
  92–93, 96
Swing, Joseph M., 466

T

Tabler, R. C., 178
Tacovsky, Charles, 266

tai-atari (body-crash)
  attack, 335
Taiho (aircraft carrier),
  66, 179, 196, 197,
  216
Taka (Chamorro chief),
  335
Takagi, Sokichi, 309,
  310, 403, 422
Takamatsu, Prince, 309
Takashina, Takeshi, 260,
  312
Talafofo (Saipan), 265
Tanapag Harbor
  (Saipan), 32, 75, 77,
  91, 105, 106, 117,
  268, 274, 281, 283,
  285, 339
Tang (SS-306), 33
tanks
  Guam invasion, 314
  Saipan, Japanese
    counterattack, 106
  Satan flame-thrower
    tank, 248–49
Tapotchau, Mount. *See*
  Mount Tapotchau
Tarawa Atoll, 4, 15, 20,
  38, 40, 302, 319
Tarr, Thomas, 199, 200
Task Force 38, 102, 356,
  442, 454, 463, 465,
  469
Task Force 51, 338
Task Force 52, 143
Task Force 53, 261
Task Force 58, xix, 34,
  76, 77, 78, 82, 100,
  102, 103, 145, 147,
  150, 151, 171, 172,
  174, 178, 182, 229,
  232, 329, 339, 376,
  394, 397, 398

Tate, Benjamin C., 215,
  216, 224
Tawi Tawi, 66, 86, 87
Taxis, Samuel G., 367
Taylor (DD-468), 465
Taylor, Joe, 395
TBF/TBM Avenger. *See*
  Avenger
Tennessee (BB-43), 84,
  88, 89, 96, 107, 124,
  133, 149, 322, 333
Tenth Army, 398
Tenth Marines, 334
Tepas, Paul E., 16
tetratol, 45, 138
Thach, John S.
  "Jimmie," 8, 9, 175,
  185
Thach Weave, 8, 187,
  220
Third Amphibious
  Corps, 50, 261, 398,
  400
Third Amphibious
  Force, 168
Third Fleet, 102, 340,
  416, 431, 432, 462
  ceases offensive
    operations against
    Japan, 454
Third Marine Division,
  261, 312, 337, 379,
  464
Thomas, Buzz, 226
Thomas, Norman K.,
  157
Thomas E. Fraser (DM-
  24), 465
Thorburn, Don, 465
313th Bombardment
  Wing, 373, 398, 426
314th Bombardment
  Wing, 373

315th Bombardment Wing, 373
318th Fighter Group, 236, 316, 329, 361
320th Troop Carrier Squadron, 412
393rd Heavy Bombardment Squadron, 351, 410
Thunderbolt fighter aircraft (P-47), 236, 254, 316, 319, 321
Tibbets, Enola Gay, xxv, 437, 440
Tibbets, Lucy, 363, 381–83
Tibbets, Paul, xviii, xix, 347
    atomic bomb, 348–51, 363–65, 380–83, 425–27, 436–39, 493
    B-29 Superfortress development, xxviii, 111–13
    childhood, xxi–xxii, xxvii
    court-martial threatened, xxiv–xxv
    Doolittle and, xxiii, xxv
    early career, xxii–xxiii, 111
    Hiroshima mission, 438–47
    Homestead (Miami) reassignment, xv
    Nebraska reassignment, 112, 385
    piloting transport planes, 111
    retirement, 502
    at Wendover (Utah), 350–51, 363
    at White House, 494
    Wichita (Kansas) reassignment, 111–12
    wife Lucy, 363, 381–83
tides, 32, 38, 40, 57
"Tigers" (261st Air Group), 68
Timmes, Joseph, 474
Tinian, battle of, 50, 77, 254, 315, 317, 318–19, 366
    casualties, 326, 328, 340
    J Day, 261
    Japanese civilians on Tinian, 333
    Japanese troops, number of, 326
    landing beach, 301–4
    map: plans for landing, 320
    napalm, 316, 317, 319, 333
    naval power, 319
    Ogata's last stand, 332–34
    ritual suicides, 333, 334
    storm of July 30, 332
    typhoon, 321
    White beaches, 302–4, 319, 411
Tinian Island, xviii, 30, 31, 88, 134, 145, 146, 206, 247, 261, 262, 301, 302, 339, 362, 373, 488
    as atomic bomb site, 382–83, 410, 448
Tinian Town, 201, 301, 318, 321, 327, 328, 332, 335, 373, 412
"Tiny Tims," 395
Togo, Heihachiro, 145, 152, 478
Togo, Shigenori, 403, 424, 425, 447, 449, 453
Tojo, Hideki, 308–9, 310, 317, 429, 456, 471, 473
tokko units, 335
Tokyo
    aerial view of destruction, 459, 460
    antiaircraft defenses, 387
    central air headquarters ceases scrambling fighters, 387
    Doolittle Raid on, 1942, xxiii
    fire raid, March 1945, 386–89
    Hirohito visits, 390–91
    Omori prisoner of war camp, 465
    POW camps near, 467
    post surrender, 455
    propaganda leaflets dropped, 376–77, 394, 409, 430
    raids in 1944, 359, 362, 375, 385
    rebuilding, 462
    U.S. warships entering harbor, 465, 466
"Tokyo Rose," 476

Tompkins, Rathvon "Tommy," 239, 244

Tone (heavy cruiser), 432, 499

Top Secret (B-29), 442

Torpedo Squadron Eight (VT-8), 372

Torpedo Squadron Fourteen (VT-14), 95

Torpedo Squadron Seventeen (VT-17), 83

Torpedo Squadron Sixteen (VT-16), 84

torpedoes, 146, 168, 179, 195, 202

torture, fear of, 289

Towers, John H., 22, 23, 306, 489

Toyoda, Soemu, 67, 69, 70, 86, 144, 208, 300, 403–4, 449

tracer control, 184

training exercises, 48–49

Tripartite Pact, 309

Trout (SS-202), 71

Truk Atoll, 4, 5, 7, 86

Truk strike (Operation Hailstone), 5, 6–18, 22, 30, 34, 101, 231, 343, 483

Truman, Harry S., xx, 416, 424, 427, 428, 432, 435, 436, 438, 446, 451–52, 453, 454, 461, 494–95, 497, 531, 534

order to drop atomic bomb, confusion over, 534

Tsunoda, Kazuo, 309

Tsushima, battle of, 145

Turnage, Allen H., 312

Turner, Harriet, 498

Turner, Richmond Kelly, xviii, xix, 25, 34, 39, 261, 306

alcoholism of, 28, 62, 498

amtracs, 60, 97

contributions of, 29–30

D Day, 116, 127

early career, 26–27

exhaustion, 404

"heavy power," 29

innovations, 54–57

Iwo Jima, 376, 379

Japanese occupation, 464

Kaho'olawe gunnery school, 85

Kauffman and, 41, 457

landing assault rehearsal, 58

live-fire exercises, 56

Marianas battle, 30

napalm development, 316

nickname, 26

on Noda, 299–300

offensive firepower added to amphibious force, 54–55

old battleships (OBBs), 89

personality, 25–26, 29

Philippine Sea, 202

promotion, 28

Saipan battle, 50, 52, 54–55, 56, 57, 58, 64, 84, 88, 107, 115, 116, 134, 141, 146,

150, 154, 166, 176, 204, 241

Savo Island, battle of, 27, 28

shore bombardment, 29–30, 57

Spruance and, 26, 28, 29, 375

Task Force 51, 338

"technical equipment," 29

Tinian, battle of, 326, 335

Tinian landing, 301, 302, 304–5

Underwater Demolition Teams (UDTs), xix, 41, 44–48, 60, 90–97, 115

West Loch explosion, 61

Tweed, George Ray, 429

Twelfth Air Force, xxiii

Twelves, Wendell, 198

Twentieth Air Force, xviii, xix, 113, 114, 353, 354, 358, 386, 435, 469

21st Marines, 314

23rd Marines, 155, 285, 334

24th Marines, 285, 326, 328, 333

25th Marines, 132, 272, 285, 326

27th Division (U.S. Army), 37, 50, 153, 204, 234, 236, 237, 240, 241, 251, 262, 266, 282, 283, 307, 472

Twining (DD-540), 465
Twining, Nathan
    Farragut, 435
Twitty, Joseph, 32
typhoons, 99, 303, 321,
    397, 413, 475–76

U

UDTs. *See* Underwater
    Demolition
    Teams
Ulithi Island, 374, 375,
    376, 396, 397
Ultra crypto intelligence
    project, 417, 420,
    447, 495
Umahachi, Ano, 484
Umezu, Yoshijiro, 403–4,
    414, 429, 430, 449,
    468, 469, 480
Underwater Demolition
    Teams (UDTs), xix,
    40, 41, 44, 45, 47,
    92–93, 96, 160, 315
  Guam, 311
  Iwo Jima, 379
  Saipan battle, 90–97,
    115, 160
  Saipan
    reconnaissance,
    48–49, 92–94, 98,
    115
  Tinian
    reconnaissance,
    303–4
  training, 45–47
UDT 5, 49, 50, 56, 92,
    96, 491
UDT 6, 92, 326
UDT 7, 49, 92, 95, 96,
    97, 107
UDT 15, 379

UDT 18, 467
UDT 21, 467
underwater
    reconnaissance,
    Japanese, 47
United Nations, 463
Urakaze (destroyer), 196
uranium
  "Little Boy" bomb,
    423, 434, 437
  See also atomic bomb
U.S. Army
  27th Infantry
    Division, 37, 50,
    153, 204, 234, 236,
    237, 240, 241, 251,
    262, 266, 282, 283,
    305, 472
  77th Infantry
    Division, 314, 398
  81st Infantry Division,
    351
  96th Infantry
    Division, 398
  105th Infantry, 155,
    234, 236, 274, 281,
    283
  106th Infantry, 237,
    241, 281, 285–86
  165th Infantry, 155,
    266, 283
  708th Amphibian
    Tank Battalion, 55,
    118, 135
  engineer amphibian
    soldiers, 39–40
  Eighth Army, 416,
    462, 464, 466
  Saipan airfield
    construction, 207
  Seventh Infantry
    Division, 4, 18–19,
    63, 155, 398

Sixth Army, 342, 378,
    416, 462, 470
Tenth Army, 398
XXIV Corps, 398,
    462
XXIV Corps Artillery,
    50
U.S. Army Air Forces
  Eighth Air Force, 435
  Far East Air Forces,
    462
  Twentieth Air Force,
    xviii–xix, 113, 114,
    353, 354, 358, 386,
    435, 469
  XX Bomber
    Command, 113,
    354
  XXI Bomber
    Command, xix,
    354, 358–59, 373,
    374, 377, 383, 435
  XXII Bomber
    Command, 354
U.S. Marine Corps
  10th Marines, 334
  21st Marines, 314
  23rd Marines, 155,
    285, 334
  24th Marines, 285,
    326, 328, 333
  25th Marines, 132,
    272, 285, 326
  amphibious landings,
    51
  Eighth Marines, 131,
    155, 244, 327, 366
  Fifth Division, 464,
    479
  First Marines, 398
  First Provisional
    Marine Brigade,
    261, 329, 330

U.S. Marine Corps (*cont.*)
  Fourth Division,
    4, 18–19, 37, 49,
    50, 51, 54, 55, 91,
    117, 118, 120, 123,
    125, 132, 135, 142,
    204–5, 233, 236,
    245, 250, 261, 263,
    282, 304, 321, 326,
    328, 373, 379, 466,
    479
  Kauffman's
    personality
    and, 97
  LVT and, 51–2
  pilots, 254
  Saipan mission,
    37–38, 91, 97, 98,
    117, 118
  Second Division, 4,
    37, 38, 39–40, 50,
    51, 54, 91, 97, 98,
    117, 118, 120, 125,
    130, 132, 142, 154,
    159, 233, 243, 266,
    268, 270, 273, 304,
    326, 328, 366
  Second Marines, 464,
    483
  Sixth Marines, 127,
    130, 134, 155, 158,
    266, 334, 366, 398
  Third Amphibious
    Corps, 50, 261, 398,
    400
  Third Marine
    Division, 261, 312,
    337, 379, 464
  training for Operation
    Forager, 37–38
U.S. Navy
  amphibious
    rehearsals, 51

antiaircraft gunnery,
  13, 17, 31, 141, 167,
  175, 183–84, 201,
  401
bomb disposal school,
  42–43
ceases offensive
  operations against
  Japan, 454
fighter direction, 6,
  17, 141, 175, 184–85
frogmen, 40, 49, 92,
  96, 160, 379, 479,
  491
Joint Board, 26
Naval Combat
  Demolition Units
  (NCDUs), 40
Rainbow Five,
  development of, 27
Underwater
  Demolition Teams
  (UDTs), xix, 41,
  44, 45
War Plans
  Division, 26
Ushi Point (Tinian), 77,
  321
Ushi Point Airfield
  (North Field), 327,
  328, 373
Ushijima, Tatsukua, 309

V
Val dive-bombers, 67,
  167, 198
Van Kirk, Theodore J.
  "Dutch," 348, 364,
  427, 436, 440, 443,
  445
"variable-timed" fuzes.
  See VT fuzes

venereal infection, in
  Japan, 477
Versailles Treaty, 433
VF-3. *See* Fighter
  Squadron Three
VF-5. *See* Fighter
  Squadron Five
VF-6. *See* Fighter
  Squadron Six
VF-15. *See* Fighter
  Squadron Fifteen
VF-16. *See* Fighter
  Squadron Sixteen
VF-31. *See* Fighter
  Squadron 31
"victory flags," 16
Victory ships, 470
Victory Through Air Power
  (movie), 385
Volcano Island, 462
"voluntary deaths," 406
VP-16. *See* Patrol
  Squadron Sixteen
Vraciu, Alex, 7, 8, 17,
  35, 102, 185, 186,
  191–93, 201, 214,
  215, 220, 222, 223,
  225–28, 351, 355,
  358
Vrana, Leo, 89
VT fuze ("variable-
  timed" fuze;
  proximity fuze),
  184, 431, 532–33
VT-8. *See* Torpedo
  Squadron Eight
VT-14. *See* Torpedo
  Squadron Fourteen
VT-16. *See* Torpedo
  Squadron Sixteen
VT-17. *See* Torpedo
  Squadron
  Seventeen

W

W Day (Guam), 261
Waco Model 9, xxi, xxii
Wakayama (Japan), 470,
    475–76, 479
Waldron (DD-699), 465
Wallace, Clarence R.,
    244
war
    American way of war,
        496, 500
    horrors of, 351
    justice in war, 501
    Kauffman on, 497
    military ethics,
        xviii–xix, 316, 317
    ministering to enemy
        after defeat, 496
    Nimitz and, 502
    "proportionality in
        killing," 16, 422
    realism and, 501–2
    Spruance on, 286,
        351, 422, 470, 502
    tactics of
        extermination, 317
war crimes, 476, 482–83
war planning (Japan)
    "Big Six," 403, 414,
        422, 434
    ending the war, 414,
        415, 424–25
    Ketsu-Go (war
        policy), 399
    Plan Z (Operation
        A-Go), 66, 67, 69,
        86, 144, 145
    possibility of
        surrender, 379, 403,
        425
    Supreme War
        Direction Council,
        403, 414, 424, 430

war planning (U.S.),
    26–27, 50
    air offensive, 114
    Cairo Conference, 21,
        358
    China's importance,
        114
    invasion of Japan,
        406, 416–22
    meeting July 1944:
        Roosevelt, Nimitz,
        MacArthur,
        330–31
    Nimitz on, 62–63
    Octagon conference,
        340–42, 343
    Saipan, 50–51, 147
    San Francisco
        conference, 352,
        353–54
"war wearies," 488–89
Warren, Stafford, 492
Washington (BB-56), 85,
    171, 201, 375
Washington Navy Yard,
    bomb disposal
    school, 42–43
Wasp (CV-18), 95, 193,
    230, 356, 396
Watson, Thomas E., 38,
    60, 97, 98, 117, 120,
    127, 128, 132, 141,
    266, 304
Wedderburn (DD-684),
    465
Weidner, Albert G., 96,
    107
Weinberg, Gerhard L.,
    534
Weller, Donald, 314,
    340
Weller, George, 474
Wendover Army Air

Base (Utah), 349,
    350, 363–65, 381
West Field (Tinian), 373
"West of Tokyo
    Missionary
    Society," 34–35
West Virginia (BB-48),
    318
Westervelt, Norman,
    360
whale hunting, 489
White beaches (Tinian),
    302–4, 319
white phosphorus, 316
Whitehead, Richard F.,
    96, 121, 255
Wichita (CA-45), 17, 190,
    474
Widhelm, Gus, 35, 147,
    193, 210–11
Wildcat (Grumman FM-
    2), 121, 166–67
Willcutts, David, 400,
    401–2, 403, 413,
    490
Williams, Maxie, 273
Willoughby, Charles,
    463
Willow Run (brothel),
    477
Wilpers, John, 473
Winchester Model 12,
    132
Winston, Robert A., 183,
    226, 231
Woleai Atoll, 34, 67,
    483
Wolfe, Kenneth B., 113
Wolin, Robert E., 154
Wood, Phil, 272
Wotje Atoll, 20, 484
Wright 3350, xxvi, 20
Wyoming (BB-32), 52

X

XB-29 (bomber), xxvi
XX Bomber Command.
    See U.S. Army Air
    Forces
XXI Bomber Command.
    See U.S. Army Air
    Forces
XXII Bomber
    Command. See U.S.
    Army Air Forces
XXIV Corps (U.S.
    Army), 398, 462

Y

Yahagi (light cruiser),
    196
Yamagata (Japan), 486
Yamamoto, Isoroku, 23,
    431
Yamaoka, Michiko,
    443–44
Yamashiro (battleship),
    300, 356
Yamato (superbattleship),
    66, 399, 400

Yano, Hideo, 274
Yap Island, 34, 67, 165,
    343
Yawata raid, 114,
    144
YE-ZB beacons, 225
Yellow Beach (Saipan),
    95, 120, 124, 125,
    135, 139, 142
Yokohama (Japan), 413,
    467, 472, 477
Yokosuka (Japan),
    occupation of,
    466–67, 477
Yokosuka D4Y Suisei.
    See "Judy"
Yokosuka Harbor
    (Tokyo Bay),
    208
Yokosuka JIN "Irving"
    nightfighters. See
    "Irving"
Yokosuka Navy Yard
    (Japan), 431, 466,
    478
Yokosuka PIY. See
    "Frances"

Yokosuka Wing, 210
Yonai, Mitsumasa,
    309–10, 403, 434,
    449
Yorktown (CV-5), 6n
Yorktown (CV-10), 5, 6,
    7, 17, 23, 31, 104,
    183, 215, 217, 230,
    354, 372

Z

Z flag, 145
Zamami Island, 407
"Zeke" (Mitsubishi A6M
    Model Zero), 8, 10,
    68, 77, 78, 79, 166,
    178, 179, 183, 184,
    188–92, 197–98,
    200, 206, 210, 217,
    219, 220, 221, 222,
    357, 361
Zuiho (light carrier), 66,
    179
Zuikaku (aircraft carrier),
    66, 179, 196, 202,
    216, 217, 222

About the Author

JAMES D. HORNFISCHER is the author of four works of World War II naval history, the culmination of a lifelong interest in World War II in the Pacific. He is the author of *The Fleet at Flood Tide: America at Total War in the Pacific, 1944–1945; Neptune's Inferno: The U.S. Navy at Guadalcanal; Ship of Ghosts: The Story of the USS* Houston, *FDR's Legendary Lost Cruiser, and the Epic Saga of Her Survivors*; and *The Last Stand of the Tin Can Sailors: The Extraordinary World War II Story of the U.S. Navy's Finest Hour.*

Hornfischer has given keynote lectures at venues from the U.S. Naval Academy to the Marine Corps University to the National World War II Museum in New Orleans, and frequently addresses veterans' organizations, youth and civic groups, and professional military organizations on the inspiring stories found in his books. He has also appeared in numerous television documentaries on the History Channel, on Fox News Channel's *War Stories with Oliver North,* and on C-SPAN's *BookTV.*

A native of Massachusetts and a graduate of Colgate University and the University of Texas School of Law, Hornfischer is a member of the Texas Institute of Letters, the Naval Order of the United States, and the Navy League. A former New York book editor, he is president of Hornfischer Literary Management, a literary agency. He lives in Austin, Texas, with his wife and their three children.

jameshornfischer.com
@navy1944

About the Type

This book was set in Granjon, a modern recutting of a typeface produced under the direction of George W. Jones (1860–1942), who based Granjon's design upon the letterforms of Claude Garamond (1480–1561). The name was given to the typeface as a tribute to the typographic designer Robert Granjon (1513–89).